Discovering
the Internet
Complete Concepts and Techniques

Discovering the Internet
Complete Concepts and Techniques

Gary B. Shelly
Thomas J. Cashman
H. Albert Napier
Philip J. Judd
Emily Kaufmann

THOMSON

COURSE TECHNOLOGY

COURSE TECHNOLOGY
25 THOMSON PLACE
BOSTON MA 02210

SHELLY
CASHMAN
SERIES®

Australia • Canada • Denmark • Japan • Mexico • New Zealand • Philippines • Puerto Rico • Singapore
South Africa • Spain • United Kingdom • United States

THOMSON
COURSE TECHNOLOGY

Discovering the Internet
Complete Concepts and Techniques

Gary B. Shelly
Thomas J. Cashman
H. Albert Napier
Philip J. Judd
Emily Kaufmann

Executive Editor:
Cheryl Costantini

Senior Product Manager:
Alexandra Arnold

Product Manager:
Erin Runyon

Associate Product Manager:
Reed Cotter

Editorial Assistant:
Selena Coppock

Print Buyer:
Laura Burns

Signing Representative:
Cheryl Costantini

Director of Production:
Becky Herrington

Production Editor:
Debbie Masi

Production Assistant:
Jennifer Quiambao

Development Editor:
Ginny Harvey

Copy Editor:
Lori Silfen

Proofreader:
Nancy Lamm

Interior Design:
Betty Hopkins

Cover Design:
Kenny Tran

Illustrators:
Phillip Hajjar
Andrew Bartel
Richard Herrera
Betty Hopkins

Compositors:
Betty Hopkins
Andrew Bartel

Indexer:
Sharon Hilgenberg

Printer:
Banta Menasha

Discovering the Internet
Complete Concepts and Techniques

CONTENTS

CHAPTER 1

CHAPTER 2

CHAPTER 2

CHAPTER 3
Searching the Web

CHAPTER 3

CHAPTER 4

CHAPTER 4
Communicating Online

CHAPTER 5

CHAPTER 6

CHAPTER 9

PREFACE

The Shelly Cashman Series Æ offers the finest textbooks in computer education. We are proud of the fact that our textbook series has been the most widely used series in educational instruction. We are pleased to announce the addition of Internet and World Wide Web concepts textbooks to the series with *Discovering the Internet: Complete Concepts and Techniques*. This book continues with the innovation, quality, and reliability that you have come to expect from the Shelly Cashman Series.

In *Discovering the Internet: Complete Concepts and Techniques*, you will find an educationally sound, highly visual, and easy-to-follow pedagogy that combines Internet concepts with step-by-step projects and corresponding screens. The Internet and the World Wide Web (Web) have changed the way people find information, communicate with others, and conduct business activities. The chapters and exercises in this book are designed to help students understand how the Internet and the Web have changed today's world; understand the structure of the Internet and the Web; and understand how to use both to enrich their personal and professional lives.

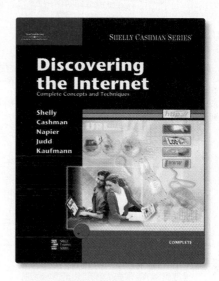

Objectives of This Textbook

Discovering the Internet: Complete Concepts and Techniques is intended for a course that provides thorough coverage of Internet and Web concepts. No experience with the Internet or the Web is assumed. The objectives of this book are:

- To teach Internet and Web concepts

- To introduce different types of online personal and business communications

- To demonstrate how to use a Web browser and Web search tools

- To explain Internet and Web technologies

- To illustrate how business is conducted over the Internet and the Web

- To develop an exercise-oriented approach that allows learning by doing

- To encourage independent study and help those who are working alone

The Shelly Cashman Approach

Features of the Shelly Cashman Series *Discovering the Internet* books include:

Figure 8-31

Figure 8-32

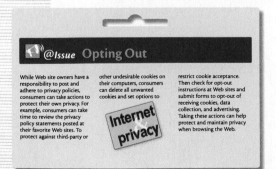

- **Chapter Orientation:** Each chapter in the book presents Internet or Web concepts accompanied by ample margin tips, figures, and multiple step-by-step projects all of which reinforce the concepts discussed in the chapter.

- **Step-by-Step, Screen-by-Screen Instructions:** Each step-by-step project is clearly identified. Full-color screen shots accompany the steps.

- **Thoroughly Tested Chapters:** Every figure in the book illustrates an Internet or Web concept and every step-by-step screen shot must pass Course Technology's award-winning Quality Assurance program.

- **Facts@Hand:** Each chapter contains multiple Facts@Hand tips that provide industry statistics or usage information relevant to the Internet and Web concepts discussed in the chapter.

- **@Issue:** Each chapter includes one or more @Issue sections that provide additional discussion of important Internet and Web issues.

- **@Source:** Each chapter includes multiple @Source tips that direct students to the *Discovering the Internet* Web page where they will find links to useful information.

Organization of this Textbook

Discovering the Internet: Complete Concepts and Techniques provides thorough coverage of Internet and Web concepts. The material is divided into nine chapters and two appendices.

CHAPTER 1 – Into the Internet In Chapter 1, students are introduced to basic Internet and Web terminology, learn how the Internet and Web are used, and become familiar with the history of the Internet and the Web.

CHAPTER 2 – Browsing the Web In Chapter 2, students are introduced to Web sites, Web pages, Web portals, Web servers, and Web browsers; learn to use Web browser features; and learn about online risks and safeguards.

CHAPTER 3 – Searching the Web In Chapter 3, students learn how to follow the search process and use various search tools to perform basic and advanced Web searches.

CHAPTER 4 – Communicating Online In Chapter 4, students learn how to send and receive e-mail using both an e-mail client and a Web-based e-mail service. Students also learn about participating in other types of communication, such as mailing lists, newsgroups, Web-based discussion groups, text and instant messaging, and virtual meetings.

CHAPTER 5 – Getting More Out of the Internet   In Chapter 5, students explore getting more out of the Internet and the Web including getting news, weather, and sports information; listening to the radio; using online reference tools; exploring special interest sites; managing their personal finances; and downloading and uploading files.

CHAPTER 6 – Understanding Internet Technologies and Security   In Chapter 6, students learn about the networking technologies and communication services that make communicating over the Internet and accessing the Web possible. Students also learn more about online security risks and safeguards.

CHAPTER 7 – Creating Web Pages   In Chapter 7, students are introduced to Web site and Web page planning and design concepts; then students plan a Web site, plan a basic Web page, and create the page using the Hypertext Markup Language (HTML).

CHAPTER 8 – Understanding E-Business   In Chapter 8, students use real-world e-business examples to explore different e-business models.

CHAPTER 9 – Managing a Web Site   In Chapter 9, students expand their knowledge of portals; learn how portals and other complex Web sites manage their Web page content; and learn how organizations and e-businesses promote their Web sites and evaluate their sites' performance.

APPENDICES   The book includes two appendices. Appendix A presents alternate step-by-step instructions for Netscape browser users. Appendix B describes HTML tags and attributes.

End-Of-Chapter Student Activities

A notable strength of the Shelly Cashman Series *Discovering the Internet* books is the extensive student activities at the end of each chapter. Well-structured student activities can make the difference between students merely participating in a class and students retaining the information they learn. The activities in the Shelly Cashman Series *Discovering the Internet* books include the following.

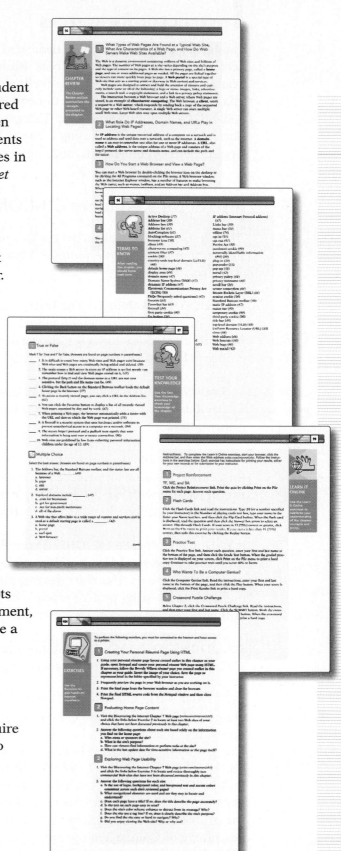

- **CHAPTER REVIEW** A review of the Internet and Web concepts discussed in the chapter.

- **TERMS TO KNOW** A listing of the keywords emphasized in the chapter including a page number reference for each keyword.

- **TEST YOUR KNOWLEDGE** Ten true/false and ten multiple choice questions including a page number reference for each question.

- **LEARN IT ONLINE** Five online exercises that reinforce the Internet and Web concepts discussed in the chapter: Project Reinforcement, Flash Cards, Practice Test, Who Wants to be a Computer Genius, and Crossword Puzzle Challenge.

- **EXERCISES** Ten in-depth exercises that require students to use the Internet and the Web to research issues or solve problems.

Instructor Resources

The Shelly Cashman Series is dedicated to providing you with all of the tools you need to make your class a success. Information on all supplementary materials is available through your Course Technology representative or by calling one of the following telephone numbers: Colleges and Universities, 1-800-648-7450; High Schools, 1-800-824-5179; Private Career Colleges, 1-800-347-7707; Canada, 1-800-268-2222; Corporations with IT Training Centers, 1-800-648-7450; and Government Agencies, Health-Care Organizations, and Correctional Facilities, 1-800-477-3692.

Instructor Resources CD-ROM

The Instructor Resources for this textbook include both teaching and testing aids. The contents of each item on the Instructor Resources CD-ROM (ISBN 0-7895-6834-9) are described below.

INSTRUCTOR'S MANUAL   The Instructor's Manual is made up of Microsoft Word files, which include detailed lesson plans with page number references, lecture notes, teaching tips, classroom activities, discussion topics, projects to assign, and transparency references. The transparencies are available through the Figure Files described below.

SYLLABUS   Sample syllabi, which can be customized easily to a course, are included. The syllabi cover policies, class and lab assignments and exams, and procedural information.

FIGURE FILES   Illustrations for every figure in the textbook are available in electronic form. Use this ancillary to present a slide show in lecture or to print transparencies for use in lecture with an overhead projector. If you have a personal computer and LCD device, this ancillary can be an effective tool for presenting lectures.

POWERPOINT PRESENTATIONS   PowerPoint Presentations is a multimedia lecture presentation system that provides slides for each chapter. Presentations are based on chapter objectives. Use this presentation system to present well-organized lectures that are both interesting and knowledge based. PowerPoint Presentations provides consistent coverage at schools that use multiple lecturers.

SOLUTIONS TO EXERCISES   Solutions are included for the end-of-chapter exercises, as well as the Chapter Reinforcement exercises.

TEST BANK & TEST ENGINE   The ExamView test bank includes 110 questions for every chapter (25 multiple-choice, 50 true/false, and 35 completion) with page number references, and when appropriate, figure references. A version of the test bank you can print also is included. The test bank comes with a copy of the test engine, ExamView, the ultimate tool for your objective-based testing needs. ExamView is a state-of-the-art test builder that is easy to use. ExamView enables you to create paper-, LAN-, or Web-based tests from test banks designed specifically for your Course Technology textbook. Utilize the ultra-efficient QuickTest Wizard to create tests in less than five minutes by taking advantage of Course Technology's question banks, or customize your own exams from scratch.

ADDITIONAL ACTIVITIES FOR STUDENTS   These additional activities consist of Chapter Reinforcement Exercises, which are true/false, multiple choice, and short answer questions that help students gain confidence in the material learned.

Online Content

Course Technology offers textbook-based content for Blackboard, WebCT, and MyCourse 2.1

BLACKBOARD AND WEBCT   As the leading provider of IT content for the Blackboard and WebCT platforms, Course Technology delivers rich content that enhances your textbook to give your students a unique learning experience. Course Technology has partnered with WebCT and Blackboard to deliver our market-leading content through these state-of-the-art online learning platforms. Course Technology offers customizable content in every subject area, from computer concepts to PC repair.

MYCOURSE 2.1   MyCourse 2.1 is Course Technology's powerful online course management and content delivery system. Completely maintained and hosted by Thomson, MyCourse 2.1 delivers an online learning environment that is completely secure and provides superior performance. MyCourse 2.1 allows nontechnical users to create, customize, and deliver World Wide Web-based courses; post content and assignments; manage student enrollment; administer exams; track results in the online gradebook; and more. With MyCourse 2.1, you easily can create a customized course that will enhance every learning experience.

Acknowledgments

The Shelly Cashman Series would not be the leading computer education series without the contributions of outstanding publishing professionals. First, and foremost, among them is Becky Herrington, director of production and book designer. She is the heart and soul of the Shelly Cashman Series, and it is only through her leadership, dedication, and tireless efforts that superior products are made possible.

Under Becky's direction, the following individuals made significant contributions to these books: Debbie Masi, production editor; Jennifer Quiambao, production assistant; Ken Russo, senior Web and graphic designer; Betty Hopkins, interior designer; Kenny Tran, cover designer; Phillip Hajjar, Andrew Bartel, Betty Hopkins and Richard Herrera, interior illustrators; Betty Hopkins and Andrew Bartel, QuarkXPress compositors; Lori Silfen, developmental editor; Ginny Harvey, copy editor; Nancy Lamm proofreader; and Sharon Hilgenberg, indexer.

We also would like to thank Kristen Duerr, executive vice president and publisher; Cheryl Costantini, executive editor; Alexandra Arnold, senior product manager; Erin Runyon, product manager; Heather McKinstry, online product manager; Reed Cotter, associate product manager; and Selena Coppock, editorial assistant.

Gary B. Shelly
Thomas J. Cashman
H. Albert Napier
Philip J. Judd
Emily Kaufmann

Shelly Cashman Series – Traditionally Bound Textbooks

The Shelly Cashman Series presents the following computer subjects in a variety of traditionally bound textbooks. For more information, see your Course Technology representative or call 1-800-648-7450. For Shelly Cashman Series information, visit Shelly Cashman Online at scseries.com.

COMPUTERS	
Computers	Discovering Computers 2005: A Gateway to Information, Web Enhanced, Complete Edition
	Discovering Computers 2005: A Gateway to Information, Web Enhanced, Introductory Edition
	Discovering Computers 2005: A Gateway to Information, Web Enhanced, Brief Edition
	Discovering Computers 2005: Fundamentals Edition
	Teachers Discovering Computers: Integrating Technology in the Classroom 3e
	Exploring Computers: A Record of Discovery 4e
	Study Guide for Discovering Computers 2005: A Gateway to Information, Web Enhanced
	Essential Introduction to Computers 5e (40-page)

WINDOWS APPLICATIONS	
Microsoft Office	Microsoft Office 2003: Essential Concepts and Techniques (5 projects)
	Microsoft Office 2003: Brief Concepts and Techniques (9 projects)
	Microsoft Office 2003: Introductory Concepts and Techniques (15 projects)
	Microsoft Office 2003: Advanced Concepts and Techniques (12 projects)
	Microsoft Office 2003: Post Advanced Concepts and Techniques (11 projects)
	Microsoft Office XP: Essential Concepts and Techniques (5 projects)
	Microsoft Office XP: Brief Concepts and Techniques (9 projects)
	Microsoft Office XP: Introductory Concepts and Techniques, Windows XP Edition
	Microsoft Office XP: Introductory Concepts and Techniques, Enhanced Edition (15 projects)[1]
	Microsoft Office XP: Advanced Concepts and Techniques (11 projects)
	Microsoft Office XP: Post Advanced Concepts and Techniques (11 projects)
Integration	Integrating Microsoft Office XP Applications and the World Wide Web: Essential Concepts and Techniques
PIM	Microsoft Outlook 2002: Essential Concepts and Techniques
Microsoft Works	Microsoft Works 6: Complete Concepts and Techniques[2] • Microsoft Works 2000: Complete Concepts and Techniques[2]
Microsoft Windows	Microsoft Windows XP: Complete Concepts and Techniques[3]
	Microsoft Windows XP: Brief Concepts and Techniques
	Microsoft Windows 2000: Complete Concepts and Techniques (6 projects)[3]
	Microsoft Windows 2000: Brief Concepts and Techniques (2 projects)
	Microsoft Windows 98: Essential Concepts and Techniques (2 projects)
	Microsoft Windows 98: Complete Concepts and Techniques (6 projects)[3]
	Introduction to Microsoft Windows NT Workstation 4
Word Processing	Microsoft Word 2003[3] • Microsoft Word 2002[3]
Spreadsheets	Microsoft Excel 2003[3] • Microsoft Excel 2002[3]
Database	Microsoft Access 2003[3] • Microsoft Access 2002[3]
Presentation Graphics	Microsoft PowerPoint 2003[3] • Microsoft PowerPoint 2002[3]
Desktop Publishing	Microsoft Publisher 2003[2] • Microsoft Publisher 2002[2]

PROGRAMMING	
Programming	Microsoft Visual Basic.NET: Complete Concepts and Techniques[3] • Microsoft Visual Basic 6: Complete Concepts and Techniques[2] • Programming in QBasic • Java Programming 2e: Complete Concepts and Techniques[3] • Structured COBOL Programming 2e

INTERNET	
Concepts	Discovering the Internet: Brief Concepts & Techniques • Discovering the Internet: Complete Concepts & Techniques
Browser	Microsoft Internet Explorer 6: Introductory Concepts and Techniques • Microsoft Internet Explorer 5: An Introduction • Netscape Navigator 6: An Introduction
Web Page Creation and Design	Web Design: Introductory Concepts and Techniques • HTML: Complete Concepts and Techniques 2e[3] Microsoft FrontPage 2003[3] • Microsoft FrontPage 2002[3] • Microsoft FrontPage 2002: Essential Concepts and Techniques • Java Programming: Complete Concepts and Techniques 2e[3] • JavaScript: Complete Concepts and Techniques 2e[2] • Macromedia Dreamweaver MX: Complete Concepts and Techniques[3]

SYSTEMS ANALYSIS	
Systems Analysis	Systems Analysis and Design 5e

DATA COMMUNICATIONS	
Data Communications	Business Data Communications: Introductory Concepts and Techniques 4e

[1] Available running under Windows XP or running under Windows 2000,

[2] Also available as an Introductory Edition, which is a shortened version of the complete book,

[3] Also available as an Introductory Edition, which is a shortened version of the complete book and also as a Comprehensive Edition, which is an extended version of the complete book.

Discovering the Internet

Brief Concepts and Techniques

CHAPTER 1
Into the Internet

Introduction

Internet. E-mail. Online. Web. Whether you are an experienced Internet user or you have never accessed the Internet, you most likely have heard these terms. Over the past decade, these terms have rocketed into common use, changing the way people talk about communicating with others, accessing information, or purchasing products and services.

In this chapter, you will learn the precise meaning of these terms and discover the many ways the Internet is used. You will also review the exciting history of the Internet and learn how the Internet is managed today. Finally, you will learn how individuals and businesses connect to the Internet.

OBJECTIVES

After completing this chapter, you will be able to:

1. Define the Internet

2. Describe how the Internet is used

3. Discuss the history of the Internet and the World Wide Web

4. Describe how individuals and businesses connect to the Internet

CONTENTS

Defining the Internet

The **Internet** is a worldwide network of computers that allows individual and business users around the world to share information and other resources and to conduct business transactions. More specifically, the Internet is an interconnected network of networks, and each **host** — any computer directly connected to the Internet — has a number of other computers connected to it (Figure 1-1). When an Internet user connects to the Internet to access information and services, the user is considered to be **online**.

The Internet works because different types of computers — from personal computers used at home and in the office to supercomputers used by government and researchers — share a common method of communicating known as a protocol. A **protocol** is a standard or set of

hosts

Figure 1-1   The Internet is a worldwide network of networks. Each computer connected directly to the Internet, called a host, can have a number of other computers connected to it.

rules that computer network devices follow when transmitting and receiving data. Every computer connected to the Internet uses the **Transmission Control Protocol/ Internet Protocol** (**TCP/IP**). The TCP/IP protocol suite makes it possible for different types of computers using a variety of operating systems to communicate. You will learn more about TCP/IP and other Internet technologies in later chapters.

Internet communications are transmitted across high-speed fiber-optic networks that connect other networks around the world. These high-speed networks, which provide the Internet backbones, are operated by a number of communication carriers, such as AT&T, MCI, and Qwest in the U.S.; Global TeleSystems in Europe; Telstra in Australia; and various telecommunications carriers in Asia.

Although these communication carriers play an important role, they do not control the Internet. In fact, no one organization owns or controls the Internet. Several organizations, such as the National Science Foundation, InterNIC, and the Internet Society (ISOC), attempt to oversee and standardize the development of Internet technologies and manage some Internet processes.

Using the Internet

Without a doubt, the Internet has profoundly changed nearly every aspect of life. For example, the Internet has revolutionized the way people access information for personal or business use; the way individual shoppers or commercial buyers purchase products and services; the way students do their school work; and the way people communicate with friends, family, colleagues, and others. Additionally, the Internet has also overwhelmingly changed the way businesses interact with their customers, vendors, and business partners (Figure 1-2).

Figure 1-2   People use the Internet for many different purposes.

Facts@Hand

A survey by the Pew Internet & American Life Project reveals that 73 percent of Americans between the ages of 12 and 17 use the Internet.

Who Uses the Internet?

Students, business people, homemakers, retirees — people in all occupations and stages of life — find that using the Internet enhances their world. For example, students often rush home from school and use their computers and the Internet to send instant messages to their friends. Colleges and universities use the Internet to host online classes and instructors use the Internet to find scholarly articles and data for their research, make instructional material available outside class time, post grades, and publish electronic class announcements.

Individuals of all ages use the Internet to search for information on almost any topic — entertainment, sports, politics, science, art, history, and so forth. For example, medical professionals use the Internet to research new drugs, current treatments, and trends in medical practice. Students use the Internet to find information on assigned topics.

Adults with similar interests or hobbies interact and exchange information by participating in online discussions. Consumers shop online, pay bills, reconcile bank statements, and even complete their taxes online. Senior citizens use the Internet to keep in contact with family and friends. People also use the Internet to publish their résumés, photos, or travel journals. Some enjoy publishing an Internet diary, known as **weblog** or **blog**.

Business people and professionals use the Internet to communicate with clients and colleagues whether at home or on the road; check the status of work in progress, view up-to-the-minute business news, and check stock prices. New uses of the Internet are evolving continually, making the Internet increasingly valuable to individuals and businesses.

Internet Activities

The Internet supports a wide range of activities, including:

- Browsing and searching for information on the World Wide Web
- Communicating with others via e-mail, chat, newsgroups, and mailing lists
- Downloading and uploading files
- Logging on to remote computers
- Conducting business activities

The following sections define and describe each of these activities.

THE WORLD WIDE WEB The **World Wide Web**, commonly called the **Web,** is a subset of the Internet that supports a vast collection of documents that combine text with pictures, sound, and even animation and video. These documents, called **Web pages**, are

 @Source

For more information about weblogging, visit the Discovering the Internet Chapter 1 Web page (**scsite.com/ internet/ch1**) and click a link below Weblogs. (Note: you will learn the skills to access these Web pages in Chapter 2.)

stored in Web sites all over the world. A **Web site**, or **site**, is a collection of related Web pages managed by an individual or organization. Web site examples (Figure 1-3) include college and university Web sites, such as the University of Tampa site; corporate Web sites such as the BP site; Web sites that sell products or services, such as the PETs-MART site; Web sites for non-profit organizations, such as the Girl Scouts of the USA; and personal Web sites.

Figure 1-3   Web sites include college and university, corporate, retail, non-profit, and personal sites.

Web pages are created using **Hypertext Markup Language** (**HTML**), a set of special codes or tags that define the layout of Web page content. A Web page can be created using HTML tags in a simple text editor program, such as Notepad. Today, however, most Web pages are created with **Web authoring software**, such as Macromedia Dreamweaver or Microsoft FrontPage, which automatically generate the HTML tags as a page is being created. After a Web page is created, it must be uploaded or **published** to a **Web server** in order to be accessed by others.

To access and view Web pages, you use a software program called a **Web browser** or **browser**. Two widely used browsers are Microsoft Internet Explorer and Netscape Navigator. A Web page is connected to other Web pages by hyperlinks. A **hyperlink,** or **link**, is text or a picture on a Web page that you click with the mouse pointer to view a different location in the same Web page, another Web page at the same Web site, or a Web page at a different Web site (Figure 1-4).

Figure 1-4 A hyperlink is Web page text or a picture that you click with the mouse pointer to view a different location in the same Web page, another Web page at the same Web site, or a Web page at a different Web site.

Exploring the Web by clicking links from one Web page to another is sometimes called **browsing** or **surfing** the Web. For example, when planning a trip, you might first visit an airline Web page and book a flight; then click a link on the airline page to visit a hotel Web page and book your accommodations; and, finally, click a link on the hotel page to view a page containing yet more links to restaurants and entertainment venues near the hotel. In other circumstances, you might simply click from page to page in a more undirected way to learn what kind of information is available at different Web sites. With little effort, you can spend a great deal of time browsing the Web. In Chapter 2, Browsing the Web, you will learn how to use a Web browser to access Web pages and how to click hyperlinks to view other Web pages.

A **search tool** is a Web-based resource that helps you find specific information on the Web. One type of search tool is a search engine, such as Google, that is used to search for Web pages that contain specific keywords or phrases. Another type of search tool is a directory, such as Yahoo!, that maintains a searchable index by category. Figure 1-5 illustrates a search results page at Google and a directory page at Yahoo!. You will learn how to use Google, Yahoo!, and other search tools in Chapter 3, Searching the Web.

Figure 1-5 Search tools allow users to find information on the Web.

Just as no one entity controls the Internet, no one entity controls the Web, although some organizations, such as the **World Wide Web Consortium (W3C)** founded in 1994 by Tim Berners-Lee, support the Web by developing and promoting Web technologies and standards.

E-MAIL AND OTHER COMMUNICATIONS TOOLS   **E-mail**, short for **electronic mail**, allows Internet users to send messages and files over a local computer network or the Internet. By far the most popular Internet activity, e-mail offers several advantages over other means of communication, such as sending letters or making telephone calls. Sending an e-mail message is less expensive and faster than regular mail or express delivery services, such as UPS and FedEx. E-mail also can be more convenient than making a telephone call, especially to others in different time zones around the world. You can send e-mail when it is convenient for you, and the recipient can read it and respond when it is convenient for him or her. You use an **e-mail program**, such as Microsoft Outlook, Outlook Express, or Netscape Mail, to create, send, receive, and manage e-mail.

@Source

To learn more about the W3C and its role in promoting Web standards and technologies, visit the Discovering the Internet Chapter 1 Web page (**scsite.com/ internet/ch1**) and click a link below W3C.

In addition to e-mail, the Internet offers several other ways for individuals and groups to communicate (Figure 1-6). These communications tools allow Internet users to connect with others online to converse about a topic or activity of interest, share information, conduct business, and play. You will learn more about e-mail and other online communications tools in Chapter 4, Communicating Online.

Online communication	Description	Must users be online at the same time?
E-mail	Users send text with or without attached files	No
Instant messaging (IM)	Users take turns exchanging brief messages; only two users can exchange instant messages	Yes
Internet Relay Chat (IRC) or chatting	Users type text into a chat window; all users can see what other users type	Yes
LISTSERVs and mailing lists	Users subscribe to a list on a certain topic and receive messages from every other member of the group	No
USENET or newsgroups	Users post topical messages to a public electronic bulletin board	No

Figure 1-6   The Internet offers several ways for people to communicate.

🖐 Facts@Hand

Perhaps the first person to send e-mail who was not a computer scientist was Queen Elizabeth II, who sent an e-mail message on March 26, 1976.

Figure 1-7   FTP is used to download and upload files.

DOWNLOADING AND UPLOADING FILES   One of the most useful Internet activities is downloading files from a server or uploading files to a server. A **server** is a computer on a network used to store files. As you learned earlier, a Web server stores Web pages. Other server examples are a mail server that stores e-mail messages and a file server that stores electronic files. To **download** is to copy or transfer files from a server to your computer; to **upload** is to copy or transfer files from your computer to a server (Figure 1-7). The Internet standard or protocol that allows you to download from or upload files to a server connected to the Internet is the **File Transfer Protocol** (**FTP**). Music, software, word processing, photograph, and other files can be downloaded or uploaded using FTP. You will learn more about using FTP to download and upload files in Chapter 5, Getting More Out of the Internet.

LOGGING ON TO A REMOTE COMPUTER **Telnet** is the standard or protocol that allows users to log in and to use the processing power of a remote computer. While the public typically does not use Telnet, it still has many valuable uses. Computer system administrators, for example, can use Telnet to log in to a remote computer to troubleshoot problems, and researchers use Telnet to employ the computing power of supercomputers at distant institutions.

CONDUCTING BUSINESS ACTIVITIES Businesses and organizations that use the Internet to generate a profit or to maintain goodwill with their partners, members, or customers are engaged in **e-business**. **E-commerce**, the act of conducting business transactions over the Internet, is a subset of e-business. E-commerce may take the form of electronically transmitting financial transactions, such as placing orders, sending invoices, or paying by credit card online. E-business goes beyond e-commerce to include the functions of supporting and enhancing business relationships by sharing information with customers, suppliers, and employees.

E-business can take a variety of forms or models (Figure 1-8). When a consumer uses the Internet to interact with an online business, the e-business model being followed is **business-to-consumer** (**B2C**). Customers checking airfares on Southwest Airline's Web site or tracking packages on the UPS Web site are examples of B2C e-business in action. When one business uses the Internet to purchase goods and services or complete other transactions with another business, the e-business model being followed is **business-to-business** (**B2B**). An example of a B2B activity is when a company's purchasing manager goes online to buy materials using a vendor's Web site. An organization may also use the Internet for **business-to-employee** (**B2E**) functions, such as connecting its employees to its Human Resources system. Finally, when a consumer uses the Internet to conduct business with another consumer, the e-business model being followed is **consumer-to-consumer** (**C2C**). A collector purchasing a collectible item from another individual through an auction site is an example of C2C e-business activity.

Figure 1-8 E-business models can be classified by the parties involved in the transaction.

@Issue   The Dark Side of the Internet

In addition to its many valuable uses, the Internet also has a dark side. The qualities that make the Internet and the Web so powerful also make them vulnerable to misuse. Because anyone can publish Web pages and make his or her page content appear credible, even ideas that may be illegitimate, biased, or unfounded may garner a huge audience.

The vast informational resources of the Web also include adult-oriented Web sites and hate sites. Adults and children may stumble across them or other Web pages with objectionable material. The ease of communicating over the Internet also makes it easy for destructive computer programs to spread quickly and widely. The anonymity provided by the Internet makes it possible for

criminals to steal credit card numbers, break into computers, engage in identity theft, or frighten others by cyberstalking, which is using threatening or harassing behavior over the Internet.

For more information on the dark side of the Internet, visit the Discovering the Internet Chapter 1 Web page (**scsite.com/internet/ch1**) and click a link below The Dark Side of the Internet.

History of the Internet

Although the Internet and the Web are based on relatively new technologies, millions of people now consider both to be indispensable. In this section, you will learn about the origins of the Internet, the process of growth, and the factors that drove the Web's rapid ascent.

Origins in ARPANET

The Internet traces its origins to the early 1960s, when several seemingly unrelated circumstances led to the development of the world's first computer network. The development of this network resulted from a collaboration among academia, industry, and government.

At that time, computers had been used for only a little over ten years, but not by the general public. Roughly 10,000 computers existed, many of which were mainframes used by the U.S. government to perform specific, mission-critical work for the Census Bureau, the Pentagon, and other government agencies.

The Soviet Union's success in launching Sputnik, the first space satellite, fueled concerns that the United States was falling behind its Cold War competitors in the realm of science and technology in 1958. Further, the government was concerned that existing computer systems were vulnerable to nuclear attack. The government felt that, for the sake of national security, it was important to connect computers so they could distribute computing power and data to more than one location, rather than having them centralized and thus vulnerable to attack.

The U.S. government initiated a push for scientific advances and charged the Department of Defense (DoD) with creating the Advanced Research Projects Agency (ARPA). In 1962 J.C.R. Licklider, formerly of the Massachusetts Institute of Technology (MIT), was appointed to head up ARPA's computer and information processing research efforts. Licklider wrote a series of memos outlining his vision of a Galactic Network of interconnected computers, where users could share data and resources from around the world. His memos were the first published references to the idea of the Internet as it is now known.

In the early sixties, the telephone system's vast network of cabling covered all parts of the United States. Telephone systems work by using a technology known as circuit switching. **Circuit switching** allows a caller to dial a number to establish and maintain a private circuit across the wires from the time the receiver is lifted until one of the parties hangs up. At the time, circuit switching seemed to be the only method to connect two or more remote computers and exchange data.

In 1961, Leonard Kleinrock (Figure 1-9), a scholar at the University of California, Los Angeles (UCLA), wrote his doctoral dissertation and outlined the idea of data networking and packet switching, in contrast to circuit switching. Instead of sending data in a continuous stream over a dedicated circuit like the telephone company, **packet switching** involves separating data from a sending computer into small units known as **packets**, sending each packet independently over cables, and then reassembling the packets on the receiving computer. Each packet can even follow different routes to its destination at the receiving computer. According to Kleinrock, packet switching would make the network more robust and less vulnerable to attack because the data would move in individual packets over different routes, rather than over a single dedicated connection.

A brief experiment in 1965 connected a computer in Massachusetts to a computer in California. The experiment demonstrated two things: (1) that running programs and sharing data on a remote computer was feasible, and (2) that telephone circuits were too slow and unreliable to support data and resource sharing. Kleinrock convinced ARPA to use packet switching instead, and, in 1966, the effort to create the new network of computers known as **ARPANET** was launched.

With government funding, the ARPANET team began work in earnest. Because of Kleinrock's

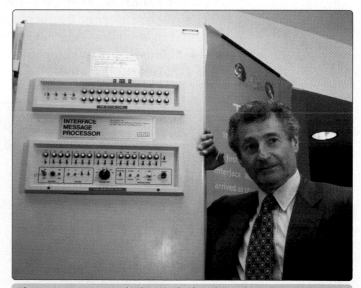

Figure 1-9 Leonard Kleinrock developed packet switching technology.

research, the team chose the computer at UCLA to be the first computer on ARPANET. The team then selected the computer at the Stanford Research Institute (SRI) in Menlo Park, California, headed by Douglas Engelbart, as the second. Next, the government awarded a contract to Bolt Beranek and Newman (BBN), a company in Cambridge, Massachusetts, to create the programming, design, and hardware for the refrigerator-sized switches called IMPs (Interface Message Processors) that would be used to send the packets of data.

On September 2, 1969, representatives from BBN delivered the first IMP to the UCLA lab. Too large to fit into the elevator, the IMP had to be hoisted through a window to the third-floor computer room. About twenty people from the government, the telephone company, and the university watched as a gray cable connected the mainframe to the IMP, and the packets flowed perfectly. Kleinrock said later, "We didn't think of this as a key event in any historical sense. We didn't even have a camera."

@Source

ARPA was renamed DARPA (Defense Advanced Research Projects Agency) in 1972. To read more about DARPA and its current work, visit the Discovering the Internet Chapter 1 Web page (scsite.com/internet/ch1) and click a link below DARPA.

@Source

To learn more about Leonard Kleinrock, visit the Discovering the Internet Chapter 1 Web page (scsite.com/internet/ch1) and click a link below Kleinrock.

On October 29 of the same year, the second IMP was delivered to SRI and the connection was initiated over telephone lines. At UCLA, a student named Charley Kline began to log on, as Kleinrock watched. Kline typed the letters, L-O-G — and then the new network crashed. After a quick fix, the first packets were flowing from computer to computer.

By December 1969, the University of California, Santa Barbara, and the University of Utah joined the ARPANET network, making those four universities the foundation of the global network known today as the Internet.

Growth and Development

As quickly as BBN could create the necessary hardware, more computers, or hosts, were connected to ARPANET. Thirteen research centers had joined ARPANET by the end of 1970. It grew steadily over the next 15 years, roughly doubling in size every year. The first international connections were made to England and Norway in 1973, and other nations came online in the late 1980s and early 1990s.

During those early years, programmers had to make constant changes to programs and hosts on the new network, because no common communications protocol was in use. In 1972, Robert Kahn and Vinton Cerf (Figure 1-10) developed two new protocols for ARPANET, TCP and IP, which solved these and other problems. **Transmission Control Protocol** (**TCP**) provided flow control over the network and error checking for lost packets; **Internet Protocol** (**IP**) addressed and sent the packets. In 1983, DARPA mandated the use of this suite of communications protocols, referred to as TCP/IP. Since then, every computer and device connected to the Internet has been required to use TCP/IP to communicate.

Figure 1-10   Internet pioneers Vinton Cerf (from left), Lawrence Roberts, Robert Kahn, and Tim Berners-Lee.

Originally, researchers used ARPANET to log in to and use the computing power of remote computers and to share files. It was not long, however, before the network was used more significantly for interpersonal communication. In 1971, the first live computer-to-computer chat took place between Stanford University and BBN in

Massachusetts. Late in 1971, Ray Tomlinson, a scientist at BBN, developed the first e-mail program that would send and receive messages to and from remote computers (Figure 1-11). He also devised the use of the @ symbol in e-mail addresses. E-mail instantly became popular as it allowed researchers to collaborate on the continual development of ARPANET. By 1973, e-mail composed 75 percent of the data traffic over ARPANET.

In 1975, the first mailing list, titled SF-Lovers for science fiction fans, was created. A mailing list allows participants to send a single message to the list, which then automatically routes the message to every other participant.

Beyond Research, To the Public

Several factors led to the burgeoning growth of the new network. The Internet became easier for people to use when the long series of numbers originally used to identify computer hosts were replaced with English-language names, such as scsite.com. At the same time, the academic community established networks such as USENET and BITNET, which were open to all members of the academic community and were not restricted just to the computer science researchers involved in the Internet. Furthermore, with the introduction of the Apple II, Macintosh, and IBM PC computers, many more people began to use computers daily. The general public had no access to the Internet until 1979, when CompuServe first offered a subscription service for sending electronic mail (as it was then called). The following year, CompuServe also made real-time chat available to subscribers.

In 1985, the National Science Foundation (NSF) established a new network called NSFnet. NSFnet connected five regional supercomputer centers, at Princeton University, University of Pittsburgh, University of California, San Diego, University of Illinois, and Cornell University, using high-speed connections. In 1987, Senator Al Gore called for a national computer network for research, and sponsored a bill to fund the Internet to enhance the speed of the Internet **backbone**, the main long-distance lines and the hardware that connect computers to the Internet. By 1990, NSFnet superseded ARPANET as the main government network linking universities and research facilities, and the military portion became a separate network called MILNET. When NSFnet made its connections open to the entire academic community, the number of universities, K–12 schools, and community colleges connected to the Internet increased significantly.

The NSF continued to exclude businesses from the network until 1992, when the U. S. Congress lifted the ban against commercial use of the Internet. Beginning then, most of the growth of the Internet came from businesses, not universities, and e-business started to grow. In 1995, the NSF moved the connections from the original NSFnet backbone to a commercial Internet backbone supported by commercial network providers, such as AT&T (Figure 1-12).

Figure 1-11 Ray Tomlinson developed the first e-mail program.

To learn more about the early days of e-mail, visit the Discovering the Internet Chapter 1 Web page (**scsite.com/ internet/ch1**) and click a link below E-Mail.

To learn more about the history of the Internet, visit the Discovering the Internet Chapter 1 Web page (**scsite.com/ internet/ch1**) and click a link below History.

Figure 1-12 AT&T backbone.

The Beginnings and Rise of the Web

Two other pivotal events occurred in 1991. Paul Lindner and Mark McCahill, graduate students at the University of Minnesota, invented a new protocol to form a hierarchical directory-based system to deliver information across the Internet. They named the system **Gopher** after the university's mascot. For the first time, users could navigate easily through online text resources by clicking a directory link to open folders and access files stored in those folders (Figure 1-13). McCahill commented that Gopher was "the first Internet application my mom can use." Many universities quickly followed suit and created Gopher systems to catalog their online resources. A search engine was soon developed for finding documents stored on the numerous Gopher servers.

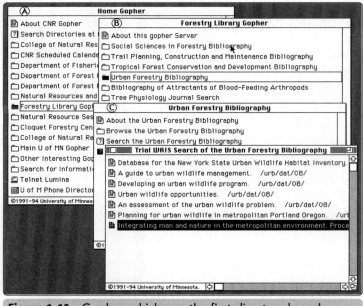

Figure 1-13   Gopher, which was the first directory-based Internet system, provided ease of navigation.

That same year, Tim Berners-Lee (Figure 1-14), who was working at CERN in Switzerland, envisioned the use of hyperlinks to make connections between related ideas in separate documents. **Hypertext**, which is a system of hyperlinks that allows users to click on a word to jump to another location within the same file, was already in use. Hypertext also allowed users to link to different files in the same location, but only when an index of the links was kept in a central database. Frustrated with these limitations, Berners-Lee visualized a system in which all of the various projects at CERN could cross-reference each other easily. He wrote a proposal outlining his vision, noting that hyperlinked resources were not restricted to text, but could include graphics, video, or other document elements.

Figure 1-14   Tim Berners-Lee originated the World Wide Web.

With the help of his CERN colleague Robert Cailliau, Berners-Lee created three technologies to make his ideas about hyperlinked documents a reality. First, he created the Hypertext Markup Language (HTML) which is used to create a document whose layout and content — text, graphics, and links — can be read by a special software program. Berners-Lee then created the special software program, the first browser known as WorldWideWeb (spelled with no spaces), to provide a way to view the HTML documents. Finally, because document links had to refer to a specific server where the linked documents were stored, Berners-Lee devised a Web addressing system and the **Hypertext Transfer Protocol (HTTP)**, a protocol that defines how HTML documents are transmitted to a browser. Figure 1-15 shows an early version of Berners-Lee's WorldWideWeb browser and HTML documents.

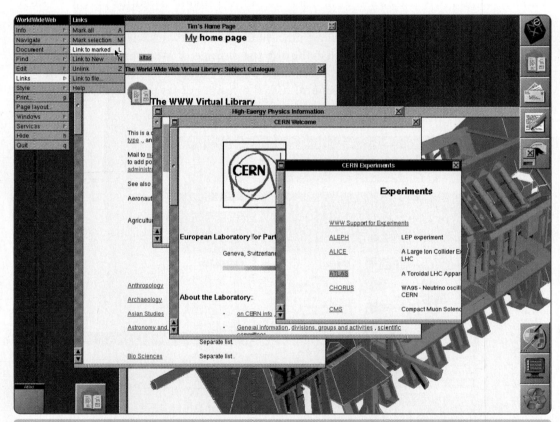

Figure 1-15 Berners-Lee's original WorldWideWeb browser and HTML documents.

Programmers began developing a number of other browsers, but the most widely used at universities and colleges was Mosaic. The Mosaic browser was created in March 1993 by Marc Andreessen and Eric Bina, two University of Illinois graduate students employed at the university's National Center for Supercomputing Applications (NCSA). Mosaic was easy to install and use, and free to university faculty and students, so it instantly became popular.

The next year, with businesses clamoring for a browser to use, Andreessen broke ties with the University of Illinois, which claimed ownership of the Mosaic browser. He joined with Silicon Valley entrepreneur Jim Clark to found a new company, Netscape Communications. Over the summer of 1994, the company created the first commercial browser called Netscape Navigator.

@Source

To learn more about Tim Berners-Lee and the early development of the Web, visit the Discovering the Internet Chapter 1 Web page (**scsite.com/ internet/ch1**) and click a link below Berners-Lee.

By 1994, the Internet was growing exponentially. The growth largely was fueled by increased usage of the new World Wide Web, named by Berners-Lee. Commercial and individual Web sites proliferated, radio stations began broadcasting over the Internet, and companies posted the first banner ads and sent the first bulk advertising by e-mail, now called **spam**. By the end of 1994, the Web had 10 million users and 10,000 hosts, of which 2,000 were commercial. Today, there are approximately a billion worldwide Web users and many thousands of hosts.

As commercial use of the Internet continued to grow, universities wanted to regain a high-speed network reserved specifically for research and education, much like the original Internet. In 1996, a new initiative called **Internet2** (**I2**) was born. I2 is a collaboration among universities, government, and industry to develop advanced network technologies and new uses for the Internet. I2 and its Canadian counterpart, CANARIE, (Figure 1-16) now have enlisted nearly 300 universities and firms to collaborate on developing several new technologies: an ultra high-speed network, new streaming video technologies, an infrastructure for distributing the storage of Web resources closer to the user, and standardized software to enhance security and operation of the I2 network. While I2 is not available for general use, the results of its research eventually will affect the general population of Internet users.

@Source

To learn more about Marc Andreessen and his role in the early development of commercial Web browsers, visit the Discovering the Internet Chapter 1 Web page (**scsite.com/ internet/ch1**) and click a link below Andreessen.

@Source

To learn more about Internet2 and its role in the future of the Internet, visit the Discovering the Internet Chapter 1 Web page (**scsite.com/ internet/ch1**) and click a link below Internet2.

Figure 1-16 Internet2 (I2) and its Canadian counterpart, CANARIE, are collaborations by universities, government, and industry to develop high-speed networking technologies.

Connecting to the Internet

To enjoy the benefits of e-mail, the Web, and the rest of the Internet, individuals and business must first connect their computers to the Internet. Many individuals rely on organizations, such as libraries, schools, and businesses, to provide access to the Internet. For example, most public libraries now have Internet-connected computers that anyone can use. Most businesses of any size now provide an Internet connection so their employees can use e-mail and the Web to complete their tasks. College and university students may have access to the Internet through campus networks and computer labs. Travelers can connect to the Internet using kiosks at airports or train stations and computers provided at cyber cafés.

Libraries, schools, businesses, and other organizations typically connect their computers via cables into a **local area network** (**LAN**). A LAN connects computers within a building or campus so users can share data and resources, such as printers. When an organization connects its local area network directly to the Internet, all the computers on the local area network have access to the Internet.

Connection Methods

Generally, local area networks are connected to the Internet via high-speed telephone lines or cable. A home computer is generally connected to the Internet using a telephone line or cable connection. Other connection methods include satellite, microwave, and wireless connections. In the following sections, you learn about different ways to connect to the Internet.

DIAL-UP The method for connecting to the Internet using a regular telephone line is known as **dial-up access**. Dial-up access works just like a standard phone connection, except that the call connects computer devices rather than people. To use a dial-up connection, a computer must have a **modem**, which is a card or device that converts a computer's digital data to an analog signal that can be sent over telephone lines. All of the wiring in the telephone system supports digital data, except for the short distance between the switching station and a customer's home, which is often called the last mile. Because the last mile is analog, a modem (Figure 1-17) still is required for dial-up access.

internal modem

notebook phone jack

Figure 1-17 A modem is required for dial-up Internet access.

Dial-up access is a common means of connecting to the Internet. Dial-up access is also the slowest connection option. Its maximum speed is 56.6 Kbps, but connection speeds typically range from 33 to 45 Kbps. A dial-up service is the least expensive Internet connection option, costing approximately $22 a month.

Another disadvantage to dial-up access is that you cannot use the telephone while the computer remains connected to the Internet. To get around this problem, you can install an additional telephone line so that you have a separate line designated for the computer. Also, it is possible to get a busy signal if a significant number of customers are trying to connect during peak hours and some inactive dial-up connections can disconnect after a certain period of time. A dial-up connection is considered a temporary connection.

DIGITAL SUBSCRIBER LINE (DSL)   A high-speed alternative to dial-up access is a **Digital Subscriber Line** (**DSL**). DSL is a sophisticated technology that condenses digital data and then sends it at high speeds over standard telephone wires. Just like dial-up, DSL uses existing telephone lines, but requires a special type of modem, a DSL modem. DSL comes in several variations; however, the DSL type used in most homes is ADSL, or asymmetric DSL, so called because it downloads data faster than it uploads data.

The main advantage of DSL is its fast speed, which is significantly faster than that of a dial-up connection. Using DSL at speeds ranging from 256 Kbps to 1.5 Mbps, Web pages appear quickly, and downloading music, software, and video is much faster than with a dial-up connection. DSL uses **broadband** transmission, which means it divides the telephone wire into separate channels for sending data, receiving data, and transmitting voice calls. Because it is broadband, you can talk on the telephone while the computer is online. In contrast, **baseband** transmission, like dial-up access, allows only one channel at a time.

Another advantage to using DSL is its dedicated connection. With a **dedicated connection**, the computer is always connected to the Internet. Unlike dial-up access, there is no waiting while the computer dials-up and there is no risk of getting a busy signal. A dedicated connection, however, also makes a computer more vulnerable to intruders. For this reason, many DSL services include a **firewall**, which is a security system that uses hardware and/or software to protect the computer from intruders.

One DSL disadvantage is lack of availability in some areas. DSL is available only in areas close to the telephone company's local exchange, called the central office (CO). DSL also is more costly than dial-up, at about $40 to $50 per month, although it saves the cost of an extra telephone needed for dial-up access. In addition, there may be an activation fee.

CABLE   Another high-speed Internet connection option is cable, which connects to the Internet using the same cable connection used by a cable television service. Cable access is a popular Internet connection option with many consumers who already have a cable television service in their homes. Cable access, like DSL, uses a dedicated connection to achieve maximum speeds of about 1.5 Mbps.

Cable Internet connections require a coaxial cable, a **line splitter** that divides the television signals from the data signals, a cable modem, and a network expansion card inside the computer (Figure 1-18). A **cable modem** is a particular type of modem used for high-speed cable connections.

line from cable company

television

computer

cable modem

Figure 1-18   Cable Internet access requires a line splitter and cable modem.

Like DSL, cable is asymmetric, meaning that it offers faster download speed than upload speed. Unlike DSL, however, the Internet connection is made over a cable shared with others in the neighborhood. As more people get online, the shared connection has less bandwidth available and becomes slower for everyone. Two major companies providing cable Internet service are AOL and Road Runner, although other local cable TV providers also may provide cable Internet service. Home service costs around $45 each month and may require an installation fee.

FIXED WIRELESS   People who live in a rural area where neither DSL nor cable service is offered must use a wireless connection to get high-speed Internet access. Wireless Internet access offers the additional benefit of having access to bandwidth that may not be limited by the capacity of the wires or cabling.

In a home or office, wireless Internet access is probably a **fixed wireless connection**, that is, a connection from a permanent, stationary location. Fixed wireless connections can use one of two technologies: satellite and microwave. Using satellite technology for an Internet connection requires specialized outside equipment: an antenna and a small dish or receiver. From these devices runs a cable to a specialized device connected to a computer. In addition to the purchase of this expensive equipment, satellite Internet service costs approximately $60 to $100 in monthly service fees.

Satellite Internet access comes in two varieties: one-way and two-way (Figure 1-19). One-way satellite access uses the satellite to download data and a slow, regular telephone line and modem for uploading data. A better alternative is two-way satellite access, which uses the faster satellite connection for both uploading and downloading data. The speed for a two-way digital satellite transmission is comparable to a cable transmission, around 1 Mbps. DirecWay, from the Hughes Electronic Corporation that offers DirecTV satellite television, is an example of a major two-way satellite Internet provider.

One-Way

Two-Way

Figure 1-19   Satellite Internet access can be one-way or two-way.

Like other types of Internet connections, digital satellite has some disadvantages. Snow, rain, wind, or even clouds also may affect the clarity of the signal. Further, the lengthy distance to the orbiting satellites can create a significant lag in the response time. The lag is not noticeable while browsing Web pages, but for communications such as instant messaging or chat, which take place simultaneously, or in **real time**, the lag may be noticeable.

Multipoint Microwave Distribution System (MMDS), also known as **microwave access**, is a fixed wireless means of Internet access by use of high-frequency radio waves. Connecting to the Internet using microwaves requires a receiver, similar to that used for satellite access. Microwave access depends on a rotating frequency of radio waves, and its speed ranges from 128 Kbps to 1.5 Mbps, depending on the traffic. While it is available in rural areas, microwave access is limited because the Internet user's location must be within 35 miles of the microwave tower. Further, the Internet user's location must have a clear line of sight to the microwave tower, because mountains or tall buildings will interfere with the microwave signal (Figure 1-20). Because microwave Internet access depends on local microwave towers, no nationwide or global providers yet exist.

Figure 1-20   Microwave Internet access must be within line of sight to prevent signal interference.

MOBILE WIRELESS   As you have learned, individuals access the Internet in other places besides at home or in the office. Public libraries often make Internet-connected computers available for the public to use. Travelers can access the Internet by using Internet kiosks at airports and other public places for approximately 25 cents per minute. Individuals can access the Internet at cyber cafés around the world for approximately $5 for 30 minutes of use (although access may be free to customers who purchase a beverage or snack). Business people often access the Internet while traveling by using wireless connections available for notebook computers and handheld devices, such as cell phones, personal digital assistants (PDAs), and tablet PCs.

One way to connect a notebook computer while on the road is to rely on one of the wireless networks that use Wi-Fi technologies. **Wi-Fi**, which is short for **wireless fidelity**, is a wireless networking standard (also known as IEEE 802.11b) that uses radio waves to allow a computer to communicate with other computers on a local area network or the Internet. A **hotspot** is a specific geographic location in which a wireless access point provides public Internet access. Hotspots can be found in hotels, airports, restaurants, coffee shops, convention centers, and other venues where people with notebook computers or handheld wireless devices are likely to need Internet access. A hotspot typically covers a 100- to 300-foot range from the wireless access point, although some may extend up to 15 miles. A **wireless access point** is a hardware device with an antenna that is connected to a wired network and is used to send and receive radio waves to notebook computers or other wireless devices.

To connect to a wireless access point in a hotspot, a notebook computer must have a Wi-Fi card and the correct software installed (Figure 1-21). After the computer is turned on, the software searches for a hotspot, and, if it finds one, connects to the Internet at speeds up to 11 Mbps. Wi-Fi connections may suffer interference from nearby microwave ovens and cordless telephones, because those devices use the same radio frequency.

@Source

To learn more about wireless Internet access and wireless hotspots, visit the Discovering the Internet Chapter 1 Web page (scsite.com/internet/ch1) and click a link below Hotspots.

Facts@Hand

The Gartner Group estimates that more than two million people currently use Wi-Fi Internet connections and that the number soon will double. According to International Data Corp., the number of hotspots will soar from 3,000 to 40,000 in the next several years.

As common as cell phones have become, it is not surprising that technologies are available to connect them to the Internet. Although not offered everywhere, these technologies quickly are becoming available in more locations. For example, a computer can connect to the Internet with a cable to a cell phone. Software installed on the computer then automatically connects to the Internet through the cell phone. Alternatively, a special **GSM/GPRS** (Global System for Mobile Communications and General Packet Radio Service) card can be installed in a computer. A GSM/GPRS card, such as the Sierra Air Card, allows the computer to connect automatically to a cellular phone network without using the cell

Figure 1-21   A notebook computer with a Wi-Fi card and special software installed can connect to a wireless access point in a hotspot.

phone (Figure 1-22). Further, many cell phones, PDAs, and tablet PCs now have wireless Internet access. Users can send and receive e-mail with attached files and photos, and browse the Web using these devices and a wireless Internet connection (Figure 1-23).

Figure 1-22   Computers can connect to the Internet using a cellular phone system.

Figure 1-23   Cell phones and PDAs can connect to the Internet using a wireless Internet connection.

Cell phone and PDA connection speeds range up to 115 Kbps, about double that of standard dial-up, but 50 Kbps is more typical. Depending on the cell phone calling plan, the cost is based on either the number of airtime minutes or the number of kilobytes of data transmitted. Per-kilobyte costs typically range from one to three cents per kilobyte. Given that one e-mail message online requires about 15 KB of data transfer, heavy usage can be expensive.

HIGH-SPEED BUSINESS CONNECTIONS   As more people use a single connection, the more bandwidth is required. For this reason, businesses, even small businesses, generally need higher-speed connections than individuals and thus typically choose a high-speed Internet connection, such as DSL or cable. Companies generally pay more for their Internet connections than individuals, beginning at $60 to $200 a month for cable or DSL access. While more expensive, these connections typically offer higher-speed connections than those for individuals.

As businesses grow and their demand for bandwidth increases, the technology requirements also increase. Typical medium to large businesses may lease or install a fiber-optic loop directly into their building. A **fiber-optic loop** is a dedicated, high-speed telephone line that uses fiber-optic cable with T1 or other fiber-optic technology. A leased **T1 line**, also called a DS1 line, is a type of fiber-optic line that supports data transfer rates of 1.5 Mbps for hundreds of users simultaneously and costs about $1,000 per month. Expanded options include T3 or DS3 lines, which offer a 10 Mbps line (the equivalent of 28 T1 lines) for about $25,000 to $30,000 per month. The largest firms requiring the highest capacity and speed use high-speed fiber-optic networks which cost well over $100,000 a month.

Internet Service Providers (ISPs)

A company that provides Internet access for homes and businesses is called an **Internet Service Provider (ISP)**. Thousands of local, regional, and national ISPs (Figure 1-24) offer a wide variety of services. An individual or a business must weigh several considerations when choosing an ISP, including:

- The speed or bandwidth of the connection
- The type of connection and cost of service
- Availability of customer service and technical support

Figure 1-24 Thousands of local, regional, and national ISPs offer a variety of services.

@Source

To review various
ISPs and learn
more about
Internet
connection
speeds, visit the
Discovering the
Internet Chapter 1
Web page
(**scsite.com/
internet/ch1**) and
click a link below
Broadband.

 @Source

To read Federal
Trade Commission
tips about ISPs
and their free
offers, visit the
Discovering the
Internet Chapter 1
Web page
(**scsite.com/
internet/ch1**) and
click a link below
ISP Alert.

The speed of an Internet connection depends on **bandwidth**, which is the capacity of the communications channel. Just as the speed of travel depends on the capacity of a road — for example, whether the road is a multilane freeway or an unpaved road — the bandwidth of an Internet connection defines the amount of data that can be transmitted in a fixed amount of time.

The bandwidth of an Internet connection is measured in **bits per second** (**bps**). A **bit**, short for binary digit, is the smallest unit of electronic data. A bit is represented as the digit one (1) or zero (0), which is why computers are described using the term, digital. Thousands of bits flow each second, even over the slowest connection. Connection speeds can range from a thousand bits per second, called **kilobits per second** (**Kbps**), to a million bits per second, called **megabits per second** (**Mbps**), to a billion bits per second, called **gigabits per second** (**Gbps**).

As noted above, the speed of the transmission is just one factor to consider when choosing an ISP. You also need to consider how you will physically connect your computer to the Internet, whether through dial-up, DSL, cable, or wireless connections. As you have learned, each of these Internet connection methods has advantages and disadvantages, related to speed, cost, features, and convenience. Figure 1-25 summarizes the features for the Internet connection methods discussed earlier.

Many ISPs offer premium services, including a unique interface, special content, e-mail, instant messaging, and space to store Web pages or photographs online. By contrast, a free ISP offers free Internet access with basic features, but requires users to view on-screen advertisements as they use the service. In the middle are many other ISPs that offer simple packages with e-mail and Web page hosting services for a monthly fee.

Customer service and technical support offered by an ISP are always important factors and should be available 24 hours a day, seven days a week. When comparing price, note that while a national ISP may cost more than a comparable local provider, the national ISP provides the added advantage of having local access numbers for major cities available if you travel frequently and require Internet access while traveling.

Method	Advantages	Disadvantages	Speed	Cost per month
Dial-up	• Least expensive • Available wherever there is a telephone connection	• Slowest • Cannot make telephone calls while connected • May encounter busy signals • May be disconnected after set amount of time	Up to 56.6 Kbps	Ranges from free to approximately $25
DSL	• High speed • Dedicated connection so no busy signals • Always connected • No need for extra line for voice telephone calls	• Available only near telephone company central office	256 Kbps to 1.5 Mbps	$40 to $50, plus possible activation fee of approximately $100
Cable	• High speed • Dedicated connection so no busy signals • Always connected	• Available only where cable TV is offered • Slows down when too many neighbors are online	1.5 Mbps downstream, 256 Kbps upstream	$45, plus possible installation fee of approximately $100
Satellite	• High speed • Available everywhere	• Expensive equipment needed • Weather may interfere with signal • Potential lag time	1 Mbps downstream, 256 Kbps to 1 Mbps upstream	$60 to $100, plus cost of installing dish and cabling
Microwave	• High speed • Only available locally	• Line of sight to tower required • Range must be within 35 miles of tower	From 128 Kpbs to 1.5 Mbps	$200 and up per month, including equipment
Wi-Fi	• High speed • Wireless • Mobile use	• Limited availability • Must remain within 300 feet of receiver • May have interference from cordless phone or microwave oven • Requires Wi-Fi card	Up to 11 Mbps	$75, though prices may come down as it becomes more available
Cell phone	• Mobile use • Wireless	• Limited availability • Requires cell phone or GSM/GPRS card	Up to 115 Kbps	Depends on cell phone contract

Figure 1-25 Comparison of major Internet connection methods.

CHAPTER REVIEW

The Chapter Review section summarizes the concepts presented in the chapter.

1 What Is the Internet?

The **Internet** is a worldwide network of networks. The Internet allows individual and business users to communicate, share information, and conduct business transactions. Businesses, governments, academic institutions, non-profit organizations, and other organizations and individuals can use their computers to communicate across the Internet because their computers use a common suite of communications **protocols** called **TCP/IP**.

2 Who Uses the Internet and How Do They Use It?

People of all ages and stations in life find that using the Internet enriches their lives. Many people use the Internet to find information on a vast range of topics for school, work, hobbies, or personal enrichment. Internet users send and receive **e-mail**, send instant messages, participate in online chat, and use mailing lists and newsgroups to communicate with loved ones, colleagues, and clients. Other users **download** and **upload** music, software, and images over the Internet and **publish** Web pages that include personal **links**, photos, or a **weblog**. Businesses conduct business transactions with their customers, vendors, and employees over the Internet.

The **Web** is a subset of the Internet that supports **Web pages**, which can include text, graphics, animation, sound, or video. Related Web pages are part of a **Web site**. Web pages are interconnected by **hyperlinks**, which enable a user to move from one page to another, perhaps on the same or another **site**. A **browser**, such as Microsoft Internet Explorer and Netscape Navigator, allows users to access and view Web pages, while a **search engine** allows users to find specific resources.

Businesses use the Internet for a variety of purposes. **E-business** is the use of the Internet for marketing, offering information, and maintaining partnerships with key constituents. **E-commerce**, the act of conducting business transactions over the Internet, is a subset of e-business. E-business may connect a business with other businesses (**B2B**), with consumers (**B2C**), or with employees (**B2E**), or it may connect individuals with each other (**C2C**) for doing business.

3 What Are the Key Events in the History of the Internet?

The Internet has its roots in **ARPANET**, a research and defense initiative of the U.S. government in collaboration with technology firms and universities. In 1969, the ARPANET network connected four computers at different universities for the first time. The computers used the **packet switching** technology developed by Leonard Kleinrock of UCLA. As the network connected more computers, the TCP and IP protocols developed by Vinton Cerf and Robert Kahn became the standard. In 1971 Ray Tomlinson developed and sent the first e-mail; within two years, e-mail accounted for 75 percent of the traffic on the Internet.

In 1990, the NSFnet superseded ARPANET as the main government network linking universities and research facilities. The U.S. Congress opened the Internet to commercial use in 1992, and e-business grew. The NSF maintained the major Internet backbones until 1995, when the NSF migrated the connections to commercial networks.

The general population began to take an interest in the Internet in the mid- to late 1980s when personal computers came into wide use and BITNET, USENET, and Gopher were developed. Tim Berners-Lee's development of the Web in 1991 caused Internet usage to explode. Berners-Lee developed the use of hyperlinks between different files, HTML to create Web documents, the addressing scheme and the WorldWideWeb browser. In 1993, Marc Andreessen released the Mosaic browser to universities; in 1994, he created a new commercial browser, called Netscape Navigator. Businesses and individuals soon discovered the possibilities available online, and the use of the Internet expanded rapidly.

 4 How Do Individuals and Businesses Connect to the Internet?

Computers connected to the Internet are available in libraries, schools, or cyber cafés, either for free or for a small fee or at the office through an employer's local area network. The Internet can be accessed with a dial-up connection via a telephone line; with a DSL connection via a telephone line; with a cable connection; or by satellite or microwaves for a wireless connection.

Mobile users can connect their notebooks or handheld wireless devices via their cell phones or using **Wi-Fi**. Wi-Fi users can find a hotspot and connect to a wireless access point. Handheld devices such as PDAs and cell phones offer limited e-mail and Web browsing as well. Businesses require high speeds and large capacity, so they typically connect a **fiber-optic loop** directly to their building.

Individuals and businesses use a telephone line, cable, or wireless connection to access the Internet through an **Internet Service Provider** (**ISP**). When choosing an ISP, key considerations include the cost of the equipment and monthly subscription, as well as the connection speed.

CHAPTER REVIEW

The Chapter Review section summarizes the concepts presented in the chapter.

TERMS TO KNOW

After reading this chapter, you should know each term.

ARPANET (*13*)
backbone (*15*)
bandwidth (*26*)
baseband (*20*)
bit (*26*)
bits per second (bps) (*26*)
blog (*6*)
broadband (*20*)
browser (*8*)
browsing (*8*)
business-to-business (B2B) (*11*)
business-to-consumer (B2C) (*11*)
business-to-employee (B2E) (*11*)
cable modem (*21*)
circuit switching (*13*)
consumer-to-consumer (C2C) (*11*)
cyberstalking (*12*)
dedicated connection (*20*)
dial-up access (*19*)
Digital Subscriber Line (DSL) (*20*)
download (*10*)
e-business (*11*)
e-commerce (*11*)
electronic mail (*9*)
e-mail (*9*)
e-mail program (*9*)
fiber-optic loop (*25*)
File Transfer Protocol (FTP) (*10*)
firewall (*20*)
fixed wireless connection (*21*)
gigabits per second (Gbps) (*26*)
Gopher (*16*)
GSM/GPRS (*23*)
host (*4*)
hotspot (*23*)
hyperlink (*8*)
hypertext (*16*)
Hypertext Markup Language (HTML) (*7*)
Hypertext Transfer Protocol (HTTP) (*17*)

Internet (*4*)
Internet Protocol (IP) (*14*)
Internet Service Provider (ISP) (*25*)
Internet2 (I2) (*18*)
kilobits per second (Kbps) (*26*)
line splitter (*21*)
link (*8*)
local area network (LAN) (*19*)
megabits per second (Mbps) (*26*)
microwave access (*22*)
modem (*19*)
online (*4*)
packet switching (*13*)
packets (*13*)
protocol (*4*)
published (*7*)
real time (*22*)
search tool (*8*)
server (*10*)
site (*7*)
spam (*18*)
surfing (*8*)
T1 line (*25*)
TCP/IP (Transmission Control Protocol/Internet Protocol) (*5*)
Telnet (*11*)
Transmission Control Protocol (TCP) (*14*)
upload (*10*)
Web (*6*)
Web authoring software (*7*)
Web browser (*8*)
Web pages (*6*)
Web server (*7*)
Web site (*7*)
weblog (*6*)
Wi-Fi (*23*)
wireless access point (*23*)
wireless fidelity (*23*)
World Wide Web (*6*)
World Wide Web Consortium (W3C) (*9*)

True or False

Mark T for True and F for False. (Answers are found on page numbers in parentheses.)

_____ 1. While Internet usage is very popular among teenagers and young adults, it is not used by senior citizens. (*6*)

_____ 2. The Internet is a collection of Web pages and other information stored on computers. (*4*)

_____ 3. The terms, World Wide Web, Web, and Internet, are interchangeable and refer to the same thing. (*4, 6*)

_____ 4. The most popular Internet activity is e-mail. (*15*)

_____ 5. Telnet is used to log in to remote computers. (*11*)

_____ 6. E-commerce specifically refers to completing business transactions, such as buying and selling goods, over the Internet. (*11*)

_____ 7. The person who first outlined the idea of packet switching was Leonard Kleinrock. (*13*)

_____ 8. Telecommunications firms, governments, and online businesses own the Internet. (*5*)

_____ 9. The speed of an Internet connection typically is measured in bits per second. (*26*)

_____ 10. Most large businesses connect to the Internet using a dial-up connection. (*24*)

Multiple Choice

Select the best answer. (Answers are found on page numbers in parentheses.)

1. People use the Internet for _____ . (*5-6*)
   a. researching for school and personal interests
   b. doing business and shopping
   c. communicating with friends, clients, and colleagues
   d. all of the above

2. Different types of computers can communicate across the Internet because they follow the same set rules or standards called _____ . (*5*)
   a. FTP
   b. hosts
   c. TCP/IP
   d. Telnet

3. A(n) _____ is a software program used to view Web pages. (*8*)
   a. browser
   b. FTP client
   c. search engine
   d. Web authoring package

(continued)

TEST YOUR KNOWLEDGE

Use the Test Your Knowledge exercises to check your knowledge of the chapter.

TEST YOUR KNOWLEDGE (continued)

4. FTP is used for _____ . (*10*)
   a. e-mail
   b. chatting and instant messaging
   c. Web conferencing
   d. none of the above

5. Web pages are created using _____ codes or tags. (*7*)
   a. backbone
   b. FrontPage
   c. HTML
   d. Wi-Fi

6. E-business takes a number of forms, including _____ . (*11*)
   a. B2C, in which businesses stay in contact with consultants
   b. B2B, in which firms do business online with other firms and businesses
   c. B2E, which connects businesses in North America with those in Europe
   d. all of the above

7. The Internet began with **ARPANET** in _____ . (*13*)
   a. 1951
   b. 1969
   c. 1975
   d. 1991

8. The person who is credited with inventing the Web is _____ . (*16*)
   a. Marc Andreessen
   b. Tim Berners-Lee
   c. Vincent Cerf
   d. all of the above

9. A telephone Internet connection that provides a high-speed, dedicated, and always-on connection to the Internet is _____ . (*20*)
   a. cable
   b. dial-up
   c. DSL
   d. all of the above

10. When choosing an ISP, you should consider _____ . (*25-27*)
   a. whether or not you need local access numbers nationwide
   b. access to technical support
   c. whether you prefer low cost or high-speed connectivity
   d. all of the above

Instructions: To complete the Learn It Online exercises, start your browser, click the Address bar, and then enter the Web address **scsite.com/internet/ch1**. Follow the instructions in the exercises below. Each exercise has instructions for printing your results, either for your own records or for submission to your instructor.

1 Chapter Reinforcement

TF, MC, and SA
Click the Chapter Reinforcement link. Print the quiz by clicking Print on the File menu for each page. Answer each question.

2 Flash Cards

Click the Flash Cards link and read the instructions. Type **20** (or a number specified by your instructor) in the Number of playing cards text box, type your name in the Enter your Name text box, and then click the Flip Card button. When the flash card is displayed, read the question and then click the Answer box arrow to select an answer. Flip through Flash Cards. If your score is 15 (75%) correct or greater, click Print on the File menu to print your results. If your score is less than 15 (75%) correct, then redo this exercise by clicking the Replay button.

3 Practice Test

Click the Practice Test link. Answer each question, enter your first and last name at the bottom of the page, and then click the Grade Test button. When the graded practice test is displayed on your screen, click Print on the File menu to print a hard copy. Continue to take practice tests until you score 80% or better.

4 Who Wants To Be a Computer Genius?

Click the Computer Genius link. Read the instructions, enter your first and last name at the bottom of the page, and then click the Play button. When your score is displayed, click the Print Results link to print a hard copy.

5 Crossword Puzzle Challenge

Below Chapter 1, click the Crossword Puzzle Challenge link. Read the instructions, and then enter your first and last name. Click the SUBMIT button. Work the crossword puzzle. When you are finished, click the Submit button. When the crossword puzzle is redisplayed, click the Print Puzzle button to print a hard copy.

EXERCISES

Use the Exercises to gain hands-on Internet experience.

To perform the following exercises, you must be connected to the Internet and have access to a printer.

1 Student Use of the Internet

1. According to a study by the Pew Internet & American Life Project, many students rely on the Internet to help them in their academic work. Survey five students, asking how they use the Internet for their studies. Listen for their answers to see if they mention items a through e, as outlined in Step 2.

2. Tabulate how many of the five students use the Internet for each of the following purposes:
   a. To look up information, to act as a reference library, or to get sources for reports, presentations, and projects
   b. To plagiarize content or cheat
   c. To collaborate with classmates on projects, or to study or share class notes with classmates
   d. To keep track of class schedules, assignments, and syllabi
   e. To choose a university, major, or future career path

3. Ask the students whether they have access to the Internet during class time under teacher direction or only outside of class or lab time. As a follow-up question, ask how effective they think that approach is.

4. Find out whether they feel there is a difference between students who have Internet access at home and those who do not. Write a paragraph explaining what those differences are and how they might impact academic work.

5. Summarize the importance of the Internet to students, according to the results of your survey.

2 Use of the Internet

1. Survey five people who have Internet access in their homes. Try to survey both men and women and people of all ages.

2. Ask them to define the Internet and tell what year they first began to use the Internet.

3. Ask them to estimate how much time each week they spend online for each of the following purposes:
   a. To browse the Web for work or school
   b. To browse the Web for entertainment or leisure
   c. To send e-mail
   d. To chat or send instant messages
   e. To play games
   f. To download music, software, or other files
   g. To create and publish their own Web pages, photos, or weblogs
   h. To compare prices and look for product information
   i. To buy or sell items

4. Ask them what browser they use. After you have completed the survey, calculate the total number for each browser.

5. Ask them how they access e-mail and how many e-mail addresses each person has.

6. Ask them if the time they spend using the Internet has affected the time spent other activities, such as watching television, reading books, shopping in stores, and so on.

7. Summarize the differences in how various age groups and sexes use the Internet.

3 ISP Satisfaction

1. Survey five people who use various ISPs, asking the questions below to determine their level of satisfaction.
   a. Do you ever get busy signals during peak hours?
   b. How satisfied are you with the speed of your connection?
   c. Was the software or connection easy to install and set up?
   d. Have you ever had to contact technical support or billing services? Did you contact them by telephone or e-mail? Was your problem answered promptly and solved to your satisfaction?
   e. Have you had any billing troubles? How much effort did it take for them to be resolved?
   f. With what aspects of your ISP are you most satisfied? Most dissatisfied?

2. Compare the results. Determine where ISP users seem to experience the most problems and where they have the best experience.

3. Summarize whether these users are satisfied with their ISPs overall or would prefer to change to another ISP.

4. Write a paragraph analyzing which ISP seems to give the best customer service and satisfaction.

4 History of Internet

1. Use written resources to learn more about the Internet's history. If you prefer, you can use links to online resources located on this book's companion Web site. To do so, follow this optional step: visit the Discovering the Internet Chapter 1 Web page (**scsite.com/internet/ch1**) and click a link below Exercise 4.

2. Find the names and accomplishments of three individuals not mentioned in this chapter who played key roles in the development of the Internet and the Web.

3. Write a paragraph on the origin or development of one of the following elements of the Internet:
   a. USENET
   b. LISTSERV or mailing lists
   c. BITNET
   d. IRC
   e. hypertext
   f. any computer hardware or device used in the Internet

(continued)

EXERCISE (continued)

4. Make a set of trivia questions about the history of the Internet from your reading, either in this book or from other research. Ask several friends the questions and record how many of them correctly answer each question.

5 Who Owns the Internet

1. Look for an article or opinion piece on who owns the Internet, using print or electronic sources. If you prefer, you can use links to online resources located on this book's companion Web site. To do so, follow this optional step: visit the Discovering the Internet Chapter 1 Web page (**scsite.com/internet/ch1**) and click a link below Exercise 5 to access an article on Internet ownership.

2. Print or photocopy the article. Underline or highlight the sentences that express the author's view of Internet ownership.

3. Summarize the article in a paragraph or two. Include an analysis of the author's view of Internet ownership.

6 Defining the Internet

To perform the following exercise, you must be connected to the Internet and know how to browse. You also must have access to a printer and know how to print Web pages.

1. Visit the Discovering the Internet Chapter 1 Web page (**scsite.com/internet/ch1**) and click the Definitions link below Exercise 6 to access the Webopedia Web site.

2. Type the following keywords into the Webopedia Search box and press Enter. Write down the core part of the definition for each word.
   a. Internet
   b. Web
   c. TCP/IP
   d. protocol
   e. host

3. Click the Did You Know link on the left side of the page. Scroll to display the heading, Internet, and then click a link for one of the topics related to this chapter. Print the article.

4. Write a paragraph to evaluate how effective the Webopedia site is as a resource for learning about the Internet.

7 Global Internet Use

To perform the following exercise, you must be connected to the Internet and know how to browse.

1. Visit the Discovering the Internet Chapter 1 Web page (**scsite.com/internet/ch1**) and click the CyberAtlas link below Exercise 7.
   a. Read the article.
   b. Read the introductory remarks to determine the number of nations who account for 90 percent of the global online users. List the names of the countries.
   c. List two countries that have surprisingly few ISPs and people online relative to their overall population.

2. Visit the Discovering the Internet Chapter 1 Web page (**scsite.com/internet/ch1**) and click the How Many Online link below Exercise 7. Write down the continents from highest to lowest population of Internet users.

3. Visit the Discovering the Internet Chapter 1 Web page (**scsite.com/internet/ch1**) and click the World Total link below Exercise 7. View the historical growth of the Internet and analyze whether you see growth in the total percentage of the world's online population.

4. Visit the Discovering the Internet Chapter 1 Web page (**scsite.com/internet/ch1**) and click the Global Reach link below Exercise 7. Click the global Internet statistics link. Write down how much of the online population is non-English speaking. Sketch a pie chart that shows the most common languages used by Internet users. Include labels and percents.

 8 Finding ISPs

To perform the following exercise, you must be connected to the Internet and know how to browse.

1. Visit the Discovering the Internet Chapter 1 Web page (**scsite.com/internet/ch1**) and click the The List link below Exercise 8 to access the Web site for an Internet services buyer's guide.

2. Click the link to display the list by Location/Area Code. List four ISPs for your area that offer dial-up access. List one that offers a dedicated or high-speed connection. List one specializing in being a low-cost provider.

3. Click the link to display the list by U.S. Nationwide. List an ISP for each of the following categories: dial-up, business and dedicated, DSL/cable, and fixed wireless.

4. Click the link to display the list by Country Code. Select a small country and examine the ISPs. Write down how many exist, and describe what sort of connections are available.

5. Look in the telephone directory to find the telephone numbers of three ISPs that provide service in your area. Contact the ISPs to learn about their prices and services. Make a comparison chart of prices and services.

EXERCISES

Use the Exercises to gain hands-on Internet experience.

(continued)

EXERCISES

Use the
Exercises to
gain hands-on
Internet
experience.

EXERCISE *(continued)*

 9 Connection Speed

To perform the following exercise, you must be connected to the Internet and know how to browse.

1. Visit the Discovering the Internet Chapter 1 Web page (**scsite.com/internet/ch1**) and click the links below Exercise 9 to view connection speed tests.

2. Try the bandwidth tests and record the results.

3. Summarize the results of the tests and explain whether the connection speeds are considered slow, average, or fast, according to the bandwidth speed test sites.

4. At the direction of your instructor, repeat the tests at different times of the day over several days. Write a brief paragraph explaining any variation in connection speeds over the different days and times of day.

10 Wireless Connections

To perform the following exercise, you must be connected to the Internet and know how to browse.

1. Visit the Discovering the Internet Chapter 1 Web page (**scsite.com/internet/ch1**) and click the Hotspots link below Exercise 10. Use the Web site search tools to find the following information:
    a. List the locations of hotspots closest to your home.
    b. Find a hotspot for a travel destination you might enjoy visiting.
    c. List three countries that offer hotspots for wireless access.

2. Visit the Discovering the Internet Chapter 1 Web page (**scsite.com/internet/ch1**) and click the Cyber Cafés link below Exercise 10. Find answers for the following items:
    a. List the number of cyber cafés that are located in the largest city near your hometown.
    b. Describe the Internet facilities provided by cruise ship lines.
    c. Write down the names of five businesses that offer public Internet access.
    d. Find the location of a cyber café on each continent (except Antarctica).

3. At the direction of your instructor, visit a cellular phone or electronics store for a demonstration of how a cell phone or PDA can be used to access the Internet. Write a paragraph summarizing your visit and describing how easy or difficult it is to connect to the Internet using a cell phone or PDA. Discuss whether or not you would use a cell phone or PDA to access the Internet and give the reasons for your answer.

NOTES

CHAPTER 2
Browsing the Web

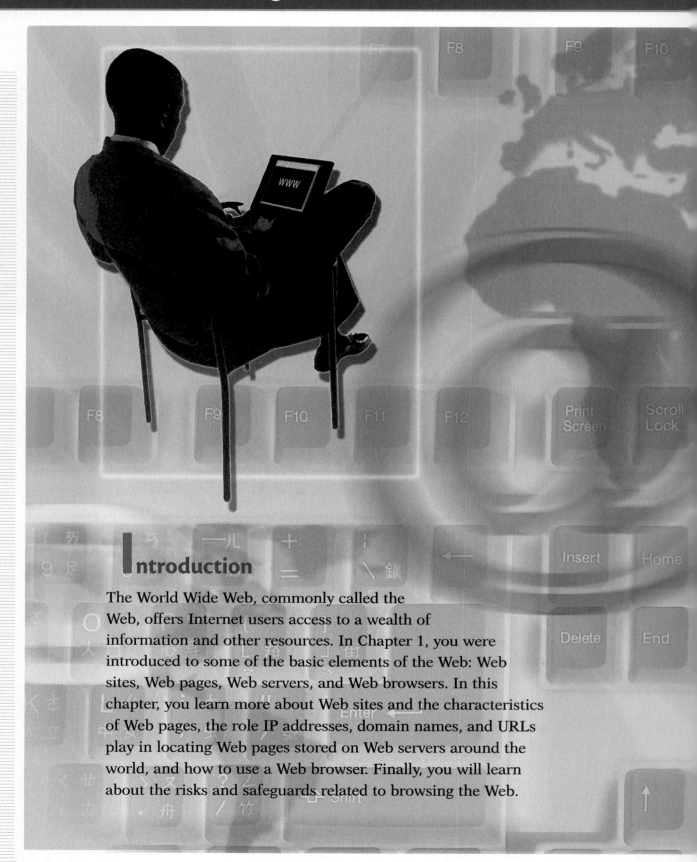

Introduction

The World Wide Web, commonly called the
Web, offers Internet users access to a wealth of
information and other resources. In Chapter 1, you were
introduced to some of the basic elements of the Web: Web
sites, Web pages, Web servers, and Web browsers. In this
chapter, you learn more about Web sites and the characteristics
of Web pages, the role IP addresses, domain names, and URLs
play in locating Web pages stored on Web servers around the
world, and how to use a Web browser. Finally, you will learn
about the risks and safeguards related to browsing the Web.

OBJECTIVES

After completing this chapter, you will be able to:

1. Describe a Web site, common Web page characteristics, and Web servers

2. Explain the role IP addresses, domain names, and URLs play in locating Web pages

3. Start a Web browser and view Web pages

4. Revisit Web pages using browser and desktop shortcuts

5. Describe ways to save online information for later use

6. Demonstrate how to change Web browser options

7. Discuss the risks and safeguards related to using the Web

CONTENTS

Web Sites, Web Pages, and Web Servers

Since its beginnings in the early 1990s, the Web has grown at an exponential rate. Today, the Web consists of millions of Web sites and billions of pages. Getting an accurate and up-to-date count of Web sites and Web pages is virtually impossible because of the dynamic nature of the Web. New pages are continually being added to existing Web sites and old pages removed. Additionally, new Web sites are being published at an amazing pace. In this section, you learn about the types of Web pages included at these Web sites, the general characteristics of a Web page, and the role Web servers play in making these sites and pages available to people around the world.

@Source

For the latest statistics on the number of Web sites available to the public, visit the Discovering the Internet Chapter 2 Web page (**scsite.com/ internet/ch2**) and click a link below Growth.

Web Sites

The number of pages at a Web site can vary, based on the site's purpose and the type of content and services the site provides. A personal Web site, for example, might consist of a single Web page, called a home page, containing relevant information about an individual. A **home page** is the primary page at a Web site. Alternatively, the site might also include additional pages containing photos of friends and family, a résumé, a portfolio of school projects, a list of hobbies, or other content. All of the pages are then linked together so viewers can move quickly from page to page.

Typically, the Web site for an e-business or other organization includes multiple pages: a home page with general, introductory information and links to a variety of related Web pages containing information about products and services, employment opportunities, the organization's history, contact information, and so forth (Figure 2-1). Many organizations also include one or more Web pages listing **FAQs (frequently asked questions)**. FAQ pages provide answers to questions commonly asked by Web site viewers.

@Source

To learn more about Web portals, visit the Discovering the Internet Chapter 2 Web page (**scsite.com/ internet/ch2**) and click a link below Portals.

A **Web portal**, or simply a **portal**, is a special type of Web site that offers a doorway to a wide range of content and services. Some Web portals are created specifically to serve as an all-encompassing starting point for viewers when they start their browsers. These types of portals generally offer local, national, and international news; weather and sports scores; access to references tools, such as online white or yellow pages; market information and stock tickers; maps and driving instructions; links to other general-purpose sites; and a search tool. Web sites such as Yahoo!, Lycos, and MSN are general-interest portals.

Other portals, such as Golf.com or The Dog Portal.com, focus on a more narrow range of information and services and appeal to viewers with specific interests, such as golf or pets and pet care. Figure 2-2 illustrates examples of both general-interest and specific-interest portals.

Figure 2-1 A multi-page Web site consists of a home page and linked subsidiary pages.

Figure 2-2 Web portals can provide a broad range of information and services or can focus on a specific interest.

Web Pages

A Web page is designed to attract and hold viewers' attention so that they spend time at that Web page and others at the Web site. A well-designed Web page draws viewers to items of potential interest and includes links to lead viewers to investigate other Web pages. Most commercial Web pages and many non-commercial Web pages share some or all of the following characteristics (Figure 2-3) that make the pages more attractive and easier to use.

- A logo and Web site name generally appear at or near the top-left corner of a Web page to help viewers identify the site.
- Various images, including photographs, graphics, and animations are used to make a site more interesting and attractive.
- Links to related pages, often grouped into categories with headings, are included to make the site's content more useful.
- Advertisements, which may be images or links on a Web page, are included to generate revenue for the Web site.
- A search tool that allows viewers to locate specific information at the site or at other sites on the Web is often included.
- A copyright statement notifying viewers that all the content at the site is protected by copyright law is usually included.
- A link to a privacy policy statement informing viewers about the type of information collected from them at the site and how it is used. It is commonly found at the bottom of a commercial Web page.

Figure 2-3   Most commercial Web pages share common characteristics such as logos, images, links, advertisements, search tools, a copyright statement, and a privacy statement.

As you have learned, Web sites and individual Web pages are dynamic. New Web pages are constantly being added to sites and old ones removed. The content on most individual Web pages and the pages' layout and design are also constantly changing; thus, the Web pages you see on your screen as you work through the projects in this text may not look exactly like the Web page illustrations.

Web Servers

Before a Web browser can display a Web page, it must first send a request for a copy of the page to the Web server where the page is stored. The Web server responds to the request by sending a copy of the page to the browser. This process is an example of **client-server computing**, in which a client, the Web browser, requests services from another computer, the Web server (Figure 2-4).

Figure 2-4 The interaction between a Web browser and a Web server is an example of client/server computing.

Typically, a **client** is an application that runs on a computer, such as a personal computer, and requests resources or services from another computer. A server is a computer that *serves up*, or provides, the requested resources or services. A server might be located in the same building, in a nearby building, or, in the case of a Web server, anywhere in the world.

A single Web server can store or host many small Web sites (Figure 2-5). For example, hundreds of students at a college or university can create personal Web sites and store them on the university's Web server. Larger Web sites, such as those created by e-businesses or other organizations, often are stored across multiple Web servers (Figure 2-6).

Figure 2-5　A single Web server can host several small Web sites.

Figure 2-6　Large Web sites can span several Web servers.

IP Addresses, Domain Names, and URLs

In order for a Web browser to request a Web page, it must know where that page is stored. IP addresses, domain names, and URLs all play a role allowing a browser to locate Web pages. In this section, you learn how an IP address is structured, how the Domain Name System and domain names are used, and the components of a URL.

IP Addresses

An **IP address (Internet Protocol address)**, is a number that uniquely identifies each computer or device connected to the Internet. Just as a postal service relies on mailing addresses to ensure that mail is delivered to the correct recipient, the Internet relies on a computer's unique IP address to ensure that data is sent to the correct computer or device. An IP address consists of four groups of numbers, each separated by periods, or dots. For example, the IP address 198.80.146.30 is the IP address of a Course Technology Web server. Course Technology is the publisher of this book.

A personal computer at home or at the office must have an IP address when it is connected to the Internet. Computers that are always connected to the Internet, such as Web servers or personal computers with a broadband connection, typically have a permanent or **static IP address** that seldom changes. Computers that connect to the Internet via a temporary connection, such as a dial-up connection to an ISP, generally are assigned a temporary or **dynamic IP address** for the duration of the connection.

Domain Names

Because complex, numeric IP addresses are difficult for people to remember, Web servers typically are referenced by a domain name. A **domain name** is a text alias for one or more IP addresses. The domain name, course.com, for example, corresponds to the IP address 198.80.146.30. When a domain name, such as course.com, is entered in a browser, the browser must look up the corresponding IP address by requesting the IP address from a Domain Name System (DNS) name server. The **Domain Name System (DNS)** consists of name servers that contain databases with domain names and the numeric IP addresses to which they correspond. The DNS translates, or *resolves*, the domain name to its IP address and returns the IP address to the browser so that the request for a Web page then can be sent to the Web server where the page is stored.

✋ Facts@Hand

You can find the numeric IP address that corresponds to a domain name by using the nslookup command. To use the nslookup command, click the Start button, click Run on the Start menu, type `nslookup` in the Open text box, and then click the OK button. Type a domain name after the > prompt. The window will display the IP address for your computer, as well as the one for the domain name you entered.

Because domain names must be unique, domain names are registered, much like trademarks. The organization that manages the DNS and controls the domain name registration system is The **Internet Corporation for Assigned Names and Numbers (ICANN)**. ICANN is a non-profit organization that operates under the auspices of the U.S. Department of Commerce.

 @Source

To learn more about ICANN, visit the Discovering the Internet Chapter 2 Web page (**scsite.com/ internet/ch2**) and click a link below ICANN.

Domain names are grouped by **top-level domain** (**TLD**), which is an abbreviation that identifies the type of organization associated with the domain. Originally, only seven generic top-level domains, such as .com, .edu, and .org, were created. Today, there are a number of additional top-level domains as shown in Figure 2-7. Each nation of the world also has its own **country-code top-level domain** (**ccTLD**), such as .us for the U.S., .ca for Canada, and .uk for the Great Britain (the United Kingdom).

TLD Abbreviation	Type of Domain	TLD Abbreviation	Type of Domain
.com	Commercial firms	.aero	Aviation industry
.edu	Educational institutions	.biz	Businesses
.gov	Government entities	.coop	Cooperatives
.mil	Military groups	.info	All uses
.net	Major networking centers	.museum	Museums
.org	Non-profit organizations	.name	Individuals
.int	International organizations	.pro	Professionals

Figure 2-7   Domains in the DNS are grouped by type of organization.

 Facts@Hand

The South Pacific island nation of Tuvalu will reap more than $50 million in royalties for the lease of its popular ccTLD, .tv.

Uniform Resource Locators (URLs)

Each Web page also has its own unique address. A **Uniform Resource Locator** (**URL**) is a unique address, sometimes called a **Web address**, which identifies an individual Web page or other Web-based resource. A URL has several components as shown in Figure 2-8.

protocol   domain name   path   file name

http://www.scsite.com/internet/ch2/survey.htm

Figure 2-8   A URL includes a protocol and a domain name. Some URLs also include the path and file name.

The first part of the URL is *http://*, the protocol or set of rules, used to transmit a Web page from a Web server to a Web browser. The second part of the URL is the name of the server hosting the Web page and consists of the *www* (Web server) designation and the server's domain name, *scsite.com*. A URL also can contain the path to and the file name of a specific Web page. For example, in Figure 2-8, the path is */internet/ch2/* and the file name is *survey.htm*. When entering a URL in a browser, the http:// protocol and the www designation are optional. For example, entering *http://www.scsite.com* or entering *scsite.com* in a browser loads a copy of the Shelly Cashman Series Instructional Web Site home page. When a URL is entered without a specific path and file name, the page returned to the browser is generally the site's home page.

Domain names are not case sensitive, meaning they can be entered in a browser in either uppercase or lowercase characters. For example, entering any of these three domain names — scsite.com or SCsite.Com or SCSITE.COM — in a browser accesses the same Shelly Cashman Series Instructional Web site home page. On some Web servers, however, the path and file name may be case sensitive, which means a Web page will not be located if the path and file name are entered in the browser incorrectly.

Web Browsers

As you learned in Chapter 1, a Web browser is a software program used to access and view Web pages. The most widely used browser for personal computers at home or at the office is Microsoft Internet Explorer. Other browsers include Netscape Navigator (commonly called Netscape), Opera, and Mozilla. Figure 2-9 illustrates the Internet Explorer browser window.

Figure 2-9 The Internet Explorer Web browser contains a number of features that make browsing the Web easy.

The Internet Explorer window includes a number of features that make browsing the Web easy:

- A starting page when the browser opens, called the **default home page**.
- The **display area** contains the Web page requested from a Web server.
- The **title bar** displays the title of the Web page shown in the display area.

- The **menu bar**, located below the title bar, contains a list of menu names from which you can choose commands to perform various actions, such as saving the Web page.

- The **browser icon** located on the right side of the menu bar shows animation while a Web page is being loaded in the browser.

- The **Standard Buttons toolbar**, located below the menu bar, contains buttons for commonly used menu commands.

- The **Address bar** displays the URL of the Web page in the display area.

- The **Address box** on the Address bar is a text box in which a URL is typed.

- The **Go button** sends the URL request to a Web server when clicked with the mouse pointer. Pressing the ENTER key also sends the URL request to a Web server.

- The **status bar** displays the URL for a link to which the mouse pointer is pointing or other information about the Web page loading process.

- A **scroll bar** appears whenever a Web page is too long or wide to fit in the display area.

Other toolbars, such the customizable **Links bar** that contains Web page shortcuts or toolbars for Web browser plug-ins also may appear in the browser window. A Web browser **plug-in** is software added to a browser to make specific features available, such as special toolbars that make searching the Web easier. Also, the Standard Buttons toolbar can be customized by adding or removing buttons; therefore, as you work through the projects in this text, your browser window may not look exactly like Figure 2-9 on the previous page or other browser illustrations.

 In Netscape

The Netscape toolbars include the Navigation Toolbar, the Personal Toolbar, and the Component Bar. URLs are entered in the Location Bar. My Sidebar is a tabbed, customizable area in the Netscape window.

Starting the Browser and Loading a Web Page

You start your Web browser by clicking the browser icon on the Windows desktop or by displaying the Start menu, pointing to All Programs, and then locating and clicking the browser's program icon or name. The browser opens with its default starting or home page. The default home page for the Internet Explorer browser is the MSN portal. However, the default home page can be changed to be any Web page. For example, many colleges, universities, and businesses use their organization's Web site home page as their default home page. Many individuals use a portal site for their home page. You learn more about changing the default home page later in this chapter.

After the browser starts, you then type the URL of the Web page you want to load in the Address box on the Address bar and click the Go button or press ENTER. Depending on the speed of your Internet connection and the contents of the Web page, the page may load very quickly or it may take several seconds to load. While the Web page is loading, the browser icon on the far right side of the menu bar is animated indicating a page is being loaded. The status bar at the bottom of the browser window also displays information about the loading process: the URL of the page being loaded and a progress bar showing duration of the loading process.

In the following steps, you start your Web browser, type a URL in the Address box, and click the Go button to load a Web page in the browser window.

Facts@Hand

The steps in this book use Microsoft Internet Explorer, which is included with the Microsoft Windows operating system and Microsoft Office software or can be downloaded from the Microsoft Web site. Alternate information is provided for Netscape users in tips or in Appendix A.

Steps: To Start the Browser and Load a Web Page

1 **If necessary, view the Windows desktop. Point to the Internet Explorer icon on the Windows desktop (Figure 2-10).**

Because the Windows desktop can be customized, your desktop may look different than the desktop shown in Figure 2-10.

Internet Explorer icon

Figure 2-10

2 **Double-click the Internet Explorer icon. Point to the Address box on the Address bar.**

Address bar

Address box

The Internet Explorer browser starts and displays the default home page (Figure 2-11). Your default home page may be different than the MSN portal page shown in Figure 2-11.

Figure 2-11

(continued)

3 Click the Address box on the Address bar.

The current page URL is selected and the mouse pointer, when placed in the Address box, become an I-beam (Figure 2-12).

Figure 2-12

4 Type scsite.com/ internet/ as the URL. Point to the Go button.

The browser displays the URL in the Address box (Figure 2-13). As you type the URL, the Address box list appears below the Address bar. You will more about using this list to revisit Web pages later in this chapter.

Figure 2-13

5 Click the Go button.

The browser icon in the upper-right corner of the browser window is animated while the browser locates and loads the requested page. The Discovering the Internet Web site home page appears in the browser window (Figure 2-14).

Figure 2-14

Clicking a Link and Using Web Page Features

A simple way to load another Web page in the browser window is to click a link on the current Web page. Web page links may be text, a graphic image, or a photo. Text links generally appear underlined in a different color from other text on the page. It may be difficult to determine whether or not a graphic image or photo is also a link. To determine if a Web page element, such as a photo, is a link, point to the element with the mouse pointer. The mouse pointer changes to a pointing hand pointer and a URL appears in the status bar if the element is a link.

@Issue Ad Filters

As you browse the Web, you soon notice the barrage of advertisements. Web advertisements are no longer simple banner graphics on a Web page. Ads now crop up in pop-up windows that appear in front of the Web page currently displayed or in pop-under windows that appear behind the browser window. Some advertisements with attention-grabbing sounds and animation even appear right in the middle of the Web page you are viewing. Some consumers consider these new approaches to Web advertising increasingly invasive and distracting.

While many consumers dislike these ads, they serve the purpose for advertisers. Marketing companies say that banner ads have lost some effectiveness and that

consumers are more likely to respond to these new types of ads. While many consumers would prefer to avoid banner ads and pop-up ads, most simply ignore them or patiently click the Close button on the pop-up or pop-under window that displays the ad.

Several companies have created software and other solutions to help you block or limit the display of online ads as you browse the Web:

- Free ad-blocking software, such as Ad-aware, AdSubtract, Guidescope, WebWasher, or Zeroclick

- Commercial ad-blocking software, such as AdDelete, Internet Watcher, PopUpCop, or Pop-Up Stopper

Some ISPs also allow users to set preferences to limit the display of pop-up ads. AOL subscribers, for example, can restrict pop-up ads by entering the keyword Marketing Preferences and then clicking Pop-up.

Using an ad filter is particularly important if children are browsing the Web. According to research, children are less able than adults to distinguish between Web ads and content. When they see a cartoon character in an ad, for example, they likely will click the ad and expect to see more cartoons, not realizing they have clicked an ad. Using an ad filter can help reduce the likelihood that children will click ads and navigate to Web pages selling products and services.

For more information about ad filters, visit the Discovering the Internet Chapter 2 Web page (**scsite.com/internet/ch2**) and click a link below Ad Filters.

In the following steps, you use a link to load a new Web page in the browser window. Pop-up or pop-under advertising windows may open as you load a Web page in the browser. You can close these windows by clicking the Close button on a window's title bar or by right-clicking a window's button on the taskbar and clicking Close.

Steps: To Load a New Web Page in the Browser Window

1 **If necessary, start the browser. Visit the Discovering the Internet home page (scsite.com/internet/ch2). Point to Chapter 2.**

The shape of the mouse pointer changes to a pointing hand indicating that the mouse pointer is pointing to a link and the link's URL appears on the status bar (Figure 2-15).

Figure 2-15

2 **Click Chapter 2. Point to the Weather Channel link.**

The Discovering the Internet Chapter 2 Web page appears (Figure 2-16). The page's URL appears in the Address box on the Address bar. This page contains links to the online resources discussed in Chapter 2.

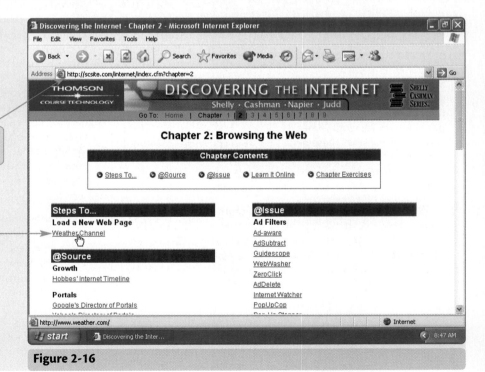

Figure 2-16

3 **Click Weather Channel. If a pop-up or pop-under advertising window appears, close it by clicking the Close button on the window's title bar or by right-clicking the window's button on the taskbar and clicking Close. Point to the Enter city or US zip text box in the local forecast area near the top of the page.**

The Weather Channel home page appears (Figure 2-17). The Web page content on your screen may be different than that shown in Figures 2-17 through 2-23 on pages 55 through 59.

Enter city or US zip text box

Figure 2-17

After a Web page loads in the browser, you then can click various links to locate additional information or use other features presented on the page. For example, the Weather Channel home page offers weather headlines and links to stories about current weather situations, links to related topics such as travel, driving, and so forth, and a feature that allows you to check the weather for any city or zip code. In the following steps, you check the weather for Colorado Springs, Colorado by entering the city's zip code in a text box on the Weather Channel page and then loading the local weather page for that zip code. In the steps on the next page and for the remainder of the chapter, close any pop-up or pop-under advertising windows that appear.

⟫ Steps: To Load a Local Weather Page

1 Click the Enter city or US zip text box. Type 80995 as the entry.

The insertion point appears in the text box when you click it so that you can type the 80995 zip code (Figure 2-18).

80995 zip code for Colorado Springs, CO

Figure 2-18

2 Press the ENTER key. Leave the browser open with the current page.

The Local Forecast for Colorado Springs, CO (80995) page appears (Figure 2-19).

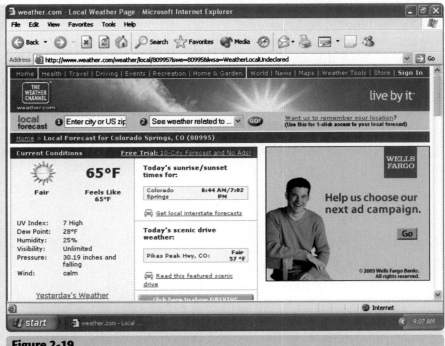

Figure 2-19

Navigating Recently Viewed Web Pages

Buttons on the Standard Buttons toolbar (Figure 2-20) allow you to move back and forth between recently viewed pages, reload the default browser home page, reload the current page, and stop the loading process. You also can use buttons on the Standard

Buttons toolbar to search the Web, create a shortcut to a favorite Web page, listen to the radio, revisit a page viewed several days ago, print a Web page, send e-mail, send an instant message, and communicate with others by posting discussion notes on a server. In this section, you learn about navigating recently viewed Web pages using the Back, Forward, Home, Stop, and Refresh toolbar buttons. Later in this chapter and in Chapters 3 and 4, you learn how to use the other toolbar buttons.

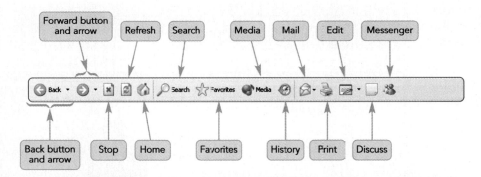

Figure 2-20 The Internet Explorer Standard Buttons toolbar provides buttons to navigate recently viewed Web pages.

BACK AND FORWARD BUTTONS The Back and Forward buttons on the Standard Buttons toolbar maintain a list of the last few pages you viewed since you started the browser. Clicking the Back button once returns to the page you viewed immediately before the current page. Clicking the Forward button once returns to the page you viewed before you clicked the Back button. You can click the Back or Forward arrows to view the list and then click a Web page title in the list to return to that page. When you close the browser, the Back and Forward button lists are cleared.

HOME BUTTON The Home button on the Standard Buttons toolbar reloads the default home page. You can click the Home button to view the default home page at any time while browsing the Web.

STOP AND REFRESH BUTTONS The Stop button on the Standard Buttons toolbar allows you to stop loading a Web page. For example, if you change your mind about viewing the Web page currently being loaded in the browser, you can click the Stop button to stop the loading process.

The Refresh button on the Standard Buttons toolbar loads a fresh copy of the current Web page. The Refresh button is useful when you want to reload a Web page for which you stopped the transfer or when you need to reload Web pages with content that changes every few minutes, such as stock quotes, weather, and news.

In the following steps, you use the Back, Forward, Refresh, and Home buttons on the Standard Buttons toolbar.

 In Netscape
The Refresh button is called the Reload button.

Steps: To Navigate Through Recently Viewed Pages

1 Verify that the browser is open with the Local Forecast for Colorado Springs, CO (80995) page. Point to the Back button on the Standard Buttons toolbar.

The Back button is used to return to the immediately viewed page (Figure 2-21).

Figure 2-21

2 Click the Back button. Point to the Forward button on the Standard Buttons toolbar.

The Back button returns you to the previously viewed Weather Channel home page (Figure 2-22).

Figure 2-22

3 **Click the Forward button. Point to the Refresh button on the Standard Buttons toolbar.**

The Forward button returns you to the page you were viewing before you clicked the Back button, the Local Weather Page for Colorado Springs (Figure 2-23). This page contains time-sensitive temperature information.

Figure 2-23

4 **Click the Refresh button. Point to the Home button on the Standard Buttons toolbar.**

A fresh copy of the Local Weather Page for Colorado Springs loads from the server. You now may be able to see updated temperature information on the page (Figure 2-24). The content of the Web page on your screen may be different than that shown in Figure 2-24.

Figure 2-24

(continued)

5 **Click the Home button. Point to the Back button arrow on the Standard Buttons toolbar.**

The default home page loads (Figure 2-25).

Back button arrow

Figure 2-25

6 **Click the Back button arrow. Point to the Discovering the Internet - Home link.**

A list of recently viewed Web pages appears (Figure 2-26).

Back button list

Discovering the Internet - Home link

Figure 2-26

7 **Click the Discovering the Internet – Home link. Leave the browser open with the current page.**

The previously viewed Discovering the Internet - Home page loads (Figure 2-27).

Figure 2-27

Using Browser and Desktop Shortcuts to Revisit Web Pages

As you learn to navigate the Web and become more familiar with Web pages and the information and services they provide, you likely will want to return to certain Web pages frequently. Your Web browser provides several ways to revisit Web pages, such as:

- Using the Address box list
- Creating and using favorites
- Using the History list
- Creating a Web page desktop shortcut.

Using the Address List

You can revisit a Web page by clicking a URL in the Address list. The **Address list** displays a list of previously viewed Web pages. The browser's **AutoComplete** feature saves URLs for previously viewed Web pages, as well as anything you type in an online form field, such as your name or a password. An online form, much like a paper form, is used to gather viewer information at Web sites. When you start to type a URL or information in an online form field, AutoComplete suggests possible matches. Thus, when you begin typing a URL in the Address box, the AutoComplete feature displays a list of recently visited URLs in the Address list. You then can scroll down the Address list and click the URL you want.

The following steps revisit the Weather Channel home page (weather.com) using the Address list on the Address bar.

Steps: **To Use the Address List to Revisit a Web Page**

1 **Click the Address box to select the URL. Type w (the letter). Point to the http://www.weather .com URL.**

The Address list opens and displays recently visited Web pages. Your Address list may contain different URLs than those shown, but should include the URL for the Weather Channel, http://www.weather.com (Figure 2-28).

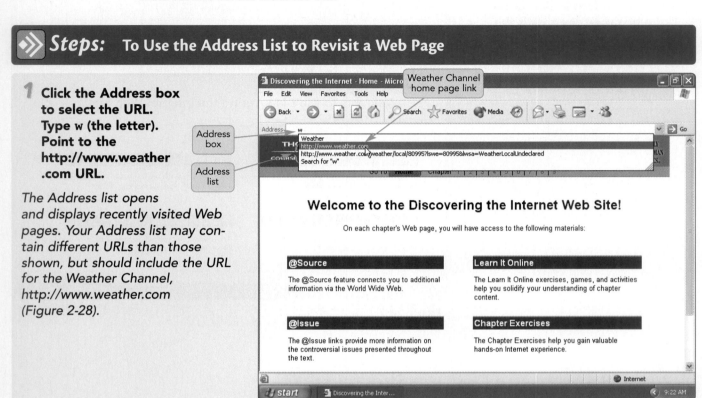

Figure 2-28

2 **Click the http://www.weather .com URL. Leave the browser open with the current page.**

The Weather Channel home page appears (Figure 2-29).

Figure 2-29

Creating and Using a Favorite

A **favorite** is a shortcut to a frequently viewed Web page. You can create a favorite, which includes the page's title and URL, for the current Web page using the Favorites menu or the Favorites list in the **Favorites bar**. When you want to revisit the page, you simply open the Favorites menu or Favorites bar containing the Favorites list and click the favorite. Favorites are stored in a Favorites folder, by default; however, you can create a folder inside the Favorites folder, if necessary, to organize your favorites. As you create a favorite, you can replace the page title with a more meaningful name, if desired. When you no longer need a favorite, you can delete it. You also can delete a Favorites folder and its contents.

 In Netscape

A favorite is called a bookmark in Netscape. You create bookmarks in Netscape using the Bookmarks menu commands or the Bookmarks tab on My Sidebar.

In the following steps, you create a favorite for the Weather Channel home page (weather.com) and save it in a new folder inside the Favorites folder. Next, you use the Weather Channel favorite to view the Weather Channel home page and then you delete the new folder and favorite.

 Facts@Hand

According to StatMarket, the majority of Web users access a Web page by entering the URL in the Address bar or by clicking a favorite or bookmark, rather than relying on search tools and links.

⟫⟫ Steps: To Create a Favorite

1 **Verify that the browser is open with the Weather Channel home page. Point to the Favorites button on the Standard Buttons toolbar.**

The Favorites button opens and closes the Favorites bar (Figure 2-30).

Figure 2-30

(continued)

2 **Click the Favorites button. Point to the Add Favorite button in the Favorites bar.**

The Favorites bar opens and contains the Favorites list. Your Favorites list may be different than that shown in Figure 2-31.

Figure 2-31

3 **Click the Add Favorite button. Point to the New Folder button.**

The Add Favorite dialog box opens (Figure 2-32). The Name text box contains the Weather Channel home page's URL.

Figure 2-32

4 **Click the New Folder button. Type Weather in the Folder name text box. Point to OK.**

You create a new folder named Weather in which to store the Weather Channel favorite (Figure 2-33).

Create New Folder

Internet Explorer will create the following folder for you. You can use this folder to organize shortcuts on your Favorites menu.

Folder name: Weather

OK button

OK   Cancel

Folder name

Figure 2-33

5 **Click OK to create the Weather folder. Select Weather.com in the Name text box and then type Weather Channel as the entry. Point to OK.**

The Weather Channel favorite will be stored in the Weather folder (Figure 2-34).

OK button

Add Favorite

Internet Explorer will add this page to your Favorites list.

☐ Make available offline   Customize...

OK   Cancel

Name: Weather Channel

new favorite name

Create in: Favorites
    Links
    Weather ← Weather folder

Create in <<

New Folder...

Figure 2-34

6 **Click OK. Click the Weather folder in the Favorites list to view the Weather Channel favorite. Click the Home button to reload the default home page. Point to the Weather Channel favorite link in the Favorites list.**

The Weather Channel favorite link appears inside the Weather folder in the Favorites list (Figure 2-35).

Figure 2-35

(continued)

7 **Click the Weather Channel favorite. Point to the Weather folder.**

The Weather Channel home page reloads in the browser (Figure 2-36).

Weather folder

reloaded Weather Channel page

Figure 2-36

8 **Right-click the Weather folder. Point to Delete.**

When you no longer need a favorite or a folder, you can delete them using a shortcut menu (Figure 2-37).

9 **Click Delete. Click Yes to send the deleted folder and its contents to the Recycle Bin. Click the Favorites button on the Standard Buttons toolbar. Click the Home button on the Standard Buttons toolbar. Leave the browser open with the current page.**

The Weather folder and its contents are deleted, the Favorites bar and Favorites list close, and the browser's default home page again appears.

shortcut menu

Delete command

Figure 2-37

 In Netscape

To accomplish this task in Netscape, see To Create and Use Bookmarks in Appendix A.

SHARING FAVORITES   You can share your favorites between different browsers and computers. When you install the Internet Explorer browser on a computer that already has the Netscape Navigator browser installed, Internet Explorer automatically imports the Netscape bookmarks and stores them in a folder named Imported Bookmarks.

You also can import and export favorites manually to make them accessible in another browser or on another computer. To export your favorites from Internet Explorer, click File on the menu bar and then click Import and Export to start the Import/Export Wizard. Follow the Import/Export Wizard steps to select an option to export either the entire contents of the Favorites folder or the contents of a single folder. The favorites are saved as an HTML file. You then can import the favorites into Netscape on the same computer or into a browser on another computer. To import favorites into Internet Explorer, click File on the menu bar, click Import and Export, and then follow Import/Export Wizard steps.

 In Netscape

To import or export bookmarks in Netscape, click Manage Bookmarks on the Bookmarks menu. When the Manage Bookmarks dialog box opens, click Import or Export on the Tools menu. Netscape stores the favorites imported from Internet Explorer in a folder named Imported IE Favorites.

Using the History List

Another easy way to revisit a Web page is to use the History list. You can display the History list by click the History button on the Standard Buttons toolbar to open the **History bar**. The History list is a list of Web site folders and Web page links for the sites and pages visited during the past several days. By default, the History list maintains this information for 20 days; therefore, the History list may contain icons for sites visited Three Weeks Ago, Two Weeks Ago, Last Week, and for every day of the current week including Today. When you click one of these icons, a list of Web page folders appears — each folder represents a Web site visited during that time period. You can expand each Web site folder to view links to the individual Web pages viewed at the site.

In the following steps, you use a link in the History list to revisit a Web page. Because the History list can be cleared or changed to reflect a different number of days of browsing history, the icons, folders, and links you see in your History list will vary from those in the following illustrations. Additionally, these steps assume all the previous hands-on projects in this chapter have been completed on the same day. If that is not the case, your instructor may modify the following instructions. Remember to close any pop-up or pop-under windows as you complete the steps on the next page.

Steps: To Revisit a Web Page Using the History List

1 Verify that the browser is open with the default home page. Point to the History button on the Standard Buttons toolbar.

Your default home page may be different from the one shown in Figure 2-38.

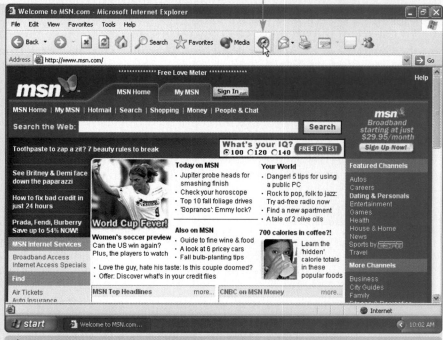

Figure 2-38

2 Click the History button. Point to the weather folder link.

The History bar containing the History list opens (Figure 2-39). The History list may contain multiple collapsed or expanded week and day icons and Web site folders. The Today folder is expanded to display a list of Web sites you visited today. The folder containing the current Web site is expanded and the current Web page link is highlighted.

Figure 2-39

3 **Click the weather folder icon in the History list. Point to the weather.com link.**

The weather folder expands and displays a list of pages viewed today at the Weather Channel Web site (Figure 2-40). The list of page links you see may vary from that shown in Figure 2-40.

expanded weather folder

Weather Channel home page link

Figure 2-40

History button

4 **Click the weather.com link. Point to the History button on the Standard Buttons toolbar.**

The Weather Channel home page appears (Figure 2-41).

5 **Click the History button. Leave the browser open with the current page.**

The History bar and History list close.

Figure 2-41

 In Netscape

To accomplish this task in Netscape, see To Use the History List to Revisit a Web Page in Appendix A.

Creating a Web Page Desktop Shortcut

Sometimes a frequently visited Web page needs to be even handier than a shortcut in the Favorites or History list. For example, some people such as boaters, farmers, fishermen, and others who work or play outdoors may need to check weather frequently. Students may need to create a shortcut to a frequently viewed Web page when completing assignments. Placing a Web page shortcut on the Windows desktop provides quick access to a needed page without first opening the browser. A desktop shortcut for the current Web page can be created using the Send command on the File menu.

Facts@Hand

You also can drag the current Web page icon from the browser's Address box to the desktop to create a shortcut to the Web page.

In the following steps, you create a shortcut to the Discovering the Internet Web site's home page, use the shortcut to access the page, and then delete the shortcut.

Steps: To Create a Web Page Desktop Shortcut

1 **Verify that the browser is open. Type** `scsite.com/ internet/` **in the Address box. Press ENTER. Click File on the menu bar, point to Send, and then point to Shortcut to Desktop on the Send submenu.**

The Discovering the Internet - Home page appears and the File menu and the Send submenu open (Figure 2-42).

Figure 2-42

2 **Click Shortcut to Desktop. Point to the Close button on the browser's title bar.**

The shortcut to the Local Weather Page Web page is placed on the Windows desktop. You close the browser to view the shortcut (Figure 2-43).

Figure 2-43

3 **Click the Close button. Point to the Discovering the Internet – Home shortcut on the desktop.**

You can use this shortcut to open the browser and load the Web page (Figure 2-44).

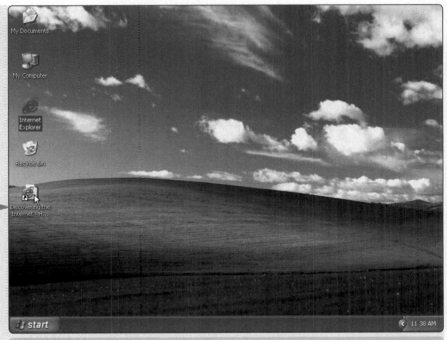

Figure 2-44

(continued)

4 **Double-click the shortcut on the Windows desktop. Point to the Minimize button on the browser title bar.**

The browser opens and the Discovering the Internet - Home page loads (Figure 2-45). You mini-mize the browser window to view and delete the desktop shortcut.

5 **Click the Minimize button. Drag the Discovering the Internet – Home page desktop shortcut to the Recycle Bin. Click the Discovering the Internet button on the taskbar. Click the Home button on the Standard Buttons toolbar.**

The desktop shortcut is deleted, the browser window is maximized, and the default browser home page loads.

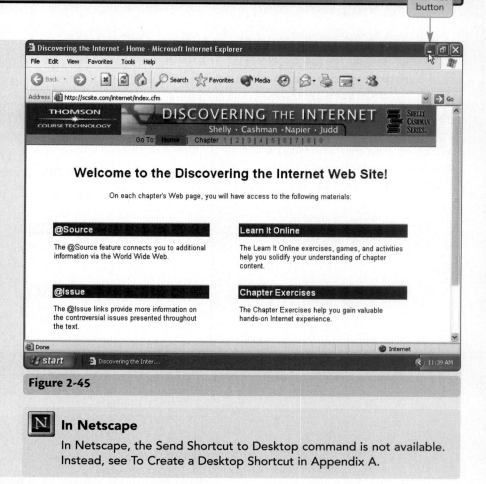

Minimize button

Figure 2-45

N **In Netscape**

In Netscape, the Send Shortcut to Desktop command is not available. Instead, see To Create a Desktop Shortcut in Appendix A.

Saving Online Information

As you browse the Web, you may want to print a **hard copy** of a Web page in order to reference its contents later. Web pages also can be saved in a variety of formats. For example, you can save a snapshot of the page or the complete HTML page with all its associated files. You also can save just a Web page image. You can send a Web page to someone via e-mail and you can add Web page content to the desktop. In the following sections, you learn more about printing, saving, and e-mailing a Web page and adding Web page content to the Active Desktop.

Printing a Web Page

You can print a Web page by clicking the Print button on the Standard Buttons toolbar to send the entire Web page to the default printer. If you need to specify a differ-ent printer or change print options, you must open the Print dialog box by clicking the Print command on the File menu. The hard copy printout of a Web page includes a header on each page showing the Web page title and page number. A footer on each page shows the URL and the date on which the page was printed. To print part of a Web page — for example, a single picture or a selected portion of the text — use one of the following methods:

- Select the information to be printed by dragging across it with the mouse pointer, click Print on the File menu, and then click Selection in the Print dialog box.
- Right-click the selected information and then click Print.

You also can preview Web pages to see how they will look when printed by clicking Print Preview on the File menu. You can use buttons on the Print Preview toolbar to view specific pages, zoom the view in or out, or open the Print dialog box and print the pages. Figure 2-46 illustrates a Web page in Print Preview.

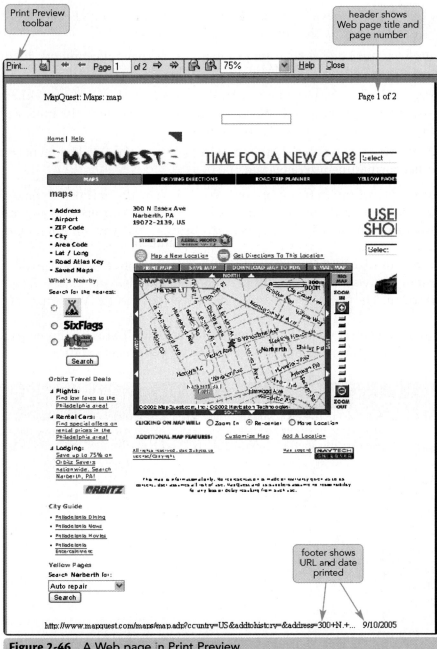

Figure 2-46 A Web page in Print Preview.

Saving a Web Page

You can save a Web page by clicking the Save As command on the File menu to open the Save As dialog box. The Save as type list in the Save As dialog box offers four options for saving a Web page:

- *Web Page, complete* saves not only the HTML Web page, but also all of the other files needed to display the complete page, such as graphics.
- *Web Archive, single file* saves a snapshot of the page and its contents, including graphics, in one file.
- *Web Page, HTML only* saves the HTML Web page, but does not save other related files such the page's graphics. When you view this page later, the links will work, but an icon appears in place of any graphics.
- *Text File* saves the text on the Web page in plain text format. The links, graphics, and other formatting are not saved.

If you use either of the first two options, you can view the entire Web page, including graphics, while you are working offline. Working **offline** means that you are viewing previously loaded or saved Web pages in the browser but you are not connected to the Internet.

Another way to save a Web page is to save it directly from a link. If you see a link to a Web page that you want to save, right-click the link and then click Save Target As on the shortcut menu. The browser saves the linked Web page in the Web Page, HTML only format.

In the following steps, you save a snapshot of the default browser home page to the My Documents folder (or other folder as specified by your instructor.)

Steps: To Save a Web Page

1 **Start the browser, if necessary, and view the default home page. Click File on the menu bar. Click Save As. Point to the Save as type box arrow.**

The Save Web Page dialog box appears and displays the contents of the My Documents folder. Your folder contents may be different. Because your default home page may be different, the file name in the File name text box also may be different (Figure 2-47).

Figure 2-47

2 Click the Save as type box arrow. Point to Web Archive, single file (*.mht).

The list of Web page file types appears (Figure 2-48).

Figure 2-48

3 Click Web Archive, single file (*.mht). Point to Save.

The Web Archive, single file (.mht) saves the HTML page and related files together in one file (Figure 2-49).*

4 Click Save.

In a few seconds, the Web page is saved in the My Documents folder on the hard drive.

Figure 2-49

 In Netscape

When you use the Save Page As command to save a Web page in Netscape, the Save As dialog box includes three Save as type options: Web Page, complete; Web Page, HTML only; and Text File. To save a page directly from a link in Netscape, right-click the link and then click Save Link Target As on the shortcut menu.

E-Mailing a Web Page

When you find a Web page that might interest others, you can share it by sending it to them via e-mail. You can send a Web page via e-mail by pointing to Send on the File menu and clicking the Page By E-mail command. The recipient receives an e-mail message with the Web page in the body of the e-mail message. You also can send a link to a Web page by pointing to Send on the File menu and clicking Link By E-mail. The recipient receives an e-mail message with an attachment containing a shortcut to the Web page. When the recipient clicks the link, the browser starts and loads the Web page. You learn more about sending and receiving e-mail with and without attachments in Chapter 4.

 In Netscape

The commands to e-mail a page or a link in Netscape are Send Page and Send Link on the File menu.

Saving a Web Page Image

While browsing the Web, you may find a picture that you want to save, such as a picture of a landscape or a sports personality, perhaps to use as the wallpaper on your Windows desktop. You can save and print an image or send it to someone using buttons on the Image toolbar that appears when you point to some Web page images (Figure 2-50).

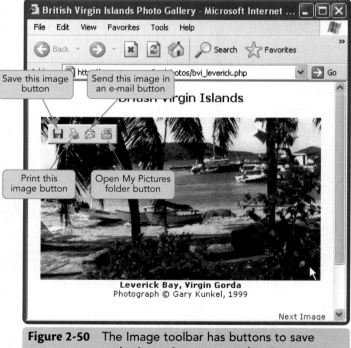

Figure 2-50   The Image toolbar has buttons to save and print an image or send an image to someone via e-mail.

When the Image toolbar is not available, such as when the image is a link, you can save an image by right-clicking the image and then clicking the Save Picture As command on the shortcut menu (Figure 2-51). The shortcut menu also includes commands for printing the image as well saving the image as the Windows desktop background wallpaper.

Figure 2-51   You can use a shortcut menu to save, print, or e-mail an image.

 In Netscape

To save a picture in Netscape, right-click the image and select Save Image As from the shortcut menu. To print or e-mail the image, select View Image from the shortcut menu. This opens the image in a separate window. Then, you can choose Send Page, Send Link, or Print from the File menu.

Adding Web Content to the Active Desktop

Printing or saving a Web page or image works well to make the content available offline when the Web page content does not need to be updated. Sometimes, however, you want to save a Web page so that new content is available on a regular basis when you are online, but not browsing the Web.

The Windows **Active Desktop** feature supports the display of dynamic Web content on the desktop. You can use the Set As Desktop Item on the shortcut menu to create an area on the desktop that displays static information when the computer is offline and displays dynamic Web page content when the computer is online. For example, news enthusiasts can add live news-headlines, investors can add a stock price ticker, and sports fans can add updated scores to their desktops based on content delivered via the Web. You can find out more about using the Active Desktop and adding Web content to the desktop in Windows online Help.

In Netscape
Placing Web pages on the Active Desktop is called subscribing in Netscape.

Remember that all Web page content is protected by copyright law, even if no copyright notice is found on the page. This means you cannot use any Web page content without the specific permission of the owner, except for your own private use. For example, if you use the ideas from a Web page or copy the text into a research paper, be sure to include a proper citation to avoid plagiarism. You will see examples of proper citation methods in Chapter 3, Searching the Web.

Changing Browser Options

The browser window and some browser features can be customized in a number of ways. For example, the browser window can be customized to show or hide toolbars and the Address bar using a shortcut menu. As you have learned, the default home page can be changed and the History list can be changed to show a different number of days of history or be cleared completely. You also can set options to make Web pages download faster when using a slow dial-up Internet connection. You change the default home page, set the number of history days, clear the History list, and set other options in the Internet Options dialog box. In the following sections, you show and hide the Links bar, change the default home page, and view options that allow Web pages to load faster over a dial-up connection.

Showing and Hiding Toolbars

The Links bar is a customizable toolbar to which you can add Web page shortcuts by dragging the current Web page icon from the Address box to it. You can turn on or off the view of the Links bar, the Standard Buttons toolbar, the Address bar, and other plug-in toolbars using the Toolbars submenu on the View menu or with a shortcut menu. In the following steps, you show and hide the Links bar and view its menu of Web page shortcuts.

Steps: To Show and Hide the Links Bar

1 **Start the browser, if necessary, and view the default home page. Right-click the Standard Buttons toolbar. Point to Links.**

The toolbar shortcut menu appears (Figure 2-52). The visible toolbars have a checkmark to the left of the toolbar name. Your shortcut menu may include toolbar names other than those shown in Figure 2-52. Your Links toolbar may have a checkmark indicating it is already visible in the browser window.

Figure 2-52

2 **Click Links, if necessary, to show the Links bar. Point to the Links bar expansion button.**

The Links bar appears to the right of the Address bar. The Links bar has an expansion button you can click to show the available Web page shortcuts (Figure 2-53).

Figure 2-53

(continued)

3 **Click the Links bar expansion button. If necessary, point to the Links bar expansion button again.**

The menu of available Web page shortcuts appears (Figure 2-54). Because the Links bar is customizable, your list of shortcuts may be different than the shortcuts in Figure 2-54.

4 **Click the Links bar expansion button to close the menu. Right-click the Standard Buttons toolbar and click Links to hide the Links bar. Redisplay the Links bar, if desired.**

Figure 2-54

 In Netscape

To show and hide toolbars in Netscape, see To Show and Hide Toolbars in Appendix A.

Changing the Default Home Page

The default home page can be changed so that a favorite Web page, such as a portal page, loads when the browser starts or when you click the Home button. In the following steps, you change the browser's default home page to the Yahoo! portal page and then return it to the previous default home page. As you work through the steps in this project, be certain to make a note of the current default home page's URL.

 In Netscape

To accomplish this task in Netscape, see To Change the Default Home Page in Appendix A.

Steps: To Change the Default Home Page

1 Start the browser, if necessary, and view the default home page. Click Tools on the menu bar. Point to Internet Options (Figure 2-55).

Figure 2-55

2 Click Internet Options. Write down the current URL in the Address text box.

The Internet Options dialog box opens. The URL for the current default home page appears selected in the Address text box (Figure 2-56). Write down the URL, if necessary, so that you can restore it in a subsequent step. The Use Current button inserts the URL of the current Web page as the default home page; the Use Default button inserts the URL of the MSN home page; the Use Blank button allows the browser to open with a blank page. The Clear History button clears the History list. The Days to keep pages in history box contains the number of days of browsing history currently being retained.

Figure 2-56

3 **Type www.yahoo.com in the Address text box. Point to OK.**

The address for the Yahoo! portal page appears in the Address text box (Figure 2-57). The browser will supply the http:// portion of the URL.

Figure 2-57

4 **Click OK. Click the Home button on the Standard Buttons toolbar.**

The dialog box closes and the browser loads the Yahoo! portal page, the new default home page (Figure 2-58).

Figure 2-58

5 Click Tools on the menu bar. Click Internet Options. Type the URL of the original default home page or click the Use Default button to insert the MSN portal page URL. Point to OK.

The URL in the Address text box is returned to the original browser default page URL (Figure 2-59).

6 Click OK. Click the Home button on the Standard Buttons toolbar.

The browser's default home page is again its original default home page.

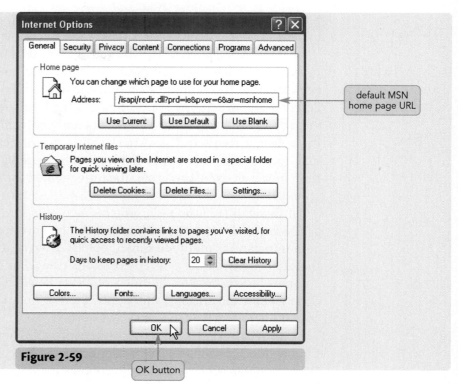

Figure 2-59

Loading Web Pages Faster

When you have a slow Internet connection, Web pages with multimedia content such as sound, video, large images, and animation can take some time to load in the browser. You can set browser options to limit the display of these items, so that only the Web page text appears and the Web pages load faster. The Advanced tab in the Internet Options dialog box contains a number of advanced browser setting options including Multimedia options, such as playing Web page animations, sounds, and video or downloading pictures (Figure 2-60). You can turn off or on these Multimedia options by clicking each option's check box.

Figure 2-60 The Advanced tab in the Internet Options dialog box contains options to turn off or on multimedia content.

Using the Web: Risks and Safeguards

As you browse the Web, you access information stored on servers located anywhere in the world. Thus, even as you use the Web from the privacy of your home or office, you are venturing into a very public arena that connects thousands of computers and people from around the globe. While this global connectivity has many positive aspects, it also creates the possibility that you could be exposed to unethical people or objectionable material. In the next few sections, you will learn about the risks of using the Web and safeguards that can protect you from these risks.

Is My Computer Protected from Hackers?

Anyone connected to the Internet should take precautions to protect their computer by hackers. A **hacker** is an individual who uses his or her computer skills to access a network and the computers on that network without authorization. A hacker typically accesses a computer by connecting to it and then logging on as a legitimate user. Once logged on, the hacker can access data and programs, save files, or highjack its computing power, all without the owner's knowledge or permission. Exposure to hackers with a dial-up connection is somewhat limited because of the temporary nature of the connection; however, exposure is significantly greater with an always on DSL or cable Internet connection.

A **firewall** (Figure 2-61) protects a computer or a network from unauthorized access by hackers. A firewall, which can be hardware or software, can examine network communications and then directly block or warn the user about those communications that do not meet a set of predetermined rules. For example, a firewall on a home computer connected to the Internet might be set to block certain outgoing communications from a specific software application or operating system utility or incoming communications from an unknown source.

The Windows XP operating system provides a personal firewall utility, the Internet Connection Firewall, useful for protecting home computers with Internet connections. Other popular personal firewall products include BlackICE Defender, McAfee Personal Firewall, Norton Personal Firewall, and ZoneAlarm Pro. Businesses use a variety of sophisticated firewalls for their local area networks.

Figure 2-61 A firewall helps to protect your computer against hackers.

Will My Computer Get a Computer Virus?

A computer **virus** is a small, potentially damaging computer program that can infect a computer and then be passed to other computers. Browsing the Web typically does not expose a computer to damaging viruses. More often, a computer can be infected with a virus via an e-mail message or attachment, when software and utility programs are downloaded, or when infected word processing or spreadsheet files are exchanged with other users. One way to guard against viruses is to never open an e-mail attachment unless you can trust the source *and* you are expecting the attachment. You will learn more about the risks and safeguards for using e-mail in Chapter 4. Another way to guard against viruses is to install virus protection software, such as Symantec's Norton AntiVirus software, and keep the virus definitions updated regularly.

Is It Safe to Shop Online?

Shopping online is convenient because consumers can read quickly about product features, view pictures, and compare prices. In most circumstances, shopping online is a safe activity; however, there are some risks. The risks in online shopping come in not knowing with whom you are doing business and in making payments online. By following a few guidelines, you can enjoy safe and successful shopping online.

Before purchasing from an online vendor, determine if the business is reputable. For example, by purchasing products or services from well-known companies, such as Dell, Inc., Barnes & Noble, or Delta Airlines, consumers can feel more confident about the purchase and that the company will not use their customer information or payment information illegally. On the other hand, purchasing a collectible doll from an anonymous seller at an online auction Web site is inherently more risky because the seller does not have a well-known reputation. The Better Business Bureau (BBBOnline) Web site (Figure 2-62) is a great resource to learn about shopping online safely and to see whether a vendor has agreed to follow the Better Business Bureau's high standards for ethical online business practices.

Figure 2-62 The BBBOnline Web site offers a wealth of information about shopping safely online.

In addition to choosing an online vendor carefully, consumers should be careful in handling payments over the Internet. Most online vendors accept credit cards, currently the most popular online payment method, which limits the consumer's liability. Other payment methods include electronic checks and third-party payment services, such as PayPal and BidPay (Figure 2-63), which allow consumers to send money to anyone via e-mail or money order. Third-party payment services are a popular means of paying for C2C transactions.

Figure 2-63   Third-party payment services are a popular way to pay for C2C transactions.

When paying for an online purchase using a credit card, be sure the Web page is accessed with a secure connection. A **secure connection** uses *https://* rather than *http://* as its connection protocol and a locked padlock icon appears on the browser's status bar. The secure https:// protocol and the locked padlock icon signify that the information is being sent over the secure connection using Secure Sockets Layer. **Secure Sockets Layer (SSL)** is a commonly used protocol for managing the security of message transmissions on the Internet. Using a secure connection (Figure 2-64) for transactions means that only the intended recipient will see the payment information, such as the mailing address and credit card number.

Figure 2-64   The http:// protocol and a locked padlock icon indicate a secure Internet connection.

Finally, never send a credit card number by e-mail, as there is no control over who sees the e-mail message as it could be forwarded or possibly intercepted. By following these simple guidelines, you can shop online safely and confidently.

Will I Be Exposed to Objectionable Content Online?

Web users may mistakenly access objectionable material, such as offensive language, sexually explicit or violent material, or hate propaganda while browsing the Web. One of the Web's greatest strengths is that it is unregulated and open to all; however, that also means that the Web is an unprotected environment that contains material some may find objectionable. The prevalence of objectionable content can be particularly problematic for children browsing the Web (Figure 2-65).

Figure 2-65 Young people using the Internet need supervision.

Blocking software can protect Web users against accidentally viewing objectionable material. **Blocking software**, also called an **Internet filter** or **content filter**, is software that filters the display of Web content based on user settings. For example, parents can use blocking software to protect their children from objectionable material. Employers can use blocking software to prevent their employees from viewing objectionable material at work.

Some blocking software, such as N2H2, NetNanny, and FamilyClick, includes predefined filters that block certain Web pages based on keywords or a predefined database of objectionable Web sites. In addition, Internet Explorer and Netscape have built-in content filter features that block objectionable material.

The content filter included in the Internet Explorer browser, called Content Advisor, allows you to specify filters or rating levels for language, nudity, sex, and violence. To turn on the Content Advisor, use options in the Content tab in the Internet Options dialog box. Content Advisor works by checking ratings that Web content providers voluntarily post on their sites. When someone tries to access a page that contains objectionable content, the Content Advisor prevents the Web page from being displayed, presents a warning dialog box (Figure 2-66), and allows a designated supervisor to enter a password to override the block when appropriate.

Unfortunately, many inappropriate sites post no ratings, so the Content Advisor's usefulness is limited. Even with the best blocking software, however, no system is foolproof, and adults must keep a watchful eye on children and teens browsing the Web.

Is My Personal Information Kept Private?

Information privacy refers to the right of individuals and companies to deny or restrict the collection and use of personal information. In the past, information privacy was easier to maintain, because information was kept in separate locations. Today, personal information entered in Web page forms

 @Source

To read the Internet Education Foundation's Online Safety Guide for Kids, visit the Discovering the Internet Chapter 2 Web page (**scsite.com/ internet/ch2**) and click a link below Kids' Safety.

Figure 2-66 The browser displays a Content Advisor warning when a site with blocked content is accessed.

@Source

For a review of blocking software products, visit the Discovering the Internet Chapter 2 Web page (**scsite.com/ internet/ch2**) and click a link below Reviews of Blocking Software.

@Source

The filtering software for Netscape is called NetWatch. After you install it, you can customize its settings to filter out objectionable material. To learn more about NetWatch, visit the Discovering the Internet Chapter 2 Web page (**scsite.com/ internet/ch2**) and click a link below NetWatch.

@Source

To read more about the privacy issues raised by an ISP's customer tracking activities, visit the Discovering the Internet Chapter 2 Web page (**scsite.com/ internet/ch2**) and click a link below Comcast.

is tracked by Web sites and stored in their databases. While this information may be accessible only to authorized users, some people question whether this data really is private. Some companies and individuals collect and use your personal information and record your online activities without your authorization. Entities such as your employer, your Internet service provider (ISP), the government, the companies whose Web sites you visit, and third-party advertisers all may be tracking your online activities.

Some people, who are less concerned about protecting their personal information, enjoy the benefits of targeted marketing, personalized e-mail messages, and direct mail such as catalogs that they receive as a result of information gathered about them while they use the Web. Others are very concerned that their private information is not protected from entities such as third-party advertisers. The following sections discuss the entities that may be collecting and using your private information and the laws that protect your information privacy.

EMPLOYERS   An employer may legally monitor employee use of its computer equipment and time spent on the Web at the workplace. Many employers publish policies explaining that they have the legal right to monitor employees' computer usage and require that their employees acknowledge that right before accepting employment. Most employers, however, do not abuse their right to monitor employees; employers only want to protect themselves from any illegal or harmful use of their network and computer systems.

INTERNET SERVICE PROVIDERS   An Internet service provider (ISP) is capable of tracking online usage, because all of its customers' Web traffic goes through the ISP's system. Unlike an employer, however, an ISP has no legitimate reason to track online behavior. Most ISP customers responded negatively to any revelations that an ISP is gathering their private information. Thus, although an ISP has the ability to record online activities, many ISPs publish and adhere to a **privacy policy** which specifically describes what information they collect, how they use it, and whether they share this information with third parties. The terms of such a privacy policy then are made available to their customers in the form of a **privacy statement**, usually posted at the ISP's Web site.

GOVERNMENT   The concern about privacy has led to federal and state laws being passed regarding the storage and disclosure of personal data. Several of these laws protect certain kinds of information, such as medical records and financial data, from being revealed to anyone without permission. Other laws limit the U.S. government's right to track online activities to specific circumstances.

For example, the **Electronic Communications Privacy Act** (**ECPA**), which grew out of the Watergate scandal of the 1970s, prohibits access to stored communications or transmitted messages such as e-mail or voice mail without consent or a court order, and then only in the course of a criminal investigation. (One exception under this law is an employer, which can legally monitor its employees, as you learned in the previous section.) The **Patriot Act**, which grew out of the post-September 11 terrorist attacks, increases the scope of government investigations to electronic communications. Under the guidelines stated in the ECPA and the Patriot Act, the FBI can use its Carnivore software program to monitor e-mail and online activity relevant to ongoing terrorist or criminal activity. With regard to commercial Web sites, the ECPA requires that companies adhere to their stated privacy policies, as discussed in the next section.

COMPANY WEB SITES   A company can, at its Web site, collect personal information, such as name, address, telephone number, or credit card information and then store that information in a database. Consumers visiting Web sites should be aware of what information is collected, how it is used, and how it is protected. Consumers can learn how a company handles personal information collected at its Web site by reading the site's privacy statement.

Like ISPs, many commercial Web sites publish their privacy policies in an easily accessible privacy statement posted at their Web sites. You typically can find a link to a privacy statement at the bottom of a site's home page.

Many companies demonstrate a commitment to privacy by applying to be part of the TRUSTe program. The TRUSTe program is a voluntary program in which a company's Web site and business practices are reviewed by TRUSTe to ensure that the site adheres to established privacy principles and complies with ongoing TRUSTe review and consumer resolution procedures. Once approved, the site can display the TRUSTe trustmark, a seal displayed by TRUSTe member sites.

In general, to be an informed consumer and Web user, everyone should make a practice of viewing the privacy statement at frequently visited Web sites to see exactly what information is collected and how it is used. The privacy statement should indicate how the company handles **personally identifiable information** (**PII**), such as an e-mail address, name and address, or even more sensitive personal information, such as health, financial, political, or religious information. Figure 2-67 illustrates the privacy statement and TRUSTe trustmark at the Microsoft Web site.

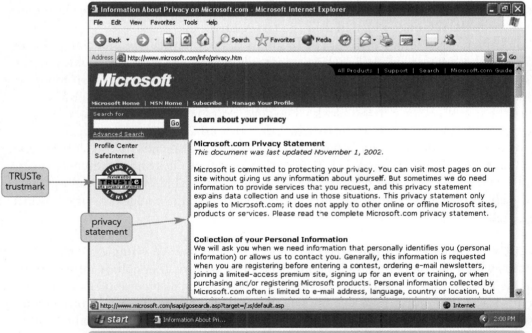

Figure 2-67   A privacy statement explains a company's privacy policy.

Web sites are prohibited from collecting personal information from children under the age of 13. The Children's Online Privacy Protection Act (COPPA), which went into effect in April 2000, requires that Web sites get explicit permission from parents before marketing to or collecting personal data from children. The explicit permission is often in the form of a credit card number.

 @Source

To read the specifics of the Electronic Communications Privacy Act, visit the Discovering the Internet Chapter 2 Web page (scsite.com/internet/ch2) and click a link below ECPA.

 @Source

To learn more about the TRUSTe program, visit the Discovering the Internet Chapter 2 Web page (scsite.com/internet/ch2) and click a link below TRUSTe.

 @Source

To learn more about the Children's Online Privacy Protection Act, visit the Discovering the Internet Chapter 2 Web page (scsite.com/internet/ch2) and click a link below COPPA.

COOKIES   E-businesses and other Web sites often rely on cookies to identify users and customize Web pages. A **cookie** is a small text file stored on a computer's hard drive, which can contain data such as a user name, password, shipping address, or viewing preferences. E-businesses then can use the information stored in cookies to customize Web pages, to remember a user name and password, or to present targeted advertisements on a Web page. E-businesses also use cookies to track which Web site pages are visited most often and other Web site viewer statistics.

Cookies come in several varieties: temporary or persistent, and first-party or third-party. A **temporary cookie**, or **session cookie**, is used to store information during a single session or visit to a Web site. A temporary cookie typically is used to store data such as any items you want to purchase or graphic elements that repeat from page to page. Temporary cookies pose little privacy risk and help make your browsing experience more efficient.

A **persistent cookie** is stored on a computer's hard disk and remains there even after the browser is closed. On the next visit to the Web site, the site can access the cookie to customize Web pages or automatically log in the user. A **first-party cookie** is a persistent cookie placed on the hard disk by the Web page currently being viewed. First-party cookies permit a customized browsing experience based on a set of preferences. These cookies also can store any personal information entered at the Web site. For example, a log in profile that contains a user ID and password, an e-mail address, or name and address, can be stored in a cookie. A **third-party cookie** is a temporary or persistent cookie that originates from a Web site different from the one you currently are visiting. For example, a third-party cookie might be stored on a computer's hard drive when a Web user visits a site that includes advertisements from a third-party e-business. Many online advertising firms, such as DoubleClick, 24/7, and Advertising.com, use third-party cookies to track Web page usage in order to target their advertisements.

You can change the browser's privacy settings in the Internet Options dialog box by specifying whether to accept all cookies, accept temporary or first-party cookies only, or refuse all cookies. Cookies from specific Web sites also can be blocked. When modifying browser privacy settings, you might not want to refuse all cookies. Some Web sites require the use of cookies; if you block all cookies, you may not be able to purchase merchandise, tickets, or services or benefit from customized content at such sites.

Cookies can be deleted from a hard drive; however, deleting all cookies also deletes those that are useful, such as cookies that store personal profiles and preferences for frequently visited sites. Deleting cookies one at a time is preferable, because it allows you to specify which ones to delete. For more information on deleting cookies, see the browser's online Help.

WEB BUGS   In addition to using cookies, some Web sites use **Web bugs** or **Web beacons**, which are hidden graphics embedded in Web pages that collect information about visitors to the site. Web bugs gather information such as a computer's IP address, the type of browser used to retrieve the bug, the Web address of the page from which the user came, and the time the page was viewed. Unlike cookies which can be located on a hard drive and deleted, Web bugs are invisible. Although Web sites commonly use Web bugs to customize a user's experience or to gather statistics on the site, the invisible nature of Web bugs fuels privacy debates. To protect yourself from Web bugs, you can install and use software such as Bugnosis or Ad-aware.

@Source

To learn more about Web bugs, visit the Discovering the Internet Chapter 2 Web page (**scsite.com/ internet/ch2**) and click a link below Web Bugs.

 Facts@Hand

According to a random sample by Cyveillance, eight of the top 50 Web sites use Web bugs to track visitors' behavior on their Web sites.

How Can I Protect My Privacy?

Maintaining privacy is an important issue for Web users. Organizations such as the Electronic Privacy Information Center (EPIC) and Center for Democracy and Technology (CDT) are dedicated to informing consumers about privacy issues and maintain information about privacy issues at their Web sites.

As a result of the influence of EPIC and CDT and other consumer protection organizations, the U.S. Senate is considering new laws to protect the privacy of consumers. The new laws will focus on the following four main principles:

- *Notice*: Web sites must give clear notice as to what information they collect, how that data will be used, and whether it will be released to third parties.

- *Consent*: Web sites must get consumers to specifically **opt in,** or give consent to, having their personally identifiable information collected.

- *Opt out*: Companies must offer a way for consumers to **opt out**, or refuse consent, before any personally identifiable information is collected.

- *Permanence*: If a new company takes control of a Web site as a result of merger or acquisition, the consumer's original opt in or opt out preference still remains in effect.

As discussed earlier, Web users also can take steps to protect and maintain their privacy as they browse the Web by modifying the browser privacy settings using options on the Privacy tab in the Internet Options dialog box. In the following steps, you open the Internet Options dialog box and view the browser's current privacy settings. You will not permanently change the privacy settings unless instructed to do so by your instructor.

 @Source

To visit the EPIC or CDT Web site, visit the Discovering the Internet Chapter 2 Web page (**scsite.com/ internet/ch2**) and click a link below Privacy.

Steps: To View the Browser's Privacy Settings

1 If necessary, start the browser. Click Tools on the menu bar. Click Internet Options. Click the Privacy tab. Point to the slider button. Make a note of the current privacy setting.

The Privacy tab in the Internet Options dialog box displays options for privacy settings. Your original privacy setting may be different than that shown in Figure 2-68.

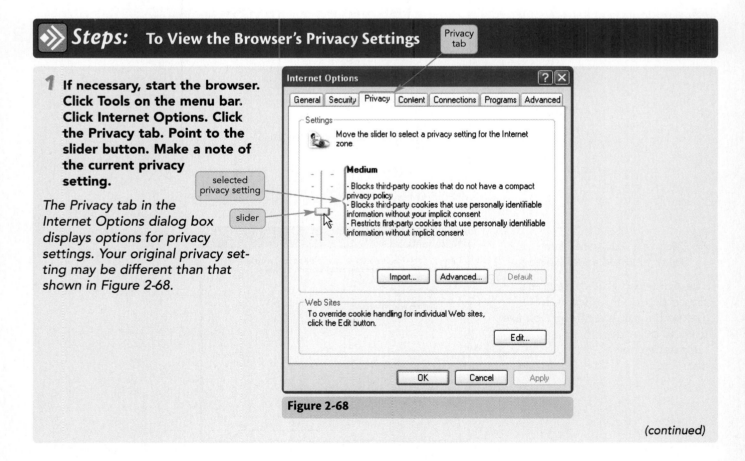

Figure 2-68

(continued)

2 Drag the slider to the bottom to view the lowest privacy setting, Accept All Cookies. Drag the slider up to the next tick mark to view next, highest privacy setting, Low. Point to the slider.

As you drag the slider, the privacy settings change and a description of the current setting appears to the right of the slider (Figure 2-69). Available privacy settings from lowest to highest are Accept All Cookies, Low, Medium, Medium High, High, and Block All Cookies.

Figure 2-69

3 Continue dragging the slider up until you have reviewed all privacy settings. Drag the slider back its original position. Point to the Advanced button.

The privacy setting is returned to its original setting (Figure 2-70).

Figure 2-70

4 Click the Advanced button. Point to the Cancel button.

The Advanced Privacy Settings dialog box opens (Figure 2-71). The settings in this dialog box are used to override automatic cookie handling.

Figure 2-71

5 **Click the Cancel button. Point to the Cancel button in the Internet Options dialog box (Figure 2-72).**

6 **Click the Cancel button.**

The Internet Options dialog box closes and no changes to the browser's privacy settings are made.

Internet Options

General | Security | Privacy | Content | Connections | Programs | Advanced

Settings

Move the slider to select a privacy setting for the Internet zone.

Medium

- Blocks third-party cookies that do not have a compact privacy policy
- Blocks third-party cookies that use personally identifiable information without your implicit consent
- Restricts first-party cookies that use personally identifiable information without implicit consent

Import... | Advanced... | Default

Web Sites

To override cookie handling for individual Web sites, click the Edit button.

Cancel button

Edit...

OK | Cancel | Apply

Figure 2-72

@Issue Opting Out

While Web site owners have a responsibility to post and adhere to privacy policies, consumers can take actions to protect their own privacy. For example, consumers can take time to review the privacy policy statements posted at their favorite Web sites. To protect against third-party or other undesirable cookies on their computers, consumers can delete all unwanted cookies and set options to restrict cookie acceptance. Then check for opt-out instructions at Web sites and submit forms to opt-out of receiving cookies, data collection, and advertising. Taking these actions can help protect and maintain privacy when browsing the Web.

 @Source

For more information on opting-out, visit the Discovering the Internet Chapter 2 Web page (**scsite.com/ internet/ch2**) and click a link below Opt-Out Forms.

CHAPTER REVIEW

The Chapter Review section summarizes the concepts presented in the chapter.

 What Types of Web Pages Are Found at a Typical Web Site, What Are Characteristics of a Web Page, and How Do Web Servers Make Web Sites Available?

The Web is a dynamic environment containing millions of Web sites and billions of Web pages. The number of Web pages at a site varies depending on the site's purpose and the type of content on its pages. A Web site has a primary page, called a **home page**, and one or more additional pages as needed. All the pages are linked together so viewers can move quickly from page to page. A **Web portal** is a special type of Web site that acts as a starting point or doorway to Web content and services.

Web pages are designed to attract and hold the attention of viewers and typically include some or all of the following: a logo or name, images, links, advertisements, a search tool, a copyright statement, and a link to a privacy policy statement.

The interaction between a Web browser and a Web server, where Web pages are stored, is an example of **client/server computing**. The Web browser, a **client**, sends a request to a Web **server**, which responds by sending back a copy of the requested Web page or other Web-based resource. A single Web server can store multiple small Web sites. Large Web sites may span multiple Web servers.

 What Role Do IP Addresses, Domain Names, and URLs Play in Locating Web Pages?

An **IP address** is the unique numerical address of a computer on a network and is used to address and send data over a network, such as the Internet. A **domain name** is an easy-to-remember text alias for one or more IP addresses. A **URL**, also called a **Web address**, is the unique address of a Web page and consists of the http:// protocol, the server name and domain name, and can include the path and file name.

 How Do You Start a Web Browser and View a Web Page?

You can start a Web browser by double-clicking the browser icon on the desktop or by clicking the All Programs command on the File menu. A Web browser window, such as the Internet Explorer window, has a number of features to make browsing the Web easier, such as menus, toolbars, and an Address bar and Address box. When you start a Web browser, the default starting or home page loads in the browser window.

You can load other Web pages by typing each page's **URL** in the **Address box** on the **Address bar** and clicking the **Go button** or pressing ENTER. You also can load a Web page by clicking a Web page link or using a Web page feature. You can navigate between recently loaded Web pages during the current browser session, load a fresh copy of the current page, stop loading a page, and load the default home page by clicking buttons on the **Standard Buttons toolbar**.

 How Can You Revisit Web Pages Using Browser and Desktop Shortcuts?

You can click a **URL** in the **Address list**, click a **favorite** in the Favorites list or on the Favorites menu, or click a link in the History list to revisit a Web page. The

Address list appears when you begin typing a URL in the **Address box**. The Favorites list appears in the **Favorites bar** when you click the Favorites button on the Standard Buttons toolbar. You can create a favorite by adding it to the Favorites list. You also can share favorites between browsers and different computers by importing and exporting them.

The History list appears in the **History bar** when you click the History button on the Standard Buttons toolbar. The History list contains a number of pages of browsing history organized by week and day. You can use a command on the File menu to send the current page as a shortcut to the Windows desktop.

 5 How Can Online Information Be Saved for Later Use?

You can print a copy of the current Web page in order to reference its contents later. You also can save a Web page in a variety of formats that include or exclude the page's related files, such as graphics. You can send a snapshot of a Web page or a link to a page to someone via e-mail. Individual Web page images can be saved for private use such as the Windows desktop background image.

 6 How Can You Change Web Browser Options?

The browser window can be customized by showing and hiding toolbars. Browser features such as the default home page, the number of days of browsing history, the contents of the history list, the display of multimedia content, and privacy settings can be changed in the Internet Options dialog box.

 7 What Are the Risks and Safeguards Related to Using the Web

A computer connected to the Internet can be exposed to unauthorized access by **hackers** who may attempt to damage files or steal information. A damaging computer **virus** can infect an Internet-connected computer through e-mail or downloading files. **Firewalls** and virus protection software are used to protect computers from unauthorized access and virus infections.

In most circumstances, shopping online is a safe activity; however consumers should make purchases from reputable online vendors and take care when making online payments to mitigate the risks in online shopping. Most online shoppers pay by credit card and only make purchases and payments over a **secure connection** that uses the **Secure Sockets Layer (SSL)** security protocol.

Another concern is filtering out objectionable content. **Blocking software** such as Content Advisor allows a supervisor to set a limit on the language, nudity, sex, and violent content that are allowed on Web pages displayed in the browser. In addition to using blocking software, children always should be supervised when using the Web.

Web users can protect their privacy by understanding how Web sites they visit gather and use personal information via online forms, **cookies**, and **Web bugs**. Web users can review a company's **privacy policy** by reading a **privacy statement** posted at the company's Web site. Restricting the acceptance of cookies by modifying browser privacy settings and opting out of receiving cookies and advertising from Web sites also can help protect privacy when browsing the Web.

CHAPTER REVIEW

The Chapter Review section summarizes the concepts presented in the chapter.

TERMS TO KNOW

After reading this chapter, you should know each term.

Active Desktop (77)
Address bar (50)
Address box (50)
Address list (61)
AutoComplete (61)
blocking software (87)
browser icon (50)
client (45)
client-server computing (45)
content filter (87)
cookie (90)
country-code top-level domain (ccTLD) (48)
default home page (49)
display area (49)
domain name (47)
Domain Name System (DNS) (47)
dynamic IP address (47)
Electronic Communications Privacy Act (ECPA) (88)
FAQs (frequently asked questions) (42)
favorite (63)
Favorites bar (63)
firewall (84)
first-party cookie (90)
Go button (50)
hacker (84)
hard copy (72)
History bar (67)
home page (42)
information privacy (87)
Internet Corporation for Assigned Names and Numbers (ICANN) (47)
Internet filter (87)

IP address (Internet Protocol address) (47)
Links bar (50)
menu bar (50)
offline (74)
opt in (91)
opt out (91)
Patriot Act (88)
persistent cookie (90)
personally identifiable information (PII) (89)
plug-in (50)
pop-under (53)
pop-up (53)
portal (42)
privacy policy (88)
privacy statement (88)
scroll bar (50)
secure connection (86)
Secure Sockets Layer (SSL) (86)
session cookie (90)
Standard Buttons toolbar (50)
static IP address (47)
status bar (50)
temporary cookie (90)
third-party cookie (90)
title bar (49)
top-level domain (TLD) (48)
Uniform Resource Locator (URL) (48)
virus (84)
Web address (48)
Web beacons (90)
Web bugs (90)
Web portal (42)

True or False

Mark T for True and F for False. (Answers are found on page numbers in parentheses.)

_____ 1. It is difficult to count how many Web sites and Web pages exist because Web sites and Web pages are continually being added and deleted. (50)

_____ 2. The main reason a Web server is given an IP address is so that people can remember how to find and view Web pages stored on it. (47)

_____ 3. The protocol (http://) and the domain name in a URL are not case sensitive, but the path and file name can be. (49)

_____ 4. Clicking the Back button on the Standard Buttons toolbar loads the default home page in the browser. (57)

_____ 5. To access a recently viewed page, you can click a URL in the Address list. (61)

_____ 6. You can click the Favorites button to display a list of all recently viewed Web pages organized by day and by week. (67)

_____ 7. When printing a Web page, the browser automatically adds a footer with the URL and date on which the Web page was printed. (73)

_____ 8. A firewall is a security system that uses hardware and/or software to prevent unauthorized access to a computer on a network. (84)

_____ 9. The secure https:// protocol and a padlock icon signify that your information is being sent over a secure connection. (86)

_____ 10. Web sites are prohibited by law from collecting personal information from children under the age of 13. (89)

Multiple Choice

Select the best answer. (Answers are found on page numbers in parentheses.)

1. The Address bar, the Standard Buttons toolbar, and the status bar are all features of a Web _____ . (49)
   a. browser
   b. page
   c. site
   d. server

2. Top-level domains include _____ . (47)
   a. .com for businesses
   b. .gvt for government
   c. .net for non-profit institutions
   d. all of the above

3. A Web site that offers links to a wide range of content and services and is often used as a default starting page is called a _____ . (42)
   a. home page
   b. portal
   c. surf spot
   d. Web browser

(continued)

TEST YOUR KNOWLEDGE

Use the Test Your Knowledge exercises to check your knowledge of the chapter.

TEST YOUR KNOWLEDGE *(continued)*

4. To revisit a page without having to type the entire URL, _____ . *(61)*
   a. click the URL in the Address list
   b. click a link in the History list
   c. click a favorite in the Favorites list
   d. all of the above

5. To add a Web page shortcut to the desktop, _____ . *(70)*
   a. click the Favorites button and then click the Add to Favorites button
   b. double-click the Address box, type the URL, and then click OK
   c. drag the Web page icon from the Address bar to the desktop
   d. all of the above

6. When you add a favorite to the Favorites list, you can specify _____ . *(63)*
   a. the name of the favorite
   b. the existing folder in which to store it
   c. a new folder in which to store it
   d. all of the above

7. To print a selected portion of a Web page, _____ . *(72)*
   a. select it with the mouse pointer, click Print on the File menu, and then click Selection
   b. select it with the mouse and then click the Print button
   c. use Print Preview to specify which page or pages you want to print
   d. choose Print as HTML from the File menu

8. When you see an image on a Web page that you want to save, _____ . *(74)*
   a. point to the image and then click the Save button on the Standard Buttons toolbar
   b. right-click the image and then click Save Picture As
   c. right-click the image and then click E-mail Picture
   d. all of the above

9. Laws prohibit _____ from monitoring your online behavior. *(88)*
   a. your employer
   b. your ISP
   c. the Web sites you visit
   d. none of the above

10. A _____ cookie is used to store information during a single browser session. *(90)*
    a. first-party
    b. third-party
    c. temporary
    d. permanent

Instructions: To complete the Learn It Online exercises, start your browser, click the Address bar, and then enter the Web address **scsite.com/internet/ch2**. Follow the instructions in the exercises below. Each exercise has instructions for printing your results, either for your own records or for submission to your instructor.

1 Chapter Reinforcement

TF, MC, and SA

Click the Chapter Reinforcement link. Print the quiz by clicking Print on the File menu for each page. Answer each question.

2 Flash Cards

Click the Flash Cards link and read the instructions. Type 20 (or a number specified by your instructor) in the Number of playing cards text box, type your name in the Enter your Name text box, and then click the Flip Card button. When the flash card is displayed, read the question and then click the Answer box arrow to select an answer. Flip through Flash Cards. If your score is 15 (75%) correct or greater, click Print on the File menu to print your results. If your score is less than 15 (75%) correct, then redo this exercise by clicking the Replay button.

3 Practice Test

Click the Practice Test link. Answer each question, enter your first and last name at the bottom of the page, and then click the Grade Test button. When the graded practice test is displayed on your screen, click Print on the File menu to print a hard copy. Continue to take practice tests until you score 80% or better.

4 Who Wants To Be a Computer Genius?

Click the Computer Genius link. Read the instructions, enter your first and last name at the bottom of the page, and then click the Play button. When your score is displayed, click the Print Results link to print a hard copy.

5 Crossword Puzzle Challenge

Below Chapter 2, click the Crossword Puzzle Challenge link. Read the instructions, and then enter your first and last name. Click the SUBMIT button. Work the crossword puzzle. When you are finished, click the Submit button. When the crossword puzzle is redisplayed, click the Print Puzzle button to print a hard copy.

EXERCISES

Use the Exercises to gain hands-on Internet experience.

To complete these exercises you must be connected to the Internet and have access to a printer.

1 Compare Portals and Change the Browser Home Page

1. Visit the Discovering the Internet Web page (**scsite.com/internet/**) and click Chapter 2.

2. Click a link below Exercise 1 to view a Web portal home page and examine the features on the page.

3. Click the Back button on the Standard Buttons toolbar to return to the Chapter 2 Web page and then continue to click the links below Exercise 1 until you have reviewed all the portals.

4. Revisit the portal of your choice using the Back or Forward buttons on the Standard Buttons toolbar.

5. Click Tools on the menu bar and click Internet Options to open the Internet Options dialog box. Click the General tab, if necessary. Important! Write down the URL of the current default home page as shown in the Address box. Click Use Current to set the portal page as your browser's home page and click OK.

6. Click the Back button on the Standard Buttons toolbar to revisit a previously viewed page. Then click the Home button on the Standard Buttons toolbar to view the new browser home page.

7. Open the General tab in the Options dialog box and reset the browser's home page back to its default home page. (**Hint:** type the URL of the default home page in the Address box or click Use Default, if the home page is the MSN portal page, and then click OK.)

2 Identify Characteristics of a Web Page

1. Visit the Discovering the Internet Chapter 2 Web page (**scsite.com/internet/ch2**) and click a link below Exercise 2 to review a Web site that allows you to send electronic greeting cards. Click File on the menu bar and click Print to print the Web page.

2. Examine the site's home page in the browser window. On the home page printout, label each of the following items:
   a. Logo or name of the site
   b. Image as a link
   c. Text as a link
   d. Advertisement for another company's product or service
   e. Copyright statement or link
   f. Privacy policy link
   g. Link to a FAQ page

3. Click various links on the site's home page to browse other pages at the site. Use the Back and Forward buttons on the Standard Buttons toolbar to revisit the recently viewed pages.

4. Use the Address list to revisit recently viewed pages.

3 Copy, Paste, and Print Web Page Text

1. Visit the Discovering the Internet Chapter 2 Web page (**scsite.com/internet/ch2**) and click Dictionary.com below Exercise 3.

2. Type URL in the Dictionary.com search text box and click the Look it up button.

3. Using the mouse pointer, drag to select the first definition for the acronym URL. Click File on the menu bar and click Print. Click the Selection option button and click Print to print the selected definition.

4. Verify that the URL definition text is still selected. Click Edit on the menu bar and click Copy to copy the selected text to the Clipboard.

5. Click the Start button on the taskbar, point to All Programs, point to Accessories, and click WordPad to open the WordPad application.

6. Click Edit on the WordPad menu bar and click Paste to paste the copied text into a WordPad document.

7. Click File on the menu bar and click Save As. Save the document as URL with the Rich Text Format file type in the folder specified by your instructor. Close the WordPad window.

4 Use the History List

1. Start the browser, if necessary. Click the History button on the Standard Buttons toolbar to open the History bar and view the History list.

2. Click the Today icon or text link in the History list, if necessary, to view a list of folders for Web sites visited by anyone using the computer today.

3. Click a folder in the Today list to expand it, if necessary, and view the links to individual Web pages visited at that site today. Click a link to any Web page to revisit it.

4. Verify that the History list is still open. Click the same folder expanded in Step 3 to collapse it so that only the folder icon is visible and not its contents.

5. Click the Last Week icon or text link, if necessary, to view the folders for Web sites visited last week. Open a folder, revisit a Web site, and close the folder.

6. Click the Last Week icon or text link and the Today icon or text link to collapse the lists of Web site folders.

7. Click the History button on the Standard Buttons toolbar to close the History list.

5 Create Web Page Shortcuts

1. Start the browser, if necessary. Type `scsite.com/internet/` in the Address box on the Address bar and press Enter to load the Discovering the Internet – Home page in the browser window.

(continued)

EXERCISES

Use the Exercises to gain hands-on Internet experience.

EXERCISES *(continued)*

2. Click the Favorites button on the Standard Buttons toolbar to display the Favorites list in the Favorites bar.

3. Click the Add button in the Favorites bar and click Create in>> in the Add Favorite dialog box. Click New Folder, type your name in the Folder name text box, and click OK to create a new folder in which to save the scsite.com/internet/favorite. Click OK in the Add Favorite dialog box to save the Discovering the Internet – Home favorite in your new folder.

4. Click the new folder in the Favorites list to view the saved favorite link.

5. Right-click the new folder in the Favorites list, click Delete, and click Yes to delete the folder and its contents. Click the Favorites button on the Standard Buttons toolbar to close the Favorites bar and Favorites list.

6. Verify that the Discovering the Internet – Home page is displayed in the browser. Show the Links bar, if necessary, by right-clicking the Standard Buttons toolbar and clicking Links. Right-click the Links bar and click Lock the Toolbars to remove the checkmark and unlock the toolbars, if necessary. Drag the Links bar to the left with the mouse pointer.

7. Drag the Web page icon in the Address box on the Address bar to the Links bar to add a shortcut button to the Discovering the Internet – Home page on the Links bar.

8. Right-click the Discovering the Internet – Home page button on the Links bar, click Delete, and click Yes to remove the shortcut.

9. Right-click the Links bar and click Lock the Toolbars to lock them. Right-click the Standard Buttons toolbar and click Links to turn off the Links bar, if desired.

 6 Send a Web Page via E-Mail and Save a Web page

This exercise requires you to use send a Web page via e-mail and save a Web page to the computer's hard drive. Check with your instructor for the recipient's e-mail address and in which folder to save the page.

1. Visit the Discovering the Internet Chapter 2 Web page (**scsite.com/internet/ch2**) and click ESPN below Exercise 6.

2. Browse the ESPN Web site to find a page you think is interesting.

3. Click File on the menu bar, point to Send, and click Page by E-mail to open your e-mail program. Enter the recipient's e-mail address provided by your instructor and click Send. If necessary, close the e-mail application window.

4. Verify that the ESPN page is open in the browser. Click File and click Save As to open the Save Web Page dialog box. Switch to the folder specified by your instructor, verify that the Save as type is Web Page, complete (*.htm, *.html), and click Save.

7 Visit the Better Business Bureau and Amazon.com Web Sites

1. Visit the Discovering the Internet Chapter 2 Web page (scsite.com/internet/ch2) and click Better Business Bureau Online below Exercise 7 to load the BBBOnline home page in the browser.

2. Review the BBBOnline home page to find links to information and services are available at the site.

3. Click the Education link, scroll down, and then click the Online Shopping Tips link. Follow the links on the Online Shopping Tips page to answer the following questions:
   a. How can I tell if a transaction is secure?
   b. What is the safest way to pay for an online purchase?
   c. To whom can I complain if I am not satisfied with an online purchase?

4. Use the Back button list to revisit the BBBOnline home page and click the For Businesses link. Click OK to view pages over a secure connection, if asked. Use links on the BBBOnline Programs page to answer the following questions:
   a. What is the BBBOnline Privacy Seal Program?
   b. What requirements must companies meet to earn the BBBOnline privacy seal?

5. Visit the Discovering the Internet Chapter 2 Web page (scsite.com/internet/ch2) and click Amazon below Exercise 7 to load the Amazon.com home page in the browser. Click Yes, if asked about leaving a secure connection.

6. Click the See More Stores link to display a directory of stores at the Web site. Click the Home & Garden link to load the Home and Garden page in the browser. Scroll the page to view its content.

7. Use the Standard Buttons toolbar or Web page links to return to the Amazon.com home page and locate a link to the company's returns policy. Click the Returns Policy link and answer the following questions:
   a. How soon should you return an item for the price to be fully refundable?
   b. Who pays the shipping costs if an item was shipped in error?
   c. Can you return a CD, DVD, or VHS tape that has been opened?

8 Visit the eBay and PayPal Web Sites

1. Visit the Discovering the Internet Chapter 2 Web page (scsite.com/internet/ch2) and click eBay below Exercise 8 to load the eBay home page in the browser.

2. Use a link to view the eBay Motors Web page listing autos, trucks, and auto parts for sale. Use the Browse Cars by Make list to locate Bentley automobiles (or other auto of your choice).

3. Click the Price link in the All Models section on the Bentleys page to arrange the listings from highest to lowest price and answer the following questions:
   a. What are the price, mileage, and model year of the highest-priced car in the list?
   b. What are the price, mileage, and model year of the lowest-priced car in the list?

(continued)

EXERCISES

Use the
Exercises to
gain hands-on
Internet
experience.

EXERCISES (continued)

4. Click the eBay home link. Scroll to the bottom of the Web page and click the Help link. Use links on the eBay Help Center page to answer the following questions, then close the eBay Help Center window.
   a. How can I register to buy items at eBay?
   b. How can I register to sell items at eBay?
   c. How can I trade safely at the eBay site?

5. Visit the Discovering the Internet Chapter 2 Web page (scsite.com/internet/ch2) and click PayPal below Exercise 8 to load the PayPal home page in the browser.

6. Scroll to the bottom of the PayPal home page and click the Accounts link. Write a brief summary of the three types of PayPal accounts.

9 | Privacy Policies

1. Navigate to the following e-commerce Web sites by entering the URL in the Address box on the Address bar. Locate and click the link to each company's privacy policy statement.
   a. Amazon.com (http://www.amazon.com/)
   b. Wal-Mart (http://www.walmart.com/)
   c. Dell, Inc. (http://www.dell.com/)

2. Answer the following privacy issue questions for each Web site:
   a. What information is collected from viewers? Is any of the information collected personally identifiable information?
   b. Why is the information collected?
   c. Does the company share the collected information with its business partners?
   d. How long is the information retained?
   e. Can a viewer opt-out of the information collection, and if so, how?
   f. Does the Web site post any privacy guarantees, such as TRUSTe or BBBOnline.
   g. Does the site use cookies and, if so, why?

10 | Research Carnivore on the Web

1. Visit the Discovering the Internet Chapter 2 Web page (scsite.com/internet/ch2) and click FBI below Exercise 10.

2. Click the Search link to view the site's search page. When the search page appears, type Carnivore in the For: text box, and then click the Go button.

3. Click a link to display the FBI Press Room - Congressional Statement - 2000 - Carnivore Diagnostic Tool. Use information on the page to:
   a. List the types of cyber-crime threats against which Carnivore is used.
   b. Explain the types of information Carnivore collects and the types of information it filters out.
   c. Write a few sentences explaining what prevents the FBI from using Carnivore to spy on the activities of normal citizens.

NOTES

CHAPTER 3
Searching the Web

Introduction

Information on demand. Being able to
search for information stored on the Web
is one of the most powerful features of the
Internet and the most popular Internet activity after e-mail.
In this chapter, you will learn how to describe and follow the
steps in the search process, search Web page text, perform
basic and advanced searches using different types of search
tools, perform browser searches, and use special search tools
to locate people, businesses, and current news stories. Finally,
you will learn about the hidden information resources on the
invisible Web.

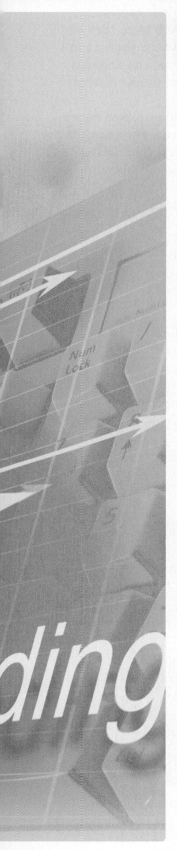

OBJECTIVES

After completing this chapter, you will be able to:

1. Describe the search process

2. Use different types of search tools and compare search results

3. Use search engine advanced search features including Boolean operators

4. Perform browser searches

5. Search for people, businesses, and news and use online research alternatives to search tools

6. Describe the invisible Web

CONTENTS

The Search Process

Many people now rely on the Web when looking for specific information. As you learned in Chapter 2, when Web users know the URL for a familiar Web page, they can enter the URL in their browser's Address box or click a favorite to load the page. In this way, sports fans can get the latest scores or team standings, an executive can keep up with the latest industry news and trends, and consumers can purchase products or services from their favorite online store.

At other times, Web users seeking specific information may not know a Web page's URL or may not be aware of a site that offers the information they need. For example, suppose you want to learn more about the origin of Valentine's Day and want to visit a Web site that can provide that information. One way could be to guess an appropriate URL — something like www.valentinesday.com — and enter that guess in the browser's Address box. If no appropriate Web page is loaded, you could guess again. Instead of trying to guess a valid URL, a more effective and direct way to find information about the origins of Valentine's Day is to search the Web for sites and pages containing the desired information. Figure 3-1 illustrates a specific process that can be followed when searching the Web. In the next sections, you learn more about this process.

1. Choose the best search tool.

2. Formulate the search query.

3. Perform the search.

4. Examine the search results.

5. Evaluate the credibility of the search results.

Figure 3-1   The Web search process.

Choosing the Best Search Tool

Searching the Web effectively starts with selecting the best search tool to use for a particular search. Different types of search tools, such as Yahoo!, Google, LookSmart, and WiseNut (Figure 3-2) are prevalent on the Web. You will learn more about these and other search tools and how to use them later in the chapter. It is important to consider, however, that search tool features and performance vary from tool to tool and change over time. Additionally, new search tools continue to be developed. The best plan is to become familiar with and use multiple search tools. This allows you to evaluate search tools and then choose the tool best suited for a particular search. In general, when evaluating search tools, look for tools that:

- Are easy to use
- Return search results quickly
- Maintain a large index of Web pages and other Web-based files, such as images, movies, and videos
- Update their indexes continually to keep them fresh
- Present the most relevant search results for a keyword search
- Limit or exclude advertisements and clearly indicate paid or sponsored links in their search results list

(a) Yahoo!

(b) Google

(c) LookSmart

(d) WiseNut

Figure 3-2 A number of search tools, such as Yahoo!, Google, LookSmart, and WiseNut are available on the Web.

Facts@Hand

According to the Pew Internet & American Life Project, on any given day 29 percent of Web users use a search tool.

Formulating the Search Query

The next step in the process of searching the Web is formulating a search query. A search **query** or question defines the information you seek. A query should include at least one **keyword**, a specific word that describes that information. To get the best results, choose keywords carefully and use specific rather than general keywords, whenever appropriate. For example, suppose you recently visited an animal shelter and are considering adopting one of two dogs you saw at the shelter. But before you adopt the new pet, you want to use the Web to learn more about the nature, personality, and care requirements of your two adoption possibilities: a sheltie and a golden retriever. The search keywords *sheltie* or *golden retriever* will generate more relevant results than the search keyword *dog*.

Search keywords are entered in a search tool's **search text box**. A search tool then uses the keywords to identify relevant Web pages and return a **search results list** containing the URL, title, and description of and links to Web pages deemed to be the most relevant to the keywords. Each Web page item listed in a search results list is called a **hit**. Figure 3-3 illustrates a search using the keyword *sheltie* and the resulting search results list.

The more keywords used in a query, the more focused the results will be. For example, assume you are planning a vacation and want to find information

Figure 3-3 Search keywords entered in a search tool's search text box are used to return a search results list containing relevant Web page hits.

about a specific national park. Searching for Web pages using the keyword *park* will return a list of more than 70 million pages, far more than you can or want to review and most of which are irrelevant to the information you seek. Using the keywords *grand canyon national park* returns more relevant hits because the search process returns only pages that contain all of those keywords.

To narrow a search further, use a phrase as a query and surround the phrase with quotation marks. A search for *James Dean*, for example, may return results including pages containing information about James Taylor and Dean Guitars. Using quotation marks around the phrase — "James Dean" — narrows the results to hits that contain only that exact phrase.

While it is always better to spell search keywords correctly, some search tools either may list search results for correctly spelled keywords or suggest the correct spelling. For example, searching for information about a musical instrument using the keyword *accordian*, may return a list of Web pages based on the correct spelling *accordion* depending on which search tool is used.

Some search tools allow you to put the query in the form of a statement or question, such as, *What is the population of Iowa?* A search that uses complete sentences is a **natural language search** (Figure 3-4). Small, unimportant words in a natural language query, called **stop words**, are ignored and only the more important words are used. Examples of stop words include what, where, is, the, of, in, and how.

Figure 3-4 The Ask Jeeves search tool performs natural language searches.

Some search tools allow you to include keywords in the query, by preceding them with a plus sign — for example, *queen elizabeth +I* or to exclude keywords from a query by using a minus sign — for example, *diamonds –baseball*. Different search tools have various methods for including and excluding keywords, however, so it is a good idea to review a search tool's FAQ pages or online Help section for information about formulating queries. Examples of effective queries that can be used with most search tools include the following:

- To look up a specific company, product, or school, enter the specific name as a keyword, such as *Cisco Systems*, *Toyota Camry*, or *Ohio State*.
- To shop for a product or service, enter the word, shop, followed by the name of the product or service: for example, *shop digital cameras*.
- To check stock quotes, enter the word, quote, followed by the ticker symbol, such as *quote MSFT*.
- To find information about restaurants, movies, concerts, news, sports, or weather in a city, type the name of the city followed by one of those keywords: for example, *Philadelphia sports*.

Examining the Search Results

Different search tools actually perform a search and then display hits in the search results list in different ways; thus it is very important to become familiar with and use a variety of search tools. As you have learned, the hits in a search results list are presented in a certain order, usually with more relevant hits at the top of the list. Some search tools place hits for recommended sites at the top of a search results list because a human editor has determined that the sites are the most relevant to the keywords. Other search tools may place hits for affiliated sites, called featured sites or sponsored listings, near or at the top of a search results list because the affiliated sites pay the search tools to do so. Although listed at or near the top, affiliated site hits may not provide the best information for a query. For this reason, it is important to scroll further down a search results list to review other, possibly more relevant hits.

The number of the hits returned in a search results list depends on a query's structure and keywords. For example, a targeted search might seek answers to a specific question such as, *What is the average rainfall in the Amazon rainforest?* This type of targeted search requires examining only a few Web pages until locating the specific information. An open-ended search asks open-ended questions such as, *What is a rainforest?* An open-ended search like this typically generates millions of hits and requires reviewing multiple Web pages to gather appropriate information. Scholarly research often involves open-ended searches.

 Facts@Hand

Studies show that 70 percent of the time that people use search tools, they are seeking a single, targeted answer.

Because a Web search can return thousands or millions of hits, most people typically look only at the first 10 or 20 hits in a search results list. If no relevant pages are found, they then reformulate the query and search again using the same search tool or a different search tool. When a search results list with possibly relevant pages is returned, the next step is to click the links associated with relevant hits and review each Web page to find the desired information.

Sometimes it is difficult to locate specific information on a Web page, especially when the page contains large text paragraphs. Visually scanning a long Web page with densely worded paragraphs can take some time. You can perform a keyword search on the page's contents to locate specific information more quickly on the page. In the following steps, you load a Web page in the browser and then perform a keyword search on the page's contents to find specific information.

Steps: To Search a Web Page

1 **If necessary, start the browser. Visit the Discovering the Internet Chapter 3 Web page (scsite.com/internet/ch3). Click Grand Canyon National Park. Point to Edit on the menu bar.**

The Grand Canyon National Park Nature and Science page appears (Figure 3-5). The content of the Web pages on your screen may vary from that in Figures 3-5 through 3-9 on pages 113 and 114.

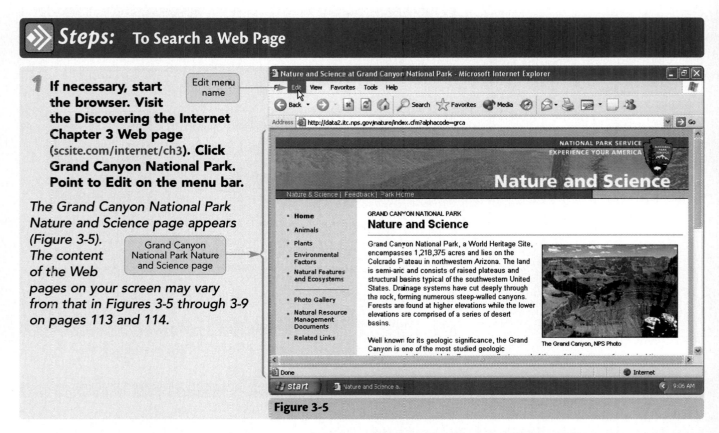

Figure 3-5

2 **Click Edit. Point to Find (on This Page).**

The Edit menu opens (Figure 3-6).

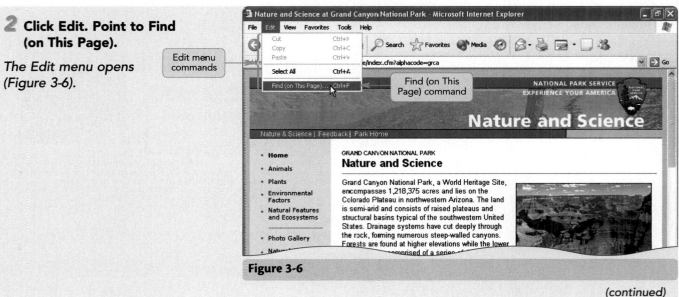

Figure 3-6

(continued)

3 Click Find (on This Page). Type **Colorado River** in the Find what text box. Point to the Find Next button.

The Find dialog box appears (Figure 3-7). You type the keywords for the Web page search in this dialog box.

Figure 3-7

4 Click the Find Next button. Scroll the page to view the Colorado River selected Web page text. Point to the Find Next button.

The first instance of the keywords, Colorado River, is found in the page (Figure 3-8). You can continue to search for other instances of the keywords until the entire page is searched.

Figure 3-8

5 Click the Find Next button. Point to OK.

When no other instances of the keywords are found, a message window appears indicating the search is complete (Figure 3-9).

6 Click OK. Click Cancel in the Find dialog box.

Figure 3-9

In Netscape
To search Web page contents in Netscape, click Find in This Page on the Edit menu. Type a keyword in the Find text box and click Find to locate each instance of the keyword in the page.

Evaluating the Credibility of Search Results

A key step in the search process is to evaluate the credibility of the hits listed in a search results list. A list of hits can contain an assortment of pages; and while all may contain information related to the query, not all will contain accurate or useful information. Because the Internet offers anyone the opportunity to publish information, careful assessment of the credibility Web page content is important. To do this, look at the authority of the source, the objectivity of the text, the scope and quality of the content, and the site's design and functionality.

AUTHORITY The first step in determining the quality of the information on a Web page is to examine its authority. To do this, determine who owns or sponsors the Web site of which the page is a part and, if possible, who authored the Web page content. Try to determine if the content's author and/or the site's sponsor has the appropriate expertise to present the information authoritatively. To do this, look for and read any background information posted about a page's author or the site's sponsoring organization.

Some search tools give extra weight to governmental and education Web pages, listing these hits at or near the top of a search results list. Look past the top-level domain to the country-code top-level domain, however, when evaluating the authority of these sites. For example, information presented by agencies of a totalitarian government that limits free speech or free access to the Internet and the Web may not be unbiased or completely accurate. Sites with the .edu top-level domain represent educational institutions, but a Web page at an educational site may be the work of a student rather than a scholar. The highest quality and more authoritative results come from primary sources. A primary source is any document, item, or other data that provides firsthand information about a particular topic. For example, when searching for the history of the Web, an authoritative primary source would be a Web page with an account written by Tim Berners-Lee, who experienced the beginnings of the Web firsthand.

OBJECTIVITY When examining a Web site's objectivity, determine whether the Web page information is fair, whether any biases are stated clearly, or whether the information is skewed toward commercial interests. For example, when looking for information about vitamins or nutritional supplements, determine whether a Web page bases its recommendations on scientific evidence or whether it is part of a commercial site that profits by promoting the sale of its particular formulas. One way to assess objectivity is to look for high-quality links on the Web page to other related sites.

SCOPE AND QUALITY Evaluating the scope of Web page content — that is, the depth of coverage and the amount of detail provided — can help determine its value. The intended audience, whether for children or adults, professionals or enthusiasts, often determines the scope of a Web site. Additionally, high-quality Web page content should be accurate and up-to-date.

One technique for determining scope and quality is to compare several Web page sources that discuss the same topic. Different Web pages may offer different information on the same topic. For example, in searching for the origin of pizza, the name of

Queen Margherita appears in a number of documents. If several Web pages refer to her but one Web page spells her name incorrectly or omits a reference to her entirely, you may consider that page to be a less valuable source of information. Some Web page authors publish information gathered from others without careful research. Web page content that has been carefully researched typically offers more details and depth, as well as citations or references to other sources. Therefore, comparing Web page coverage of the same topic can be helpful in evaluating the scope and quality of information on the pages. In addition, look for dates on Web pages indicating when the information was published or last updated. Out-of-date pages may not present the most recent information.

DESIGN AND FUNCTIONALITY   A first impression of the site also offers insight to its credibility. Web Pages with grammar or spelling errors, poor organization, missing images, or broken links — links that no longer work — at best indicate a poor attention to detail and at worst may indicate the page is a poor-quality source. Be aware, however, that an attractive and professional-looking Web page is no guarantee of high-quality, credible content.

Figure 3-10 lists several key questions to ask as you evaluate the credibility of Web page content. Using these questions and the guidelines outlined above can help you identify valuable information resources from among the many hits listed in a search results list.

Area	Questions
AUTHORITY	• Is this a primary source document? • Is the Web page's sponsoring organization or author a noted authority? • Are the Web pages up-to-date?
OBJECTIVITY	• Is the page objective? • Is any bias clearly stated?
SCOPE	• What is the intended audience for this site? • How does the information on the Web page compare with others on the same topic?
DESIGN AND FUNCTIONALITY	• Does the page have a professional appearance? • Do all parts of the page work correctly?

Figure 3-10   Questions to ask when evaluating the credibility of Web pages.

🌐 @Source

To learn more about evaluating Web pages, visit the Discovering the Internet Chapter 3 Web page (**scsite.com/ internet/ch3**) and click a link below Evaluation Checklists.

Search Tools

In the early 1990s, before the Web, Internet users needed a way to find specific files stored on FTP servers and Gopher servers. In 1990, three students at McGill University in Montreal, Canada — Alan Emtage, Bill Heelan, and Peter Deutsch — developed a search tool called **Archie** to find files on FTP sites. In 1992, the search engine **Veronica** was developed at the University of Nevada to help people search the information stored on Gopher servers. A third search engine, **Jughead**, was created to allow users to search resources within a single Gopher site. By the mid-1990s, new Web-based search tools were being created to help users more easily find resources on the growing Web.

Web-based search tools help users around the world locate all types of information including informational Web pages, e-businesses, people, and multimedia files. Web-based search tools include general-purpose search tools, such as Lycos, HotBot, AltaVista, and MSN Search (Figure 3-11). Additionally, specialty search tools, such as BizRate (shopping), Yahooligans! (kid-friendly searches), AllExperts (fee Q & A service), Switchboard.com (white and yellow pages), and Business.com (B2B listings) abound (Figure 3-12 on the next page).

(a) Lycos

(b) HotBot

(c) AltaVista

(d) MSN Search

Figure 3-11 Search tools include major general-purpose search tools, such as Lycos, HotBot, AltaVista, and MSN Search.

Figure 3-12   Specialty search tools abound on the Web.

Some search tools, such as Inktomi, AlltheWeb, Teoma, and Open Directory (Figure 3-13) are search providers for other popular and well-known search tools. For example, Inktomi provides search results for both Yahoo! and MSN Search. HotBot's search results are provided by AlltheWeb, Inktomi, Google, and Teoma.

Search tools are generally classified as directories, search engines, and metasearch engines. In the following sections, you learn how to identify directories, search engines, and metasearch engines and how to use them to perform basic searches.

(a) Inktomi

(b) AlltheWeb

(c) Teoma

(d) opendirectory

Figure 3-13 Some search tools are search providers for other, popular search tools.

Using Directories

A human-compiled, hierarchical list of Web pages in categories is called a **directory**. One of the first directories was created by Chih-Yuan "Jerry" Yang and David Filo (Figure 3-14), two doctoral students at Stanford, who began to keep a list of interesting Web pages for their personal use. Their Stanford classmates and friends soon began asking to share the list, originally called Jerry's Guide. Before long, the list became long and unwieldy, so Filo and Yang divided the list into categories and then later, as the number of Web pages continued to grow, into subcategories. By late 1994, the Jerry's Guide directory was renamed Yahoo!, and is today one of the most widely used and popular search tools.

Figure 3-14 Jerry Yang and David Filo created Yahoo!, the first widely popular Web directory.

Directories, compiled and indexed by a staff of human editors, are useful search tools that present links to Web sites organized into easy-to-understand categories. Directories offer a way to locate Web-based information by browsing from a general category to an ever more specific category until the desired information is located. For example, using the Yahoo! directory to locate the Guggenheim Museum Web site can involve clicking a number of links to move from a general category, Arts & Humanities, through additional subcategories, to the Guggenheim Museum Web page link and, finally, through to the Guggenheim Museum Web site (Figure 3-15). This process is sometimes called **drilling down** the directory categories.

Figure 3-15 Directories use human editors to organize Web sites into hierarchical categories that can be browsed, or drilled down, by clicking links.

Some directories show, at the top of a page, a horizontal list of links to categories and subcategories through which you have drilled down to reach the current page. This list of category and subcategory links is called a breadcrumb trail. A **breadcrumb trail**, which shows the hierarchical arrangement of categories and subcategories through which you have clicked, makes it easy to navigate back and forth between categories and subcategories and return to the home page by clicking a link.

Using human editors to compile a directory's index of Web resources is both a strength and a weakness. Human editors can organize lists of Web resources in a logical way, making browsing or drilling down through a directory's categories an organized process. Using human editors also is a weakness, however, because of the time it takes for human editors to review new Web pages and add them to a directory's index. Additionally, human editors determine what pages are accepted for the index and what pages are not accepted. Using a directory, therefore, may not provide links to a number of appropriate and useful pages on any particular topic simply because the pages have not yet been indexed or were selected *out* by the editors. In addition to Yahoo!, major directories include LookSmart and the Open Directory.

In the following steps, you drill down the LookSmart directory to find Civil War maps and then return to the LookSmart home page using the breadcrumb trail.

@Source

To review different directories, visit the Discovering the Internet Chapter 3 Web page (scsite.com/internet/ch3) and click a link below Directories.

Steps: To Use a Directory

1 **Start the browser, if necessary. Visit the Discovering the Internet Chapter 3 Web page (scsite.com/internet/ch3). Click LookSmart. If necessary, click the DIRECTORY tab. Point to the Reference & Education link.**

The LookSmart directory Web page appears (Figure 3-16). The contents of the Web pages on your screen may vary from that in Figures 3-16 through 3-23 on pages 121 through 125.

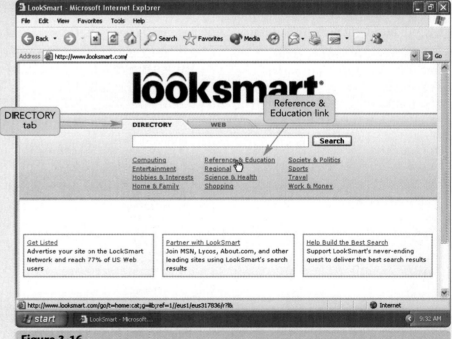

Figure 3-16

(continued)

2 **Click the Reference & Education link. Point to the Reference link.**

The Library page with a Directory Categories list appears (Figure 3-17). You continue to drill down through the Reference category.

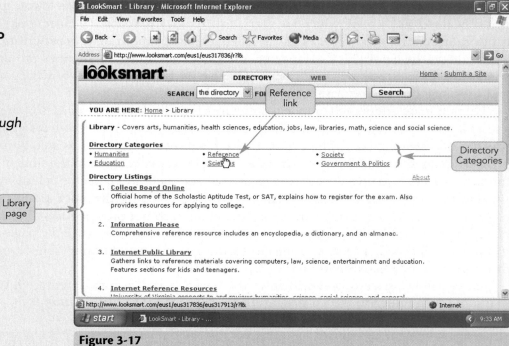

Figure 3-17

3 **Click the Reference link. Point to the Maps & Atlases link.**

The Reference page appears and the Directory Categories list is expanded to show links to different types of reference pages (Figure 3-18). You can see the path of the links you have clicked to reach the current page in the breadcrumb trail.

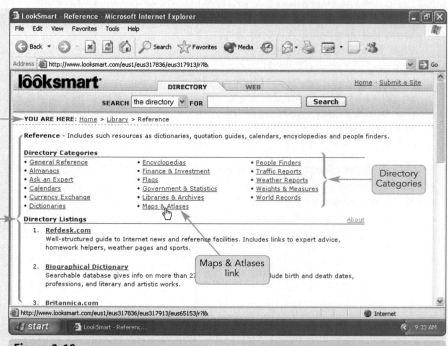

Figure 3-18

4 Click the Maps & Atlases link. Point to the Historic Maps link.

The Maps and Atlases page appears and the Directory Categories list contains map and atlas categories (Figure 3-19).

Maps and Atlases page

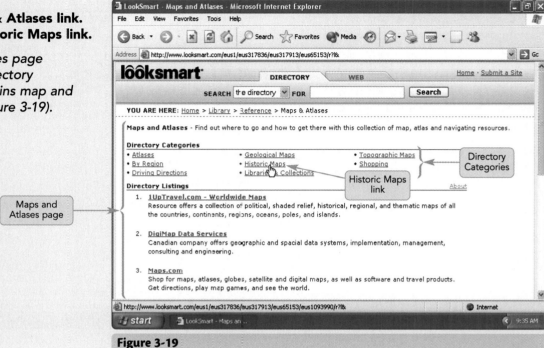

Figure 3-19

5 Click the Historic Maps link. Point to Eras & Events link.

The Historic Maps page appears and the Directory Categories list narrows to include special map and atlas categories (Figure 3-20).

Historic Maps page

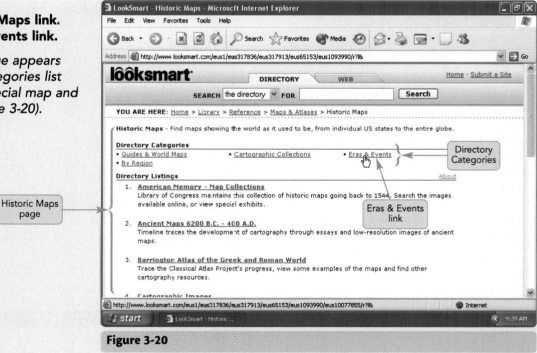

Figure 3-20

(continued)

6 **Click the Eras & Events link. Point to the Civil War link.**

The Early and Historical Maps by Era and Event page appears and the Directory Categories list now contains map and atlas categories by era or event (Figure 3-21).

Early and Historical Maps by Era and Event

Figure 3-21

7 **Click the Civil War link. Point to the Home link in the breadcrumb trail.**

The Civil War page appears and contains directory listings to Web pages with links to Civil War map collections (Figure 3-22). The breadcrumb trail provides a visual cue to the categories and subcategories through which you have drilled down to locate the Civil War maps Web page links. You can click a link in the breadcrumb trail to return to that category page or to the home page.

Civil War page

Figure 3-22

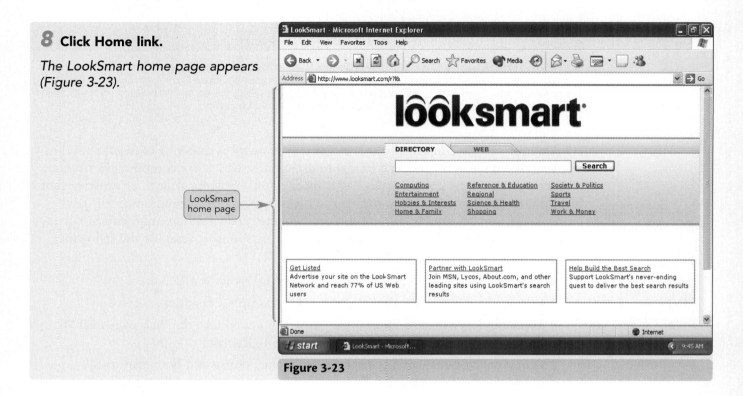

8 Click Home link.

The LookSmart home page appears (Figure 3-23).

LookSmart home page

Figure 3-23

Most directories partner with powerful search tools, called search engines, to enable users to search the directory's index by keywords instead of drilling down through categories and subcategories. Through these search engine partnerships, many directories allow users to search the entire Web in addition to searching the directory's own index. You learn more about search engines in the next section.

Using Search Engines

In early 1995, researchers at Digital Equipment Corporation developed a computer program that could store every word on every Web page in an index that could be searched easily. This program evolved into AltaVista, which was one of the first search engines for the Web and the most powerful one of its kind for many years. Today, popular and useful search engines include Google, AlltheWeb, MSN Search, Yahoo! Search, Ask Jeeves, HotBot, WiseNut, and Lycos.

In terms of sheer audience size, the most popular search tools in the U.S. are Yahoo! and MSN Search. Their popularity reflects the fact that these sites function as portals as well as search tools. In addition, MSN Search functions as the default search engine when users click the Search button in Internet Explorer, thus increasing its popularity. Globally, Google is one of the most widely used search tools.

Google and AlltheWeb are known for their ability to search for items in other file formats and archives from the online discussion groups that pre-date the existence of the Web. These files, which have few or no links to and from the main core of the Web, are considered to be part of the invisible Web, because they are not accessed easily by normal browsing or search engines. (You learn more about the invisible Web later in this chapter.)

Facts@Hand

Studies show that Google and Inktomi (which powers MSN Search, HotBot, and other search tools) have the freshest or most up-to-date indexes. In a study conducted for the Search Engine Showdown, Google found the most unique hits. Other search engines, including AlltheWeb, WiseNut, Teoma, and MSN Search, each returned unique hits that none of the other search engines listed in their search results.

 @Source

To learn more about different search tools and how they work, visit the Discovering the Internet Chapter 3 Web page (scsite.com/internet/ch3) and click a link below Search Tool Comparison.

A search engine consists of three major components: a spider or crawler, an index, and search engine software. In contrast to directories, which are compiled by humans, a **search engine** uses a program called a **spider**, **bot** (short for robot), or **crawler** that browses the Web automatically adding the URLs and other information about new pages to a searchable index. Different search engines collect different kinds of information about each Web page, but search engine spiders typically scan for the following information to create their indexes:

- Page title — specifically the title shown on the browser title bar
- URL — specifically the domain name (for example, cheaptickets.com)
- **Meta tag keywords** — descriptive keywords coded into the Web page's HTML that are readable by the spider but invisible to the user
- Occurrence of keywords — both the frequency of use and how near to the top of the page they appear
- All of the words on the page, which is known as **full-text searching**
- Links within the page
- Number and names of other pages that link to the page

The Web page information received from the spiders is stored in a database on one or more servers creating an **index** similar to the index at the back of a book. Spiders continually scan pages on the Web to update their indexes with modified Web page content or new, previously unknown Web pages. Google and AlltheWeb maintain two of the largest indexes with several billion Web pages and other Web-based resources indexed.

When a user enters keywords into a search engine's search text box, **search engine software** compares the keywords to its index, compiles a list of Web pages for which the keywords are relevant, and arranges the list in a specific order. Each search engine uses its own unique software and formula or algorithm to determine the relevance of a Web page to specific keywords and the order in which to rank or order the pages in the search results list.

Most search engines attempt to present the most useful and relevant hits at or near the top of a search results list in order to make their search engine more useful and to attract more users. As discussed earlier in this chapter, however, some search engines also accept payment from affiliated sites to list Web pages based on certain search keywords. These paid listings may be highlighted and positioned in a prominent place on a search results page or may be included in a search results list.

 Facts@Hand

According to comScore Media Metrix, Google users spend an average of 26 minutes using the search engine. Yahoo! users spend just over 10 minutes.

One search tool, Google, relies solely on its unique ranking algorithm to determine which pages to rank first in a search results list. Paid links do not influence the ranking of hits in a Google search list. Instead, Google lists any sponsored links at the top and right side of the page, separated from the search results. Furthermore, Google does not include any images, banner ads, and pop-up advertisements, to reduce download times and clutter. Other search engines are following this example.

Finally, many search engines today have become hybrids — basing their results on indexes created both by spiders and by human editors. For example, along with its own directory listings, Yahoo! search results include pages from the Google search engine, and Google search results include directory listings from the Open Directory.

In the following steps, you use three different search engines, Google, WiseNut, and AlltheWeb to find Web pages that contain information about lighthouses. As you use each search engine, carefully review each search results list to note the differences in the first ten hits listed, the inclusion of category links, and the position of sponsored listings.

@Source

To review different search engines, visit the Discovering the Internet Chapter 3 Web page (**scsite.com/ internet/ch3**) and click a link below Search Engines.

⟩⟩⟩ *Steps:* To Use a Search Engine

1 **If necessary, start the browser. Visit the Discovering the Internet Chapter 3 Web page (scsite.com/internet/ch3). Click Google. Type** `lighthouses` **in the search text box. Point to the Google Search button.**

The Google home page appears (Figure 3-24). You enter the search query in the search text box. The contents on the Web pages on your screen may vary from that shown in Figures 3-24 through 3-30 on pages 127 through 129.

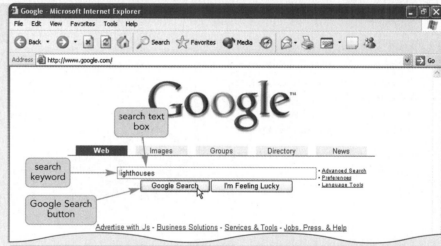

Figure 3-24

2 **Click the Google Search button. Point to the scroll box on the scroll bar.**

The Google search engine displays a list of categories, Sponsored Links (sponsored listings), and the first 10 hits (Figure 3-25).

Figure 3-25

(continued)

3 Scroll the page to review the hits and their ranking in the list, the category links, and the sponsored listings.

Each hit includes the Web page title as a link, the page URL, a brief description, highlighted keywords, the page size, links to older, cached pages (pages stored by Google), and a link to similar pages (Figure 3-26).

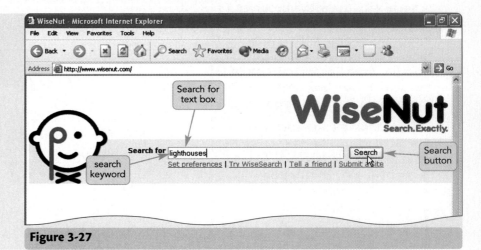

Figure 3-26

4 Visit the Discovering the Internet Chapter 3 Web page (scsite.com/internet/ch3). Click WiseNut. Type lighthouses in the Search for text box. Point to the Search button.

The WiseNut home page appears (Figure 3-27).

Figure 3-27

5 Click the Search button. Scroll the page to review the category links, sponsored listings, and first ten hits.

The WiseNut search results page appears (Figure 3-28). While containing some of the same Web pages, the WiseNut search results list is not identical to the Google search results list in content or hit ranking. Additionally, the WiseNut category links and sponsored listings are different.

Figure 3-28

6 **Visit the Discovering the Internet Chapter 3 Web page (scsite.com/internet/ch3). Click AlltheWeb. Type** lighthouses **in the search text box. Point to the SEARCH button.**

The AlltheWeb home page appears (Figure 3-29).

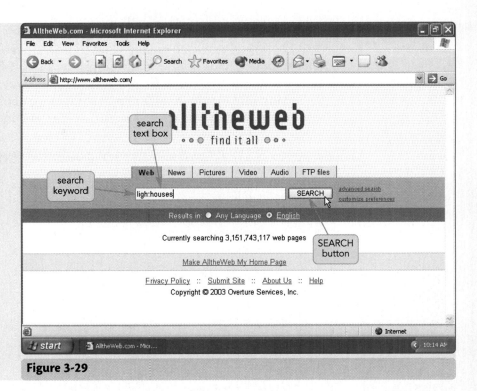

Figure 3-29

7 **Click the SEARCH button. Scroll the page to review the hits, category links, and sponsored listings.**

The AlltheWeb search results page appears (Figure 3-30). Again, the list of hits, sponsored sites, and category links are not identical.

Figure 3-30

Reviewing the search results lists returned by each of the search engines shows that a search results list based on the same search query will not be identical — either in pages listed or in the ranking of those pages — when using different search engines. Also, other features such as directory links may be different and each search engine may offer special tools and features. For example, some search engines offer searches in multiple languages, allow users to customize search results pages, or provide separate search tools for news, images, and multimedia items. Additionally, some search engines, such as Google and Yahoo! Search, allow users to download a search toolbar

(Figure 3-31) as a free browser plug-in. These toolbars are designed to make searching with that specific search engine easier. Finally, paid or sponsored listings may not be as clearly indicated on some such results pages as others. For these reasons, it is important to become familiar with and comfortable using more than one search engine. Reviewing a search engine's online help feature can provide a number of tips for using a search engine and its special features more effectively.

Figure 3-31   Some search engines allow users to download a search toolbar as a browser plug-in to make using their search engines easier.

@Issue Kid-Friendly Searches

The Web makes sitting down with school-aged children to do research for a report seem so easy, now that you do not have to trudge to the library and look through heavy volumes of *Encyclopedia Americana*. It is so easy to use a search tool to locate information for the report. Allowing children to use a general search engine, however, might result in some hits that link to objectionable content. A seemingly innocuous search query can result in hits that link to Web pages that include offensive language, sexually explicit or violent material, or hate propaganda.

For this reason, many search tools include a feature to block objectionable content. Examples of these features include Google's SafeSearch feature, AlltheWeb's Offensive Content Reduction filter, and WiseNut's WiseWatch feature. By default these options typically are enabled, but parents should check this before children use a general search tool.

A number of other search tools are designed specifically for children. These search tools return search results that include only sites that are appropriate for school-aged young people, and they specifically exclude from the results any sites that feature sexually explicit text or images, violence, hate speech, gambling, or information on illicit drugs. Search tools for kids also may serve the needs of children and young teens better by offering search results focused on their level of reading and understanding. Some return only sites selected by an editorial staff that reviews the content of each site.

Several of the major search tools sponsor search engines for children. Some of the more widely used children's search tools include the following:

- Ask Jeeves For Kids
- Yahooligans!
- LycosZone
- KidsClick!
- CyberSleuth-Kids
- Family Friendly Search (a metasearch engine)

To view kid-friendly search engines, visit the Discovering the Internet Chapter 3 Web page (**scsite.com/internet/ch3**) and click a link below Kid-Friendly Searches.

Using Metasearch Engines

Performing the same search multiple times using different search tools can be cumbersome. If you need to perform a basic search and do not need to use any special search tool features, you can combine your searching efforts by using another type of search tool, called a **metasearch engine**. Metasearch engines were developed to compile the search results for multiple search tools into a single search results list. An early example of a metasearch engine is MetaCrawler, which was developed in 1994 by Erik Selberg, a graduate student at the University of Washington, and his professor, Oren Etzioni. Today, metasearch engines include Dogpile, KartOO, SurfWax, and IxQuick (Figure 3-32 on the next page).

Figure 3-32   Metasearch engines submit a search query to multiple search tools and compile the search results in one search list.

@Source

To learn more about metasearch engines, visit the Discovering the Internet Chapter 3 Web page (scsite.com/internet/ch3) and click a link below Metasearch Engines.

When you enter search query keywords in a metasearch engine's search text box, the metasearch engine submits the search query to a number of search engines at one time and then compiles the results from all of them into a single list of hits. A good metasearch engine will eliminate any duplicate entries, categorize the hits based on topic, order the hits by relevance, and indicate which search tools provided the search results. Like search engines, metasearch engines may rely heavily on sponsored listings when listing pages in a search results list.

In the following steps, you use a metasearch engine to search for Web pages containing information about night vision.

Steps: To Use a Metasearch Engine

1 If necessary, start the browser. Visit the Discovering the Internet Chapter 3 Web page (scsite.com/internet/ch3). Click IxQuick. Type `night vision` in the Search text box. Point to the Search button.

The IxQuick home page appears (Figure 3-33).

Figure 3-33

2 Click the Search button. Point to the scroll box on the scroll bar.

The IxQuick search results page appears. The search results page includes links to related searches, sponsored listings, and a checklist of the search engines and directories used in the search (Figure 3-34).

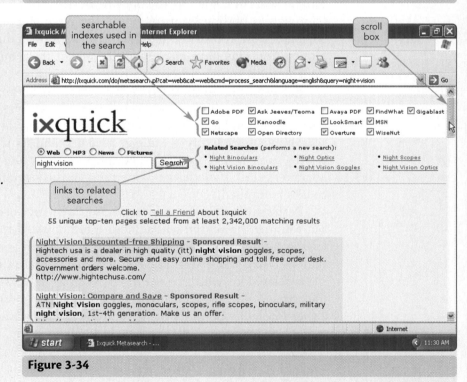

Figure 3-34

(continued)

3 **Scroll the page to view the hits below the sponsored listings.**

Each hit includes a link to the page, a brief description, and the URL (Figure 3-35). IxQuick ranks hits with stars indicating how many search engines rank that hit in a top ten list. For each hit, one or more search engine sources are listed, along with the rank each search engine gave the site.

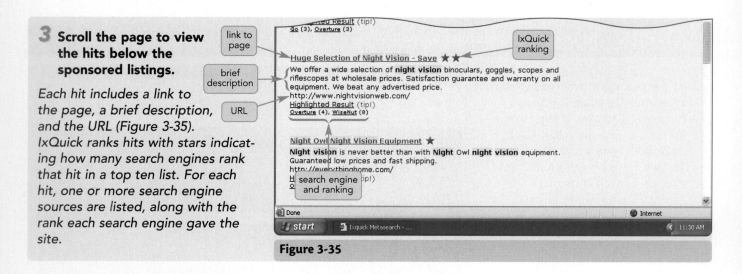

Figure 3-35

In the previous sections, you performed simple keyword searches using a directory, a search engine, and a metasearch engine. For more complex searches, however, you may need to use advanced search techniques to locate Web-based resources.

Advanced Search Techniques

Simple searches, such as the ones demonstrated so far in this chapter, offer a basic approach to finding information on the Web. More complex searches require additional consideration in formulating the query, as well as understanding advanced search techniques. You may have already used some of these advanced search techniques, such as Boolean operators, without realizing it.

For example, suppose you are researching an answer to the following question: How many college students play sports and why? After selecting a search tool to use, the next task is to formulate the search query by selecting the keywords that will perform the search most efficiently — *college*, *students*, and *sports*. There is no need to include stop words, such as *how* and *from*, because a search tool likely will ignore them. There is also no need to include the word, *why*, in the search query, because the question of causes is implied.

Performing the search using those three keywords in the query will get good results, but refining the search will achieve more targeted results. For example, grouping college and students together in a single phrase surrounded by quotation marks indicates that Web pages in the search results must contain the phrase *college students*. Adding more related keywords to the query, such as *university*, however, may further narrow the scope of the search, potentially eliminating good resources. An alternative is to use either Boolean operators or the search engine's advanced search feature to more clearly target good results.

Using Boolean Operators

When given multiple keywords in a query, a search tool uses a **Boolean operator**, such as AND, OR, and NOT (typed in all capital letters), to specify which keywords should be included or excluded from the search results. Figure 3-36 lists several typical methods for using Boolean operators to perform an advanced search; however, be aware that not all search tools handle Boolean operators in the same way.

The AND operator indicates a keyword must be found in a search results hit. Many search tools assume that a list of several keywords entered into the search text box are connected by the AND operator; thus the search tools return a search results list in which all of the hits include all of the words in the query. Some search tools permit the inclusion of multiple keywords in a query by preceding them with a plus sign instead of the AND operator.

Task	Procedure
Search for all the words in any order	Type AND between keywords. Example: Canada AND nickel AND mines
Search for at least one of the words	Type OR between keywords. Example: ocean OR sea
Search for a phrase in the given order	Surround the phrase with quotation marks. Example: "Catalina yachts"
Exclude a concept from the search results	Type NOT before the excluded word. Examples: orange NOT Florida or sometimes: kayak AND NOT inflatable

Figure 3-36 Typical methods for advanced searches using Boolean operators.

Suppose you want the search results in the previous research example to include Web pages that refer to students from either a university or a college. To find Web pages that include either *university* or *college* requires the use of an **OR** operator. To specify an either-or condition, you must specifically enter **OR** between the keywords to indicate that hits should include either of the keywords rather than both of the words.

To exclude a keyword from a search, some search tools require you to use the NOT operator before the excluded term, for example, *diamonds NOT baseball*. Other search tools may require a minus sign before the excluded term, for example, *diamonds – baseball*. The best way to understand how any search engine handles Boolean operators is to review the search engine's online Help page.

Using Search Engine Advanced Search Features

An alternative to entering Boolean operators in a search query is to rely on the advanced search features provided by most search engines. These advanced search features offer prompts to help you specify AND, OR, NOT, and other criteria for a more complex search. In addition to making it easy to do a complex search without specifically entering Boolean operators, the advanced search features also may offer a way to filter the results by language, geographic region, or IP address. Some search engines allow you to restrict the search results according to date, document size, and how many layers deep the page is from the site's home page. Furthermore, advanced search options allow you to search for a keyword found only in specific elements of a Web page, such as the page title.

The most powerful search engines also can search for specific file types. For example, if you wanted to find a video clip of a space shuttle launch, you could use a search tool that restricts search results to only video file formats. Other search tools can

 @Source

To review search tool comparison, visit the Discovering the Internet Chapter 3 Web site (scsite.com/ internet/ch3) and click a link below Search Tool Comparisons.

restrict search results to only MP3 files to help you locate music online. The file formats available for searching vary by search engine, but may include the following:

- Images, such as GIF, JPEG, or PNG
- Audio, such as MP3 or RealAudio
- Video, such as RealVideo or MPEG
- Macromedia Flash
- Word documents
- Excel spreadsheets
- PowerPoint presentations
- Adobe Acrobat (PDF)
- ActiveX
- Java applets
- JavaScript
- VBScript

In addition, some search tools allow you to target specific sites or domains. For example, Google's Advanced Search offers options to restrict the search results to only U.S. government sites with a .gov domain, university sites with an .edu domain, or a specific Web site, such as microsoft.com. In the following steps, you use Google's Advanced Search page to search for Web pages referring to NASA space shuttle launches that do not involve the International Space Station. You begin with a simple search and then continue to refine the search using the Advanced Search page options until the search results include only the desired information.

◈》 Steps: To Use Search Engine Advanced Search Features

1 **If necessary, start the browser. Visit the Discovering the Internet Chapter 3 Web page (scsite.com/internet/ch3). Click Google. Type** NASA launch **in the search text box.**

The Google home page appears and the query keywords are entered in the search text box (Figure 3-37).

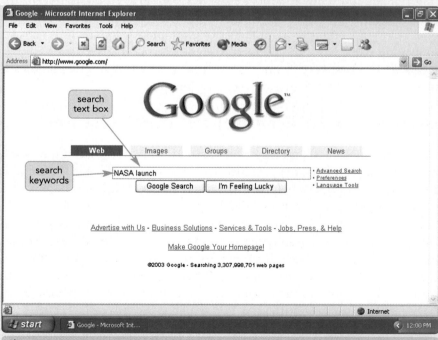

Figure 3-37

2 Press the ENTER key. Observe the number of hits returned in the search results list.

Because this search is not well-focused, Google returns more than a million hits in the search results (Figure 3-38). The contents of the Web pages on your screen may vary from that in Figures 3-38 through 3-48 on pages 137 through 142.

Figure 3-38

3 Type NASA liftoff in the search text box. Press the ENTER key. Point to the Advanced Search link.

Although liftoff is a synonym for launch, the new query returns very different search results containing fewer than 100,000 hits (Figure 3-39).

Figure 3-39

(continued)

4 **Click the Advanced Search link.**

Google's Advanced Search page appears and includes text boxes in which to enter a complex query without entering Boolean operators. NASA liftoff appears in the Find results with all of the words text box (Figure 3-40).

Google Advanced Search criteria

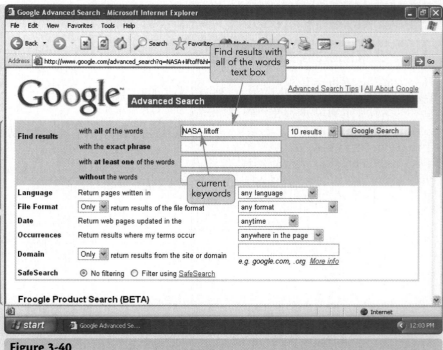

Figure 3-40

5 **Type NASA in the Find results with all of the words text box. Type** `liftoff launch` **in the Find results with at least one of the words text box.**

This query asks Google to use the Boolean operator AND to include the keyword NASA and the Boolean operator OR to include either keyword — liftoff or launch (Figure 3-41).

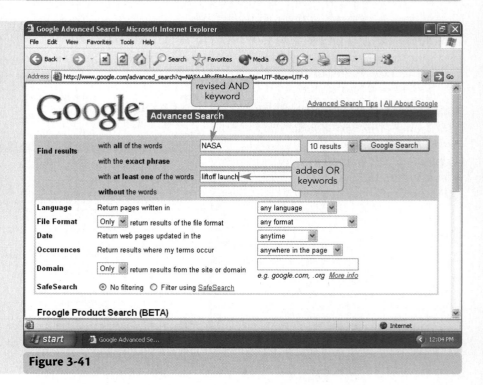

Figure 3-41

6 Press the ENTER key. Point to the Advanced Search link.

The search results list now lists pages that contain NASA and liftoff or launch (Figure 3-42).

query

search results list

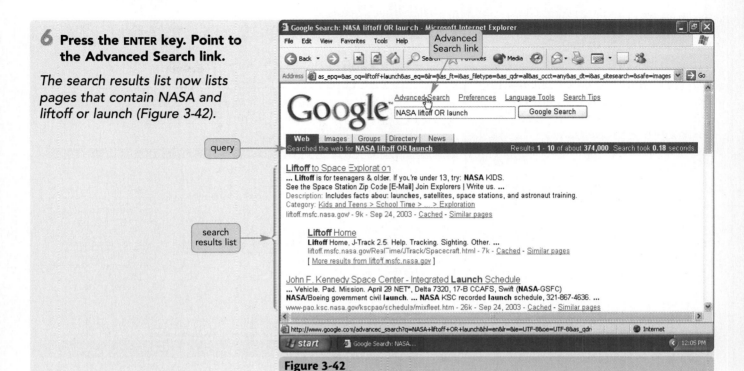

Figure 3-42

7 Click the Advanced Search link. Type space shuttle in the Find results with the exact phrase text box.

The advanced search now includes the keyword phrase, space shuttle (Figure 3-43).

Figure 3-43

(continued)

8 **Press the ENTER key. Point to the Advanced Search link.**

The search results now include Web pages containing NASA, liftoff or launch, and space shuttle. Google displays the phrase, space shuttle, in the search text box to indicate that the search results now include pages containing that exact phrase (Figure 3-44).

query

search
results list

Figure 3-44

9 **Click the Advanced Search link. Type station in the Find results without the words text box.**

The query now excludes pages containing the keyword station (Figure 3-45).

Figure 3-45

10 **Press the ENTER key. Point to the Advanced Search link.**

The further refined search results appear (Figure 3-46). By eliminating the keyword, station, the search results no longer contain Web pages about the launch of the International Space Station. The keyword, space, was not eliminated so that pages about the space shuttle would appear in the search results list.

Figure 3-46

11 **Click the Advanced Search link. Type nasa.gov in the Domain Only return results from the site or domain text box.**

The Advanced Search page includes all the advanced search criteria you have used in the previous steps plus the new criteria to restrict the search to the nasa.gov domain (Figure 3-47).

Figure 3-47

(continued)

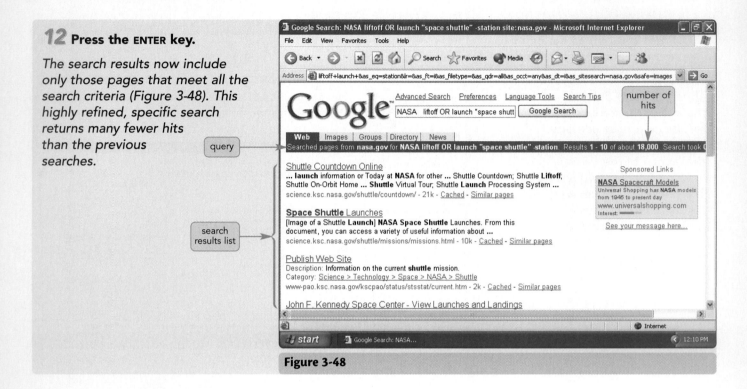

Figure 3-48

12 Press the ENTER key.

The search results now include only those pages that meet all the search criteria (Figure 3-48). This highly refined, specific search returns many fewer hits than the previous searches.

Using a search engine's advanced search features can be very useful when constructing a complex search query. It is a good practice, however, to become familiar with Boolean operators and how the search engines you use most frequently handle them.

Browser Searches

The Internet Explorer browser provides search capabilities through the Address bar and the Search bar. In the following sections you learn how to search from the Address bar, how to open the Search bar and search using the Search Companion, and how to customize the Search Companion.

Searching the Web Using the Address Bar

You can search the Web by entering keywords in the Address box on the Address bar. Internet Explorer uses MSN Search as the default search engine for an Address bar search. Like many other search engines, MSN Search offers features of both a search engine and a directory; therefore, the search results include a list of hits as well as category links. In the following steps, you use the Address bar to search for Web pages containing information about protein diets.

Steps: To Search the Web Using the Address Bar

1 If necessary, start the browser. Click the Address box on the Address bar. Type protein diets in the Address box.

As you type the keywords, protein diets, the Address list appears and contains Search for "protein diets" (Figure 3-49). The content of the Web pages on your screen may vary from that shown in Figures 3-49 and 3-50.

Figure 3-49

2 Press the ENTER key.

An MSN Search search results page appears. The search results page includes Featured Sites chosen by editors, paid sponsored sites, MSN Web directory sites, and Web pages generated by searching the Web using a spider (Figure 3-50).

Figure 3-50

 In Netscape

To search using Netscape, type the keywords in the Location Bar and then press the ENTER key or click the Search button. For more techniques on how to search using the Netscape browser, see To Search Using the Browser in Appendix A.

Searching from the Address bar is convenient; however, it does not offer as much user control as other search methods. For example, searching from the Address bar provides none of the advanced searching functionality available from search tools like Google or AlltheWeb and is limited to MSN Search. You can turn on or off searching from the Address bar and modify other Address bar search options in the Advanced tab in the Internet Options dialog box.

Searching the Web Using the Search Companion

The **Search Companion** can be used to search for files and folders saved on a computer, as well as for Web-based resources. The Search Companion is displayed, by default, when the **Search bar** is opened by clicking the Search button on the Standard Buttons toolbar. The Search Companion includes a search text box, options for performing different types of searches, links to the Search Companion online help, and an animated character you can turn on or off.

You can use a natural language query, search phrases, or search keywords when searching with the Search Companion. The more relevant words you enter, the better focused the results will be. In the following steps, you use the Search Companion to search for Web pages with information on the fastest growing jobs.

❖❖ Steps: To Search the Web Using the Search Companion

1 If necessary, start the browser. Point to the Search button on the Standard Buttons toolbar.

The Search button (Figure 3-51) opens and closes the Search bar. The contents of the Web pages on your screen may vary from that in Figures 3-51 through 3-55 on pages 144 through 146.

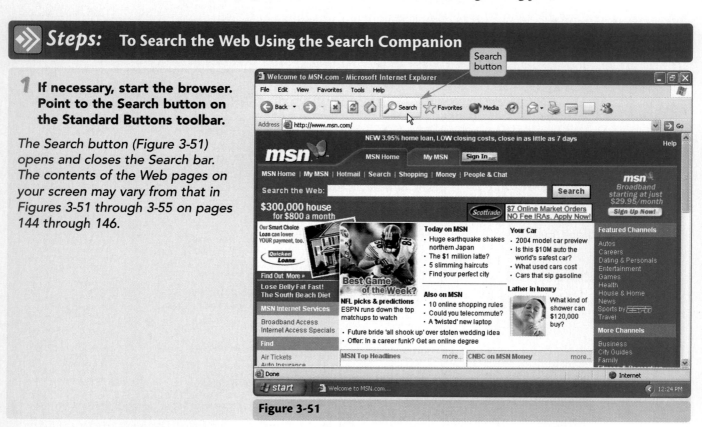

Figure 3-51

2 Click the Search button. Type **What are the fastest growing jobs?** in the Search Companion's search text box. Point to the Search button in the Search Companion.

The Search bar opens with the Search Companion (Figure 3-52). You type the natural language query in the search text box. The Search Companion has a scroll bar you can use to view various options.

Figure 3-52

3 Click the Search button in the Search Companion. Scroll to view the search results list. Point to the Automatically send your search to other search engines link.

By default, the Search Companion uses MSN Search. MSN Search ignores the stop words and displays a search results list (Figure 3-53). The Search Companion displays additional options including a Back button to return to previously viewed Search Companion options.

Figure 3-53

(continued)

4 Click the **Automatically send your search to other search engines** link. Point to AltaVista Advanced Search in the Search Companion.

The Search Companion lists other search engines and a search results page based on results from the first search engine in the list, HotBot (Figure 3-54). You can continue to search using the other search engines in the list, send the search to yet more search engines, and highlight keywords on the search results page using options in the Search Companion.

Figure 3-54

5 Click **AltaVista Advanced Search**. Point to the Search button on the Standard Buttons toolbar.

The AltaVista search results page appears (Figure 3-55).

6 Click the Search button on the Standard Buttons toolbar.

The Search bar closes.

Figure 3-55

✋ Facts@Hand

The **Show Related Links** command on the browser's Tools menu opens a Related Info page in the Search bar. This page displays additional links related to the search keywords used to return the current search results page.

Customizing the Search Companion

The Search Companion can be customized to make it a more useful tool. For example, you can change the animated character or hide it from view and designate a different default search tool. You also can change the Search Companion to Classic Internet search which uses the search characteristics and appearance of older Internet Explorer versions. In the following steps, you change Internet Explorer's default search engine and then change it back to its original default.

Steps: To Change the Search Companion's Default Search Engine

1 **If necessary, start the browser. Click the Search button on the Standard Buttons toolbar. Point to the Change preferences link in the Search Companion.**

You can turn on or off the animated character and change the Search Companion's local and Internet search behaviors by changing preferences (Figure 3-56).

Change preferences link

Figure 3-56

2 **Click Change preferences. Point to the Change Internet search behavior link.**

You can specify a different default search engine for the Search Companion when you change Internet search behavior (Figure 3-57).

Change Internet search behavior link

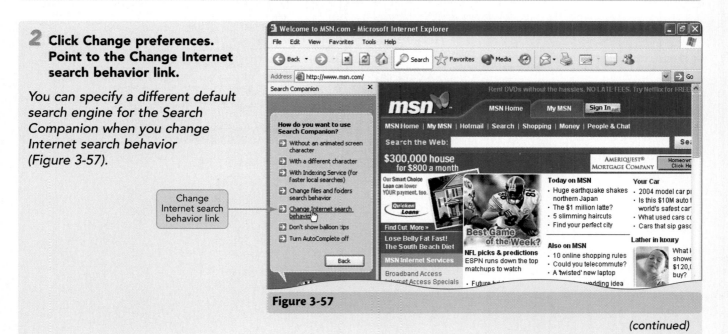

Figure 3-57

(continued)

3 Click Change Internet search behavior. Scroll to view the search engine list. Point to Google.

You can select a different search engine from the default search engine list (Figure 3-58).

search engine options

Figure 3-58

4 Click Google. Point to the OK button.

The Google search engine is selected (Figure 3-59).

selected search engine option

OK button

Figure 3-59

5 Click OK. Type stock pick in the Search Companion search text box.

You perform a new search using these keywords (Figure 3-60).

search keywords

Figure 3-60

6 Press the ENTER key. Point to the Back button in the Search Companion.

The Search Companion returns results from the Google search engine (Figure 3-61) and offers additional options to refine the search. The content of the Web page on your screen will vary from that shown in Figure 3-61.

additional search options

7 Click the Back button. Repeat Steps 2 through 4 to reset MSN Search as the Search Companion's default search tool. Close the Search bar.

Back button

Google search results

Figure 3-61

 In Netscape

My Sidebar contains the Search Tab, which offers a side-by-side view of the list of search results and the corresponding Web pages. Netscape's Search Tab also can be customized to use a different default search engine. See To Customize Browser Search Options in Appendix A.

@Issue Privacy in Searching

Microsoft collects data to track how individuals are using the Search Companion, so that the company can enhance and improve the tool. In an effort to disclose fully what information it collects and how it uses the information, Microsoft has published the Search Companion Privacy Statement, which indicates that Microsoft can collect the following information when you use the Search Companion:

- Any text you type in the search text box

- Grammatical information about the search

- List of Recommended Sites presented at the top of the list of hits

- Any Recommended Sites links that you click

Microsoft will not identify you personally, but it will retain the information it collects about the search for a year. If you want to use the Search bar and protect the privacy of your search, you can use the Classic Internet search setting, which does not gather the information.

Google and other search tools use cookies to record search behavior. While the search information typically does not correspond to personal information, such as name or address, it does correspond to the IP address of your computer. Because broadband users generally have a static IP address that seldom changes, this is tantamount to collecting personal identification.

Web sites such as Google Watch are dedicated to examining and publicizing privacy policies of Google and other search tools.

To learn more about Google Watch and other search tool privacy issues, visit the Discovering the Internet Chapter 3 Web page (scsite .com/internet/ch3) and click a link below Search Tool Privacy.

Specialized Searches

Searching for people, news, magazine or journal articles, or performing other specialized searches is best done by using the correct search tool. The following section explains how to search for individuals, businesses, and current news stories, as well as how to find and use specialized electronic sources.

Searching for People and Businesses

Web users often search for information about an individual or a business for either professional or personal reasons. One way to find Web pages containing information about an individual or a business is to use the individual's name or the company name as search keywords. Looking for other information such as an e-mail address or telephone number is more efficient when a specialized directory, such as an online **white pages directory** or **yellow pages directory** is used. Named for their similarity to telephone directories, white pages and yellow pages directories include Bigfoot, Canada411, InfoSpace, Lycos WhoWhere, SuperPages, and WhitePages (Figure 3-62).

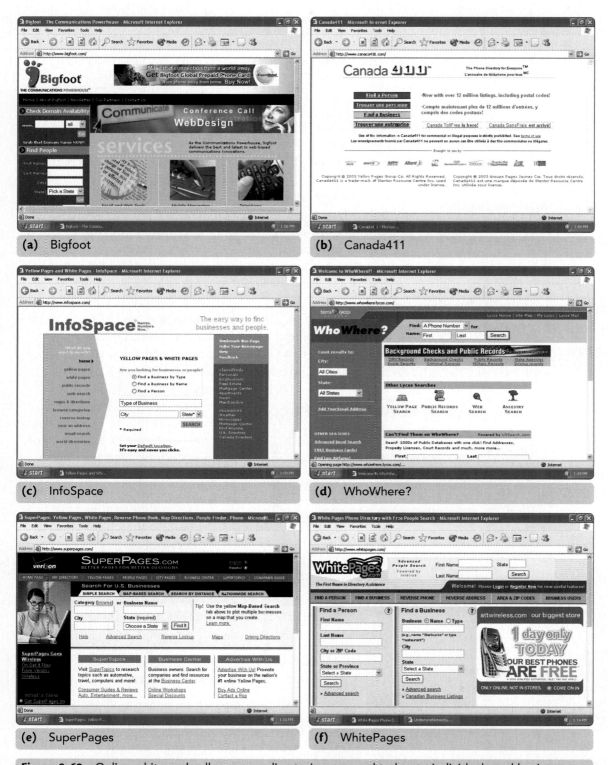

(a) Bigfoot

(b) Canada411

(c) InfoSpace

(d) WhoWhere?

(e) SuperPages

(f) WhitePages

Figure 3-62 Online white and yellow pages directories are used to locate individuals and businesses.

@Source

To review search tools that focus on finding information about people and businesses, visit the Discovering the Internet Chapter 3 Web page (**scsite.com/ internet/ch3**) and click a link below People and Business Search.

Some white page directories, such as AOL White Pages and Yahoo! People Search, list the e-mail addresses only for their own subscribers or people who specifically register. White pages directories often allow individuals to opt out to prevent their names from being listed. Therefore, to find a current e-mail address for an individual, you may have to search several directories.

Facts@Hand

According to the Pew Internet & American Life Project, nearly a third of Internet users have done a vanity search, entering their own names into a search engine to see the results.

Some white and yellow pages directories offer additional services, such a reverse lookup, which is useful when you know a telephone number and want to discover the name associated with it. Numbers for cell phones typically are excluded from reverse directories, however.

Find-People.net and other specialized search tools offer not only white pages directories, but also links to sources for military records, alumni databases, criminal information, and other governmental records. To protect privacy, many of these records are open only to authorized people. For example, Classmates.com and other alumni databases require you to register and include yourself in the list, after which you are given access to names of others who also have voluntarily made their information available. Several sites, such as ChoiceTrust, Docusearch, KnowX.com, US Search.com, and USAFind (Figure 3-63), require payment for compiled information, ranging from $10 for an instant, simple search of a person's address history to more than $100 for an exhaustive background search. Many of these sites have a no match-no charge policy.

Figure 3-63 Some e-businesses provide database searches for individuals and businesses for a fee.

Searching for News

Because search engines and directories may update their indexes only every few weeks, a simple search may not return information on current events. Searching for news on a topic requires a specialized search. Online news sources are diverse. For example, headlines often appear on the home pages of portal sites such as MSN and Yahoo!. Current news is available on the Web sites for broadcast television and radio stations, and you can read the online version of various newspapers. Because most news is distributed through one of the major news wire services, such as the Associated Press (AP), United Press International (UPI), or Reuters, headlines tend to be repeated at various sites.

Major search tools, such as Google and Yahoo! (Figure 3-64) now offer headlines and the ability to search for news stories. Google, for example, presents up-to-the-minute headlines from thousands of news sources, categorizing the stories into major areas, such as Top Stories, World, and Business. For each news story link, Google offers one or more related links to other news sources providing coverage of the event, thus making contrasting viewpoints on the same event available to the reader. Because Google keeps archives of the news for 30 days and provides an archive search engine, you can follow a story over time.

@Source

To review search tools that focus on news, visit the Discovering the Internet Chapter 3 Web page (scsite.com/internet/ch3) and click a link below News.

Figure 3-64 Major search tools also offer current news pages.

@Issue Search Engines Censored

China restricted its citizens' Internet use in September 2002 when it blocked the use of Google and AltaVista search engines. When citizens tried to access those and other sites, the Chinese government redirected the browsers to a blank screen or to a government-sanctioned site.

China previously had banned sites containing information on the forbidden Falun Gong movement. Now, the government successfully has filtered out other non-sanctioned sites, such as those focused on news, human rights, or Tibet. While the Chinese government asserts that it blocks such sites to protect its citizens from harmful information on the Internet, well-known adult sites like Playboy.com are not blocked. The government specifically targeted Google and AltaVista because they offered searches in both English and Chinese languages and because a simple search

gave citizens access to forbidden content.

Google was singled out because of its cached pages feature. While the government-owned routers blocked a Web site relating to Falun Gong, for instance, an individual could access a cached or saved version of the Web pages stored on Google's server without having to access the banned Web site. AltaVista was targeted for its feature known as Babelfish, which translates a Web page into a different language. By entering the Web address of a banned Web site into Babelfish and making the translation into Chinese, Chinese citizens could view the content with an AltaVista address, thus getting around the governments block on the original site.

News of the ban caused immediate protests from journalist groups, as well as from the management

of Google and AltaVista. Ten days later, the Chinese government lifted the ban. While China supports Internet use for business, it still maintains strict control over its 45 million Internet users. For example, the government closed a third of China's Internet cafés in 2002, purportedly to achieve fire safety after students set fire to one to protest the censorship.

Software has been created that can bypass firewalls set up by authoritarian governments. One example is Triangleboy, formerly managed by SafeWeb. In addition, a Web page on the Harvard University site can be used to test whether a given Web site is filtered in China.

To learn more about China's search engine censors, visit the Discovering the Internet Chapter 3 Web page (**scsite.com/internet/ch3**) and click a link below China.

BANNED

Using Research Alternatives to Search Tools

Search engines produce links to vast resources, but it may take a while to sift through the search results to find the information you seek. For in-depth or scholarly research, a more effective strategy is to access specialized collections of electronic resources. While many such collections offer online access to information, knowing where to find them is not always obvious.

In this section, you learn about a few of the more powerful and well-known services, such as Lexis/Nexis, ingenta, FindLaw, Hoover's Online, Dun and Bradstreet, and Dialog (Figure 3-65), which offer access to specialized information collections. Many higher educational institutions subscribe to these services; therefore, students and faculty may have free access. If a school is not a subscriber, individuals still may use these services through a public library that subscribes, by paying for an individual subscription, or with a pay-as-you-go fee.

(a) LexisNexis

(b) ingenta

(c) FindLaw

(d) Hoover's Online

(e) Dun and Bradstreet

(f) Dialog

Figure 3-65 Several companies offer online access to specialized collections.

The Lexis/Nexis service offers a Web-based interface to find abstracts and articles on business, news, government, medical, and legal topics from a vast database of information. Lexis/Nexis provides access to U.S. congressional and state government documents, statistics produced by governmental agencies and organizations, and primary and secondary sources of historical documents. It offers many sources of information on current issues and events, including organizational newsletters and governmental briefings not published commercially. Ideal for both academic scholars and students, Lexis/Nexis is the first stop for many researchers.

Ingenta, formerly called UnCover, provides full-text online articles from over 5,000 academic and professional publications. Any researcher can search and view summaries of articles. To obtain the full article either online or by fax requires a subscription or fee.

Hoover's Online and Dun and Bradstreet are two widely used resources used to find information on small and large businesses. Hoover's offers profiles on both public and private businesses, as well as extensive financial statements and analyses, management team information, and lists of competitors and market information. Dun and Bradstreet offers similar types of business and market information. It offers information that even small businesses can use to find prospective customers, research suppliers, and check the credit risk of a potential partner or customer.

FindLaw is a portal for legal resources. It offers separate channels for legal professionals, students, businesses, the public, and news agencies. This site is useful for finding information about laws and court cases, as well as for locating an attorney in your area or an attorney with a specific area of expertise. Whether you are dealing with a property complaint, a traffic ticket, criminal law, or a personal injury, this site offers an abundance of legal information.

Dialog offers in-depth information on news, business, chemistry, engineering, environment, government, intellectual property, medicine, and pharmaceuticals. The depth of information comes from source materials such as journals, books, newspapers, magazines, trade journals, newsletters, and citation bibliographies, as well as market research reports. No subscriptions or passwords are required, although a subscription service is available and more cost-effective for heavy research. Non-subscription users may search and see a list of results for no charge; to read or download the entire article, users must pay a small fee per article.

Government resources also can serve as excellent sources of information. For example, consumers can profit from information supplied by the Federal Consumer Information Center, while taxpayers can download forms and publications from the Internal Revenue Service Web site. The Census Bureau Web site supplies census bureau statistics, the Bureau of Labor Statistics Web site offers government information on employment and labor economics, and the Library of Congress's Web site (named THOMAS, after Thomas Jefferson) provides searchable databases of legislative information. The Small Business Administration Web site has many resources for entrepreneurs and small business owners, and the National Park Service Web site contains excellent travel advice. An easy-to-use portal for the U.S. federal government is FirstGov.

@Source

To review search tools useful for specific types of research, visit the Discovering the Internet Chapter 3 Web page (**scsite.com/internet/ch3**) and click a link below Research.

@Source

To access government resources, visit the Discovering the Internet Chapter 3 Web page (**scsite.com/internet/ch3**) and click a link below Government Resources.

Facts@Hand

According to the Pew Internet & American Life Project, 61 percent of adult American Internet users have used government agency sites.

Avoiding Plagiarism by Citing Web Sources

@Issue

In a research paper, scholars and students often quote another's writing and ideas. This is acceptable as long as certain rules are followed. The quote must be set apart, either with quotation marks (if the quotation is short) or by indentation (if it is long). Furthermore, you must cite the author and source of the quote, using an appropriate citation. Using more than a few lines of a person's writing or not crediting the source constitutes plagiarism and is wrong.

This holds true not only for printed materials such as books and magazines, but also for Internet sources such as Web pages or online books. The only exception is if you use information based on common knowledge or facts that are in a number of sources; in this case, you do not need to cite the specific source from which you got the information.

Various colleges and universities have differing requirements for citing sources, typically adhering to one of the following styles: Modern Language Association (MLA), American Psychological Association (APA), Chicago Manual of Style (Chicago), or Council of Biology Editors (CBE). Figure 3-66 illustrates an example of how to cite a Web page for each style.

To learn more about the comprehensive treatment of citing electronic resources, visit the Discovering the Internet Chapter 3 Web page (**scsite.com/internet/ch3**) and click a link below Citations.

Citation Style	Example
MLA style	Harnack, Andrew, and Eugene Kleppinger. Citation Styles. *Online! A Reference Guide to Using Internet Sources.* Boston: Bedford/St. Martin's, 2001. 28 Sept. 2002. <http://www.bedfordstmartins.com/online/citex.html>.
APA style	Harnack, A. & Kleppinger, E. (2001). Citation Styles. *Online! A Reference Guide to Using Internet Sources.* Retrieved September 28, 2002, from Bedford/St. Martin's Web site http://www.bedfordstmartins.com/online/citex.html.
Chicago (Turabian) style	Andrew Harnack and Eugene Kleppinger, "Citation Styles," in *Online! A Reference Guide to Using Internet Sources* 2001, <http://www.bedfordstmartins.com/online/citex.html> (28 September 2002).
CBE style	Harnack A., Kleppinger E. 2001. Citation Styles. Online! A reference guide to using Internet sources. <http://www.bedfordstmartins.com/online/citex.html>. Accessed 2002 Sep 28.

Figure 3-66 Sample methods for citing Web page sources in a research paper.

@Issue Research Papers Online

With a deadline approaching, many students turn to the Web, not only to do research on the topic, but also to take a shortcut right to the completed research paper. More than 250 sites — sometimes referred to as paper mills — offer completed papers and assignments on a vast number of topics and from a variety of viewpoints. Some are free, some require an exchange (post a paper to take a paper), and some charge a fee of $25 or more, depending on the length.

Just as quoting a few lines without citing the source is plagiarism, so is turning in a paper from a paper mill. The consequences for plagiarism may be grave.

Instructors often can detect if a student turns in a paper from one of these sites. A writing style that is above or below the student's ability, formatting that indicates it has been printed from a browser rather than a word processor, out-of-date citations, references to sources that are not in the local library, or citations to defunct Web sites — all of these are warning signs to the instructor. When students cannot answer questions about sections of their papers, the evidence is stronger. Online resources such as plagiarism.com also help instructors detect whether papers are fraudulent.

Students can use search tools to assist in the research process, but should resist the temptation to avoid the work of writing the research paper altogether. Not only are the consequences grave when cheating is caught, but turning in one's own work is a matter of honor.

For more information on plagiarism, visit the Discovering the Internet Chapter 3 Web page (scsite.com/internet/ch3) and click a link below Plagiarism.

The Invisible Web

The Web is usually conceived as a spherical set of interconnected sites, all linked together, something like a vast Tinkertoy structure. Following this model, a search engine eventually might be able to catalog and index the majority of pages online. A concept introduced by Chris Sherman and Gary Price in 2000, however, portrays the Web in the shape of a bow-tie (Figure 3-67). The center knot represents the core of the Web, the spherical set of interconnected sites. The theory states that search engines typically index only the core of the Web, leaving a huge number of Web-based resources untapped or invisible.

On one side of the bow-tie, **origination sites** may have links to the core body of the Web, but nothing in the core points back to those sites. Examples of origination sites are personal Web pages or weblogs. Because no sites from the core point outward to these pages, search engine spiders typically will not access these pages. On the other side of the bow-tie are **termination pages** that can be accessed by links from the core, but have no links back to the core. Business Web sites are examples of termination pages, which link only to pages on their own site.

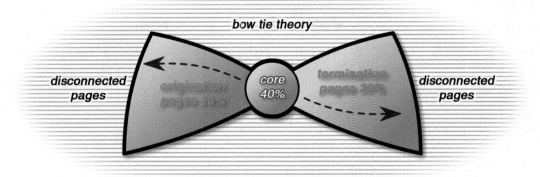

Figure 3-67 Sherman and Price depict the invisible Web in the shape of a bow-tie.

Completely outside of the bow-tie are disconnected pages that may link to or from the origination sites and termination pages at either side of the bow, but have no direct links to the core or have no direct links at all. As previously noted, Web pages with few or no links to and from the main core of the Web are labeled the **invisible Web** because they are not accessed easily by normal browsing or search engines.

Current estimates state that, with so much information outside the core, search engines and directories have cataloged only 20 to 50 percent of the Web, leaving an enormous amount of information untapped or inaccessible. Examples of such untapped information include statistical data or information available only to authorized users or protected by passwords, even if the passwords are freely available. For example, academic materials for university classes or subscription-only databases such as InfoTrac and FirstSearch are restricted from the public, although students typically have free access through the university's library system. Search tools often do not index or catalog these types of information resources.

Other elements of the invisible Web are only beginning to be indexed, such as information saved in other file types. While the major search tools now catalog images and multimedia, most overlook items created in Adobe Acrobat (PDF files), Macromedia Flash, and Java. Even Microsoft Word, Excel, and PowerPoint files are only beginning to be indexed by standard search tools. Electronic books, product catalogs, library catalogs, government records, and other databases typically must be accessed directly from a specialized search tool within the resource.

Another area of the invisible Web is **streaming media**, which includes audio and video files sent to a user's browser in a continuous data stream, instead of requiring the user to download the entire file before viewing it. For example, news sources such as CNN.com often provide scrolling headlines to supplement online news stories. These items may or may not be stored on the originating server but are not readily accessible to search tools. Search tools also are only beginning to find ways to catalog the information generated in online discussion groups and other elements of the invisible Web.

@Source

To learn more about finding information on the invisible Web, visit the Discovering the Internet Chapter 3 Web page (scsite.com/ internet/ch3) and click a link below Invisible Web.

CHAPTER REVIEW

The Chapter Review section summarizes the concepts presented in the chapter.

1 What Are the Steps in the Search Process?

The search process involves choosing the best search tool for the job, formulating the search **query**, examining the search results, and evaluating the credibility of the Web pages listed in a search results list.

2 What Are the Different Types of Search Tools and How Do They Display Search Results?

Search tools are generally classified as directories, search engines, and metasearch engines. A **directory** is a human-compiled index of Web pages organized into hierarchical categories and subcategories. A user clicks links to **drill down** from category to subcategory until a list of relevant Web pages appears. Directory examples include Yahoo!, Open Directory, and LookSmart.

In contrast, a **search engine** uses a software program called a **spider**, **bot**, or **crawler** to browse the Web and compile a searchable **index** without human intervention. A search **query** can be one or more **keywords**, a phrase, or a **natural language search** query entered in a search engine's **search text box**. The search engine then returns a **search results list** of **hits** from its index of pages that are relevant to the search query. Examples of search engines include Google and AlltheWeb.

A **metasearch engine** sends a search query to several search engines simultaneously and then compiles the results into a single list, eliminating duplicates. IxQuick and Vivisimo are examples of metasearch engines. Today, most search tools are hybrids, offering both directory categorization and the ability to search via a search query.

3 How Are Boolean Operators and Other Advanced Search Features Used?

Boolean operators, such as AND, OR, and NOT, or a symbolic equivalent, such as plus sign (+) or a minus sign (–) are used to include or exclude Web pages from a search results list. Search engines also allow users to enclose phrases in quotation marks to indicate a search for an exact phrase. Each search engine has its own requirements for how a user should enter queries to complete advanced searches including the use of quotation marks and Boolean operators.

Many search engines provide advanced search features that make creating a complex search query easier. Advanced search features allow the user to restrict the results not only by what keywords are included or excluded, but also by the date, language, geographic region, domain, file types, and so forth.

4 How Can You Perform Browser Searches?

Internet Explorer permits searches by entering keywords in the Address box on the Address bar and by opening the **Search bar** and using the **Search Companion**. Address bar searches are performed using MSN Search. You can enter a query in the Search Companion search text box to perform a search. The Search Companion also provides other search options and can be customized.

 5 How Can You Find Information on People, Businesses, and News and Use Online Research Alternatives to Search Tools?

Specialized search tools are useful for finding people, businesses, or news stories. A good resource for finding people is an online **white pages directory** and for finding businesses is an online **yellow pages directory**. Examples of white and yellow pages directories are WhoWhere and SuperPages. Some search tools, such as Google and Yahoo!, offer news-related search pages. Other specialized search tools offer access to military records, alumni databases, criminal information, and so on. Some specialized search tools require a small fee or authorization.

To find more scholarly or in-depth information, you can use specialized electronic databases and collections. University libraries offer many of these collections to students, but others are available either by subscription or for a small per-use fee. Some of the collections in this category are Lexis/Nexis, Ingenta, First-Search, and Dialog. Government agency sites are a good source of information about government policies and services.

 6 What Is the Invisible Web?

Web pages and files that have few or no links to and from the main core of the Web are considered to be part of the **invisible Web,** because they are not accessed easily by normal browsing or search tools. The invisible Web concept depicts the main core of the Web as an interconnected sphere in the center of a bow-tie, with two vast sets of Web pages, called **origination sites** and **termination pages**, not well-linked to the core. Because search engines do not index these pages readily, perhaps only 20 to 50 percent of the Web is accessible by using search engines. Included in the invisible Web are statistical data, electronic databases, information requiring a password or subscription, scholarly journals, electronic books, and unpublished information such as catalogs and industry newsletters.

TERMS TO KNOW

After reading this chapter, you should know each term.

Archie (*116*)
Boolean operator (*134*)
bot (*126*)
breadcrumb trail (*121*)
crawler (*126*)
directory (*119*)
drilling down (*120*)
full-text searching (*126*)
hit (*110*)
index (*126*)
invisible Web (*159*)
Jughead (*117*)
keyword (*110*)
meta tag keywords (*126*)
metasearch engine (*131*)
natural language search (*111*)

origination sites (*158*)
query (*110*)
Search bar (*144*)
Search Companion (*144*)
search engine (*126*)
search engine software (*126*)
search results list (*110*)
search text box (*110*)
spider (*126*)
stop words (*111*)
streaming media (*159*)
termination pages (*158*)
Veronica (*116*)
white pages directory (*151*)
yellow pages directory (*151*)

True or False

TEST YOUR
KNOWLEDGE

Use the Test
Your Knowledge
exercises to
check your
knowledge of
the chapter.

Mark T for True and F for False. (Answers are found on page numbers in parentheses.)

1. A query should include at least one keyword, a specific word that describes the information you are seeking. (*110*)

2. The first hit in the list of search results is always the Web page most relevant to the search query. (*112*)

3. You should try to determine the credibility of the Web pages included in the search results list when evaluating the results of a search. (*115*)

4. Yahoo! is an example of a metasearch engine. (*119*)

5. Search engines use spiders that collect information about Web pages automatically for the engine's index. (*126*)

6. A metasearch engine uses human editors to compile an index of Web pages. (*131*)

7. The default search engine used by Internet Explorer for an Address bar search is Google. (*142*)

8. An advanced search technique that requires a user to type AND, NOT, and OR to include or exclude keywords uses Boolean logic. (*134*)

9. A good way to find a friend's e-mail address, street address, or telephone number is to use Hoover's. (*151*)

10. The invisible Web is so called because its Web pages have many invisible links to the core of the Web. (*159*)

Multiple Choice

Select the best answer. (Answers are found on page numbers in parentheses.)

1. For most effective search results, choose keywords that are _____ . (*110*)
   a. Boolean
   b. general
   c. specific
   d. stop words

2. To search for a Web page that contains a specific phrase, _____ . (*111*)
   a. surround the phrase with brackets
   b. surround the phrase with quotation marks
   c. insert the word AND between every word
   d. no special action is required

3. A list of hits typically contains _____ . (*128*)
   a. a link to each Web site
   b. a description of the page or a sample of text from the page
   c. Web sites that are sponsored or have paid to have their pages placed at the top of the list
   d. all of the above

(continued)

TEST YOUR KNOWLEDGE *(continued)*

TEST YOUR KNOWLEDGE

Use the Test Your Knowledge exercises to check your knowledge of the chapter.

4. To evaluate a Web page's credibility, make sure that _____ . *(115)*
   a. the author or sponsor has expertise in the area
   b. it is limited in scope
   c. the information is sponsored by a well-known business
   d. all of the above

5. _____ is one of the earliest Web-based search engines. *(125)*
   a. AltaVista
   b. Google
   c. Yahoo!
   d. None of the above

6. A _____ compiles results from several search engines into a single list. *(131)*
   a. Boolean search engine
   b. directory search engine
   c. metasearch engine
   d. spider

7. To add a Web page to its index, search engine spiders typically scan for
   _____ . *(126)*
   a. page titles
   b. all of the words on the page
   c. meta tags
   d. all of the above

8. To search using the browser, _____ . *(142)*
   a. type keywords in the Address box on the Address bar
   b. click the Find button and then type keywords in the Search Companion
   c. click the Tools menu and click the Use Search Companion command
   d. all of the above

9. For academic research, specialized information collections, such as
   Lexis/Nexis, are good resources because they _____ . *(154)*
   a. are free
   b. can provide information on business, news, government, medical, and legal
      topics
   c. are available only to librarians
   d. none of the above

10. The invisible Web theory states that _____ . *(159)*
    a. many Web pages have few or no links to and from the main core of the Web
    b. the core of the Web constitutes about half of the total online information
    c. search engines typically index only information in the core
    d. all of the above

Instructions: To complete the Learn It Online exercises, start your browser, click the Address bar, and then enter the Web address **scsite.com/internet/ch3**. Follow the instructions in the exercises below. Each exercise has instructions for printing your results, either for your own records or for submission to your instructor.

 Chapter Reinforcement

TF, MC, and SA

Click the Chapter Reinforcement link. Print the quiz by clicking Print on the File menu for each page. Answer each question.

 Flash Cards

Click the Flash Cards link and read the instructions. Type **20** (or a number specified by your instructor) in the Number of playing cards text box, type your name in the Enter your Name text box, and then click the Flip Card button. When the flash card is displayed, read the question and then click the Answer box arrow to select an answer. Flip through Flash Cards. If your score is 15 (75%) correct or greater, click Print on the File menu to print your results. If your score is less than 15 (75%) correct, then redo this exercise by clicking the Replay button.

 Practice Test

Click the Practice Test link. Answer each question, enter your first and last name at the bottom of the page, and then click the Grade Test button. When the graded practice test is displayed on your screen, click Print on the File menu to print a hard copy. Continue to take practice tests until you score 80% or better.

 Who Wants To Be a Computer Genius?

Click the Computer Genius link. Read the instructions, enter your first and last name at the bottom of the page, and then click the Play button. When your score is displayed, click the Print Results link to print a hard copy.

 Crossword Puzzle Challenge

Below Chapter 3, click the Crossword Puzzle Challenge link. Read the instructions, and then enter your first and last name. Click the SUBMIT button. Work the crossword puzzle. When you are finished, click the Submit button. When the crossword puzzle is redisplayed, click the Print Puzzle button to print a hard copy.

LEARN IT ONLINE

Use the Learn It Online exercises to reinforce your understanding of the chapter concepts and terms.

To perform the following exercises, you must be connected to the Internet and have access to a printer.

 Online Scavenger Hunt

EXERCISES

Use the Exercises to gain hands-on Internet experience.

Find solutions to three of the following scenarios using online resources. Even if you already know the answer or can ask someone who knows, search the Web to find the answer. For each scenario, complete the following steps.

1. Visit the Discovering the Internet Chapter 3 Web page (scsite.com/internet/ch3) and click a link below Search Engines, or Directories, or Metasearch Engines to choose a search tool.

2. Determine the keywords you will use in the search query.

3. Time how long it takes you to find the information you are seeking.

4. Evaluate how well you performed the search.

Scenario 1: A friend's grandmother recently has moved to a new condominium in Sun City, Arizona, for the warmer climate. Your friend wants to send her a nice green plant as a housewarming gift. Give your friend the name and telephone number of a local florist. Also, give the URL for a site where she can order a plant online, as well as an approximate range of prices.

Scenario 2: Your professor assigns some independent reading for a business class. The professor could not remember the title or author of the book, but told you that a former CEO of Scandinavian Airlines wrote it. Find the title and author of the book and find out how much it costs at an online bookstore. If possible, see whether the book is available in your school's library or the local library or obtain the library telephone numbers so you can call to ask about availability.

Scenario 3: Your sister tells you that her coworker recently had a baby, and she wants you to see if you can find a picture online. Check the local hospital to see if it has a virtual or Web nursery, choose a baby with a first name you like, and view the picture.

Scenario 4: Your boss is a diehard Chicago Cubs fan, and you would like to impress him by finding something positive to say about the baseball team. Find the first and last time the team won the World Series, and list the names of a few notable players who have been inducted into the Hall of Fame. Also, find the name of the current manager.

Scenario 5: You decide to go to the movies. Find out what film is the current number one box-office hit. Read a critic's review of the movie. See whether it is playing at a local theater and the times of the showings.

Scenario 6: A friend wants to go on a whitewater rafting trip through the Grand Canyon and wants you to go along. Find out what time of year is best, what experience is necessary, what river rafting companies are available, how much such a trip costs, and how early you have to make a reservation for the trip.

Scenario 7: You and your fiancé or fiancée decide to have your wedding in Hawaii. Price the airfare and determine a range of prices for such a wedding. List the requirements for a marriage license. Find the name of a person to officiate the ceremony in Hawaii.

Scenario 8: You and your friends have been discussing roller coasters and now you want to know more about them. Find the origins of roller coasters; the oldest one in the U.S., Canada, and Europe; as well as the highest and fastest ones.

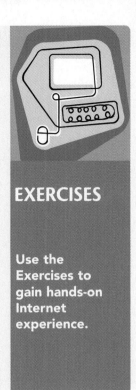

2 Evaluate Credibility of Online Health Information

1. Display the Search Companion.

2. Choose a disease or health condition to research.

3. Determine the keywords you will use in the search query.

4. Time how long it takes you to find the information you are seeking.

5. Evaluate how well you performed the search.
   a. Record how many sites you visit.
   b. For each site you visit, evaluate the quality of information and credibility of the site. List the qualities that make the site more or less credible.
   c. For the health condition that you choose, find out the symptoms, cause, duration, and treatment.
   d. Find the name of one medication used in the treatment of the disease. Look up any side effects and the contraindications that indicate when not to take that medication.
   e. Write down what further steps you should take to evaluate the quality of the information.

3 Job Hunting and Relocating

1. Search for jobs in your chosen field.

2. Visit the Discovering the Internet Chapter 3 Web page (**scsite.com/internet/ch3**) and click a link below Search Engines, or Directories, or Metasearch Engines to choose a search tool.

3. Determine the keywords you will use in the search query.

4. Time how long it takes you to find the information you are seeking.

5. Evaluate how well you performed the search.
   a. List several occupations and some information about each.
   b. Research average salaries for each occupation.
   c. Find out whether your chosen field is a fast-growing one.
   d. Select a city to which you would like to relocate. Determine the climate by researching the average temperatures, rainfall, and snowfall.
   e. Research school districts in the area and find out which one seems the best.
   f. Find the prices of a two-bedroom apartment and a four-bedroom home in that community.
   g. Find the difference in the cost of living between your current location and the destination.
   h. Get an estimate of how much it would cost to move the contents of a two-bedroom apartment from your current location to the destination.

(continued)

EXERCISES

Use the
Exercises to
gain hands-on
Internet
experience.

EXERCISES *(continued)*

4 Best Sites about Search Engines

1. Several sites offer quality information on search engines. These include Search Engine Watch, Search Engine Showdown, and Search Engine Guide. Visit the Discovering the Internet Chapter 3 Web page (scsite.com/internet/ch3) and click the links below Exercise 4 to examine each of these sites. Using information you find at the sites, answer the following questions.
   a. Which of the sites offers particularly good tips for efficient searching?
   b. Which of the sites offers a newsletter?
   c. Which of the sites offers ratings, rankings, and reviews of various search engines?
   d. Which of the sites offers usage statistics?

2. Use the information from one of the sites to read current issues regarding search engines. Write a paragraph summarizing one of these issues.

3. Visit the Discovering the Internet Chapter 3 Web page (scsite.com/Internet/ch3) and click Wayback Machine below Exercise 4 to research the search capability of the Wayback Machine. Write down where this archive is found, why it is important, and how it might be used.

5 Search Engine Statistics

1. Visit the Discovering the Internet Chapter 3 Web page (scsite.com/internet/ch3) and click the links below Exercise 5 to find current statistics on search engines.
   a. Which search engines have the largest number of pages indexed?
   b. Which search engines offer the freshest information?
   c. Which search engines are most widely used in the U.S. and around the world or have the largest audience size?

2. Visit the Discovering the Internet Chapter 3 Web page (scsite.com/internet/ch3) and click a link below Search Engines, or Directories, or Metasearch Engines to select a search tool.
   a. Use the search tool to find a list of the day's most-searched-for keywords. This data is available on several Web sites, including search tool sites. Some sites offer a real-time listing, while others have a daily or monthly listing.
   b. Write a short paragraph describing the most used keywords and why you think people are searching for topics related to those keywords.

3. Visit the Discovering the Internet Chapter 3 Web page (scsite.com/internet/ch3) and click a link below Search Engines, or Directories, or Metasearch Engines to select a search tool. Use the search tool to research the Open Directory Project. Summarize the purpose of the project, how large the Open Directory is, and how many people are involved.

4. Visit the Discovering the Internet Chapter 3 Web page (scsite.com/internet/ch3) and click links below Search Engines, or Directories, or Metasearch Engines to select three search tools. Choose any topic and perform a search using three different search tools and the same keywords.
   a. Time how long it takes for each search engine to return results.

b. Note how many hits each search engine finds.

c. Note which sites are listed by more than one search engine and which hits are unique. Evaluate only the first 10 hits.

d. For one of the three search engines, repeat the search on the same topic using different keywords. Evaluate the differences in the search results list.

6   Using Google

1. Visit the Discovering the Internet Chapter 3 Web page (scsite.com/internet/ch3) and click Google below Exercise 6.
   a. Research how Google performs a search. Find out what happens from the time you enter the query to the time Google returns the results.
   b. One reason Google is used so widely is that it offers the most relevant hits first. Write a brief summary of the method Google uses to rank pages.
   c. Write down other features that make Google a user-friendly and powerful search engine.

2. Find information on downloading the Google toolbar and, if you want, download and install it (if you are working in a computer lab, consult your instructor first). List the capabilities of the Google toolbar and the benefits it provides. Use the toolbar to search for information on any topic of interest.

3. Research the search engine game called Googlewhacking. Challenge a few friends to play and write down the combination of words that returns the fewest hits.

7   Using White Pages and Yellow Pages Directories

1. Visit the Discovering the Internet Chapter 3 Web page (scsite.com/internet/ch3) and click the links below Exercise 7 to answer the following questions.
   a. Is your name or the name of a relative listed in an online white pages directory?
   b. Which white pages directories list your or your family member's information?
   c. Which white pages directories list your information correctly with the most current street address and telephone number and which ones list outdated information?
   d. Approximately how many other people share your name?

2. Write down your feelings about having your name, street address, and e-mail address listed in the white pages directories.

3. Visit the Discovering the Internet Chapter 3 Web page (scsite.com/internet/ch3) and click SuperPages below Exercise 7.
   a. Review and list the resources offered at the SuperPages site.
   b. Compare SuperPages with other white pages directories you have used.
   c. Use a reverse lookup to find the owner of a telephone number using the telephone number of your choice.

(continued)

EXERCISES

Use the
Exercises to
gain hands-on
Internet
experience.

EXERCISES *(continued)*

4. Visit the Discovering the Internet Chapter 3 Web page (**scsite.com/internet/ch3**) and click the links below Exercise 7 to identify the online resources available for consumers trying to find a business.
   a. Review each online yellow pages directory.
   b. Search for businesses of your choice by name, by type of business, by location, or other criteria using two different directories.
   c. Write down the information you find.

8 Searching and Browsing News

1. Visit the Discovering the Internet Chapter 3 Web page (**scsite.com/internet/ch3**) and click a link below Search Engines, or Directories, or Metasearch Engines to select a search tool. Use the search tool to find other search tools that offer the ability to search for news stories.
   a. List the general search engines that offer a way to browse headlines.
   b. Write down the number of news sources available at or indexed by each search engine.
   c. Find a Web site that provides local news for your community.

2. Visit the Discovering the Internet Chapter 3 Web page (**scsite.com/internet/ch3**) and click the links below Exercise 8 to visit the WorldNews Network and WorldHeadlines Web sites. Write down the sponsors for each of these sites and describe how the content on these sites is similar or different.

9 Government Sites

1. Visit the Discovering the Internet Chapter 3 Web page (**scsite.com/internet/ch3**) and click a link below Search Engines, or Directories, or Metasearch Engines to select a search tool. Search for information on one of the following topics. In the list of results, examine only government-sponsored Web pages (from the .gov TLD).
   a. Government jobs
   b. Filing taxes online
   c. Consumer protection information
   d. Environmental regulations for small businesses
   e. Postal service
   f. Import and export regulations for small businesses
   g. National Weather Service

2. Visit the Discovering the Internet Chapter 3 Web page (**scsite.com/internet/ch3**) and click a link below Search Engines, or Directories, or Metasearch Engines to select a search tool. Use the search tool to find an article on how people use government agencies' Web sites. Write a brief summary of the article.

10 Library Collections and Electronic Resources

To complete all the parts of this exercise you must have both electronic and physical access to a school or public library.

1. Visit your school's Web site and examine the resources available at the school's online library page.
   a. List the main electronic collections and the topic each covers.
   b. List the resources that are restricted to faculty, staff, and students at your institution.
   c. List items that are available via the Internet versus the ones that must be accessed within the library.

2. Visit the Web site for your local public library. List the main electronic collections and the topic each covers. List items that are available via the Internet versus the ones that must be accessed within the library.

3. Schedule an interview with a school or public librarian, if possible, to discuss the online research capabilities offered through the library that go beyond those available to any user on the Web.

4. Visit a school or public library and use FirstSearch, Ingenta, InfoTrac, or another electronic resource to search for articles on search engines.
   a. Write or print a list of available articles.
   b. Print the abstract from one of the articles.

CHAPTER 4
Communicating Online

Introduction

Internet users around the world now rely on online tools such as e-mail, chat, mailing lists, newsgroups, and messaging to communicate with friends, family members, fellow employees, and others. For example, business people use e-mail to exchange data and arrange appointments with business colleagues; students use e-mail to correspond with teachers and instant messaging to stay in touch with classmates; hobbyists subscribe to hobby-related mailing lists; and adults join chat rooms to discuss topics of interest with others. In this chapter, you will learn about several online communications tools, including e-mail, mailing lists, newsgroups, Web-based discussion groups, text and instant messaging, chat, and virtual meetings.

OBJECTIVES

After completing this chapter, you will be able to:

1. Describe the components of an e-mail system and discuss e-mail etiquette

2. Demonstrate how to use the Outlook Express e-mail client to send, receive, and organize e-mail messages

3. Demonstrate how to set up a Web-based e-mail account and use Web-based e-mail services

4. Describe mailing lists, newsgroups, Web-based discussion groups, and text messaging

5. Discuss real-time online communications including chat, instant messaging, and virtual meetings

CONTENTS

E-Mail Systems

E-mail still is the most popular online communication tool used by Internet-connected individuals. In addition, e-mail communications are now indispensable for businesses and other organizations as well. As recently as the late 1990s, businesses used the telephone as their primary means of communicating with customers, business partners, and vendors. Today, businesses of all sizes rely heavily on e-mail. For example, a study by the Pew Internet & American Life Project indicates that approximately 40 percent of employees have Internet access at work and use e-mail daily in their jobs, and the number is growing by almost 20 percent a year!

The volume of personal and business e-mail messages sent daily is staggering, exceeding the number of pieces of paper mail handled by major national postal systems. A significant portion of personal e-mail messages consists of non-original, forwarded e-mail, including jokes, inspirational messages, or virus warnings. Many e-mail messages are **spam**, which is unsolicited, junk e-mail sent as part of an electronic mass mailing, usually to advertise a product or service.

Facts@Hand

Studies indicate individuals receive on average 34 e-mail messages each day, although 60 percent receive 10 or fewer messages on an average day and only 6 percent receive 50 or more. Analysts at IDC, a marketing research company, predict that, within the next few years, the average number of messages received each day will quadruple.

Using e-mail has several distinct benefits, including speed of delivery, low cost, accessibility, convenience, and ease of management.

- *Speed of delivery* — E-mail messages can be composed by the sender, sent, and received by the recipient in mere moments. The recipient can send a reply just as quickly, thus providing rapid feedback.

- *Low cost* — E-mail is a cost-effective way to communicate with others and to share documents quickly. For example, sending an e-mail message is much less expensive than the paper, envelope, and stamp required for writing and sending a letter. And sending an electronic file attached to an e-mail message is much less expensive than sending a printed document via a courier service.

- *Accessibility* — Some e-mail messages can be accessed from any computer with Internet access, not from just a single fixed location.

- *Convenience* — E-mail messages can be sent when it is convenient for the sender and read when it is convenient for the recipient. Because e-mail messages are much less formal than paper-based communications, using e-mail can promote increased collaboration among employees or the members of a social group.

- *Ease of management* — Users can manage their e-mail messages by storing them in folders on their computers or mail servers where the messages can be arranged and viewed by date, sender, or other criteria or deleted.

In the next sections, you learn about the components of an e-mail system: addresses, clients, servers, and protocols.

E-Mail Addresses

In order to be delivered to the correct destination, an e-mail message must have a unique delivery address consisting of two components: a user ID and a host name, as shown in Figure 4-1.

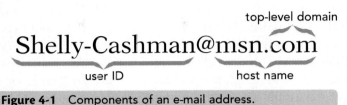

Shelly-Cashman@msn.com

top-level domain

user ID   host name

Figure 4-1 Components of an e-mail address.

The **user ID** is a unique identifier for the recipient and the **host name** identifies the server where the recipient's e-mail account or mailbox resides. In Figure 4-1, the host name is msn.com, a domain name. The user ID and host name are separated by the @ symbol. An e-mail address is entered in a message window provided by an e-mail client.

E-Mail Clients, Servers, and Protocols

The steps in the transmission of an e-mail message from origin to destination parallel those followed in the delivery of a letter by a traditional postal service, often called **snail mail**. A letter arrives at post office, either directly or via a mail carrier or drop box. At the receiving post office, the letter's delivery address is checked and then the letter is routed to the destination post office, either directly or though a series of interim post offices. Once at the destination post office, the letter's delivery address is again checked and the letter is delivered to its recipient's mailbox. A similar process occurs when sending and receiving e-mail messages. An e-mail message has a unique delivery address, is routed from server to server over the Internet until it reaches its destination, and then is delivered to its recipient's mailbox.

E-MAIL CLIENTS An **e-mail client** is a program used to create, send, and receive e-mail messages. Microsoft Outlook, Microsoft Outlook Express, and Netscape Mail are all examples of an e-mail client. Microsoft Outlook is available with the Microsoft Office suite; Microsoft Outlook Express is available with the Internet Explorer browser, and Netscape Mail is available with the Netscape Navigator browser. Other e-mail clients, such as QUALCOMM Eudora, are available as stand-alone programs users can download from vendor sites.

Many colleges and universities provide e-mail services for their students, and these services often require a particular e-mail client. For example, Pine is a text-only e-mail client that allows schools to provide e-mail services to large numbers of students while requiring only modest resources.

E-mail clients typically offer tools to:

- Create and send outgoing e-mail messages.
- Read, save, and print incoming e-mail messages and their attachments.
- Sort, archive, and delete messages.
- Create folders in which to organize messages.

In the past few years, Web-based e-mail services have become widely used by individuals at home, at school, and at work. You learn more about using a Web-based e-mail service later in this chapter.

E-MAIL SERVERS AND PROTOCOLS   E-mail messages are sent over the Internet using the same packet-switching technology and TCP/IP suite that govern all communications over the Internet. An e-mail client uses a number of protocols to interact with e-mail servers when sending and receiving messages. When a user sends an e-mail message, the first server to handle it is a **SMTP (Simple Mail Transfer Protocol) server** (Figure 4-2) usually located at the sender's ISP. This SMTP server contacts a DNS name server to resolve the host name (domain name) portion of the e-mail address to an IP address. The message may then be routed through multiple SMTP servers until it reaches its final destination server, called a **mail server**. The mail server receives the message and stores it in the recipient's mailbox, a folder on the server, identified by the user ID portion of the e-mail address. Upon request from the user's e-mail client, the mail server sends the new message to the client.

Several different types of mail servers are in use today. The three most common mail servers are POP (Post Office Protocol), IMAP (Internet Message Access Protocol) and HTTP (Hypertext Transfer Protocol) mail servers. E-mail clients, such as Outlook, Outlook Express, or Mail, use POP or IMAP mail servers. Web-based e-mail services, such as Hotmail and Yahoo! Mail, use HTTP servers. While each type of server handles incoming messages, each server does so in a different way.

All mail management functions take place using the e-mail client when incoming messages are stored on a **POP (Post Office Protocol) server**. For example, an e-mail client sends a request to a POP server, downloads all new messages, and stores the messages on the user's computer. The main disadvantage of a POP server is that after messages are downloaded to a user's computer, only that computer can be used to view and manage the messages.

In contrast, an **IMAP (Internet Message Access Protocol) server** provides mail management functions on the server. The user's messages are stored and managed on the server.

Sender sends
message using
an e-mail client.

SMTP Server

Via Internet

Recipient receives
a message using
an e-mail client

Mail Server
(POP, IMAP, or HTTP)

Figure 4-2   Several types of servers are involved in handling e-mail.

Although the user reads, deletes, or sorts the messages using his or her e-mail client, the action actually takes place on the IMAP server. The user also can work with messages locally on his or her computer by downloading the messages and reading them, marking them for deletion, or by composing new messages. The next time the user's e-mail client connects to the IMAP server, the server synchronizes with the e-mail client, sending out any new mail messages and deleting messages on the server that were marked for deletion in the e-mail client. Unlike POP servers, where the messages are downloaded to a specific machine, a user can access an IMAP server from different computers to view his or her messages.

An **HTTP (Hypertext Transfer Protocol) server** provides Web-based e-mail services that can be accessed by any Internet-computer and a Web browser. A Web site provides access to an e-mail account and e-mail services. The main advantage of an HTTP server and Web-based e-mail is that access to e-mail is available wherever access to the Internet and the Web are available. One disadvantage is that Web-based e-mail services are very popular, which may mean a slow response times during peak hours when the HTTP servers are processing many requests.

Anatomy of an E-Mail Message

Most e-mail clients provide the same basic message window features, including the following elements illustrated in Figure 4-3:

- The **To line** contains one or more e-mail addresses of the message's recipient or recipients. The e-mail addresses for multiple recipients are typically separated with semi-colons or commas.

- The **Cc line** lists the e-mail addresses of recipients who will receive a courtesy copy of the message. A **courtesy copy** is a copy of the message that is sent as a courtesy to someone other than the recipients in the To line.

- The **Bcc line** contains the e-mail addresses of recipients who will receive a blind courtesy copy of the message. A **blind courtesy copy**, is a copy of a message that is sent to a recipient without that recipient's name or e-mail address appearing in the message header. The Bcc line is visible only to the sender and the Bcc recipient.

- The **Subject line** contains a description of the message content.

- The **Attach line** contains the file names of any attachments. An **attachment** is a file that is transmitted along with the e-mail message.

- The **message body** contains the actual text of the message. In addition to text, a message body can include graphics, links to Web pages, or the contents of Web pages.

- The signature can be automatically inserted via a small **signature file** containing standard content, such as the name, title, and contact information of the sender.

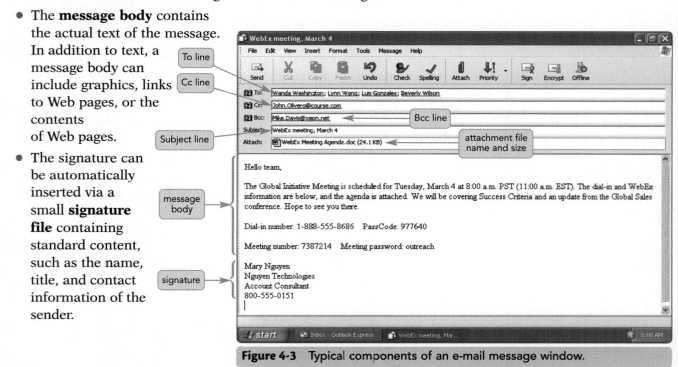

Figure 4-3 Typical components of an e-mail message window.

E-Mail Etiquette

The very characteristics of e-mail that make it so popular and easy to use can also be disadvantages. For example, because e-mail is informal, messages may not be written clearly or worded carefully. The speed and ease with which an e-mail message can be sent creates another potential problem. An individual might send an e-mail message when upset or angry without carefully thinking through the message's contents. Additionally, the recipient of an e-mail message can easily forward the message on to others making the message's contents public information without the sender's permission. Finally, because e-mail is so easy to send, some individuals may send too many unnecessary, and often unwanted, e-mail messages to their friends, family, and co-workers.

One of the major drawbacks of e-mail, and of most text-based communications in general, is the potential for a message to be misunderstood. The composer of an e-mail message may write something with sarcasm in mind. The reader, however, may not interpret the language as sarcasm, instead reading the message as entirely sincere. The reader sees only the content of the message, and does not see the facial expressions, hear the tone of voice, or observe the body language of the sender. Following some basic e-mail etiquette guidelines can help get an idea across clearly and avoid accidentally insulting someone or hurting feelings. E-mail etiquette guidelines include:

- When composing an e-mail message, do not use all capital letters for the entire message. All caps represent SHOUTING and are read and interpreted as such.

- When responding to a message about which you have strong negative feelings, it is often a good idea to save your response for a few hours or a day before you send it. Responding with strong language or insults via e-mail (and other online communication tools) is called **flaming** and is considered improper in most online venues.

- When you want to convey a particular feeling or emotion in an e-mail message, you can make use of an **emoticon** — such as :-) — at appropriate points in the message to convey the emotion you are trying to convey. Some programs contain a set of buttons that allow you to insert picture emoticons — such as ☺ — by clicking a button. These really can help the message recipient get the full flavor of a message. Be careful, however, not to overuse emoticons: a message that contains one or more emoticons per sentence loses its appeal and impact. Additionally, emoticons are generally not used in business e-mail messages.

@Issue Spam

Spam — along with its browser counterpart, pop-up advertisements — is the bane of Internet users. Because e-mail is inexpensive to send and easy to use, it is a perfect medium for bulk e-mail advertisements, and many people now suffer from inboxes stuffed with unwanted messages.

The monstrous volume of unsolicited e-mail strains computing resources and technical support, and consumes bandwidth. According to estimates from Ferris Research, spam costs corporate America and European companies billions of dollars each year in increased hardware costs, bandwidth loss, and lost productivity. Studies show that around 15 percent of spam is pornographic in nature; 25 to 30 percent deals with financial services such as loans, insurance, investments, and real estate; and around 30 percent consist of advertisements for products. Fraudulent spam, such as messages proposing pyramid schemes or messages asking for help in secretly moving large amounts of money into bank accounts, constitute another 6 percent.

Although one percent of consumers say they enjoy receiving spam, consumers overwhelmingly are annoyed by spam, particularly pornographic spam. According to studies by Harris Interactive, 75 percent of Americans who use the Internet would like to make spamming illegal, although 12 percent oppose a ban.

For more information about spam and its costs, visit the Discovering the Internet Chapter 4 Web page (scsite.com/internet/ch4) and click a link below Spam.

Using Outlook Express

As you have learned, e-mail clients provide tools to send and receive messages, reply to and forward messages, and print, organize, and delete messages. In this section, you review the Microsoft Outlook Express e-mail client window and then receive, read, and reply to an e-mail message, open an attachment, compose and send a message with an attachment, and organize e-mail messages.

Reviewing the Outlook Express Window

The Outlook Express window includes common e-mail client elements such as menus, toolbars, and viewing panes. At the top of the window are the menu bar and the Toolbar. You click menu commands or toolbar buttons to create and send an e-mail message; reply to, forward, print, and delete an incoming e-mail message; view the Address Book, and find messages or people, called contacts, listed in the Address Book or in one of the several white pages directories you learned about in Chapter 3.

The Outlook Express window (Figure 4-4 on the next page) also has, by default, two viewing panes — the Folders Bar and Contacts — on the left side of the window. The **Folders Bar** contains the **Folder List**, a tree-style hierarchy of the Outlook Express folders used to store e-mail messages: the Inbox, Outbox, Sent Items, Deleted Items, and Drafts folders. These folders are subfolders under Local Folders in the Folder List indicating that the folders are stored on the computer's hard drive. If you have an e-mail account on an HTTP server, you may see an additional set of folders stored on the server.

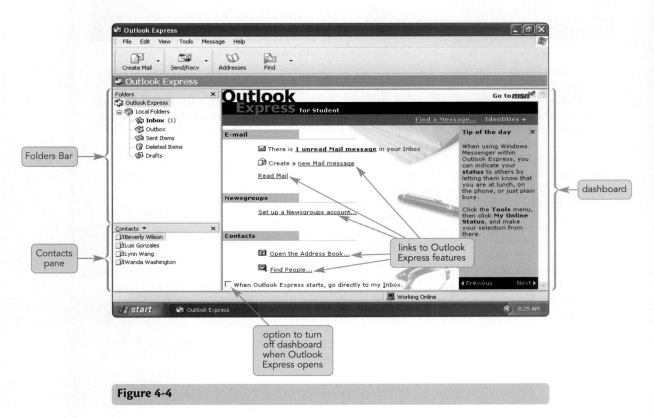

Figure 4-4

The **Inbox** folder contains incoming messages. The **Outbox** is a temporary storage folder for outgoing messages. Once an outgoing message has been sent, a copy is placed, by default, in the **Sent Items** folder. The **Deleted Items** folder contains deleted messages. Just as you can restore deleted files sent to the Windows operating system's Recycle Bin until you empty it, you can retrieve deleted messages from the Deleted Items folder until you empty it. The **Drafts** folder contains messages that you create and save without sending. The number in parenthesis to the right of the Inbox folder is the number of unread messages currently in the folder. Because the Folder List can be customized to add or delete folders, the folders you see in your Outlook Express Folders Bar may vary from those shown in the illustrations in this chapter.

Below the Folders Bar is the **Contacts pane**, which contains a list of **contacts**, or frequently used names, e-mail addresses, and other contact information saved in the **Address Book**. You can add contacts manually by keying the information in the Address Book or by adding the basic e-mail information to the Address Book from an incoming e-mail message.

Outlook Express may open with a page, called a **dashboard** (Figure 4-4), which has links to common Outlook Express functions such as reading or sending e-mail, reviewing newsgroups, or looking for people in the Address Book or in an online white pages directory. The dashboard page is often turned off, however, as many users prefer to view the contents of the Inbox when Outlook Express starts. You can view the dashboard by clicking the Outlook Express folder in the Folder List.

Selecting one of the e-mail folders in the Folder List changes the contents of the viewing area by splitting it into two panes in which you can view the folder's contents. For example, clicking the Inbox folder in the Folder List displays the **messages pane** containing a list of incoming messages and the **preview pane**, which displays the contents of the message selected in the messages pane. As new e-mail messages are received, you may also see an **e-mail notification icon** in the notification area on the taskbar (Figure 4-5).

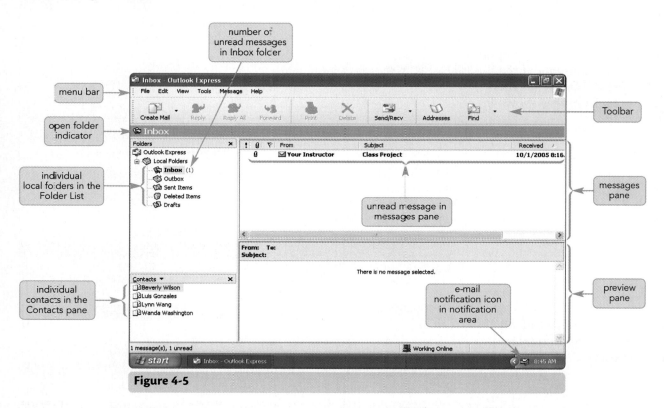

Figure 4-5

🖐 Facts@Hand

Before sending and receiving e-mail using Outlook Express, a user must first set up an Outlook Express e-mail account including user ID, password, and names of the POP, IMAP, HTTP, and SMTP servers to be accessed. For the projects in this section, it is assumed your e-mail account has already been set up. For more information about setting up an Outlook Express e-mail account, see Outlook Express online Help.

Reviewing an Incoming E-Mail Message

Most e-mail clients check for new e-mail messages on the assigned mail servers at regular intervals. At any point, however, you can click the Send/Recv button on the Outlook Express Toolbar to check for new e-mail messages. In the steps on the next page, you open Outlook Express, check for incoming e-mail, and review an e-mail message sent to you by your instructor. In the Outlook Express projects in this chapter, Outlook Express appears with the Inbox folder opened and uses a POP server for incoming e-mail messages. If your Outlook Express or server configuration is different, your instructor may modify the steps in the projects.

Steps: To Open Outlook Express and Receive an E-Mail Message

1 **Click Start on the taskbar, point to All Programs, and click Outlook Express. Point to the Send/Recv button on the Toolbar.**

The Outlook Express window appears with the Inbox folder open (Figure 4-6). The contents of the Outlook Express window on your screen will vary from that shown in the figure.

Send/Recv button

Figure 4-6

2 **Click the Send/Recv button. Point to the message from your instructor.**

Outlook Express connects to its assigned POP mail servers and the e-mail messages stored on the servers are downloaded into the Inbox folder (Figure 4-7). Each unread message has a closed envelope icon to the left of the sender's name. By default, each message's subject and date received information also appears. If a message has an attached file, a paper clip icon also appears to the left of the message. The messages that appear in your messages pane will vary from those shown in the figure.

paper clip icon   sender   subject   date received

new unread messages

message from instructor   closed envelope icon

Figure 4-7

3 **Click the message from your instructor. Leave Outlook Express open and the message from your instructor selected.**

The content of the message from your instructor appears in the preview pane (Figure 4-8). The message contents you see may be different from that shown in the figure.

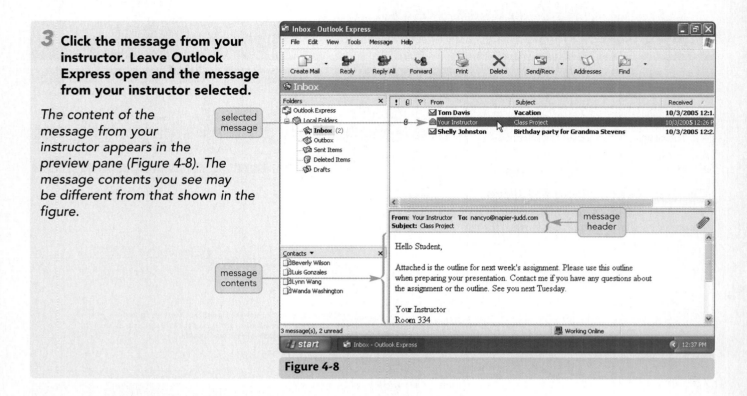

selected message

message header

message contents

Figure 4-8

For short messages, like the one from your instructor, you may be able to read all or most of the message in the preview pane. If the message is long, however, you can double-click the message line in the messages pane to open the e-mail message in its own window.

 Facts@Hand

The Reply All button on the Outlook Express Toolbar allows you to send your reply to all the addresses in the original message's header.

REPLYING TO AN E-MAIL MESSAGE A standard e-mail client feature is the reply feature, which allows you to respond to a message. Replying creates a new message automatically addressed to the sender of the original e-mail message and includes, on the Subject line, a reference to the subject of the original message. By default, the text of the original message is included for reference. In the steps on the next page, you reply to your instructor's e-mail message.

Steps: To Reply to an E-Mail Message

1 Verify that the Outlook Express window is open, the Inbox is open, and the message from your instructor is selected. Point to the Reply button on the Toolbar.

The Reply button (Figure 4-9) allows you to create a new message that references the original message.

Figure 4-9

2 Click the Reply button. If necessary, maximize the message window. Type `Received.` at the insertion point on the blank line above the original message. Press the ENTER key. Type your name as the entry. Press the ENTER key. Point to the Send button on the Toolbar.

The message window appears with a blank line above the text of the original message (Figure 4-10). The e-mail header contains the recipient's name as an alias for his or her e-mail address in the To text box. Re: precedes the Subject line text in the Subject text box indicating the message is a reply. You may not see the Bcc line in the message window on your screen. The Bcc line is displayed by clicking the All Headers command on the View menu in the message window.

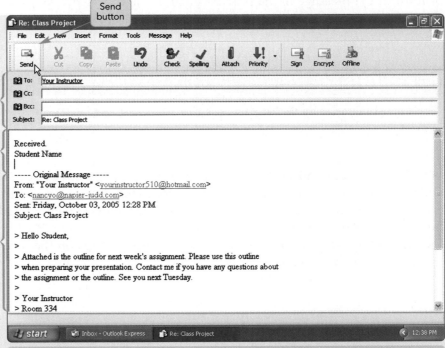

Figure 4-10

3 **Click Send. Leave the Outlook Express window open and the message from your instructor selected.**

The reply is sent and the message window closes (Figure 4-11). Your instructor's message line in the messages pane now shows an open envelope icon indicating the message has been read and a left-pointing arrow icon indicating you have replied to the message. Your instructor's name and address are automatically added to the list of contacts in the Contacts pane.

Figure 4-11

VIEWING AND SAVING ATTACHMENTS The message from your instructor has an attached file indicated by the paper clip icon. You can view, save, and print an attachment by first opening the message with the attachment in a message window and then using a shortcut menu or menu commands to open, save, or print the attachment. When you open an attachment, the application associated with the attachment's file type automatically starts. You must use caution, however, when opening attachments. Because of the risk of receiving attachments that contain damaging viruses, you should never open an attachment from an unknown source. Because some viruses are spread by messages with attachments automatically sent from an infected computer's Address Book, you should not open an attachment even from a trusted source unless you are expecting the attachment.

In the following steps, you view the file attached to your instructor's message and then save the attached file in a folder specified by your instructor.

⟩⟩ *Steps:* **To View an Attachment**

1 **Verify that the Outlook Express window is open and the message from your instructor is selected in the messages pane. Double-click the message from your instructor. If necessary, maximize the message window. Point to the file name in the Attach text box.**

The message from your instructor appears in its own window (Figure 4-12). You can use a short-cut menu to open, save, or print the attached file. The message contents and attachment file name in your message window may vary from that shown in the figure.

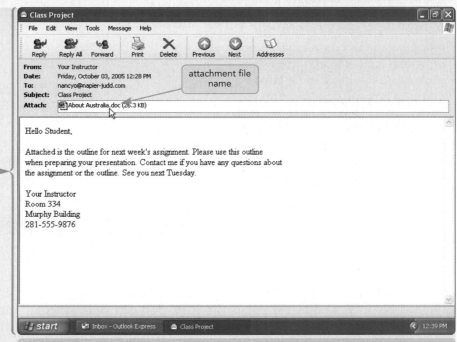

Figure 4-12

2 **Right-click the attachment's file name. Point to Open.**

A shortcut menu appears with commands to open, save, and print the attachment (Figure 4-13).

Figure 4-13

3 **Click Open. Point to the Open it option button.**

A warning message dialog box appears (Figure 4-14). Because some files can contain viruses, you must be certain that the attachment comes from a trusted source and you should be expecting to receive the attachment from the source before opening it.

Figure 4-14

4 **Click the Open it option button. Point to OK.**

Because this message is from your instructor and you knew that your instructor was sending you an attachment, you can open it (Figure 4-15).

OK button

Open Attachment Warning

Opening:
About Australia.doc

Some files can contain viruses or otherwise be harmful to your computer. It is important to be certain that this file is from a trustworthy source.

What would you like to do with this file?
⊙ Open it
○ Save it to disk

☑ Always ask before opening this type of file

OK   Cancel

Figure 4-15

Close button

5 **Click OK. Point to the Close button on the application's title bar.**

The attachment appears in its application window (Figure 4-16). The attachment's contents and application you see on your screen may vary from that shown in the figure.

attachment opened in application window

Figure 4-16

6 **Click Close. Point to File on the menu bar.**

File menu name

The File menu (Figure 4-17) contains commands that allow you to save the attachment.

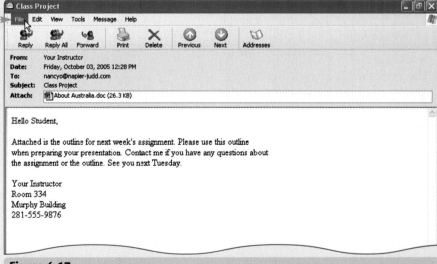

Figure 4-17

(continued)

7 **Click File. Point to Save Attachments.**

The File menu commands appear (Figure 4-18).

File menu

Save Attachments command

Save Attachments dialog box

Figure 4-18

8 **Click Save Attachments. Browse to select the folder specified by your instructor. Point to the Save button.**

The Save Attachments dialog box appears (Figure 4-19). You can browse to select the folder specified by your instructor. The path and folder name you select will be different from that shown in the figure.

attachment

Save button

9 **Click Save. Close the message window. Leave Outlook Express and the Inbox open.**

The attachment is saved in the folder specified by your instructor and you are again viewing the contents of the Inbox.

Save Attachments

Attachments To Be Saved:

About Australia.doc (26.3 KB)

Save
Cancel
Select All

Save To
C:\Documents and Settings\orivers\My Documents\   Browse...

Figure 4-19

path to specified folder

Browse button

FORWARDING AN E-MAIL MESSAGE   You may receive an e-mail message that contains information that needs to be shared with other users. For example, a message sent to one person with information about a rescheduled meeting needs to be shared either in part or in total with all meeting attendees. To **forward** a message means to send a message you receive on to someone else.

You can forward a message by selecting the message in the messages pane and then clicking the Forward button on the Toolbar (Figure 4-20). You then type the recipient's e-mail address in the To text box, type your message text in the message body area above the original message, and then click the Send button. By default, a forwarded message includes the original message and any attached files. Remember to use your best judgment when forwarding messages to ensure that you include enough of the original message to preserve its integrity, but do not forward information not meant to be distributed freely. If only part of the original message is appropriate for forwarding, you can select and delete that portion of the original message that should not be shared before forwarding the message.

PRINTING AN E-MAIL MESSAGE   Although e-mail messages are stored and read electronically, many people still prefer to work with paper and pen for certain tasks. Outlook Express and other e-mail clients provide printing capabilities that allow users to create a hard copy of an e-mail message. To print a message, select the message in the messages pane and click the Print button on the Toolbar (Figure 4-20).

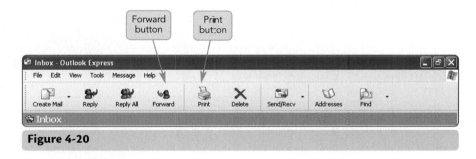

Figure 4-20

Composing and Sending an E-Mail Message

As you compose a message, keep in mind the following guidelines to ensure that your messages are reader-friendly.

- Put a meaningful phrase in the Subject line. Gain the reader's attention, or identify the request by using a key phrase.

- Add a greeting line. Although the e-mail header shows the recipient's e-mail address or name, it still is considered good form to include a greeting on the first line. The greeting can be a formal one (Dear Mr. Chung:) or a casual one (Hi, Bob!), depending on the nature of the message.

- Keep your message brief, but make sure it is clear. Make your point quickly, but provide enough information so the recipient understands the required background information. If possible, make requests in the first sentence or two.

- For replies, leave the message to which you are replying at the bottom of your e-mail. Keeping the thread of e-mails will provide background information and make it easier for the recipient to understand your request or comments.

- Use a personalized closing and include a signature file in case the recipient needs to know alternative ways to contact you.

CREATING A SIGNATURE FILE   As you have learned, Outlook Express allows you to create a signature file, a file that includes standard information inserted at the end of e-mail messages. For example, you often may need to provide your contact information and title, particularly with business e-mail. A signature file can contain basic contact information, such as your name, company, telephone number, fax number, and e-mail address; a confidentiality agreement; an inspirational quotation or motto; or any text that you wish to add to the end of e-mail messages. In the following steps, you create a signature file for your messages. If you are working in a computer lab, check with your instructor before setting up a signature file.

Steps: To Create a Signature File

1 **Verify that Outlook Express and the Inbox are open. Point to Tools on the menu bar.**

The Tools menu contains commands to send and receive messages, open the Address Book, and set user options (Figure 4-21).

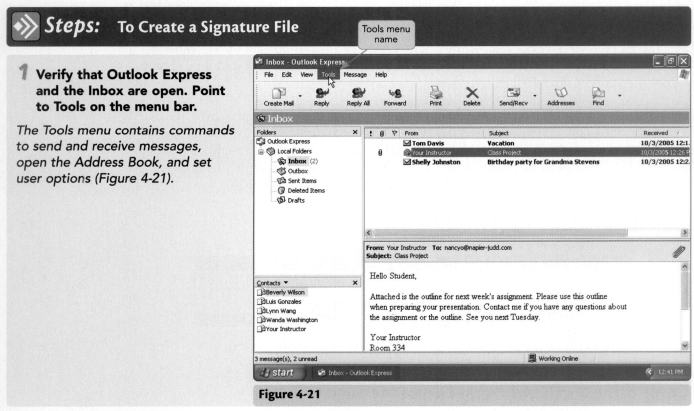

Figure 4-21

2 **Click Tools. Point to Options.**

The Options command (Figure 4-22) opens the Options dialog box.

Figure 4-22

3 **Click Options. Click the Signatures tab. Point to the New button.**

The Options dialog box and the Signatures tab appear (Figure 4-23). If no current signatures exist, only the New button will be active. The contents of your Signatures tab may be different than that shown in the figure.

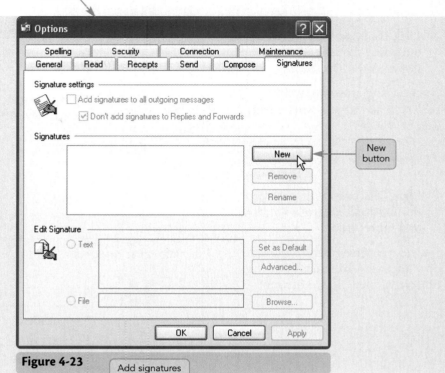

Options dialog box

New button

Figure 4-23

4 **Click New. Type** `your name` **and** `telephone number` **in the Edit Signature text box. Point to the Add signatures to all outgoing messages check box.**

The options in the dialog box are activated and the new signature, named Signature #1, appears (Figure 4-24). Your new signature may have a different number. The signature text you type should be similar to but not exactly like that shown in the figure.

Add signatures to all outgoing messages check box

new default Signature #1

signature file text

Figure 4-24

(continued)

5 Click the Add signatures to all outgoing messages check box. Point to the OK button.

The new signature file will be added to all outgoing messages except Replies and Forwards (Figure 4-25).

option to exclude signature file from Replies and Forwards

6 Click OK. Leave the Outlook Express window and Inbox open.

The text in the signature file will now appear automatically at the bottom of each new message.

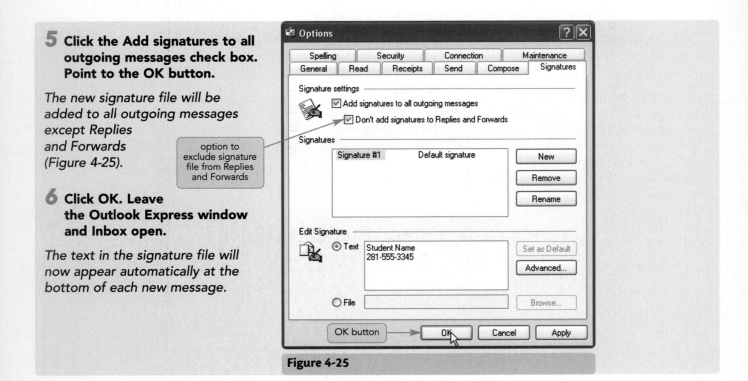

Figure 4-25

Now, whenever you create a new message, Outlook Express automatically appends the signature file to the message. When deciding whether to create and include a signature in your e-mail messages, consider how you usually use e-mail. If most messages you create do not need a signature, then you might prefer to include a signature on a message-by-message basis, instead of automatically for all e-mail messages. Some e-mail clients, including Outlook Express, also allow you to set up multiple signatures so that you can use one for business communications, one for personal messages, and so on. If you want to insert a signature file on a message-by-message basis or be able to select from multiple signatures, do not turn on the option to add the signature file to all new messages. Instead, create the signature file or files. Then, after composing a new message, click Insert on the new message window's menu bar and select the desired signature from the Signature File submenu.

COMPOSING A NEW MESSAGE WITH AN ATTACHMENT You can send an electronic file — such as a document, spreadsheet, or photo — to someone by attaching the file to an e-mail message. Be aware, however, that some mail servers limit attachment sizes to ensure that extremely large files do not bog down the e-mail system. Additionally, some networks block incoming e-mail messages that have certain types of attachments to reduce the risk of viruses.

In the following steps, you compose a new e-mail message and attach the small file sent to you by your instructor which you saved earlier. To send e-mail to someone, you need to know their e-mail address. As you have learned, you can look up an e-mail address in an online white or yellow pages directory. In most cases, however, the best way to find out an e-mail address is to simply ask the intended recipient. Assume that you have asked a classmate, John Olivero, for his e-mail address. Now, you compose a new e-mail message to John Olivero, attach the file, and send the message.

Steps: To Compose and Send a Message with an Attachment

1 **Verify that the Outlook Express window and Inbox are open. Point to the Create Mail button on the Toolbar.**

The Create Mail button (Figure 4-26) opens a new message window. If you click the Create Mail button arrow, you will see a menu of decorative stationery from which to choose.

Figure 4-26

2 **Click Create Mail. If necessary, maximize the message window. Type John.Olivero@course.com in the To text box. Type appropriate subject text in the Subject line. Type a greeting and a short message applicable to the subject in the message area. Point to the Attach button on the Toolbar.**

When you start typing the subject, the message's subject line becomes the name of the message window (Figure 4-27). A formatting toolbar appears in the message window because the default formatting option is HTML mail. HTML mail permits HTML formatting including the bold, underline, italic font styles for emphasis, graphics, bulleted and numbered lists, and hyperlinks in a message. If a recipient's e-mail client cannot read HTML mail, the message's contents appears as plain text. Your message should be similar to Figure 4-27.

Figure 4-27

(continued)

3 Click Attach. If necessary, switch to the folder in which you saved your instructor's attachment. Select the attachment file. Point to the Attach button.

The Insert Attachment dialog box appears (Figure 4-28). The selected file will be attached to the message.

Figure 4-28

4 Click Attach. Point to the Send button on the Toolbar.

Your message and attachment are ready to send (Figure 4-29).

5 Click the Send button. Leave Outlook Express and the Inbox open.

The message is sent. In a short while, you should receive John's reply.

Figure 4-29

Managing Messages

As the number of e-mails you receive from friends, family members, business associates, and others grows, you may need to better organize the messages in order to find messages more quickly, delete messages you do not need, and indicate which new messages need your immediate attention. Outlook Express allows you to create folders in which you can store your messages, options for deleting messages, and a method of flagging messages for follow-up.

CREATING MESSAGE FOLDERS   The first step in organizing your incoming e-mail messages is to create message folders. You then can move messages into the folders. Creating and using message folders with meaningful names can make finding a particular message much easier. In the following steps, you create a new folder for incoming messages about class assignments.

◆》 *Steps:*   To Create a New Message Folder

1 **Verify that Outlook Express and the Inbox are open. Right-click the Inbox folder in the Folder List. Point to New Folder.**

A shortcut menu appears (Figure 4-30). Note that as you work in Outlook Express, you can select different messages in the messages pane to view them. The selected message you see on your screen will vary from that shown in the figure.

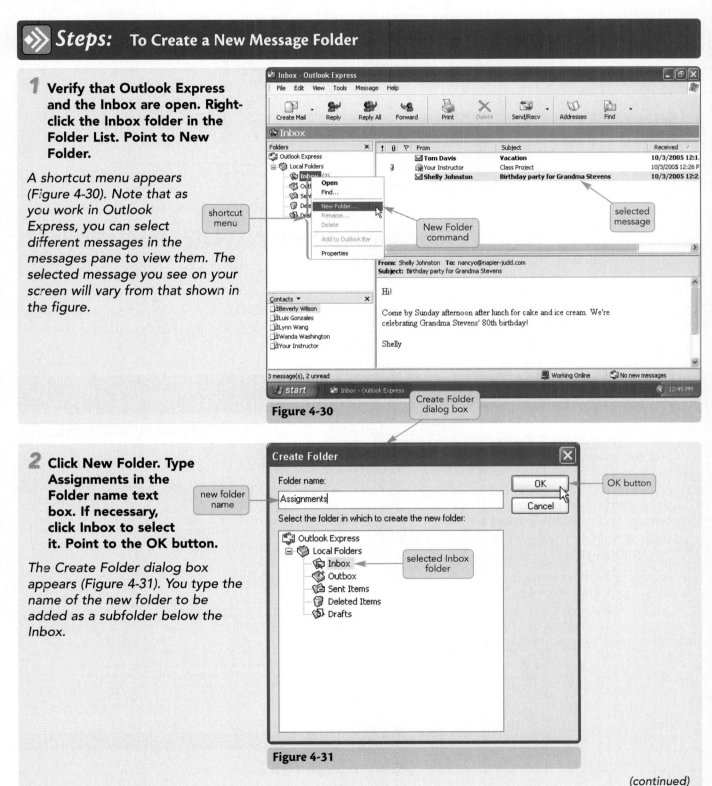

2 **Click New Folder. Type Assignments in the Folder name text box. If necessary, click Inbox to select it. Point to the OK button.**

The Create Folder dialog box appears (Figure 4-31). You type the name of the new folder to be added as a subfolder below the Inbox.

Figure 4-30

Figure 4-31

(continued)

3 **Click OK. Leave Outlook Express and the Inbox open.**

The new Assignments subfolder appears in the Folder List below the Inbox folder (Figure 4-32).

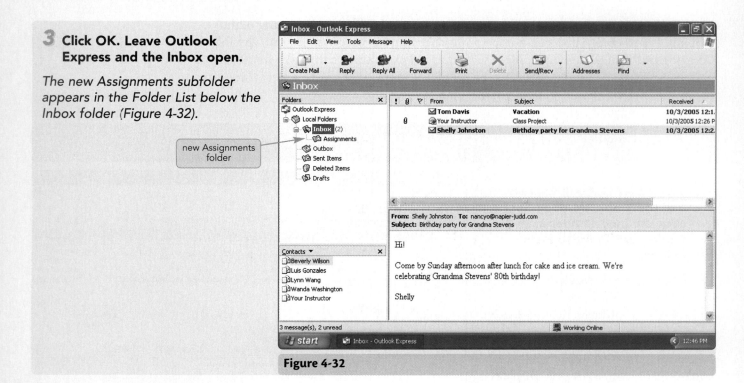

new Assignments folder

Figure 4-32

MOVING A MESSAGE After you create message folders, you can move incoming messages into the appropriate folder. In the following steps, you move the message from your instructor into the Assignments folder.

Steps: To Move an Incoming Message into a Folder

1 **Verify that Outlook Express and the Inbox are open. Click the message from your instructor in the messages pane, hold down the mouse button, and drag the message to the Assignments folder in the Folder List.**

As you drag the message to the Assignments folder, the folder name is selected indicating that when you release the mouse button the message will be moved to this folder (Figure 4-33).

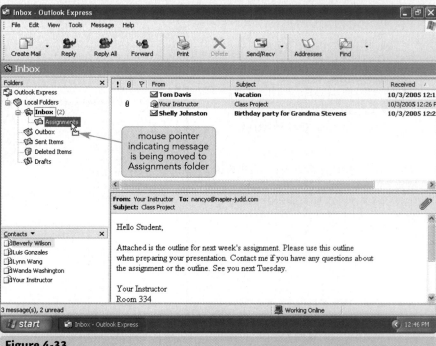

mouse pointer indicating message is being moved to Assignments folder

Figure 4-33

2 **Release the mouse button. Click the Assignments folder in the Folder List. Point to the Inbox in the Folder List.**

The Assignments Folder opens (Figure 4-34) and contains the message from your instructor.

3 **Click the Inbox. Leave Outlook Express and the Inbox open.**

The message from your instructor no longer appears in the Inbox.

Figure 4-34

DELETING A MESSAGE   In addition to keeping messages organized using folders, you can keep the number of incoming messages manageable by deleting messages when you no longer need them. Deleted messages are moved to the Deleted Items folder. You can delete selected messages by clicking the Delete command on the Edit menu or shortcut menu; by clicking the Delete button on the Toolbar; by pressing the DELETE key; or by dragging the messages to the Deleted Items folder.

You can retain messages in the Deleted Items folder and then retrieve them, as necessary. You can empty the Deleted Items folder manually with a shortcut menu or automatically each time you exit Outlook Express by turning on an option in the Maintenance tab in the Options dialog box. Once you empty the Deleted Items folder, however, you no longer can retrieve any of the messages stored in the folder. In the following steps, you delete a message from your Inbox.

Steps: To Delete a Message

1 **Verify that Outlook Express and the Inbox are open. Click the Send/Recv button on the Toolbar, to download new messages. Select a message of your choice. Point to the Delete button on the Toolbar.**

The Delete button (Figure 4-35) moves selected messages to the Deleted Items folder.

2 **Click Delete. Leave Outlook Express and the Inbox open.**

The selected message now is moved to the Deleted Items folder.

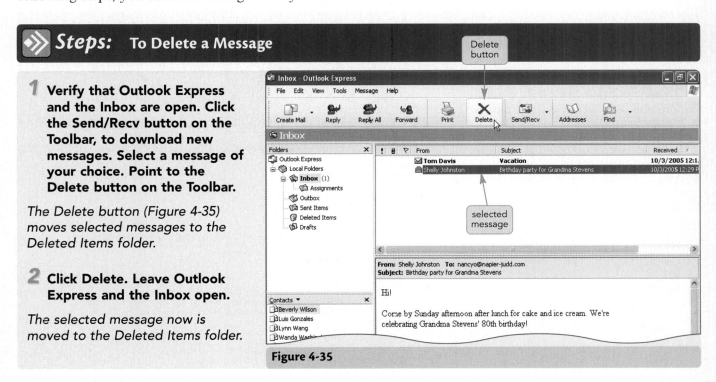

Figure 4-35

FLAGGING A MESSAGE   Some messages require further action. You can mark an incoming e-mail with a **flag** icon, indicating the message requires your attention. You then can leave the flagged message in your Inbox until you have completed the required action. To flag or unflag a message, simply click in the flag column to the left of the message in the messages pane.

Managing Contacts

When corresponding with large numbers of people via e-mail, keeping track of everyone's e-mail address can become overwhelming. E-mail clients, therefore, provide electronic address books to help users keep track of e-mail addresses. You can use the Outlook Express Address Book to enter names, addresses, e-mail addresses, and other important information about those with whom you frequently correspond via e-mail.

CREATING CONTACTS   As you have seen, when you reply to an e-mail message, the original sender's e-mail address and name information are automatically added to the Address Book and the sender's name as an alias for his or her e-mail address appears in the Contacts list in the Contacts pane. You can open the Outlook Express Address Book by clicking the Addresses button on the Toolbar or by clicking the Address Book command on the Tools menu. When the Address Book opens, you can add a contact or modify an existing contact.

✋ Facts@Hand

You also can create a new contact by right-clicking a message in the messages pane and clicking Add Sender to Address Book.

In the following steps, you open the Address Book and add John Olivero as a contact.

⧁⧁ *Steps:*   To Create a Contact

1 **Verify that Outlook Express and the Inbox are open. Point to the Addresses button on the Toolbar.**

The Addresses button (Figure 4-36) opens the Address Book.

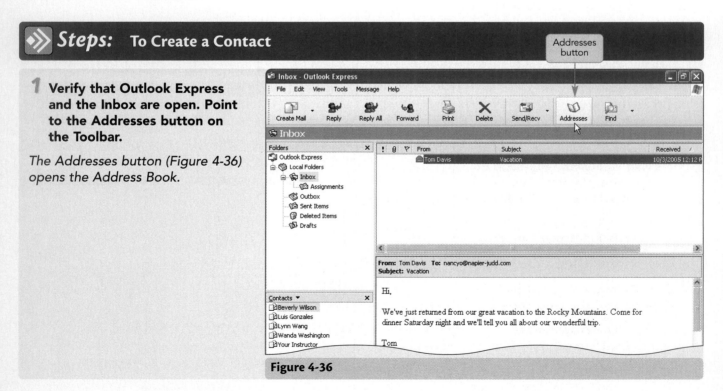

Figure 4-36

2 Click Addresses. If necessary, maximize the window. Point to the New button on the Toolbar in the Address Book.

The Address Book window appears (Figure 4-37). You can select an existing contact to modify the contact's information or create a new contact in this window. The contents of your Address Book will vary from that shown in the figure.

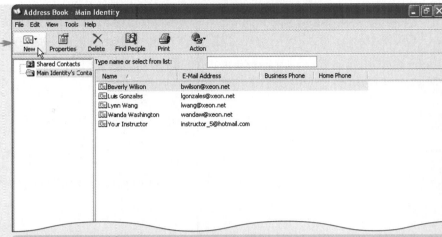

Figure 4-37

3 Click New. Point to New Contact.

The New menu appears (Figure 4-38).

Figure 4-38

4 Click New Contact. Click the Name tab, if necessary. Type John in the First text box. Type Olivero in the Last text box. Type John.Olivero@course.com in the E-Mail Addresses text box. Point to the Add button.

The Name tab in the Properties dialog box appears (Figure 4-39). You enter the name and e-mail address of the new contact in this dialog box.

Figure 4-39

(continued)

5 **Click Add. Point to the OK button.**

John Olivero is added as a contact (Figure 4-40).

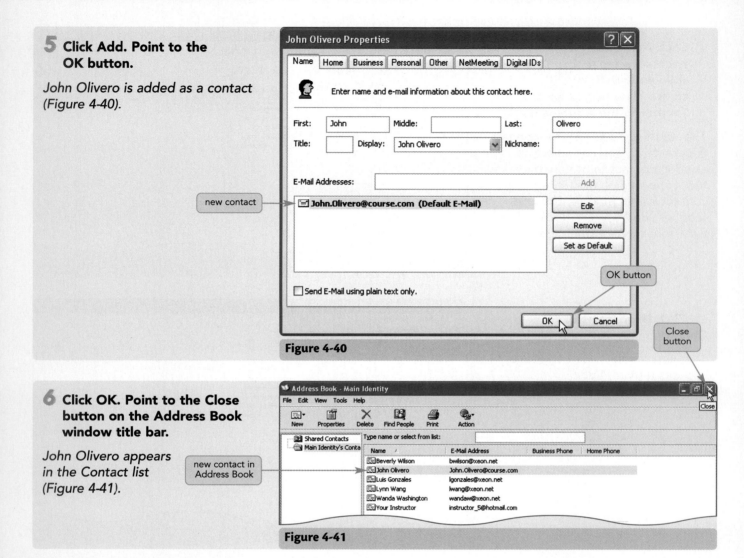

Figure 4-40

6 **Click OK. Point to the Close button on the Address Book window title bar.**

John Olivero appears in the Contact list (Figure 4-41).

Figure 4-41

7 **Click Close. Leave Outlook Express and the Inbox open.**

The Address Book closes and John Olivero appears in the Contacts list in the Contacts pane (Figure 4-42).

Figure 4-42

USING CONTACTS   You can send an e-mail message to a contact by double-clicking the contact in the Contacts list in the Contacts pane to open a new message window containing the contact's e-mail address in the To text box. You also can right-click a contact and click the Send E-Mail command on the shortcut menu to open a new message window containing the contact's e-mail address in the To box. Finally, you can create a new message and click the To button to open the Address Book and select a contact's e-mail address. In the following steps, you send an e-mail message to John Olivero using the Contacts list.

Steps: **To Send an E-Mail Message to a Contact**

1 **Verify that Outlook Express and the Inbox are open. Double-click John Olivero in the Contacts pane. If necessary, maximize the New Message window. Compose the message of your choice by typing a subject in the Subject text box and a short message in the message body area. Point to the Send button on the Toolbar.**

The Presentation window with your new message appears and John Olivero's name as an alias for his e-mail address is in the To text box (Figure 4-43). Your message should be similar to that shown in the figure.

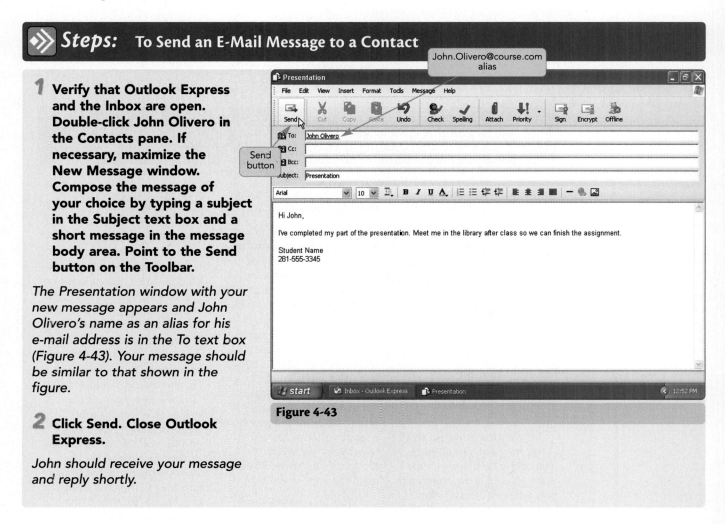

Figure 4-43

2 **Click Send. Close Outlook Express.**

John should receive your message and reply shortly.

EDITING AND DELETING CONTACTS   You may need to edit a contact's information or to delete a contact. You can view a contact's properties quickly and then edit the information — for example, to update his or her e-mail address or telephone number — by right-clicking the contact's name in the Contacts list and clicking Properties. You can delete a contact by selecting the contact's name in the Contacts list and then clicking the Delete button on the Toolbar; by right-clicking the contact's name in the Contacts list and clicking Delete; or by selecting the contact's name in the Contacts list and pressing the Delete key. In each case, you will be asked to confirm the deletion before the contact is removed.

CREATING A DISTRIBUTION LIST   A **distribution list** or **group** is a list of e-mail addresses to which you can refer collectively by a single name. For instance, a distribution list named Team could contain the e-mail addresses and contact information for everyone involved in a specific school or work project. When you need to send an e-mail to everyone on the team, you use the Team distribution list name in the To text box instead of individual e-mail addresses. Everyone you want to include in an Outlook Express group must be a contact in the Address Book. To create a group in Outlook Express, open the Address Book, click the New button, and click New Group. Next, type a name for the group and select the contacts to be included in the group. After you create the group, the group's name appears in the Contacts list in the Contacts pane. Sending an e-mail message to a group follows the same process as sending an e-mail message to an individual contact.

@Issue E-Mail Viruses

E-mail, for all its benefits, has the distinction of being a primary method of spreading computer viruses. Viruses often are sent via e-mail in Word document attachments containing macro viruses (Melissa, for example), other infected attachments (including Klez and Yaha), and commands embedded in HTML messages (such as Exploit.IFrame).

Viruses that arrive via an e-mail message may damage files on the hard disk or copy themselves to other computers on a network. Viruses often replicate themselves by sending new messages addressed to all the names in the victim's e-mail client's address book. An e-mail message also may include, as an attachment, a program that appears to be something useful, but actually does something harmful such

as creating a way for a hacker to breach network security.

Because of the risk of e-mail viruses, you always must be cautious when opening attachments, particularly those with an executable file extension (.exe) or a script extension such as .vbs. Remember that some viruses send themselves to everyone in the victim's address book, so even if you know the sender of an e-mail, the message could contain a virus. If you are not expecting an attachment from a sender who is a trusted source, or if you do not recognize the sender, do not open the attachment.

When you receive e-mail from a sender unknown to you, use extra caution, especially if the Subject line seems unusual. The message may be as innocuous as an advertisement, but it may contain a vicious program, such as the Nimda worm, that resides within the HTML coding of a formatted

message. Web-based e-mail clients, Microsoft Outlook, Outlook Express, or any e-mail client that allows formatted messages may enable the spread of these HTML viruses. Outlook and Outlook Express users are particularly vulnerable because of the preview pane. By merely selecting the message — even to delete it immediately — displays the message in the preview pane. For this reason, Outlook and Outlook Express users may decide that safety is more important than convenience and turn off the handy Reading or preview pane by clicking View on the menu bar, clicking Layout, and then removing the checkmark from the Show preview pane check box.

For more information on e-mail viruses, visit the Discovering the Internet Chapter 4 Web page (scsite.com/internet/ch4) and click a link below E-Mail Viruses.

Using Web-Based E-Mail Services

A **Web-based e-mail service** is an e-mail service available to a user via a browser and a Web site. Web-based e-mail services make e-mail available to people who do not own a computer but have access to public computers connected to the Internet or individuals who have Internet access at work, but want to receive personal mail via an account other than one supplied by their employer. In addition, some individuals set up separate Web-based e-mail accounts to use for specific types of e-mail, such as one for correspondence with family and friends and another for buying and selling via auction sites.

Web-based e-mail services typically offer basic e-mail functions such as sending and receiving messages, maintaining an address book, sending messages with attachments, and so forth. Most Web-based e-mail services are free; these services, however, may have mailbox limits that restrict the number of e-mails that can be stored and may provide only basic features. Some Web-based e-mail services will allow you to upgrade for more services and additional e-mail storage space for a small fee.

The primary advantages of using a Web-based e-mail service are portability and low cost. Because Web-based e-mail can be sent and received from any computer, users can stay in touch when traveling by accessing the Internet at cyber cafés, libraries, and other public venues. Since basic Web-based e-mail services are generally free, e-mail access no longer is tied to owning a computer and contracting with an ISP for e-mail services or relying on school or work to provide e-mail services.

Web-based e-mail services do have some disadvantages, however. The Web page interface contains advertising messages that some users may find annoying. Additionally, a Web-based e-mail service's registration process may require that the user provide more personal information than an ISP, increasing the risk of invasion of privacy.

Two of the most popular Web-based e-mail services are MSN Hotmail and Yahoo! Mail. Both provide the same basic services to the user, and both allow users to enhance their e-mail service for a fee.

 Facts@Hand

According to a study by Vault.com, many e-mail users have more than one e-mail account: nearly 40 percent have two, 30 percent have three, 20 percent have four, and 10 percent manage five accounts or more.

Creating a Yahoo! Mail Account

To create a Yahoo! Mail account, you must have access to a computer with an Internet connection and an installed browser. The computer can be in a public facility such as a library, because setting up a Yahoo! Mail account does not store account-specific information on the computer. You access Yahoo! Mail by clicking the Mail icon or link on pages at the Yahoo! Web site.

The Yahoo! Mail features are similar to the features found in e-mail clients, such as Outlook Express, including tools to compose, send, and receive mail and an address book. A Yahoo! Mail account's main page displays a notice of any new, unread messages and their folder location(s), information about mailbox capacity and use, numerous clickable ads, and links to information on upgrading to various fee-based features.

With a Yahoo! Mail account, you can set general preferences, such as how your name and e-mail address appears to recipients of your e-mails; how sent and received messages are organized in the Inbox and other folders; and how the various components of a message appear on the screen. You can also create signature files, set up an automatic response, specify filters to block certain e-mail addresses; and specify how Yahoo! Mail deals with actions such as message deletion, forwarding, and replying.

To use Yahoo! Mail, you must first set up an e-mail account with a user ID and password. When you create a new Yahoo! Mail account you automatically receive a new Welcome message in your account's Inbox. In the following steps, you access the Yahoo! Mail Web site and create a new Yahoo! Mail account. Then you open the Inbox and read your Welcome message. If you already have a Yahoo! Mail account, your instructor may modify these steps.

Steps: To Create a Yahoo! Mail Account

1 **If necessary, start the browser. Visit the Discovering the Internet Chapter 4 Web page (scsite.com/internet/ch4). Click Yahoo! Mail. Point to the Sign up now link.**

The Yahoo! Mail Web page displays the welcome screen, where you can sign up for a Yahoo! Mail account or log in if you already have established an account (Figure 4-44). If a Yahoo! ID is stored on your computer, you may need to click the Sign in as a different user link and then click the Return to Yahoo! Mail link to view the Web page shown in Figure 4-44. The contents of the Web pages on your screen may from that shown in Figures 4-44 through 4-52 on pages 204 through 208.

Figure 4-44

2 **Click the Sign up now link. Point to the Sign Up Now link in the Free Yahoo! Mail section.**

Yahoo! Mail offers three different services (Figure 4-45). You want to set up a free mail account.

Figure 4-45

3 **Click the Sign Up Now link. Type a Yahoo! ID, password, and other requested information in the online form fields. Scroll the page as necessary to see all the online form fields. Point to the Submit This Form button.**

The Yahoo! Mail registration page appears and includes fields for a user ID and password; hints for recalling a forgotten password; and customization features that determine which types of ads display when you use Yahoo! Mail (Figure 4-46). You also need to complete the Word Verification, which guards against automated sign-ups. Warning! You may have to try a number of Yahoo! ID and password combinations to find one that is not already in use by someone else.

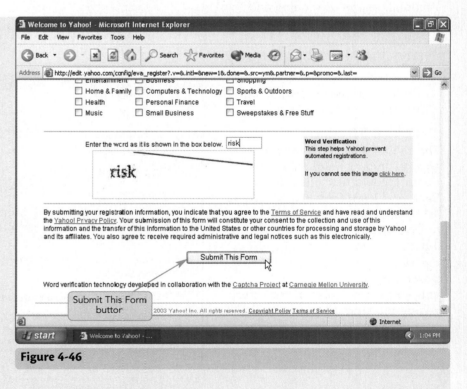

Figure 4-46

(continued)

4 **Click Submit This Form. Point to the Continue to Yahoo! Mail button.**

If the user ID and password are not available or if you failed to complete any required information, you will see a Web page prompt asking you to re-enter the required information or a different user ID and password. If you see the prompt page, make the necessary changes and click the Submit This Form button again. When your data is accepted, a confirmation page appears, listing your Yahoo! ID and new Yahoo! Mail address (Figure 4-47). Yahoo! Mail assigns the e-mail address using your Yahoo! ID as the user name and Yahoo.com as the domain name.

Figure 4-47

5 **Click Continue to Yahoo! Mail. Point to the Inbox in the Folders list.**

The Yahoo! Mail Welcome page appears (Figure 4-48). Your new e-mail account has Inbox, Draft, Sent, and Trash folders in a Folders list. These folders are used to receive incoming mail, store messages composed but not yet sent, store copies of sent messages, and store deleted messages. Your account also has an Address Book.

Figure 4-48

6 **Click the Inbox in the Folders list. Point to the unread message from Yahoo! Mail link in the Inbox.**

Your Inbox folder page appears (Figure 4-49). You can read and delete messages or move them to different folders on this page.

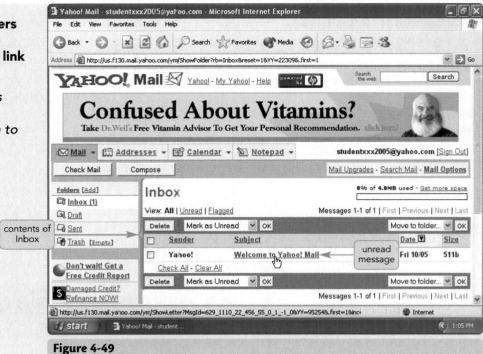

Figure 4-49

7 **Click the message link. Scroll the page to read the message. Point to the Delete button on the message toolbar.**

The message opens and you can read the message header and text (Figure 4-50). You can delete, reply, or forward the message as desired with buttons on the message toolbar.

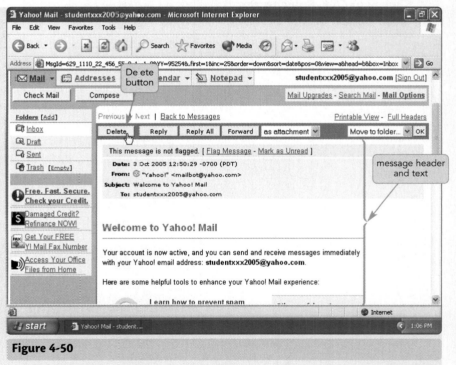

Figure 4-50

(continued)

8 **Click Delete. Point to the Sign Out link.**

The message is deleted and you return to the Inbox page (Figure 4-51). When you are finished using your Yahoo! Mail account, you should sign out.

9 **Click Sign Out. Point to the Close button on the browser title bar.**

The Yahoo! Mail sign out page appears (Figure 4-52).

10 **Click Close.**

The browser closes.

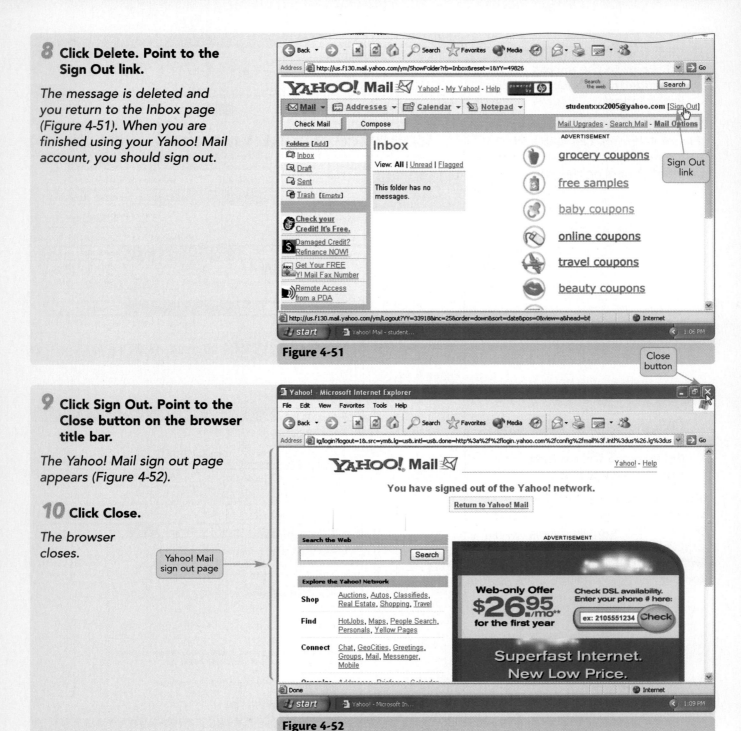

Figure 4-51

Figure 4-52

Sending and Receiving Messages

You can log in to your Yahoo! Mail account at any time to send and receive e-mail messages. The messages you receive and copies of messages you send are stored on the Yahoo! Mail servers. Sending and receiving Web-based e-mail is very similar to sending and receiving e-mail using an e-mail client. When you log in to Yahoo! Mail, the HTTP servers are immediately checked for any new incoming mail and new mail is directed to the Inbox. You can check for new incoming mail at any time by clicking the Check Mail button on the Inbox page.

In the following steps, you start the browser, access the Yahoo! Mail page, log in, compose and send a message, and check for new incoming mail.

Steps: To Send a Message and Check for New Mail

1 **If necessary, start the browser. Visit the Discovering the Internet Chapter 4 Web page (scsite.com/internet/ch4). Click Yahoo! Mail. Type your Yahoo! ID and password in the appropriate text boxes. Point to the Sign In button.**

The Yahoo! Mail page appears (Figure 4-53). You type your Yahoo! ID and password to sign in.

Figure 4-53

2 **Click Sign In. Point to the Compose button.**

Your Yahoo! Mail account page appears (Figure 4-54). The contents of the Web pages on your screen may vary from that in Figures 4-54 through 4-63 on pages 209 through 214.

Figure 4-54

(continued)

3 Click Compose. Type John.Olivero@course.com in the To text box. Type Class Project in the Subject text box. Point to the Attach Files link.

The Yahoo! Mail Compose page appears (Figure 4-55). You type the e-mail address, subject line, message body, and attach a file with options on this page.

Figure 4-55

4 Click Attach Files. Point to the first Browse button.

The Yahoo! Mail Attach Files page appears (Figure 4-56). You can attach up to three files to this message.

Figure 4-56

5 Click Browse. Switch to the folder in which you saved the attachment from your instructor. Select the file. Point to the Open button.

The Choose file dialog box appears (Figure 4-57). You select the attachment file in this dialog box.

Choose file dialog box

attachment file name

Open button

Figure 4-57

6 Click Open. Point to the Attach Files button.

The path and file name of the selected attachment appears in the File 1 text box (Figure 4-58).

attachment's path and file name

Attach Files button

Figure 4-58

(continued)

7 Click Attach Files. Point to the Done button.

In a few seconds, the Files Attached page appears (Figure 4-59) and the file is attached to the message. Your attached file may be different.

Figure 4-59

8 Click Done. Type a short, appropriate message. Point to the Send button.

The Yahoo! Mail Compose page appears (Figure 4-60). Now you are ready to send your message.

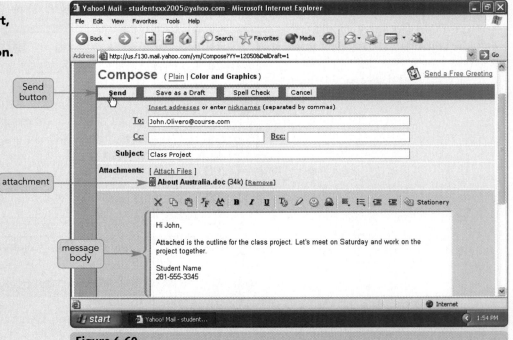

Figure 4-60

9 **Click Send. Point to the Back to Inbox link.**

The Yahoo! Mail Message Sent page appears (Figure 4-61) with a confirmation message indicating that the message has been sent.

message sent confirmation

Back to Inbox link

Figure 4-61

10 **Click the Back to Inbox link. Point to the Check Mail button.**

The Yahoo! Mail Inbox page appears (Figure 4-62). You can check for new mail on this page.

Check Mail button

Figure 4-62

(continued)

11 Click Check Mail. Point to the Sign Out link.

You may now see the reply from John Olivero or other messages in the Inbox (Figure 4-63).

12 Click Sign Out. Close the browser.

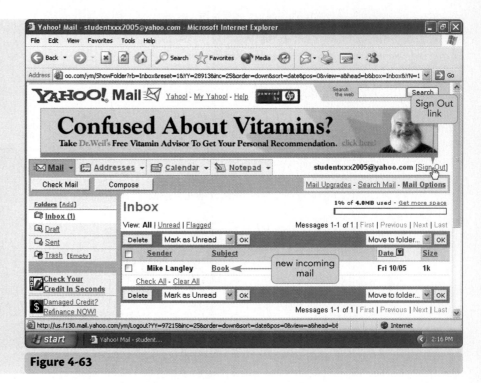

Figure 4-63

Using Other Yahoo! Mail Features

Yahoo! Mail and other Web-based e-mail services provide the same basic features offered by the e-mail clients you learned about earlier in the chapter, such as replying to and forwarding a message, using folders to organize your messages, creating and appending signature files, and managing your contacts.

Figure 4-64   Click the Reply and Forward buttons to reply to or forward an open message.

REPLYING TO AND FORWARDING A MESSAGE To reply or forward a Yahoo! Mail message, the message must be open. To reply to a message, click the Reply button and type a reply. To forward a message, click the Forward button and then type a forwarding message and e-mail address. Figure 4-64 illustrates the Reply and Forward buttons for an open message.

When you forward a message, the original message may be included either as an attachment or as inline text, which means it appears in the message body. If you select the *as attachment* option, keep in mind that some users may not know to look in the attachment for the original e-mail and that some Web-based e-mail services impose size restrictions on attachments. After you send a reply or forward a message, the original message is marked with a Reply icon or Forward icon. Message replies that you receive typically have Re: on the Subject line, preceding the original subject text and forwarded messages have Fwd: preceding the original subject text.

PRINTING A MESSAGE Because Yahoo! Mail is Web-based, printing an e-mail message in Yahoo! Mail is different from printing an e-mail message when using an e-mail client, such as Outlook Express. If you click the browser's Print button or choose the Print command on the File menu while viewing the message, the hard copy will include everything on the screen, including ads, the Folders list, and so forth. To print only the message, first open it and then click the Printable View link (Figure 4-64). The message page appears in a printable view (Figure 4-65) that contains just the header and text of the message; large ads and the Folder list are not included. Finally, click the Print link to open the Print dialog box, select the print options, and print the message.

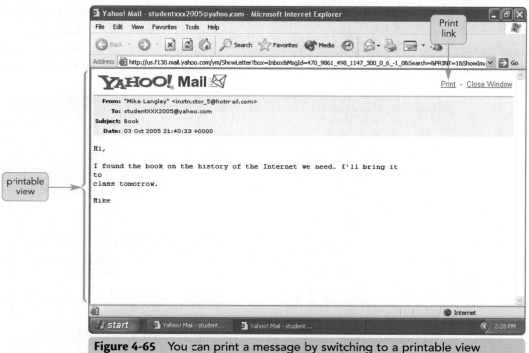

Figure 4-65 You can print a message by switching to a printable view containing the message header and body.

USING FOLDERS Folder organization is just as important when using Web-based e-mail services as it is when using an e-mail client. To create a new folder, click the Add link above the Folders list. When prompted, enter a name for the new folder and then click the OK button. The new folder is added in the My Folders section (Figure 4-66 on the next page).

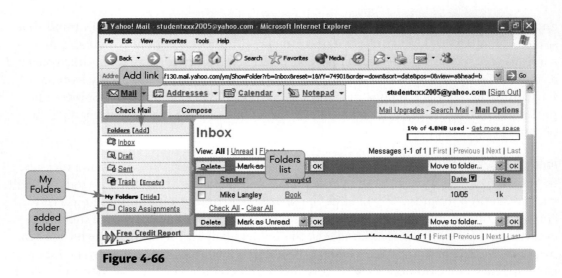

Figure 4-66

MOVING AND DELETING MESSAGES   Yahoo! Mail also allows you to move a message from the Inbox into a different folder. To move a message, click the check box next to the message (or messages) to be moved. Then click the Move to folder list arrow and select the folder in which you want to store the message (Figure 4-67). Yahoo! Mail moves the message from the current folder into the selected folder. Note that you can select multiple messages at one time to move the messages into the same folder.

Figure 4-67   You can move selected messages from the Inbox to other folders.

To delete messages that you no longer need, click the check box next to each message to be deleted and then click the Delete button. This moves the selected messages to the Trash folder. Deleted messages normally remain in the Trash folder until you click the Empty link, which permanently deletes the contents of the folder. Note, however, that Yahoo! Mail reserves the right to delete messages in the Trash folder at any time. Because Yahoo! Mail limits the amount of space you can use to store your messages, you will want to empty the Trash folder often.

SIGNATURE FILES   Yahoo! Mail allows you to configure signature files to append standard text automatically to the end of every message. To create a signature file in

Yahoo! Mail, click the Mail Options link in the upper-right corner of a page, click the Signature link on the Mail Options page (Figure 4-68), and create the signature file. You can add or remove the signature from a specific message by clicking the Use my signature check box in the Compose window.

Figure 4-68   You can create a signature file and set other mail options on the Mail Options page.

MANAGING CONTACTS   Yahoo! Mail allows you to save names and e-mail addresses in an Address Book and create a distribution list. When composing an e-mail message, you can refer to a contact by his or her **nickname** or alias, which is a shorter name associated with the full e-mail address of the contact in the Address Book. To work with the Yahoo! Mail Address Book click the Addresses button list arrow at the top of the Inbox page and click the desired link (Figure 4-69). To create a contact, for example, click the Add Contact link in the Addresses list, complete the Add Contact form, and save the contact.

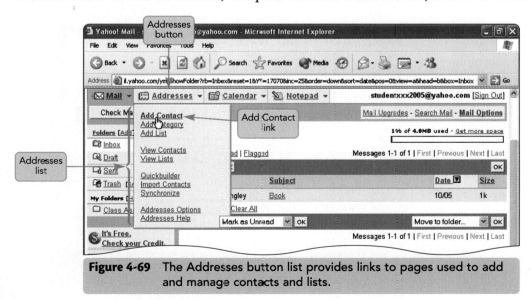

Figure 4-69   The Addresses button list provides links to pages used to add and manage contacts and lists.

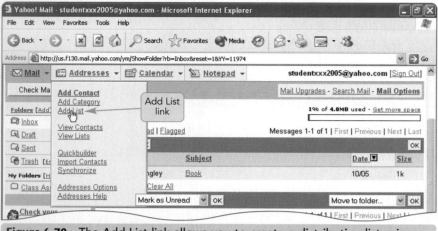

Figure 4-70 The Add List link allows you to create a distribution list using contacts from the Address Book.

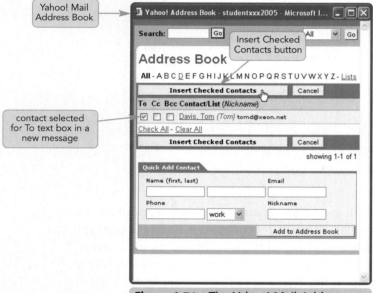

Figure 4-71 The Yahoo! Mail Address Book.

A **Yahoo! Mail list** is a list of contacts referred to collectively by a single name and it fulfills the same purpose as an Outlook Express group. Anyone you want to add to a Yahoo! Mail list first must be included as a contact in the Address Book. To create a list, click the Add List link in the Addresses list (Figure 4-70), then complete the Edit List form to name the list, add individuals from your contacts to the list, and save the list.

To use a contact or list when composing a message, click the To button in the Compose window to open the Address Book (Figure 4-71). Select individual contacts or a list name from the Address Book for the To, Cc, and Bcc lines as appropriate. Then click the Insert Checked Contacts button.

You also can delete contacts and lists once they no longer are needed. To delete contacts and lists first click the Addresses button to open the Address Book, click the check boxes next to the contacts or lists to be deleted and then click the Delete button, as shown in Figure 4-72.

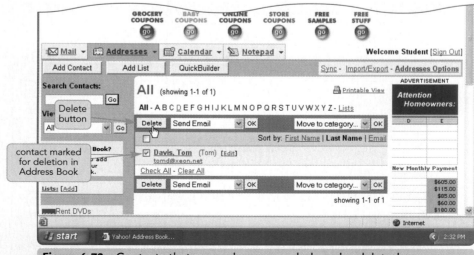

Figure 4-72 Contacts that are no longer needed can be deleted.

Online Communities and Text Messaging

In addition to exchanging e-mail with specific recipients, many people enjoy communicating with others over the Internet using mailing lists, USENET newsgroups, and Web-based discussion groups. E-mail, mailing lists, and newsgroups are all examples of **asynchronous communication**, because they do not require users to be online at the same time. Instead, a user can send an e-mail message to an individual, a newsgroup, or a mailing list at any time; other users can receive and respond to the e-mail message when it is convenient for them — possibly later in the day or even later that week.

Mailing Lists

Mailing list participants use e-mail to exchange information, opinions, and ideas about particular subjects with other participants who may be located anywhere in the world. A large number of mailing lists are available, as are some excellent resources for finding lists that may be of interest. Many users find mailing lists through work, professional associations, or while searching the Web. Some Web sites provide mailing list directories and most of these sites have a search tool you can use to find mailing lists on specific topics. None of these directories are exhaustive, however, so you may have to search several directories to find mailing lists of interest.

Unlike regular e-mail, where the sender must know the recipients' e-mail addresses, mailing lists require that the sender know only the e-mail address of the list itself. Figure 4-73 illustrates the difference between sending an e-mail message to a mailing list and sending a personal e-mail message to multiple recipients. A server, called a **list server**, handles the job of directing the e-mail messages to all subscribers. In addition to the list server, a mailing list requires special software, referred to as **LISTSERV** or **Majordomo**, to facilitate the exchange of e-mail between members; and a **moderator** or **list owner**, who handles various administrative tasks to keep the list running.

@Source

To see Web sites that offer a mailing list directory, visit the Discovering the Internet Chapter 4 Web page (**scsite.com/ internet/ch4**) and click a link below Mailing Lists.

(a) Message sent to mailing list.

(b) Message sent to distribution list or group.

To: mailing list

Member 1
Member 2
Member 3
Member 4

list server

To: group

Member 1
Member 2
Member 3
Member 4

Member 1
Member 2
Member 3
Member 4

SMTP server

Figure 4-73 E-mail and mailing lists use different methods for sending messages to multiple recipients.

To receive e-mail from a mailing list, you first must join, or **subscribe** to, the list. To subscribe to a mailing list, you send an e-mail message to the list's administrative address asking to subscribe. The **administrative address** is an e-mail address used for administrative requests, such as subscribing to and unsubscribing from a list. E-mail sent to the administrative address is not sent on to list members. Subscribing to an **open list** is automatic upon receipt of the subscription e-mail message. Subscribing to a **closed list**, however, requires approval by the list moderator. In either case, an accepted subscription is acknowledged by an e-mail reply. Figure 4-74 illustrates the sequence of events in subscribing to a mailing list.

1 Send subscribe message to list administrative address.

2 List administrator responds with message.

3 Confirm the subscription, if asked to do so.

Figure 4-74   The process of subscribing to a mailing list includes sending an e-mail to a list administrator to subscribe. Some mailing lists require replying to a confirmation e-mail before the subscription is accepted.

After you subscribe to a mailing list, you begin to receive messages. Most lists offer two formats to the user. The **individual messages format** sends each message to members as a single e-mail message. The **digest format** appends messages to a single file called a digest, and then sends the digest when it reaches a certain size or message number or when a certain period has passed since the last digest was sent. You determine the format in which to receive the mailing list by the way you subscribe to the list.

You also can send messages to the list. To send a message to a list, you simply compose a message and send it to the list address. The **list address** is an e-mail address used to send messages for distribution to list subscribers. If the list is an **unmoderated list**, the message goes out immediately to all subscribers who receive messages in individual message format and is appended immediately to the digest to be sent later. If the list is a **moderated list**, the moderator reviews the message and either approves the message, edits and approves the message, sends the message back to the sender with comments, or discards the message.

SUBSCRIBING TO A MAILING LIST   To subscribe to a mailing list, you first must know the administrative address for the list and the name of the list. You can use search tools to search for mailing lists or use an online directory of mailing lists, such as L-Soft, to find appropriate mailing lists. In the following steps, you send a subscription e-mail to the Spam-L mailing list, which is a list for spam prevention discussions. However, you do not confirm the subscription unless told to do so by your instructor.

》 Steps: To Subscribe to a Mailing List

1 **Start Outlook Express, if necessary. Click the Create Mail button to open a new message window. If necessary, maximize the message window. Type** `listserv@peach.ease .lsoft.com` **in the To text box. Type** `Subscribe Spam-L anonymous` **in the message body. If necessary, delete the signature file. Point to Send.**

The message is addressed to the administrative address and the body text requests a subscription to the Spam-L list (Figure 4-75). You do not add subject text when subscribing to a mailing list.

Figure 4-75

2 **Click the Send button. Click OK if a warning message appears telling you the message has no subject. Click the Send/Recv button on the Toolbar to check for new mail. Click the L-Soft list server message when it arrives in the Inbox. Point to the Close button on the title bar.**

The e-mail message is sent to the list server at peach.ease.lsoft.com requesting subscription to the Spam-L list. The L-Soft list server responds with a confirmation message (Figure 4-76).

3 **Click Close.**

Outlook Express closes.

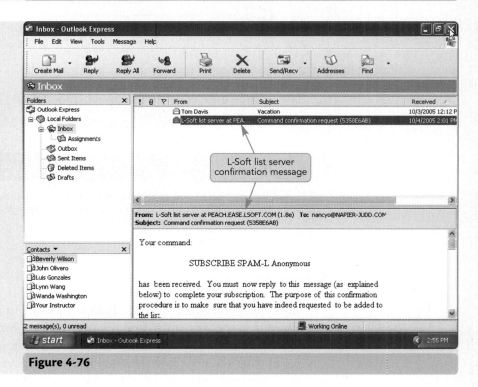

Figure 4-76

To confirm a subscription request, you simply follow the instructions in the e-mail from the list server. Confirmation may require you to send another e-mail message or to access a Web site to confirm your subscription. After you successfully subscribe to a mailing list, you will receive administrative e-mails from the list administrator explaining how to send messages to the list. Sending messages to the list is called **posting**.

Each mailing list may follow different rules for posting messages; therefore, you should take time to become familiar with a mailing list's rules and instructions before posting to the list. Mailing list rules are intended to ensure that new subscribers are able to contribute to the list in a productive manner and do not offend other subscribers by sending inappropriate material to the list.

After you subscribe to a list, you should spend some time reading the list messages to get a feeling for the list, its tone, and its character. Reading a mailing list's messages without posting to the list is called **lurking** and it is considered good form, at least until you become familiar with how the list operates. It is also a good plan to become familiar with a list's FAQs to learn more about how the list operates.

You may decide that the information in the list does not meet your needs or that the volume of mail is too high, even in digest format, after reading a mailing list's postings for awhile. Therefore, you can choose to unsubscribe, or leave, the list. Unsubscribing from the list again requires you to send an e-mail message to the administrative address. For example, to unsubscribe to the Spam-L list, you would send an e-mail message with the text Signoff Spam-L in the message body. Figure 4-77 illustrates an e-mail message sent to unsubscribe to the L-Spam list.

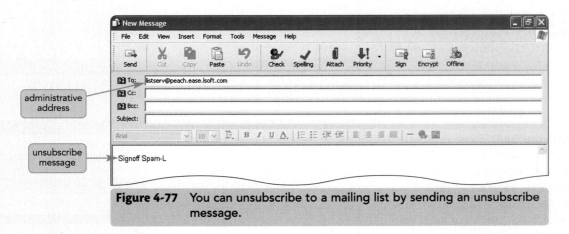

Figure 4-77   You can unsubscribe to a mailing list by sending an unsubscribe message.

Facts@Hand

Many mailing lists keep a copy, or archive, of the posts sent to them. These archives are available online and can be accessed by e-mail or the list's Web site. For more information on reviewing archived postings for a list, check the list's FAQs or instructions.

Newsgroups

Most local communities have bulletin boards in public places: for example, a laundromat, a grocery store, and a student union building often have bulletin boards on which individuals can post notices about events, items for sale, properties for rent, want ads, and posters about causes or issues they support. These bulletin boards provide a venue where people can drop in to post information or read what others have posted. You do not have to belong to a group to read or post bulletin board messages; you just need access to the bulletin board. Newsgroups are electronic bulletin boards.

USENET, an electronic bulletin board system, was developed in the late 1970s to provide students at several universities with the ability to communicate with large numbers of people on a wide range of topics in close-to-real time. USENET topic groups are called **newsgroups**. USENET consists of a number of servers utilizing the

Network News Transfer Protocol (**NNTP**) to make information available via newsgroups. To read newsgroup messages, a user needs an NNTP client. An **NNTP client**, or news client, is any software that allows a user to read newsgroup messages. An NNTP client is included as part of many browsers, including Netscape and Internet Explorer; you also can use a separate program called a newsreader.

Each USENET server, also called a news server or an **NNTP server**, acts as host to a number of newsgroups. In addition, each NNTP server subscribes to any number of newsgroups from other NNTP servers. Figure 4-78 shows the relationships between the servers and the other groups to which the servers subscribe.

Figure 4-78   News servers host their own newsgroups and subscribe to newsgroups on other servers.

Each NNTP server stores the messages of the newsgroups it hosts; the server also polls the other NNTP servers at fixed intervals to find the new messages for its subscribed newsgroups from those servers. The servers then download the new messages to be able to provide them locally. Each group exists in a permanent home on one server, and copies of messages in other groups appear on other servers that subscribe to those groups. Most ISPs maintain a news server, or provide access to a news server, for their subscribers. Educational institutions usually provide access to news servers as well. A user has access to all the newsgroups to which his or her NNTP server either hosts or subscribes.

An e-mail client, such as Outlook Express or Netscape Mail, can be configured as a newsreader. For example, you can configure Outlook Express as a newsreader by using the Internet Connection Wizard used to set up a new e-mail account. To configure an e-mail client, such as Outlook Express, as a newsreader, you must know the name of the news server at your ISP. Users who spend a lot of time reading newsgroups may wish to download a newsreader program with more features than the browser clients provide.

The basic organization behind newsgroups is simple. Each newsgroup has a unique name that identifies it, such as rec.pets.dogs or humanities.lit.authors.shakespeare. The names are multilevel, and each level provides more detail about the purpose of the newsgroup. The multilevel hierarchy is based on content. The top-level categories in the USENET news hierarchy are .alt (alternative topics), .biz (business), .comp (computers), .humanities (art and literature), .misc (miscellaneous), .news (USENET information), .rec (recreation and entertainment), .sci (science), .soc (social issues and culture), and .talk (current issues and debates). Within each top-level category, additional levels are specified to define the group further. For example, within the .rec category are subcategories, such as pets, sports, crafts, and music, to specify different types of recreational topics.

Tens of thousands of newsgroups exist, so finding a specific newsgroup can be a bit overwhelming. If you are new to newsgroups, using newsgroups also may be intimidating. Two newsgroups designed specifically to help new newsgroup users are news.announce.newusers and news.newusers.questions. A good way to become more familiar with newsgroups before subscribing is to read archived postings from the news.announce.newusers newsgroup. Google provides users with access to USENET newsgroups and newsgroup archives dating from 1980 through its Google Groups pages. To post or reply to a newsgroup, users must register with Google, but registration is not required for reading postings.

Facts@Hand

The oldest USENET article in the Google Groups archive of the original USENET is dated May 11, 1981.

In the following steps, you use Google Groups to read archived postings in the news.announce.newusers newsgroup.

Steps: To Read Newsgroup Postings

1 If necessary, start the browser. Visit the Discovering the Internet Chapter 4 Web page (scsite.com/internet/ch4). Click Google Groups. Point to the news.newsgroup link.

The Google Groups page appears (Figure 4-79). You can drill down to find a specific group of interest starting with the top-level group names on this page.

Figure 4-79

2 Click the news. link. Point to the news.announce. link.

The Group: news page appears (Figure 4-80). You can view postings to different news. groups by clicking links on this page.

Group.news links

Figure 4-80

3 Click the news.announce. link. Point to the news.announce .newusers link.

The Group: news. announce page appears (Figure 4-81). This page contains links to postings about newsgroup announcements.

Group: news.announce links

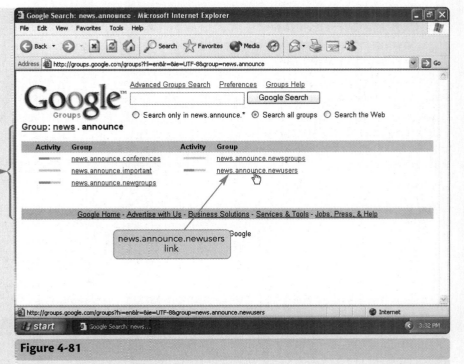

Figure 4-81

(continued)

4 Click the news.announce.newusers link. Scroll the page to view the links. Point to the Common questions about using newsgroups link or another link of your choice that offers answers to common questions about newsgroups.

This page contains links to postings about how to use newsgroups (Figure 4-82).

Common questions about using newsgroups link

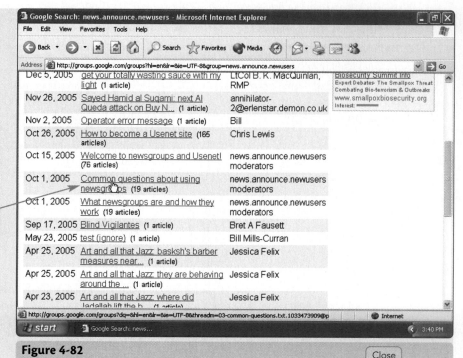

Figure 4-82

5 Click the link. Read the posting. Point to the Close button on the title bar.

Postings to the newsgroup appear (Figure 4-83). You can click a posting in the left pane to view its contents in the right pane.

6 Click the Close button.

The browser closes.

Close button

right pane

left pane

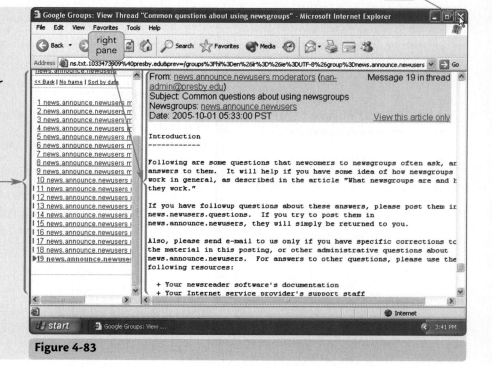

Figure 4-83

Web-Based Discussion Groups

In recent years, interest in participating in online communities called Web-based discussion groups has grown. A **Web-based discussion group**, which provides features of both mailing lists and newsgroups, usually is hosted by a portal, such as Yahoo! or

Lycos. To join a Web-based discussion group, you must register with the group's host. Once you join a group, you then can determine how to receive messages from the group: individually or in digest form, like a mailing list; or via a Web site and a browser.

To find a group, you can browse through the group host's directory or search for a group using a keyword or phrase. Once you have located a group of interest, you can join by clicking a link and filling in preferences. In the following steps, you use Yahoo! Groups to search for a group that discusses organic gardening. The Yahoo! ID you created for Yahoo! Mail allows you to sign in to use Yahoo! Groups as well. You will not join a group unless told to do so by your instructor.

Steps: To Find a Web-based Discussion Group

1 **If necessary, start the browser. Visit the Discovering the Internet Chapter 4 Web page (scsite.com/internet/ch4). Click Yahoo! Groups. Point to the Sign in! link.**

The Yahoo! Groups home page appears (Figure 4-84). The content of the Web pages you see on your screen will vary from that shown in Figures 4-84 through 4-88 on pages 227 through 229.

Figure 4-84

2 **Click the Sign in! link. Type your Yahoo! ID and Password in the text boxes. Point to the Sign In button.**

The Yahoo! Groups welcome page appears (Figure 4-85). You can sign in, if you have an existing Yahoo! ID and password, or create a new account on this page.

Figure 4-85

(continued)

3 Click Sign In. Type organic gardening in the Search text box. Point to the Search button.

The Yahoo! Groups page appears. This page provides a directory of groups and a search tool; a series of Editor's Picks highlighting specific groups; and links for starting a group, accessing account info, and signing out of Yahoo! Groups. The left side of the screen lists any groups to which you already have subscribed (Figure 4-86).

subscribed groups

links to featured groups

Search text box

keywords

Search button

Figure 4-86

4 Click Search. Scroll the page and review the listed groups. Point to the first group in the list.

The search results list appears (Figure 4-87). Each group in the list is described and the number of members noted. Your search results list may be different.

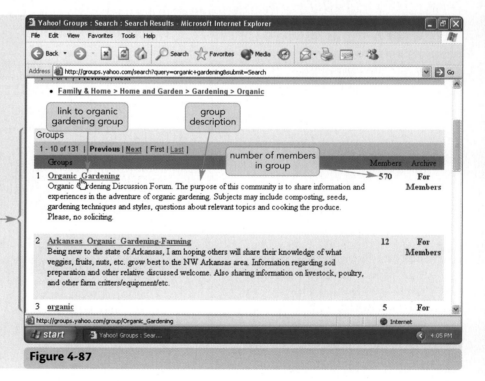

link to organic gardening group

group description

number of members in group

search results

Figure 4-87

5 Click the link to the first group in the list. Scroll the page and review its contents. Point to the Close button on the browser title bar.

The group's home page displays information and an introductory description about the group (Figure 4-88). If you join the group, you can exchange messages and participate in online chat with other members.

6 Click Close.

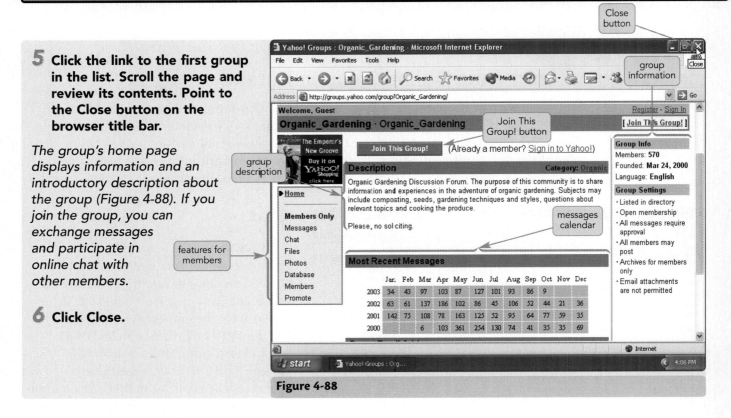

Figure 4-88

When you join a group, you have access to the features on the group's home page which typically include reading and posting messages and managing your membership in the group. The home page may contain links to messages, organized by month, along with a search facility for searching the message archives using keywords or phrases; links to edit membership options; and access to photos, databases, and other features. Instructions for reading and posting messages to the group also are available.

Text Messaging

The past few years have seen a dramatic surge in the use of a different type of asynchronous communication, called text messaging. **Text messaging**, also called **Short Message Service (SMS)**, allows users to send short messages to and from cell phones. An individual can use an e-mail client or a Web page to send a message to a cell phone (Figure 4-89). The cell phone user also can initiate a message, but typing the message is a little more cumbersome. Text messaging limits the size of messages to 160 characters, including the address and Subject line. Because the amount of text is so limited, short abbreviations are used to save space such as *shrt abbr R used 2sav spc.*

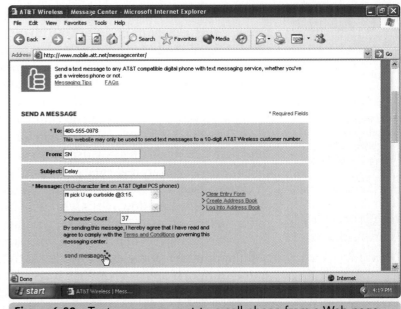

Figure 4-89 Text messages sent to a cell phone from a Web page typically use abbreviations.

Real-Time Online Communications

As you have learned, e-mail, mailing lists, and newsgroups are all examples of asynchronous communication, because they do not require users to be online at the same time. By contrast, chat, instant messaging, and virtual meetings allow for **synchronous communication**, or **real-time communication**, in which two or more users are online at the same time communicating with each other.

Figure 4-90   IRC uses only text for chatting.

Chat

Chat is a facility that allows two or more people to exchange text or multimedia messages in real time, using either a special client or a Web interface. Prior to the Web, the earliest type of chat facility was **IRC**, or **Internet Relay Chat**, a text-based communications tool (Figure 4-90). To chat, users need a special client application on their computers and access to the Internet. Users connect to an IRC server, and, from that server, can chat with any other user on that IRC network. Several IRC networks exist; users cannot chat between networks.

Once connected to an IRC network, the user can view a list of available channels or chat rooms and join one to chat with others. A **channel** or **chat room** is a specific chat discussion that may be on a given topic or with a certain set of participants. Users also can set up private channels in which access is by invitation only, thus restricting who can participate.

The Web has made Web-based chat possible. **Web-based chat** allows for real-time communication using a Web browser instead of a special client. Opening a chat session is as simple as connecting to the Internet, starting your browser, and clicking a link on a Web page. Many portals and entertainment sites sponsor Web-based chat and offer chats with celebrities. Some commercial sites are using chat facilities for real-time customer service, providing the user with a chance to talk to a customer service representative electronically in real time.

Web-based chat allows users to exchange both text and multimedia messages. Some chat facilities also allow users with a microphone to exchange voice messages in a chat room instead of, or in addition to, text messages. Some Web-based chat sites provide the ability to share video between two participants who have Web cameras. Chat is very popular, but new users may find that it takes some time to learn how to follow a conversation online. If a chat room has many participants, many conversations may be going on at once, which makes following one particular chat thread very difficult.

Before jumping into a chat room discussion, a new user — referred to as a **newbie** — should read the rules and (FAQs) pages. Because many chat rooms have regular participants, a new member can become familiar with the group by lurking, remaining quiet, and not participating in the chat discussion at first. Because the exchange of text often is rapid, participants use many abbreviations and shorthand — for example,

@Source

To learn more about IRC chat, visit the Discovering the Internet Chapter 4 Web page (**scsite.com/ internet/ch4**) and click a link below IRC Chat.

@Source

For a list of chat directories, visit the Discovering the Internet Chapter 4 Web page (**scsite.com/ internet/ch4**) and click a link below Chat Directories.

typing LOL instead of the phrase, laughing out loud, to express laughter in response to another's post. Flaming also can occur in a chat room, just as it does in asynchronous discussions taking place via e-mail, mailing lists, or newsgroups.

To learn more about common abbreviations used in chat, visit the Discovering the Internet Chapter 4 Web page (**scsite .com/internet/ch4**) and click a link below Chat Abbreviations.

Facts@Hand

Studies show that workers in North America prefer to communicate important information using asynchronous communications such as voice mail or e-mail, whereas Europeans use those tools to request a real-time conversation, which they prefer to use for collaboration.

To maintain privacy and security, chat participants should consider these guidelines:

- Do not disclose your real name and address or any information of a sensitive nature. Use a nickname rather than your real name.
- Avoid using sites that display your IP address along with your nickname.
- Remember that other participants may misrepresent themselves — she may not be a woman and he may not be a teen — and that some predators are online, seeking the unwary. Therefore, be careful about arranging to meet online chat participants in person

Instant Messaging

A newer form of chat is **instant messaging (IM)**, a private means of exchanging real-time messages with one or several friends via the Internet. Several IM programs are in popular use, including AOL Instant Messenger (AIM), ICQ, MSN Messenger, and Yahoo! Messenger (Figure 4-91 on the next page). While all of these IM programs offer similar features, an individual using one IM program, such as AOL Instant Messenger, generally cannot communicate with another individual using a different IM program, such as Yahoo! Messenger. For this reason, many people choose to install and use several different IM programs so they can send instant messages to all of their friends. Alternatively, users can install and use Trillian (Figure 4-91), a unique instant messaging program that consolidates messages from these dissimilar IM programs into a single interface.

According to some studies, nearly 30 percent of Internet users use instant messaging to communicate with friends, family, and colleagues. The use of IM is greatest among teenagers and young adults, whose informal communication style and ability to focus on many things at once are particularly useful. Businesses and other organizations also have begun to incorporate the use of IM at work. While some find IM pop-up windows distracting, others find IM a valuable way to get quick, immediate answers to a focused question or to collaborate on a particular project.

To learn more about instant messaging programs, visit the Discovering the Internet Chapter 4 Web page (**scsite .com/internet/ch4**) and click a link below Instant Messaging.

Figure 4-91   Instant messaging is a popular form of real-time communications over the Internet.

Virtual Meetings

The most media-rich means of communicating online is through the use of virtual meeting software. A **virtual meeting**, also called **rich media online communication**, is a private channel for communicating by text, audio, whiteboard, and video. Three of the major virtual meeting providers are MeetingPlace, Microsoft (Office Live Meeting and NetMeeting), and WebEx (Figure 4-92). Virtual meetings can save time and improve productivity by allowing participants at various geographic locations to come together online to communicate as though they were all sitting around the same physical conference table.

Figure 4-92 Virtual meetings can save time and improve productivity.

@Issue Internet Addiction

Compulsive Internet use — in which people feel preoccupied with cyber-relationships and cannot control the impulse to get online — can be characterized as Internet addiction. Falling within this scope are viewing pornography online, engaging in online gambling, or suffering from online auction fever, and although those behaviors may be serious compulsions for some people, they are not the most addictive Internet behaviors.

The activities that clinical research has found to be most addictive are chat, e-mail and interactive online gaming. In these interpersonal online activities, people make relationships quickly and can become too involved in the lives of online friends to the detriment of real-life relationships with family and friends nearby. Research shows that the average age for Internet-addicted males is 29 and for females is 43. The vast majority of those suffering from Internet addiction are either non-technical white-collar workers or people who are not employed (students, homemakers, retired, or disabled).

How can you tell if you or someone you know is addicted to the Internet? The first sign is that the time spent on the Internet interferes with other things, such as school, work, home, or personal relationships. Other signs include spending an excessive amount of time preoccupied with the Internet, keeping Internet usage a secret, withdrawal from social activities, or feeling closer to online friends than those in the real world.

For more information about Internet addiction, visit the Discovering the Internet Chapter 4 Web page (**scsite.com/internet/ch4**) and click a link below Internet Addiction.

1 What Are the Components of an E-Mail System and What Is E-Mail Etiquette?

The components of an e-mail system include unique e-mail addresses, e-mail clients, mail servers, and the communications protocols that make the delivery of messages over the Internet possible.

An e-mail address consists of a **user ID** and a **host name**, which identify an e-mail message recipient's mailbox and the server on which that mailbox is stored. An **e-mail client** is a software program that sends, receives, and manages e-mail messages. The communication protocols used to send and receive e-mail messages are **SMTP**, **POP**, **IMAP**, and **HTTP**. E-mail messages are routed over the Internet through SMTP servers until they reach their final destination **mail servers** which may be POP, IMAP, or HTTP servers.

E-mail etiquette involves following a few simple guidelines — such as not typing in all capital letters, not **flaming** others with e-mail messages, avoiding sending unnecessary messages, and taking care to be certain message content is clear and concise.

2 How Does Outlook Express, Send, Receive, and Organize E-mail Messages?

Outlook Express interacts with SMTP servers to send e-mail messages and POP, IMAP, or HTTP servers to receive e-mail messages. Outlook Express contains basic e-mail client features including folders in which to organize incoming and outgoing messages: **Inbox**, **Sent Items**, **Outbox**, **Drafts**, **Deleted Items**, plus custom folders. Outlook Express also provides an **Address Book** containing the names, e-mail addresses, and other important information for frequently contacted individuals or **groups** of individuals. The Outlook Express Toolbar and menus contain commands to check for incoming e-mail messages and read them; compose and send e-mail messages with and without **attachments**; reply to and forward e-mail messages; create and append signature files to outgoing messages; **flag**, print, and delete incoming messages; and view and edit the contents of the Address Book.

3 What Are Web-Based E-Mail Services and How Do You Set Up a Web-Based E-Mail Account?

A **Web-based e-mail service** is an e-mail service available via a Web site and Web browser. Many portals such as Yahoo! Mail and MSN Hotmail, offer free basic e-mail services. These services include composing, attaching files to, sending, replying, and forwarding e-mail messages; creating and appending signature files; maintaining an Address Book; organizing messages in folders; and printing and deleting messages. Other services may be offered for a fee. Anyone with access to the Internet and a Web browser can sign up for an e-mail account at the service provider's Web site by establishing a **user ID** and **password**. Once an account is created, a user then can log on to the Web site using his or her user ID and password, and access the e-mail services.

4 ## What Are Mailing Lists, Newsgroups, Web-Based Discussion Groups, and Text Messaging?

Like e-mail, mailing lists and newsgroups are examples of **asynchronous communication**, communication in which the people involved are not necessarily online at the same time. **Mailing lists** allow subscribers to use e-mail to send newsletters or postings on a specific topic to all subscribers using a single mailing address and a **list server**.

Newsgroups use the **Network News Transfer Protocol** (**NNTP**) to coordinate the many topics and postings from newsgroup users. You can use an **NNTP client** to read the newsgroup postings, which are arranged in a hierarchy of topics and organized into threads of comments or questions and replies.

A **Web-based discussion group** provides features of both mailing lists and newsgroups, allowing individuals to participate in discussions by receiving mailing list-style messages or digests or using a Web site and browser. **Text messaging** or **SMS** allows users to send a short message to and from cell phones.

 5 ## What Are Real-Time Online Communications: Chat, Instant Messaging, and Virtual Meetings?

Chat, instant messaging, and virtual meetings are all examples of **synchronous communication**, in which conversations take place online at the same time. **Chat** is a **real-time communication** forum, sometimes focused on a particular topic, often public, although it also can be restricted to subscribers only. With perhaps dozens of people participating in a single **chat room**, the conversations are unorganized and may be difficult to follow.

In contrast, **instant messaging** (**IM**) is a private means of communicating with specific contacts or buddies, one or a few at a time. IM programs allow users to share files and photos and to use audio as well as text messages.

Virtual meetings feature the use of video as well as audio and bring individuals at different physical locations together to communicate and share resources in an online meeting. Typically used by businesses, these **rich media communications** tools include MeetingPlace, Office Live Meeting, and WebEx.

CHAPTER REVIEW

The Chapter Review section summarizes the concepts presented in the chapter.

TERMS TO KNOW

After reading this chapter, you should know each term.

Address Book (*180*)
administrative address (*219*)
asynchronous communication (*219*)
Attach line (*177*)
attachment (*177*)
Bcc line (*177*)
blind courtesy copy (*177*)
Cc line (*177*)
channel (*230*)
chat (*230*)
chat room (*230*)
closed list (*220*)
contacts (*180*)
Contacts pane (*180*)
courtesy copy (*177*)
dashboard (*180*)
Deleted Items (*180*)
digest format (*220*)
distribution list (*201*)
Drafts (*180*)
e-mail client (*175*)
e-mail notification icon (*181*)
emoticon (*178*)
flag (*198*)
flaming (*178*)
Folder List (*179*)
Folders Bar (*179*)
forward (*189*)
group (*201*)
host name (*175*)
HTTP (Hypertext Transfer Protocol) server (*177*)
IMAP (Internet Message Access Protocol) server (*176*)
Inbox (*180*)
individual messages format (*220*)
instant messaging (IM) (*231*)
Internet addiction (*233*)
Internet Relay Chat (IRC) (*230*)
list address (*220*)
list owner (*219*)
list server (*219*)
LISTSERV (*219*)

lurking (*222*)
mail server (*176*)
mailing list (*219*)
Majordomo (*219*)
message body (*177*)
messages pane (*181*)
moderated list (*220*)
moderator (*219*)
Network News Transfer Protocol (NNTP) (*222*)
newbie (*230*)
newsgroups (*222*)
nickname (*217*)
NNTP client (*222*)
NNTP server (*223*)
open list (*220*)
Outbox (*180*)
POP (Post Office Protocol) server (*176*)
posting (*221*)
preview pane (*181*)
real-time communication (*230*)
rich media online communication (*232*)
Sent Items (*180*)
Short Message Service (SMS) (*229*)
signature file (*177*)
SMTP (Simple Mail Transfer Protocol) server (*176*)
snail mail (*175*)
spam (*174*)
Subject line (*177*)
subscribe (*219*)
synchronous communication (*230*)
text messaging (*229*)
To line (*177*)
unmoderated list (*220*)
USENET (*222*)
user ID (*175*)
virtual meeting (*232*)
Web-based chat (*230*)
Web-based discussion group (*226*)
Web-based e-mail service (*203*)
Yahoo! Mail list (*218*)

True or False

Mark T for True and F for False. (Answers are found on page numbers in parentheses.)

_____ 1. E-mail is the most popular online communication tool. (*174*)

_____ 2. You must have an HTTP mail server to handle incoming e-mail messages. (*176*)

_____ 3. To read e-mail, you must have access to either an e-mail client, such as Yahoo! Mail, or a Web-based e-mail service, such as Outlook or Outlook Express. (*179, 203*)

_____ 4. You either can type a recipient's e-mail address in the message window To line or can select it from the Outlook Express Address Book. (*193, 201*)

_____ 5. NNTP is a type of mail server used to send e-mail messages over the Internet. (*222*)

_____ 6. A file that is sent with an e-mail message is called an attachment. (*192*)

_____ 7. A distribution list allows you to send messages to multiple people at one time. (*201*)

_____ 8. A newsgroup is an electronic bulletin board. (*222*)

_____ 9. Yahoo! Messenger is an example of a chat room program. (*231*)

_____ 10. Virtual meetings are popular with businesses because they can save time and increase productivity. (*232*)

TEST YOUR KNOWLEDGE

Use the Test Your Knowledge exercises to check your knowledge of the chapter.

Multiple Choice

Select the best answer. (Answers are found on page numbers in parentheses.)

1. E-mail is _____ . (*174*)
   a. nearly instantaneous
   b. inexpensive
   c. convenient
   d. all of the above

2. The communications protocol used to send e-mail from its source to its destination is _____ . (*176*)
   a. HTTP
   b. IMAP
   c. POP
   d. SMTP

3. To keep e-mail organized in your Inbox, you can _____ . (*195*)
   a. print out each message
   b. create folders for different topics and move messages to them
   c. color-code the Subject line according to topic, sender, or date received
   d. attach electronic sticky notes to the messages

4. A valid e-mail address includes _____ . (*175*)
   a. http://, the user ID, an @ symbol, and the host name
   b. http://, the user ID, the password, and the mail server name
   c. the user ID, an @ symbol, the password, and the mail server name
   d. the user ID, an @ symbol, and the host name

(continued)

TEST YOUR
KNOWLEDGE

Use the Test
Your Knowledge
exercises to
check your
knowledge of
the chapter.

TEST YOUR KNOWLEDGE (continued)

5. Examples of asynchronous communications include all of the following except _____ . (219)
   a. e-mail
   b. IRC chat
   c. mailing lists
   d. newsgroups

6. A(n) _____ handles the job of directing messages to all mailing list subscribers. (219)
   a. HTTP server
   b. list server
   c. IMAP server
   d. none of the above

7. NNTP servers _____ . (222)
   a. host newsgroups
   b. provide chat rooms
   c. store and forward e-mail
   d. host instant messaging

8. .comp, .news, .rec, .sci, .soc, .talk, .misc, and .alt are associated with _____ . (223)
   a. USENET newsgroups
   b. list servers
   c. IRC chat
   d. IM

9. A form of chat that involves exchanging real-time messages with one or several friends via the Internet is called instant _____ . (231)
   a. spamming
   b. flaming
   c. messaging
   d. flagging

10. Sending short messages to and from cell phones is called _____ . (229)
    a. chatting
    b. instant messaging
    c. text messaging
    d. posting

Instructions: To complete the Learn It Online exercises, start your browser, click the Address bar, and then enter the Web address **scsite.com/internet/ch4**. Follow the instructions in the exercises below. Each exercise has instructions for printing your results, either for your own records or for submission to your instructor.

1 Chapter Reinforcement

TF, MC, and SA
Click the Chapter Reinforcement link. Print the quiz by clicking Print on the File menu for each page. Answer each question.

2 Flash Cards

Click the Flash Cards link and read the instructions. Type **20** (or a number specified by your instructor) in the Number of playing cards text box, type your name in the Enter your Name text box, and then click the Flip Card button. When the flash card is displayed, read the question and then click the Answer box arrow to select an answer. Flip through Flash Cards. If your score is 15 (75%) correct or greater, click Print on the File menu to print your results. If your score is less than 15 (75%) correct, then redo this exercise by clicking the Replay button.

3 Practice Test

Click the Practice Test link. Answer each question, enter your first and last name at the bottom of the page, and then click the Grade Test button. When the graded practice test is displayed on your screen, click Print on the File menu to print a hard copy. Continue to take practice tests until you score 80% or better.

4 Who Wants To Be a Computer Genius?

Click the Computer Genius link. Read the instructions, enter your first and last name at the bottom of the page, and then click the Play button. When your score is displayed, click the Print Results link to print a hard copy.

5 Crossword Puzzle Challenge

Below Chapter 4, click the Crossword Puzzle Challenge link. Read the instructions, and then enter your first and last name. Click the SUBMIT button. Work the crossword puzzle. When you are finished, click the Submit button. When the crossword puzzle is redisplayed, click the Print Puzzle button to print a hard copy.

LEARN IT ONLINE

Use the Learn It Online exercises to reinforce your understanding of the chapter concepts and terms.

EXERCISES

Use the
Exercises to
gain hands-on
Internet
experience.

To perform the following exercises, you must be connected to the Internet and have access to a printer. You also need an e-mail address for some of the exercises.

1 Surveying Online Communications Choices

1. Survey five friends and ask them the following questions about their choices for online communications. Summarize the results, and include yourself in the summary.
   a. How often do you check for incoming e-mail messages?
   b. Do you use IM to communicate with friends, family, co-workers, and classmates?
   c. How often do you participate in an IRC chat room or Web-based chat?
   d. Do you subscribe to mailing lists and newsgroups? How many?
   e. Do you use interactive video or audio to communicate online with friends or family?
   f. How often do you send text messages to or from a cell phone?
   g. How often do you engage in playing online fantasy games with others?

2. Answer the following questions related to your own choice of online communications tools.
   a. Are there some people with whom your primary means of communication is e-mail? IM?
   b. Are there some people with whom you never use any online communication? Why?
   c. When do you prefer to use an online communications tool and when do you prefer to communicate with others by telephone or in writing?

3. Use the results of your survey to describe how the survey group makes online communication choices.

2 Surveying E-Mail Use

1. Survey five friends and ask them the following questions about their general e-mail use. Summarize the results. Include yourself in your summary.
   a. How many e-mail accounts do you use?
   b. How many messages do you receive daily, on average?
   c. How many messages do you send daily, on average?
   d. Do you access your e-mail accounts using multiple computers or a single computer?

2. Survey five friends and ask them the following questions about their use of folders in organizing mail. Summarize the results. Include yourself in your summary.
   a. Approximately how many messages are currently in your Inbox?
   b. Do you organize e-mail messages into folders or leave them all in the Inbox?
   c. If you use custom folders, how many custom folders do you have?
   d. How often do you delete unwanted messages?
   e. How often do you retrieve deleted messages?

3. Survey five friends and ask them the following questions about their experience with spam. Summarize the results. Include yourself in your summary.
   a. On average, how many spam messages do you receive daily?
   b. What proportion of the spam messages deal with pornography, financial fraud, and advertising?
   c. How often do you read spam messages?
   d. Do you receive chain letters and forwarded messages from friends, and do you consider those to be spam? Do you forward these types of messages on to others?

4. Survey five friends and ask them the following questions about their experience with e-mail viruses. Summarize the results. Include yourself in your summary.
   a. How many e-mail viruses has your computer gotten this year?
   b. What virus protection do you use?
   c. How do you handle attachments on incoming messages?

5. Use the results of your survey to describe how the survey group uses e-mail.

3 CAPTCHA

1. Visit the Discovering the Internet Chapter 4 Web page (**scsite.com/internet/ch4**) and click a link below Exercise 3 to search for information about CAPTCHA. Use your research to answer the following questions:
   a. What is a CAPTCHA?
   b. Where are CAPTCHAs being developed?

2. Print an example of a CAPTCHA.

4 Children's Chat

1. Visit the Discovering the Internet Chapter 4 Web page (**scsite.com/internet/ch4**) and click Kidchatters below Exercise 4. Review the Web site and answer the following questions:
   a. For what age group is this site appropriate?
   b. What safety features are provided for the protection of children?

2. Visit the Discovering the Internet Chapter 4 Web page (**scsite.com/internet/ch4**) and click Yahoo! Chat below Exercise 4.
   a. Use your Yahoo! ID and password to sign in and enter one or more public chat rooms. Based on what you see, do you think these chat rooms are appropriate for children?
   b. Locate and read the Help/FAQs page to review Yahoo! Chat's rules regarding participation by children.

3. Write a paragraph comparing and contrasting children's use of KidChatters and Yahoo! Chat's public chat rooms.

(continued)

EXERCISES

Use the
Exercises to
gain hands-on
Internet
experience.

EXERCISES *(continued)*

 Newsgroups

1. Visit the Discovering the Internet Chapter 4 Web page (**scsite.com/internet/ch4**) and click Google Groups below Exercise 5. Think of a topic which you would enjoy discussing with others, and then:
   a. Search Google Groups for that topic.
   b. Locate and read the rules for posting on Google Groups. Does this information encourage you to post a message or discourage you from doing so?
   c. Register for Google Groups and post a new thread or a reply.
   d. Read the Google help information on how to delete your posting and then delete it.

2. Visit the Discovering the Internet Chapter 4 Web page (**scsite.com/internet/ch4**) and click EzBoard below Exercise 5. Think of a topic you would enjoy discussing with others. Use EzBoard to search for discussion groups related to the topic.

6 **Instant Messaging**

1. Visit the Discovering the Internet Chapter 4 Web page (**scsite.com/internet/ch4**) and click the links below Exercise 6 to research Yahoo! Messenger, MSN Messenger, and AOL Instant Messenger. Make a list of the features of each program and select the service you would most like to use. Give the reasons for your choice.

2. Visit the Discovering the Internet Chapter 4 Web page (**scsite.com/internet/ch4**) and click Trillian below Exercise 6 to research the Trillian instant messaging service. Compare the benefits of using Trillian with the other IM programs you researched in Step 1.

7 **Chat**

1. Visit the Discovering the Internet Chapter 4 Web page (**scsite.com/internet/ch4**) and click Yahoo! Chat below Exercise 7.
2. Use your Yahoo! ID and password to sign in and browse the Yahoo! Chat topics.
3. Select several chat rooms whose topics are of interest to you. Enter the chat rooms and answer the following questions.
   a. How many people are in the room? How many are participating in the discussion?
   b. Do the participants seem to know each other? Are they friendly? What is their reaction to newcomers: welcoming, ignoring, or rejecting?
   c. How much of the discussion is on topic?

4. Visit the Discovering the Internet Chapter 4 Web page (**scsite.com/internet/ch4**) and click Business.com below Exercise 7. Search the Business.com directory for two companies that sell chat programs and services used for customer support. Describe the companies and their products.

8 Virtual Meetings

1. Visit the Discovering the Internet Chapter 4 Web page (scsite.com/internet/ch4) and click the links below Exercise 8 to research the virtual meeting services provided by MeetingPlace, Microsoft Office Live Meeting, and WebEx.

2. Write a one-page paper describing these three virtual meeting services and how using these services might benefit a business or organization.

9 Text Messaging

1. Visit the Discovering the Internet Chapter 4 Web page (scsite.com/internet/ch4) and click the links below Exercise 9 to research the text messaging capability of two major cellular phone networks. Answer the following questions for both networks:
   a. What is the limit on the amount of text that can be received?
   b. How much does it cost to receive text messages on the phone?
   c. How much does it cost to send text messages?

2. Compare the two networks' text messaging services and describe the advantages text messaging offers over other forms of Internet communication.

10 Internet Addiction

1. Visit the Discovering the Internet Chapter 4 Web page (scsite.com/internet/ch4) and click the links below Exercise 10 to research Internet addiction. In your opinion, do the behaviors discussed constitute Internet addiction?

2. Visit the Discovering the Internet Chapter 4 Web page (scsite.com/internet/ch4) and click Center for Online Addiction below Exercise 10. Locate and read the FAQs page. Read at least one referenced article and write a one-paragraph summary of the article.

3. Visit the Discovering the Internet Chapter 4 Web page (scsite.com/internet/ch4) and click Virtual Addiction Information below Exercise 10. Read the personal experiences of individuals impacted by Internet addiction. Summarize one of the stories.

EXERCISES

Use the
Exercises to
gain hands-on
Internet
experience.

CHAPTER 5
Getting More Out of the Internet

Introduction

Do you want to get immediate notification of breaking news from a major news source or learn about traffic snarls that might make you late for school or work? Listen to a radio broadcast? Look up the definition of a new technical term or verify your bank balance and pay a few bills?

Download the latest version of a software program or relax by working a crossword puzzle? With Internet access and a Web browser, you can complete all of these tasks — and many more — while working on your computer.

In this chapter, you learn how to get even more out of the Internet and the Web, by using them to keep up-to-date with current events; access research and reference tools; explore special-interest sites; manage your personal finances; advance your education; shop for a variety of consumer goods; play online games; and download files.

In the following sections, you will learn the reasons behind the popularity of the Web as a major information source as you explore several interesting and useful Web sites.

OBJECTIVES

After completing this chapter, you will be able to:

1. Identify and use online news, weather, and traffic resources

2. Discuss streaming media and listen to streaming audio using a Web browser

3. Utilize online research and reference tools

4. Explore health, entertainment, hobby, and other special-interest Web sites

5. Discuss online tools for managing personal finances

6. Describe online educational resources

7. Shop the Web effectively using shopping guides and shopping bots

8. Locate and play online games

9. Download and upload files over the Internet

CONTENTS

News, Sports, Weather, and Traffic Resources

In today's fast-paced environment, it can be difficult to keep up with the local, national, and international events that affect everyday lives. Before the Internet, most people used newspapers, magazines, radio, and television to stay informed about current events, follow their favorite sports teams, keep an eye on the weather, or learn about traffic problems. Today, you can supplement these traditional print and broadcast news media sources with Web sites you quickly can access at home, school, or work (Figure 5-1).

In Chapter 3, you learned how to use online search tools to locate and read news stories. Most major U.S. newspapers, such as *The New York Times*, *The Washington Post*, the *Los Angeles Times*, and the *Houston Chronicle*, publish Web sites. If you have an interest in international news, you quickly and easily can view Web sites published by newspapers from around the world, such as the *Sydney Morning Herald* (Sydney, Australia), *The Globe and Mail* (Toronto, Canada), the *Daily Mirror* (London, U.K.), *The Telegraph* (Calcutta, India), *The Japan Times* (Tokyo, Japan), and *The Jerusalem Post* (Jerusalem, Israel). Web sites published by newspapers commonly include the same type of content found in the corresponding print versions: headline news, top stories,

Figure 5-1   News, news magazine, traffic, and weather sites.

Facts@Hand

According to the *Counting on the Internet* report by the Pew Internet & American Life Project, approximately 66 percent of all Americans now expect the Internet to be a reliable source for news, health care information, government information, and e-business.

feature articles, current weather, sports scores, entertainment reviews, classified ads, editorials and opinion columns, and so forth. Many general news and business news magazines, such as *Time*, *Newsweek*, *Fortune*, *Forbes*, *Barron's*, *BRW* (Australia), *Maclean's* (Canada), and *The Economist* (U.K.), also have Web sites that contain content similar to that in their print magazines.

As you learned in Chapters 2 and 3, television and radio networks, such as National Public Radio (NPR), NBC, CBC, BBC, and local television network affiliates, publish Web sites that provide a combination of headline news, sports, weather, and other news and entertainment features. Often these Web sites include content that promotes their broadcast programming and on-air personalities.

While sports, weather, and traffic reports usually are available at news-oriented Web sites, you also can find a number of Web sites devoted specifically to sports, weather, and traffic. Web sites such as the online versions of ESPN, FOXSports, and Sports Illustrated cover a wide range of sports around the world. Web sites such as weather.com, accuweather.com, and Intellicast.com provide local and worldwide weather forecasts, weather-related travel advisories, and weather maps. Web sites such as Traffic.com, SmarTraveler, and local or state Web sites provide updated traffic reports that highlight routes with congestion, construction, or accidents that might cause delays.

✋ Facts@Hand

A report by the Pew Internet & American Life Project suggests that more and more Americans are getting their political and election news from the Web. For example, the report indicates that while television is still the primary source for election information, almost 80 percent of U.S. Internet users used online news sources to get information about political candidates and their positions.

Characteristics of News-Oriented Web Sites

The four primary reasons for the growing popularity of news, sports, weather, and traffic Web sites are the following:

1. Availability — these Web sites are accessed easily from almost anywhere, at any time.

2. Immediacy — these Web sites can be updated quickly with breaking news, sports scores, or weather and traffic updates.

3. Interactivity — these Web sites provide features that allow their viewers to interact with the editorial staff or other viewers.

4. Customizability — these Web sites can provide information customized for each viewer's locality and interests.

The following section reviews each of these characteristics in detail.

AVAILABILITY Today, thousands of local, national, and international news-oriented Web sites often are more readily available than broadcast news sources. For example, if you are away from home, you may have no convenient access to television or radio, but you may have access to the Internet via a computer at work, or at school, or perhaps via a wireless device. The ready availability of Internet access from multiple locations makes it very easy for you to check the latest news, sports scores, or changing weather quickly.

 @Source

To review the news, sports, weather, and traffic Web sites discussed in this section, along with others, visit the Discovering the Internet Chapter 5 Web page (**scsite.com/ internet/ch5**) and click a link below Newspapers, Magazines, Television, Radio, Sports, Weather, or Traffic.

IMMEDIACY News-oriented Web sites are updated quickly with breaking stories — often as the actual events unfold — thus providing you with immediate access to the latest information. Print news media, of course, cannot be updated constantly and can contain only information about events that occurred prior to the last publication.

INTERACTIVITY Interactive features help to make a Web site more interesting and stickier. A **sticky Web site** is one that users visit often and browse for long periods of time. Many news-oriented Web sites provide interactivity by allowing you to submit questions and comments to their editorial staff, commentators, and reporters via e-mail or join other users in posting questions and comments in Web-based discussion groups. If the Web site is associated with print or broadcast media, these questions and comments also may be addressed in print or on the air. Another way in which these Web sites provide interactivity and create stickiness is by allowing users to participate in an online survey on a current topic and then quickly see how their opinions compare with those of other viewers. Sports-oriented Web sites often use a similar technique to allow you to vote for a league's most popular players or to vote for members of an All-Star team. Additionally, many of these Web sites allow you to subscribe to a mailing list, so that you will receive brief e-mail messages about breaking news and a link to the Web site for more details.

CUSTOMIZABILITY The ability to customize Web site content plays a major role in the growing popularity of news-oriented Web sites. For example, the Web sites for MSNBC, CNN, and BBC allow you to customize content based on a series of preferences. These preferences can include the following:

- ZIP code or locality — used to customize content for local news, weather, and traffic.
- News region preference — used to customize content for a specific geographic area such as the U.S., Europe, or Asia.
- Sports preferences — used to include news and scores for favorite sports.
- Stock portfolio — used to include activity reports and current quotes on the individual investments in your personal portfolio.

Most of the information available at these Web sites is free, although some sites, such as The New York Times on the Web, require that you register with a user name and password to access certain features. Other online news sources, such as The Wall Street Journal Online or HoustonChronicle.com, charge a fee or require you to subscribe to the corresponding print version to access certain articles, features, and archived material. A number of sites, such as CNN.com, contain premium content in the form of videos and special reports that you can view for a small per-item or monthly fee.

The following steps explore several news and traffic Web sites to view the latest news and traffic information, along with the interactive and customizable features of the Web sites.

◆》 *Steps:* To Explore News and Traffic Web Sites

1 Start your Web browser and visit the Discovering the Internet Chapter 5 Web page (scsite.com/internet/ch5). Click The New York Times on the Web. If necessary, close any pop-up windows. Scroll down the page and review its layout, content, and navigational links. Point to the Editorials/Op-Ed link in the Opinion section.

The New York Times on the Web home page appears (Figure 5-2). Because the news content is updated continually, the content in the Web page on your screen may vary from that shown in Figures 5-2 through 5-11 on pages 249 through 253.

Figure 5-2

2 Click the Editorials/Op-Ed link. Scroll down the page to review the brief introductory text for each editorial and Op-Ed column, as well as the list of contributors' forums. Point to the Readers' Opinions link in the Opinion section.

The Editorials/Op-Ed page appears (Figure 5-3). You can read an introduction to editorials and columns written by the editorial staff and columnists and then click a link to view the page containing the complete editorial or column.

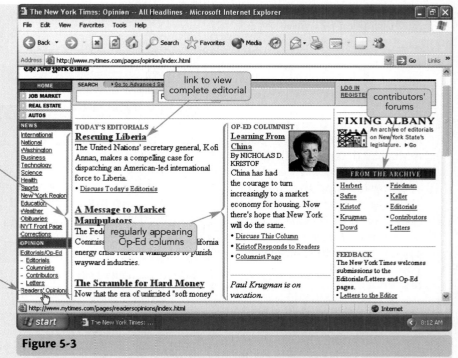

Figure 5-3

(continued)

3 **Click the Readers' Opinions link. Scroll down the page and review the current hot topics and the list of available readers' forums. Point to the Classifieds link in the Services section.**

The Readers' Opinions page appears (Figure 5-4). From this page, you can link to readers' forums on various topics and then review comments made by other readers and post your own.

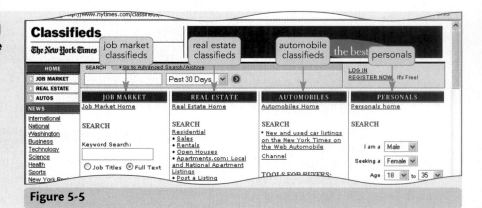

Figure 5-4

4 **Click the Classifieds link. Scroll down the page and review the different categories of classifieds ads.**

The Classifieds page appears (Figure 5-5). You can link to or start a search for classified ads by category from this page.

Figure 5-5

5 **Next, visit the Discovering the Internet Chapter 5 Web page (scsite.com/internet/ch5). Click CNN.com. If necessary, close any pop-up windows. Scroll to view the QuickVote area of the page. Read the online survey question and point to the option button that indicates your preferred response.**

The CNN.com home page appears, listing updated new stories, financial market information, and weather that can be customized to the user's location (Figure 5-6). The QuickVote section of the page allows users to participate in an online survey by clicking an option button to select a response.

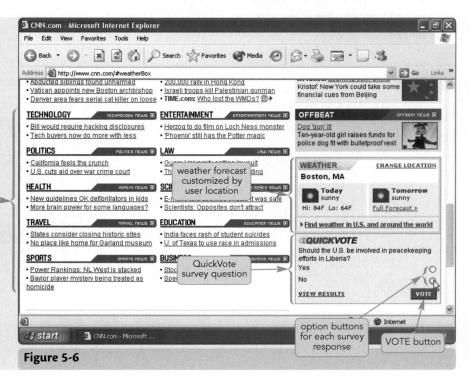

Figure 5-6

6 **Click your preferred response option button and then click the VOTE button.**

Clicking the VOTE button registers your survey response and opens the CNN.com QuickVote page in a new pop-up window (Figure 5-7). This chart shows the cumulative survey results at this point in time.

7 **Click the Close button on the QuickVote pop-up window.**

The browser continues to display the CNN.com home page.

Figure 5-7

8 **Next, visit the Discovering the Internet Chapter 5 Web page (scsite.com/internet/ch5). Click Traffic.com. Point to the link for your city in the Select A City list. If your city is not in the list, point to the Phoenix link.**

The Traffic.com home page appears (Figure 5-8). Clicking a link for one of the various cities listed allows you to view the current traffic patterns and problems for that city.

Figure 5-8

(continued)

9 Click your city link or the Phoenix link. Scroll down the page to view the traffic map, the types of alert indicators, and the positions of the traffic alert indicators on the map. Observe the Last Updated date and time listed below the map. Continue viewing the map for several seconds, then point to the Refresh button on the Standard Buttons toolbar.

Either your city traffic map or the Phoenix traffic map appears (Figure 5-9). Incident, advisory, event, and alert indicators are posted to the map where necessary.

Figure 5-9

10 Click the Refresh button on the Standard Buttons toolbar. When your city traffic map or the Phoenix traffic map page appears again, point to any alert icon on the map.

The traffic map is refreshed and the Last Updated date is updated to the new date and time (Figure 5-10). Note that after several seconds, the traffic map page automatically refreshes and updates the map and alert icons as needed. You can click any of the alert icons on the map to view the details of the alert.

Figure 5-10

11 Click the alert icon and review the location and reason for the alert. Point to the close window button in the pop-up window.

The Traffic.com alert details page appears in a pop-up window and contains information about the location and type of alert (Figure 5-11).

12 Click the close window button.

The browser continues to display the traffic map page for the selected city.

Figure 5-11

Use of Streaming Media

Audio and video at a Web site enhance viewers' enjoyment and add excitement to the way in which information at the site is delivered. Many news Web sites, such as CNN.com, provide video clips of timely news commentaries or important newsmaker interviews, while sports Web sites provide video clips of game highlights. Radio Web sites provide short audio clips of interviews or make entire broadcasts available as audio over the Internet.

Audio and video files used on the Web are available in several different formats, including:

- WAV (Microsoft/IBM Waveform sound) audio
- MIDI (Musical Instrument Digital Interface) audio
- MPEG (Motion Picture Experts Group) audio and video
- MP3 (MPEG) audio
- Windows Media (Microsoft) audio and video
- RealAudio (RealNetworks) audio
- RealVideo (RealNetworks) video
- QuickTime (Apple) audio and video

The last six audio and video formats listed above can be used as **streaming media**, which is audio or video transmitted continuously from a Web server to a Web browser. Most major news, sports, weather, and traffic sites use streaming media, because it provides the advantage of allowing users to hear and watch audio and video content as it is being transmitted.

To enjoy streaming media, your computer must have a sound card, speakers, and a media player installed. The Windows operating system comes with the Windows Media Player; other media players, such as RealNetworks' RealOne player and Apple's QuickTime player, are available as free downloads from the vendors' Web sites.

A fun way to experience streaming media is to listen to a radio broadcast using your Web browser. In addition to the traditional radio stations that broadcast over the Internet via their Web sites, a number of Internet-only radio stations broadcast over the Internet. The radio broadcasts are converted into a streaming media format, such as RealOne or Windows Media Player format, and then made available via the Web. You can listen to a radio broadcast by starting your media player and clicking a link to the server or by starting your browser and clicking a link on a radio station Web page.

The following steps illustrate the use of streaming media to allow users to listen to a radio broadcast using a Web browser.

Steps: To Listen to Radio Broadcasts Using a Web Browser

1 If necessary, start your Internet Explorer Web browser and then click the Media button on the Standard Buttons toolbar. When the Media bar opens, point to the Media Options button.

Internet Explorer displays the WindowsMedia.com Web page on the Media bar, as shown in Figure 5-12. The WindowsMedia.com Web page provides links to music videos, movie previews, and radio.

Figure 5-12

2 Click the Media Options button and then point to Radio Guide on the Media Options menu.

The Media Options menu appears (Figure 5-13). The Radio Guide command is selected.

Figure 5-13

3 **Click Radio Guide. When the MyRadio Web page appears, point to a featured radio station link in the Featured Stations list.**

The browser displays the MyRadio Web page, which includes a list of featured stations and links to other stations, organized by category (Figure 5-14). The list of featured stations in Figure 5-14 through Figure 5-16 may vary from those on your screen.

Figure 5-14

4 **Click the featured radio station link. Point to the Play link.**

The radio station selection expands (Figure 5-15). The available links allow you to add the station to your list of favorite radio stations, visit the station's Web site, or play the a broadcast. (Some featured radio stations do not have a separate play link requiring you to play a broadcast from their Web site.)

Figure 5-15

(continued)

5 Click the Play link. If the Media Bar Setting dialog box displays to ask if you want to play the item in the Internet Explorer window, click the No button.

The Windows Media Player window opens (Figure 5-16). After a few seconds, the audio of the radio station's broadcast plays. The station's Web page opens in a new browser window, which is minimized. Depending on the settings, the appearance of the Windows Media Player on your screen may vary from that shown.

6 After you have finished listening to the radio broadcast, click the Close button to close the Windows Media Player window. Maximize the browser window displaying the radio station's home page and then click the Close button.

The Windows Media Player closes and the audio broadcast stops playing.

Figure 5-16

Windows Media Player Close button

streaming broadcast now playing

player control buttons

 In Netscape

To find and listen to a radio broadcast using Netscape, click the Radio button on the Personal Toolbar. You may be asked to install a plug-in after clicking the Radio button. When the Radio@Netscape window appears, scroll through the Stations list to find a broadcast category. After you click a category name, an expanded list of radio stations in that category appears. Click a station link to start playing the audio broadcast.

As shown in Figure 5-16, Windows Media Player provides several player control buttons that allow you to play, pause, and stop the audio broadcast; to change or mute the volume; and to go to the next or previous track when you are listening to a CD. Streaming media is used on a wide range of Web sites to provide entertaining, up-to-the-minute content.

Research and Reference Tools

As you learned in Chapter 3, the Web includes numerous sites that provide access to specialized information collections, such as Lexis/Nexis, Find-Law, and Hoover's, and government Web sites, such as the Library of Congress and the Bureau of Labor Statistics. In addition to these specialized information collections, the Web also includes numerous general reference sites such as online encyclopedias, dictionaries, reference desks, and trip planners (Figure 5-17).

(a) Encyclopedia Britannica

(b) Dictionary.com

(c) Librarians' Index to the Internet

(d) FreeTrip.com

Figure 5-17 Reference sites.

 Facts@Hand

An Internet tracking survey by the Pew Internet & American Life Project indicates that 19 percent of online Americans access the Internet daily to find an answer to a specific question and that 17 percent use the Internet for research as part of their jobs.

Using Online Encyclopedias

It is likely that you are very familiar with the process of looking up a topic in a printed encyclopedia at home, at your school, or at a public library. With Internet access you now have a quick and easy way to research topics using online encyclopedias, such as Encyclopedia.com (Columbia Encyclopedia), the Encyclopædia Britannica, the MSN Learning & Research-Encyclopedia Center, The Encyclopedia of World History, and the Encyclopedia Smithsonian.

 @Source

To review the encyclopedia, dictionary, reference desk, and trip planner Web sites discussed in this section, visit the Discovering the Internet Chapter 5 Web page (**scsite .com/internet/ch5**) and click a link below **Encyclopedias, Dictionaries, Reference Desks,** or **Trip Planners.**

The following steps explore using an online encyclopedia to perform a keyword search for a specific topic.

Steps: To Explore an Online Encyclopedia

1 **If necessary, start your Web browser. Visit the Discovering the Internet Chapter 5 Web page (scsite.com/internet/ch5). Click Encyclopedia.com. Click the Enter Keyword(s) text box.**

The Encyclopedia.com home page appears (Figure 5-18). You can click a letter to browse through topics alphabetically or search for topics using keywords on this page. The content of the Web page on your screen may vary from that shown in Figures 5-18 through 5-21 on this and the next page.

Figure 5-18

2 **Type mummy and point to the Search button.**

Clicking the Search button will execute a search for pages on the Web site that contain the keyword, mummy (Figure 5-19).

Figure 5-19

3 **Click the Search button. Scroll down the page and review the first page of the search results. Point to the mummy –> Mummification in Other Parts of the World link or any other link on the search results page.**

A search results page appears, listing the first 10 search results hits for the keyword, mummy (Figure 5-20). The page also lists the total number of hits returned as a result of the search.

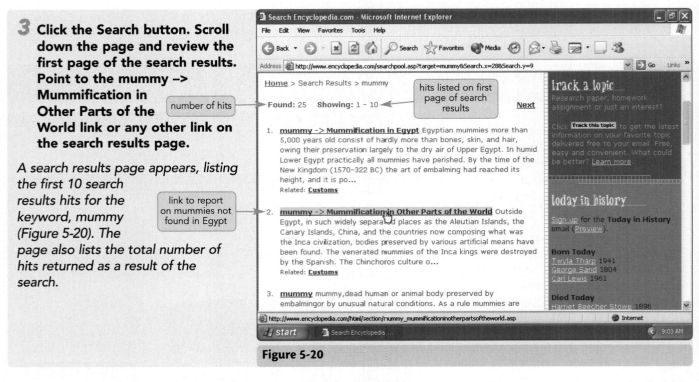

Figure 5-20

4 **Click the mummy –> Mummification in Other Parts of the World link and then read the short article.**

The article on mummification in other parts of the world appears (Figure 5-21). The article includes links to other Encyclopedia.com articles on related topics and links to related Web sites.

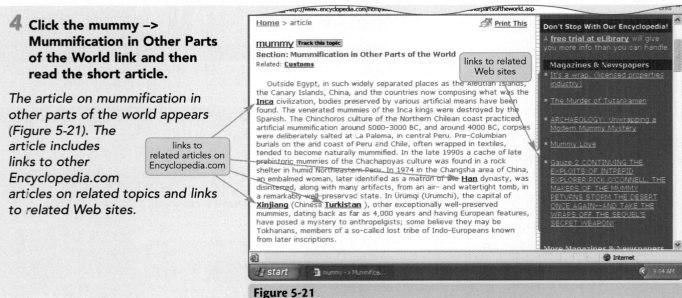

Figure 5-21

Using Online Dictionaries

Checking the spelling and meaning of words or finding synonyms for words has never been easier. You can find online dictionaries and thesauruses in a number of languages, including Merriam-Webster Unabridged, Dictionary.com, the Cambridge Dictionaries Online, and Roget's Thesaurus. You also can find dictionaries devoted to specific topics, such as law, biology, or technology. The NetLingo and the ComputerUser High-Tech Dictionary, for example, provide definitions of thousands of computer and Internet terms.

The following steps explore using an online dictionary to search for the definition, part of speech, and phonetic pronunciation of a specific word.

◈▶ Steps:　To Explore an Online Dictionary

1 **If necessary, start your Web browser. Visit the Discovering the Internet Chapter 5 Web page (scsite.com/internet/ch5). Click Cambridge Dictionaries Online.**

The Cambridge Dictionaries Online home page appears (Figure 5-22). From this page, you can enter a search keyword to search for a specific word in the English dictionary. You also can select another dictionary to search. The content of the Web page on your screen may vary from that shown in Figures 5-22 through 5-24 on this and the next page.

Figure 5-22

2 **Type** clone **in the Search our dictionaries text box. Click the Show phonetics check box. Point to the Search button.**

Clicking the Search button will execute a search for the word, clone, in the English dictionary (Figure 5-23). Clicking the Show phonetics check box will cause the search results to display the pho-netic pronunciation of the word, along with the definition.

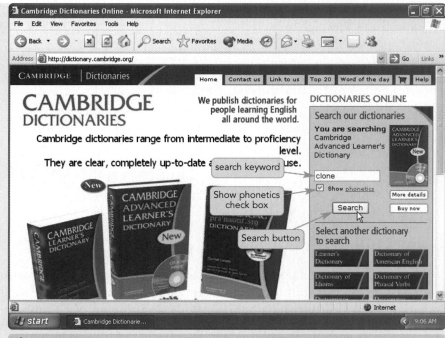

Figure 5-23

3 Click the Search button. When the Definition page displays, review the definitions, part of speech, and phonetic pronunciation for the word, clone.

A definition of the word, clone, as both a noun and a verb and its phonetic pronunciations appear (Figure 5-24).

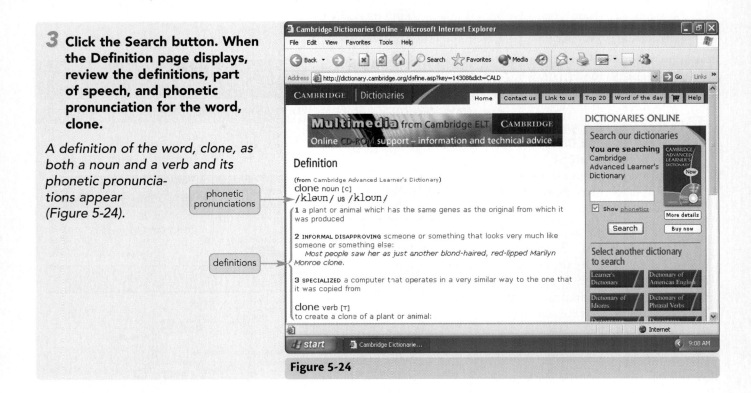

phonetic pronunciations

definitions

Figure 5-24

Using Online Reference Desks

Do you need to know what time it is in Hong Kong? What important event took place on today's date in history? How to translate text into another language? In the past, solving these information problems likely required that you call or drop by the reference desk at your local library. Today, you can connect to the Internet and find this information at an online reference desk Web site, such as the Internet Public Library, Librarians' Index to the Internet, InfoPlease.com, Refdesk.com, LibrarySpot, or iTools.

Online reference desks offer links to dictionaries, thesauruses, language translators, fast fact finders, and other traditional library reference desk information. Additionally, many college, university, public, and government libraries offer online reference desk resources. Examples include the Michigan eLibrary Reference Desk, the Duke University Reference Resources, and the Chicago Public Library Selected Internet Resources Web sites.

@Source

One of the most comprehensive collections of online maps can be found in the Perry-Castañeda Library Map Collection at The University of Texas at Austin General Libraries Web site. To find a link to this map collection, access the Discovering the Internet Chapter 5 Web page (**scsite.com/internet/ch5**) and click a link below Maps.

The following steps explore an online reference desk.

Steps: To Explore an Online Reference Desk

1 If necessary, start your Web browser. Visit the Discovering the Internet Chapter 5 Web page (scsite.com/internet/ch5). Click Refdesk.com. Point to the World Clock link.

The refdesk.com home page appears (Figure 5-25). This online reference desk lists a huge variety of online resources, including links to date and time references; headline news; reference tools such as almanacs, maps, and writing guides; a Web site of the day; and more. The content of the Web page on your screen may vary from that shown in Figures 5-25 through 5-29 on pages 262 through 264.

Figure 5-25

2 Click the World Clock link. Point to the Australia — New South Wales — Sydney link.

The World Clock page at the Web site, timeanddate.com, appears (Figure 5-26). This page lists the current day and time for worldwide locations. Links to more detailed information about each location also are available.

Figure 5-26

3 **Click the Australia — New South Wales — Sydney link. Point to the Back button on the Standard Buttons toolbar.**

The current local time in Sydney page appears (Figure 5-27). This page shows the date, day, and current time in Sydney, Australia, based on the location's number of hours from Greenwich Mean Time (GMT) and a daylight savings time adjustment, if necessary. Other information includes Sydney's latitude and longitude, international telephone country code, and links to other relevant information.

Back button

Sydney date and time details

Figure 5-27

4 **Click the Back button twice to return to the Refdesk.com home page. Scroll down the page and then point to the Canadian Statistics link in the Facts-at-a-Glance section.**

The refdesk.com home page again appears (Figure 5-28). The Facts-at-a-Glance section includes an alphabetical list of links to numerous reference sites.

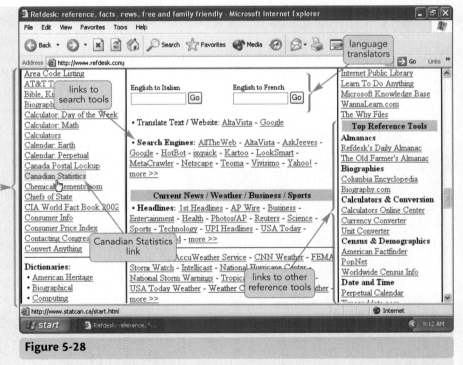

language translators

links to search tools

links to quick facts

Canadian Statistics link

links to other reference tools

Figure 5-28

(continued)

5 Click the Canadian Statistics link. Scroll down the page and review the latest general statistical indicators: the Population estimate, Consumer Price Index (CPI), Unemployment rate, and Gross Domestic Product (GDP).

The Statistics Canada home page appears (Figure 5-29). This site is published by Canada's national statistical agency and is available in both an English-language and a French-language version.

Figure 5-29

Most online dictionary, reference desk, and encyclopedia sites, such as the sites you explored in the previous sections, offer free information. Some sites, such as the Encyclopædia Britannica or Merriam-Webster Unabridged, however, are premium sites requiring a subscription fee to access some or all of the information available at the site.

Using Online Trip Planners

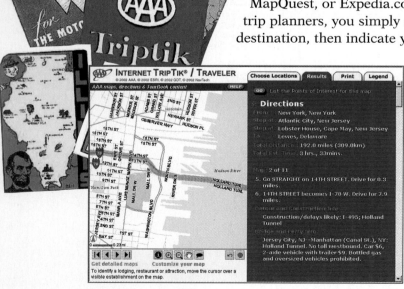

Planning an automobile trip used to require that you pore over printed maps and manually calculate the distance between your starting location and your destination. Often it was not clear where you would find overnight accommodations along the way. Now, you can plan your automobile trip in a snap with online trip planners such as those at FreeTrip.com, MapQuest, or Expedia.com. When you use one of these online trip planners, you simply specify a starting location and ending destination, then indicate your preference for either a scenic route or the shortest-distance route. Some trip planners also provide information about restaurants; shopping; and motel, hotel, and bed-and-breakfast accommodations along the desired route.

The following steps explore an online trip planner.

 Steps: To Explore an Online Trip Planner

1 **If necessary, start your Web browser. Visit the Discovering the Internet Chapter 5 Web page (scsite.com/internet/ch5). Click Expedia.com. Click the maps tab at the top of the page. Point to the Get Driving Directions link.**

The Expedia.com Maps page appears (Figure 5-30). From this page, you can search for detailed maps from around the world or get specific driving instructions for locations in North America and Europe. The content of the Web page on your screen may vary from that shown in Figures 5-30 through 5-35 on pages 265 through 267.

Figure 5-30

2 **Click the Get Driving Directions link.**

The Expedia.com Get driving directions page appears (Figure 5-31). You enter the starting location and ending destination and specify your route preferences for an automobile trip on this page. Note that your page may contain information remaining from the last time driving directions were requested from Expedia.com using this computer.

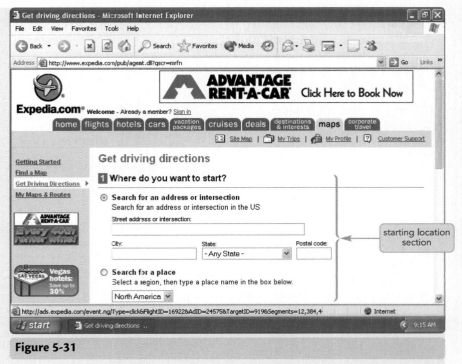

Figure 5-31

(continued)

3 In the Where do you want to start? section, click the Search for an address or intersection option button, type your street address in the Street address or intersection text box, type the name of your city in the City text box, select your state in the State list, and then type your postal code in the Postal code text box. (If you do not have a U.S. address, use 11767 Katy Freeway, Houston, Texas, 77079 as your starting location.)

Your street address, city, state, and postal code provide the trip planner with a starting location (Figure 5-32).

Figure 5-32

4 Click the Search for an address or intersection option button, in the Where do you want to end? section, and then enter `900 Ohio Drive, SW, Washington, D.C., 20024` as the address. Point to the Route type box arrow in the Select route options section.

The Washington, D.C. address provides the trip planner with a destination location (Figure 5-33).

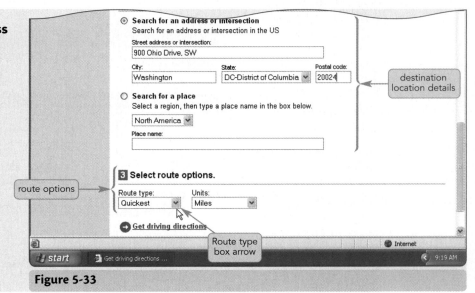

Figure 5-33

5 Click the Route type box arrow and then click Shortest in the Route type list. If necessary, select Miles in the Units list. Point to the Get driving directions link.

You have selected the shortest driving route from your city, state, and postal code (or from the Houston location) to the Washington, D.C., destination (Figure 5-34).

Figure 5-34

6 **Click the Get driving directions link. Scroll down the page and view the driving directions, then view the map.**

In a few seconds, a map highlighting the route between the starting and destination locations and a list of driving directions appear (Figure 5-35). You can save and print the map and directions, if desired.

Figure 5-35

Health, Entertainment, Hobby, and Other Special-Interest Web Sites

No matter what your interest, you likely can find a Web site with information on that topic. For example, hundreds of Web sites with health, diet, and fitness information are available to provide a wide range of information and advice, as are Web sites to provide entertainment news and movies reviews. If you have a specific hobby or special interest, such as cooking, museums, or genealogy, you can visit one of hundreds of Web sites on those topics. The next few sections explore just a few of the wide range of health, entertainment, hobby, and other special-interest Web sites available to you.

Finding Health, Diet, and Fitness Information

The epidemic of obesity in the U.S., coupled with rising health care costs, may have you thinking about ways to ensure that you are eating a healthy diet, getting the proper exercise, and staying informed on health, diet, and fitness issues. From time to time, you also may want to review information about a specific illness or medical condition. Your primary source of health, diet, and fitness information should be your doctor or another health care professional. If you are looking for health, diet, and fitness information online, however, you can choose from hundreds of Web sites such as eDiets, eFitness, Cancer.gov, WebMD, MedScape, and Yahoo! Health (Figure 5-36 on the next page).

Facts@Hand

A study by the Pew Internet & American Life Project indicates that two-thirds of Americans with Internet access get health and medical information via the Web. A similar study by Ipsos-Reid indicates that two-thirds of Canadians with Internet access also visit health-oriented Web sites.

(a) eDiets

(b) eFitness

(c) cancer.gov

(d) WebMD

(e) Medscape

(f) Yahoo! Health

Figure 5-36   Health-related sites.

Several popular commercial diet and fitness Web sites, such as eDiets.com, eFitness, and WeightWatchers.com, are available for a monthly fee to help you plan and execute a personal diet and fitness program. These sites offer a variety of features, including:

- Restricted-calorie meal plans
- Grocery shopping lists
- Exercise plans complete with text and graphic instructions
- Daily food and exercise diaries
- Support discussion groups

In short, everything you need to create a personal diet and fitness plan — plus support groups to help you stay on track — is available at one of these commercial Web sites. For more general diet and fitness information, you can turn to government Web sites such as Fitness.gov, which is sponsored by the President's Council on Physical Fitness and Sports (PCPFS), and Nutrition.gov.

In addition to researching specific health, medical, diet, and fitness topics, you may be one of thousands of Internet users who now review hospital Web sites to check out services; go to health insurance provider Web sites to evaluate enrollment options and coverage; and fill prescriptions at online drugstores. You also can go online to learn about and sign up for medical clinical trials or to locate a doctor in your area. Web sites such as Veritas Medicine, ClinicalTrials.gov, Yahoo! Health Find a Doctor, or AMA Physician Select offer these services. Many health care organizations, such as the National Cancer Institute (Cancer.gov), also provide online information about how to find support groups for a particular disease or disability.

The following steps explore several health, diet, and fitness Web sites.

⟫ *Steps:* To Explore Online Health, Diet, and Fitness Sites

1 **If necessary, start your Web browser. Visit the Discovering the Internet Chapter 5 Web page (scsite.com/internet/ch5). Click MayoClinic.com. Point to the Allergy link in the Health Centers list.**

The MayoClinic.com home page appears (Figure 5-37). You can find links to information about specific diseases and healthy lifestyle options on this page. You also can customize the page for your particular health and medical interests and respond to an online survey. The content of the Web page on your screen may vary from that shown in Figures 5-37 through 5-45 on pages 269 through 272.

Figure 5-37

(continued)

2 **Click the Allergy link. Point to the Medical tests for allergies link.**

The MayoClinic.com Allergy Center page appears (Figure 5-38). This page contains links to allergy-related topics, along with a relevant Ask a Specialist question.

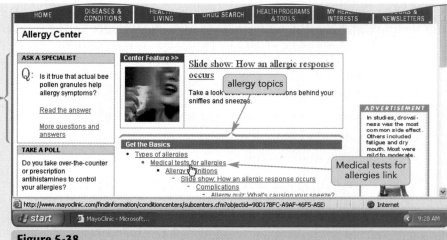

Figure 5-38

3 **Click the Medical tests for allergies link. Point to the Allergy skin tests: Diagnosing your allergies link.**

The MayoClinic.com Medical tests for allergies page appears (Figure 5-39).

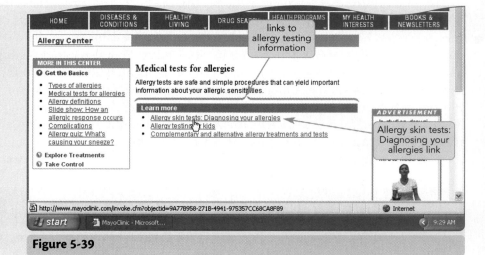

Figure 5-39

4 **Click the Allergy skin tests: Diagnosing your allergies link. Scroll down the page to review its content on allergy tests.**

The Allergy Center Allergy skin tests: Diagnosing your allergies page appears (Figure 5-40). On this page, you can learn about testing for allergies using a skin test.

Figure 5-40

5 Next, visit the Discovering the Internet Chapter 5 Web page (scsite.com/internet/ch5). Click NUTRITION.gov. Point to the Healthy Eating link in the Food Facts section.

The NUTRITION.gov home page appears (Figure 5-41). On this page, you can find links to various health, diet, and fitness pages, as well as links to pages containing information about related government programs.

Figure 5-41

6 Click the Healthy Eating link. Point to the CDC's Healthy Eating Tips link.

The Healthy Eating page opens (Figure 5-42). This page contains links to additional articles and other Web sites containing information about specific healthy eating topics.

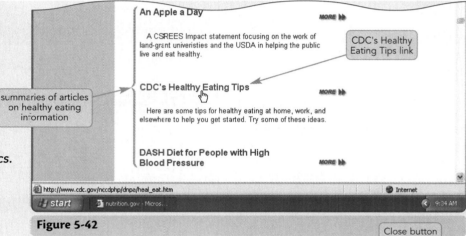

Figure 5-42

7 Click the CDC's Healthy Eating Tips link. Scroll down the page and read the healthy eating tips.

A new browser window opens, and the Centers for Disease Control and Prevention (CDC) Healthy Eating Tips page appears (Figure 5-43). This page contains useful tips about eating a healthy diet and links to related sources.

8 Click the Close button to close the new browser window.

The NUTRITION.gov Healthy Eating page again appears in the browser window.

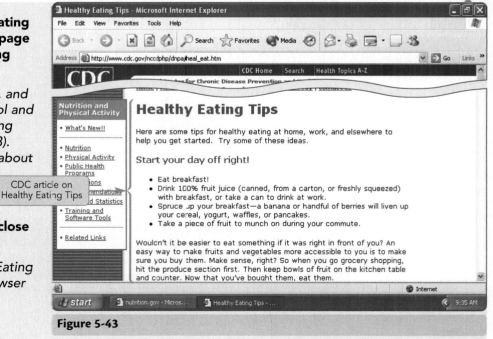

Figure 5-43

(continued)

9 Next, visit the Discovering the Internet Chapter 5 Web page (scsite.com/internet/ch5). Click PCPFS. Point to The Active Life link.

The PCPFS Fitness.gov home page appears (Figure 5-44). This page offers links to information about the President's Council on Physical Fitness and Sports (PCPFS), its reports and publications, and special programs.

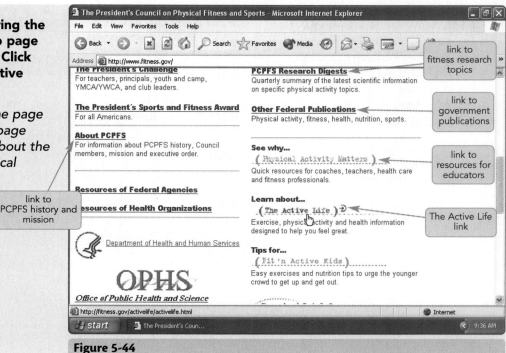

Figure 5-44

10 Click the The Active Life link. Scroll down the page and review its layout, its content, and the available government publications on physical fitness.

The Active Life page opens (Figure 5-45). This page contains links to fitness publications. You can view these publications as Web pages (HTML) or in Adobe Acrobat format (PDF).

Figure 5-45

 Facts@Hand

Just like consumers, health care professionals are turning to the Web in increasing numbers. For example, a study by the American Medical Association reports that more than 75 percent of U.S. physicians have Internet access; more than 67 percent of these physicians use the Internet more than four hours per week.

Credibility of Online Health Information

@Issue

Many health care professionals and Internet users are concerned about the credibility of online health information. These concerns are legitimate, as some health-oriented Web sites may not be reviewed professionally. For example, a survey of 400 health-oriented Web sites by a group from the University of Michigan reported that 50 percent of the surveyed sites had not been reviewed for scientific accuracy and that 6 percent of the sites published incorrect information. More recent surveys conducted by the Birmingham Women's Hospital (U.K.), the University of Texas (U.S.), and the Instituto di Ricerche Farmacologiche (Italy) indicate an improvement in the overall credibility of surveyed Web sites — but some problems still exist.

With these concerns in mind, how should you evaluate health-oriented Web sites? The credibility of the content at these Web sites first should be evaluated using the steps you learned in Chapter 3, including identifying the sponsoring organization or author, establishing that the content is timely and objective, and comparing the content with

that from other, similar sites. Most people who go online to find health information rely on popular search tools to locate health-oriented Web sites; however, some health care professionals suggest that you ask a trusted source, such as your doctor or medical information professional, to recommend health-oriented Web sites. Another resource to help you evaluate health-oriented Web sites is the CAPHIS (Consumer and Patient Health Information Section) Web site. The CAPHIS Web site is sponsored and published by medical information professionals from the non-profit Medical Library Association. CAPHIS evaluates health-oriented Web sites based on a number of criteria, including credibility, disclosure, sponsorship and authorship, and design, and then lists the top 100 highest evaluated Web sites as part of the CAPHIS Top 100.

Another alternative is to look for accredited Web sites. Two agencies that offer accreditation for health-oriented Web sites are the American Accreditation

HealthCare Commission (URAC) and the Health On the Net Foundation (HON). The Web site standards required by these agencies include the full disclosure of financial relationships; an editorial review process to ensure content accuracy; and internal processes to ensure privacy, security, and Web site quality. Web sites that adhere to the standards established by these agencies are entitled to display the URAC or HONcode symbols on their Web sites.

Finally, you should beware of false health care reports and health hoaxes. Unfortunately, it is all too easy to circulate false information via the Internet. You can find a list of current false health reports and health hoaxes at the Centers for Disease Control and Prevention (CDC) Web site.

For more information, visit the Discovering the Internet Chapter 5 Web page (scsite.com/internet/ch5) and click a link below Credibility of Online Health Information.

 @Source

Medscape, the U.S. National Library of Medicine Web site, and the American Medical Association Web site are all examples of Web sites of interest to U.S. health care professionals. To review these Web sites, visit the Discovering the Internet Chapter 5 Web page (**scsite.com/internet/ch5**) and click a link below Health.

Exploring Entertainment, Hobby, and Other Special-Interest Web Sites

Thousands of entertainment, hobby, and other special-interest Web sites offer something for everyone, whether your interest is cooking, learning about your family's genealogy, finding a job, making new friends, reading a movie review or the latest celebrity gossip, visiting the world's museums, or building toy trains. For example, using one of the numerous entertainment, hobby, and other special-interest Web sites, you can do the following:

- Learn to make hummus at VegWeb.com.
- Exchange family history with distant cousins at FamilySearch.org.
- Review résumé writing tips and post your résumé at Monster.
- Check out colleges, universities, graduate schools, and financial aid choices at Peterson's.
- Enjoy movie reviews at Rotten Tomatoes.
- Discover the splendors of ancient imperial China at the Asian Art Museum of San Francisco.

FOOD AND COOKING   Just as news media publish related Web sites, food and cooking print and broadcast media also publish Web sites to promote their magazines and television shows, while providing valuable information. Sites such as Emerils.com (Emeril Lagasse, world-famous chef and TV host), Epicurious (Gourmet and Bon Appétit magazines), VegetarianTimes (Vegetarian Times magazine), and FoodNetwork.com (Television Food Network) tempt you with recipes, easy-to-follow cooking tips, products to purchase at online stores, and information about associated restaurants (Figure 5-46).

If you love to cook but want to try something different, you can find a wide variety of food and cooking Web sites that offer recipes and cooking tips from around the world. For example, you can learn how to make vegetarian and non-vegetarian Indian dishes with recipes at the Bawarchi - Your Indian Cook site or learn to cook specialties from Italy's Lombardy region at the Delicious Italy Web site (Figure 5-46).

@Source

To review the special-interest Web sites discussed in this section, visit the Discovering the Internet Chapter 5 Web page (**scsite.com/ internet/ch5**) and click a link below Special Interest.

Facts@Hand

The *Parents Online* report published by the Pew Internet & American Life Project notes that 77 percent of Internet-connected American adults go online to look for information about a hobby and more than 65 percent go online just for fun.

Figure 5-46   Food-related sites.

MUSEUMS Perhaps you enjoy touring museums and viewing natural science exhibits, paintings, sculpture, or ancient artifacts from around the world. With Internet access, many of the world's museums — great and small — are at your fingertips (Figure 5-47). At museum Web sites, you can learn about current exhibits, operating hours, and membership opportunities. You also can view portions of ongoing special exhibits at many museum Web sites. Examples of online museum exhibits include the following:

- Archaeological and anthropological exhibits at the American Museum of Natural History in New York.
- An art history timeline at The Metropolitan Museum of Art in New York.
- An animated tour of treasures from the world's greatest libraries at The National Library of Australia.
- A virtual tour of western Canada's landscape, as interpreted by several landscape painters, at the University of Alberta Museums.
- A virtual exhibit of African artifacts in the Sainsbury African Galleries at The British Museum.

Figure 5-47 Museum sites.

GENEALOGY If you are interested in learning more about your family's history, the Internet is an amazing resource. For example, you can find U.S. census data, federal land grant information, state and county court records, death and cemetery records, marriage records, immigrant ship manifests, diary transcripts, historical and genealogical society records, and other genealogical information online (Figure 5-48). Similar information from other countries around the world is becoming increasingly available online as well.

For a small subscription fee, commercial Web sites such as Ancestry.com allow you to access a variety of databases. Data recorded in these databases includes the U.S. and U.K. censuses, U.S. county and U.K. parish records, the U.S. Social Security Death Index, and family tree submissions by other subscribers to these Web sites. RootsWeb.com is a free genealogy site that focuses on surname searches and general information on how to research family history. Hobbyist-supported Web sites, such as Cyndi's List of Genealogy Sites on the Internet, publish free directories of online genealogical information from around the world. Many government archives, such as the National Archives of Canada, FamilyRecords.gov.uk, the National Archives of Australia, and the U.S. National Archives and Records Administration (NARA), publish Web sites offering a wealth of tips on how to gather genealogy information, including how to order copies of archived military pension, naturalization, and immigration documents. Some Internet analysts suggest that, because of the extensive selection of family history and genealogy resources now available via the Internet, family history and genealogy research is becoming one of the world's fastest growing hobbies.

Figure 5-48 Genealogy sites.

SENIORS   Seniors use the Internet to enrich their lives by staying connected to family and friends, keeping up-to-date with world and local events, staying informed about health and aging issues, and having fun interacting with other seniors via discussion groups and online chats (Figure 5-49). A number of Web sites, such as the AARP site and SeniorNet, cater exclusively to the interests of older adults. Senior-oriented Web sites offer a variety of content, including articles on aging, continuing education courses, book clubs, retirement planners, and updates on legislation that affect seniors. Government sites such as the U.S. government's FirstGov for Seniors site, the Health Canada Division of Aging and Seniors site, and the Australian Seniors.gov.au site (Figure 5-49) offer information about health and aging and about government programs designed for seniors.

Facts@Hand

According to a study by eMarketer, 46 percent of U.S. seniors have been using the Internet for more than five years. Other surveys indicate that seniors (often defined as adults 50+ and older) around the world are accessing the Internet on a regular basis in greater and greater numbers.

Figure 5-49   Senior-oriented sites.

As you can see, the range of informative and useful special-interest Web sites is virtually unlimited. Regardless of your age or interest, you likely can find any number of Web sites to enjoy. The following steps explore two special-interest Web sites, one focused on food and cooking, and the other on genealogy.

❖❖ Steps: To Explore Special-Interest Web Sites

1 If necessary, start your Web browser. Visit the Discovering the Internet Chapter 5 Web page (scsite.com/internet/ch5). Click epicurious. Type gazpacho in the Recipe Search box and then point to the Go button.

The epicurious home page appears and gazpacho is entered as a search keyword (Figure 5-50). You can search for recipes and restaurants, review feature articles from the Bon Appétit and Gourmet magazines, shop for cooking-related items, or subscribe to print magazines on this page. The content in the Web page on your screen may vary from that shown in Figures 5-50 through 5-55 on pages 278 through 280.

Figure 5-50

2 Click the Go button. Point to the SHRIMP GAZPACHO WITH BASIL CROUTONS link.

The epicurious Search Results page appears (Figure 5-51). This page contains links to different recipes for gazpacho, a tomato-based soup typically served chilled.

Figure 5-51

3 Click the SHRIMP GAZPACHO WITH BASIL CROUTONS link. If necessary, close any pop-up windows. Scroll down the page to review the recipe's ingredients, instructions for preparation, and reviews from other cooks.

The selected recipe page appears (Figure 5-52). You can save this recipe to your personal recipe box at the epicurious site, view the contents of your recipe box, e-mail the current recipe to a friend, or print it from this page.

links to save recipe, e-mail recipe, print recipe, or view recipe box

recipe

Figure 5-52

4 Next, visit the Discovering the Internet Chapter 5 Web page (scsite.com/internet/ch5). Click NARA. Point to the Research Topics link.

The National Archives and Records Administration (NARA) Genealogy Main Page appears (Figure 5-53). On this page, you can learn about genealogy research, find out more about specific research topics, review a list of upcoming NARA-sponsored genealogy workshops, and access the forms to order archived records.

Sections list of genealogy information

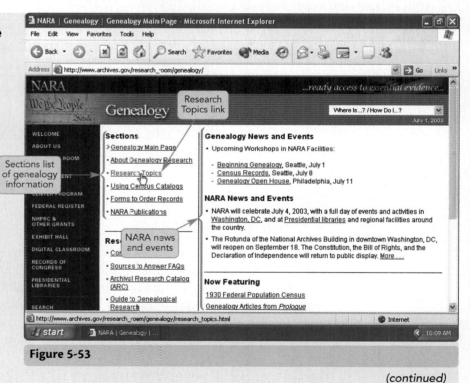

Figure 5-53

(continued)

5 Click the Research Topics navigational link to view a list of links to research topics. Point to the African Americans link in the Sections list.

An expanded list of research topics appears (Figure 5-54). You can select a research topic from the Sections list on the left side of the page or the Research Topics list on the right side of the page.

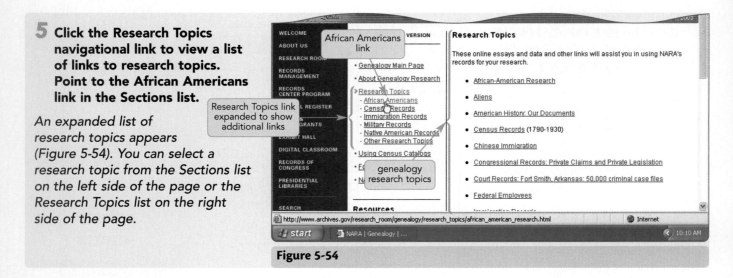

Figure 5-54

6 Click the African Americans Research link. Scroll down the page and review the list of links.

A list of African-American Research links appears (Figure 5-55). On this page, you can follow links to African-American history and archived records.

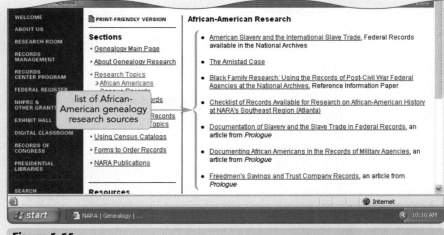

Figure 5-55

Personal Finances

Carefully managing your personal finances — from checking your bank balance and paying your monthly bills to financing a new car or reviewing investment opportunities — often is time-consuming and sometimes frustrating. You can use online tools to make managing your personal finances easier, faster, and more convenient. In this section, you learn about online personal financial management tools and why these online tools are becoming more and more popular.

Banking, Bill Presentment, and Bill Payment Services

Using online banking allows you to complete traditional time-consuming and paper-based banking activities, such as those required to transfer money from one account to another, with a few quick mouse clicks. If your bank or financial institution provides online banking, you already may be familiar with how easy it is to go online and check your bank balance or view a list of paid items from your account.

Facts@Hand

 @Source

According to a survey by eMarketer, more than 30 million U.S. households are expected to be banking online in the next few years.

To review the online personal finance-oriented Web sites discussed in this section, visit the Discovering the Internet Chapter 5 Web page (**scsite.com/internet/ch5**) and click a link below Online Banking, Bill Presentment and Payment, Credit, Insurance, or Investing.

In the past, a bank was largely a **bricks-and-mortar business**, meaning that customers conducted transactions primarily in person at a physical location, over the phone, or using paper-based transactions. Today, large banks, such as Bank One, Citibank, the RBC Royal Bank (Canada), and the National Australia Bank, and smaller regional banks, local banks, and credit unions (Figure 5-56) are becoming brick-and-click businesses — that is, they offer online banking in addition to the services offered at the physical banking facilities. A **brick-and-click business** is any business that allows customers to conduct business or complete transactions at a physical location as well as online at a Web site. By contrast, a **cyberbank**, such as NetBank (Figure 5-56c), is a virtual bank that has no physical facilities and offers products and services solely on the Internet.

(a) RBC Royal Bank

(b) National Australia Bank

(c) NetBank

(d) Bank One

Figure 5-56 Online banking sites.

At both brick-and-click banks and cyberbanks, you usually can complete some or all of the following banking tasks using online banking:

- View real-time account balances and recent transactions.
- View a history of account activity.
- Search for individual transactions.
- Pay your bills.
- Transfer funds between accounts.
- Download transactions into personal financial management software such as Quicken and Microsoft Money.
- Issue a stop payment on a check.
- Order checks.
- Report a lost or stolen ATM card and request a replacement.
- Change personal information such as your address, telephone number, and e-mail address.

Fees for online banking services vary from one bank or credit union to another. For example, some banks offer free online checking with no minimum account balance requirement, while other banks may require that you maintain a minimum balance to avoid paying service fees. Some banks also charge additional fees for specific types of online transactions, such as transferring money from account to account. If you are thinking about banking online, you should consider some of the advantages and disadvantages of online banking as illustrated in Figure 5-57. Before you open an online bank account, you should shop several online banks to compare services and fees.

Online Banking Advantages	Online Banking Disadvantages
An online bank is never closed; therefore, your account is available 24 × 7. Also, an online bank is available everywhere Internet access is available, so you can access your account when you are traveling out of the city or even out of the country.	Although online banks use strong security methods such as transaction encryption and password protection, you, like many other consumers, still may have concerns about the privacy and security of your online banking transactions.
You can manage all your bank accounts, including checking, savings, and money market accounts, from one Web site. You usually can download your banking transactions into personal financial management software on your computer.	Poorly designed online banking Web sites may be difficult to navigate. Additionally, Web site content changes frequently, which may make finding new services or features more difficult for a new user.
Cyberbanks have no physical buildings; therefore, they can save money on overhead costs. As a result of these cost savings, cyberbanks may charge lower fees for online services or lower interest rates on loans than standard banks.	Cyberbanks have no ATM machines of their own. Using other bank or network ATM machines for withdrawals and deposits may incur additional fees.

Figure 5-57   Advantages and disadvantages of online banking.

A common concern about online banking is related to the security of online banking transactions. While no online transactions are 100 percent secure and instances of online banking fraud have occurred, the banking industry has been involved with the security of electronic transactions for more than 40 years, starting with the electronic funds transfer (EFT) systems of the 1960s. Today, you can expect your online bank to use sophisticated security technologies to protect your personal information and to secure your online transactions. When shopping for an online bank, you carefully should review a bank's privacy policies and any security statements it provides.

Many financial industry analysts think the most valuable use of online banking is online bill payment services. A **bill payment service** allows you to log on to a Web site and pay any number of bills from a range of vendors. In addition to online banks, e-businesses such as CheckFree, PayTrust, and Yahoo! Bill Pay offer bill payment services. Even the United States Postal Service (USPS) now offers online bill payment services (Figure 5-58).

(a) CheckFree

(b) Paytrust

(c) USPS

(d) Yahoo! Bill Pay

Figure 5-58 Bill payment sites.

When you are ready to pay a bill online using an online bill payment service, you simply follow these steps:

1. Log on to your online bank or payment service's Web site.

2. Access your account by entering your username and password.

3. Select a vendor from a list of vendors you created when your first established your account.

4. Enter a payment amount and specify the payment date.

On the scheduled payment date, your payment is debited from your bank account and transmitted to the vendor either by an electronic funds transfer or via a paper check. You also can set up recurring monthly bills, such as your cellular phone bill or car payment, to be paid automatically on a specific day each month.

Facts@Hand

Surveys by the Gartner Group suggest that more than 40 percent of U.S. adults will be using online bill payment services by 2005, while a 2002 report by Jupiter Research estimates that more than three billion bills will be presented to U.S. consumers online by 2006.

More and more utilities, credit card companies, auto finance companies, and other businesses are using **bill presentment**, the process of sending bills electronically instead of mailing their customers paper bills or statements. Using bill presentment to send electronic bills, also called **e-bills,** can reduce a company's billing costs substantially. For example, the cost to send a paper bill can be more than $2 per bill; the cost to send an e-bill is about 50 cents per bill. You can arrange to receive e-bills and then pay them electronically through your online bank account or bill payment service. Consumers enjoy the convenience of receiving bills online. For example, assume you are on vacation. You still need to pay your credit card bill by its due date even though you are not at home to open your mail. If you receive an e-bill, you can log onto your bill payment service from your laptop or other computer and pay the bill on time.

Some online banks now offer online bill payment and bill presentment services for free, while other banks and payment services charge from $5 to $7 a month for a limited number of transactions, plus a per-transaction fee of about 50 cents for each additional transaction. If you are considering receiving and paying your bills online, you should shop several online banks and bill payment services and compare their fees before making your decision.

One way to take advantage of the ease and speed of online bill presentment and payment without paying a fee is to pay your bill directly at the vendor's Web site. Many utility and credit card companies now allow you to set up payment information that includes a user ID, password, and bank account information at the company's own Web site. Then, you simply log on to the Web site each month, view your monthly statement, and make your payment. While this method is less expensive than paying for a bill presentment and payment service, it lacks the advantage of using just one Web site to pay all your bills. For example, to pay bills directly at credit card company or utility company Web sites, you must remember multiple user IDs and passwords.

The steps on the following page view an online banking demo to allow you to review online banking features and services available at the Citibank Web site.

In Netscape

To accomplish this task in Netscape, see Viewing an Online Banking Demo in Appendix A.

Steps: To View an Online Banking Demo

1 If necessary, start your Web browser. Visit Discovering the Internet Chapter 5 Web page (scsite.com/internet/ch5). Click Citibank. Point to the learn more take a tour link.

The Citibank home page appears (Figure 5-59). This page includes links to apply to open an account, view Citibank's personal or business banking services, or view an online banking demonstration. The content on the Web page on your screen may vary from that shown in Figures 5-59 through 5-63 on pages 285 through 287.

Figure 5-59

2 Click the learn more take a tour link. When the opening page animation is complete, point to the next navigation button.

The Citibank Online Banking Demo opening page appears and, in a few seconds, the welcome page appears (Figure 5-60).

Figure 5-60

(continued)

3 **Click the next navigation button. Point to the green underlined word, accounts.**

The My Citi — Your Home Page example page appears, showing a typical customer home page (Figure 5-61). When you point to any of the green underlined words, the demo page displays zoomed-in views of different areas on the page.

4 **Point to each of the green underlined words, bill payments, markets, portfolios, and headlines, to zoom in on these sections of the page. When you are finished, click the next navigation button.**

Citibank also provides bill payment services, market information, an investment portfolio, and investment news headlines from the customer's home page.

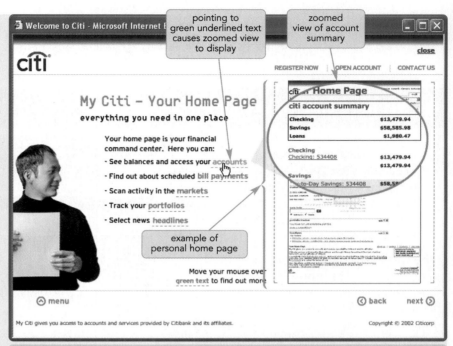

Figure 5-61

5 **Review the page layout and contents. Point to the green underlined words, customize this page and edit, to display a zoomed-in view of these sections of the page. Click the show me how to customize link.**

The See Things Your Way page appears (Figure 5-62). You can zoom in on the customization sections on this page and view a customization demo. A brief auto-mated example of changing the source of stock market information appears.

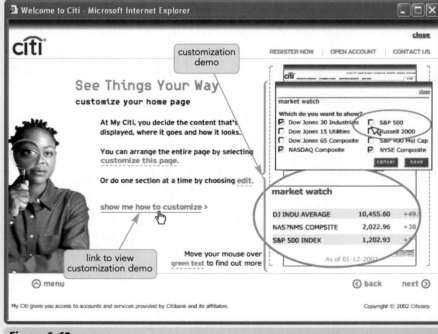

Figure 5-62

6 Continue to review the online banking demo by clicking the next navigation button to view the next page. Point to the green underlined words, if any, on each remaining page and click any links to view automatic how-to demonstrations. When the Thanks for Taking the Tour! page appears, point to the Close button on the Welcome to Citi window title bar.

The Thanks for Taking the Tour! page appears at the completion of the online banking demo (Figure 5-63).

7 Click the Close button.

The Citibank home page again appears.

Figure 5-63

Financial Calculators, Insurance, and Credit

Online information sources can help you make important personal financial decisions such as buying a new auto, selecting the right home mortgage, getting the best insurance value for your money, or accepting a credit card offer (Figure 5-64 on the next page). For example, online mortgage loan calculators and auto loan calculators can help you decide how much you can afford to pay each month for a home mortgage or how big a down payment you should make when buying an auto. Savings calculators can help you plan for a major purchase or your eventual retirement. Financial calculators are available at a number of financial institution Web sites, such as the Citibank Web site, or at financial information sites, such as Bankrate.com.

If you own a car, auto insurance is likely one of your major expenses. Shopping for auto insurance offline often requires that you personally contact several different insurance agents and then manually compare each agent's policies, terms, and quoted rates. Web sites such as Insweb, Insure.com, or Insurance.com make it easier to comparison shop for auto insurance by providing competing quotes from multiple insurance companies in just a few seconds. All you have to do is submit your auto and personal information, along with the insurance coverage you want, using an online form. You also can get online comparative quotes on other types of insurance such as homeowners, renters, and life insurance.

Figure 5-64   Online brokers, financial calculators, insurance agencies, and credit reporting agencies.

Web sites provide similar comparison shopping for credit cards. Because a wide range exists in payment terms, fees, and services associated with different credit cards, it is a good idea to shop for a credit card in the same way that you shop for other products and services. You can compare credit card offers at comparison shopper sites, such as BillSaver.com, or credit card information sites, such as CardRatings.com. Additionally, before you accept a credit card offer, you may want to learn more about the advantages and disadvantages of using credit cards; learn how to protect yourself from credit card fraud; and learn how to budget your credit card spending. Online credit card education is provided by many credit card issuers, such as on the Student Financial Services Web pages provided by Wells Fargo Bank and the Credit Education Web pages provided by J.P. Morgan Chase.

Protecting your credit also involves being aware of your credit history maintained by credit reporting agencies and knowing what to do if you are a victim of credit card fraud or identity theft. The three major U.S. consumer credit reporting agencies — TransUnion, Experian, and Equifax — now allow you to review your credit reports online for an annual fee. By quickly and conveniently reviewing your credit reports online, you easily can detect an error or an instance of possible fraud and take immediate action to have the error corrected or the fraud uncovered. If you are a victim of credit card fraud or identity theft, the U.S. Federal Trade Commission (FTC) Web site provides useful information on what steps you should take to protect yourself and correct your credit records.

 Facts@Hand

According to the U.S. Federal Trade Commission (FTC), more than 40 percent of fraud complaints received by the FTC, the FBI, and consumer groups involve identity theft — stealing credit card numbers or Social Security numbers in order to commit fraud.

Online Investing

Quick access to online investment information and the proliferation of investment-oriented Web sites empower many people to handle their own stock portfolios and other investments. Online sources such as CBSMarketWatch, Hoover's, CNNMoney, Morningstar.com, MSN Money, and The Motley Fool provide investors with current market information and stock quotes. Online brokers such as E*Trade and Charles Schwab offer a variety of investment accounts, some with low startup costs and small per-trade transaction fees. Most online brokers also offer premium financial services, including financial planning and market research. Increasingly, online brokers are offering a full line of financial services, including e-bill presentment and payment from your investment account. If you are considering online investing, Web sites such as the Investing Online Resource Center (IORC) can help by providing tips on how to select an online broker and how to open an online account. The IORC site also provides an online investing simulation in which you can practice managing an investment account before you actually open one. Many investor information Web sites also offer a portfolio feature that you can use to create a mock portfolio and practice managing it over time.

Education

For years, anytime, anywhere educational programs have been made available to students using the best technology at the time — from telephone and radio to television and videoconferencing. Today, ubiquitous Internet access is the leading technology behind an explosion in the popularity of online education. **Web-based learning**, or **online learning**, involves the delivery of educational material via the Internet to users, who view the material using a Web browser.

You can find Web-based learning opportunities in virtually every educational venue, from K–12 schools to adult continuing education at colleges and universities. Online adult professional development courses and employee training courses abound. Additionally, you can enjoy non-credit online courses on almost any topic for your personal enrichment or just for fun. In this section, you learn how the Internet and Web-based learning is changing the face of K–12 schools, colleges, and universities; employee training and professional development; and adult continuing education.

K–12, College, and University Education

Web-based learning programs open up a broad vista of educational opportunities for K–12, college, and university students. Rural schools with limited enrollment and resources can offer their students more curriculum choices via Web-based learning. Web-based learning also enables home-bound students to enjoy an enriched curriculum. According to a survey by the American Federation of Teachers, U.S. high school students in more than 20 states take online courses in public schools. Many of these students also use Web-based learning to complete freshmen college courses while still in high school or to explore possible careers by taking courses in special areas such as engineering or computer technology.

Perhaps you are one of the millions of students who are enjoying the advantages of Web-based learning: courses that are available 24 × 7, courses in which you can participate from anywhere you have an Internet connection, and courses that are self-paced. Today, hundreds of colleges and universities offer online courses in which students interact with their instructors and other students via e-mail, chat rooms, and online discussion groups (Figure 5-65). These online courses are becoming increasingly popular, especially with nontraditional adult students who must work full-time while getting their degrees. Web-based learning allows colleges and universities to offer these working adults courses that are flexible enough to fit into their busy lives. Increasingly, some colleges and universities are offering complete degree programs online. You can use online directories, such as those provided by WorldWideLearn, classesUSA, or USNews.com, to locate online courses and degree programs.

Figure 5-65   Online learning offered by colleges and universities.

@Source

To review the education Web sites discussed in this section, visit the Discovering the Internet Chapter 5 Web page (**scsite.com/ internet/ch5**) and click a link below K–12, College, and University Education; Training and Professional Development; or Continuing Education.

Employee Training and Professional Development

Organizations such as Motorola, Circuit City, Merck, McDonald's, General Motors, and the U.S. Army are using Web-based learning to deliver employee training programs. Using Internet, satellite, and videoconferencing technologies, these organizations save millions of training dollars each year by reducing travel costs, keeping their employees on the job, and reducing the need for trainers and centralized training facilities. For example, General Motors uses Web-based learning to introduce new vehicle models to auto dealership salespersons and to train dealership mechanics on how to repair them. By delivering new vehicle training online, General Motors avoids the expenses involved in sending thousands of trainers to auto dealerships around the country each new model year. Sales representatives for Merck learn about new pharmaceutical products in interactive, online sessions — saving them a trip to Merck's training center for a traditional product introduction session. New Circuit City salespersons can take self-paced online courses to become familiar with the consumer electronic products Circuit City sells, such as digital cameras and high-definition TVs, instead of spending several days at the Circuit City training center. The U.S. Army offers enlistees the chance to enroll in more than 2,000 online courses and 90 online degree programs from colleges and universities around the country, through the Army's eArmyU Web-based learning program. The eArmyU program is designed to encourage new enlistments and keep enlistees in the service longer — thus reducing recruitment and turnover costs.

Thousands of busy accountants, doctors, and other professionals also are going online to meet their professions' continuing education requirements (Figure 5-66 on the next page). For example, e-businesses such as Positive Systems, Inc. (PASSonline) (Figure 5-67 on the next page) offer online continuing professional education (CPE) courses for accounting and financial professionals, who are required by state licensing agencies to take several courses each year. Doctors and other health professionals can log on to the Medscape CME Center site (Figure 5-67) and take free online courses to complete their continuing medical education (CME) requirements.

Technical certification enhances career opportunities for information technology (IT) professionals and helps keep their skills up-to-date in today's highly dynamic technological environment. IT professionals increasingly are turning to online courses provided by colleges and universities and training companies such as Skillsoft and NETg (Figure 5-67) to prepare for CompTIA A+ and Net + network certification; the Microsoft Certified System Engineer (MCSE) certification; the Cisco Certified Network Associate (CCNA) certification; and other technical certification examinations.

Figure 5-66   Online employee training and professional development.

Figure 5-67   Professional certification and continuing professional development sites.

Adult Continuing Education

Learning for personal growth, lifestyle enrichment, and just plain fun has never been easier for Internet-connected busy adults. Perhaps you would like to learn how to write a mystery novel, study the history of film, or learn to speak a second language, but do not have time for a traditional on-campus course. If so, online courses on these and thousands of other topics may be ideal. Many colleges and universities, such as the University of California, Berkeley, offer a variety of credit and non-credit courses online. Additionally, e-businesses such as Suite101.com, Learnthat.com, and FamilyEdge offer online courses on a wide range of topics, from ecological gardening to making salsa to getting your music compositions recorded and published (Figure 5-68). Fees for online courses at e-business Web sites such as these can range from free for short, non-interactive courses to around $100 for interactive, instructor-led courses. Fees for college- and university-sponsored online continuing adult education courses vary by the length of the course and whether or not you earn college credit.

(a) UC Berkeley

(b) Learnthat.com

(c) FamilyEdge

(d) Suite 101.com

Figure 5-68   Adult continuing education sites.

Shopping

Consumer electronics. Specialty food items. Computers and printers. Autos. Flowers. Hotel reservations. Personalized cosmetics. If you want it, you can find it on the Web, where shelf space is infinite, product choices are boundless, and the stores never close. Consumers around the world are shopping for and buying products online more and more frequently for several reasons. For one, widespread high-speed Internet access allows consumers to view feature-rich Web stores and permits online inquiries and transactions to be processed more quickly. Further, most online store sites now are designed with shoppers' needs in mind and are easier to use. Finally, as consumers make more frequent online purchases, they increasingly trust the online purchasing process and are satisfied with the results. In this section, you learn about the online consumer marketspace, shopping guides and shopping bots, and online auctions.

Online Consumer Marketspace

The term **marketspace** is used to distinguish the virtual location in which e-business is conducted — such as an online bookstore — from the conventional physical marketplaces in which business takes place — such as the bookstore in the local mall. One of the fastest growing e-business marketspaces is the worldwide business-to-consumer (B2C) marketspace, or online consumer marketspace.

In the U.S., more and more consumers are turning to the Web to purchase goods and services from online-only retailers, such as Amazon.com, and brick-and-click retailers, such as Best Buy, Wal-Mart, and J. Crew. According to a survey by the Business Software Alliance, more than 90 percent of Internet-connected Americans already have bought something online, while more than 60 percent are more likely to shop online today than they were a few years ago. A few of the key reasons for these increased numbers include the savings, efficiency, and selection offered on the Web. For example, if you want to buy a personal CD player, you can use a Web site to compare CD player features and prices at multiple online retailers, avoiding traffic hassles and long checkout lines at brick-and-mortar stores. Additionally, online retailers may offer discounted prices, free shipping, and other incentives that could make your online CD player purchase a real bargain (Figure 5-69).

Figure 5-69   Online stores and shopping guides.

Books, music, videos and DVDs, apparel, and consumer electronics account for more than two-thirds of online consumer spending, according to a report issued by Harris Interactive and Nielsen/NetRatings. Travel-related online spending — airline tickets, auto rentals, hotel accommodations, and so forth — accounts for approximately 25 percent of online consumer spending. The remaining 7 to 8 percent includes spending on thousands of other items such as toys, pet supplies, and specialty food items. Buying consumer products, however, is only part of the online shopping story.

Thousands of consumers shop online to compare product features and prices and then buy the products at brick-and-mortar locations. Using the Internet and the Web to gather product information before making a buying decision leads to a power shift away from sellers and toward buyers. One example of this power shift is occurring in new or used auto and truck sales. Online shoppers in the market for a new or used vehicle increasingly are using third-party automotive Web sites such as Edmunds.com, Autobytel, and CARFAX to get information on factory and dealer pricing, trade-in values, financing deals, auto ownership histories, and other factors that go into buying a new or used vehicle. Armed with this kind of information, vehicle buyers then are better able to negotiate with sellers at the point of sale — either online or at a dealership. According to research reports by J.D. Power and Associates, more than 83 percent of online shoppers in the market for a new auto or truck spent two or more months shopping third-party automotive, manufacturer, or dealer Web sites before actually going to a dealership to take a test drive.

Shopping Guides and Shopping Bots

Saving time is one of the primary reasons consumers shop online. Therefore, when shopping online for a new book or music CD, you may go directly to well-known sites such as Amazon.com or Barnes&Noble.com, rather than spend time shopping at multiple Web sites. Because the buying decision is simple, it may not be worth your time to comparison shop: new books or music CDs have the same features regardless of where you buy them and price variances on these products generally are small.

If you want to purchase a gift online but do not know which online store to use, you can try an online shopping guide. A **shopping guide**, such as MSN Shopping, Yahoo! Shopping, and AOL Shopping, categorizes featured online stores. You either can search the shopping guide's index by keyword or click category links to drill down through the directory until you find featured stores selling the type of gift you want. Some shopping guides, such as Epinions, offer product reviews submitted by other consumers.

What if you are shopping for a more expensive and complex item, such as a new printer or camcorder? In this instance, your buying decision is made more complicated because features for these types of products vary from model to model, and price variances between stores may be substantial. One way to make your buying decision easier is to use an online comparison shopper or shopping bot to locate and compare different products from different manufacturers and retailers.

In Chapter 3, you learned about search engine spiders or bots, computer programs that browse the Web to examine text, links, and keywords on various pages and then send the information to an index stored on the search engine's server. Like a search engine, a **shopping bot** has computer programs that search the Web to build an index or database. When a user enters a search keyword or phrase, the shopping bot searches its database to find products that match the search request. The shopping bot then displays a results list of products, usually compared or rated on the basis of price, and where to buy the item. Examples of shopping bots include NexTag, MySimon, Dealtime, Price.com, and BizRate.com.

@Source

To review the shopping Web sites discussed in this section, visit the Discovering the Internet Chapter 5 Web page (**scsite.com/ internet/ch5**) and click a link below Shopping.

@Source

As you learned in Chapter 2, shopping online generally is safe if you take a few simple precautions. For a quick review of the Better Business Bureau (BBB) tips on shopping safely online, visit the Discovering the Internet Chapter 5 Web page (**scsite .com/internet/ch5**) and click a link below Shopping Safely Online.

The following steps use a shopping bot to comparison shop for a product.

Steps: **To Use a Shopping Bot**

1 If necessary, start your Web browser. Visit the Discovering the Internet Chapter 5 Web page (scsite.com/internet/ch5). Click BizRate.com. Point to the Electronics navigation tab.

The BizRate.com home page appears (Figure 5-70). The content on the Web page on your screen may vary from that shown in Figures 5-70 through 5-74 on pages 296 through 297.

Figure 5-70

2 Click the Electronics navigation tab. Scroll down the page and review the numerous categories in the Browse section. Point to the Camcorders link under Photography.

The BizRate.com Electronics page appears (Figure 5-71). You can view the top-selling items in Electronics, click a link to browse a subcategory of Electronics such as camcorders, or search for a specific item on this page.

Figure 5-71

3 **Click the Camcorders link. Point to the first camcorder link in the Top Sellers section.**

The Camcorders page includes information on pricing and availability for specific camcorders (Figure 5-72). This page also provides additional links so you can browse by brand, price range, and features.

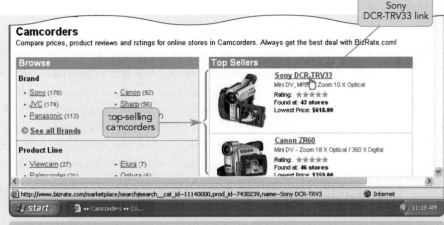

Figure 5-72

4 **Click the first camcorder product link. Scroll down the page to view the table of stores and then type your ZIP code in the ZIP Code text box. If you do not have a U.S. ZIP code, use 02210. Point to the Calculate total price button.**

The selected camcorder page appears (Figure 5-73). You can review the technical details for the camcorder; read consumer reviews; and view a table listing the stores that sell the camcorder, consumer reviews of these stores, and the availability and price of the camcorder at each store. The ZIP Code text box allows you to calculate the total price of the camcorder, including estimated tax and shipping.

Figure 5-73

5 **Click the Calculate total price button. Scroll down the page and review the different prices and shipping costs for each store.**

Any applicable tax and estimated shipping charges are added to the selling price for each store (Figure 5-74).

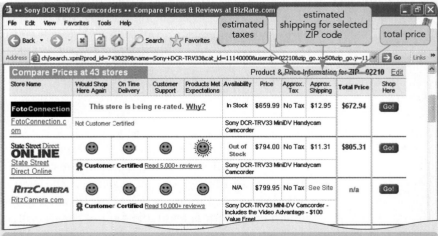

Figure 5-74

Online Auctions

Online auction sites continue to attract millions of individuals with something to sell or a desire to buy. Computer equipment and collectible items account for about half of sales at online auctions sites, but you also can find autos, books, jewelry, and numerous other items at online auction sites, such as eBay, Yahoo! Auctions, or Amazon Auctions (Figure 5-75). In addition to these major auction sites, some companies such as Dell or CompUSA conduct online auctions of refurbished, marked-down, and closeout computer equipment at their own Web sites.

Figure 5-75 Auction, overstock, and discount/coupon Web sites.

Facts@Hand

According to Forrester Research, U.S. online auction sales are expected to grow to $54 billion (or about 25 percent of all online retail sales) by 2007.

Even at different online auction sites, the general processes for selling and buying items are similar. First, you register at the Web site as a seller, a buyer, or both. As a seller, you post the items you want to sell and indicate the specific time period during which each item is available for purchase. Sellers also can set a **reserve price**, which is the lowest price at which a seller is obligated or willing to sell an item. As a buyer, you search the site for an item you want to buy. When you find the item, you indicate how much you are willing to pay for it, an amount called a **bid**. At the end of the specified timeframe, the item is sold to the highest bidder. Finally, the seller and buyer arrange for payment and shipping.

The main advantages of buying items at an online auction include access to a variety of items, some of which may be hard to find elsewhere, and the opportunity to get products at lower prices. Unfortunately, a darker side to online auctions also exists. A U.S. Federal Trade Commission (FTC) study indicates auction fraud — including non-payment, non-delivery of merchandise, and fraudulent third-party escrow services — accounted for more than 10 percent of all FTC complaints. Because of the risk of fraud, some auction sites provide mechanisms to hold payment in **escrow** — that is, they hold the payment until the buyer has received the purchased item or service — or to mediate problems between the buyer and seller. Most reputable auction sites provide tips for their prospective sellers and buyers on how to reduce the risk of auction fraud; the FTC Web site also provides helpful tips on reducing this risk.

Online Gaming

Online gaming is extremely popular around the world. More than 40 percent of Internet users in China play online games. In Europe, more than 3 million U.K. Internet users, 1.5 million Spanish users, and 2 million French users logged on to online gaming sites in a single month. In the U.S., interactive online gaming is one of the fastest-growing entertainment venues, with more than 68 million online gamers.

Early online gamers were likely to be males aged 15 through 30 involved in role-playing games. Today, online gaming appeals to a much wider group of participants, including young women and older adults of both sexes. Whether you want to relax alone or play with friends, you likely can find an online game you will enjoy playing. For example, you can play card games, arcade games, and word games or you can log on to an online game room and join a friend — from across town or across the world — in playing a board or tile game. You can test your gaming skills by competing with other players in online game tournaments or you can experience an exciting alternate universe by participating in a strategy or role-playing game (Figure 5-76 on the next page). Figure 5-77 on the next page illustrates just a few of the games you can find online.

Many online games are free. For example, some non-gaming Web sites offer free word or trivia games as an incentive for viewers to return to their sites frequently. Gaming portals such as Yahoo! Games and MSN Zone offer free online and downloadable games for players who register at their sites. Sites such as Yahooligans! and PBSKids offer free online games targeted to children. Some sites, such as Uproar, offer premium casino games and chances to win money and prizes.

Other Web sites, however, offer subscription-based games. With a **subscription-based game**, you first purchase a CD-based game, such as EverQuest or The Sims. Then, for a small monthly subscription fee ranging from about $10 to $13, you can play the game online with thousands of other players from around the world. Some online gaming analysts expect the popularity of subscription-based games to drive online gaming revenues from $635 million in 2003 to more than $2.5 billion by 2005.

 @Source

Online bargain hunters also can shop a number of Web sites that specialize in manufacturers' overstocks, remainders, and other discounted items. Sites that offer online coupons for products you can purchase online or at brick-and-click stores are useful as well. To view links to some of these sites, visit the Discovering the Internet Chapter 5 Web page (**scsite .com/internet/ch5**) and click a link below Overstocks and Coupons.

 @Source

To learn more about the FTC tips on reducing the risk of auction fraud, visit the Discovering the Internet Chapter 5 Web page (**scsite .com/internet/ch5**) and click a link below Shopping Safely Online.

Figure 5-76   Types of games available online.

Category	Name
Arcade games	Alchemy, Diamond Mine, Noah's Ark, Bounce Out
Board and tile games	Backgammon, Bingo, Chess, Checkers, Dominoes, MahJongg
Casino games	Blackjack, Poker, Baccarat, Roulette, Slots
Children's games	Math Baseball, Grammar Gorillas, Connect the Dots
Classic card games	Solitaire, Bridge, Canasta, Cribbage, Gin, Hearts, Pinochle, Spades
Sports games	Fantasy Auto Racing, Football, Golf, Baseball, Basketball, Sports Trivia
Strategy and role-playing games	Sims! Online, EverQuest, Star Wars Galaxies, Civilization II, Asheron's Call
Word and trivia games	Crossword, Spelldown, Literati, Word Racer, Pop Trivia, Text Twist

Figure 5-77   Online games.

@Issue Online Gambling

Online gaming should be about fun — enjoying the challenge of the game and interacting with other players in multi-player games. When it comes to online gambling, however, the stakes and consequences can be much higher than simply losing a game to a friend. As losses mount, online gambling can have a detrimental effect on personal lives.

You may or may not think gambling online is appropriate. Hundreds of gambling sites — offering everything from virtual poker to betting on college football games — already exist on the Web. Fifty countries now authorize Internet gambling; however,

an ongoing controversy in the U. S. rages about the legality of online gambling, and it may be illegal in your area.

Many Internet analysts and social scientists are concerned about the addictive quality of online gambling, specifically because gambling on the Web makes gambling more convenient; provides access to children, who are not allowed to gamble legally; and is not regulated like other forms of legal gambling and thus is more open to fraud. Some U.S. legislators are moving to restrict online gambling, while some financial

institutions and online payment e-businesses also now are refusing to process credit card transactions from online gambling sites.

Before you begin gambling online, you should consider the ethical, social, and financial ramifications for you and your family.

If you or someone you know needs help with an online gambling addiction, you may want to visit the Discovering the Internet Chapter 5 Web page (**scsite.com/ internet/ch5**) and click a link below Online Gambling.

Download and File-Sharing Sites

One of the most popular Internet activities is transferring text, graphics, music, and software files from one Internet-connected computer to another. In Chapter 4, you learned how to transfer a file by attaching it to an e-mail message. Two other ways to transfer files over the Internet are using FTP (File Transfer Protocol) and using a peer-to-peer (P2P) file-sharing network. In this section, you learn where to find download sites, how to use FTP to download and upload files, and how people use P2P file-sharing networks.

Download Sites

The Internet has numerous resources where you can search for and download freeware or shareware programs, including games, utilities, and screen savers, or upgrades to commercial software products. **Freeware** is software that the author allows you to download and use without charge; however, the software is protected by copyright law, meaning you can use it only in the ways proscribed by the author. For example, you cannot distribute it to someone else, unless the author gives you permission to do so. **Shareware** is software that you can download and try out, but you are expected to pay for the software if you decide to use it on a permanent basis. You can search

 @Source

To review the online gaming Web sites discussed in this section, visit the Discovering the Internet Chapter 5 Web page (**scsite .com/internet/ch5**) and click a link below Online Gaming.

sites such as FreewareWeb.com, Tucows, CNET Download.com, Kids Freeware, and CNET Shareware.com for freeware or shareware screen savers, games, utilities, file compression programs, and more. You also can purchase and download software and software updates from vendor sites such as Microsoft, Adobe, and Macromedia.

File Transfer Protocol (FTP) Sites

As you learned in Chapter 1, FTP is an Internet standard that allows you to download or upload files to and from other computers connected to the Internet. You can use FTP to view a directory of files located on a remote computer, called an **FTP site**, and then open or download a file. You also can upload a file to an FTP site.

To access an FTP site, you log on with a user name and a password. Public FTP sites, such as those provided by government agencies, some colleges and universities, and other organizations, are called **anonymous FTP sites** because anyone can log on to these sites using anonymous as their user name. As a courtesy to the site administrator, anonymous users often enter their e-mail addresses at the password prompt, although a password is not required for a public FTP site. Private FTP sites, such as those operated by a private company for its employees' use, restrict access to authorized users, who must enter a unique user name and a unique password.

You can download or upload files using FTP in three ways: by typing instructions using a command-line interface, by using an FTP client program, or by using your Web browser. A **command-line interface**, such as the Command Prompt window included with the Windows operating system, provides a non-graphical interface in which you can enter commands at a command prompt (Figure 5-78). To use FTP via the Command Prompt window, click the Run command on the Start menu to open the Run dialog box and then enter the command, ftp. You then enter a series of commands to log on to the FTP site and download or upload your files.

Figure 5-78   Command-line interface.

An **FTP client**, such as CuteFTP or WS_FTP Pro, is a program that offers an easy-to-use graphical user interface containing menu commands and toolbar shortcuts (Figure 5-79). FTP clients generally use an interface similar to other file management programs with which you already may be familiar, such as Windows Explorer. To upload or download files, you simply:

1. Start the FTP client. Select or enter the information for the FTP site to which you want to connect.

Figure 5-79   FedWorld FTP site in CuteFTP window.

2. Enter your user name and password and connect to the site.

3. Specify the source location (where the file is stored) and the destination location (where the file is to be downloaded or uploaded).

4. Select a file or files.

5. Click a menu command or toolbar button to begin the download or upload process.

The FTP client automatically issues the necessary FTP commands to download or upload the selected file(s).

As you learned in Chapter 1, you also can use your Web browser to download files from FTP sites. To navigate to an FTP site, you type the FTP site's URL in the Address box in the same way in which you type a Web site's URL. FTP sites' URLs start with ftp://, to represent the File Transfer Protocol (FTP), instead of the http:// used for Web sites' URLs.

When you enter an FTP site's URL to access an anonymous FTP site using your Web browser, the browser automatically logs you on as an anonymous user. You can upload a file to an FTP site using a command-line prompt or an FTP client. You can also upload a file to an FTP site by logging onto the site from your Web browser and then using drag-and-drop to drag a file from another open window, such as My Computer, to the FTP site.

The following steps access the Library of Congress FTP site and download two files: a text document and a compressed file.

@Source

To read the Internet Education Foundation's Online Safety Guide for Kids, visit the Discovering the Internet Chapter 2 Web page (**scsite.com/ internet/ch2**) and click Kids' Safety.

 In Netscape

To accomplish this task in Netscape, see Accessing the Library of Congress in Appendix A.

Steps: To Access the Library of Congress FTP Site

1 If necessary, start your Web browser. Type `ftp://ftp .loc.gov` in the Address box, and click the Go button or press ENTER. Point to the pub folder.

The FTP site's URL is displayed in the Address box (Figure 5-80). The Web browser automatically logs you on to the anonymous FTP site hosted by the Library of Congress. The root directory at the Library of Congress public FTP site contains several subfolders.

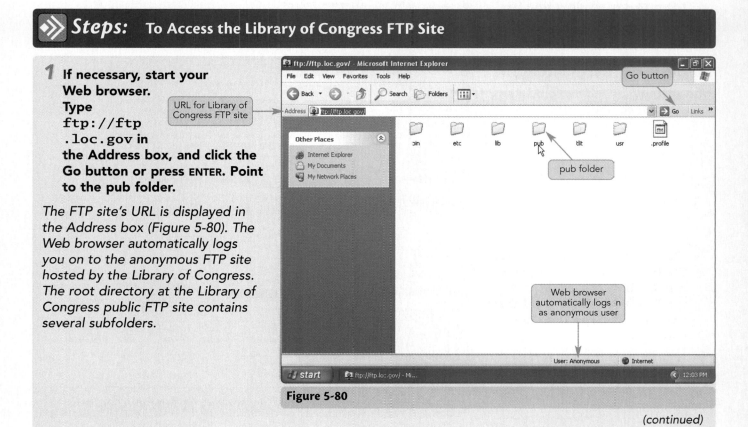

Figure 5-80

(continued)

2 **Double-click the pub folder icon and view the folder's contents. Point to the README file icon.**

FTP site URL indicates pub directory contents displayed

The pub folder has several subfolders containing files on various topics of public interest, in addition to individual documents that you can open and view from the site or download (Figure 5-81).

Figure 5-81

3 **Double-click the README file icon and scroll down the document to view its contents. Point to the Close button on the browser window title bar.**

FTP site URL indicates README file displayed

The README file opens in its own browser window (Figure 5-82). The README file lists the contents of the various files and subfolders in the /pub directory.

LIBRARY OF CONGRESS
FILES AVAILABLE THROUGH FTP

ftp.loc.gov (140.147.2.69)

The Library of Congress has placed a variety of files on a central computer for anonymous file transfer by Internet users. The address of this FTP host is FTP.LOC.GOV (140.147.2.69).

Once connected to this address, look in the /pub directory to find the various files and directories described below:

/pub/american.memory

Figure 5-82

4 **Click the Close button to close the browser window displaying the README file. Right-click the README file icon and then point to the Copy To Folder command.**

You can download a copy of this document by copying it to a folder on your hard disk or a floppy disk (Figure 5-83).

Figure 5-83

5 **Click the Copy To Folder command. When the Browse For Folder dialog box displays, point to the OK button.**

The Browse For Folder dialog box allows you to specify the destination folder (Figure 5-84). The default folder is the My Documents folder on your hard disk.

Browse For Folder dialog box

Browse For Folder

Copy the selected item(s) to the folder:

- Desktop
  - My Documents
  - My Computer
  - My Network Places

default destination

Folder: My Documents

Make New Folder   OK   Cancel

OK button

Figure 5-84

6 **Click the OK button. Point to the american.memory subfolder.**

The README file is copied to the My Documents folder on your hard disk (Figure 5-85). The american.memory folder contains information about the Library of Congress American Memory Project.

american.memory subfolder

Figure 5-85

(continued)

7   **Double-click the american.memory subfolder icon and then double-click the docuview subfolder icon. Point to the libcong.zip file icon.**

*The docuview folder contains two compressed files, both with a .zip extension (Figure 5-86). Very large files or sets of files often are **compressed** to save storage space.*

Figure 5-86

8   **Double-click the libcong.zip file icon. When the File Download dialog box appears, point to the Save button.**

The File Download dialog box appears (Figure 5-87). Clicking the Save button downloads and saves the file to a hard disk or floppy disk. Clicking the Open button opens the file directly from the FTP site.

Figure 5-87

9 Click the Save button. When the Save As dialog box appears, click the My Documents icon and then click the Save button.

The Save As dialog box (Figure 5-88) opens. The compressed file, libcong.zip, is saved to the My Documents folder on your hard disk.

Figure 5-88

If you download a compressed file, as in the previous steps, you then must decompress it using a file compression utility. A **file compression utility** is a program that compresses one or more files so that they require less storage space, and decompresses compressed files to restore them to their original sizes. WinZip is one of the most widely used file compression utilities; files compressed using WinZip have a **.zip** file extension. For this reason, compressing a file often is referred to as **zipping** a file, while decompressing a file often is referred to as **unzipping** a file.

As shown in the previous steps, FTP sites use a directory structure of folders and subfolders. Depending on whether you log on to the site at the root folder or a subfolder, you may see a directory as a list of linked folder names or as a group of folder icons. You can click a linked folder name or double-click a folder icon to open a folder and view its contents. You can double-click a file icon to open the file at the site. Double-clicking some file icons, such as that for a compressed file, opens a dialog box that allows you to either open the file at the FTP site or download it.

 @Source

To review the Web sites discussed in this section, visit the Discovering the Internet Chapter 5 Web page (**scsite .com/internet/ch5**) and click a link below Downloading/ Uploading Files.

 In Netscape

When you log on to an FTP site using Netscape Navigator, you see both a folder icon and a linked folder name. You can click the icon or name to open the folder. You click a file icon to open it at the site or to download it.

P2P File-Sharing Networks

Another way to share or transfer files is via a peer-to-peer (P2P) file-sharing network. A **peer-to-peer (P2P) file-sharing network** allows files to be transferred between individual personal computers located on the same local area network (LAN) or between individual personal computers connected via the Internet. P2P file-sharing networks, such as Kazaa, Grokster, Morpheus, and Napster, exploded in popularity as a means for individuals to share music, video, and other files stored on their personal computers. Unfortunately, many users of these P2P file-sharing networks are sharing material — music, movies, and software — that is protected by U.S. copyright law. In fact, the music and movie industries, through the Recording Industry Association of America (RIAA) and the Motion Picture Association of America (MPAA), are working to stop the piracy of copyrighted material by such P2P file-sharing networks.

Music and video file sharing, while popular, are not the only uses of P2P networks. Commercial applications of P2P file-sharing networks include sharing product information between several thousand employees and researchers and distributing training materials to employees. The SETI@Home project (based at the University of California, Berkeley) uses P2P file-sharing technologies to harness the unused capacity of thousands of home computers to perform radio-telescope data analyses. Many Internet analysts expect more and more organizations to use P2P technologies in the future to distribute network processes to individual users.

@Issue Responsible Internet Access

It is nearing the end of the work day and you are thinking about Aunt Sophie's birthday next week. You quickly access an online bookstore and order a book by her favorite author. Or you need a mid-morning work break, so you spend a few minutes at a news-oriented Web site reviewing today's news headlines. Or you only have slow dial-up Internet access at home, so as soon as you get to work, you log on to a P2P file-sharing network and use your company's high-speed Internet access to download music files by your favorite artist.

Most workers assume that no one gets hurt if you spend time on the Internet at the office for personal reasons. The staggering statistics, however, show that is far from the case. A 2002 survey by Websense International, Ltd., indicates that, while at work, more than 65 percent of U.S. workers access news sites for personal reasons; more than 35 percent shop online for personal items; and about 2 percent admit to viewing pornography or gambling online. Sending and receiving personal e-mail and

instant messaging at work also contribute to the problem. And U.S. workers are not alone. More than 60 percent of workers in the U.K. lose at least two hours of work time per week by accessing the Internet and the Web for personal reasons at work.

Cyberslacking, or using the Internet and the Web for personal use at work, costs companies around the world billions of dollars in lost productivity each year. Further, downloading music and video files eats away at a company's expensive Internet access bandwidth, slowing down legitimate business activities. Sending and receiving personal e-mail and downloading files can expose a company's network to viruses and other security breaches. Viewing pornography sites or hate sites at work creates a hostile work environment and increases a company's liability for expensive and embarrassing lawsuits.

Increasingly, companies are protecting themselves from cyberslacking in several ways, including:

- Formulating clear Internet use policies.

- Educating employees about Internet use policies and then following through with appropriate action when an employee violates those policies.

- Controlling which employees have Internet access.

- Installing monitoring software that provides information on individual employees' Internet activities.

- Installing filtering software that blocks access to non-business sites and filters e-mail.

What should you do to access the Internet at work responsibly? Carefully read and understand your company's Internet access policies and follow them. When in doubt, ask your supervisor for clarification on the policies. Resist the urge to shop, chat, play online games, send personal e-mail, or send instant messages to friends during work hours, unless your company permits these kinds of activities. Remember that downloading copyrighted music, videos, and software — either at work or at home — without paying for the downloaded material is piracy and therefore against the law.

CHAPTER REVIEW

The Chapter Review section summarizes the concepts presented in the chapter.

1 Why Are More Individuals Using Online Information Sources?

More Internet users are going online to get news, weather, sports, and traffic information from news-oriented Web sites because these sites share four primary characteristics: availability, immediacy, interactivity, and customizability. You can access hundreds of news-oriented Web sites from home, work, or school. These sites are updated quickly with breaking stories as events happen; many also include interactive features and customization to make the sites interesting and tailored to a user's specific interests.

2 What Is Streaming Media?

Some Web sites, such as news-oriented Web sites, use streaming media to deliver on-the-spot news stories or commentary. **Streaming media** is audio and video transmitted continuously from a Web server to your browser. By using a streaming media player, you can view and hear streaming media content as it is being transmitted.

3 What Types of Research and Reference Tools Are Available Online?

Online dictionaries, encyclopedias, reference desks, and trip planners provide you with convenient 24 × 7 access to information on specific topics, fast facts, word definitions, and driving directions — all without having to make a trip to the local library.

4 Where Can Users Find Health, Entertainment, Hobby, and Other Special-Interest Information?

You can find health, diet, and fitness information at thousands of Web sites. The information presented at a health or fitness Web site, however, always should be evaluated carefully. Thousands of Internet users, including more and more seniors, are turning to special-interest Web sites to enjoy entertainment information, practice their hobbies, look for jobs, make new friends, trace their family tree, and a host of other activities.

5 What Web Resources Are Available for Managing Your Personal Finances?

Managing your personal finances with online tools is fast, easy, and convenient. Online banking services provided by **brick-and-click businesses** and **cyberbanks** allow you to complete most common banking transactions, such as reviewing your account balance and details and paying your bills. **Bill presentment** and **bill payment services** are offered by banks, e-businesses devoted to bill payment, and even the U.S. Postal Service. Many utility and credit card companies also allow you to set up a payment account and then pay your monthly bill at their Web sites.

When you are considering a major purchase such as a new home or auto, Web-based financial calculators help you determine how much you can afford to spend and estimate a monthly mortgage or auto payment. The Web provides a wide variety of information sources to help you evaluate credit card offers and manage credit card usage. You also can manage your own investments using investment-oriented Web sites or practice managing your investments at sites that offer online investment simulations and mock portfolios.

 What Education Resources Are Available on the Web?

CHAPTER REVIEW

The Chapter Review section summarizes the concepts presented in the chapter.

Millions of people around the world are taking advantage of **Web-based learning** opportunities made possible by the Internet and the Web. K–12 public schools, colleges, and universities use Web-based learning to enrich their curriculums and offer online instructor-led credit and non-credit courses. Employers and professionals are embracing Web-based learning as an efficient, cost-effective way to deliver employee training programs, complete continuing education courses, or prepare for technical certification exams. Other people are taking online courses for personal growth or for enrichment of their lives.

 Why Is Shopping Online So Popular and What Online Tools Can You Use to Shop Online More Effectively?

Consumers increasingly are shopping online because of the availability of Internet access, the improved design of online stores, a growing trust in the online purchasing process, and increasing satisfaction with their shopping results. The two primary reasons consumers shop online are to save time and to save money. **Shopping guides** help consumers locate online stores. **Shopping bots** help consumers search for a specific item and then compare the item's price and features at multiple online stores at one time. Online auctions provide a mechanism for buyers and sellers to agree on a price for an item and then work together to arrange payment and delivery.

 What Kinds of Games Can You Play Online?

Today, the audience for online games includes children, young men and women, and adults of all ages. You can play card games, board games, casino games, word games, trivia games, arcade games, and strategy or role-playing games online — either alone, with a friend, or with thousands of other players.

 How Can You Download or Upload Files over the Internet?

Several popular Web sites offer **freeware** and **shareware** software downloads. You also can download software from vendors' Web sites. Some of these download sites use FTP to allow you to log on to a remote computer, called an **FTP site**, and transfer files. You can enter FTP commands at a command-line prompt, use an **FTP client**, or use your Web browser to access an FTP site. Public FTP sites are called **anonymous FTP sites** because anyone can log on using anonymous as their user name and no password is required. Private FTP sites require you to log on with a unique user name and password. Once you log on to an FTP site, you can view and navigate its directory structure of folders and subfolders and download or upload files.

Another way to transfer files is over a P2P file-sharing network, where files can be transferred from one computer to another over a local area network (LAN) or the Internet. While commercial applications for P2P technologies do exist, today, P2P file-sharing networks are used most widely to transfer music and video files between individual users over the Internet.

TERMS TO KNOW

After reading this chapter, you should know each term.

anonymous FTP sites (*302*)
bid (*299*)
bill payment service (*283*)
bill presentment (*284*)
brick-and-click business (*281*)
bricks-and-mortar business (*281*)
command-line interface (*302*)
compressed (*306*)
cyberbank (*281*)
cyberslacking (*309*)
e-bills (*284*)
escrow (*299*)
file compression utility (*307*)
freeware (*301*)
FTP client (*302*)
FTP site (*302*)

marketspace (*294*)
online learning (*289*)
peer-to-peer (P2P) file-sharing network (*308*)
reserve price (*298*)
shareware (*301*)
shopping bot (*295*)
shopping guide (*295*)
streaming media (*253*)
sticky Web site (*248*)
subscription-based game (*299*)
unzipping (*307*)
Web-based learning (*289*)
.zip (*307*)
zipping (*307*)

TEST YOUR KNOWLEDGE

Use the Test Your Knowledge exercises to check your knowledge of the chapter.

 True or False

Mark T for True and F for False. (Answers are found on page numbers in parentheses.)

_____ 1. A Web site that viewers visit often and browse for longer periods of time is a shopping bot. (*295*)

_____ 2. Many news-oriented Web sites provide the ability to customize content, which means they can display information tailored to the user's locality and interests. (*248*)

_____ 3. To find out what time it is in Berlin or what important event took place on today's date in history, you can use an online reference desk Web site. (*261*)

_____ 4. All health information on the Web has been evaluated and certified as accurate by health care professionals. (*273*)

_____ 5. A cyberbank has both online and physical banking facilities. (*281*)

_____ 6. Bill presentment is the process of sending bills electronically instead of mailing paper bills or statements. (*284*)

_____ 7. A command-line interface, such as CuteFTP or WS_FTP Pro, offers an easy-to-use graphical user interface containing FTP commands and toolbar shortcuts. (*302*)

_____ 8. Consumers often shop online for a major purchase, such as an auto, but then buy at a brick-and-mortar location. (*295*)

_____ 9. The term marketspace is used to distinguish the virtual location in which e-business is conducted from the conventional physical marketplaces in which business takes place. (*294*)

_____ 10. Software you can download and use for free on a permanent basis is called shareware. (*301*)

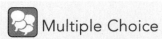 Multiple Choice

Select the best answer. (Answers are found on page numbers in parentheses.)

1. File-sharing networks that allow users to transfer files between individual personal computers located on the same LAN or between Internet-connected individual computers are called _____ networks. (*308*)
   a. FTP
   b. C2C
   c. P2P
   d. NPR

2. A business that allows customers to conduct business or complete transactions at a physical location, as well as online at a Web site is a _____ business. (*281*)
   a. cyberbank
   b. brick-and-click
   c. bricks-and-mortar
   d. dealership

3. _____ gaming allows you to pay a small monthly fee to play strategy or role-playing games online with thousands of other players. (*299*)
   a. Subscription-based
   b. Casino
   c. Virtual reality
   d. None of the above

4. When shopping online for a specific item, you can compare prices from multiple online stores by using a shopping _____ . (*295*)
   a. cart
   b. bot
   c. list
   d. report

5. Kazaa, Grokster, and Morpheus are examples of _____ . (*308*)
   a. subscription-based games
   b. cyberbanks
   c. FTP clients
   d. P2P file-sharing networks

6. Using bill presentment to send _____ can reduce a company's billing costs substantially. (*284*)
   a. data files
   b. e-bills
   c. Web pages
   d. none of the above

7. Web-based learning is being used effectively for _____ . (*289*)
   a. high school courses
   b. employee training
   c. continuing professional development
   d. all of the above

8. Because of the risk of fraud, some auction sites hold payment in _____ until the buyer has received the purchased item or service. (*299*)
   a. reserve accounts
   b. non-delivery
   c. escrow
   d. all of the above

9. A public FTP site also is called a(n) _____ . (*302*)
   a. open FTP site
   b. anonymous FTP site
   c. nameless FTP site
   d. unknown FTP site

10. Audio and video content transmitted continuously from a Web server to a Web browser is called _____ . (*253*)
    a. anonymous file transfer
    b. P2P file sharing
    c. streaming media
    d. none of the above

LEARN IT ONLINE

Use the Learn It Online exercises to reinforce your understanding of the chapter concepts and terms.

Instructions: To complete the Learn It Online exercises, start your browser, click the Address bar, and then enter the Web address **scsite.com/internet/ch5**. Follow the instructions in the exercises below. Each exercise has instructions for printing your results, either for your own records or for submission to your instructor.

1 Chapter Reinforcement

TF, MC, and SA
Click the Chapter Reinforcement link. Print the quiz by clicking Print on the File menu for each page. Answer each question.

2 Flash Cards

Click the Flash Cards link and read the instructions. Type 20 (or a number specified by your instructor) in the Number of playing cards text box, type your name in the Enter your Name text box, and then click the Flip Card button. When the flash card is displayed, read the question and then click the Answer box arrow to select an answer. Flip through Flash Cards. If your score is 15 (75%) correct or greater, click Print on the File menu to print your results. If your score is less than 15 (75%) correct, then redo this exercise by clicking the Replay button.

3 Practice Test

Click the Practice Test link. Answer each question, enter your first and last name at the bottom of the page, and then click the Grade Test button. When the graded practice test is displayed on your screen, click Print on the File menu to print a hard copy. Continue to take practice tests until you score 80% or better.

4 Who Wants To Be a Computer Genius?

Click the Computer Genius link. Read the instructions, enter your first and last name at the bottom of the page, and then click the Play button. When your score is displayed, click the Print Results link to print a hard copy.

5 Crossword Puzzle Challenge

Below Chapter 5, click the Crossword Puzzle Challenge link. Read the instructions, and then enter your first and last name. Click the SUBMIT button. Work the crossword puzzle. When you are finished, click the Submit button. When the crossword puzzle is redisplayed, click the Print Puzzle button to print a hard copy.

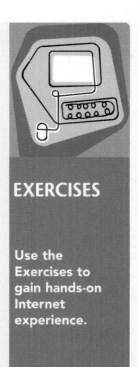

To perform the following exercises, you must be connected to the Internet and have access to a printer. You also need an e-mail address for some of the exercises.

1   Subscribing to and Unsubscribing from a Mailing List

1. Visit the Discovering the Internet Chapter 5 Web page (**scsite.com/internet/ch5**) and click The New York Times on the Web below Exercise 1.

2. If the membership pop-up window opens, follow the instructions and links to create a membership account with your own user name, password, e-mail address, and other information. Accept the default options for e-mail preferences. If the membership pop-up window does not open, click the REGISTER NOW link on the home page and create your account. A membership account is free of charge and gives you access to certain features at the Web site. Close all advertisement pop-up windows that might appear.

3. On the home page, click the E-Mail Preferences link in the Member Center section of the left navigation bar. When the Your E-Mail Preferences page appears, modify your e-mail preferences in the Today's Headlines section to change the number of headlines and major sections for which you want to receive a daily e-mail message as desired. Click the Save Selections button at the bottom of the page to save your new e-mail preferences. Click the Home navigation button at the top left of the page to return to the home page.

4. Click the Editorials/Op-Ed link in the Opinion section of the left navigation bar. Review three editorial/opinion articles of your choice. Write a brief summary of each article, including why you do or do not agree with the author.

5. Click the Readers' Opinions link in the Opinion section of the left navigation bar. Review three opinion forums. Respond to other readers' comments in the forum of your choice.

6. Navigate to the home page. On the home page, click the E-Mail Preferences link in the Member Center section of the left navigation bar. In the E-mail Delivery Options area, click the To unsubscribe from all e-mail products, click here link. Click the Unsubscribe button at the bottom of the page to cancel your subscription to NYTimes.com e-mail services.

2   Customizing a News-Oriented Web Site

1. Visit the Discovering the Internet Chapter 5 Web page (**scsite.com/internet/ch5**) and click MSNBC News below Exercise 2.

2. Scroll down the page and locate the Zip Code and Enter your favorite stock symbol text boxes. Type your U.S. ZIP code in the Zip Code text box. If you do not have a U.S. ZIP code, type 19610 as the Zip code. Type the following stock symbols in the Stock Symbol text boxes: TOC, DELL, and BA. Click the GO button.

(continued)

EXERCISES

Use the Exercises to gain hands-on Internet experience.

EXERCISES *(continued)*

3. Scroll down the MSNBC home page to view how the page now is customized with your local weather and news, selected stock quotes and information, and sports. Click the Change my sports choices link to open the Personalize My News pop-up window. Modify your sports preferences as desired and then click the Save & Exit button. Scroll down the MSNBC home page to view the changes to your sports preferences.

4. Click the Remove weather from my page link in the Weather section to remove that section. Remove the Local News, Business, and Sports sections.

3 Using Online Resources to Research a Report Topic

1. Visit the Discovering the Internet Chapter 5 Web page (**scsite.com/internet/ch5**) and click any of the online encyclopedia and reference desk links below Exercise 3 to find answers to the following questions.
   a. Where is Afghanistan located? Who are its geographical neighbors? Where can I find a map of Afghanistan and its geographical neighbors? What are its major cities and towns?
   b. What is Afghanistan's political and religious history?
   c. What is the current population of Afghanistan? Into what ethnic groups is the Afghanistan population divided?
   d. What is the basis of Afghanistan's economy?

2. Write a short, one- or two-page report describing the geography, history, population, and economy of Afghanistan. Follow the directions provided by your instructor on how to cite your online sources.

4 Planning an Automobile Trip Using Online Resources

1. Visit the Discovering the Internet Chapter 5 Web page (**scsite.com/internet/ch5**) and click FreeTrip.com below Exercise 4.

2. Plan a road trip from your location to Vancouver, British Columbia. If you do not live in North America, plan a trip from Dallas, Texas, to Vancouver, British Columbia. Select options to include scenic routes and references to camping locations along the way.

3. Use the personal itinerary created by FreeTrip.com to answer the following questions:
   a. How many miles will I drive?
   b. What is the total driving time to arrive at my destination?

4. Print the itinerary page.

5. Plan the trip a second time, but do not select scenic routes. Use the personal itinerary created by FreeTrip.com to compare the new itinerary's miles and hours driven with the original itinerary.

6. Print the new itinerary page.

5 Evaluating the Credibility of Online Health Information

1. Visit the Discovering the Internet Chapter 5 Web page (**scsite.com/internet/ch5**) and click URAC below Exercise 5.

2. Use the navigational links at the URAC Web site to answer the following questions:
   a. What is the URAC mission and how is the organization structured?
   b. What services does URAC provide?
   c. Which of the following health-oriented Web sites is accredited by URAC: VegetarianCentral.org, Health & Fitness Tips, Shape Up America, WebMD, or MDAdvice.com? (***Hint***: Use the Directory navigation button on the home page to find a link to a list of accredited organizations.)

3. Visit the Discovering the Internet Chapter 5 Web page (**scsite.com/internet/ch5**) and click HON below Exercise 5.

4. Use the information and the navigational links at the Health On The Net (HON) Web site to answer the following questions:
   a. Where is HON located and what is its mission?
   b. Who are the HON sponsors?
   c. What global organization is affiliated with HON?
   d. Which of the following health-oriented Web sites is accredited by HON: Body Positive, WebMD, Medscape, or DrWeil.com? (***Hint***: Use the MedHunt search feature on the home page to search for each site.)

5. Visit the Discovering the Internet Chapter 5 Web page (**scsite.com/internet/ch5**) and click CAPHIS below Exercise 5.

6. Follow various navigational links to identify at least five Web sites that meet the CAPHIS standards. Print each Web site's home page.

6 Exploring Special-Interest Web Sites

1. Visit the Discovering the Internet Chapter 5 Web page (**scsite.com/internet/ch5**) and click Monster below Exercise 6.

2. Click the Search Jobs navigation button. When the Job Search page appears, click the Career Advice link at the top of the page.

3. Click the Get Resume Advice link in the Resume Tips section of the Career Advice page. Use the links on the Resume Center page to answer the following questions:
   a. Dos and Don'ts link: What are three common résumé blunders?
   b. Dilemmas link: What are four tips for creating a concise résumé?
   c. Cover Letters and More link: What are three things to avoid in a cover letter?
   d. Dilemmas link: How can a recent graduate solve the dilemma of structuring a résumé to compensate for limited work experience?

4. Visit the Discovering the Internet Chapter 5 Web page (**scsite.com/internet/ch5**) and click RootsWeb.com below Exercise 6.

(continued)

EXERCISES

Use the
Exercises to
gain hands-on
Internet
experience.

EXERCISES *(continued)*

5. Enter your last name in the Search RootsWeb Last Name text box and click Search. Use the Search Results page to respond to the following:
   a. List the featured databases that contain your last name.
   b. List at least three vital records indexes that contain your last name.
   c. List two additional Web site searches that include your last name.

6. Click several of the links and review the content on the linked pages. Click the Back button to return to the Search Results page.

7. Visit the Discovering the Internet Chapter 5 Web page (scsite.com/internet/ch5) and click Peterson's Education Portal below Exercise 6.

8. Use the information on the Peterson's home page and the navigational links to learn which online practice tests are available for graduate admissions. Create a list of the available tests.

7 Managing Your Personal Finances Online

1. Visit the Discovering the Internet Chapter 5 Web page (scsite.com/internet/ch5) and click Citibank below Exercise 7.

2. Click the Planning & Tools link near the top of the page. Click the Calculators drop-down list arrow and then click Savings in the Calculators list. Click OK if you are advised that you are viewing pages over a secure connection. Use the Savings calculators to answer the following questions:
   a. At what age will I become a millionaire if I immediately start saving or investing $150 per month at an expected 8 percent return? (Enter your age in the Your Current Age text box; enter zero (0) in the Amount You Now Have text box; enter 150 in Amount You Can Save Monthly text box and 8 in the Return You Can Earn text box; use the calculator's default values for all other values.)
   b. What monthly investment should I make to become a millionaire by age 65 at an expected 8 percent return?

3. Visit the Discovering the Internet Chapter 5 Web page (scsite.com/internet/ch5) and click FTC below Exercise 7.

4. Click the Consumer Protection link and then click the Identity Theft link. Using information and links at this site, answer the following questions:
   a. What are four ways in which an identity thief works?
   b. How can you minimize your risk of identity theft?
   c. What should you do if you are a victim of identity theft?

5. Visit the Discovering the Internet Chapter 5 Web page (scsite.com/internet/ch5) and click Wells Fargo below Exercise 7.

6. Search the Wells Fargo site using the keywords credit cards 101, and then click the Well Fargo Student – Credit card 101 link.

7. Follow the links to complete Lesson 1 of Credit Cards 101. Use the information in this lesson to answer the following questions:
   a. What is a credit card's APR?
   b. What does the phrase, available credit, mean?
   c. What are some types of charges you may incur on a credit card?

8. Visit the Discovering the Internet Chapter 5 Web page (**scsite.com/internet/ch5**) and click IORC below Exercise 7.

9. Click the Investing Simulator Center link and then complete the Find Out What It's Like To Trade Online simulation. Using the information in the simulation, answer the following questions:
   a. What are market orders?
   b. What are limit orders?

EXERCISES

Use the Exercises to gain hands-on Internet experience.

8 Continuing Your Education Online

1. Visit the Discovering the Internet Chapter 5 Web page (**scsite.com/internet/ch5**) and click WorldWideLearn below Exercise 8.

2. Use the links on the WorldWideLearn page to research technical writing courses. Then compare at least three online technical writing courses. Include the following information in your table:
   a. Institution's name, address, telephone number, and e-mail address.
   b. Type of course: credit, non-credit, certificate, or adult continuing education.
   c. Duration of the course.
   d. Major topics covered in the course.
   e. How the course is conducted: instructor-led, e-mail, discussion groups, and so forth.
   f. Cost for the course.
   g. Any other characteristics of the course that you find important.

3. Using the comparison table you created in Step 3, select a course and explain in two or three short paragraphs why you would choose this course over the others.

9 Shopping for a Laptop Computer Online

1. Visit the Discovering the Internet Chapter 5 Web page (**scsite.com/internet/ch5**) and click online auction, shopping bot, and overstock links below Exercise 9 to shop for a new or used notebook computer priced under $1,200.

2. Create a list of at least three available laptops, including the online store, manufacturer, model, features, and price.

3. Use your shopping research to answer the following questions:
   a. Which online shopping sites offered you the most laptop computer choices?
   b. Which online shopping site(s) provided useful product or consumer reviews for the laptop computer listings?
   c. Which laptop is the best bargain, and why?

(continued)

EXERCISES

Use the
Exercises to
gain hands-on
Internet
experience.

EXERCISES (continued)

10 Downloading Files and File Sharing

1. Visit the Discovering the Internet Chapter 5 Web page (**scsite.com/internet/ch5**) and click the download site links below Exercise 10 to locate a freeware screen-saver program and download the file. If you are working in a computer lab or on a school computer, ask your instructor's permission before you download the file.

2. Visit the Discovering the Internet Chapter 5 Web page (**scsite.com/internet/ch5**) and click TechWeb TechEncyclopedia below Exercise 10.

3. Search the TechWeb TechEncyclopedia for information you can use to answer the following questions:
   a. What is peer-to-peer computing?
   b. What is a peer-to-peer network?

4. Visit the Discovering the Internet Chapter 5 Web page (**scsite.com/internet/ch5**) and click AlltheWeb below Exercise 10.

5. Search for anonymous FTP sites that have the WinZip file compression utility. Print the search results Web page.

CHAPTER 6
Understanding Internet Technologies and Security

Introduction

The Internet and the Web are dramatically changing the way individuals around the world work, play, and communicate with others. At the heart of these changes are the technologies that make it possible to connect to the Internet and then send an e-mail, download a file from a server, or shop safely online for the latest music CD. In Chapters 1 and 2, you were introduced to circuit switching, packet switching, the TCP and IP protocols, the Domain Name System (DNS), IP addresses, URLs, and other fundamental networking and internetworking technologies. In this chapter, you will learn about local, metropolitan, and wide area networks and the devices that connect them together; how IP addresses are structured; how the DNS server hierarchy resolves domain names to IP addresses; and how network service providers facilitate the exchange of data across the Internet backbone. You also will learn about the wireless Web; how the Internet is converging with traditional telephony, television, and conferencing; and about network security threats and security technologies.

OBJECTIVES

After completing this chapter, you will be able to:

1. Discuss basic networking technologies

2. Describe the infrastructure of the Internet, including network service providers, the TCP/IP stack, IP addresses, and the Domain Name System (DNS)

3. Identify wireless services and describe wireless Web protocols

4. Describe the convergence of the Internet with telephony, television, and conferencing

5. Discuss internal and external network security threats, transactional risks, and network security technologies

CONTENTS

Networking Basics

As you have learned, a computer network connects two or more computers, printers, or other devices together with cables or wireless media, making it possible for users to share data, expensive equipment, and other network resources such as an Internet connection. A simple computer network for a small business or home office may have only two or three computers and a single printer connected via cables. A large, complex computer network may have thousands of computers in a number of worldwide locations communicating with each other using a combination of transmission media.

Local, Metropolitan, and Wide Area Networks

Modern networks can be categorized by the physical area they cover: a local area, a metropolitan area, or a wide area.

LOCAL AREA NETWORKS   As discussed in Chapter 1, a local area network (LAN) is a computer network supporting users in a small geographical area such as a home, an office, a single building, or several buildings such as on a college campus. Each computer or other device on a LAN is called a **node**; these nodes communicate with each other via cables or wireless media, such as radio waves. LANs are configured in one of two basic structures: peer-to-peer or client/server.

✋ Facts@Hand

In Chapter 5, you learned about peer-to-peer (P2P) file-sharing networks that allow Internet-connected users to transfer files between individual computers. The term peer-to-peer also is used to describe the way in which computers and other devices are connected in a simple LAN.

A **peer-to-peer LAN** consists of a small number of personal computers (generally 10 or fewer) connected together. One or more of the computers also may have a printer, a scanner, or an external storage device attached to it (Figure 6-1). To connect to the peer-to-peer LAN, each computer must have a network interface card. A **network interface card** (**NIC**), sometimes called a **network card**, is an internal expansion card

hub

shared printer

individual
network node

desktop operating
system on each
computer

Figure 6-1   A small number of personal computers connected together in a peer-to-peer LAN.

that enables a computer or other device to access a network. The computers on a peer-to-peer LAN can be connected to each other via one main cable. More commonly, however, the computers on a peer-to-peer LAN are connected at a common connection point on the network, using a hub. A **hub** is an inexpensive hardware device used to connect multiple nodes on the same network.

Users on a peer-to-peer LAN can access files stored on any of the networked computers and use any peripheral devices connected to the computers. For example, if your computer is part of a peer-to-peer LAN, you can open a file stored on another user's computer, save it to your hard drive, and then send the file to a printer attached to a different user's computer. You control access to files and printers by setting options in the desktop operating system of the individual computers connected to the peer-to-peer LAN.

A peer-to-peer LAN is an attractive networking choice for a home office or for a small business or other organization just getting started with computer networking, because it is simple to configure and inexpensive to use. A peer-to-peer LAN is not a practical option to connect more than a few computers, however. An organization thus may outgrow a peer-to-peer LAN quickly, as more computers need to be added or file- and device-sharing becomes more complex. Additionally, a peer-to-peer LAN lacks robust security options.

When a peer-to-peer LAN structure is not appropriate, an alternative LAN structure called a client/server network is used. In Chapter 2, you were introduced to client/server computing, in which client computers request resources from servers. A **client/server network** consists of multiple personal computers or workstations (clients), one or more servers, and other devices such as printers (Figure 6-2). The servers enable the clients to share data, file storage space, peripheral devices, and an Internet connection. A client/server LAN uses a **network operating system** to manage data storage, printer access, communications, Internet connections, security, and network administration. Examples of network operating systems include Microsoft Windows XP, Microsoft Windows 2000, UNIX, and Novell NetWare. Figure 6-3 on the next page describes the different types of services provided by a network operating system.

Figure 6-2   Multiple personal computers, servers, and printers can be connected on a client/server network.

Network Service	Importance
File Services	Permit the centralized storage of files on a file server, which can be accessed by any authorized user on the network. Maintaining backup copies of critical files protects against accidentally deleted files, damaged files, or files lost to natural or man-made disasters. Files stored centrally on a file server are backed up more easily than files stored on individual computer hard drives.
Print Services	Enable users to share printers across a network. Replacing multiple individual printers with one or two high-speed networked printers can reduce equipment costs and increase productivity.
Mail Services	Manage the sending, receiving, routing, and storage of e-mail messages. E-mail is now a critical component of any organization's communications with employees, clients, and vendors. Mail services enable e-mail communications to flow smoothly.
Communications Services	Allow authorized users to connect to the network when out of the office. Network users may need to keep up with their e-mail messages or work with their data files when they are not in the office. Communications services permit remote users to connect to the network.
Internet Services	Manage internal Web-based services, external Internet access, and other Internet-based services such as Web servers, Web browsers, and Internet-based e-mail. Organizations today use Internet-based e-mail to send and receive messages from clients or vendors outside the organization. Many organizations also use internal Web pages to support internal business operations. Additionally, external Web pages are used to sell products and services and provide customer support. Internet services help manage these critical operations.
Management Services	Enable network administrators to perform a variety of tasks important to the health and operation of the network. Network administrators perform a number of important tasks such as determining the level of network activity, detecting and solving network hardware and software problems, and distributing software to users. These and other complex management tasks are made easier with management services.

Figure 6-3 A network operating system provides a variety of services on a client/server network.

The ability of a client/server LAN to support shared data storage, provide network maintenance tools, and promote more efficient data backups offers advantages over a peer-to-peer LAN. The extensive security features built into a client/server network operating system provide another advantage. Setting up and maintaining a client/server network, however, can be more difficult and more expensive, and can require much more technical expertise to manage than a peer-to-peer LAN. For these reasons, a client/server LAN is the best networking choice for an organization with multiple users and the technical staff and financial resources to develop and maintain the LAN.

METROPOLITAN AREA NETWORKS   A **metropolitan area network (MAN)** connects clients and servers in a region that is larger than a single office or building (Figure 6-4). A MAN might connect multiple buildings across a city or multiple educational, research, or government facilities across a state. MANs generally are owned by a consortium of users or by a single network provider who sells high-speed network services to the multiple users.

Figure 6-4   A metropolitan area network connects LANs across a city or region.

WIDE AREA NETWORKS   A **wide area network** (**WAN**) — a network covering a very wide geographical area — can be a single network or multiple connected LANs located across the country or around the world (Figure 6-5). For example, a business with branch offices in England, Australia, Canada, and the U.S. may use a WAN to connect the individual LANs in each branch office. Most WANs are corporately owned, private WANs. The Internet, which is the world's largest WAN, is a public WAN.

Network Topologies, Access Methods, and Transmission Media

A network's **physical topology** is the layout in which its computers, printers, and other devices are arranged. A network's **access method** specifies how data is transmitted from node to node across the network, and its **transmission media** are the communication media — physical or wireless — used to carry these transmissions. These three characteristics help define a network's **throughput** — that is, the amount of data that can be transferred from one node to another node in a specified amount of time.

Figure 6-5   A wide area network can be a single network or can connect LANs around the world.

PHYSICAL TOPOLOGIES   Three basic LAN physical topologies are the bus, the ring, and the star. Today, however, many LANs use a hybrid physical topology that combines some elements of these three basic physical topologies.

The **bus topology** connects all nodes on a peer-to-peer LAN with a single cable (Figure 6-6 on the next page). This single cable, called a **bus**, is shared by all nodes, which means only one transmission is allowed at a time. To send a transmission, a node first must announce to the entire network that it will be sending a transmission.

The transmission, which includes the destination node address, is ignored by all nodes except the destination node, which accepts it. A peer-to-peer LAN with a bus topology is easy and inexpensive to install and nodes can be added or removed without difficulty. If, however, a problem occurs with the bus, the entire network becomes inoperable until that problem is solved. Adding additional nodes also can slow down the transmission process.

Figure 6-6   The bus topology connects all nodes on a peer-to-peer network with a single cable.

The **ring topology** connects each node to the next node via a single circle of cable (Figure 6-7). A transmission moves from node to node around the circle in a clockwise direction. As each node receives a transmission, it accepts any data addressed to it and forwards the transmission on to the next node. Because a transmission is passed from node to node, the failure of one node can affect all the nodes following the failed node. Adding nodes also can slow down the transmission process.

Figure 6-7   The ring topology connects each node to the next node via a single circle of cable.

The **star topology** connects each node to a central device, such as a hub (Figure 6-8). A transmission passes from the originating node, through the hub, directly to the destination node. Because each node is connected separately to the hub, the failure of a single node or its connecting cable does not make the entire network inoperable. The centralized connection point allows star topology LANs to be modified, moved, or connected to other networks easily.

Figure 6-8 The star topology connects each node to a central device, such as a hub.

ACCESS METHODS A network's access method (sometimes called its **logical topology**) is the way in which data is transmitted between nodes. The two most common network access methods are Ethernet and token ring. **Ethernet** is a network access method in which a node wanting to transmit data first must determine if any other node is sending a transmission. If so, the node waits a short period of time and then checks again. When no transmissions are being sent, the node sends its transmission. When two nodes check and then transmit at the same time, their two transmissions collide. Both nodes then stop transmitting, wait a random amount of time, check again, and then send their transmissions.

Networks using a bus or star topology commonly use the Ethernet access method, which can transmit data from 10 Mbps to 100 Mbps. High-speed networks such as MANs may use Gigabit Ethernet, which transmits data at 1,000 Mbps.

Facts@Hand

In Chapter 1, you learned that bandwidth is measured in bits per second (bps). Throughput — the amount of data that can be transferred from one node to another node in a specified amount of time — generally is measured in Kbps, Mbps, and Gbps. Modern network throughput is generally between 100 and 1,000 Mbps.

A **token ring** network uses a token-passing access method. A **token** is a small packet that moves clockwise in a circle from node to node. Only one free or unused token is available per network; a node cannot transmit until it has the token. When a node is ready to transmit, it intercepts the token, adds data and the destination node's address, and then sends the token on to the next node. The token moves from node to node around the network until it reaches the destination node, which intercepts the token and sends an acknowledgment back to the originating node. The originating node then reissues a free token and sends it to the next node. Because a node cannot transmit unless it has the token, two nodes cannot transmit at once, avoiding the transmission collisions that may occur on an Ethernet network. A token ring network generally is more expensive to install, however.

TRANSMISSION MEDIA   As you learned in Chapter 1, data is transmitted over modern networks using a variety of physical media, such as cable, and wireless media, such as microwaves. Examples of physical media used in networks include coaxial, twisted-pair, and fiber-optic cable.

Coaxial cable was the transmission medium of choice for many early networks and still is used for cable television connections. **Coaxial cable** (Figure 6-9), commonly called coax, consists of a single copper wire surrounded by insulating material, woven or braided metal, and a plastic outer covering. Coaxial cable can carry network traffic for long distances and is resistant to interference. It is not used in most modern networks, however, because it does not transmit data as fast as other media.

Twisted-pair cable (Figure 6-9) consists of insulated copper wires twisted around each other in pairs and then enclosed in a plastic covering. Twisted-pair cable originally was used for telephone transmissions; today it commonly is used as a LAN transmission medium, because it is easier to install than other types of cable and can handle the faster transmission speeds required by modern networks.

Fiber-optic cable (Figure 6-9), which contains glass fibers surrounded by a layer of glass cladding and a protective outer jacket, is used to carry voice, video, and data transmissions over very long distances. Because of its capacity and reliability, fiber-optic cable is a popular transmission medium for high-speed long-distance transmissions. While fiber-optic cable is too expensive to be used as a transmission medium for a small LAN, it is a transmission medium of choice for MANs and WANs.

Examples of wireless media used in networks include microwave, infrared, and radio frequency. As you learned in Chapter 1, microwave transmissions are used to provide high-speed connectivity to the Internet where DSL and cable are not available. Microwaves transmitted via satellite also are used for WAN transmissions.

Infrared (IR) transmissions use infrared light-wave signals as a short-range transmission medium between computers or other devices equipped with IrDA ports (Figure 6-10). IR transmissions are line-of-sight transmissions, because the sending and receiving devices must be positioned or aligned so that the infrared signal's path is unobstructed.

@Source

For information on organizations that set networking standards, visit the Discovering the Internet Chapter 6 Web page (**scsite.com/ internet/ch6**) and click a link below Networking Standards.

coaxial cable

twisted-pair cable

fiber-optic cable

Figure 6-9 Coaxial, twisted-pair, and fiber-optic cable provide the physical transmission media for networks.

Figure 6-10 Infrared (IR) light-wave signals are used as a short-range transmission medium between two handheld devices.

Radio frequency (RF) transmissions use broadcast radio waves to transmit data over short distances, such as between two handheld computers or between a notebook computer and a printer. RF transmissions are not line-of-sight transmissions, but a transmitter must exist to send the transmission and a receiver must exist to receive it. Some wireless devices send and receive RF transmissions using a **transceiver** — a single component that both sends and receives transmissions. **Bluetooth** is an example of a short-range RF technology that sends and receives wireless transmissions between devices such as personal computers, personal digital assistants (PDAs), and cell phones (Figure 6-11). A Bluetooth-enabled device contains a transceiver that sends and receives radio transmissions in the 2.4 GHz radio frequency band with a throughput of up to 1 Mbps. Bluetooth devices, designed for small **wireless personal area networks (WPANs)**, have a range of approximately 33 feet (10 meters) or less.

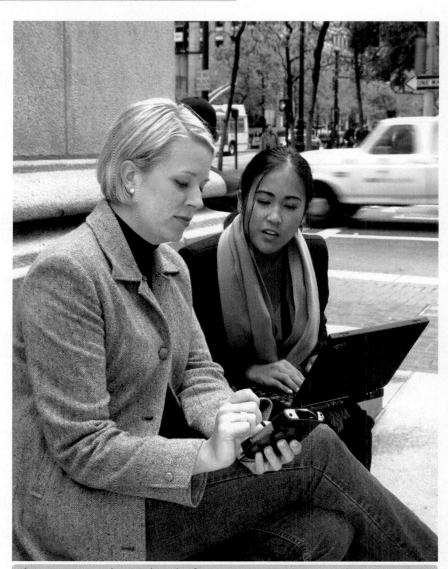

Figure 6-11 A Bluetooth radio frequency (RF) transmission between a PDA and a notebook computer.

A **wireless LAN** (**WLAN**) uses a wireless medium — such as radio frequency transmissions — to connect computers, printers, and other devices (Figure 6-12). A wireless LAN in an office, for example, can use radio frequency transmissions to allow computers and printers equipped with wireless network interface cards (NICs) to communicate. To ensure that the devices on the network communicate, wireless LANs follow IEEE 802.11 wireless networking standards, including the Wi-Fi (IEEE 802.11b) standard discussed in Chapter 1. The IEEE 802.11 family of wireless LAN standards specifies data transmission speeds and the radio frequencies over which the WLANs can communicate.

Some wired LANs also provide wireless access for notebooks, handheld computers, and other devices via wireless access points. As you learned in Chapter 1, a wireless access point is a hardware device with an antenna that sends and receives radio signals to and from a mobile device and a wired LAN.

Figure 6-12   A wired network can accept wireless transmissions from notebooks and handheld devices via a wireless access point.

 @Source

For more information on Bluetooth, Wi-Fi, IEEE 802.11 standards, and other wireless networking technologies, visit the Discovering the Internet Chapter 6 Web page (**scsite.com/ internet/ch6**) and click a link below Networking.

🖐 **Facts@Hand**

Bluetooth technologies are not compatible with the IEEE 802.11 wireless LAN technologies.

Connectivity Hardware and Software

As discussed in Chapter 1, packet switching involves breaking data up into packets at its source and then transmitting the individual packets across various networks to their destination, where the packets are reassembled. Hardware connectivity devices, such as hubs, bridges, data switches, and routers, and hardware or software gateways are at the heart of this process. These devices and software are used to connect nodes on the same network, to connect across multiple networks, and to forward packets between nodes.

Large modern networks often are broken up into **segments**, or multiple groups of computers that share a common function. For example, on a business LAN, the marketing department computers might be on one segment and the sales department computers might be on another segment. Bridges, data switches, routers, and gateways connect different network segments and control transmissions with and between segments (Figure 6-13). Most large networks use a combination of network hardware and software to help move packets efficiently and quickly to their destinations.

Figure 6-13 Large modern networks are often broken up into network segments.

HUBS As you learned earlier in this chapter, a hub is an inexpensive hardware device used to connect multiple nodes on the same network. A **passive hub** cannot determine how to direct a packet and simply sends the same signal to all the nodes or segments to which it is connected. An **intelligent hub**, however, can perform a variety of tasks, such as filtering data or permitting a network administrator to monitor hub traffic.

BRIDGES A **port** is an opening in a device that is used to connect it to another device. A **bridge** is an intelligent connectivity device with one input port and one output port that connects two segments on the same LAN or two separate LANs. Each node on a network has a unique physical address called its **MAC address**, which is assigned to its network interface card (NIC) by the card's manufacturer. A bridge creates a database of all the MAC addresses for nodes on its segment or LAN. It then uses the database to determine if a packet should be forwarded to another segment or LAN. Bridges originally were able to connect only segments or LANs that used the same access method — either Ethernet or token ring. Today, more sophisticated bridges can connect, forward packets, and translate the packets between Ethernet and token ring LANs. In some cases, however, bridges are being replaced by modern data switches and routers.

DATA SWITCHES A **data switch** is an intelligent device that also interprets MAC addresses and filters and forwards packets to other network segments. A data switch has multiple ports, with each port acting as a bridge. Using multiple ports to direct packets helps ease congestion and makes a data switch a more inexpensive choice than a bridge for networks with a large number of nodes.

 @Source

The 7-Layer OSI Model illustrates the flow of data in a network and defines the networking protocols at each step in the flow. To learn more about the 7-Layer OSI Model, visit the Discovering the Internet Chapter 6 Web page (**scsite.com/ internet/ch6**) and click a link below Networking.

ROUTERS   Like a data switch, a **router** is an intelligent device with multiple ports. A router, however, is much more powerful than a switch. In fact, a router is a specialized computer that can connect LAN segments, two LANs, or multiple LANs on a WAN — all transmitting at different speeds and using different protocols. In addition to keeping track of all the nodes on a network, a router can determine the best route for a packet to take to its destination and switch the packet to an alternate route, if necessary.

A router can use one of two methods of directing packets: static routing and dynamic routing. A router using **static routing** is programmed by a network administrator to route packets over specific paths between nodes. **Dynamic routing** allows a router to determine the best route between two nodes automatically and then store this information in a routing table. To route a packet dynamically, an incoming packet is opened, the packet's destination address is compared to the routing table, and then the packet is sent on to its destination using the route specified in the routing table. Dynamic routing also allows a router to detect trouble on a specific route and reroute packets when necessary.

The routers used to route packets on the Internet are complex, fast, and expensive devices that can search through routing tables quickly enough to forward millions of packets per second correctly. Internet routers ensure that packets reach their destination — across town or across the world — by sending packets from one router to another until the packets reach their destination network. Forwarding a packet to the next Internet router is called a **hop**. The more hops, the longer it takes for data to go from the sending computer to the destination computer.

Most operating systems provide a utility you can use to trace hops from your computer to another computer over the Internet. In the Windows operating system, this utility is called the tracert utility. The tracert utility can be used to test the path to a destination Internet site and see if any problems exist with making a connection at a particular point along the route. The following steps use the Command Prompt window and the Windows tracert utility to trace hops from your computer to the Course Technology Web server.

Steps: To Use the Tracert Utility to Trace Hops

1 **Click the Start button on the Windows taskbar, point to All Programs on the Start menu, point to Accessories, and then click Command Prompt on the Accessories submenu.**

The Command Prompt window opens (Figure 6-14). The contents of your Command Prompt window will vary from those of the Command Prompt window shown in Figures 6-14 through 6-16.

Figure 6-14

2 **Type** `tracert` `www.course.com` **at the command-line prompt.**

The tracert command will instruct the operating system to trace the number of hops between your computer and the destination computer (Figure 6-15). In this example, the destination computer, the Course Technology Web server, is indicated by the URL, www.course.com.

Figure 6-15

3 **Press the ENTER key.**

The path from your computer to the Course Technology Web server appears in the Command Prompt window as packets are sent from router to router over the Internet (Figure 6-16).

4 **Click the Close button on the Command Prompt window title bar.**

The Command Prompt window closes.

Figure 6-16

GATEWAYS A **gateway** is a hardware device or software that runs on a mainframe computer, a server, an individual workstation, or a router. Gateways are used to connect two or more networks or network segments that use different packet formatting, different communication protocols, and different access methods. Gateways not only forward packets, they also translate packets so that those packets can be read by the destination network. Because of this translation capability, gateways are more expensive than routers and transmit packets more slowly than do bridges, switches, or routers. Figure 6-17 on the next page lists different types of gateways.

Name	Description
E-mail gateway	Converts e-mail messages created by one type of e-mail system so that they can be read by a different type of e-mail system.
Internet gateway	Allows LAN users to access the Internet. May be used to define which users have Internet access or to restrict access to certain Internet services or Web sites.
LAN gateway	Connects LAN segments that use different access methods and communication protocols.
Voice/data gateway	Allows data packets to be sent over a voice network or voice to be sent over a data network by translating between voice circuit switching and data packet switching.
Wireless gateway	Allows integration of wireless devices such as laptops, PDAs, and cell phones with a wired network.

Figure 6-17 Gateways can connect two or more divergent networks.

Internet Infrastructure

From a user's perspective, accessing the Internet and downloading a file, viewing a Web page, or sending an e-mail may seem quite simple. In a few seconds, the file is downloaded, the Web page is loaded into your browser, or the e-mail message reaches its destination. The processes taking place behind the scenes, however, are quite complex and rely on the ability of your computer to communicate with computers on other networks; on the ability of your Internet Service Provider (ISP) to exchange data with other providers; and on the ability of network hardware and software to break down data into properly addressed packets that are delivered error-free and reassembled correctly at their destination.

In this section, you will learn about network service providers and how they interact to exchange data at specific points on the Internet backbone. You also will learn more about the TCP/IP suite of protocols that is instrumental in addressing and delivering data packets; how IP addresses are constructed; and how the Domain Name System (DNS) resolves domain names to IP addresses.

Network Service Providers (NSPs)

As you learned in Chapter 1, the original Internet backbone was provided by the NSFnet, which used transmission media from AT&T. In the mid-1990s, the NSFnet Internet backbone was replaced by interconnected backbones or networks provided by several telecommunications companies, including AT&T. Today, AT&T, Sprint, MCI (formerly WorldCom), Level 3 Communications, Qwest Communications, and others, called **network service providers** (**NSPs**), provide the public and private network infrastructure for the Internet. Figures 6-18 through 6-20 show the backbones from various network service providers.

Figure 6-18 AT&T backbone.

Figure 6-19 Sprint backbone.

Figure 6-20 MCI backbone.

NETWORK ACCESS POINTS The connection point on the Internet backbone where multiple NSP networks come together to exchange Internet traffic is called a **network access point** (**NAP**). Originally, NAPs were located in Pennsauken, New Jersey; Washington, D.C.; Chicago, Illinois; and San Jose, California. As Internet traffic grew, it became necessary to add more NAPs; therefore, today many NAPs are located across North America and around the world, enabling Internet users on one network to access resources on a different network.

A specific type of network access point — called a **Metropolitan Area Exchange** (**MAE**) — is a high-speed Ethernet NAP connection within a metropolitan area. Five regional MAEs exist in the United States and are now owned and operated by MCI: MAE West (San Jose), MAE East (Washington, D.C.), MAE Chicago, MAE Central (Dallas), and MAE New York. Today, the original San Jose and Washington D.C. NAPs both are considered MAEs (Figure 6-21).

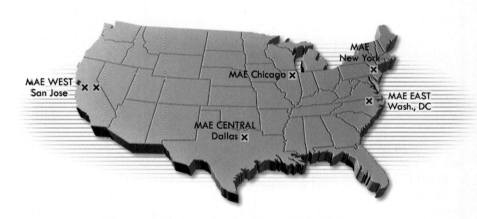

Figure 6-21 The regional MAEs are owned and operated by MCI.

Facts@Hand

Network service providers (NSPs) provide the public and private network infrastructure for the Internet. Internet Service Providers (ISPs) are companies who sell Internet access to individuals, businesses, and other organizations. An ISP may sell Internet access locally to individuals and businesses, regionally to other ISPs, or worldwide to a varied customer base. An ISP may or may not be an NSP; several NSPs, however, are also ISPs.

PEERING **Peering** is the exchange of Internet traffic and router information between NSPs and ISPs at an exchange point, such as a NAP. Peering agreements specify the terms under which NSPs exchange data and can include how much traffic can be peered or exchanged, the type of network the peering entities must have, and other requirements such as transit fees. **Public peering** involves exchanging Internet traffic at a public connection such as a NAP. Because NAPs can become very congested during the Internet's peak traffic periods, some NSPs and ISPs set up **private peering**

connections, which are dedicated connections to each other's networks. These private peering arrangements and connections enable Internet traffic to bypass congested public peering points.

TCP/IP Stack

As you learned in Chapter 1, the Transmission Control Protocol/Internet Protocol (TCP/IP) suite, also called the **TCP/IP stack**, is the de facto set of standard Internet protocols on which communications across the Internet and many private networks rely. The TCP/IP stack encompasses multiple subprotocols, several of which are shown in Figure 6-22. Of these protocols, TCP, IP, and UDP are the core subprotocols required for all TCP/IP transmissions. Other subprotocols accomplish various network communication tasks such as downloading files or sending and receiving e-mail.

Subprotocol	Description
Transmission Control Protocol (TCP)	Breaks data into packets, verifies packet integrity, and reassembles error-free packets at their destination.
Internet Protocol (IP)	Sends packets and provides routers with the address information needed to deliver the packets.
User Datagram Protocol (UDP)	Sends packets without checking for errors or verifying receipt of the packets. UDP is used to broadcast live video or audio over the Internet.
Address Resolution Protocol (ARP)	Converts a computer's IP address to its physical MAC address.
Reverse ARP (RARP)	Converts a computer's physical MAC address into its IP address.
Internet Control Message Protocol (ICMP)	Sends error messages to routers and host computers when problems occur with data transmissions.
Dynamic Host Configuration Protocol (DHCP)	Automatically assigns IP addresses to network devices.
Hypertext Transfer Protocol (HTTP)	Allows Web servers and Web browsers to communicate.
Post Office Protocol version 3 (POP3)	Manages storage of e-mail messages on a mail server and the forwarding of e-mail messages from a mail server to a user's mailbox.
Simple Mail Transfer Protocol (SMTP)	Routes e-mail messages from mail server to mail server across an IP network such as the Internet.
Internet Mail Access Protocol version 4 (IMAP4)	Provides remote access to a mail server, allowing users to manage their stored messages, and functions similar to POP3.
File Transfer Protocol (FTP)	Enables uploading and downloading of files between a local and remote computer.
Telnet	Allows a computer to act as a terminal for logging on to remote devices such as a computer or router.

Figure 6-22   The TCP/IP stack includes several subprotocols on which communications across the Internet and private IP networks rely.

Most current network operating systems use the TCP/IP stack as their default networking protocols. A network running TCP/IP often is called an **IP network**.

IP Addresses

Every network node must have its own individual and unique address to ensure that data transmitted over a private or public IP network reaches its correct destination. Earlier in this chapter, you learned that each network device has a MAC address, a physical address set in its network interface card (NIC). In addition to a physical address, each node on an IP network also has a **logical address**, called an IP address. The IP subprotocol uses this address to deliver packets to the correct destination.

The discussion of IP addresses in this chapter is based on the current and most widely used standard, called IPv4. It is expected, however, that a newer version, called IPv6, gradually will replace IPv4. IPv6 will lengthen IP addresses from 32 bits to 128 bits and thus increase the number of available IP addresses. As you learned in Chapter 2, a typical IP address — such as 202.78.173.12 — has four groups of numbers that range from 0 through 255, each separated by a period. This form of the IP address is sometimes called a dotted decimal number or dotted quad. An IP address is actually a 32-bit number made up of four 8-bit numbers. Each 8-bit number in the IP address is called an **octet.**

The IP address for any node on a network is made up of two components: one that identifies the network to which the node is connected and one that identifies the node itself. The IP addresses for nodes on the same network have the same network identification component, while each has a unique node component. Networks are classified as Class A through Class E networks, in order to maximize the number of available IP addresses for each network. The network class defines which octets in the IP address identify the network and which octets identify the specific node, as follows:

- Class A networks: The first octet identifies the network and can be a number from 1 through 126. The remaining three octets identify individual network nodes.
- Class B networks: The first two octets identify the network; the first octet can be a number from 128 through 191. The remaining two octets identify individual nodes.
- Class C networks: The first three octets identify the network; the first octet can be a number from 192 through 223. The remaining octet identifies individual nodes.
- Class D networks: Class D networks are used for multicast videoconferencing or sending packets to a group of IP addresses. The first octet can be a number from 224 through 239. The three remaining octets are used to identify the group of computers to which the packets are being sent.
- Class E networks: Class E networks are experimental networks. The first octet can be a number from 240 through 255.

Figure 6-23 on the next page summarizes IP addressing for Classes A through C. As you can see, Class A networks have more possible IP addresses than Class B networks, which in turn have more possible IP addresses than Class C networks. For this reason, Class A and Class B networks are generally very large educational, business, and government networks. Class C networks are typically found in small- to medium-sized organizations and ISPs. For example, an ISP may be assigned a block of Class C IP addresses, which it then subdivides among its small business customers. ICANN, through the Internet Assigned Numbers Authority (IANA), assigns groups of IP addresses to businesses, ISPs, and other organizations.

@Source

For more information about IPv6, visit the Discovering the Internet Chapter 6 Web page (**scsite.com/ internet/ch6**) and click a link below Internetworking.

Class	Maximum Number of Networks	Maximum IP Addresses per Network	First Octet	Sample IP Addresses for Nodes on the Same Network
A	126	16,777,214	1-126	89.34.104.15 89.62.112.23 89.70.124.77
B	16,382	65,534	128-191	150.45.34.53 150.45.78.67 150.45.80.41
C	2,097,150	254	192-223	198.88.162.12 198.88.162.13 198.88.162.14

Figure 6-23   IP addressing for Class A through C networks.

Some IP addresses are reserved for special uses. For example, 127.0.0.1 is used to troubleshoot TCP/IP-related problems on an individual computer, and 255.255.255.255 is reserved for broadcasting messages to multiple computers. Other groups of IP addresses, such as 192.168.0.0 through 192.168.255.255, 172.16.0.0 through 172.31.255.255, and 10.0.0.0 through 10.255.255.255, are internal IP addresses reserved for private networks.

As previously discussed, every computer on a network has a unique IP address. You can use the Command Prompt window and the ipconfig /all command to display your own computer's IP address. The following steps use the Command Prompt window to view the IP address of your computer. To complete the steps, your computer must be connected to a network.

Steps: To View a Networked Computer's IP Address

1   **Click the Start button on the Windows taskbar, point to All Programs on the Start menu, point to Accessories, and then click Command Prompt on the Accessories submenu.**

The Command Prompt window opens.

2   **Type** `ipconfig /all` **at the command-line prompt.**

Executing the ipconfig command with the parameter, all, instructs the operating system to display all IP information about your networked computer (Figure 6-24). The contents of your Command Prompt window on your screen will vary from those of the Command Prompt window shown in Figures 6-24 and 6-25.

Figure 6-24

3 Press the ENTER key.

The Command Prompt window displays your computer's host name, IP address, and other IP information (Figure 6-25). If your computer is not connected to a network, no IP information appears.

4 Click the Close button on the Command Prompt window title bar.

The Command Prompt window closes.

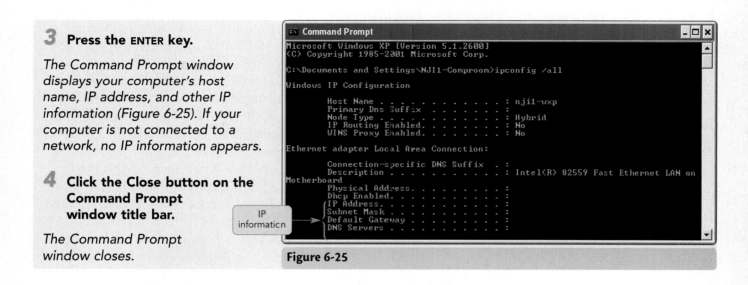

Figure 6-25

Domain Name System (DNS)

As you learned in Chapter 2, a domain name is a registered, easy-to-remember text name that can be translated into one or more IP addresses. For example, microsoft.com is the registered domain name for several IP addresses, including 207.46.249.190, 207.46.249.222, 207.46.135.155, 207.46.134.222, and 207.46.249.27. ICANN, the non-profit corporation that assigns IP addresses, also oversees the Domain Name System (DNS). The DNS consists of a hierarchy of servers used to translate domain names into IP addresses in a process called **resolving** the domain name.

DNS SERVERS   At the top of the DNS hierarchy (Figure 6-26) are 13 ICANN-managed **root servers** located in the United States, Sweden, England, and Japan. These root servers maintain directories of the next level of servers — primary and secondary **name servers** or **DNS servers** — that actually contain the IP information for the top-level domain (TLD) and country-code top-level domain (ccTLD) registrants. At the bottom of the hierarchy are local DNS servers containing domain name and IP address information about their local networks. All of the information in the DNS databases — including the top-level domain, country code top-level domain, domain name, and IP address information — collectively is called the **namespace**.

13 root servers containing directories of primary and secondary name servers

multiple primary and secondary name servers containing TLD and ccTLD domain name information

multiple local name servers at companies or ISPs

Figure 6-26   The DNS namespace consists of 13 root servers, multiple primary and secondary name servers, and thousands of local name servers.

Resolving a domain name to an IP address begins with your local name server, which may be located at your company or at your ISP. When you attempt to view a Web page, your local DNS server first tries to provide the IP address for the domain name you entered in your browser. If the domain name is external to the local network, your local DNS server may not have the IP address information and thus cannot resolve the domain name to an IP address. When this happens, the local DNS server next contacts a root server to determine which primary or secondary DNS servers have the IP address information — and then contacts these DNS servers until it finds the one that can resolve the domain name to an IP address. The local DNS server then returns the IP address to your browser, the Web server is accessed, and the Web page is loaded into your browser. Figure 6-27 illustrates the process of resolving a domain name.

Root Server

2 local name server attempts to resolve domain name and then contacts root server to determine primary or secondary name servers that can resolve the domain name

Local Name Server

Primary or Secondary Name Server

3 root server identifies primary or secondary name servers that have the IP address information for URL

1 user enters URL in browser

6 local name server sends IP address to browser

5 primary or secondary server resolves domain name and sends IP address back to local name server

4 local name server locates appropriate primary or secondary name server

Figure 6-27 The process of resolving a domain name via the DNS begins with a local name server contacting a root server, if necessary, to identify the primary and secondary name servers that have the IP address information for the domain name entered in a browser.

If you are using Windows XP or Windows 2000 on a networked computer, you can use the Command Prompt window and the nslookup command to find the numeric IP address that corresponds to a domain name and vice versa. The following steps use the Command Prompt window to look up corresponding IP addresses and domain names.

Steps: To Look Up Corresponding IP Addresses and Domain Names

1 Click the Start button on the Windows taskbar, point to All Programs on the Start menu, point to Accessories, and then click Command Prompt on the Accessories submenu.

The Command Prompt window opens.

2 Type nslookup cnn.com at the command-line prompt.

The nslookup command will display the IP address(es) for the cnn.com domain name (Figure 6-28). The contents of your Command Prompt window on your screen will vary from those in the Command Prompt window shown in Figures 6-28 through 6-30.

Figure 6-28

3 Press the ENTER key.

The cnn.com domain name corresponds to eight IP addresses (Figure 6-29). The command-line prompt appears at the bottom of the Command Prompt window.

Figure 6-29

4 Type nslookup 207.171.182.16 at the command-line prompt and press the ENTER key.

The IP address, 207.171.182.16, corresponds to the amazon.com domain name (Figure 6-30).

5 Click the Close button on the Command Prompt window title bar.

The Command Prompt window closes.

Figure 6-30

DNS REGISTRATION ICANN also manages the **Shared Registration System** (**SRS**), which is the domain name registration system that allows private companies to handle the registration of domain names. These private companies, called **accredited registrars**, ensure that an organization's unique domain name is maintained on the appropriate DNS servers, for a fee ranging from about $10 to $35 per year. Examples of accredited registrars include Network Solutions and Register.com (United States), NameSystem (Canada), and Safenames (United Kingdom) (Figure 6-31).

(a) NetworkSolutions

(b) register.com

(c) safenames.net

(d) namesystem

Figure 6-31 Accredited registrar Web sites.

The process of registering a domain name online is very easy. You simply:

1. Access an accredited registrar's Web site.

2. Enter a desired domain name including the desired top-level domain, such as .com, .net, or .biz. The Web site searches a database of registered domain names to determine if the domain name you entered is available.

3. Select an available domain name and enter the purchaser information, which usually consists of the name, address, telephone number, and e-mail address of the person responsible for the domain name.

4. Provide the IP address(es) of the primary and secondary DNS servers of the company or ISP hosting the Web site, if necessary. (See your network administrator or contact your ISP for this information, if necessary.)

5. Pay for the domain name using a credit card.

If you are considering registering a domain name, you first may want to search a domain name database to see what appropriate domain names are available. The following steps show how to search an accredited registrar's database for an available domain name.

◈❯ *Steps:* To Search for an Available Domain Name

1 If necessary, start your browser. Visit the Discovering the Internet Chapter 6 Web page (scsite.com/internet/ch6). Click Network Solutions.

The Network Solutions home page appears (Figure 6-32). You can enter a desired domain name, select from several top-level domains (TLDs), and search a domain name database to see if a domain name is available. The contents of the Web pages on your screen may vary from those shown in Figures 6-32 through 6-34 on this and the next page.

Figure 6-32

2 Type my-new-business in the www. text box and click the .biz check box to insert a check mark. Point to the SEARCH button.

You cannot use spaces in a domain name; instead, use a hyphen where you normally would use a space (Figure 6-33). You can search for your desired domain name in multiple top-level domains at one time.

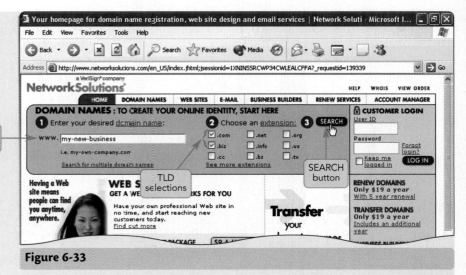

Figure 6-33

(continued)

3 **Click the SEARCH button and scroll down the search results page.**

The search results page indicates whether or not the my-new-business.com or my-new-business.biz domain names are available (Figure 6-34). The page also lists the availability of the domain name using different top-level domains, as well as similar available domain names.

available domain name

unavailable domain name

suggested domain names

Figure 6-34

✋ Facts@Hand

Careful selection of an e-business domain name is critical. E-business domain names are used both to identify and to market the e-businesses. When choosing an e-business domain name, select a short, easy-to-remember name that ties in to the products or services the e-business sells.

Wireless Internet

Handheld wireless devices, such as cell phones, personal digital assistants (PDAs), and smart phones that combine the features of both, are ubiquitous in today's modern mobile societies (Figure 6-35). You may already use one or more of these devices to communicate with friends and co-workers, connect to the Internet and check your e-mail, download games, or view wireless Web content. Many Internet analysts predict a massive explosion in the number of wireless Internet users within the next three to five years — which will drive a demand for more handheld wireless devices and wireless Web content. In this section, you will learn about the wireless services expected to drive the greater adoption of handheld wireless devices, as well as the technologies that enable you to access the Web using wireless devices.

smart phones

PDAs

cell phones

Figure 6-35 The demand for handheld wireless devices and wireless Web content is expected to grow along with the continuing growth of wireless Internet users.

Authoritative vs. Alternative Root Systems

@Source

To view the ICANN Web site and other Web sites discussed in this section, visit the Discovering the Internet Chapter 6 Web page (**scsite.com/internet/ch6**) and click a link below Internetworking.

@Source

To learn more about the companies offering domain name registration using an alternative root system, visit the Discovering the Internet Chapter 6 Web page (**scsite.com/internet/ch6**) and click a link below Internetworking.

As you learned in Chapter 2, ICANN is a non-profit entity that contracts with the Department of Commerce to manage the DNS and assign TLDs. As of this writing, the contract between ICANN and the Department of Commerce is extended to September 2003. The ICANN-managed TLD root system is not the only TLD root system, however. Several for-profit businesses, such as New.net, name.space, the Atlantic Root Network, and PacificRoot, are challenging ICANN's authoritative root system and its control over assigning TLDs by offering users registry services that support alternative root systems.

Alternative root systems are domain name systems that offer domain names with TLDs beyond those supported by ICANN such as .family, .xxx, .law, and .sport. To access a domain name registered under an alternative root system, you either must reconfigure your browser to access an ISP whose DNS server database includes non-authoritative domain names or you must download and install a plug-in provided by the alternative root system registrar.

ICANN opposes these alternative root systems on the basis that domain names registered to alternative root systems potentially may conflict with domain names in ICANN's authoritative DNS system and thereby threaten the "Internet's reliability and stability." Proponents of alternative root systems include the for-profit companies that provide the alternative root registration services, ICANN critics who think ICANN has excessive power and is too slow to introduce new TLDs, and international critics who resent a perceived U.S. domination over the DNS. As of this writing, the future impact of alternative root systems on ICANN's authoritative root system is unclear, and ICANN remains committed to providing a "single, authoritative public root system" as a means of providing a reliable way to resolve domain names to IP addresses.

For more information on ICANN's position on alternative root systems, visit the Discovering the Internet Chapter 6 Web page (**scsite .com/internet/ ch6**) and click a link below Authoritative Root System for the DNS.

ICANN

Wireless Services

In the near future, activities such as purchasing airline tickets, getting stock quotes, downloading and playing games, checking bank balances, sending e-mail, or downloading video over the Internet via a cell phone or PDA may be everyday tasks (Figure 6-36). The widespread adoption of these wireless services, however, may be driven by the availability of the latest digital cellular

MMS messaging

gaming

SMS text messaging

Internet access

Figure 6-36 Analysts predict that within the next few years millions of people around the world will be accessing the wireless Web.

technologies (called third-generation or 3G); enhanced small-screen browsers, called **microbrowsers**; and color screens. Today, wireless services such as SMS, MMS, wireless gaming, and location-based services are used increasingly and continue to drive demand for handheld wireless devices and wireless Internet access.

SHORT MESSAGE SERVICE   In Chapter 1, you were introduced to the GSM/GPRS card that allows a computer to connect automatically to the cellular phone network without even using a cell phone. GSM digital cellular technologies first were adopted widely by European wireless carriers to allow for easy exchange of wireless calls and messages across country borders. More recently, several U.S. wireless carriers, such as AT&T, have adopted GSM technologies to provide a two-way, text-messaging service called Short Message Service. The Short Message Service (SMS), you first learned about in Chapter 4, transmits short text messages between phones over a GSM wireless network via a central message service center. Today, SMS technologies are used to send a wide variety of messages — including personal messages, weather and traffic reports, stock quotes, personal banking information, and movie schedules — to cell phones. Wireless networks generally charge a small monthly fee plus additional per-message fees for SMS services.

MULTIMEDIA MESSAGING SERVICE   **Multimedia Messaging Service (MMS)** is a standard that enables users with MMS-enabled devices to send and receive messages that combine text with graphics, photographs, audio, and video clips. MMS, which is an outgrowth of SMS, supports standard image, video, and audio formats such as GIF, JPEG, MPEG, MP3, MIDI, and WAV. MMS is expected by many analysts to become a standard feature and the default messaging mode for cell phones, PDAs, and smart phones. Cell phones with built-in digital cameras are the first wave of MMS-enabled devices.

 Facts@Hand

Ovum, a United Kingdom-based research firm, estimates that Multimedia Messaging Services will generate more than $65 billion in worldwide revenues for wireless networks by 2007.

WIRELESS GAMING   As you learned in Chapter 5, playing online games is a very popular pastime with millions of online gamers around the world. Quick to recognize the revenue potential, the wireless industry is poised to exploit the latest digital cellular technologies and improved color screens on handheld devices to promote wireless gaming services. Some industry analysts anticipate wireless gaming will be the fastest-growing wireless consumer application in the world over the next several years with estimates of annual wireless gaming revenues ranging from $1 billion in 2005 to $9 billion by 2010.

LOCATION-BASED SERVICES   **Location-based services (LBS)** are wireless services offered to customers based on their physical location. An example of a non-commercial location-based service is the wireless 911 emergency service mandated by the FCC in its Enhanced 911 (E911) initiative. The E911 initiative will allow emergency call centers to use a location-based service to identify the location of the caller accurately, thus helping to eliminate the delay caused by asking users to describe their location.

At the heart of this and other LBS are the global positioning system (GPS) satellite network and receivers mounted in autos or placed in cell phones or other handheld devices. The **global positioning system (GPS)** is a navigation system that consists of one or more Earth-based receivers that accept and analyze signals sent by 24 small satellites orbiting approximately 11,000 miles above the Earth. Four to six satellites are always visible above the horizon, and each of these satellites constantly beams down a signal containing the exact time and its own position in the sky. A GPS receiver in a ship, airplane, auto, or handheld device uses these signals to calculate the receiver's own position on Earth to within a few feet.

Using the GPS satellite network, a service provider can identify the physical location of the person with a GPS-enabled device, such as a cell phone, and then offer services based on that location. Examples of commercial LBS include:

- Information services: "Where is the closest ATM?"
- Tracking services: "Your stolen auto is at 5th and Main."
- Advertising services: "Gino's Pizzeria is immediately to your left. Use the coupon code, HALF, to get any pizza at half-price."

Two areas of concern that may affect the widespread adoption of commercial LBS are privacy and unsolicited advertising. Industry and consumer groups are working with the FCC to develop the regulations that govern wireless privacy and unsolicited wireless advertising.

 Facts@Hand

Consulting companies expect a bright future for commercial LBS and wireless advertising. The Strategis Group projects annual LBS revenues to exceed $8 billion, and the Kelsey Group projects wireless advertising revenues to be more than $17 billion within the next few years.

Wireless Web

The **wireless Web** refers to using the Internet and Web through a wireless device, such as a cell phone or other handheld device. To accommodate wireless users, Web sites must provide content and services in a format that can be displayed and navigated on small wireless-device screens. Despite the current screen sizes and navigational limitations of handheld wireless devices, many wireless service providers and wireless Web content providers are continuing to develop new services and content for the wireless Web. For example, in Chapter 5, you learned how the Internet and the Web are changing the dynamics of buying a new or used vehicle. CARFAX and Edmunds.com also provide their content and services to wireless Web users. Now, using a cell phone or PDA, you can get information about vehicle pricing, reviews, and ratings from Edmunds.com and the history of a specific vehicle from CARFAX — all while sitting in the car on the dealer's lot.

 Facts@Hand

The Intermarket Group predicts wireless Web users in the U.S. will grow to more than 85 million and the number of worldwide wireless Web users will grow to more than 750 million within the next few years.

WAP AND WML   The Wireless Application Protocol (WAP) and its markup language, the Wireless Markup Language (WML), are two technologies that make the wireless Web viable. The **Wireless Application Protocol (WAP)** suite or stack makes it possible to access Internet resources on small-screen wireless devices. The WAP stack originally was developed as a wireless Web standard group of protocols by the WAP Forum, a consortium of wireless vendors such as Motorola, Nokia, and Ericsson. The WAP stack includes wireless application subprotocols that work across many different wireless devices and networks. The **Wireless Markup Language (WML)**, part of the WAP stack, is used to design Web content for small-screen wireless devices. (WML is based on the Extensible Markup Language (XML), which you will learn more about in Chapter 7.) **WMLScript**, a scripting language similar to JavaScript, is used to manipulate content and perform math functions on small-screen wireless devices.

WIRELESS WEB ACCESS   WAP-enabled devices cannot communicate directly with Web servers, because WAP is not compatible with TCP/IP. This means that a WAP-enabled device's request for a Web page first must pass through a WAP gateway server, which uses HTTP to send the request on to a Web server (Figure 6-37). The Web server returns the requested page to the WAP gateway server using HTTP, and the page is converted to WML, if necessary. The WAP gateway server then uses WAP protocols to send the page on to a microbrowser application in the WAP-enabled device.

@Source

For more information on the WAP stack, visit the Discovering the Internet Chapter 6 Web page (**scsite.com/ internet/ch6**) and click a link below Wireless Web.

Web server

WAP gateway

Wireless Network

WAP-enabled device

Figure 6-37   A WAP-enabled wireless device's request for a Web page must first pass through a WAP gateway server.

I-MODE WIRELESS DATA SERVICE   An alternative approach to WAP and WML is the i-Mode wireless data service developed by the Japanese telecommunications giant NTT DoCoMo, a subsidiary of the government-owned Nippon Telephone and Telegraph. **i-Mode** is an IP-based digital cellular phone service, which uses a simplified version of HTML instead of WAP and WML. Web content for the i-Mode service is developed using **cHTML**, a subset of the Hypertext Markup Language (HTML) used to create Web pages. cHTML leaves out the instructions for images, tables, background colors, and so forth that are difficult to view on a small screen. Launched by NTT DoCoMo in February 1999, the i-Mode service had more than 30 million subscribers sending and receiving e-mail, shopping online, accessing entertainment sites, getting stock quotes, booking airline tickets, playing games, downloading cartoons, and banking online by December 2001. In April 2002, AT&T partnered with NTT DoCoMo to offer a U.S. version of the i-Mode service called mMode. Millions more subscribers are expected to use the service as the i-Mode service expands in Europe and the U.S. (Figure 6-38).

Figure 6-38   i-Mode and mMode wireless service.

Internet Telephony, Television, and Videoconferencing

In Chapter 4, you learned how the Internet is making possible new modes of communication, such as e-mail, news-groups, and online chat. The Internet also is being used to enhance two traditional modes of communication: the telephone and television. In this section, you will learn how telephone calls are transmitted over the Internet; how you can add interactivity to a favorite television show using the Internet; and how the Internet enhances videoconferencing.

Internet Telephony

In Chapter 1, you were introduced to the circuit-switching technologies that establish and maintain private circuits for telephone calls over the public switched telephone network (PSTN). A private circuit connection is maintained for the duration of a call even during conversation pauses when neither party is talking. **Internet telephony**, also called **IP telephony** or **voice over IP** (**VoIP**), uses TCP/IP and packet switching to send voice transmissions over a private or public IP network. Using IP packet-switching technologies to make telephone calls is more efficient than old circuit-switching technologies, because packet switching minimizes the connection time for each call, thus allowing more calls to be transmitted during the same time period during which a single circuit-switched call must maintain its connection. VoIP is becoming increasingly popular as a way for organizations to take advantage of these efficiencies, centralize the management of their private voice and data networks, increase productivity, and save money by avoiding the long-distance charges of telephone carriers.

Telecommunications carriers also save money and improve productivity by using IP voice gateways and packet-switching technologies to send voice across a public IP network, such as the Internet (Figure 6-39 on the next page). When you make a telephone call across a public IP network, your call is carried by the PSTN to an IP voice gateway, where the analog voice signals are converted into digital IP packets and sent over the public IP network to another IP voice gateway near the call's destination. The receiving IP voice gateway accepts the packets, reassembles them, converts them into their original analog format, and then sends the call on to its destination phone over the PSTN.

Figure 6-39 The IP telephony process converts a call's analog signals to digital IP packets for transmission over an IP network and then converts the IP packets back to analog signals before the call reaches its destination.

In addition, you can use a private or public IP network to make computer-to-computer or computer-to-telephone calls. With a properly equipped computer, you can participate in a toll-free conversation with someone using a similarly equipped computer, or you can make low-cost calls from your computer to any telephone around the world (Figure 6-40). To make such a call over the Internet, you need a computer

Figure 6-40 Low-cost computer-to-telephone calls and toll free computer-to-computer calls are possible over an IP network.

equipped with a microphone and speakers or a headset, a sound card, special software provided by vendors such as Net2Phone, and an Internet connection.

When making computer-to-computer calls, both computers must be using the same calling software. For outgoing calls, the calling software searches a directory of other users to identify the IP address of the destination computer; converts voice into compressed, machine-readable files; breaks the files into IP packets; and routes the packets over an IP network to the destination computer. At the destination computer, the calling software reassembles and decompresses the packets so that the person receiving the files can hear them.

 Facts@Hand

The communications industry continues to develop technologies that allow voice, data, and video to be delivered simultaneously across the same network using a combination of computers, telephones, and television. Network engineers refer to these modern networks as converged networks.

Internet Television

The Internet and television are converging into an important broadcast entertainment medium much as the Internet and telephony are converging into a primary communications medium. Today, you can use your television to view Web pages, send and receive e-mail, and send and receive instant messages, using a service such as the MSN TV Internet service. With interactive television (ITV), you can view a television program and at the same time participate in chats with other viewers, take online polls, request additional information such as sports scores, play games, and so forth.

TV INTERNET SERVICE   TV Internet service provides Internet access using your television set instead of a computer. To use a TV Internet service, such as MSN TV, you first must purchase a set-top Internet receiver, similar to a cable TV box, and then connect this receiver to your television set and a telephone line. Because television screens and computer monitors use different technologies to display pictures, the TV set-top receiver converts the incoming signals from the Web into signals that can be displayed clearly on a television set. You use a handheld remote control device to browse the Web and a wireless keyboard to send e-mail and instant messages.

INTERACTIVE TELEVISION   **Interactive television (ITV)**, sometimes called enhanced television, is a two-way, interactive television technology that allows you to shop, bank, download movies, vote in surveys, play games, answer quiz show questions, and enjoy other interactive Internet activities — all while watching your favorite television program. ITV works directly with high-definition digital television (HDTV) or with a computer equipped with a TV tuner card that allows you to watch television on your computer. Examples of ITV broadcasts include Super Bowl XXXVII, ABC's Monday Night Football, the American Music Awards, ABC's "Who Wants to be a Millionaire" program, and the 75th Annual Academy Awards ceremony. In the following steps, you review a television network's ITV schedule.

 Facts@Hand

The FCC has mandated that analog television be phased out and that all television broadcasters be broadcasting digital television (DTV) signals by 2006. The FCC also has mandated that consumer electronics manufacturers build DTV tuners into all new television sets, starting with the 2004 model year.

▶▶ *Steps:* To Review a Television Network ITV Schedule

1 If necessary, start your browser. Visit the Discovering the Internet Chapter 6 Web page (scsite.com/internet/ch6). Click ABC's Enhanced TV. Point to the PROGRAM ARCHIVE link.

The ABC Enhanced Television home page appears (Figure 6-41). On this page, you can learn more about ABC Enhanced TV programming, view a list of upcoming programs, link to a program schedule, or view information about previous broadcasts. The contents of the Web pages on your screen will vary from those shown in Figures 6-41 and 6-42.

Figure 6-41

2 Click the PROGRAM ARCHIVE link and scroll down the page to review its contents.

Links to information about previous ABC Enhanced TV broadcasts appear (Figure 6-42).

Figure 6-42

Videoconferencing

Videoconferencing is the real-time transmission of video and audio between two locations. Today, most videoconferencing uses streaming video over a private or public IP network, as you learned in Chapter 5. Because of transmission quality concerns, commercial videoconferencing over an IP network (video over IP) most frequently occurs over private IP networks, which have more control over traffic and bandwidth availability. Examples of commercial videoconferencing include employee training sessions, customer support activities, and meetings involving employees who work in different locations. Government agencies, colleges, and universities with access to Internet2 use Internet2 for videoconferencing and for broadcasting instructors' lectures to numerous different classrooms.

To listen and watch a videoconference using your computer, your computer must be equipped with speakers, a monitor, a sound card, and videoconferencing software. If you are going to participate in the videoconference, your computer also must have a microphone or headset and a camera.

Network Security Issues and Technologies

Network security involves protecting network equipment and data from accidental or deliberate damage. Threats to network and Web site security can originate both internally within the organization and externally from outsiders. If business transactions are conducted over the network, fraudulent transactions and failure to protect transaction information pose additional risks. In this section, you will learn about the internal and external threats to network security, transactional security risks, and network security practices and technologies.

Internal Network Security Threats

Internal threats to network security can include management failure to support organization-wide security awareness; inadequate security policies; security procedures that are not enforced; unhappy employees or disgruntled former employees; failure to make copies of critical data or failure to store the copied data offsite; and missing or untested disaster recovery plans. These are just a few examples of the failure to protect against threats to internal network security and data security — the results of which can be catastrophic. Two important ways to protect against internal network security threats are (1) clearly articulating and enforcing network security policies and procedures and (2) ensuring that network access is restricted to authorized users. Equally important is ensuring that critical data is backed up and taken offsite and that plans for coping with a natural or human-caused disaster are in place.

 Facts@Hand

Most security analysts agree that the greatest threat to network security is, of course, from human ignorance and error. One simple but amazingly effective strategy for gaining unauthorized access to a network or network facilities is called social engineering. Social engineering simply relies on a helpful network user divulging his or her user name or password to someone or allowing someone to enter a network facilities room without the proper authorization.

SECURITY POLICIES AND PROCEDURES After a thorough assessment of an organization's network security risks, management should develop appropriate security policies and procedures and then see that the policies are understood and the procedures are enforced. All employees should receive the training necessary to understand fully an organization's network security policies and how to implement specific security procedures. These procedures might be as simple as not divulging the physical location of network facilities to visitors or more complex, such as requiring all users to encrypt sensitive e-mails sent outside the organization.

AUTHORIZED NETWORK ACCESS Network operating systems have built-in security features that allow network administrators to restrict user access to the network or to specific network functions. For example, a network administrator can configure the network so that each user must enter a unique user name and password before he or she can access the network (Figure 6-43). A **user name** is a unique name you use along with a password to log on to a network, and a **password** is a group of secret characters that identifies you as an authorized network user. When a user leaves an organization, the network administrator then eliminates that user's logon information.

Unauthorized internal users or outside intruders often attempt to guess legitimate passwords in order to break into a network. Passwords that contain a mix of at least six letters and numbers are much more difficult to guess than those with fewer characters or with only letters. Mixing uppercase and lowercase letters or adding some non-reserved special characters (such as & or $) also can help to make a password more secure. Additionally, passwords consisting of names, birth dates, and common words that might be easy to guess should be avoided. Finally, passwords should be changed regularly. Figure 6-44 illustrates some effective passwords.

Figure 6-43 Private networks are configured so that each user must enter a unique user name and password before he or she can log on.

DO THIS	DO NOT DO THIS
Z89$33	Wilson (last name)
D33f084	012664 (birthday)
66G13B	apple
7y3MF98F	user

Figure 6-44 Passwords containing a mix of letters, numbers, and special characters are harder to guess.

Other methods used to restrict network access are biometric identification and smart card identification. **Biometrics** involves using devices to measure biological data to identify a user. A user's fingerprints, voiceprints, iris or retina image, or other biological data can be read by biometric devices and software to allow network logon or permit entrance to a network's physical facilities (Figure 6-45). Authorization for a remote user to access a network or for an employee to enter a network's physical facilities can be provided by a smart card. A **smart card** (Figure 6-45), a plastic card the size of a credit card, contains memory chips that can store special access codes or biometric information.

Figure 6-45 Biometric devices measure biological data that can be used to identify a network user.

DATA BACKUP AND RESTORE Data backup and restore policies and procedures identify how and when copies of critical data and software are made and how backed-up data is restored to a network when an equipment failure or loss of data has occurred. Backup copies of critical data and software can be stored on offsite servers or copied to magnetic tape, CD-ROMs, or other media, which should be stored offsite (Figure 6-46). Data backup procedures should be a normal, regularly scheduled part of network operations, and data restore procedures should be tested periodically to ensure that the correct data is being backed up and the storage media is not damaged. Data backup and restore policies and procedures are an important part of an organization's disaster recovery planning.

@Source

To review real-world employee cybercrimes prosecuted by the U.S. Department of Justice, visit the Discovering the Internet Chapter 6 Web page (**scsite.com/internet/ch6**) and click a link below Cybercrimes.

Data

Data

Data

Offsite Server

CD-ROM

Magnetic Tape

Figure 6-46 Backup copies of critical network data and software can be stored on offsite servers, CD-ROM, or magnetic tape.

DISASTER RECOVERY PLANNING   Networks and data are also at risk for physical damage from natural causes such as fire or flood, as well as from deliberate destruction by employees or outside intruders. IT managers and network administrators use a variety of techniques to protect against accidental or deliberate physical damage to network equipment and data, including locating equipment in locked, tightly controlled, and monitored rooms; removing room numbers and door signs so that network facilities are not marked clearly; using specially designed fire suppression systems; providing backup electrical power; and following sound data backup and restore procedures. Additionally, very large organizations may maintain duplicate network facilities in different geographical areas.

Despite the use of these techniques, disasters that compromise network operations still can occur. A **disaster recovery plan** covers how an organization deals with a natural or man-made disaster to ensure the organization's viability. The portion of a disaster recovery plan that covers network operations should define how an organization plans to manage equipment failure, electrical outages, data loss, security breaches, and damage to physical facilities. Components of a disaster recovery plan should be tested periodically to make certain the plan covers new contingencies.

✋ Facts@Hand

The September 11th terrorist attack in New York provided a wake-up call for the U.S. financial industry when many affected banks, brokerage houses, and other financial firms found their disaster recovery plans were outdated and inadequate. As of this writing, the U.S. Federal Reserve is leading an effort to establish new rules for disaster recovery planning for the financial industry, including requiring firms to be able to resume normal business activities within two hours of an event; requiring duplicate data centers and network operations located several hundred miles from main facilities; and requiring comprehensive testing of backup systems, including testing communications between networks.

External Network Security Threats

External network security threats are those that originate from outside the network. Hackers who gain unauthorized access to a computer network are a threat, as are viruses, worms, and Trojan horses. To help protect against these threats, organizations should use virus protection software and perform regular security audits to ensure network security policies are in place.

UNAUTHORIZED NETWORK ACCESS   In Chapter 1, you were introduced to the term, hacker, which commonly is used to describe a person who uses his or her programming skills to gain unauthorized access to a computer network. A hacker might attack a network for any number of reasons, including accessing and perhaps stealing valuable information. For example, in February 2003, a hacker attacked a credit card processing company, thus resulting in the compromise of approximately eight million American Express, MasterCard, and Visa credit card numbers.

✋ Facts@Hand

The term, hacker, originally was used to describe any especially gifted software programmer. Today, the term refers to malicious hackers, also called crackers or black hat hackers, who compromise networks to steal information or disrupt network services. Some hackers, who voluntarily use their skills to find network vulnerabilities and publicize them, prefer to be called ethical hackers or white hat hackers.

To attack a network, a hacker might break into a home computer or break into multiple computers on a corporate network, to plant software that allows the hacked computers to launch difficult-to-trace attacks on other networks. These types of attacks, called **Distributed Denial of Service (DDoS)** attacks, involve sending a continuous stream of server requests that ultimately overload a server's capacity to respond (Figure 6-47). An example of a DDoS attack occurred in October 2002, when unknown hackers overloaded the 13 ICANN-managed root servers with requests. The flood of requests lasted for approximately one hour, resulting in some slowing of Internet service; no major outages were reported as a result of this DDoS attack, however.

@Source

To learn about cybercrime, visit the Discovering the Internet Chapter 6 Web page (**scsite.com/ internet/ch6**) and click a link below Cybercrimes.

Figure 6-47   A DDoS attack involves sending a continuous stream of server requests in an attempt to overload the server's ability to respond and to cause the server to shut down.

COMPUTER VIRUSES   Hackers often exploit well-known security vulnerabilities in popular software to spread destructive programs such as viruses, worms, and Trojan horses. As you have learned, a computer virus is a small, destructive program that infects other files on a computer by releasing its payload. The **payload** is the destructive event the program is intended to cause, such as erasing individual files or a computer's entire hard drive, preventing you from saving or printing files, or automatically sending messages to the e-mail addresses in your online address book. Viruses, which usually infect executable program files, spread to other files when the infected program is executed; viruses, however, also can be spread via e-mail headers or files attached to e-mail messages, or can be part of a worm payload.

A **worm** is a special kind of virus that spreads across a network, such as the Internet, by replicating itself. A worm does not attach itself to other programs; instead, the worm replicates continuously, ultimately consuming network resources, slowing server response, and crashing infected networks. For example, the SQL Slammer worm, released in January 2003, flew across the Internet from Asia to the United States, replicating itself so rapidly that it crashed hundreds of networks in a very short period of time.

Another type of destructive program that can be part of a virus or worm payload is a Trojan horse. **A Trojan horse** is a program that appears to be something useful or fun, but actually does something nasty, including destroying files, creating a way for a hacker to breach network security, stealing passwords, or recording user keystrokes. A Trojan horse program can be distributed as part of a standard virus, a worm, an e-mail message, or a downloaded file. An example of a Trojan horse is the Backdoor.Hitcap Trojan discovered in February 2003. The Backdoor.Hitcap Trojan, which is distributed via e-mail, affects the Windows operating system by modifying files in the operating system's registry to create a back door, a point of entry into the compromised computer that can be exploited later by a hacker.

Protecting individual home computers connected to the Internet or network computers, servers, and routers involves a combination of security tools, including hardware and software designed to guard against intruders and software designed to detect and destroy viruses, worms, and Trojan horses. Additionally, network administrators must be vigilant about installing software patches that plug security holes, and management should consider periodic security audits to detect network security vulnerabilities.

FIREWALLS AND PROXY SERVERS   In Chapter 2, you learned about personal firewalls, software such as BlackICE Defender or ZoneAlarm Pro that is used to protect home computers with DSL or cable modem Internet connections. A **network firewall** is a combination of hardware and software that filters traffic between private networks or between a private network and a public network, such as the Internet (Figure 6-48). Network firewalls can monitor and report suspicious network traffic and can filter out or block incoming or outgoing network traffic based on a set of predetermined rules established by the network administrator. For example, a network firewall might block outgoing server requests for certain Web pages or block incoming e-mail from specific sources.

Figure 6-48   Personal firewall software protects home computers with always-on Internet connections; network hardware and software filters traffic between networks.

The most common type of network firewall is a **packet-filtering firewall**, which compares information contained in an IP packet header, such as the packet's source and destination IP addresses, with a set of predetermined filtering rules. The firewall allows packets that agree with the filtering rules to pass through to the network; packets that do not agree with the filtering rules are blocked. Another security device often used in conjunction with a packet-filtering firewall is a proxy server. A **proxy server** hides an internal IP address from the outside world by substituting its own IP address for a source computer's IP address before sending outgoing e-mail or Web page requests. For example, an outgoing Web page request first would pass through the proxy server, which substitutes its own IP address for the original source's IP address (Figure 6-49). The proxy server then sends the request on to the packet-filtering firewall, which validates that the source IP address (now the proxy server's IP address) and the destination IP address meet its filtering rules before sending the request on to the Web server.

@Source

To learn more about virus, worm, and Trojan horse threats and hoaxes, visit the Discovering the Internet Chapter 6 Web page (**scsite.com/ internet/ch6**) and click a link below Viruses, Worms, and Trojan Horses.

Figure 6-49 A proxy server hides an internal IP address by substituting its own IP address and a packet-filtering firewall blocks packets that do not agree with its filtering rules.

@Source

To learn more about Internet-filtering software, visit the Discovering the Internet Chapter 6 Web page (**scsite.com/ internet/ch6**) and click a link below Internet Filtering Software.

INTERNET FILTERING SOFTWARE As you have learned, employees' inappropriate use of Internet access can increase a company's potential liabilities and network security risks. Vendors such as WebSpy, Elron Software, SurfControl, and DynaComm sell Internet-filtering software that monitors and restricts employee Internet access.

VIRUS PROTECTION SOFTWARE Several vendors, such as Symantec Corporation and Network Associates, sell software that can detect a known virus, worm, or Trojan horse program as it is being introduced and then clean the infected e-mail message or file by removing the destructive program. Virus protection software must be updated continually with information on recently discovered viruses. This usually is accomplished with virus definition and software update downloads over the Internet.

False warnings about viruses — called virus hoaxes — often are sent from person to person via e-mail. Before you take any action regarding an e-mail virus warning, you should check whether or not that warning is a hoax. To help users determine which viruses are real and which are hoaxes, major virus protection software vendors usually maintain up-to-date information on current threats and an encyclopedia of known viruses, worms, Trojan horse programs, and hoaxes at their Web sites. In the following steps, you review current virus, worm, and Trojan horse threats and hoaxes.

Steps: To Review Current Virus, Worm, or Trojan Horse Threats and Hoaxes

1 **Visit the Discovering the Internet Chapter 6 Web page (scsite.com/internet/ch6). Click Symantec. Point to the security response button on the navigation bar.**

The Symantec home page appears (Figure 6-50). You can use links on this page to review Symantec security products or review the latest virus, worm, and Trojan horse threats. The contents of the Web pages on your screen will vary from those shown in Figures 6-50 through 6-55 on pages 362 through 364.

Figure 6-50

2 **Click the security response button. Point to the first item in the latest virus threats list.**

The Symantec Security Response page appears and displays a list of the newest virus, worm, or Trojan horse programs threats (Figure 6-51). The list includes risk ratings for each threat, with 5 being very severe and 1 being very low. From this page, you can search for virus, worm, or Trojan horse programs by keyword or link to an alphabetical list of threats.

Figure 6-51

3 **Click the link to the first item in the latest virus threats list. Point to the search button in the navigation menu.**

A detail page for the specific threat appears, listing details such as discovery date, threat assessment, technical details, and removal instructions (Figure 6-52).

Figure 6-52

4 **Click the search button. Click the Search text box and type hoaxes as the keyword. Point to the search button to the right of the Search text box.**

The Symantec Search page appears (Figure 6-53). On this page, you can search the Symantec site for a list of virus hoaxes.

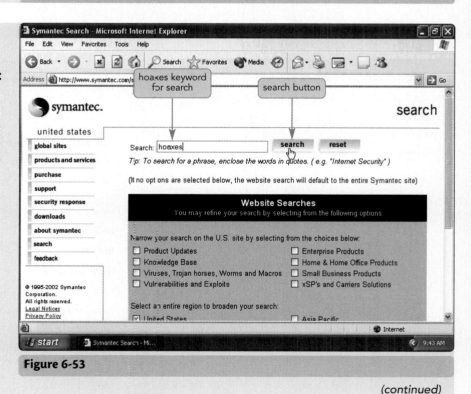

Figure 6-53

(continued)

5 **Click the search button. Scroll down the page and review the search results. Point to the first hoax item in the list.**

The hoaxes search results page appears (Figure 6-54). You can read the details behind each hoax by clicking the hoax links on this page.

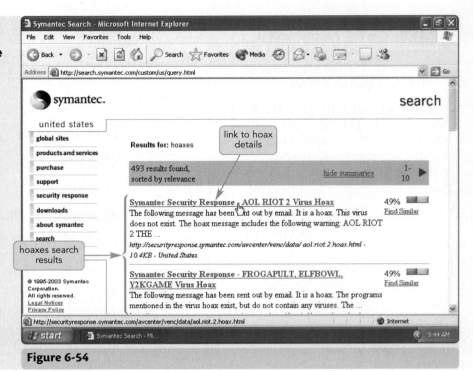

Figure 6-54

6 **Click the first hoax link. Scroll down the page and review the details about the hoax.**

The hoax details page appears (Figure 6-55). You can review the details about the selected hoax on this page.

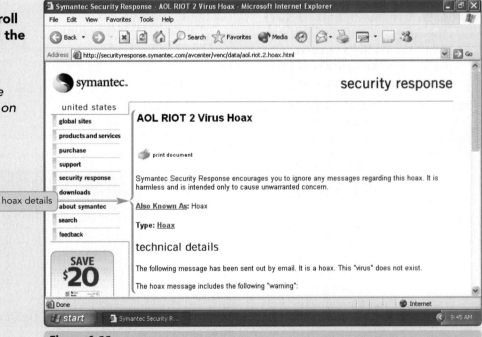

Figure 6-55

SECURITY AUDITS In addition to ensuring that all software updates and patches are installed quickly, as soon as vendors make them available, network administrators and IT managers also use network security audits to expose network vulnerabilities. A **network security audit** generally involves reviewing overall network security policies, employee security policy and procedure training, data backup and restore policies and procedures, and the physical security of the network equipment and data. Additionally, a security audit may involve **penetration testing** in which security audit personnel actually attempt to hack into the network. A network security audit often is conducted by a third-party auditing firm. The security audit results then are used to revise security policies and procedures, improve employee training, and make necessary updates to the network's hardware and software.

Transactional Risks

When a company conducts business transactions with vendors and customers over its network, transactional risks are an additional security concern. The company must ensure that all parties to a transaction are really who they say they are (authentication), that transactions cannot be intercepted or corrupted during transmission (integrity), that no party to a transaction can deny its participation (non-repudiation), and that transaction information is kept private (confidentiality). The primary tools used to provide transaction authentication, integrity, non-repudiation, and confidentiality are encryption and digital certificates.

Encryption is the process of translating readable data into unreadable data to prevent unauthorized access or use. Encrypted data is decoded at its destination using a special key, which can be created, for a fee, by a **certificate authority (CA)**, such as VeriSign, Inc. When an organization wishes to use encryption to protect its online transactions, it requests a set of associated public and private keys from a CA. The **public key** is used by others to encrypt data being sent to the organization and is posted by the certificate authority to a publicly accessible directory. The **private key** is known only to the organization and is used to decrypt the incoming data.

A **digital certificate** electronically authenticates an organization's or individual's identity. A digital certificate is issued, for a fee, by a certificate authority and contains the issuer's name, a certificate number, an expiration date, the requesting entity's public key information, and the issuer's digital signature, which validates the certificate's legitimacy (Figure 6-56). A digital certificate is posted to a public directory or registry so that interested parties can look up public keys.

Figure 6-56 Digital certificates electronically authenticate an organization's or individual's identity.

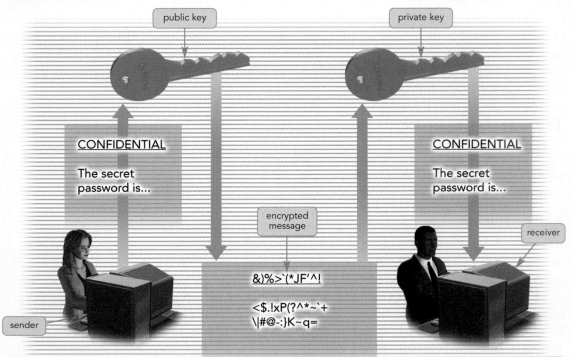

Figure 6-57 Data is encrypted by the sender using the recipient's public key and sent over a public or private IP network to its destination, where it is decrypted using the recipient's private key.

A **public key infrastructure** is the combination of organizations or individuals sending and receiving encrypted data, their public and private keys, and the certificate authorities that issue the keys and digital certificates. Figure 6-57 illustrates sending and receiving encrypted data.

Figure 6-58 A virtual private network (VPN) sends encrypted data and a special tunneling protocol inside IP packets over a public IP network, such as the Internet.

Virtual Private Networks

A **virtual private network** (**VPN**) is a private network that uses a large public network, such as the Internet, to transmit its data (Figure 6-58). **Tunneling** is a process that encapsulates one protocol inside another protocol. VPNs use tunneling to hide encrypted data, IP addresses, and a special tunneling protocol inside IP packets that are routed over the public network using the IP protocol. When the IP packets reach their destination LAN, special VPN firewall software removes the IP protocol information, and the tunneling protocol transmits the packet to its final destination computer. VPNs also use public and private key encryption, digital certificates, and special security protocols to secure their data transmissions.

@Issue Cyberterrorism

Ten minutes! That is all it took on January 26, 2003, for the SQL Slammer worm (also known as Sapphire) to speed across the Internet, rapidly replicating itself by exploiting a well-known flaw in Microsoft's SQL Server database software. The quickly replicating SQL Slammer packets slowed or brought down industry and government servers from South Korea to the U.S. and, by some estimates, caused overworked routers to drop up to 20% of their packets. In the U.S. alone, the disruption caused ATM machines to fail, overwhelmed airline Internet-based ticketing and reservation systems, interfered with publishing the Sunday morning edition of several newspapers, and created delays in accessing several government Web sites. Malicious hacking? Of course. Expensive? Certainly. Estimates of lost productivity worldwide range from $950 million to $1.2 billion. Cyberterrorism? Perhaps not.

The September 11th terrorist attack in New York was followed immediately by a heightened awareness — fueled by news media reports — of a wide range of infrastructure vulnerabilities that possibly could be exploited by terrorists, including potential vulnerabilities in computer network security. The news media often refers to this type of attack as cyberterrorism. A common definition of cyberterrorism, however, is a "politically-motivated criminal act using computers that results in loss of life and/or mass destruction." Using this definition, the SQL Slammer worm — although destructive — was not cyberterrorism.

Many network security and terrorism experts disagree about the importance and immediacy of cyberterrorism threats against the control systems used to manage a country's physical infrastructure — power grids, water and sewer systems, communications, and air traffic control systems. Some experts believe that these control systems are too difficult to compromise without years of preparation, extensive experience with the control systems, and insider information. Most network security and terrorism experts, however, do express concern about acts of cyberterrorism that might massively destroy critical data, such as that stored in Social Security databases, banking records, or airline reservation systems — the loss of which would result in chaos and huge economic losses. And, of course, experts are concerned by terrorists' increasing use of the Internet to communicate with each other and promote acts of violence.

Network security experts stress that the best protection against cyberattacks and the threat of cyberterrorism is the vigilant application of sound network security practices, including installing software patches in a timely manner and using passwords, virus protection software, firewalls, proxy servers, backup systems, and other security measures. For example, the effect of the SQL Slammer worm cyberattack would have been much less dramatic if more network administrators had installed a simple software patch to correct the SQL Server security flaw — a patch made available by Microsoft several months before the SQL Slammer attack took place.

For more information on cyberterrorism, visit the Discovering the Internet Chapter 6 Web page (scsite/internet/ch6) and click a link below National Infrastructure Protection Center.

CHAPTER REVIEW

The Chapter Review section summarizes the concepts presented in the chapter.

 1 **What Are Three Categories of Networks and What Are Common Network Topologies, Access Methods, Transmission Media, and Connectivity Devices?**

Networks are categorized by the physical area that they cover, and include local area, metropolitan area, and wide area networks. A local area network (LAN) supports users in a small geographical area such as a home or single building. A **metropolitan area network** (**MAN**) can connect two or more LANs in multiple buildings across a city or state. A **wide area network** (**WAN**) can be a single network spanning a wide geographical area or it can connect multiple LANs in a wide geographical area. The Internet is the world's largest WAN.

LANs are configured in one of two basic structures: peer-to-peer or client/server. Computers on a **peer-to-peer LAN** are connected via a single cable, and all users can access any computer or peripheral device on the network. While peer-to-peer LANs are inexpensive and easy to install, they are suitable only for a small home or business network of fewer than 10 computers. A **client/server network** consists of clients (multiple personal computers, printers, and other devices containing a NIC) and servers, computers that serve up resources upon a request from a client. Client/server networks use a special network operating system that allows for centralized administration of the network and other services.

A network's **physical topology** is the way in which its components are arranged on the network. The three most common physical topologies are the **bus topology**, the **ring topology**, and the **star topology**. A network's **access method** is the way in which data is transmitted over the network from node to node. The two most common LAN access methods are **Ethernet** and **token ring**. Networks use both physical transmission media, such as **twisted-pair** and **fiber-optic cable**, and wireless transmission media, such as **infrared** (**IR**) and **radio frequency** (**RF**) **transmissions**.

The hardware devices and software that connect network **segments** and multiple networks to each other are **hubs**, **bridges**, **data switches**, **routers**, and **gateways**. A hub is an inexpensive device that forwards packets to all nodes connected to it. Bridges and switches are intelligent devices that read packets and then use MAC addresses to route them to their destinations. Routers are more expensive specialized computers that open packets, read their destination address, compare that address with a table of best routes, and then forward the packets using the best route indicated by the routing table. Routers also can redirect packets to an alternate route, if necessary. Gateways, which can be hardware devices or software, are used to connect dissimilar network segments or networks, and translate packets so that they can be read by the destination segment or network.

 2 **What Are the Key Components and Services that Make Up the Internet Infrastructure?**

Network service providers (**NSPs**) provide the interconnected Internet backbones and networks. NSPs exchange data between networks at **network access points** (**NAPs**). Today, many NAPs are located around the world, to enable Internet traffic to move from one network to another. Other exchange points are the five regional **Metropolitan Area Exchanges** (**MAEs**) located in San Jose, Washington, D.C.,

Chicago, Dallas, and New York. **Peering** is the exchange of Internet traffic at a public or private exchange point. NAPs and NSPs create peering agreements that regulate the exchange of Internet traffic bound for each other's networks.

The **TCP/IP stack** is a group of subprotocols that provides the de facto standard protocols for communications across the Internet, and many private networks. The TCP subprotocol breaks data into packets, verifies packet integrity, and reassembles error-free packets at their destination. The IP subprotocol sends data packets and uses IP addresses to direct packets to their correct destination. Other subprotocols, including FTP, HTTP, UDP, POP3, and SMTP, provide for a variety of communications over the Internet including uploading and downloading files, communications between a Web server and Web browser, live video and audio broadcasting, and sending and receiving e-mail.

An IP address, which is used by the IP protocol to deliver a data packet, is a 32-bit number made up of four 8-bit numbers, called **octets**, which are represented by a decimal number from 0 through 255. An IP address consists of two components: one component that identifies a network and one component that identifies an individual node on the network. IP addresses for all nodes on the same network share the network identification component, and each has a unique node component. IP addresses are assigned to a network based on the network's class. A network's class defines which octets are used to identify the network itself and which are used to identify individual nodes on the network.

The ICANN-managed DNS consists of a hierarchy of servers: **root servers**, which contain directories of primary and secondary DNS servers; primary and secondary DNS servers, which contain domain name and IP address databases for TLD and ccTLD registrants; and local DNS servers, which contain domain name and IP address databases for their local networks. The DNS is used to **resolve** a domain name to its IP address.

ICANN also manages the **Shared Registration System (SRS)**, which allows private companies, called accredited registrars, to participate in the registration of domain names. Accredited registrars insure that an organization's unique domain name is maintained on the appropriate DNS servers for an annual fee.

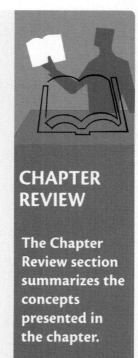

CHAPTER REVIEW

The Chapter Review section summarizes the concepts presented in the chapter.

---

3 What Devices, Services, and Web Technologies Are Driving Greater Adoption of Wireless Internet Access?

Wireless handheld devices, such as digital cellular phones, personal digital assistants (PDAs), and smart phones that combine features of both, are widely popular in Europe, Asia, and the U.S. Wireless messaging services, such as SMS and MMS, are one of the primary reasons for the growing popularity of handheld wireless devices. Analysts expect that future growth in the use of these wireless devices will be driven by messaging services, **location-based services**, and online gaming services.

The standard communication protocol for the wireless Web is the **Wireless Application Protocol (WAP)**, a stack of protocols that operate similarly to TCP/IP but are incompatible with TCP/IP. A WAP gateway is used to translate the HTML page into a **Wireless Markup Language (WML)** page and send it to a microbrowser in the WAP-enabled device.

The **i-Mode** wireless data service is a **wireless Web** alternative to WAP. i-Mode, developed by NTT DoCoMo in Japan, is an IP-based digital cellular phone service. Wireless Web content for the i-Mode service is created using **cHTML**, a subset of HTML that can create Web pages for small-screen displays.

(continued)

CHAPTER REVIEW *(continued)*

CHAPTER REVIEW

The Chapter Review section summarizes the concepts presented in the chapter.

4 How Is the Internet Converging with Traditional Forms of Communication Such as Telephone, Television, and Conferencing?

IP telephony or **voice over IP** (**VoIP**) uses TCP/IP and packet switching to send voice over an **IP network**. VoIP is more efficient than the circuit-switching technologies used by the public switched telephone network. Many organizations are using VoIP to save money on long-distance telephone calls. Telecommunication carriers also are saving money and increasing productivity by using IP voice gateways and packet-switching technologies to direct telephone calls over their networks. With a properly equipped computer, you can use the Internet to make free computer-to-computer calls or low-cost computer-to-telephone calls.

The Internet and television are merging into an important broadcast entertainment medium by allowing you to browse the Web and to send and receive e-mail and instant messages using your television and a subscription TV Internet service. **Interactive television** (**ITV**) is a two-way television technology that allows you to view a favorite television program and, at the same time, participate in interactive online activities such as banking, shopping, playing games, answering quiz show questions, or voting in an online survey.

Videoconferencing permits the real-time transmission of images and sound between two locations and is used for activities such as employee training, new product introduction, customer support activities, and employee meetings. Colleges and universities also use videoconferencing to transmit instructors' lectures to different classrooms and campuses. To participate in a videoconference, you can use a networked computer equipped with a sound card, speakers, a microphone or headset, and videoconferencing software.

5 What Are Internal and External Network Security Threats, Transactional Risks, and the Security Technologies that Mitigate Them?

Network security involves protecting network equipment and data from internal and external threats. Internal threats include failure by an organization's management to develop appropriate security policies and procedures; failure to train users properly in these policies and procedures; failure to create offsite backups of critical data; and failure to prepare for a man-made or natural disaster. External threats include hackers, who breach network security to steal information or disrupt network operations, and destructive viruses, **worms**, and **Trojan horse** programs introduced into a network by infected data files or e-mail. Transactional risks include fraud, denial of participation, interception, and failure to maintain the confidentiality of online business transactions. **Encryption** and **digital certificates** protect online business transactions.

Clearly articulated and enforced security policies and procedures, effective use of network operating system security features to restrict logon access to a network, and restricted access to a network's physical facilities are important ways to protect against internal security threats. Additionally, all critical data should be backed up on a regular basis, and the backed up data should be sent offsite. A plan should be in place that indicates how equipment failure, electrical outages, data loss, damage to physical facilities, and other factors will be handled in case of a disaster.

Employees should be cautioned against divulging their **user name** and **password** information to others, and any unauthorized attempt to enter a network's physical facilities should be challenged. **Network firewalls** and **proxy servers** can be used to protect a network against hackers. Virus protection software can be used to detect and remove viruses, worms, and Trojan horse programs introduced into the network.

Network administrators should install all software updates promptly to remove vulnerabilities that might be exploited by hackers. Additionally, network administrators and IT managers can uncover network security vulnerabilities by hiring a third party to perform a security audit, complete with **penetration testing**.

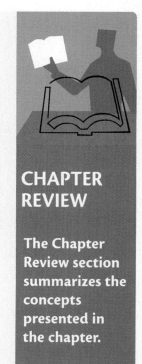

CHAPTER REVIEW

The Chapter Review section summarizes the concepts presented in the chapter.

TERMS TO KNOW

After reading this chapter, you should know each term.

access method (*327*)
accredited registrars (*344*)
alternative root systems (*347*)
authoritative root system (*347*)
biometrics (*356*)
Bluetooth (*331*)
bridge (*333*)
bus (*327*)
bus topology (*327*)
certificate authority (CA) (*365*)
cHTML (*350*)
client/server network (*325*)
coaxial cable (*330*)
cyberterrorism (*367*)
data switch (*333*)
digital certificate (*365*)
disaster recovery plan (*358*)
Distributed Denial of Service (DDoS) (*359*)
DNS servers (*341*)
dynamic routing (*334*)
encryption (*365*)
Ethernet (*329*)
fiber-optic cable (*330*)
gateway (*335*)
global positioning system (GPS) (*348*)
hop (*334*)
hub (*325*)
i-Mode (*350*)
infrared (IR) transmissions (*330*)
intelligent hub (*333*)
interactive television (ITV) (*353*)
Internet telephony (*351*)
IP network (*339*)
IP telephony (*351*)

location-based services (LBS) (*348*)
logical address (*339*)
logical topology (*329*)
MAC address (*333*)
Metropolitan Area Exchange (MAE) (*337*)
metropolitan area network (MAN) (*326*)
microbrowsers (*348*)
Multimedia Messaging Service (MMS) (*348*)
name servers (*341*)
namespace (*341*)
network access point (NAP) (*337*)
network card (*324*)
network firewall (*360*)
network interface card (NIC) (*324*)
network operating system (*325*)
network security audit (*364*)
network service providers (NSPs) (*336*)
node (*324*)
octet (*339*)
packet-filtering firewall (*361*)
passive hub (*333*)
password (*356*)
payload (*359*)
peering (*337*)
peer-to-peer LAN (*324*)
penetration testing (*364*)
physical topology (*327*)
port (*333*)
private key (*365*)
private peering (*337*)
proxy server (*361*)
public key (*365*)
public key infrastructure (*366*)

public peering (*337*)
radio frequency (RF) transmissions (*331*)
resolving (*341*)
ring topology (*328*)
root servers (*341*)
router (*333*)
segments (*333*)
Shared Registration System (SRS) (*344*)
smart card (*356*)
star topology (*329*)
static routing (*334*)
TCP/IP stack (*338*)
throughput (*327*)
token (*329*)
token ring (*329*)
transceiver (*381*)
transmission media (*327*)
Trojan horse (*360*)
tunneling (*366*)
twisted-pair cable (*330*)
user name (*356*)
videoconferencing (*355*)
virtual private network (VPN) (*366*)
voice over IP (VoIP) (*351*)
wide area network (WAN) (*327*)
Wireless Application Protocol (WAP) (*350*)
wireless Web (*348*)
wireless LAN (WLAN) (*332*)
Wireless Markup Language (WML) (*350*)
wireless personal area networks (WPANs) (*331*)
worm (*359*)
WMLScript (*350*)

True or False

Mark T for True and F for False. (Answers are found on page numbers in parentheses.)

_____ 1. The TCP/IP stack of subprotocols is the de facto set of communication protocols for the Internet and many private networks. (*338*)

_____ 2. A peer-to-peer LAN is an appropriate networking choice for a medium-sized organization with 45 users. (*324*)

_____ 3. A proxy server sits between a user and the Internet and forwards HTTP requests using its own IP address rather than the user's IP address. (*361*)

_____ 4. Ethernet uses a token that moves clockwise in a circle from node to node. (*329*)

_____ 5. A virtual private network uses a large public network, such as the Internet, to transmit its encrypted data inside regular IP packets. (*366*)

_____ 6. VoIP uses TCP/IP and packet switching to send voice over an IP network. (*351*)

_____ 7. A DDoS attack uses multiple computers to disable another computer or server by flooding it with requests. (*359*)

_____ 8. Most ISPs are also network service providers. (*337*)

_____ 9. ITV uses the Internet to add an interactive experience to passive television viewing. (*353*)

_____ 10. A WAP-enabled digital cellular phone can contact a Web server directly to request a Web page. (*350*)

Multiple Choice

Select the best answer. (Answers are found on page numbers in parentheses.)

1. The transmission media of choice for most MANs is _____ . (*330*)
   a. coaxial cable
   b. infrared (IR)
   c. radio frequency (RF)
   d. fiber-optic cable

2. The markup language used to design Web content for small-screen devices is _____ . (*350*)
   a. WAP
   b. i-Mode
   c. WXML
   d. WML

3. _____ transmissions use light-wave signals as a short-range transmission medium. (*330*)
   a. radio frequency (RF)
   b. Wi-Fi
   c. infrared (IR)
   d. none of the above

(continued)

TEST YOUR KNOWLEDGE

Use the Test Your Knowledge exercises to check your knowledge of the chapter.

TEST YOUR KNOWLEDGE *(continued)*

4. The process of translating readable data into unreadable data to prevent unauthorized access or use is called _____ . *(365)*
   a. decryption
   b. private key
   c. encryption
   d. tunneling

5. A _____ is an intelligent connectivity device with one input port and one output port that connects two network segments or two LANs. *(333)*
   a. bridge
   b. data switch
   c. router
   d. gateway

6. A _____ is not part of a public key infrastructure. *(366)*
   a. certificate authority
   b. public key directories
   c. public and private keys
   d. virtual private network

7. Networks that carry voice, data, and video simultaneously are called _____ networks. *(353)*
   a. videoconferencing
   b. converged
   c. ITV
   d. none of the above

8. Using an IP network to exchange voice, fax, and other transmissions traditionally carried over the public switched telephone network is called _____ . *(351)*
   a. streaming video
   b. IP telephony
   c. IP data services
   d. ITV

9. Also called a dotted quad, a(n) _____ is a 32-bit number used to identify an individual node on a network. *(339)*
   a. physical address
   b. network address
   c. MAC address
   d. IP address

10. A _____ is a special kind of virus that spreads across a network, such as the Internet, by replicating itself. *(359)*
    a. worm
    b. Trojan horse
    c. backdoor
    d. none of the above

Instructions: To complete the Learn It Online exercises, start your browser, click the Address bar, and then enter the Web address **scsite.com/internet/ch6**. Follow the instructions in the exercises below. Each exercise has instructions for printing your results, either for your own records or for submission to your instructor.

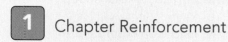

1   Chapter Reinforcement

TF, MC, and SA
Click the Chapter Reinforcement link. Print the quiz by clicking Print on the File menu for each page. Answer each question.

2   Flash Cards

Click the Flash Cards link and read the instructions. Type 20 (or a number specified by your instructor) in the Number of playing cards text box, type your name in the Enter your Name text box, and then click the Flip Card button. When the flash card is displayed, read the question and then click the Answer box arrow to select an answer. Flip through Flash Cards. If your score is 15 (75%) correct or greater, click Print on the File menu to print your results. If your score is less than 15 (75%) correct, then redo this exercise by clicking the Replay button.

3   Practice Test

Click the Practice Test link. Answer each question, enter your first and last name at the bottom of the page, and then click the Grade Test button. When the graded practice test is displayed on your screen, click Print on the File menu to print a hard copy. Continue to take practice tests until you score 80% or better.

4   Who Wants To Be a Computer Genius?

Click the Computer Genius link. Read the instructions, enter your first and last name at the bottom of the page, and then click the Play button. When your score is displayed, click the Print Results link to print a hard copy.

5   Crossword Puzzle Challenge

Below Chapter 6, click the Crossword Puzzle Challenge link. Read the instructions, and then enter your first and last name. Click the SUBMIT button. Work the crossword puzzle. When you are finished, click the Submit button. When the crossword puzzle is redisplayed, click the Print Puzzle button to print a hard copy.

LEARN IT ONLINE

Use the Learn It Online exercises to reinforce your understanding of the chapter concepts and terms.

EXERCISES

Use the
Exercises to
gain hands-on
Internet
experience.

To perform the following exercises, you must be connected to the Internet and have access to a printer.

1 Look Up Corresponding Domain Names and IP Addresses

1. Open the Command Prompt window and use the nslookup command to identify the domain names that correspond to the following IP addresses:
   a. 198.133.219.25
   b. 207.46.150.20
   c. 18.7.21.110
   d. 192.150.14.120
   e. 209.235.240.56

2. If necessary, open the Command Prompt window and use the nslookup command to identify the IP addresses that correspond to the following domain names:
   a. berkeley.edu
   b. fedworld.gov
   c. godiva.com
   d. rackspace.com
   e. pbs.org

3. Using the IP addresses you found in step 2 above, answer the following questions:
   a. Which IP addresses identify Class A networks?
   b. Which IP addresses identify Class B networks?
   c. Which IP addresses identify Class C networks?

4. Close the Command Prompt window.

2 Compare the Authoritative Root System with Alternative Root Systems

1. Visit the Discovering the Internet Chapter 6 Web page (**scsite.com/internet/ch6**) and click links below Exercise 2 to research alternative root systems and the ICANN-managed authoritative root system.

2. Using your research, write a one-page paper that compares and contrasts the ICANN-managed authoritative root system with alternative root systems. Be certain to address the following topics in your paper:
   a. Define the authoritative root system.
   b. Define and give examples of alternative root systems.
   c. Discuss ICANN's position on alternative root systems.
   d. Describe why proponents favor alternative root systems.
   e. State why you do or do not agree with ICANN's position on alternative root systems.

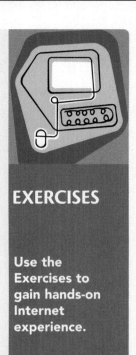

EXERCISES

Use the
Exercises to
gain hands-on
Internet
experience.

 Consider a Small Business Network

You are the owner of a small handicraft business and are thinking about ways to increase your employees' productivity. Your small business has four computers and a printer, and one of the four computers has an Internet connection. Your business operates on a very tight budget; you think, however, that a computer network might be one answer to your productivity concerns. To learn more about whether or not a computer network is a good idea for your small business, you want to learn more about networking.

1. Visit the Discovering the Internet Chapter 6 Web page (scsite.com/internet/ch6) and click 3Com below Exercise 3.

2. Scroll to view the Free online courses links and click the Networking Basics link.

3. Read the course overview and click the TAKE COURSE NOW link.

4. Follow the navigational links to proceed through Lessons 1 through 4 and answer the following questions.
   a. What are four resources your employees can share via a network?
   b. How can a computer network enable your employees to share files and software applications?
   c. How can a computer network enable your employees to share an Internet connection?
   d. How can a computer network help your employees communicate with each other more effectively?
   e. What type of LAN should you consider that would allow your employees to share your single printer and an Internet connection and still fit within your budget?

5. If instructed to do so, continue with Lessons 5 through 8 and then take the short online quiz at the end of the course.

 Search for an Available Domain Name

You want to register a domain name for your small photography supply business. The first step is to identify suitable and available domain names from which to choose. You need the domain name to be short, easy to remember, and appropriate for a photography supply business.

1. Visit the Discovering the Internet Chapter 6 Web page (scsite.com/internet/ch6) and click the links below Exercise 4 to search for an appropriate domain name that meets your criteria: short, easy to remember, and appropriate for a photography supply business. Do not forget to search in multiple top-level domains (TLDs).

2. Print the search results page that provides available, appropriate domain names and indicate which name you prefer.

(continued)

EXERCISES

Use the Exercises to gain hands-on Internet experience.

EXERCISES (continued)

5 Identify Handheld Wireless Devices and Wireless Carriers

1. Visit the Discovering the Internet Chapter 6 Web page (scsite.com/internet/ch6) and click the links below Exercise 5 to research the latest models of handheld wireless devices.

2. Identify two each of the following devices: cell phones, personal digital assistants (PDAs), and smart phones.

3. Create a table containing the following information:
   a. Vendor name
   b. Model name
   c. Model description
   d. Model price

4. Use the search tool, shopping guide, or shopping bot links below Exercise 5 to identify wireless network carriers.

5. Create a table containing the following information:
   a. Carrier name
   b. Messaging services available and pricing for those services
   c. Wireless Internet and Web services available and pricing for those services

6. Write a one- or two-paragraph summary discussing why you would or would not purchase a handheld wireless device to access the Internet and the wireless Web. If you would purchase a device and wireless Internet access, select the device and carrier based on your previous research in this exercise and explain the reasons for your choices.

6 Use the Windows Tracert Utility to Trace Hops

1. Open the Command Prompt window and use the tracert command to identify the number of hops between your computer and the following locations:
   a. www.mit.edu
   b. www.microsoft.com
   c. www.bbc.co.uk
   d. www.hometownfavorites.com
   e. www.nasa.gov

2. Which location required the most hops? Which location required the fewest hops?

7 Identify Current Virus, Worm, and Trojan Horse Risks

1. Visit the Discovering the Internet Chapter 6 Web page (scsite.com/internet/ch6) and click the links below Exercise 7 to identify 10 current viruses, worms, and Trojan horses.

2. Create a table that lists the following information:
   a. Name
   b. Risk level
   c. Description and payload
   d. Date discovered
   e. Source of information

8   Review Wireless Security Issues

1. Visit the Discovering the Internet Chapter 6 Web page (**scsite.com/internet/ch6**) and click the links below Exercise 8 to research wireless security issues.

2. Using your wireless security research, write a one-page paper that describes current wireless security issues. Be sure to include the following topics in your discussion:
   a. wireless viruses, worms, and Trojan horse risks
   b. wireless LAN security risks, including war driving

9   Understand Cyberattacks

1. Visit the Discovering the Internet Chapter 6 Web page (**scsite.com/internet/ch6**) and click the links below Exercise 9 to answer the following questions about cyberattacks:
   a. Who is Kevin Mitnick, what did he do, and what were the repercussions of his actions?
   b. Who is the single hacker who successfully breached network security at Yahoo!, Microsoft, WorldCom (now MCI), and the New York Times during the months from August 2001 to February 2002? How did he accomplish each attack? What were his motives?
   c. What unprecedented event occurred on February 7-8, 2000, that interrupted access to major Web sites, including Yahoo!, eBay, CNN.com, Amazon.com, and E*Trade? Who was responsible for the event and why?

2. Visit the Discovering the Internet Chapter 6 Web page (**scsite.com/internet/ch6**) and click the links below Exercise 9 to identify two recent cyberattacks. Write a short paragraph describing each cyberattack. Remember to identify your sources correctly.

10   Review International Standards Organizations

1. Visit the Discovering the Internet Chapter 6 Web page (**scsite.com/internet/ch6**) and click the links below Exercise 10 to identify the mission of each of the following standards organizations:
   a. ANSI   b. EIA
   c. ETSI   d. IEC
   e. IEEE   f. ISO
   g. ITU

2. Write a short paper that includes one paragraph for each organization that describes the organization and its mission.

CHAPTER 7
Creating Web Pages

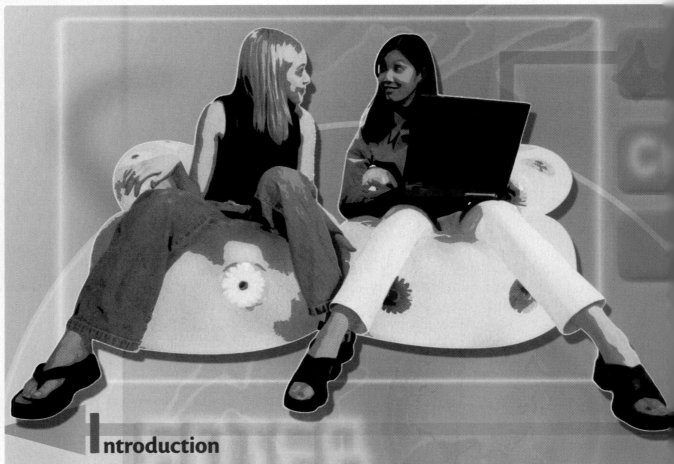

Introduction

As you explore the Web, your level of satisfaction with each Web site you visit may vary considerably. Factors that affect your level of satisfaction with each Web site may include how easy or difficult it is to navigate a site, how fast a site's pages download into your Web browser, and whether or not you were able to find useful information easily. You more likely enjoyed a positive viewing and browsing experience when the site was well-organized with attractive, easy-to-read and easy-to-navigate Web pages.

In this chapter, you will learn how to plan a Web site. You also will learn about the importance of Web site navigational elements and how to use text, color, images, and other design elements to create attractive and useful Web pages. Then you will learn about markup languages, such as HTML and XML, and how to create a simple personal résumé page using HTML. Next, you will learn about the importance of testing completed Web pages and how to publish them to a Web server. Finally, you will learn how Web authoring, scripting, and programming tools are used to create Web pages.

OBJECTIVES

After completing this chapter, you will be able to:

1. Discuss how to plan a Web site by defining its purpose, target audience, objectives and strategies, and organizational structure

2. Describe how navigational elements, text, color, images, tables, frames, and other design elements affect Web page usability

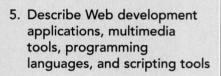

3. Identify markup languages and create a simple résumé Web page using HTML

4. Discuss the importance of Web page testing and how pages are published to a Web server

5. Describe Web development applications, multimedia tools, programming languages, and scripting tools

CONTENTS

@Source

To view examples of Web site mission statements, visit the Discovering the Internet Chapter 7 Web page (**scsite.com/ internet/ch7**) and click a link below Web Site Mission Statements.

Web Site Planning

Whether you are involved in creating your personal Web site or you are part of a team developing a large commercial Web site, effective Web site design starts with the planning process — long before you begin to create the site's pages. Web site planning involves identifying your Web site's purpose, its target audience, its objectives, the strategies used to accomplish those objectives, and its organizational structure.

Purpose

As you learned in Chapter 5, Web sites serve many different purposes. A government Web site, for example, can provide citizens with information about a government agency and its programs; an e-business Web site can sell products or services directly to consumers or to other businesses; and a non-profit organization's Web site can inform the public about the organization's operations. The first step in planning a Web site is to consider carefully the site's overall purpose, also called its **mission**. For example, a personal Web site's mission might be to support an individual's job search, to share a family's history, or to promote a particular hobby. A commercial Web site's mission might be to enable vendors to interact directly with a company's supply processes; to provide an additional sales channel for products and services; or to promote a particular company, industry, or technology. You may choose to create a formal, written mission statement for your Web site. A Web site **mission statement** is a written statement that clearly explains a site's purpose and the reason it exists. You sometimes can find a Web site's mission statement posted directly at the site so that the site's purpose is clear to its viewers. A Web site's mission statement often takes the form of a welcome paragraph on the home page. Alternatively, a Web site can use a **tag line**, which is a short, simple phrase or slogan that identifies an organization's or Web site's purpose. Figure 7-1 provides an example of a Web site mission statement at the Boeing Company's Supplier Environmental Web site. Figure 7-2 provides another example of a Web site mission statement at the University of Otago Library site.

Figure 7-1 Boeing Company's Supplier Environmental Web site.

Figure 7-2 University of Otago Library Web site.

While a Web site mission statement explains the purpose of the site, many organizations use a global mission statement to explain their overall business or organizational purpose to employees, vendors, customers, and other constituents. Often these organizations include that global mission statement at their Web sites.

Facts@Hand

The development of a complex Web site often involves a team of people, including writers who develop content for the site; Web and graphic designers, who lay out and create the Web pages; technical support personnel, who publish, test, and maintain the site; and managers, who oversee the entire project.

@Source

To view examples of business, government, and non-profit global mission statements, visit the Discovering the Internet Chapter 7 Web page (**scsite.com/internet/ch7**) and click a link below Mission Statements.

Target Audience

After establishing a Web site's mission, you next need to identify the site's target audience. A Web site's **target audience** is the group or groups of viewers to which the site's content is directed. For example, a university Web site used to provide online course catalogs and registration may have several groups in its target audience, including prospective students, enrolled students, faculty, and administration. The target audience for a personal Web site might be family members, people who enjoy the same hobby, or prospective employers in a specific industry or geographic area. After defining the target audience, you next need to identify the objectives and strategies that support the site's mission while meeting the target audience's needs and expectations.

Objectives and Strategies

Web **site objectives** define a site's aims or goals, and Web **site strategies** are those actions taken at the Web site to accomplish those goals. A small, personal Web site may have just one or two goals and supporting strategies. For example, a personal family history Web site might have two goals: to share information about a family and to share useful genealogy links with other family history researchers. Three strategies to support these two goals could include providing a list of family members and their relationships to each other in a family tree, excerpts from family Bibles or diaries, and links to various genealogy sites.

In contrast, a complex, commercial Web site generally has multiple goals and strategies. Determining objectives and strategies for a commercial Web site is more difficult in part because a commercial site's mission may be very broad. One way to develop objectives and strategies for a commercial Web site is for the development team to determine the answers to a series of questions such as:

- Is the Web site going to be used to market the company's image?
- Will customers be able to order products and services at the Web site?
- Will the Web site provide customer support?
- Is the Web site going to be used to gather information on customers and potential customers?
- Will the Web site provide additional information about a specific industry or technology?

By answering these types of questions, the Web site development team can identify the commercial Web site's objectives and plan the strategies to accomplish those objectives, including what individual Web pages should be included at the site.

With the site's mission statement, target audience, and objectives and strategies defined, you then can plan the Web site and Web page design elements such as organizational structure, navigational elements, graphics, and text.

Organizational Structure

A Web site's organizational structure should allow viewers to find what they are looking for easily, with just a few mouse clicks. In a **hierarchical structure** or **tree structure**, Web pages are ordered in a hierarchy from the home page at the top and major category pages and sub-category pages organized beneath. A simple, personal Web site likely will have no more than two or three levels of pages in its hierarchy, while a complex Web site may require several levels. A hierarchical structure is the most common Web site structure, especially for larger Web sites, because it allows Web site developers to organize related content and provide clear navigation to users.

Two other Web site structures are a **linear structure**, in which pages are linked in a straight line so that they can be read in a specific order, and a **webbed structure**, in which pages are linked in no particular order with a number of navigational options for moving between pages.

HIERARCHICAL WEB SITE At the top of a Web site's hierarchical structure is the home page, which provides an overview of the site's contents and links to other pages at the site. Additional pages in increasing level of detail are found in subsequent levels of the hierarchy.

It is important to structure a complex Web site with an appropriate number of page levels below the home page. For example, a multi-page Web site with only two levels — a home page and a second level of detail pages — creates an uninteresting, flat structure and requires the home page to provide a complete list or menu of links to the remaining pages (Figure 7-3a). A multi-page Web site with too many layers of linked pages, on the other hand, may create an unnecessarily complicated structure that confuses and frustrates viewers because they have to click many times to find detailed information (Figure 7-3b).

An effective Web site structure places as much important information as possible in the second, third, and fourth levels of linked pages, to allow most viewers to find what they need in three or fewer mouse clicks from the home page. Figure 7-4 illustrates a more balanced Web site structure.

STORYBOARDING A good way to plan a Web site's structure is to create a model of the structure using a method called storyboarding. A **storyboard** is a design model that originally was developed to plan scenes for a movie or television program. You can use the storyboarding method to plan a Web site's structure and then test that structure to see how easy or difficult it is for viewers to go from the home page to other pages in the hierarchy.

You can create a storyboard using simple office supplies such as a whiteboard and sticky notes or a bulletin board, index cards, and push pins. You use the sticky notes or index cards to represent each Web page you plan to include at the site. You then arrange the sticky notes on a whiteboard or the index cards on a bulletin board in an organized structure, beginning with the home page at the top of the hierarchy (Figure 7-5 on page 388). The second level of notes or cards represents the major Web pages that follow the home page in importance. The subsequent levels of notes or cards represent pages that provide an increasing level of detail. After you position the notes or cards on the board, you then should draw appropriate connections both vertically down the hierarchy from the home page and horizontally from page to page, with each connection representing a link that a viewer might click to access information.

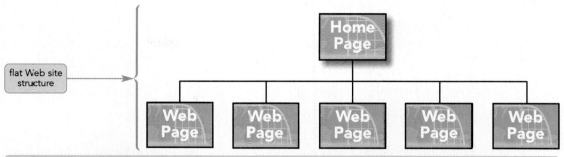

flat Web site structure

Figure 7-3(a) A too flat Web site structure can make a site uninteresting to navigate.

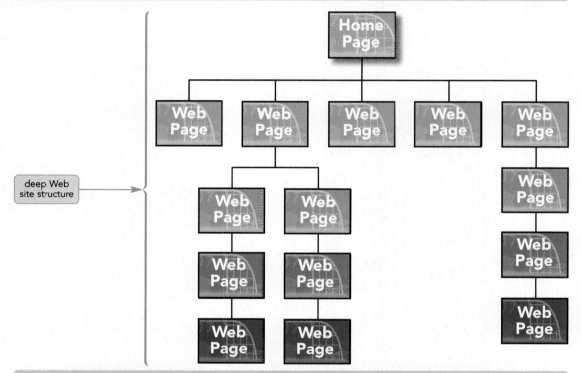

deep Web site structure

Figure 7-3(b) A too deep Web site structure can make a site difficult to navigate and create viewer frustration.

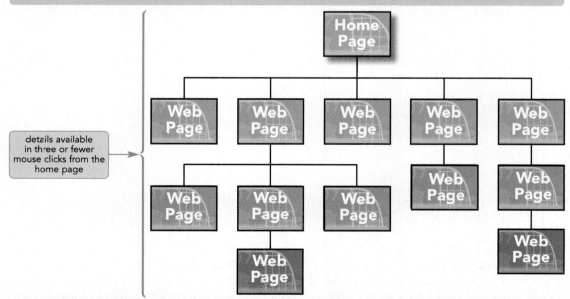

details available in three or fewer mouse clicks from the home page

Figure 7-4 Viewers will find it easier and less frustrating to navigate a Web site whose structure allows them to find important information with a minimum of mouse clicks.

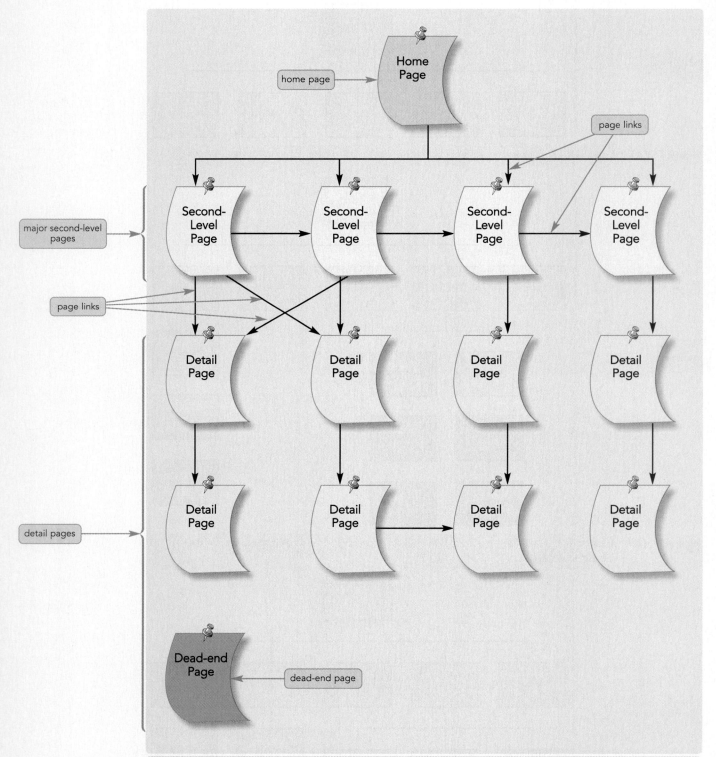

Figure 7-5   A storyboard is an excellent tool for planning a Web site's structure and linking relationships.

The storyboarding process helps you define your Web site's structure in several ways. First, it helps you identify potential navigation problems with the proposed site structure. It also provides you with an excellent tool to determine how many clicks are required to reach specific information. Finally, it helps you identify **dead-end pages**, pages without links to other pages.

In this chapter, you will complete two hands-on projects that allow you to plan your personal Web site and plan a résumé Web page for the site. The following steps show how to plan a personal Web site. You can complete the steps by using a word processing application or by handwriting the information about the Web site plan.

Steps: To Plan a Personal Web Site

1 Write a short mission statement for your personal Web site.

Figure 7-6 illustrates a sample mission statement for a personal Web site. Your mission statement will vary.

My Personal Web Site

Mission Statement

My personal Web site's mission is to share information about my life, work, hobbies, and special interests with others.

Figure 7-6

2 Define the target audience for your personal Web site.

Figure 7-7 illustrates a sample target audience definition. Your definition will vary.

Web Site Target Audience

My personal Web site's target audience consists of family members, classmates, friends, and potential employers.

Figure 7-7

3 Write at least two objectives for your personal Web site and list the strategies you will use at your Web site to accomplish those objectives, including a list of the individual pages you plan to add to your site.

Figure 7-8 illustrates sample objectives and strategies for a personal Web site. Your goals and objectives will vary. You may plan to include as many pages as you want; be sure, however, to include a résumé page.

Web Site Objectives and Strategies

Objective A: to connect with others who also enjoy my hobbies.
Objective B: to share family stories with other family members.
Objective C: to review and discuss books with other readers.
Objective D: to pursue a job as a policy analyst.

Strategies:
1. Create a Web site with three levels of pages.
    a. Include a home page with links to a hobby page, a family stories page, a book review page, and a personal résumé page.
    b. Add a separate page for each family story below the family stories page.
    c. Add a separate page for each book category below the book review page.
2. Design my personal résumé page to target policy analyst jobs in private companies or government agencies.

Figure 7-8

(continued)

4 **Use the storyboarding method to create an appropriate organizational structure for your personal Web site.**

Figure 7-9 illustrates a sample organizational structure for a personal Web site. Your organizational structure will vary.

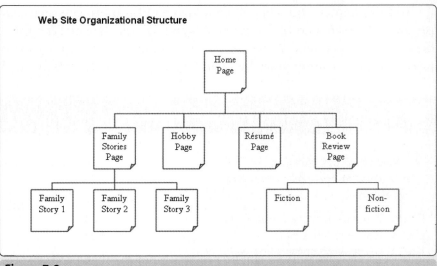

Web Site Organizational Structure

Figure 7-9

 @Source

For more information on Web site design sources, visit the Discovering the Internet Chapter 7 Web page (**scsite.com/ internet/ch7**) and click a link below Web Design.

Web Page Design

It takes only a few seconds for a viewer to form his or her first impression of your Web site — and first impressions really count when similar Web sites are just a few clicks away. If a viewer has an unpleasant or unproductive visit to your Web site, it is likely that he or she will not return for another visit. Whether you are developing pages for a small personal Web site or you are part of the Web site development team constructing a complex commercial site, you can increase the probability of a favorable first impression and a return visit by designing attractive and easy-to-use pages. Web site viewers should be able to understand a Web site's purpose and its message clearly; text, colors, images, and other features at the site should help to convey that purpose and message. This section uses a combination of simple personal Web pages and complex commercial Web pages to illustrate Web design concepts and principles.

Usability

The ease or difficulty with which your target audience members access your site and use its features is a measure of the site's **usability**. Over the past few years, Web designers and usability analysts have focused on developing design guidelines that help increase Web site and Web page usability. Following usability guidelines when designing your Web pages can help minimize potential usability issues. For example, you already have learned that structuring a Web site to reduce the number of mouse clicks required to find useful information increases usability. Other basic Web page usability guidelines include designing for the technology viewers will use to access your Web site; using the home page to communicate clearly information about who owns the Web site and its purpose; avoiding unnecessary splash pages; presenting content in a consistent manner across all pages; limiting page length; using effective page titles; and writing scannable text.

 @Source

For more information on Web site and Web page usability, visit the Discovering the Internet Chapter 7 Web page (**scsite.com/ internet/ch7**) and click a link below Usability Issues.

TECHNOLOGY When designing for Web usability, you must consider the technology viewers will use to access and view your site. An **intranet** is a private internet that uses Web pages to disseminate information to employees over an internal IP network. If you are part of the team designing Web pages for an intranet, you likely have the necessary information about the technologies, such as monitor resolution and Web browser type and version, your target audiences members are using.

If you are designing pages for the World Wide Web, however, you probably will not have access to this information. You should not simply assume that your target audience members are using the latest Web browser versions, the highest monitor resolution, and high-speed Internet connections. Instead, you should design your Web pages to work using the most common technologies employed by your target audience.

For example, you should test your Web pages in several different Web browser types and versions to ensure that the pages display correctly and that page features function correctly. For example, a Web page may look slightly different in Netscape than it does in Internet Explorer. Further, not all browsers support the same features; older versions of browsers often do not support the latest Web page technologies. You thus should test your Web pages to be sure that the pages are attractive and easy to use and that all page features work properly in the various Web browser versions likely to be used by your target audience, rather than just the latest browser versions.

The type of Internet connection used by your target audience also is important. Most viewers will wait less than 10 seconds for a page to download before becoming frustrated. Large, image-laden Web pages designed to be downloaded quickly over a high-speed Internet connection may take too long to download over a slower dialup connection. Some studies indicate that a Web page should be no larger than 30K (30,000 bytes) to download in less than 10 seconds over a 56K dialup connection.

You also must consider **monitor resolution** when designing your Web pages. A monitor's resolution is measured in pixels. A **pixel** (an abbreviated form of the term *pic*ture *el*ement) is the smallest segment of a picture on a computer's monitor. For example, a monitor with a 1024 × 768 resolution can display 1,024 pixels horizontally and 768 pixels vertically. If you design your Web pages for viewing on a monitor with a 1024 × 768 resolution or higher, viewers using monitors with a lower resolution, such as 800 × 600 or 640 × 480, may have to scroll your Web pages horizontally to view the contents — an inconvenience that most viewers dislike.

You thus should design your Web pages to be viewed at the lowest monitor resolution used by the largest portion of your target audience. Today, the lowest monitor resolution for most users is 800 x 600 resolution. Be aware, however, that if you design your Web pages for an 800 × 600 resolution, viewers using a higher resolution may see empty space at edges of your Web page. For example, Figure 7-10 illustrates the Barnes & Noble home page viewed at an 800 × 600 resolution and a 1024 × 768 resolution. At the 800 × 600 resolution, the Web page content fills the screen. When the page is viewed in 1024 × 768 resolution, however, empty space is visible on the right side of the content area.

HOME PAGE CONTENTS A Web site's home page often is the most visited page at a site, and it is the logical starting point for new Web site visitors. A home page functions much like a magazine or book cover and table of

Figure 7-10   The Barnes & Noble home page viewed at two different resolutions.

contents or a newspaper's front page. A home page should, at minimum, provide viewers with answers to four basic questions:

1. *Who* owns or sponsors the Web site?
2. *What* is the Web site's purpose?
3. *How* can viewers find information or perform tasks at the site?
4. *When* was time-sensitive content created or updated last?

🖐 Facts@Hand

The 640 x 480 monitor resolution that was the standard in the early days of the Web largely has been replaced by the 800 x 600 resolution on today's computer monitors. For example, a 2001 survey by StatMarket indicates that fewer than 6% of worldwide Internet users view Web pages at a 640 x 480 resolution, while more than 80% view Web pages at 800 x 600 or 1024 x 768 resolution. Some of those still using a 640 x 480 resolution are people with vision problems, who need to enlarge the screen's content.

Figure 7-11 illustrates how these questions might be addressed on the home page of a family history Web site. As shown in this example, when designing this Web site, you likely would place the family surname prominently on the home page. You also might add brief text that describes the family's origins, a short description of the site's purpose, and contact information. By displaying this information prominently on the home page, you allow viewers quickly to learn who owns the site, what they can find there, and, if necessary, how to contact someone at the site. Next, you would plan clearly defined links to other site pages, such as a family tree or a page of photographs, and links to other family history or genealogy sites to assist viewers in finding useful information. Finally, adding the date on which the site was updated last can help return viewers who may want to know if the site has changed since their last visit.

It is equally important to provide viewers with answers to these important questions on the home page of a commercial Web site. The home page should contain the organization's name and logo in a prominent location, as well as contact information or a link to a page that offers contact information. The home

Figure 7-11 Home page contents should inform the viewer about who owns the site, the site's purpose, how viewers can find information at the site, and when time-sensitive content was last updated.

🖐 Facts@Hand

It is important to show creation or update dates and times for a Web site's time-sensitive content such as news items or stock quotes. When adding a date, be aware that international viewers interpret numerical dates differently. For example, in the U.S., a date written as *3/4/2005* would be read as *March 4, 2005*, but in other parts of the world, it may be read as *April 3, 2005*. To avoid confusion with dates, you should write out the complete name of the month or use its common text abbreviation. You also should add the time zone for any times included in the Web page.

page of a commercial Web site often includes a link to a separate About Us page that includes details about the organization's history and current direction, information about the organization's principals, press releases, and so forth. Additionally, a date and time should be added if time-sensitive content is included. The E*TRADE Financial home page (Figure 7-12) is an example of a commercial Web site's home page that provides this information.

Figure 7-12 The E*TRADE Financial home page identifies the site's owner and provides a link to more information about E*TRADE, an update date for time-sensitive information, and a link to contact information.

As you have learned, a Web site should have a clearly defined mission that is expressed in a formal Web site mission statement or, alternatively, a welcome paragraph or tag line. In the personal family history home page example in Figure 7-11, the tag line is *GONE TO TEXAS*, a phrase that should be recognized by most members of the site's target audience as a historical reference to the U.S. westward migration into Texas in the 1800s. Tag lines on commercial Web sites often are business slogans. Figure 7-13 on the next page illustrates tag lines on the eBay, U.S. Robotics, and Visa home pages.

Figure 7-13   Web site tag lines succinctly identify each site's mission.

SPLASH PAGES A **splash page**, sometimes called a splash screen, is an introductory page that opens before a home page appears. Splash pages often use graphics and animation to interest viewers in going on to the home page. Most animated splash pages automatically redirect the viewer to a site's home page after the animations are finished; most splash pages also provide a link that allows viewers to skip the splash page and go directly to the home page. While splash pages often are visually interesting, they can be a useless distraction for many viewers who want to get to a site's useful content quickly, rather than waste time viewing animations and graphics. The final determination about whether or not to include a splash page rests on the site's purpose and target audience's expectations. For example, a Web site that sells art or graphic design services might benefit from a splash page that emphasizes creativity. The Ontario, Canada, government GOjobs site (Figure 7-14), which offers both English and French versions, effectively

uses a splash page to allow viewers to select a language version. The Coca Cola
Company (Figure 7-14) uses a splash page to direct viewers to different Web site
areas at its large site.

Figure 7-14   Two splash page examples that provide useful information to viewers.

CONSISTENCY   Consistent use of logos, background color, foreground text and accent
colors, navigation bars, and navigation menus across all pages at your Web site will
provide a coherent navigation and browsing experience as users view the Web site. It
also is less confusing to viewers if elements common to all pages at a site — such as a
company name, a logo, or a navigation bar — are positioned in the same place on each
page. For example, it is common to find a company name or logo positioned in the top-
left corner of a commercial Web site's home page; therefore, it is helpful to viewers if
the company name or logo also appears in the top-left corner of all the other pages at
the site.

Consistent positioning of navigational elements allows viewers to learn how to
navigate your site more quickly. For example, if a horizontal navigation bar is placed
at the top of a home page, it is helpful to viewers if the same navigation bar also
appears at the top of other pages at the site. Dell, Inc.'s well-designed and easy-to-
navigate Web site (Figure 7-15 on the next page) illustrates the consistent use of color
and page elements.

Figure 7-15   Dell, Inc. Web pages are well designed and easy to navigate.

PAGE LAYOUT AND LENGTH   Most viewers look first at the top center section of a new Web page and then move their eyes down the page, scanning the page's contents from left to right. Earlier in this section you learned that most viewers dislike having to scroll Web pages horizontally. Many Web sites also use long pages of text, images, and links that viewers must scroll vertically. Whenever possible, very long Web pages should be broken up into multiple, shorter Web pages whose content is visible with little or no vertical scrolling. Pages that may be printed and read from hard copy, such as news reports, technical content, product catalogs, and résumés, sometimes cannot be broken up into smaller pages effectively, however.

When long pages are necessary, viewers should be able to see the most important information on the page without vertical scrolling — just as newspaper readers see the most critical headlines and news stories in the top half of a newspaper's front page (which is referred to as being above the fold). Critical content on a Web page — Web site identification, text that defines the page's content or purpose, search features, and key navigational elements — should be positioned as close to the top of the page as possible. For example, the Chrysler Web site (Figure 7-16) places important elements at the top of each page at the site and uses Web pages that allow users to view the entire contents at the standard 800 × 600 monitor resolution without vertical or horizontal scrolling.

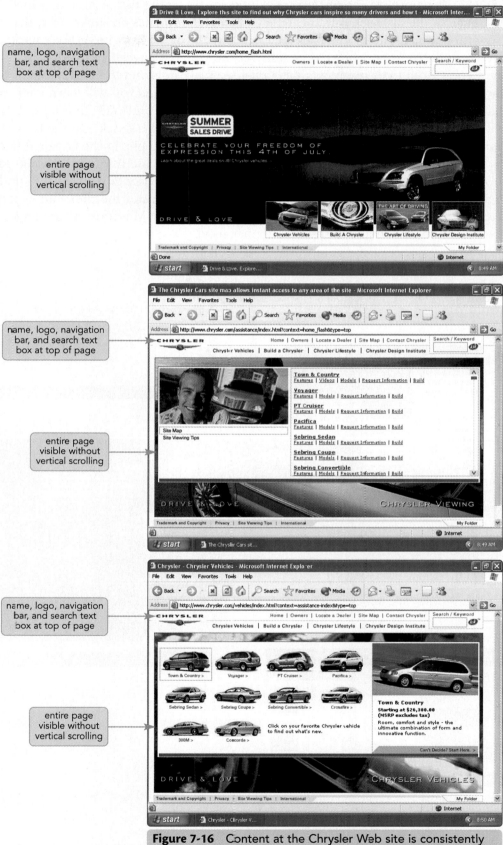

name, logo, navigation bar, and search text box at top of page

entire page visible without vertical scrolling

name, logo, navigation bar, and search text box at top of page

entire page visible without vertical scrolling

name, logo, navigation bar, and search text box at top of page

entire page visible without vertical scrolling

Figure 7-16 Content at the Chrysler Web site is consistently presented on Web pages that require no vertical or horizontal scrolling when viewed at the 800 × 600 monitor resolution.

PAGE TITLES A **page title** is text that appears in the browser title bar and identifies the Web page in the browser window. When you create favorites or bookmarks, the browser automatically stores the page title as the name of the favorite or bookmark. The browser also uses page titles to identify recently viewed pages in a history list. Finally, some search tools use page titles to list search results and to index pages.

Each page at a Web site should have a unique page title. As you will learn later in the chapter, a page title is created using the HTML <TITLE> and </TITLE> tags. A page title should be short and descriptive, so that viewers can read it quickly in the browser title bar or in a favorites, bookmarks, or history list. For example, in the personal family history page example in Figure 7-11 on page 390, an appropriate title for the home page is *Bryson Family History - Home Page*; the page title is short, easy to read, easy to understand, and it accurately describes the page. Figure 7-17 illustrates the short but descriptive page titles on the Orbitz home page, The Natural History Museum science page, and the Wal-Mart garden and hardware supplies page.

Figure 7-17 Every Web page should have a unique page title.

When possible, use the Web site name in the page title for each page on the Web site. For example, on the Wal-Mart page shown in Figure 7-17, the page title, Walmart.com - Garden, indicates to users that this page is in the Garden area of the

Wal-Mart Web site. The page title also indicates that, while this particular page is about gardening, it is still part of the Wal-Mart site.

SCANNABLE TEXT   Viewers generally do not read Web page text word for word, but instead scan the text looking for keywords or phrases that indicate important and useful information. For this reason, viewers prefer Web page text to be written in a succinct and factual style, rather than a flowery or verbose style. You easily can create **scannable text** by using short and descriptive paragraph headings; short phrases, sentences, and paragraphs; and bulleted lists. Web page text also is easier to scan when presented in narrow columns rather than in long lines across the page from the left to right margins.

 Facts@Hand

Studies by the Nielsen Norman Group and the Poynter Institute indicate that more than 75% of Web page viewers scan text on a Web page until they find something of interest; next, they read the text and then they look at graphics.

Navigational Elements

Navigational elements such as internal text and graphic links, navigation bars, navigation tabs, navigation menus, site maps, and top-of-page links all are important tools viewers can use to move from page to page at your site.

INTERNAL LINKS   A well-designed Web site should provide viewers with easy-to-use internal links. An **internal link** is a text or graphic hyperlink that connects Web pages at the same Web site. For example, you use internal links on a home page to connect to second-level pages, internal links on second-level pages to link to other detail pages, and so forth. You also may create two particular types of internal links, usually called next page and previous page links, that allow

Figure 7-18   Cisco Systems' About Cisco page provides a link to the Cisco home page.

viewers to move horizontally between pages at the same level. An internal link to the home page should appear on every page at a site because many viewers do not enter a site at the home page. Using a search results page or a link from another site, viewers may link to any Web page at a site. Having a home page link on every page allows these viewers to get to your home page with a single mouse click. The Cisco Systems About Cisco Web page (Figure 7-18) shows an internal link to the Cisco home page.

 Facts@Hand

An external link is a link to a Web page outside your Web site. For example, the Fedworld.gov site uses external links to provide viewers with quick access to other government Web sites. A personal, hobby-oriented Web site might use external links to provide viewers with quick access to popular search tools or to similar sites devoted to the same hobby.

NAVIGATION BARS AND TABS   A **navigation bar** is a group of text or graphic internal links to major pages at a Web site. Navigation bars with graphic links often are found near the top of a Web page or on the left side of a Web page. Navigation bars using text links often are found at the bottom of a Web page. Many modern sites use a series of colored tabs, called **navigation tabs**, to provide links to major Web pages below the home page in the hierarchy. Navigation tabs, which look like file folder tabs, generally are positioned at the top of a Web page. Figure 7-19 illustrates a text navigation bar at the bottom of the Amazon.com home page, a graphic navigation bar at the top of the Harry and David home page, and a set of navigation tabs at the top of the Staples home page.

Figure 7-19   Prominently displayed navigation bars and tabs help viewers navigate a Web site.

NAVIGATION MENUS   A **navigation menu** is a list of links to other pages at a site that usually appears on the left side of a Web page. A navigation menu can be a simple list of links or a complex, hierarchical arrangement of links to pages with increasing level of detail. The Novell Developers page (Figure 7-20) uses a complex, hierarchical navigation menu to provide links to other pages.

BREADCRUMB TRAILS   Another very effective way to help viewers with Web site navigation is a breadcrumb trail, which you first learned about in Chapter 3. A breadcrumb trail is a hierarchal navigational outline that helps keep viewers oriented by showing them the linking relationship between the page being viewed and the home page. Viewers can click any link in the breadcrumb trail to move quickly back in the hierarchy. While a breadcrumb trail is an excellent visual cue about the linking relationships between pages, it always should be used in addition to other navigational tools such as navigation menus and bars. Figure 7-21 illustrates a breadcrumb trail indicating the path taken from the Sun Microsystems' home page to its Products & Services page, then to its Software page, and finally to its Java & Technologies page.

SITE MAPS   Complex, multi-level Web sites often offer viewers a site map, which is similar to a table of contents. A **site map**, which may be a graphic image or text, provides viewers with a summary of a site's pages. Viewers can click a link in a site map to view a specific page quickly, without having to navigate through multiple levels of pages. Some sites, such as the U.S. Department of Labor site (Figure 7-22 on the next page), provide viewers with both a graphic and a text version of their site maps, while other sites, such as the Apple.com site (Figure 7-22), provide either a text or a graphic site map.

Figure 7-20   The Novell Developers page provides an example of a complex, hierarchical menu of links.

Figure 7-21   Breadcrumb trails help keep viewers oriented by showing the linking relationship between the current page and the home page.

Figure 7-22 Text and graphic site maps provide viewers with a summary of links to pages at a site.

TOP-OF-PAGE LINKS Another useful navigational tool is a top-of-page link. A **top-of-page link** is text or a graphic image that is linked to a position at the top of the current page. Viewers can click a top-of-page link to return quickly to the top of the current page without having to use the scroll bar. Top-of-page links usually are found at the bottom of a Web page, as shown on the NewsLink home page (Figure 7-23). Top-of-page links sometimes are found interspersed between sections of a very long Web page, which enables viewers to read a section of a Web page and then return to the top of the page without having to use the scroll bar. The U.S. Department of Agriculture Web site (Figure 7-23) uses top-of-page links between sections of a long Web page.

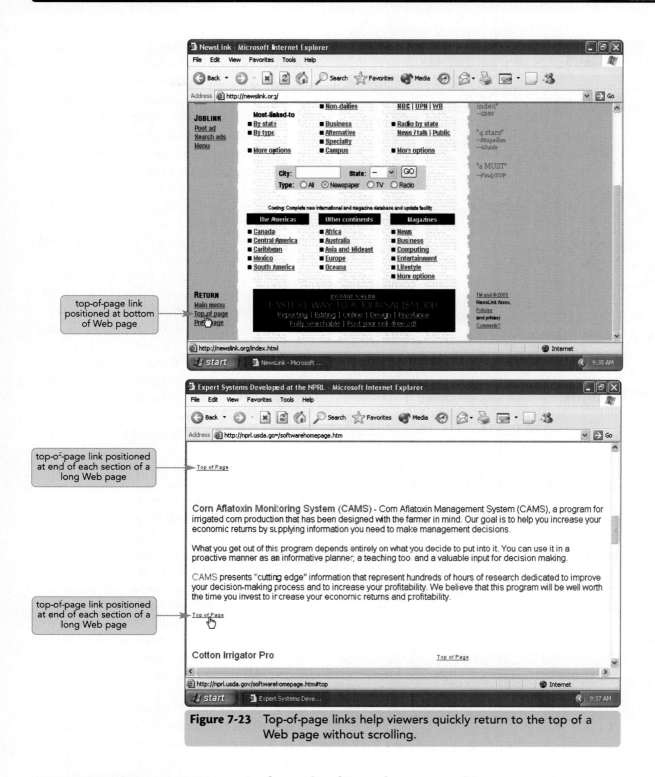

top-of-page link positioned at bottom of Web page

top-of-page link positioned at end of each section of a long Web page

top-of-page link positioned at end of each section of a long Web page

Figure 7-23 Top-of-page links help viewers quickly return to the top of a Web page without scrolling.

EASY-TO-UNDERSTAND LINKS As you learned earlier in this section, the appropriate use of navigational elements — menus, bars, tabs, and text links — ensures that viewers can navigate through a complex site successfully. The purpose of any navigational elements you use must be clear to viewers, however. Most viewers have come to expect that text links will be indicated clearly with an underline and a color. Viewers also generally expect that text links that have not been clicked will be a different color than clicked text links.

Today, many Web sites no longer use the traditional underline and color style to differentiate text links, and some eliminate text links altogether in favor of graphic links. Some Web designers and usability experts, however, think that failing to use

Figure 7-24 Hidden rollover links on the Scienceworks Museum home page may be difficult for some viewers to follow.

Figure 7-25 Easy-to-find links on the General Electric Company home page help viewers navigate the site more effectively.

traditional text link styles or failing to use text links *in addition* to graphic links can make a Web page harder to navigate.

Another area of concern for some Web designers and usability experts is hidden links. A **rollover link** (sometimes called a mouse-over link) is text or a graphic that does not appear to be a link until the mouse pointer is positioned over it — hence, the link is *hidden*. Using rollover animation for links requires viewers to move the mouse pointer several places on a page to find a specific link. Many Web designers and usability experts think using rollover links make it harder for some viewers to navigate a site. Figure 7-24 illustrates internal rollover links that some viewers may find hard to understand or navigate on the Scienceworks Museum home page. In contrast, the General Electric Company home page (Figure 7-25) uses links that are easy to find and understand.

Other Design Elements

In addition to easy-to-understand and easy-to-use navigational elements, you also should consider what fonts to use for your Web page text, how you plan to emphasize keywords, what background color and foreground accent and font colors to use, what images will support your site's message, and how to lay out elements on each page. Additionally, you carefully should consider whether or not to use frames at your Web site and whether or not you plan to gather information from viewers.

FONTS A **font** is a set of characters with the same design including size and character spacing. Two main categories of fonts exist: serif fonts and sans serif fonts. A **serif** is the small appendage or line that may be added to characters such as "B," "N," and "Z." A serif helps viewers' eyes move smoothly from character to character as they read text. Fonts containing characters without serifs are called **sans serif** (without serif) fonts. Sans serif fonts, such as Arial, often are used for paragraph heading text, while serif fonts, such as Times New Roman, often are used for paragraph body text for both printed word processing documents and Web pages designed to be printed and read offline.

Sans serif fonts, however, are easier to read online than serif fonts and studies show that mixing serif and sans serif fonts on a Web page can decrease viewers' reading speed. Many Web pages designed to be read online use sans serif fonts for both paragraph heading text and paragraph body text.

In addition, when you specify fonts for a Web page, it is important to specify commonly available fonts. Web browsers display text in the fonts available on the viewer's computer. If a Web page contains fonts not available on the viewer's computer, the browser must substitute with fonts that are available.

Because viewers are scanning for keywords, you may want to emphasize important words or phrases with the bold font style. The italic font style sometimes is used to emphasize book or magazine titles or non-English words and phrases. Beware of using underlining to emphasize Web page keywords! While underlining is an appropriate emphasis style for keywords on a printed page, Web page viewers associate underlining with links and will expect any underlined text to be a link to another page. Additionally, using colored text for emphasis also may confuse viewers who associate colored text with links. Remember to use bold and italic font style formatting for emphasis sparingly. Large blocks of bold or italicized text are more difficult to read online.

Text-intensive news-oriented Web pages such as the FOX News Channel home page and ABCNEWS.com home page (Figure 7-26) are easily scannable because they use sans serif fonts for both paragraph heading and body text, bolded keywords, frequent paragraph breaks, bulleted lists, and short phrases and sentences positioned in columns down the page.

COLOR   Color evokes an emotional response in people all around the world: "After that last conversation, I was seeing red!" "I'm really feeling blue today." Chances are you have no trouble understanding the emotions behind these two comments — anger and sadness. Color is also a powerful tool for creating an interesting and inviting Web site

Figure 7-26   The FOX News Channel and ABCNEWS.com home pages use appropriate fonts, succinct wording, bolded keywords, bulleted lists, and text in narrow columns to ensure that viewers can scan the pages' content.

and for conveying a site's message; because of viewers' emotional responses, however, the use of color on Web pages should be considered carefully.

A Web site's color scheme should reflect the site's purpose and, at the same time, take into consideration its target audiences' cultural responses to color. For example, the color scheme for an entertainment-oriented Web site could express a feeling of energy, excitement, and fun by using bright, vibrant colors. In contrast, the color scheme for a financial services company's Web site could communicate a sense of trust and professionalism by using more conservative colors. Selecting colors for a Web site targeted to an international audience is more difficult, as the site must use colors that evoke a variety of appropriate cultural responses.

You can avoid color pitfalls by keeping colors to a minimum — for example, by using a white or black background color and then adding a few harmonious accent and text colors to direct viewers to important content such as breaking news stories, navigation bars, special features, and links. Additionally, foreground font colors should contrast strongly with the background color to enhance readability. The E! Online (E! Entertainment) and Charles Schwab Web sites (Figure 7-27) demonstrate the effective use of color on pages directed toward two different target audiences.

@Source

To learn more about using color, visit the Discovering the Internet Chapter 7 Web page (**scsite.com/ internet/ch7**) and click a link below Color.

Figure 7-27   The E! Online and Charles Schwab home pages effectively use color to support the sites' message.

A Web-safe or **browser-safe palette** (Figure 7-28) is a set of 216 colors that can be viewed safely on a monitor set to display 256 colors or 8-bit color. (The other 40 colors are reserved for the computer's operating system.) When designing a Web page, you can specify one of these 216 colors by name, by a hexadecimal code, or by an RGB Triplet number — all of which specify the amount of the red, green, and blue components in the color. For example, the hexadecimal code for the color red is #FF0000, and the RGB Triplet number is 255, 0, 0. Several years ago, most monitors were capable of displaying only 256 colors. Modern monitors, however, usually are capable of displaying 24-bit or 32-bit color, a possible 16.7 million colors! While some Web designers still recommend using a browser-safe palette to ensure that your Web pages look the same on all monitors, other designers suggest it no longer is necessary to restrict a Web color scheme to the 216 colors in the browser-safe palette. When deciding whether or not to use a browser-safe palette, you first should determine the monitor color setting currently being used by the majority of your site's target audience.

#FFFFFF	#FFFFCC	#FFFF99	#FFFF66	#FFFF33	#FFFF00
#FFCCFF	#FFCCCC	#FFCC99	#FFCC66	#FFCC33	#FFCC00
#FF99FF	#FF99CC	#FF9999	#FF9966	#FF9933	#FF9900
#FF66FF	#FF66CC	#FF6699	#FF6666	#FF6633	#FF6600
#FF33FF	#FF33CC	#FF3399	#FF3366	#FF3333	#FF3300
#FF00FF	#FF00CC	#FF0099	#FF0066	#FF0033	#FF0000
#CCFFFF	#CCFFCC	#CCFF99	#CCFF66	#CCFF33	#CCFF00
#CCCCFF	#CCCCCC	#CCCC99	#CCCC66	#CCCC33	#CCCC00
#CC99FF	#CC99CC	#CC9999	#CC9966	#CC9933	#CC9900
#CC66FF	#CC66CC	#CC6699	#CC6666	#CC6633	#CC6600
#CC33FF	#CC33CC	#CC3399	#CC3366	#CC3333	#CC3300
#CC00FF	#CC00CC	#CC0099	#CC0066	#CC0033	#CC0000
#99FFFF	#99FFCC	#99FF99	#99FF66	#99FF33	#99FF00
#99CCFF	#99CCCC	#99CC99	#99CC66	#99CC33	#99CC00
#9999FF	#9999CC	#999999	#999966	#999933	#999900
#9966FF	#9966CC	#996699	#996666	#996633	#996600
#9933FF	#9933CC	#993399	#993366	#993333	#993300
#9900FF	#9900CC	#990099	#990066	#990033	#990000
#66FFFF	#66FFCC	#66FF99	#66FF66	#66FF33	#66FF00
#66CCFF	#66CCCC	#66CC99	#66CC66	#66CC33	#66CC00
#6699FF	#6699CC	#669999	#669966	#669933	#669900
#6666FF	#6666CC	#666699	#666666	#666633	#666600
#6633FF	#6633CC	#663399	#663366	#663333	#663300
#6600FF	#6600CC	#660099	#660066	#660033	#660000
#33FFFF	#33FFCC	#33FF99	#33FF66	#33FF33	#33FF00
#33CCFF	#33CCCC	#33CC99	#33CC66	#33CC33	#33CC00
#3399FF	#3399CC	#339999	#339966	#339933	#339900
#3366FF	#3366CC	#336699	#336666	#336633	#336600
#3333FF	#3333CC	#333399	#333366	#333333	#333300
#3300FF	#3300CC	#330099	#330066	#330033	#330000
#00FFFF	#00FFCC	#00FF99	#00FF66	#00FF33	#00FF00
#00CCFF	#00CCCC	#00CC99	#00CC66	#00CC33	#00CC00
#0099FF	#0099CC	#009999	#009966	#009933	#009900
#0066FF	#0066CC	#006699	#006666	#006633	#006600
#0033FF	#0033CC	#003399	#003366	#003333	#003300
#0000FF	#0000CC	#000099	#000066	#000033	#000000

Figure 7-28 Browser-safe color palette.

@Issue Web Accessibility

Web accessibility involves ensuring that people with visual, hearing, physical, and learning disabilities can access Web-based information effectively. The movement toward full Web accessibility began in the late 1990s when it became clear to many leading Internet scientists, such as Tim Berners-Lee and others at the W3C, that evolving Web design, with its emphasis on a highly graphical interface, actually was making it more and more difficult for people with disabilities to access Web content fully. In the spring of 1997, the W3C, in conjunction with leading browser vendors and the U.S. government, started its Web Accessibility Initiative (WAI) to promote technological and design changes that provide people with disabilities full access to the Web. The U.S. Congress followed suit in 1998 by amending the U.S. Rehabilitation Act to add Section 508, a directive to all federal agencies to eliminate barriers to public electronic information for people with disabilities.

Many disabled viewers use assistive technologies — software and equipment such as screen readers, magnifiers, special keyboard enhancements, and closed captioning technologies — to enable them to work with their computers.

Assistive technologies use a Web page's content and its HTML coding to make the page more accessible. For example, people who are blind can use a screen reader, which uses speech synthesizers to read Web page content aloud, or a Braille display, which presents Web page content to the touch. Screen reader technologies also allow blind users to use the keyboard to move the mouse pointer to different areas on a page. Designing a Web page with text descriptions for graphic images and text links in addition to graphic links allows the content to be read by a screen reader or a Braille display.

You may be surprised to learn that approximately eight percent of all men have some problem seeing color. Designing Web pages for accessibility includes ensuring that people with vision problems such as color blindness can see and understand Web page text and graphics. While the effective use of color can enhance a Web site, color alone should never be used to convey information. For example, using color alone to specify a link prevents viewers with color blindness from visually locating the link. Additionally, viewers with color blindness may not be able to differentiate different areas of a page if the page's color scheme does not provide a strong contrast between the background color and the foreground accent and text colors.

Using sound, scrolling text, and animations to add interest and excitement to Web pages is very tempting. People with physical or learning disabilities, however, may not be able to read and interact with scrolling text or animations quickly enough to perform a task, such as clicking a scrolling link. People with learning disabilities also may be able to understand and work with content and navigational elements better when all pages across a site have a consistent design. People with hearing problems must have a visual depiction for any sounds presented on a page. Some Web development applications, such as Macromedia Dreamweaver, have a built-in tool that checks a Web page for accessibility as it is being created.

For more information on designing for Web accessibility, visit the Discovering the Internet Chapter 7 Web page (scsite.com/internet/ch7) and click a link below Web Accessibility.

IMAGES AND MULTIMEDIA Most Web sites use some combination of pictures, graphics, animations, audio, and video to make the site more interesting and appealing. You should never add graphics, sound, animations, and other elements to a Web page simply because they look or sound terrific, however. Multimedia elements should be used sparingly and only to enhance a Web site's message or help viewers better understand content. For example, a small logo graphic helps viewers identify a Web site, while a large background graphic can be intrusive and may make it difficult for viewers to read page text. Excessive animations and sound may annoy viewers, and unnecessary graphic images can increase substantially the time it takes for a Web page to load in a browser. When designing Web page content, you should take care that any images,

Figure 7-29 The Godiva Chocolatier home page illustrates the effective use of images to support a commercial Web site's message.

animations, or multimedia elements you include support your Web site's message. For example, adding the small Georgia and Texas flag images to the simple family history home page example introduced earlier could enhance the *GONE TO TEXAS* Web site message and highlight the Bryson family's Georgia origins and its westward migration to Texas. Figure 7-29 illustrates the effective use of images to support a commercial Web site's message — buy elegant and yummy chocolate gifts from Godiva Chocolatier!

The larger an image's file size, the longer it takes for a browser to load the image. The speed with which images download in a browser is especially important to viewers using slower dialup Internet connections. To speed up the downloading process, Web pages use **GIF (Graphics Interchange Format)**, **JPEG (Joint Photographic Experts Group)**, or **PNG (Portable Network Graphics)** compressed image file types. GIF files are used most often for graphic images such as logos and icons, and a single GIF file can contain a sequence of images to create an animation effect. JPEG files commonly are used for photographs. The PNG file type is similar to GIF, but with greater file compression, and it is expected to replace the GIF file format for Web pages ultimately.

✋ Facts@Hand

One method used to improve the download time of a large image is first to download a smaller version of the image, called a thumbnail image. The thumbnail image is linked to the larger image. Viewers can see the larger version of the image by clicking the thumbnail image. Companies selling products online often use thumbnail product images in their online catalogs.

TABLES A **table** is a grid of columns and rows. The intersection of a column and a row is called a cell. You may be familiar with using tables in a word processing application, such as Microsoft Word, to organize information in a document. You also may be familiar with a worksheet arrangement of columns and rows, similar to a table, that is used to analyze numbers and perform calculations in applications such as Microsoft Excel. Tables are used to organize text and graphics on a Web page. Using tables to position navigational elements, text, and graphics allows you more control over how these elements appear on the page, giving your pages a more professional appearance. You can place navigational elements, text, or graphics in individual table cells and add color to an entire table or individual table cells. You also can position one table, called a **nested table**, inside another table.

Facts@Hand

Nested tables take longer to download than single tables; therefore, you should consider the length of time to download a page against the value of nesting a table when determining whether or not to use one in a page's design.

A Web page table can have a border, which helps draw a viewer's eye to the table's contents, or it can be borderless. Borderless tables allow you to position text and graphics precisely on a page while hiding the table structure from viewers. Figures 7-30 and 7-31 illustrate how the Bryson Family History home page looks in a browser and how the page elements were positioned on the page using tables.

Figure 7-30 The Bryson Family History home page viewed in a Web browser.

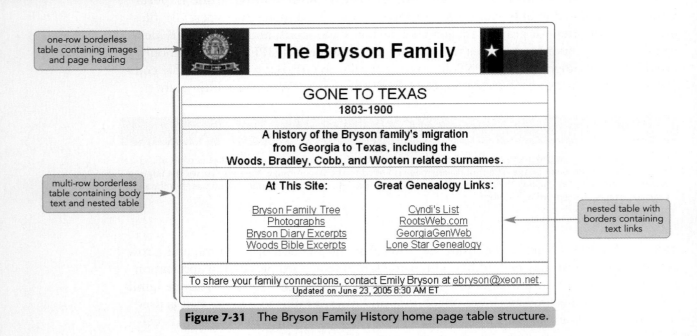

Figure 7-31 The Bryson Family History home page table structure.

FRAMES   You can divide a browser's display area into separate windows, called **frames**, and then place a different Web page in each frame. Because each frame contains a separate page, each frame can be scrolled, if necessary, without affecting the other frames. A set of frames is controlled by a master page, called a **frameset** page. For example, a frameset page might consist of three frames: a top frame, containing a name and logo page; a left frame, containing a navigation page; and a main frame, containing a content page. When a viewer clicks a link on the navigation page in the left frame, the linked page then opens in the main frame.

Frames can be useful for site maintenance. In the previous three-frame example, adding and deleting navigational links requires changing only one page — the navigation page. Problems with frames exist, however, that may outweigh their value: not all early browser versions support frames, requiring a set of no-frames alternative pages; some search engines may not index frames pages correctly; and some viewers may find frames confusing to navigate and bookmark. Frames also may make a browser's display area look overcrowded. While most modern browsers now support frames, frames should be used sparingly, if at all. Figure 7-32 illustrates the use of frames on the U.S. Pharmacopeia home page. The top frame contains a navigation bar; the left frame contains the logo, name, tag line, and navigational links; and the main frame contains the scrollable linked page.

@Source

For a closer look at the many Web page design examples in this chapter, visit the Discovering the Internet Chapter 7 Web page (**scsite.com/internet/ch7**) and click a link below Web Page Design Examples.

Figure 7-32   The U.S. Pharmacopeia frameset page contains three frames: a top frame, a left frame, and a main frame.

SEARCH TOOLS As you learned in Chapter 5, complex Web sites often add a search tool to their site to assist viewers in finding specific information at the site. A Web site search tool usually consists of a text box, in which viewers type keywords, and the button or icon to initiate the search. When viewers click the button or icon, the keywords are compared with an index of keywords maintained for the Web site, and a list of relevant site pages is returned. Web site search tools usually are found in a prominent position on a site's home page as shown on the U.S. Pharmacopeia pages in Figure 7-32 on the previous page.

COPYRIGHT NOTATION Intellectual property, such as written materials, art, music, and Web page content is protected by copyright laws from theft or use without the author's permission even if the author has not applied for a copyright. Today, most commercial Web pages include a copyright notation similar to © 2XXX, name of copyright holder, All Rights Reserved at the bottom of each page. All Web page content, however, is protected by copyright laws whether or not a copyright notation appears on a page. Figure 7-33 illustrates a copyright notice on the Wall Street Journal login page.

FORMS An **electronic form** is a device used to collect information and is similar to paper forms you may have completed when enrolling at your school, registering for a contest, or opening a bank account. Electronic forms on Web pages add the important element of interactivity to a Web page and are used for many things: to collect feedback about a Web site, to register for Web site access, to order products at an online store, to gather information via a questionnaire, and so forth. Web page electronic forms use text boxes, option buttons, check boxes, and drop-down menus to allow viewers to enter or select specific information. Web page forms also provide a button or icon viewers can click to then send the form contents to a server. Figure 7-33

Figure 7-33 Online forms are used to register for Web site access, log on to a Web site, or gather other information from viewers.

illustrates an account change form at the Amazon.com site, a membership login form at the Wall Street Journal Online site, and a Request for Catalog questionnaire at the Overton's site.

In the following step, you will design by hand the layout for a *simple* résumé page for your personal Web site. Carefully consider usability issues, navigational elements, and design elements such as fonts and color in your design. Select colors from the browser-safe color palette (Figure 7-28 on page 405).

Steps: To Design the Layout of a Personal Résumé Page

1 **Design the layout for your personal résumé page by hand or using a word processor. Use a table with three columns and several rows to lay out your page. Include your name and address information, an image, employment objectives, education and employment history sections, a home page link, links to other main pages at the site (as described in your personal Web site plan created earlier in this chapter), and an update date. A vertically scrollable page is acceptable; the text, however, should be succinct and easily scannable, with bolded keywords and bulleted lists.**

Your personal résumé page layout should be similar to, but not necessarily identical to, Figure 7-34. (You will use your personal résumé page layout later to complete Exercise 1 on page 454.)

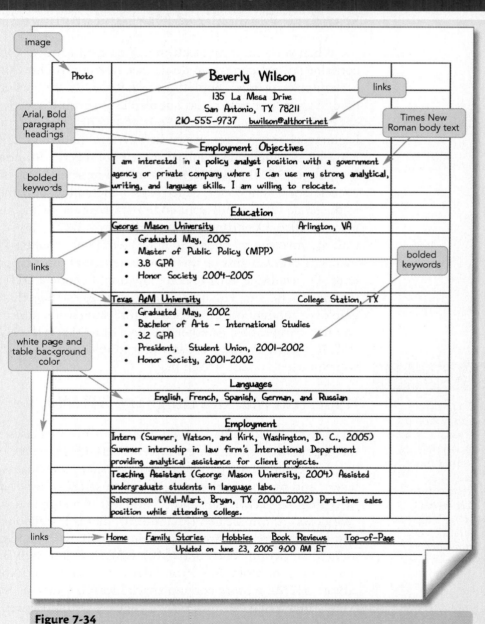

Figure 7-34

Markup Languages

Markup languages use embedded instructions called **tags** to define how text, images, and other components are displayed in a document or how a document is structured. For example, when you see a bolded word on a Web page, that word has been *marked up* by a set of tags that specify the bold format. In this section, you will learn about the SGML, HTML, DHTML, XML and XHTML markup languages. You also will create a simple résumé Web page using HTML.

Standard Generalized Markup Language (SGML)

When you create an electronic document using a word processor, that document contains special codes you do not see that control how the document is displayed on a monitor or printed. Sometimes electronic documents created with a word processor on one computer system do not display or print correctly when transported to a different computer system. In the 1960s and 1970s, scientists at IBM and other companies began working on a generic coding system that would allow documents to be portable between systems. The result of those efforts is the **Standard Generalized Markup Language (SGML)**. SGML is a standard or set of rules that describe how to create generic document codes, called tags, which allow documents to be viewed and printed in the same way on different computer systems. SGML uses a document specification format called a **document type definition (DTD)**. Users of SGML, such as large corporations, government agencies, and the military, create DTDs to define the structure of their large documents or their documents that must be portable between computer systems. For example, a large company might create a DTD specification for an employee manual document. This DTD then describes the tags that can be used to define the employee manual document's structure such as its table of contents, chapter headings, and text paragraphs. Another example of a DTD is the Hypertext Markup Language (HTML) to which you were introduced in Chapter 1. HTML specifies the codes or tags you can use to create a Web page.

@Source

To learn more about markup languages, visit the Discovering the Internet Chapter 7 Web page (**scsite.com/ internet/ch7**) and click a link below Markup Languages.

Hypertext Markup Language (HTML)

When you download a Web page, your browser uses the HTML tags embedded in the page to display it. For example, HTML tags indicate where the page begins and where it ends, where paragraph breaks occur, how text is formatted, what images to insert, and much, much more. You can use HTML to create a Web page from scratch by typing the HTML tags and related text in a simple text editor, such as Notepad (Windows) or SimpleText (Macintosh), that is installed with most operating systems. You also can create a Web page using HTML with an inexpensive HTML editor such as TextPad (from Helios Software), BBEdit (from Bare Bones Software, for the Macintosh), or HomeSite (from Macromedia). Unlike Notepad and other simple text editors, HTML editors contain special features such as line numbering and HTML tag menus that make creating HTML pages easier and faster.

HTML TAGS   HTML tags are instructions placed inside brackets, and they include **container tags**, paired tags placed before and after content to modify it, and **standalone tags**, which indicate a single page element. An example of paired container tags is the <BODY> and </BODY> tags, which define the beginning and end of the body section of a page. Note that the closing tag of a container pair always includes the forward slash. An example of a standalone tag is the <IMG> tag, which tells a browser when it should insert an image file.

HTML tags are not case-sensitive; therefore, a tag keyed as <html> or as <HTML> would be treated the same. Some HTML programmers, however, recommend using uppercase characters for your HTML tags to help you visually separate your tags from the content they modify.

Some HTML tags have special properties called **attributes** that further define the tag. For example, the attribute BGCOLOR is used with the <BODY> tag to specify a page's background color. Attributes are included inside the brackets for the tag they modify, and each attribute's value is enclosed in double quotes. The syntax for writing HTML tags is:

<TAG ATTRIBUTE="value, color, position">text</TAG>

For example, you use the <P></P> container tags to set the beginning and end of a text paragraph, and you use the ALIGN attribute to specify the paragraph's horizontal alignment on the page. Therefore, to indicate a new paragraph with a center alignment, you write:

<P ALIGN="CENTER">paragraph text</P>

To review the HTML tags used to create a complex Web page, you can use your browser. Simply open the desired page and click the Source command on the browser's View menu. In the following steps, you review the HTML source tags for the White House History & Tours page.

@Source

A comprehensive review of HTML tags, their attributes, and how to use them is beyond the scope of this chapter. See Appendix B for a list of HTML tags and their attributes.

Facts@Hand

While some HTML programmers consider including the </P> closing tag optional, many others recommend including it as part of the correct syntax for the <P> and </P> container tag set. In this chapter, you use the </P> closing tag when indicating the end of a paragraph.

Steps: To View HTML Source Tags

1 **If necessary, start your browser. Visit the Discovering the Internet Chapter 7 Web page (scsite.com/internet/ch7). Click White House History & Tours.**

The White House History & Tours page (Figure 7-35) appears.

Figure 7-35

(continued)

2 Click View and then click Source. If necessary, maximize the Notepad window. Observe the HTML tags and content.

The Notepad window opens with the page's HTML source code displayed (Figure 7-36). The HTML code you see may vary from that in Figure 7-36.

3 Close Notepad.

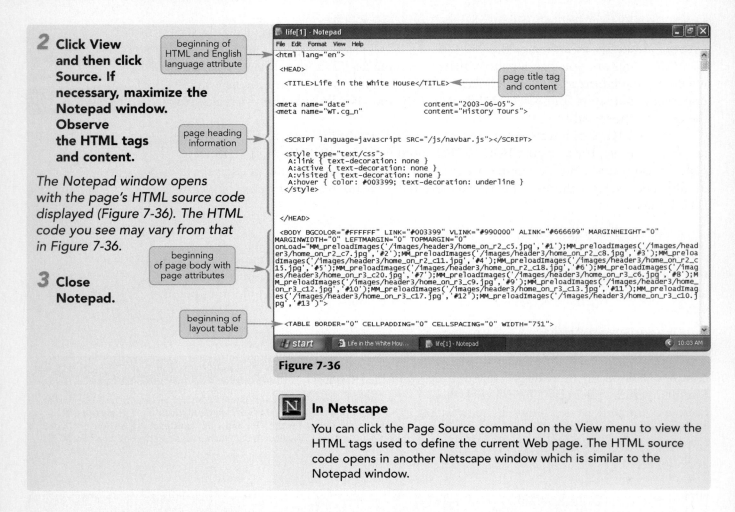

Figure 7-36

N In Netscape

You can click the Page Source command on the View menu to view the HTML tags used to define the current Web page. The HTML source code opens in another Netscape window which is similar to the Notepad window.

DOWNLOADING A PICTURE You will use HTML and Notepad to create a simple résumé page for Beverly Wilson based on the page layout illustrated in Figure 7-34 on page 411. Before you begin the page, however, you complete the following steps to visit the Discovering the Internet Chapter 7 Web page (**scsite.com/internet/ch7**) and download Beverly's picture to the folder on the hard drive specified by your instructor.

Steps: To Download a Picture File

1 Visit the Discovering the Internet Chapter 7 Web page (scsite.com/internet/ch7). Right-click the Beverly Wilson photo image and then click the Save Picture As command. Switch to the folder specified by your instructor, type bwilson in the File name text box, and select JPEG (*.jpg) in the Save as type text box. Point to Save.

The Save Picture As command opens the Save Picture dialog box (Figure 7-37). You specify the file name, file type, and folder location in this dialog box.

2 Click Save.

The Beverly Wilson photo image is saved as bwilson.jpg in the specified folder.

Figure 7-37

In Netscape

When downloading a picture from a Web page viewed in the Netscape browser, the shortcut menu command is Save Image As and the default file type is JPEG Image.

CREATING AN HTML DOCUMENT Now you are ready to begin creating Beverly Wilson's résumé HTML page. Figure 7-38 on pages 418 and 419 illustrates the HTML tags and their attributes in the order in which you will use them to create the page. As you learned earlier, HTML tags are not case-sensitive, and some HTML programmers prefer to use uppercase HTML tags to differentiate the tags from the page's content, which makes the tags easier to locate and read. You will key all HTML tags and their attributes in uppercase characters as you create the résumé page. You begin by opening a text editor such as Notepad and typing the <HTML> tag to start the page. Then you specify the heading section of the page, using the <HEAD> opening tag, and the page title, using the <TITLE> and </TITLE> tags. As you work, you save the page as resume with the .html file extension in the same folder that contains the bwilson.jpg image.

As you build your page with HTML tags and attributes, you should save your page frequently and then preview it in your browser. Frequent previewing allows you quickly to find mistakes, such as failing to add a closing tag to a set of container tags or forgetting to type a closing bracket, and then correct those mistakes before continuing. For example, if your previewed page does not look the way you expected it to look, carefully compare the HTML tags and text you entered in Notepad to the HTML instructions in the steps you just completed and the HTML tag examples provided in the accompanying figures. Make any necessary changes to your HTML tags or text, save the page, refresh the page in the browser window, and review the page again before you continue with the next step. It is important to remember to save your page in Notepad before you preview it in your browser and to refresh the page in the browser window each time you preview it to ensure you are looking at the latest version of the page.

 Facts@Hand

If you are using Notepad, you must type the .html file extension after the file name when you save the file for the first time.

HTML Tag and Attributes	Description
<HTML> </HTML>	Specifies the beginning and ending of the HTML document (Web page).
<HEAD> </HEAD>	Specifies the beginning and ending of the page's heading section where you enter the page title and other document information.
<TITLE> </TITLE>	Indicates the page title that appears in the browser title bar.
<BODY> </BODY>	Specifies the beginning and ending of a page's body section.
BGCOLOR=color	Specifies the background color.
<TABLE> </TABLE>	Specifies the beginning and ending of a table.
BORDER=value	Sets the size of the border in pixels.
COLS=value	Sets the number of columns in a table.
CELLPADDING=value	Sets the amount of space around a cell's contents in pixels.
CELLSPACING=value	Sets the amount of space between cells in pixels.
WIDTH=n or %	Sets the width of a cell in pixels (n) or as a percentage of the table's width (%).
ALIGN=position	Specifies the horizontal alignment of the table.
BGCOLOR=color	Specifies a row's background color.
<TR> </TR>	Defines the beginning and ending of a row of cells inside a table.
<TD> </TD>	Defines a table cell.
WIDTH=n or %	Sets the width of a cell in pixels (n) or as a percentage of the table's width (%).
<P> </P>	Specifies the beginning and ending of a paragraph and automatically inserts a blank link between paragraphs.
ALIGN=position	Specifies horizontal alignment: LEFT, CENTER, or RIGHT.
 	Indicates a line break within a paragraph.

Figure 7-38 HTML tags and attributes.

HTML Tag and Attributes	Description
<IMG>	Indicates an image should be inserted.
BORDER=value	Sets the image border in pixels.
SRC=URL	Specifies the image's URL, how the Web browser locates the image.
WIDTH=value	Sets the image's width in pixels.
HEIGHT=value	Sets the image's height in pixels.
ALT=text	Specifies alternative text when a browser does not display images.
<B> </B>	Applies boldface formatting.
<FONT> </FONT>	Specifies the appearance of text characters.
FACE=list	Names the font: Arial, Times New Roman, Helvetica, etc.
SIZE=value	Sets the font size as an absolute value from 1-7.
 	Indicates a line break within the existing paragraph.
Reserved Characters	Special character sets that begin with the ampersand (&) and end with the semi-colon (;).
	Non-breaking space: used between words to prevent them from being separated by a line break; used to force extra spaces.
<UL> </UL>	Specifies an unnumbered bulleted list.
TYPE=option	Sets the numbering or bulleted format for ordered and unordered lists.
<LI> </LI>	Specifies an item in a list.
<A></A>	Specifies a hyperlink.
HREF=URL	Identifies the target URL.
NAME=text	Specifies a named target for a hyperlink.

Figure 7-38 *(continued)* HTML tags and attributes.

In the steps on the next page, you start Notepad and type the HTML tags to begin the page. If you are not using Notepad, your instructor may modify the steps.

⟨⟩ Steps: To Open Notepad and Begin the Résumé Page

1 **Click Start on the taskbar, point to All Programs, point to Accessories, and click Notepad. If necessary, maximize the Notepad window. Type <HTML> and press the ENTER key twice.**

The <HTML> tag (Figure 7-39) indicates the beginning of the Web page. When you press the ENTER key twice, you add a blank line between groups of tags so that the HTML page is easier to read. A browser ignores this blank line.

2 **Type <HEAD> and press the ENTER key.**

The <HEAD> tag (Figure 7-39) starts the page's heading section which contains the page title information.

3 **Type <TITLE>Beverly Wilson - Resume</TITLE> and press the ENTER key. Type </HEAD> and press the ENTER key twice. Point to File on the menu bar.**

The <TITLE> and </TITLE> tags (Figure 7-39) surround the page title, which will appear in a browser's title bar. The </HEAD> (Figure 7-39) tag ends the heading section.

Figure 7-39

4 **Choose Save As on the File menu to open the Save As dialog box. Type `resume.html` in the File name text box. Point to Save.**

The .html file extension (Figure 7-40) ensures that Notepad saves the document as a Web page.

5 **Click Save.**

folder that contains bwilson.jpg image

file name including .html file extension

Save button

Figure 7-40

STARTING THE BODY SECTION AND LAYOUT TABLE Next, you start the body section of the page using the <BODY> opening tag and specify a white background color using the BGCOLOR attribute set to #FFFFFF (white). Then you want to use a borderless, three-column table to lay out the images and text on the page. You start the table with the <TABLE> opening tag and then specify its attributes: cell padding, cell spacing, width, number of columns, horizontal alignment on the page, and background color.

Table **cell padding** refers to the amount of space between a cell's contents and its borders. Table **cell spacing** refers to the amount of space between table cells. You do not want any extra space between your table cells' content and borders, and you do not want any extra space between your table's cells; therefore, you set the table's CELL PADDING and CELL SPACING attributes to zero.

You can specify a table's width either as an absolute width in pixels or as a percentage of the browser window. Setting a table's width in pixels keeps the table a specific size without regard to the size of the browser window. Setting a table's width as a percentage of the browser window allows the table to resize automatically when the browser window is resized. You want your table to resize with the browser window; therefore, you set the table's WIDTH attribute to 100% of the browser's window. You also want to specify three columns in the table by setting the COLS attribute to 3; align the table horizontally on the page by setting the ALIGN attribute to CENTER; and set the table's background color to white by setting the BGCOLOR attribute to #FFFFFF (white).

In the steps on the next page, you type the HTML tags to begin the page's body section and define the layout table.

Steps: To Create the Body Section and Start the Layout Table

1 Type **<BODY BGCOLOR="#FFFFFF">** **and press the ENTER key twice.**

The <BODY> tag (Figure 7-41) starts the body section of the page, and the BGCOLOR attribute specifies a white background color.

2 Type **<TABLE BORDER="0" CELLPADDING="0" CELLSPACING="0" WIDTH="100%" COLS="3" ALIGN="CENTER" BGCOLOR="#FFFFFF">** **and press the ENTER key twice.**

The <TABLE> tag (Figure 7-41) begins the layout table. The BORDER, CELLPADDING, CELLSPACING, WIDTH, COLS, ALIGN, and BGCOLOR attributes define a table that has no border, has no cell padding or cell spacing, is sized to 100% of the browser window, has three columns, is centered on the page, and has a white background color.

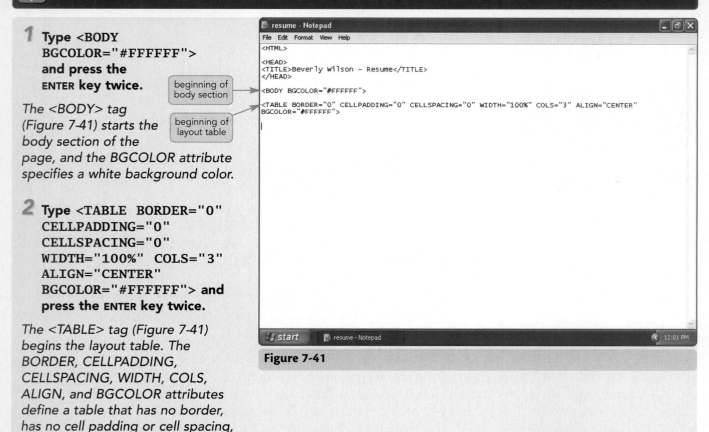

beginning of body section

beginning of layout table

Figure 7-41

Facts@Hand

Unlike a word processing application, the Notepad Word Wrap feature is turned off by default, and the text you enter on each line continues to the right until you press the ENTER key. If necessary to read more easily the HTML tags and text in the Notepad window, you can turn on the Word Wrap feature by clicking the Word Wrap command on the Format menu.

DEFINING THE FIRST TABLE ROW AND CELL   Now you must define each row in the table, each cell in the row, and the cells' contents. You begin by specifying the table's first row with the <TR> opening tag. You then define the row's first cell with the <TD> and </TD> tags. You want the first cell of each row to be 20% of the table's total width. To indicate this, you use the WIDTH attribute and set it to 20%.

The first cell in the first row contains Beverly's picture that you downloaded from the Discovering the Internet Chapter 7 Web page. You center align the contents of the cell with the ALIGN attribute and then insert the picture in the first cell using the <IMG> tag. You further define the <IMG> tag by adding attributes that specify the image's border size, its width and height, its file name, and the alternative text to be displayed by a browser that does not display images.

In the following steps, you type the HTML tags that define the first row in the table and the contents of the first cell in that row.

Steps: To Define the First Row in the Table and the First Cell in the Row

1 Type **<TR>** and press the ENTER key. Type **<TD WIDTH="20%" ALIGN="CENTER">**.

The <TR> tag (Figure 7-42) specifies a table row. The <TD> tag (Figure 7-42) specifies a table cell. The cell WIDTH attribute defines the cell's width as 20% of the table width, and the ALIGN attribute centers the contents of the cells horizontally.

2 Type **<IMG BORDER="0" SRC="bwilson.jpg" ALT="B. Wilson photo" WIDTH="84" HEIGHT="130"></TD>** and press the ENTER key.

The <IMG> tag (Figure 7-42) specifies that the bwilson.jpg image should be inserted. The SRC attribute specifies the image's file name. Because the image is stored in the same folder as the HTML page, you do not have to define a path to the image. The BORDER, WIDTH, and HEIGHT attributes specify the image's border size as 0, its width as 84 pixels, and its height as 130 pixels. The ALT attribute adds alternative text for browsers not displaying images or for screen readers. The </TD> closing tag ends the cell.

3 Choose Save on the File menu to save the page.

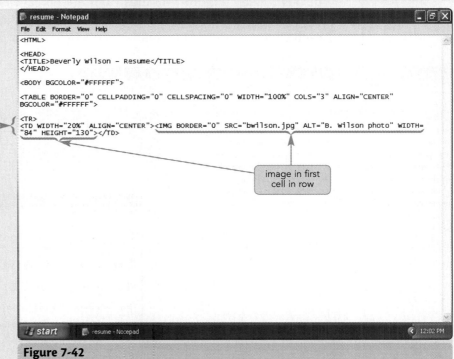

Figure 7-42

USING HEADING STYLES AND FONT FORMATTING You can format text with HTML heading style tags or with the <FONT></FONT> container tags and attributes. A **heading style** is a collection of text formats such as font face and font size that is saved with a unique name. You may have used heading styles in a word processing program to format document and paragraph headings. HTML has six heading styles, <H1> through <H6>. Figure 7-43 illustrates a Web page created in HTML using these heading styles. Note the different font sizes, the serif font, and the bold formatting included in each style.

Figure 7-43 HTML heading styles.

HTML Font Size	Point Size
Size 1	8 point
Size 2	10 point
Size 3	12 point
Size 4	14 point
Size 5	18 point
Size 6	24 point
Size 7	36 point

Figure 7-44 HTML font sizes.

You can use HTML heading styles to format page headings and paragraph headings quickly. You may want more control over heading text font and font size, however. For example, the résumé page you are creating is likely to be printed and read in hard copy by potential employers; therefore, you want to use the Arial sans serif font for the heading text and the Times New Roman serif font for the body text. To do this, you use the <FONT></FONT> container tags with the BOLD, FACE, and SIZE attributes instead of the heading style tags. Browser font sizes range from 1 (smallest) to 7 (largest) and equate to word processing font point sizes 8 to 36. Figure 7-44 lists browser font sizes and their point size equivalents.

In the following steps, you define the second and third cells of the first row. The second cell contains Beverly's name as the page heading formatted with bold and with the size 6 Arial font. The third cell should appear blank. A browser ignores empty cells; therefore, to have the browser recognize the third cell, you must put something in it. A **non-breaking space** is a space between characters that is used to keep them together on the same line. You can use the * * HTML reserved character set to force a non-breaking space in the third cell so that it is not empty and is recognized by a browser.

As you learned in the previous steps, the first cell's width is set at 20% of the table width. Now you set the second cell's width to 60% of the table width and the third cell's width to 20% of the table width, for a total of 100%.

◆◆◆ *Steps:* To Create the Second and Third Cells in the First Table Row

1 Type **<TD WIDTH="60%" ALIGN="CENTER"><B><FONT FACE="Arial" SIZE="6">Beverly Wilson</FONT></B></TD>** and press the ENTER key.

The <B> and </B> tags (Figure 7-45) turn on and off the bold formatting. The <FONT> and </FONT> tags turn on and off the font formatting defined with the FACE and SIZE attributes.

completed first row →

2 Type **<TD WIDTH="20%"> </TD>** and press the ENTER key. Type **</TR>** and press the ENTER key twice.

The </TR> tag (Figure 7-45) ends the first row in the table.

3 Save the page.

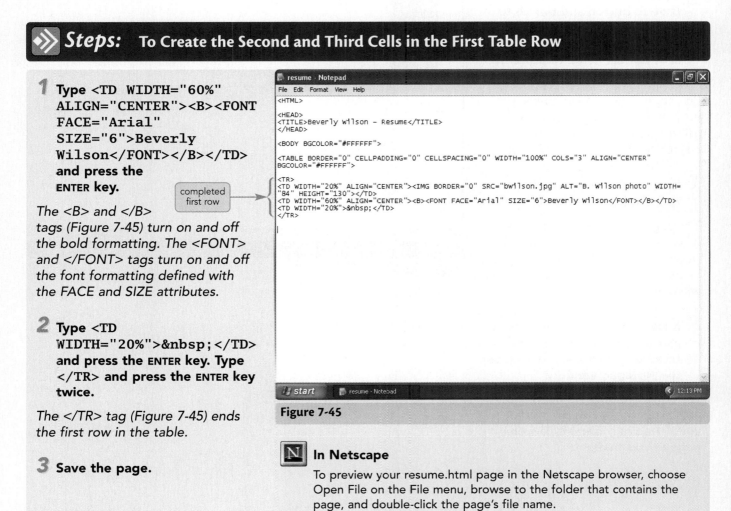

```
resume - Notepad
File  Edit  Format  View  Help
<HTML>

<HEAD>
<TITLE>Beverly Wilson - Resume</TITLE>
</HEAD>

<BODY BGCOLOR="#FFFFFF">

<TABLE BORDER="0" CELLPADDING="0" CELLSPACING="0" WIDTH="100%" COLS="3" ALIGN="CENTER"
BGCOLOR="#FFFFFF">

<TR>
<TD WIDTH="20%" ALIGN="CENTER"><IMG BORDER="0" SRC="bwilson.jpg" ALT="B. Wilson photo" WIDTH=
"84" HEIGHT="130"></TD>
<TD WIDTH="60%" ALIGN="CENTER"><B><FONT FACE="Arial" SIZE="6">Beverly Wilson</FONT></B></TD>
<TD WIDTH="20%"> </TD>
</TR>
```

start   resume - Notepad   12:13 PM

Figure 7-45

N **In Netscape**

To preview your resume.html page in the Netscape browser, choose Open File on the File menu, browse to the folder that contains the page, and double-click the page's file name.

PREVIEWING YOUR PAGE   As noted previously, it is a good idea to preview your page in your browser as you are working on it so you can make any necessary changes as you go along. In the steps on the next page, you open your browser and preview your saved page. Then you minimize the browser window to the taskbar and continue working on the page.

Steps: To Preview Your Page

1 If necessary, start your browser. Click the Open command on the File menu to open the Open dialog box. Click the Browse button and switch to the folder that contains your resume.html document. Double-click the file name to select it and then click OK.

The page (Figure 7-46) opens in your browser. Because you are using a borderless table, you cannot see the table's structure.

2 Restore the browser window to a slightly smaller size.

The page in the restored browser window still looks proportioned because you sized the layout table to be equal to 100% of the browser window size.

3 Maximize the browser window and then minimize it to the taskbar. If necessary, maximize the Notepad window.

You leave the browser open and minimized to the taskbar so that you periodically can preview the page as you create it.

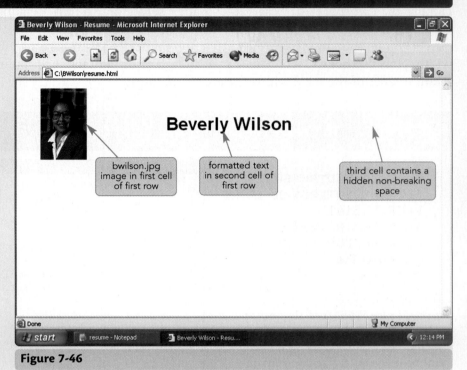

Figure 7-46

CREATING THE SECOND TABLE ROW In the following steps, you create the second row of the layout table, which contains three cells. You use the * * HTML reserved character set to force non-breaking spaces in the first and third cells. The second cell contains the centered address, telephone, and e-mail information on three separate lines within the same paragraph. A **line break** creates a new line inside a paragraph. You use the <BR> tag to create line breaks that place the street address, city, state, zip, telephone number, and e-mail address information on three separate lines within the same paragraph. You add three non-breaking spaces between the telephone number and the e-mail address in the contact information.

Steps: To Create the Second Table Row

1 Type **<TR> and press the ENTER key. Type <TD WIDTH="20%"> </TD> and press the ENTER key.**

These tags (Figure 7-47) create the first cell.

2 Type **<TD WIDTH="60%" ALIGN="CENTER"><FONT FACE="Times New Roman" SIZE="3">135 La Mesa Drive
San Antonio, TX 78211
210-555-9737   bwilson@althorit.net </FONT></TD> and press the ENTER key.**

The <BR> tag (Figure 7-47) creates a line break. The   character set forces three non-breaking spaces.

3 Type **<TD WIDTH="20%"> </TD> and press the ENTER key. Type </TR> and press the ENTER key twice.**

These tags (Figure 7-47) create the third cell and end the table row.

4 Save the page.

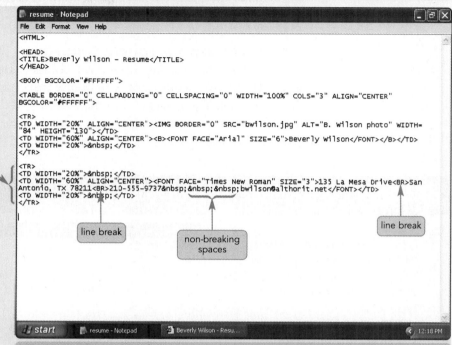

completed second table row

line break

non-breaking spaces

line break

Figure 7-47

5 Maximize the browser window and click the Refresh button on the Standard Buttons toolbar to load a copy of the most recently saved page.

The updated resume.html page appears (Figure 7-48) in the browser. Beverly Wilson's address, telephone, and e-mail address information appears below her name on three separate lines.

6 Minimize the browser window.

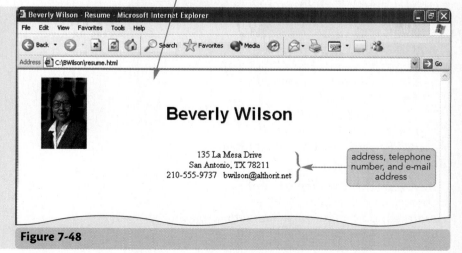

updated resume.html page in browser window

address, telephone number, and e-mail address

Figure 7-48

In Netscape

To refresh a page in the Netscape browser, click the Reload Current Document button.

CREATING THE THIRD AND FOURTH TABLE ROWS   The third row is used to add some blank space between the last line of the contact information and the next paragraph heading. In the following steps, you create three cells and add a non-breaking space to each of the cells. Then, you create the fourth row that has three cells: the first and third cells each contain a non-breaking space, and the second cell contains the Employment Objectives heading text.

Steps: To Create the Third and Fourth Rows

1 Type <TR> and press the ENTER key. Type <TD WIDTH="20%"> </TD> and press the ENTER key. Type <TD WIDTH="60%"> </TD> and press the ENTER key. Type <TD WIDTH="20%"> </TD> and press the ENTER key. Type </TR> and press the ENTER key twice.

This creates the third row of cells (Figure 7-49). The   character set forces a non-breaking space in each cell so that a browser does not ignore them.

2 Type <TR> and press the ENTER key. Type <TD WIDTH="20%"> </TD> and press the ENTER key. Type <TD WIDTH="60%" ALIGN="CENTER"><FONT FACE="Arial" SIZE="4"<B>Employment Objectives</B></FONT></TD> and press the ENTER key. Type <TD WIDTH= "20%"> </TD> and press the ENTER key. Type </TR> and press the ENTER key twice.

This step adds the Employment Objectives text (Figure 7-49) as centered, bold text formatted with the size 4 Arial font.

Figure 7-49

3 Save the page.

4 Maximize the browser window and click the Refresh button on the Standard Buttons toolbar to load a copy of the most recently saved resume.html page. Observe the formatted Employment Objectives paragraph heading.

The formatted paragraph heading (Figure 7-50) now appears two rows below the contact information.

5 Minimize the browser window.

Figure 7-50

Facts@Hand

To save time, you can select tags previously keyed and use the Copy and Paste commands on the Edit menu to copy those tags and paste them in the page. Then simply select and edit the portion that needs to change.

CREATING THE FIFTH TABLE ROW In the following steps, you create the fifth table row that has three cells: the first and third cells each contain a non-breaking space, and the second cell contains a short paragraph describing employment objectives. You use the <B> and </B> tags to bold keywords in the paragraph.

Steps: To Create the Fifth Table Row and Employment Objectives Paragraph

1 Using Figure 7-51 as your guide, create the fifth table row.

The fifth row contains three cells and a text paragraph with bolded keywords (Figure 7-51).

2 Save the page.

3 Maximize the browser window and click the Refresh button on the Standard Buttons toolbar to preview the page. Then minimize the browser window.

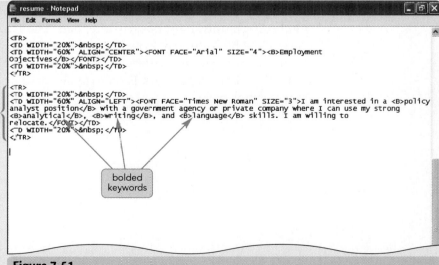

Figure 7-51

USING BULLETED AND NUMBERED LISTS   You can create numbered or bulleted lists of easily scannable text using HTML. A numbered list is called an **ordered list** and a bulleted list is called an **unordered list**. You use the <OL></OL> container tags to define an ordered list and the <UL></UL> container tags to define an unordered list. The TYPE attribute is used with ordered lists to describe the numbering scheme (1, 2, 3 or A, B, C or a, b, c) and with unordered lists to describe the bullet icon (disc, square, or circle). The <LI></LI> container tags are used to define each item in an ordered or unordered list. Figure 7-52 illustrates both ordered and unordered lists.

Figure 7-52   Ordered and unordered lists are used to itemize information on a Web page.

The Education section of the résumé page uses unordered lists to itemize information for each university Beverly attended. The Languages section itemizes the four languages in which Beverly is proficient. The Employment section provides details about Beverly's employment history. In the following steps, you add the rows that contain the Education, Languages, and Employment sections. As you add the rows, you frequently preview your page.

Steps: To Add the Education, Languages, and Employment Sections

1 Using Figure 7-53 as your guide, create a blank row; create the Education section, including the Education paragraph heading, the George Mason University paragraph heading, and the unordered list of items for the university.

These tags (Figure 7-53) create a row with a non-breaking space in each cell; a row containing three cells and the formatted Education paragraph heading; and two rows containing the George Mason University information.

2 Save the page.

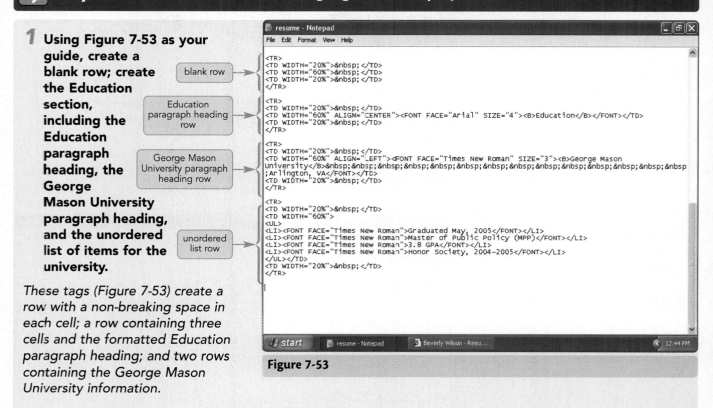

blank row

Education paragraph heading row

George Mason University paragraph heading row

unordered list row

Figure 7-53

3 Maximize the browser window and click the Refresh button on the Standard Buttons toolbar to preview the page in the browser.

Your page should look similar to Figure 7-54.

Employment Objectives paragraph

George Mason University heading

Education paragraph heading

George Mason University unordered list

Figure 7-54

(continued)

4 Using Figure 7-55 as your guide, create the Texas A&M University heading and unordered list.

Texas A&M University paragraph heading row

unordered list

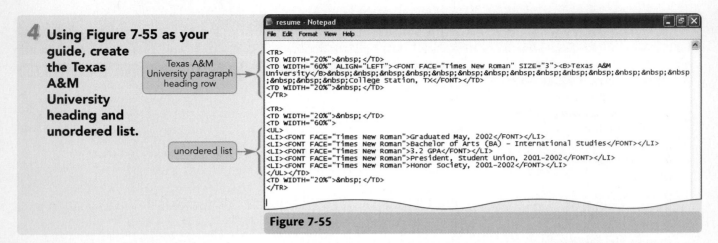

Figure 7-55

5 Using Figure 7-56 as your guide, create the Languages section.

6 Save the page.

Languages paragraph heading row

individual named languages row

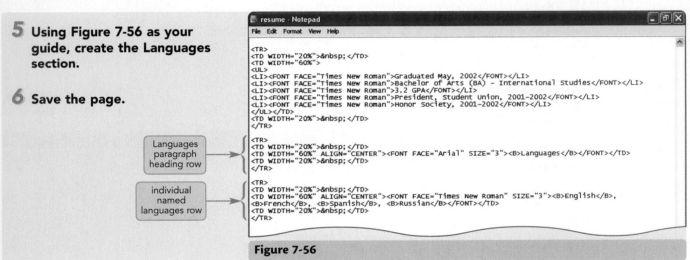

Figure 7-56

7 Maximize the browser window and click the Refresh button. If necessary, scroll down the page to review the new information.

Your page should look similar to Figure 7-57.

8 Minimize the browser window.

Employment Objectives paragraph heading and text

Education paragraph headings and unordered lists

Languages section heading and text

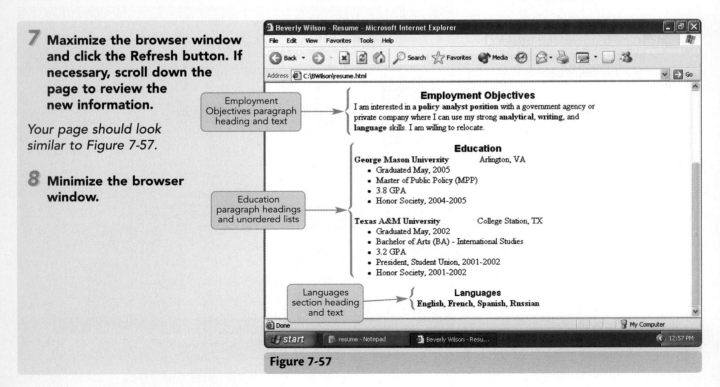

Figure 7-57

9 **Using Figure 7-58 as your guide, create the Employment section.**

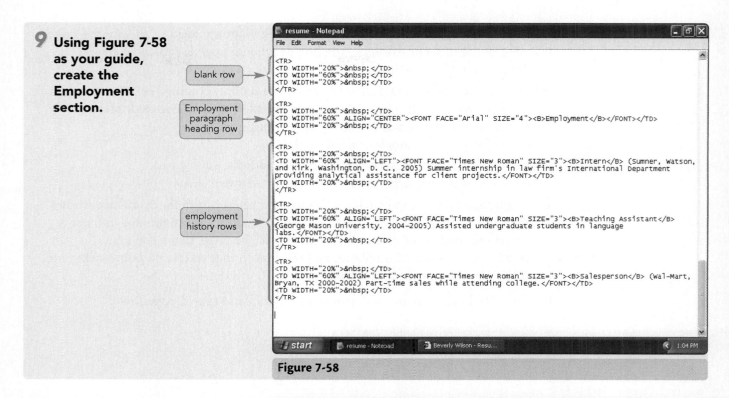

blank row

Employment paragraph heading row

employment history rows

Figure 7-58

10 **Save and preview your page.**

The Employment section on your page should look similar to Figure 7-59.

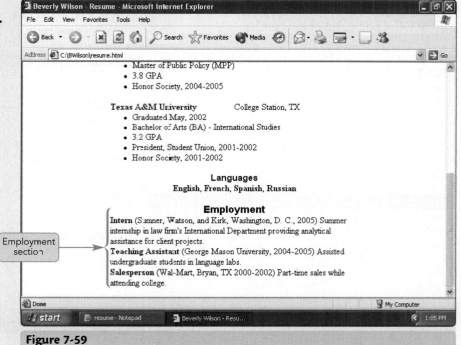

Employment section

Figure 7-59

CREATING HYPERLINKS   You can use the <A></A> container tag set, also called an anchor tag or more simply an **anchor**, and its HREF and NAME attributes to define internal, external, mailto:, and top-of-page hyperlinks. As you learned earlier in this chapter, an internal link is a link to a page at your site, and an **external link** is a link to a page outside your site. A **mailto: link** is a link that, when clicked, opens the viewer's e-mail message window. A top-of-page link is a link that viewers click to return quickly to the top of the current page. The HREF attribute specifies the link's target.

- Internal link: When creating an internal link you only need to specify the linked page's file name. For example, the link to a home page is indicated by <A HREF="home.html">Home</A>.

- External link: You must define the complete path, including the Hypertext Transfer Protocol (http://) reference, for an external link. For example, an external link to the Google search engine site is defined by <A HREF="http://www.google.com">Google</A>.

- Mailto: link: You must indicate the e-mail address, such as <A HREF="mailto:support@officesupplies.com">Support</A>.

- Top-of-page link: A top-of-page link targets a reference point or anchor at the top of the page. When you create a top-of-page link, you make two entries: a named reference point (anchor) at the top of the page, using the <A NAME="text"> tag and attribute, and the link to that reference point, using the <A HREF="#text"> tag and attribute.

Figure 7-60 illustrates internal, external, mailto:, and top-of-page links.

Figure 7-60   Internal, external, mailto, and top-of-page links.

Although it is likely that the résumé page will be printed and read in hard copy, you still need to make it more useful to online viewers by providing a mailto: link and external links to the two universities. To create these links, you use the e-mail address at the top of the page and the university names. Then, you add internal links to other pages at the site (the Home, Family Stories, Hobbies, and Book Reviews pages not yet created), and a link to the top of the résumé page. Finally, you wrap up the page by adding an update date. In the following steps, you type the HTML tags and text to create the links and update date.

Steps: To Add Links and an Update Date

1 Scroll up to view the top of the page and click in front of the bwilson e-mail address in the second cell in the second table row to position the insertion point. Type **<A HREF="mailto:bwilson@ althorit.net">**, then move the insertion point to the end of existing e-mail address and type **</A>** as the entry.

[mailto: link]

The original e-mail address at the top of the page now is surrounded by the anchor tag (Figure 7-61).

Figure 7-61

2 Scroll down to view the row containing the George Mason University paragraph heading. Click to position the insertion point in front of George and type **<A HREF="http: //www.gmu.edu">**, then move the insertion point to the end of University and type **</A>** as the entry.

[George Mason University external link]

The university's name now is surrounded by the anchor tag (Figure 7-62).

Figure 7-62

(continued)

3 Scroll down to view the row containing the Texas A&M University paragraph heading. Click to position the insertion point in front of Texas and type **<A HREF="http://www .tamu.edu">**, then move the insertion point to the end of University and type **</A>** as the entry.

The university's name now is surrounded by the anchor tag (Figure 7-63).

4 Save the page.

Figure 7-63

5 Maximize the browser window and click the Refresh button.

Your page should look similar to Figure 7-64.

6 Minimize the browser window.

Figure 7-64

7 Move the insertion point back to the bottom of the page on the second blank line below the last table row. Using Figure 7-65 as your guide, insert a blank row, create the internal links to the top of the page and the Home, Family Stories, Hobbies, and Book Reviews pages. Add the update date. End the table, end the body section of the page, and end the page.

The </TABLE> tag ends the layout table, the </BODY> tag ends the body section of the page, and the </HTML> tag ends the page (Figure 7-65).

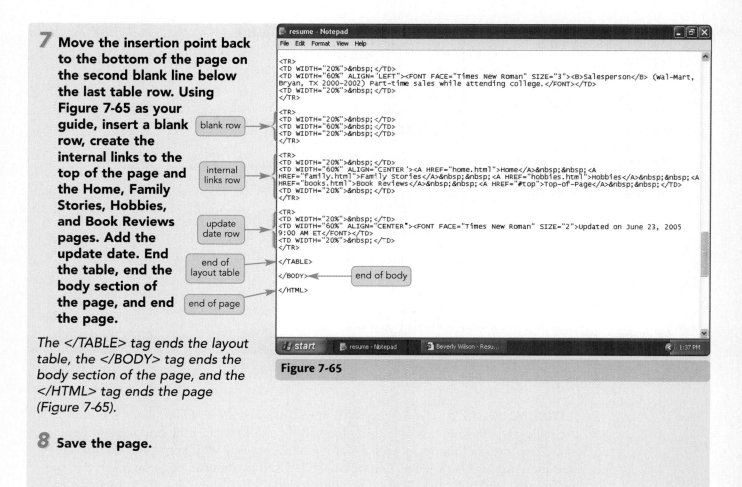

Figure 7-65

8 Save the page.

9 Maximize the browser window. Click the Refresh button on the Standard Buttons toolbar. Scroll down to view the bottom of the page.

The bottom of your page should look similar to Figure 7-66.

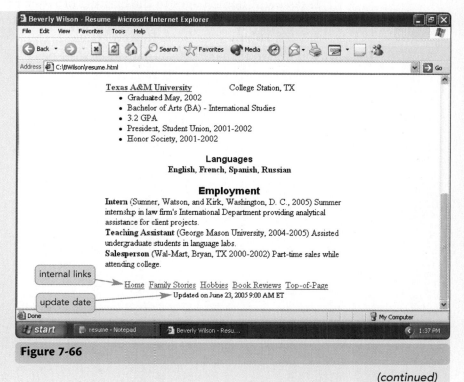

Figure 7-66

(continued)

10 Minimize the browser window.

11 Scroll up to view the top section of the page in Notepad. Move the insertion point to the end of the `<BODY>` tag and press the ENTER key twice. Type `<A NAME="top"></A>` as the entry.

This tag (Figure 7-67) creates a target for the top-of-page link created in Step 6.

12 Save the page.

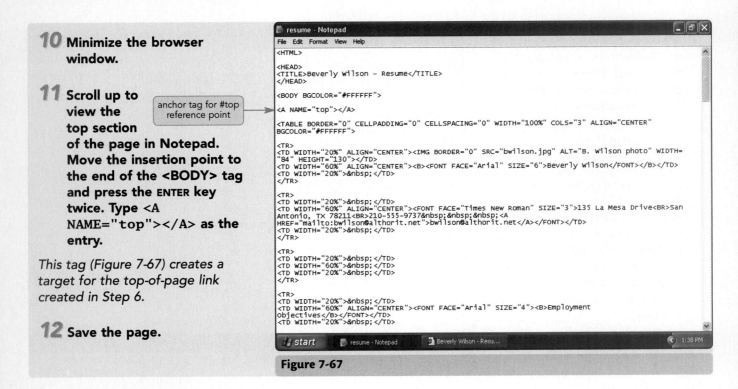

anchor tag for #top reference point

```
resume - Notepad
File  Edit  Format  View  Help

<HTML>

<HEAD>
<TITLE>Beverly Wilson - Resume</TITLE>
</HEAD>

<BODY BGCOLOR="#FFFFFF">

<A NAME="top"></A>

<TABLE BORDER="0" CELLPADDING="0" CELLSPACING="0" WIDTH="100%" COLS="3" ALIGN="CENTER"
BGCOLOR="#FFFFFF">

<TR>
<TD WIDTH="20%" ALIGN="CENTER"><IMG BORDER="0" SRC="bwilson.jpg" ALT="B. Wilson photo" WIDTH=
"84" HEIGHT="130"></TD>
<TD WIDTH="60%" ALIGN="CENTER"><B><FONT FACE="Arial" SIZE="6">Beverly Wilson</FONT></B></TD>
<TD WIDTH="20%"> </TD>
</TR>

<TR>
<TD WIDTH="20%"> </TD>
<TD WIDTH="60%" ALIGN="CENTER"><FONT FACE="Times New Roman" SIZE="3">135 La Mesa Drive<BR>San
Antonio, TX 78211<BR>210-555-9737   <A
HREF="mailto:bwilson@althorit.net">bwilson@althorit.net</A></FONT></TD>
<TD WIDTH="20%"> </TD>
</TR>

<TR>
<TD WIDTH="20%"> </TD>
<TD WIDTH="60%"> </TD>
<TD WIDTH="20%"> </TD>
</TR>

<TR>
<TD WIDTH="20%"> </TD>
<TD WIDTH="60%" ALIGN="CENTER"><FONT FACE="Arial" SIZE="4"><B>Employment
Objectives</B></FONT></TD>
<TD WIDTH="20%"> </TD>
```

start   resume - Notepad   Beverly Wilson - Resu...   1:38 PM

Figure 7-67

TESTING YOUR LINKS   The Beverly Wilson résumé page now is complete. You are ready to preview the page in your browser and test the mailto:, external, and top-of-page links. The mailto: link opens your default e-mail message window. If you do not have an e-mail application such as Outlook installed and configured on your computer, the mailto: link will not work. The external links open the George Mason University and Texas A&M home pages in the existing browser window. The top-of-page link returns you to the top of the page. You cannot test the internal links to the Home, Family Stories, Hobbies, or Book Reviews pages because you have not created these pages. You test your mailto:, external, and top-of-page links in the following steps.

Steps: To Preview and Test the Beverly Wilson Résumé Page Links

1 Maximize the browser window and click the Refresh button on the Standard Buttons toolbar. Point to the mailto: link.

The completed Beverly Wilson résumé page (Figure 7-68) appears.

completed resume.html page with links

mailto: link

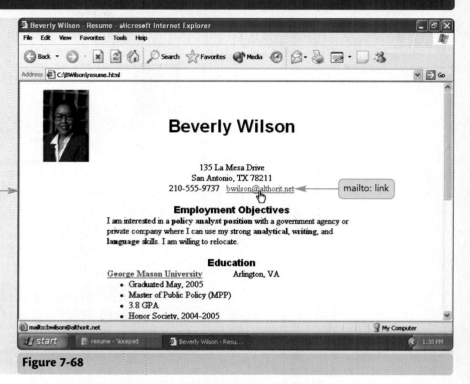

Figure 7-68

2 Click the mailto: link.

The mailto: link opens your e-mail message window (Figure 7-69). It may take a few seconds for the e-mail message window to open. Your e-mail message window may vary from that shown in Figure 7-69.

Outlook Express e-mail message window

mailto: e-mail address inserted in To: address box

Figure 7-69

(continued)

3 Close your e-mail message window. Click No if asked to save the message. Point to the George Mason University link (Figure 7-70).

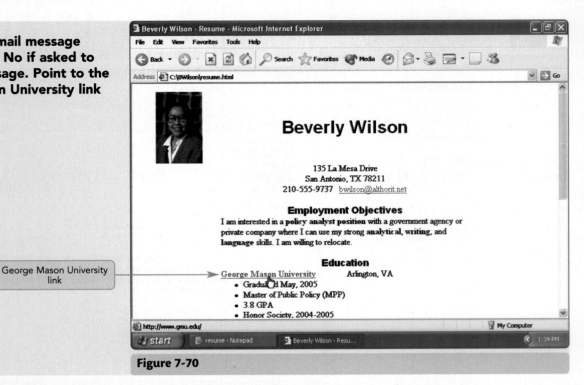

George Mason University link

Figure 7-70

4 Click the George Mason University link. Point to the Back button on the Standard buttons toolbar.

This external link loads the George Mason University home page (Figure 7-71). The Web pages on your screen may vary from those shown in Figures 7-71 and 7-73.

Back button

Figure 7-71

5 Click the Back button on the Standard Buttons toolbar. Point to the Texas A & M University external link (Figure 7-72).

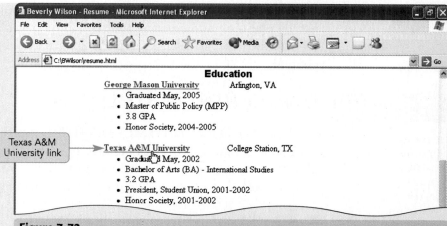

Texas A&M University link

Figure 7-72

6 Click the Texas A&M University link. Point to the Back Button on the Standard Buttons toolbar.

This external link loads the Texas A&M home page (Figure 7-73).

Back button

Figure 7-73

7 Click the Back button on the Standard Buttons toolbar. If necessary, scroll down to view the bottom of the page. Point to the Top-of-Page link (Figure 7-74).

8 Click the Top-of-Page link.

You now are viewing the top of the page.

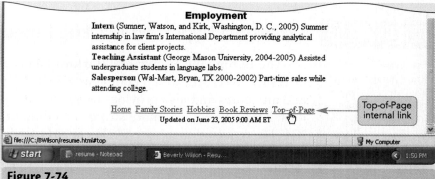

Top-of-Page internal link

Figure 7-74

9 Close the browser and close Notepad.

 In Netscape

To view the previous page in the Netscape browser, click the Back button.

Now that you have created and tested the résumé page, you could complete the Web site by planning and creating the remaining pages and then publishing all the pages and their related files to a Web server. You learn about publishing Web pages later in the chapter.

Dynamic HTML (DHTML)

@Source

For more information about DHTML, visit the Discovering the Internet Chapter 7 Web page (scsite.com/internet/ch7) and click a link below Markup Languages.

Dynamic HTML (**DHTML**) uses HTML tags, style sheets that control the format of a Web page, and a scripting language to make animations and interactive features available after a page is downloaded from the server. An animation that occurs after a page is downloaded, such as a scrolling menu or banner, is an example of DHTML in action.

Extensible Markup Language (XML)

Unlike HTML, which uses strictly defined tags to format a Web page, the **Extensible Markup Language** (**XML**) uses customizable tags to describe a document's structure and its content. Like SGML, XML tags are defined in a document type definition (DTD) specification. XML can be used to define any type of data — as long as both the sender and receiver of the data agree on the XML format called a **schema**. For example, two e-businesses can exchange purchase order, product shipment, and billing data using XML (Figure 7-75). Other current uses of XML include tracking shipping and packages and updating different types of business databases.

Figure 7-75   XML documents can be used to exchange business data.

Extensible Hypertext Markup Language (XHTML)

@Source

For more information about XHTML, visit the Discovering the Internet Chapter 7 Web page (scsite.com/internet/ch7) and click a link below Markup Languages.

The **Extensible Hypertext Markup Language** (**XHTML**) is the "next generation" of HTML. XHTML, which combines HTML 4.0 with XML, supports existing HTML tags and attributes and also provides users with the flexibility to define new tags and attributes. XHTML requires more stringent coding rules or syntax than HTML. For example, XHTML requires opening and closing tags, and tags must be written in lowercase.

Publishing and Testing Web Pages

After you create a Web page, you can save it and any related files, such as image files, to a folder on your computer's hard drive, a network drive, or directly to a folder on a Web server. If you save your pages and related files to a folder on your hard drive or a network drive, they then must be uploaded to a Web server using either the FTP or HTTP protocols. This uploading process is called **publishing** to a Web server. Some large organizations operate a **staging server**, a Web server that is used to store new Web pages and their related files temporarily while the pages are being created and tested. After the pages are tested thoroughly, they then are published to a final destination or *live* server.

When testing your Web pages, you should view the pages in different browser versions and at different monitor resolutions to ensure that they have a quality appearance across all commonly used browsers and monitor resolutions. You also should make certain that all your links work correctly. As you learned in the previous section, you can test pages that are stored on your hard drive or a network drive; you *must* retest them, however, after the pages and all related files are uploaded to a Web server. For example, the folder structure on the Web server may be different from that on your hard disk or network drive, and your HTML instructions may need to be modified to indicate the new locations of linked items and images. Retesting your pages on a live server allows you to make certain all links work correctly and that a browser can find and download all images properly.

After your review and testing, you then should have your Web pages tested by others not involved in creating them, such as members of your target audience. For example, you could ask classmates or friends to test all the pages at your personal Web site. The Web site development team working on a commercial Web site may have employees, suppliers, customers, or other target audience members test the new site's pages. Some large organizations employ outside firms that specialize in Web site usability to test their Web pages.

Web Authoring Tools

As you learned in the previous section, creating a Web page by manually typing all the HTML tags can be very time-consuming. Additionally, it is very easy to make a mistake by failing to include the appropriate attributes for a tag or by failing to follow the correct syntax when typing the tags. In this section, you will learn about another, easier way to create Web pages — using Web development applications. You also will learn how Web multimedia tools such as Adobe Photoshop and Macromedia Flash, Fireworks, and FreeHand are used. Finally, you will learn about the programming and scripting tools used to create interactive Web pages.

Web Development Applications

Web development applications such as Microsoft FrontPage, Adobe GoLive, and Macromedia Dreamweaver allow you to work in a more familiar WYSIWYG (What You See Is What You Get) working environment with menu commands, toolbars, and dialog boxes — while having the HTML tags automatically generated for you while you work!

Facts@Hand

While Web development applications can save time by generating HTML code, they sometimes cannot produce exactly what a Web designer wants. When this happens, professional Web designers modify the automatically generated HTML tags by manually adding new tags, editing existing tags, or removing tags to get just the right results.

FRONTPAGE Creating a Web page in Microsoft FrontPage is very similar to creating a text document in Microsoft's word processing application, Microsoft Word. The FrontPage window opens with a blank document similar to the blank Word document that appears when you open the Word application. The FrontPage window also contains a menu bar and toolbars similar to those in the Word application.

Before you create a Web page in FrontPage, you first create a **FrontPage Web**, which is a folder on your hard drive, on a network drive, or on a Web server in which all the related pages and images for your Web site are stored. You use the FrontPage menu commands and toolbar buttons to format text; to create internal, external, mailto:, and top-of-page links; to insert and format images; and to create and format tables. Meanwhile, as you work, FrontPage inserts the appropriate HTML tags. Figure 7-76 shows the BWilsonWeb FrontPage Web folder open in the FrontPage window and the resume.html page being created in FrontPage.

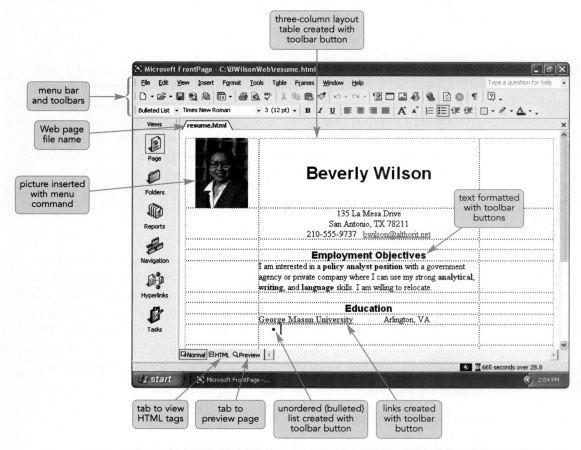

Figure 7-76 Creating a Web page in FrontPage and other WYSIWYG Web development applications involves using menu commands and toolbar buttons to create links, format text, and insert images.

Facts@Hand

Like Microsoft Word, Microsoft FrontPage also provides special tools, called wizards and templates. In Word, these tools are used to create new documents quickly. In FrontPage, these tools are used to create a new FrontPage Web and to create and customize individual Web pages.

You quickly can view the HTML tags that FrontPage automatically inserts (Figure 7-77) and preview how the page looks in your browser (Figure 7-78) as you are creating your page by clicking the HTML or Preview tabs at the bottom of the FrontPage window.

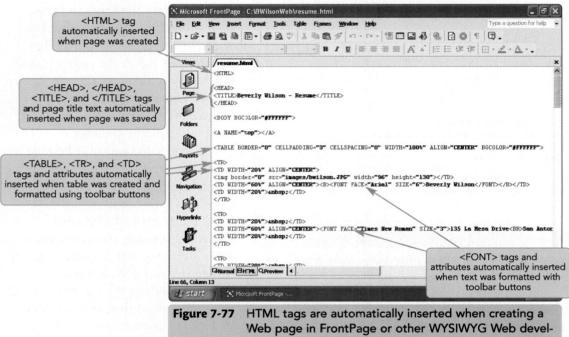

<HTML> tag automatically inserted when page was created

<HEAD>, </HEAD>, <TITLE>, and </TITLE> tags and page title text automatically inserted when page was saved

<TABLE>, <TR>, and <TD> tags and attributes automatically inserted when table was created and formatted using toolbar buttons

<FONT> tags and attributes automatically inserted when text was formatted with toolbar buttons

Figure 7-77 HTML tags are automatically inserted when creating a Web page in FrontPage or other WYSIWYG Web development applications.

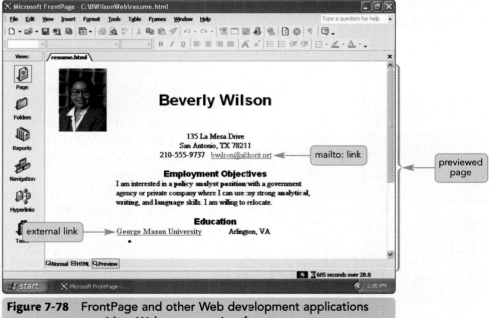

mailto: link

previewed page

external link

Figure 7-78 FrontPage and other Web development applications provide a Web page preview feature.

It is very easy to create a simple Web page in FrontPage. A Web page created in FrontPage, however, may appear best in Microsoft Internet Explorer and may not always appear exactly the same in other, non-Microsoft Web browsers. For example, the bullet icon used for the bulleted list in the page created in FrontPage displays differently in the Netscape Navigator browser (Figure 7-79) than it does in the Internet Explorer browser.

Additionally, you may be able to implement special features using FrontPage that only work well when viewed in Internet Explorer. Although Microsoft's Internet Explorer currently has more than 90% of the browser market, you still should use other Web browsers to test carefully any Web pages created

Figure 7-79 A Web page created in FrontPage may display differently in the Netscape browser.

in FrontPage. Some FrontPage features work only when the page is stored on a Web server that has FrontPage Server Extensions installed. Finally, FrontPage may not offer the robust features needed to create complex, commercial Web sites that require cross-platform compatibility with Linux and other operating systems and the ability to integrate easily with customer and vendor databases.

GOLIVE Adobe Systems GoLive (Figure 7-80) is another WYSIWYG Web development application. GoLive has a very easy-to-use interface that displays a Web page's WYSIWYG view and a special Source Code window that simultaneously displays the automatically generated HTML tags. Like FrontPage, GoLive also uses a wizard to create a new Web site and menu commands and toolbar buttons to create or format content. In addition, GoLive uses a special window, called an Inspector, to add and format page elements such as tables.

Figure 7-80 Adobe GoLive is another WYSIWYG Web development application.

DREAMWEAVER Macromedia Dreamweaver (Figure 7-81) is another very popular WYSIWYG Web development application that is similar to FrontPage and GoLive. You use a combination of menu commands, toolbar buttons, dialog boxes, and special panels called inspectors to insert and format Web page content while Dreamweaver automatically generates the appropriate HTML tags. Because of its flexibility and outstanding features, Dreamweaver is the Web authoring tool of choice for many professional Web designers.

@Source

You can download a trial version of the Adobe and Macromedia products at their Web sites. To learn more about the Web development tools discussed in this section or to download a trial version of a Web development tool, visit the Discovering the Internet Chapter 7 Web page (**scsite.com/internet/ch7**) and click a link below Web Authoring Tools.

Figure 7-81 Macromedia Dreamweaver is a WYSIWYG Web development application.

Multimedia Tools

Web designers can use several popular tools, including Adobe Photoshop and Macromedia Flash, Fireworks, and FreeHand (Figure 7-82), to create and edit images and add multimedia and animations to Web pages.

Figure 7-82 Multimedia tools are used to create and edit images and add animation to Web pages.

FLASH **Vector graphics** are created with lines and curves, while **bitmap graphics**, also called **raster images**, are created with pixels. Vector graphics download quickly over the Internet and maintain their visual quality when enlarged. Macromedia Flash originally was developed as an animation technology that uses vector graphics. Today the Flash application has evolved into a tool that is used to create interactive Web sites with animation, sound effects, and other stylish elements. To view Flash content, your browser must have the Flash Player Web browser plug-in installed. When you access a page that contains Flash content, you will be prompted to install the Flash player if necessary.

 Facts@Hand

Some estimates suggest that more than 95% of all computers now have Flash Player installed.

FIREWORKS You can use Macromedia Fireworks to create vector graphics, edit bitmap graphics, and create animated GIF files. Animated GIF files are a popular way to add interest to a Web page because the files are generally small and download quickly and because the animations play automatically when the page is downloaded into a browser.

FREEHAND Macromedia FreeHand is a design tool that allows you to plan a graphic-oriented layout for a printed document, such as a brochure, or for a Web page. You can use FreeHand to organize graphics, create a Web site storyboard, or plan a Web page to be created in Flash.

PHOTOSHOP Adobe Photoshop is another very popular image-editing application that has features similar to those in Macromedia Fireworks. You can use Photoshop to edit bitmap graphics, draw vector graphics, and create animated GIFs. For example, with Photoshop you can edit an image by adjusting its colors and removing scratches and other flaws. You also can scale and rotate the image. You can draw vector shapes (lines, rectangles, and so forth) and then add layers of shadow or other special effects.

Programming and Scripting Tools

For more information on JavaScript and other Web programming and scripting tools, visit the Discovering the Internet Chapter 7 Web page (scsite.com/internet/ch7) and click a link below Web Authoring Tools.

Features that make Web pages interactive — scrolling text, mouse rollover effects, popup windows, forms, games, shopping carts, and more — are made possible by applets, servlets, scripts, and ActiveX controls. An **applet** is a small program that downloads with a Web page and executes in your Web browser. A **servlet** is an applet that executes at the server before a page is loaded. A **script** is a series of instructions or a small program that executes inside another program such as your Web browser. **ActiveX controls**, which are similar to applets, are small programs that download and execute on your computer. In this section, you will learn about the programming and scripting technologies used to create applets, servlets, scripts, and ActiveX controls.

JAVA AND ACTIVEX Object-oriented programming languages focus on how to manipulate objects such as clickable buttons and scroll bars rather than focusing on the linear *input-process-output* logic behind earlier programming languages. Applets and servlets are created using Java, an object-oriented programming language developed by Sun Microsystems. Programming instructions in a Java applet must be compiled into a form your browser can interpret, called bytecode, before the applet executes.

JavaScript is a scripting language developed by Netscape. JavaScript instructions are embedded in a Web page and executed in a Web browser.

ActiveX technologies are object-oriented technologies developed by Microsoft that use small programs called ActiveX controls to provide Web page interactivity. ActiveX controls, like Java applets, are downloaded with a Web page and executed in your Web browser. ActiveX controls can be created using a variety of programming languages, such as C++ and Visual Basic.

CGI SCRIPTING AND ASP Scripts, applets, servlets, and ActiveX controls can use the Common Gateway Interface (CGI) or Active Server Pages (ASP) technologies to communicate between a Web server and other applications such as databases. The **Common Gateway Interface (CGI)** standard is part of the HTTP protocol and specifies the rules for how a Web server communicates with databases and other outside applications. A **CGI script** or program provides the actual instructions for sending and receiving information between a Web server and the outside application. For example, when you submit information in an online form, it is likely that a CGI script provides the instructions to add your information to a database. CGI scripts are written in a number of programming languages, such as C++, C, Perl, and Pascal.

An **Active Server Page (ASP)** is a Microsoft-developed technology that embeds server-side scripts in a Web page stored on a Microsoft Internet Information (IIS) Web server. The scripts then are executed in much the same way as CGI scripts are executed. ASP scripts can be created using the VBScript or JScript (Microsoft's scripting language similar to JavaScript) scripting language or using ActiveX controls.

1   How Do You Plan a Web Site?

You plan a Web site by identifying the site's purpose or **mission**, its **target audience**, its objectives and strategies, and its organizational structure. A Web site **mission statement** is a short, written statement of the site's purpose or reason to exist. A Web site's target audience is the group or groups of viewers toward which the Web site's message is directed. A personal Web site may have only one or two goals, while a complex, commercial Web site may have several goals. The most common Web site structure is a hierarchy of Web pages with the home page at the top of the hierarchy and subsequent levels of pages in increasing level of detail. An effective method of designing a Web site's structure is to create a **storyboard**.

2   What Are Elements of Effective Web Page Design?

Design guidelines to ensure Web site **usability** include designing for the appropriate technologies; clearly identifying the site's owner and purpose on its home page; avoiding **splash pages**; consistently applying color, images, and navigational elements across all pages; creating pages that require little or no scrolling; adding **page titles**; and writing **scannable text**.

All pages at a site should use easily recognizable navigation elements — **navigation bars**, menus, breadcrumb trails, **site maps**, and text links — to create **internal**, **external**, **mailto:**, and **top-of-page links**. Text **font** and font sizes, colors, images, and multimedia must be considered carefully so that these elements support the Web site's message.

Using **tables** to lay out Web page elements allows you more control over the pages' appearance. **Frames**, which divide a browser's window into multiple individual Web pages, should be avoided.

3   What Are Markup Languages?

Markup languages use embedded instructions called **tags** to define how document elements are displayed, how a document is structured, or the contents of a document. **SGML** is the standard that describes how to create markup tags. **HTML** and **XML** both are based on the SGML standard. HTML tags define how a Web browser displays Web page elements, such as images, text fonts, and links, while XML tags are used to define a document's contents.

4   How Can You Make Your Web Pages Available for Viewing by Others?

You can save your Web pages to a Web folder on your hard drive, on a network drive, or directly on a Web server. Some organizations save Web pages temporarily to a **staging server** while they are being developed and tested. After you create and save your Web pages, they should be tested thoroughly on a live server by classmates, friends, customers, vendors, and others in your target audience. You use FTP or HTTP to publish the pages to their final destination Web server.

5 What Are Web Authoring Tools?

Web development applications such as FrontPage, GoLive, and Dreamweaver allow you to create a Web page's content in a familiar WYSIWYG environment while automatically inserting the appropriate HTML tags in the page. You can add multimedia to Web pages and create and edit images using tools such as Flash, Fireworks, FreeHand, and Photoshop. Programming and scripting languages such as Java, ActiveX, JavaScript, and JScript are used to add interactivity to Web pages with **applets**, **servlets**, and **ActiveX controls**. Sending information between a Web server and an outside application is controlled with **CGI scripts** or **Active Server Pages** (**ASPs**).

CHAPTER REVIEW

The Chapter Review section summarizes the concepts presented in the chapter.

TERMS TO KNOW

After reading this chapter, you should know each term.

Active Server Page (ASP) (*447*)
ActiveX controls (*447*)
anchor (*431*)
applet (*447*)
assistive technologies (*406*)
attributes (*413*)
bitmap graphics (*446*)
browser-safe palette (*405*)
cell padding (*419*)
cell spacing (*419*)
CGI script (*447*)
Common Gateway Interface (CGI) (*447*)
container tags (*412*)
dead-end pages (*386*)
document type definition (DTD) (*412*)
Dynamic HTML (DHTML) (*440*)
electronic form (*410*)
Extensible Hypertext Markup Language (XHTML) (*440*)
Extensible Markup Language (XML) (*440*)
external link (*431*)
font (*402*)
frames (*409*)
frameset (*409*)
FrontPage Web (*442*)
GIF (Graphics Interchange Format) (*407*)
heading style (*422*)
hierarchical structure (*384*)
internal link (*397*)
intranet (*388*)
JPEG (Joint Photographic Experts Group) (*407*)
line break (*424*)
linear structure (*384*)
mailto: link (*431*)
markup languages (*412*)
mission (*382*)

mission statement (*382*)
monitor resolution (*389*)
navigation bar (*398*)
navigation menu (*399*)
navigation tabs (*398*)
nested table (*408*)
non-breaking space (*423*)
ordered list (*428*)
page title (*396*)
pixel (*389*)
PNG (Portable Network Graphics) (*407*)
publishing (*441*)
raster images (*446*)
rollover link (*402*)
sans serif (*402*)
scannable text (*397*)
schema (*440*)
script (*447*)
serif (*402*)
servlet (*447*)
site map (*399*)
site objectives (*383*)
site strategies (*383*)
splash page (*392*)
staging server (*441*)
standalone tags (*412*)
Standard Generalized Markup Language (SGML) (*412*)
storyboard (*384*)
table (*407*)
tag line (*382*)
tags (*412*)
target audience (*383*)
top-of-page link (*400*)
tree structure (*384*)
unordered list (*428*)
usability (*388*)
vector graphics (*446*)
Web accessibility (*406*)
webbed structure (*384*)

True or False

Mark T for True and F for False. (Answers are found on page numbers in parentheses.)

_____ 1. A Web site mission statement describes the site's organizational structure. (382)

_____ 2. A Web site's target audience is the group or groups of viewers toward which its message is directed. (383)

_____ 3. Big graphics and lots of color are hallmarks of a well-designed Web page. (407)

_____ 4. Structuring a Web site so that viewers can reach most of its important information in three or fewer mouse clicks improves the site's usability. (384)

_____ 5. A well-designed Web site always includes a splash page that appears before the site's home page opens. (392)

_____ 6. A breadcrumb trail is a graphic image or text that provides viewers with a list of links to all the pages at a Web site. (399)

_____ 7. All HTML tags are container tags that surround a page element and define it. (412)

_____ 8. An HTML unordered list is a numbered list. (428)

_____ 9. Vector graphics are created with lines and curves in multimedia applications such as Photoshop and Fireworks. (446)

_____ 10. Applets are small applications created in the Java programming language that download with a Web page and execute in a browser. (447)

Multiple Choice

Select the best answer. (Answers are found on page numbers in parentheses.)

1. ActiveX technologies are object-oriented technologies developed by _____ . (447)
   a. Adobe
   b. Microsoft
   c. Sun Microsystems
   d. Macromedia

2. The communication standard that defines how a Web server communicates with outside applications such as databases is _____ . (447)
   a. FTP
   b. HTTP
   c. ASP
   d. CGI

3. The most common Web site structure is a _____ structure. (384)
   a. linear
   b. webbed
   c. hierarchal
   d. none of the above

(continued)

TEST YOUR
KNOWLEDGE

Use the Test
Your Knowledge
exercises to
check your
knowledge of
the chapter.

TEST YOUR KNOWLEDGE *(continued)*

4. A Web site's home page should answer which of the following questions: _____ ? *(390)*
   a. Who owns the site
   b. What is the site's purpose
   c. How can viewers find information or perform tasks
   d. all of the above

5. The appropriate format for an update date is _____ . *(390)*
   a. 2/3/05
   b. February 5, 2005 9:00 PM CST
   c. Feb 5, 2005 9:00 PM
   d. none of these formats is appropriate

6. Scannable Web page text includes _____ . *(397)*
   a. short, descriptive paragraph headings
   b. brief phrases and sentences
   c. bolded keywords and bulleted or numbered lists
   d. all of the above

7. Which of the following are the correct syntax and tags for defining a table cell that is 30% of the entire table width and contains centered, bolded text? *(423)*
   a. <TD WIDTH="30%"ALIGN="CENTER"><B>Text</B></TD>
   b. <TD WIDTH=20%><B>Text</TD>
   c. <TR WIDTH=30 ALIGN="LEFT"><B>Text</B></TR>
   d. <TD ALIGN="CENTER"><B>Text</B></TR>

8. The <FONT> tag attribute used to specify the type of font is _____ . *(422)*
   a. SIZE
   b. ALIGN
   c. FACE
   d. BGCOLOR

9. The special reserve character set used to create a non-breaking space is _____ .
   (423)
   a.
   b.
   c. <IMG>
   d. SRC

10. The HTML container tags used to define each item in an unordered or ordered list are _____ . *(428)*
    a. <OL></OL>
    b. <LI></LI>
    c. <A></A>
    d. none of the above

Instructions: To complete the Learn It Online exercises, start your browser, click the Address bar, and then enter the Web address **scsite.com/internet/ch7**. Follow the instructions in the exercises below. Each exercise has instructions for printing your results, either for your own records or for submission to your instructor.

1 Chapter Reinforcement

TF, MC, and SA
Click the Chapter Reinforcement link. Print the quiz by clicking Print on the File menu for each page. Answer each question.

2 Flash Cards

Click the Flash Cards link and read the instructions. Type 20 (or a number specified by your instructor) in the Number of playing cards text box, type your name in the Enter your Name text box, and then click the Flip Card button. When the flash card is displayed, read the question and then click the Answer box arrow to select an answer. Flip through Flash Cards. If your score is 15 (75%) correct or greater, click Print on the File menu to print your results. If your score is less than 15 (75%) correct, then redo this exercise by clicking the Replay button.

3 Practice Test

Click the Practice Test link. Answer each question, enter your first and last name at the bottom of the page, and then click the Grade Test button. When the graded practice test is displayed on your screen, click Print on the File menu to print a hard copy. Continue to take practice tests until you score 80% or better.

4 Who Wants To Be a Computer Genius?

Click the Computer Genius link. Read the instructions, enter your first and last name at the bottom of the page, and then click the Play button. When your score is displayed, click the Print Results link to print a hard copy.

5 Crossword Puzzle Challenge

Below Chapter 7, click the Crossword Puzzle Challenge link. Read the instructions, and then enter your first and last name. Click the SUBMIT button. Work the crossword puzzle. When you are finished, click the Submit button. When the crossword puzzle is redisplayed, click the Print Puzzle button to print a hard copy.

To perform the following exercises, you must be connected to the Internet and have access to a printer.

1 Creating Your Personal Résumé Page Using HTML

1. Using your personal résumé page layout created earlier in this chapter as your guide, open Notepad and create your personal résumé Web page using HTML. If necessary, follow the Beverly Wilson résumé page you created earlier in this chapter as your guide. Insert the image of your choice. Save the page as myresume.html in the folder specified by your instructor.

2. Frequently preview the page in your Web browser as you are working on it.

3. Print the final page from the browser window and close the browser.

4. Print the final HTML source code from the Notepad window and then close Notepad.

2 Evaluating Home Page Content

1. Visit the Discovering the Internet Chapter 7 Web page (scsite.com/internet/ch7) and click the links below Exercise 2 to locate at least two Web sites of your choice *that have not been discussed previously in this chapter.*

2. Answer the following questions about each site based solely on the information you find on the home page:
   a. Who owns or sponsors the site?
   b. What is the site's purpose?
   c. How can viewers find information or perform tasks at the site?
   d. What is the last update date for time-sensitive information or the page itself?

3 Exploring Web Page Usability

1. Visit the Discovering the Internet Chapter 7 Web page (scsite.com/internet/ch7) and click the links below Exercise 3 to locate and review thoroughly two commercial Web sites *that have not been discussed previously in this chapter.*

2. Answer the following questions for each site:
   a. Is the use of logos, background color, and foreground text and accent colors consistent across each site's reviewed pages?
   b. What navigational elements are used and are they easy to locate and understand?
   c. Does each page have a title? If so, does the title describe the page accurately?
   d. Is the text on each page easy to scan?
   e. Does the site's color scheme enhance or detract from its message? Why?
   f. Does the site use a tag line? If so, does it clearly describe the site's purpose?
   g. Do you find the site easy or hard to navigate? Why?
   h. Did you enjoy viewing the Web site? Why or why not?

4 Evaluating the Effectiveness of Splash Pages and Frames

1. Visit the Discovering the Internet Chapter 7 Web page (**scsite.com/internet/ch7**) and click the links below Exercise 4 to search for articles on using splash pages and frames.

2. Write a one-page paper describing splash pages and frames and how they are used. Include the reasons you would or would not add a splash page to a Web site or use frames to create a Web page. In your discussion, include at least two real-world splash page and frame examples *that have not been discussed previously in this chapter*.

5 Writing Scannable Web Page Text

1. Open Notepad and use HTML tags and the text in Figure 7-83 to create a Web page with black text and a white background color. Save the page as markup.html in the folder specified by your instructor.

> Markup languages use embedded instructions called tags to define how text, images, and other components are displayed in a document or how a document is structured. For example, when you see a bolded word on a Web page, that word has been marked up by a set of tags that specify the bold format. The Standard Generalized Markup Language (SGML) is a standard (or set of rules) that defines how to create a set of generic document codes, called tags, which allow documents to be portable between computer systems. The Hypertext Markup Language (HTML) tags are used to create Web pages by indicating where the page begins and where it ends, where paragraph breaks occur, how heading paragraph text is formatted, what images to insert, and much, much more. The Extensible Markup Language (XML) uses customizable tags to describe a document's structure and its content. Like SGML, XML tags are defined in a document type definition (DTD) specification. XML can be used to define any type of data — as long as both the sender and receiver of the data agree on the XML format.

Figure 7-83   Exercise 5.

(continued)

EXERCISES (continued)

2. Edit the text in Figure 7-83 on the previous page to use descriptive page and paragraph headings, short phrases or sentences, bolded keywords, and unordered lists as appropriate to make the text easily scannable and then enter the text on the page.

   a. Format the page and paragraph headings with the HTML heading styles. Format the paragraph text with the Times New Roman, size 4 font.

   b. Remember to add an appropriate page title.

   c. Frequently save and preview the page in your Web browser as you create it.

   d. Print the final HTML source code from the Notepad window, save the page, and then close Notepad.

   e. Print the final Web page from your browser and close your browser.

6 Planning a Personal Hobby Web Site

Select a classmate to work with you on this exercise. You and your classmate want to plan a small personal Web site where you can share your hobbies with other hobby enthusiasts.

1. Visit the Discovering the Internet Chapter 7 Web page (scsite.com/internet/ch7) and click the links below Exercise 6 to locate and review several needlework and hobby Web sites.

2. Working with your classmate:

   a. Write a brief mission statement for your Web site.

   b. Identify the site's target audience.

   c. List two goals and two strategies for your Web site.

   d. List the Web pages you want to have at the site.

3. Use the storyboard method to lay out the organizational structure of your Web site.

4. Lay out your home page and note the following design elements:

   a. table structure

   b. background and foreground colors

   c. font face and size

   d. image placement

   e. navigational elements

7 Creating a Home Page

1. Using the home page layout you created in Exercise 6, open Notepad and use HTML tags to create the page. Save the page as hobby.html in the folder specified by your instructor.

2. Use available images as specified by your instructor. (Be sure to store the images in the same folder as the Web page.)

3. Test all mailto:, external, and top-of-page links.

4. Print the final HTML source code and the final Web page.

8 Researching Web Accessibility Issues

1. Visit the Discovering the Internet Chapter 7 Web page (**scsite.com/internet/ch7**) and click the links below Exercise 8 to research Web accessibility issues.

2. Using your research, write a one-page paper discussing the history of the Web accessibility initiative and the importance of making Web pages accessible to viewers with visual, hearing, physical, or learning disabilities.

9 Reviewing HTML Source Code

1. Visit the Discovering the Internet Chapter 7 Web page (**scsite.com/internet/ch7**) and click the Candy USA link below Exercise 9 to view the site's home page.

2. Open the page's HTML source code and print it from the Notepad window.

3. Review the printed HTML source code and, starting at the top of the page, identify each HTML tag and its attributes and describe how they affect the Candy USA home page. (*Note:* If necessary, use Figure 7-38 on pages 416 and 417 and the HTML appendix in the back of the book.)

10 Reviewing Navigational Elements

1. Visit the Discovering the Internet Chapter 7 Web page (**scsite.com/internet/ch7**) and click the links below Exercise 10 to locate at least five Web site examples *that have not been discussed previously in this chapter* that illustrate the effective use of:
   a. navigation bars
   b. navigation menus
   c. breadcrumb trails
   d. graphic and text site maps
   e. easy-to-understand internal and external text links
   f. mailto: links
   g. top-of-page links

2. Write a one-page paper describing each of the five pages and their effective use of navigational elements.

EXERCISES

Use the Exercises to gain hands-on Internet experience.

CHAPTER 8
Understanding E-Business

Introduction

As you learned in Chapter 1, the term *e-commerce* is sometimes used to describe the process of conducting business transactions over the Internet while the term *e-business* is sometimes used to describe the broader scope of maintaining partner, customer, and employee business relationships using the Internet. Be aware, however, that many analysts use *e-commerce* and *e-business* interchangeably. This chapter uses *e-business* to describe business activities of all types supported by Internet technologies.

In this chapter, you learn about the early origins of e-business and the unique factors that underlie e-business's amazing growth and individual e-business successes. Multiple real-world examples help you learn about different e-business models. Finally, you focus on business-to-consumer retailing by learning about online store software, merchant accounts, and how credit card transactions are authorized and processed.

After completing this chapter, you will be able to:

1. Describe the origins of electronic business transactions including the Electronic Funds Transfer (EFT) system, the Electronic Data Interchange (EDI) standard, and value-added networks (VANs)

2. Discuss unique e-business factors and identify e-businesses that exploit them

3. Define common e-business models and explain how each model generates revenues

4. Describe the e-retailing storefront software, merchant accounts, and payment-processing services needed to create and operate an online store

CONTENTS

E-Business Origins

You may be surprised to learn that some types of business transactions have been conducted electronically for more than 30 years — long before the Internet became a popular and useful business channel. Electronic business activities actually originated in the 1960s and 1970s with the banking industry's Electronic Funds Transfer (EFT) system and the Electronic Data Interchange (EDI) networks used by large companies.

Electronic Funds Transfer

The **Electronic Funds Transfer (EFT)** system allows money to be transferred between banks electronically — without the exchange of paper money. In the 1960s, banks began exchanging money electronically through a network that connects all U.S. financial institutions called the **Automated Clearing House (ACH)** network. The EFT system continues to pay an increasingly important role in business today. Having your payroll check deposited directly to your bank account, paying your federal income taxes, utility bills, or credit card bills online, and using an ATM machine are all examples of the EFT system (Figure 8-1) in action.

Figure 8-1   Paying bills online, having a paycheck deposited directly into an account, and using an ATM are examples of the Electronic Funds Transfer (EFT) system in action.

Electronic Data Interchange

The **Electronic Data Interchange** (**EDI**) standard specifies the layout or format a company uses to exchange electronic business data with its suppliers and customers. The participants in an EDI exchange of business data are called **trading partners**. Before the Internet became a viable alternative for transmitting data, EDI transmissions between trading partners occurred over private telecommunication networks called **value-added networks** (**VANs**). VANs are very expensive to set up and maintain. Additionally, it is very expensive to create a standard interface to be used by trading partners when exchanging data. For these reasons, EDI (Figure 8-2) primarily has been used only by very large companies. The Internet is a much less expensive network alternative to VANs; therefore, today many small, medium, and large companies use the Internet to exchange business data, such as purchase orders and invoices, with their trading partners.

Trading Partner A

Trading Partner B

Figure 8-2 Value-added networks (VANs) allow trading partners to exchange business data.

Unique E-Business Factors

Companies that conduct their business activities online enjoy a host of business advantages including worldwide sales opportunities, reduced transaction and purchasing costs, and access to small, niche markets. At the same time, individual and business consumers also enjoy similar advantages: access to a global electronic marketspace, wider product availability, improved customer and product support, and easy comparison shopping.

Beyond these advantages, other factors unique to conducting business activities online play an important role in the ongoing growth and success of e-business. In this section, you learn about some of these factors including the effect of geography, time, and space on the online marketspace, the network effect, the ability of individual e-businesses to redefine a market, and the power of personalization and customization.

Geography, Time, and Space

Geography, time, and space are limiting factors for any bricks-and-mortar business. The following is a look at the role geography, time, and space can play in the operation of a bricks-and-mortar store, such as a bookstore.

- Geography — A bricks-and-mortar bookstore must be physically located within a modest driving distance of its targeted customer base. In addition, the store must be located in a high traffic area to increase its visibility and attract new customers.

- Time — A bricks-and-mortar bookstore is likely to maintain the same operating hours as other stores in its area, which may be only peak shopping hours. In most areas, it is uncommon to find a bricks-and-mortar bookstore open 24 hours a day.

- Space — The inventory of books available at a bricks-and-mortar bookstore is limited to the amount of the store's available storage and shelf space. Because of space restrictions, a bricks-and-mortar bookstore may stock only the most recently published books in the most popular categories.

Now consider the affect of geography, time, and space on the online bookstore marketspace. Suppose you just read a review of the latest book by your favorite British mystery author and you want to purchase a copy of the book. The book currently is available only in the U.K. and will not be available in U.S. bookstores for several months. No need to wait — geography and time no longer matter. WHSmith, one of the leading booksellers in the U.K., operates an e-business Web site (Figure 8-3). You simply can log on to the Web site and order the book anytime of the day or night.

Maybe, you need to find an inexpensive copy of a reference book about creating Web pages using HTML, but the nearest used bookstore is several miles away and has a poor selection of technical books. No problem. Infinite shelf space is available on the Web. Check out several e-business Web sites, such as Amazon.com, Abebooks.com, or Alibris (Figure 8-4), all of which aggregate information about the used, out-of-print, and rare book inventories held by individual book resellers located all over the world.

Figure 8-3 WHSmith, a U.K. bookseller, offers books and other items for sale on its Web site to its U.K. and international customers, 24 hours a day, seven days a week.

Figure 8-4 Some online bookstores aggregate the used book inventories held by individual book resellers located around the world.

As you can see, the online marketspace is not confined by geography, time, and space, where shoppers can find an unlimited product selection, offered for sale by e-businesses and individuals anywhere in the world, 24 hours a day, seven days a week.

The Network Effect

An important e-business success factor, called the **network effect**, refers to the increasing value of a network as the network grows. The analogy often used to describe the network effect is a telephone network. Assume for a moment that your telephone is the only telephone connected to a telephone network. Your single telephone and the telephone network to which it is connected have little or no value because you cannot call any one else, and no one can call you. Connect a second telephone and user to the network, however, and the value of the network increases — now you and the other user can call each other. As additional telephones and users connect to the network, the network's value continues to increase.

Facts@Hand

The network effect also is known as *Metcalf's Law* and is named for Robert Metcalf, an early pioneer in the development of the Ethernet networking technologies and the founder of 3COM Corporation, an Internet technologies provider.

The network effect (Figure 8-5) often is used to describe the growing importance of the Internet and the overall growth of e-business. For example, the value of the Internet to individual users and to the business community continues to grow as the number of people with Internet access grows. E-business continues to become an increasingly more valuable part of the global economy as more businesses and consumers participate in the online marketspace.

increasing value of the network as number of users grows

multiple users interacting over the network

single user on a network

two users interacting over a network

Figure 8-5 The network effect ensures that e-business will continue to become a more valuable part of the global economy as the number of e-businesses and their online customers grows.

Hotmail: Exploiting the Network Effect
@Issue

Perhaps one of the better known examples of the network effect in the success of an individual e-business is Hotmail. Hotmail, an e-mail service now owned by Microsoft, was launched on July 4, 1996. Because little money was available to promote Hotmail's free e-mail service, Hotmail added a text message with a link to the Hotmail Web site to the bottom of each outgoing e-mail message. The additional text encouraged the e-mail's recipient to click the link to the Hotmail Web site and subscribe to the free e-mail service.

Using the network effect to promote the Hotmail service resulted in spectacular success. Within just a few days of its launch, hundreds of new users — primarily at colleges and universities — subscribed to the Hotmail service. First, a single user from a college or university would subscribe and then, over the next several days, thousands of users from the same school would subscribe. Quickly, Hotmail spread to other colleges and universities where the process began all over again. It was not long before users all around the world began subscribing to the Hotmail service. Eighteen months after its initial launch, Hotmail had 12 million worldwide subscribers. Did the value of the Hotmail e-business increase by exploiting the network effect? Yes, indeed. Not long after acquiring 12 million subscribers, Microsoft bought Hotmail (Figure 8-6) from its founders for $400 million!

To learn more about Hotmail, visit the Discovering the Internet Chapter 8 Web page (**scsite.com/internet/ ch8**) and click a link below Hotmail Sign In.

Figure 8-6 Hotmail is an example of an early e-business that successfully exploited the network effect.

Redefining Markets

Another important e-business factor is the opportunity an individual e-business may have to redefine a market. Market redefinition generally takes place in one of two ways: (1) by removing traditional marketplace intermediaries or (2) by creating new ways to add value to business transactions, often by introducing new types of intermediaries to the marketplace.

DISINTERMEDIATION An **intermediary**, or middleman, is a business entity that brings sellers and buyers together. Examples of traditional marketplace intermediaries include:

- Sporting goods industry — a retail store
- Real estate industry — a real estate agent
- Travel industry — a travel agent
- Insurance industry — an insurance broker

An individual e-business can redefine a market by allowing consumers to bypass the market's traditional intermediaries and purchase products or services directly from the e-business's Web site. Redefining a market by removing its traditional intermediaries is called **disintermediation**. Dell, Inc. arguably is one of the more famous examples of disintermediation. Dell bypasses retail computer stores by using its Web sites to sell thousands of personal computers, printers, servers, and other computer hardware directly to consumers around the world.

The travel industry is another example of disintermediation, where the growth of travel-related e-business is redefining the market. Traditionally, planning a vacation or business trip involved calling or visiting a local travel agent who made all the arrangements including purchasing airline tickets, reserving an auto, and booking a hotel room. In turn, the agent earned a fee or commission from the airline, auto rental company, and hotel. Today, the travel agent intermediary often is bypassed by consumers who book and pay for their travel arrangements directly at e-business Web sites operated by airlines, auto rental companies, and hotels such as those illustrated in Figure 8-7.

Figure 8-7 Examples of airline, auto rental, and hotel company Web sites contributing to travel industry disintermediation.

@Issue

Dell, Inc.: Disintermediation in the Computer Hardware Industry

Michael Dell founded Dell Computer Corporation (now Dell, Inc.) in 1984 (Figure 8-8), while an undergraduate at the University of Texas. Michael Dell recognized that a business opportunity lay in the huge difference between the cost of individual personal computer components and the price of an assembled personal computer purchased from a retail store. He decided that by eliminating the retail store middleman he could sell personal computers directly to consumers for much less and still generate a profit. And he was right.

By 1993, Dell, Inc. was a Fortune 500 company and one of the top five computer manufacturers in the world. In 1996, Dell, Inc. began selling its computer hardware products directly to individual and business consumers via its many Web sites, and by 2000, these sites were generating more than $50 million a day in sales! For its fiscal year ended January 2003, Dell, Inc. generated sales of more than $35 billion. By eliminating the traditional middleman — the retail store — Dell redefined the market for computer hardware, and by moving to e-business, Dell, Inc. became the top computer seller in the world.

For more information about Dell, Inc. visit the Discovering the Internet Chapter 8 Web page (**scsite.com/internet/ch8**) and click a link below Dell, Inc.

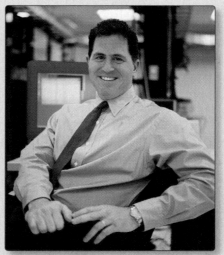

Figure 8-8   Michael Dell.

REINTERMEDIATION   Some e-businesses are eliminating traditional intermediaries and, in the process, redefining markets. Many other e-businesses also are redefining markets, however, by creating new business opportunities through a process called reintermediation. **Reintermediation** occurs when an e-business introduces a new intermediary into the marketspace. Amazon.com and other online bookstores are examples of e-business reintermediation in the book industry. While it is likely that online bookstores have contributed to the failure of some traditional book industry intermediaries — the small, local bookstores that do not have the purchasing power or shelf space to compete successfully — disintermediation is not the culprit. E-business disintermediation in the book industry occurs when book publishers such as Random House or Harcourt sell books directly to individual consumers from their Web sites. Online bookstores simply are a new type of book industry intermediary that uses Internet technologies to provide value to the marketspace in new ways.

Two examples of reintermediation in the travel industry are Orbitz and Hotels.com. Orbitz (Figure 8-9) is an e-business partnership among five major airlines: American, Continental, Delta, Northwest, and United. Orbitz, which is a travel industry intermediary that competes with other intermediaries such as bricks-and-mortar travel agents and e-businesses such as Travelocity, uses its Web site to provide consumers quick access to low fares for airline tickets and low rates on auto rentals and hotel accommodations.

Hotels.com, another travel industry intermediary, purchases large blocks of hotel rooms at a big discount from more than 7,000 hotel chains and independent hotel operators around the world. Hotels.com (Figure 8-9) then marks up the discounted room rates and resells the rooms directly to consumers from its Web site.

Figure 8-9 Online travel intermediary Web sites contribute to reintermediation in the travel industry.

Personalization and Customization

The unique interactive nature of the Web that allows buyers and sellers to communicate in new and exciting ways is another important e-business factor. E-businesses can exploit Web interactivity by personalizing and customizing Web content to increase sales, provide better customer support, and encourage customer loyalty.

While the terms personalization and customization sometimes are used interchangeably, some analysts define **personalization** as an *automatic* process that tailors Web page content to fit the profile of a specific target audience or that automatically tailors Web page content for an individual viewer based on his or her actions at a site. You experience the benefits of personalization each time you shop at an online store that acknowledges you by name and suggests new items — books, CDs, DVDs — for purchase based on your previous purchases at the site.

Customization is a *manual* process that allows a viewer to manage Web page content by selecting viewing preferences or by creating and updating a personal profile. In Chapter 5, you learned how viewers could customize the news, sports, and weather content at a major news-oriented Web site by indicating preferences or Zip codes. Customization also allows e-business customers to create custom products — clothing, skin-care products, fitness programs — designed specifically for them by indicating size, style, or other preferences. Personalization and customization work together to create a unique viewing or shopping experience by using customer databases containing purchase histories, product reviews and comments, target audience profiles, or individual viewer profiles to create Web pages with specific content; to recommend certain items to a returning customer based on his or her past purchasing history; or to promote new items.

E-businesses that sell directly to individual consumers and e-businesses that sell to other businesses use personalization and customization to develop a closer relationship with their customers that promotes increased customer loyalty. For example, Physician Sales & Service (Figure 8-10), which sells medical supplies to physicians, uses personalization to create purchasing histories, inventory reports, and replenishment purchase orders that help a physician and his or her office staff manage the office's medical supply inventory. Online office supply vendors such as Staples and Office Depot (Figure 8-10) also use personalization to provide their business customers with customized purchasing and office supply inventory control services.

Figure 8-10   E-businesses use personalization and customization to attract and keep customers.

One of the more intriguing examples of e-business personalization and customization is found at Reflect.com, which sells personal-care products directly to individual consumers. Reflect.com, nationally recognized for its effective use of e-business personalization and customization, uses customization to create customized skin- and hair-care products, cosmetics, and fragrances based on a customer's preferences. Reflect.com also maintains each customer's purchasing history and personal profile and then uses that information to personalize Web page content by suggesting new items for purchase and by automatically replenishing a customer's supply of products over time.

To see just how e-business personalization and customization might increase sales and promote customer loyalty, assume, for a moment, that you are shopping for a shampoo that is specifically tailored for your hair type, condition, length, and your scent preference. None of the bricks-and-mortar stores in your area sells exactly what you are looking for — and, of course, none allows you to create a shampoo from scratch that meets your needs. Now, experience the power of e-business personalization and customization firsthand by completing a short questionnaire and creating your own customized shampoo at the Reflect.com Web site in the following steps. (You will not have to purchase anything or provide any payment information to complete the following steps.)

Steps: To Create a Customized Shampoo at Reflect.com

1 **Start the browser and visit the Discovering the Internet Chapter 8 Web page (scsite.com/internet/ch8). Click Reflect.com. If necessary, close any pop-up windows. Point to the BEGIN button in the haircare section.**

The Reflect.com home page appears (Figure 8-11). Because Web page content is updated continually, the content in the Web page on your screen may vary from that shown in Figures 8-11 through 8-25 on pages 469 through 474.

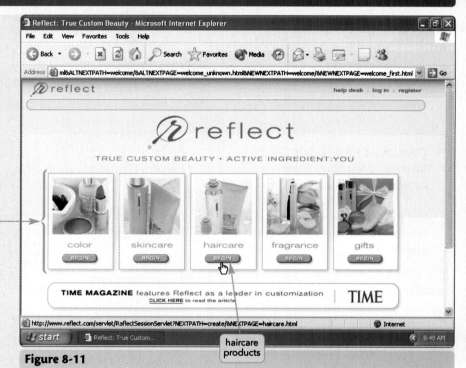

Figure 8-11

2 **Click the BEGIN button. Scroll through the page to review the text, graphics, and navigational elements and then point to the Shampoo link below DAILY ESSENTIALS in the left navigation menu.**

The custom nutrifusion haircare page appears (Figure 8-12).

Figure 8-12

(continued)

3 Click the Shampoo link. Point to the CREATE MY OWN button.

A shampoo product graphic with explanatory text appears (Figure 8-13).

Figure 8-13

4 Click the CREATE MY OWN button. Click the What is your ethnic background box arrow and select a response. Click the How would you describe the texture of your hair box arrow and select a response.

The nutrifusion haircare: formula creation page appears (Figure 8-14). Reflect.com uses your answers to the questionnaire on this page to create your own customized shampoo. Your answers may vary from those shown.

Figure 8-14

5 Scroll as necessary, to view and answer the remaining questions. After answering all the questions, point to the NEXT button.

After completing the basic questionnaire (Figure 8-15), you go to the next step in the customization process.

Figure 8-15

6 **Click the NEXT button. Review the haircare nutrients added to your customized shampoo. Point to the NEXT button.**

The nutrifusion haircare: nutrient infusion page appears (Figure 8-16). If you want, you can learn more about the nutrients added to your shampoo by clicking the nutrient graphics on this page.

Figure 8-16

7 **Click the NEXT button. Observe your personal product profile bar near the top of the page. Point to the scent you prefer for your shampoo.**

The nutrifusion haircare: sensory matching page appears (Figure 8-17). You select a scent for your shampoo on this page.

Figure 8-17

8 **Click your preferred scent.**

Your preferred scent is added to your product profile (Figure 8-18).

Figure 8-18

(continued)

9 Scroll to view the package types section. Point to the package type that most appeals to you.

Customization options on this page allow you to design the type of packaging you prefer for your shampoo (Figure 8-19).

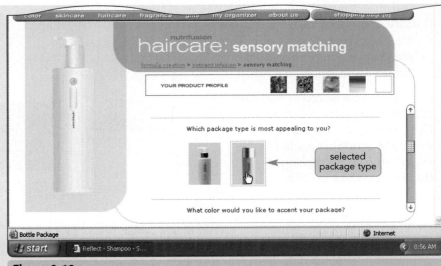

Figure 8-19

10 Click your preferred package type. Observe that the large package image on the left now illustrates your package type selection.

You choose the type of packaging for your shampoo on this page (Figure 8-20).

Figure 8-20

11 Scroll to view the packaging accent color options. Point to the accent color of your choice.

You further customize the shampoo packaging by adding an accent color to the package label (Figure 8-21).

Figure 8-21

12 **Click the accent color of your choice.**

The shampoo package graphic is modified to show your accent color selection on the label (Figure 8-22).

accent color added to package label

selected accent color

Figure 8-22

13 **Scroll to view the product name section. Type your first name in the first text box. Point to the UPDATE button.**

To customize the shampoo package further, you can add your name to the package's label. (Figure 8-23).

UPDATE button

name to be added to package label

Figure 8-23

14 **Click the UPDATE button. Point to the FINISH button.**

Your first name is added to package label (Figure 8-24).

name added to product label

FINISH button

Figure 8-24

(continued)

15 Click the FINISH button. Close the pop-up window without registering or logging in. Close any other pop-up windows that may appear. Scroll to view the details about your customized shampoo including price and ingredients.

A pop-up window appears advising that your customized shampoo is created and encouraging you to register if you are a new customer or login if you are a returning customer. You can close the pop-up window to view your customized shampoo product (Figure 8-25).

Figure 8-25

After the customized shampoo product is designed, a Reflect.com customer can log onto the site and purchase the shampoo. Data about the purchase and the formula for the customized shampoo product are stored in the Reflect.com databases. The next time the customer logs on to the Reflect.com site, he or she may see automatically generated content that suggests purchasing a hair conditioner formulated to match his or her customized shampoo exactly!

E-Business Models

As you browse the Web, you likely encounter many different types of commercial Web sites. From time to time, you may ask yourself how a site makes money, because exactly how a commercial Web site generates revenues may not be obvious. The answer lies in the business model followed by the company that publishes the site. A **business model** is the way a company operates to generate revenues, create profits (the excess of revenues over expenses), and continue as a viable business entity. The business model adopted by a company doing business online often is called its **e-business model**. Individual e-businesses exploit factors such as geography, time, space, the network effect, personalization, and customization within the framework of their e-business model. E-business models are classified in a number of ways, but the most common way is by targeted customer group such as consumers, other businesses, and government agencies.

While an individual e-business may seem to fit into one of the primary e-business model categories shown in Figure 8-26 on the next page, many e-businesses actually operate using a mix of e-business models and revenue-generation methods. For example, an e-business's primary e-business model may emphasize selling products or services directly to consumers; however, the e-business also may generate revenues by one or more of the following:

- Offering subscription-based content
- Selling advertising space at its Web site
- Earning referral fees by providing links to other e-business Web sites

- Selling proprietary e-business technologies to other companies
- Providing a channel for business partners to sell their products

In this section, you use multiple real-world e-business examples to explore common e-business models.

Targeted Customer	E-Business Model	Description
Consumers	Business-to-Consumer (B2C)	An e-business sells products or services directly to consumers.
Consumers	Consumer-to-Consumer (C2C)	A consumer sells products or services directly to another consumer.
Businesses	Consumer-to-Business (C2B)	A consumer names a price for a product or service that competing businesses accept or decline.
Businesses	Business-to-Business (B2B)	An e-business sells products or services to other businesses; brings multiple buyers and sellers together in a central online marketspace; sells e-business technologies; transacts business activities over the Internet with trading partners.
Government agencies and other businesses	Business-to-Government (B2G)	An e-business provides information about government agencies currently accepting bids for products and services; brings sellers and government agency buyers together in an online marketspace; sells bidding and procurement technologies.

Figure 8-26 E-business models can be defined by customer group.

Business-to-Consumer (B2C)

The **business-to-consumer** (**B2C**) e-business model originally described in Chapter 1 generates revenues in several ways including retail sales directly to consumers, often called **e-retail**, selling Web site advertising space, and charging subscription or membership fees for premium content.

E-RETAIL Many traditional bricks-and-mortar retailers and catalog merchants such as Sears, Williams-Sonoma, and JCPenney (Figure 8-27 on the next page) are taking advantage of their retailing experiences and existing product distribution centers to combine e-retailing Web sites successfully with their physical stores and catalog operations — in the process becoming **brick-and-click** businesses, or e-retailers. By adding e-retailing Web sites to existing operations, these companies create a new business channel mix that provides increased sales opportunities and improved customer service. Thousands of other bricks-and-mortar retailers as diverse as Circuit City (electronics), PETCO (pet supplies), Gump's (fine furniture, accessories, and gifts), and Wal-Mart (discounter) (Figure 8-28 on the next page) now sell directly to customers from their e-business Web sites.

 @Source

To learn more about the e-businesses discussed in this section, visit the Discovering the Internet Chapter 8 Web page (**scsite.com/ internet/ch8**) and click a link below E-Business Models.

 Facts@Hand

According to the U.K. research firm Ovum, global B2C revenues will approach $360 billion by 2007.

Figure 8-27 Many bricks-and-mortar retailers and catalog merchants are becoming brick-and-click e-retailers.

Figure 8-28 Diverse brick-and-mortar retailers now also sell their products directly to consumers from their Web sites.

Some early B2C e-retailers, however, moved into the online marketspace as completely new e-businesses with no existing bricks-and-mortar stores or catalog operations. These online-only retailers, called **pure-play e-retailers**, have met with mixed success. Amazon.com is, of course, the most famous examples of a pure-play e-retailer. And while Amazon.com successfully generates billions of dollars in revenues each year, profitability — the excess of revenues over expenses — continues to be elusive. Many other early pure-play e-retailers, such as Pets.com and eToys, were never able to rival Amazon.com's volume of sales or market dominance and ended in spectacular e-business failures.

Figure 8-29 Hometown Favorites is an example of a pure-play e-retailer successfully targeting a niche market.

A **niche market** is a small segment within a larger market. Some pure-play e-retailers, such as Hometown Favorites, succeed by avoiding competition with larger e-businesses and, instead, target a niche market. Founded in 1996, Hometown Favorites specializes in hard-to-find, old-time favorite foods — My-T-Fine pudding, Maypo cereal, Walnettos candy and so forth — popular in the 1950s, 1960s, and 1970s, and rarely found on grocery shelves today. With annual sales in excess of $1.5 million, Hometown Favorites (Figure 8-29) remains profitable by offering more than 1,000 nonperishable, nonrefrigerated products to a small niche market of individual and corporate customers around the world.

ADVERTISING Some B2C e-businesses offer free content — information, links, games, and so forth — and generate revenues by selling advertising at their sites. Many e-retailers also sell advertising at their sites to generate additional revenues. Web site advertising includes banner ads, pop-up ads, and Flash animation ads. A **banner ad** (Figure 8-30) is a small, rectangular area on a Web page that contains an advertising message generally composed of both text and graphics. A **pop-up ad** (Figure 8-30) is an advertising message that opens in its own small window inside the browser window often obscuring part of the Web page being viewed. Viewers must close pop-up ad windows manually to remove them from view. Some advertisers use **Flash animation ads** that appear, animate, and then disappear as a Web page is being viewed.

Figure 8-30 Example of banner and pop-up ads.

Web site ads usually are linked to the advertiser's own Web site; therefore, viewers can go directly to the advertised Web site by clicking an ad in a process called a **click-through**. The effectiveness of a particular Web site advertisement often is measured in the number of viewers who use it to click-through to the advertised Web site. Although banner, pop-up, and Flash animation ads annoy many viewers, research indicates that these ads are quite effective in driving viewers to advertised Web sites. (You learn more about how e-businesses promote their Web sites in Chapter 9.) In the following steps, you click through from a banner ad to an advertiser's Web site.

Steps: To Click Through to an Advertiser's Site Using a Banner Ad

1 **Start the browser and visit the Discovering the Internet Chapter 8 Web page (scsite.com/internet/ch8). Click Blockbuster. If necessary, close any pop-up windows. Point to the banner ad at the top of the page.**

The Blockbuster page appears (Figure 8-31). The ad and resulting page you see may vary from Figures 8-31 and 8-32 on the next page.

Figure 8-31

2 **Click the banner ad.**

The advertiser's page opens (Figure 8-32).

Figure 8-32

SUBSCRIPTION FEES   Another way the B2C e-business model generates revenues is through subscription fees for premium content. Some e-businesses that generate revenues from advertising, such as Yahoo and Classmates, also may charge subscription fees for certain premium services such as resume posting and job search, posting personals ads, or participating in an online community.

For example, Classmates (Figure 8-33) provides access to an online community with more than 35 million members that might include your friends, high-school and college classmates, family members, military members or retirees, and coworkers. While you can add your name and information to the Classmates databases free, premium services such as chatting with your long-lost classmates and friends who are also subscribers or browsing school message boards and posting messages require payment of an annual subscription fee.

Some nonprofit organizations also follow the B2C subscription e-business model. For example, the Consumers Union is an independent consumer product testing organization that publishes the Consumer Reports magazine and its online version, Consumer Reports Online (Figure 8-33). For an annual subscription fee, you can read reviews and test results on thousands of consumer products at the Consumer Reports Online Web site.

Figure 8-33   Some B2C e-businesses generate subscription-based revenues.

Facts@Hand

According to Jupiter Research, the paid content e-business market will be worth $5.4 billion by 2007, and spending on Web site advertising will grow to $14 billion by 2007.

Netflix:
Following the B2C Subscription Model

@Issue

What is the fastest selling consumer electronics device in history? No, it is not TVs, not PCs, and not VCRs. According to a report by E-Business Strategies, a technology research firm, the fastest selling consumer electronics device in history is the DVD player. Some analysts predict that more than 65 million DVD players will be in U.S. households by 2006. Introduction of inexpensive DVD players, low-cost mass-produced DVDs, the adoption of DVD technologies by the movie industry, and consumers' preference for a high-quality at-home movie experience all contributed to the explosive popularity of DVD players and DVDs.

In 1997, Reed Hastings (Figure 8-34), a computer software entrepreneur, recognized a business opportunity in the emerging popularity of DVDs. To capitalize on this popularity he cofounded the DVD rental e-business Netflix. Hastings wanted to operate a movie rental business in a very new way by having DVD rentals inexpensively delivered and then returned via the U.S. Postal Service eliminating trips to a movie rental store. Originally, Netflix charged its customers a per-movie rental fee much like its bricks-and-mortar competitors. Then, Hastings hit upon the idea of removing specific return dates and the threat of late fees. As the story goes, Hastings had rented a movie, watched it, and then forgot to return it on time, which

resulted in whopping late fees. From that costly experience was born the next Netflix e-business idea — DVDs rented on a subscription basis. Hastings envisioned Netflix customers paying a monthly subscription fee to rent as many DVDs as they wanted and keep them as long as they wanted without incurring late fees.

In September 1999, Netflix began charging customers a monthly fee of about $20 for unlimited DVD rentals. This is how it works: a Netflix customer opens an account and creates a list of movies he or she wants to rent in the order in which the movies are to be viewed. Netflix then mails the customer the first three DVDs on the list in individual postage paid

Figure 8-34 Reed Hastings.

envelopes that the customer later uses to return the DVDs. As each movie is returned, Netflix mails the customer another movie from the customer's movie list so that no more than three DVDs are out to any customer. Netflix customers are encouraged to rate the movies they rent using a five-star rating system. Netflix then uses a customer's movie ratings together with special personalization software called CineMatch to create a list of movie recommendations based on the customer's viewing preferences.

Netflix keeps inventory costs low by participating in rental revenue-sharing partnerships with a number of movie studios including DreamWorks SKG, Universal Studios, and 20th Century Fox that provide DVDs at no upfront cost to Netflix. Today, Netflix has more than 1 million customers renting DVDs from an inventory of more than 13,000 movie titles including new releases, classics, hard-to-find documentaries, and independent films. Netflix's innovative ideas and its success implementing those ideas have, of course, inspired a number of competitors. For example, Blockbuster is experimenting with an in-store DVD subscription rental plan and Wal-Mart now offers online subscription-based DVD rentals.

For more information about Netflix, visit the Discovering the Internet Chapter 8 Web page (**scsite/internet/ch8**) and click a link below Netflix.

Consumer-to-Business (C2B)

A **consumer-to-business** (**C2B**) e-business allows a buyer to name their own price for specific goods or services such as airline tickets or hotel accommodations in a process sometimes called a **reverse auction**. The C2B e-business accumulates buyer offers and then presents them to competing sellers. A buyer's offer is considered binding; therefore, when a seller accepts a buyer's offer, the buyer's credit card is charged immediately. The C2B e-business generates revenues by earning booking fees and commissions on accepted offers. Priceline.com (Figure 8-35) pioneered the C2B e-business model.

Consumer-to-Consumer (C2C)

The **consumer-to-consumer** (**C2C**) e-business model, which brings individual buyers and sellers together in an online marketspace, generates revenues in several ways, including transaction fees, sales commissions, subscription or membership fees, and personal ad fees. C2C e-businesses such as eBay and uBid

Figure 8-35 Priceline.com pioneered the C2B e-business model.

(Figure 8-36), offer the auction services you learned about in Chapter 5 and generate revenues from listing fees, sales commissions, and advertising. These auction services sometimes are called **forward auctions** because many buyers are bidding for an item offered by a single seller. Other C2C e-businesses offer reverse auctions, similar to the C2B model. In a C2C reverse auction, a single buyer makes an offer for a specific item, and multiple sellers compete to sell the item at the buyer's offer price. Another type of C2C e-business allows members to list items of equal value they want to exchange — for example, a book for a book or a DVD for a DVD. This type of C2C e-business generates revenues by charging a small subscription or membership fee. Still other C2C e-businesses, such as TraderOnline.com (Figure 8-36) sell online classified ad space to individuals trying to sell boats, cars, and other items.

Figure 8-36 C2C auction and classified ad sites allow consumers to buy from and sell to each other.

@Issue eBay: The Perfect Marketspace

In the summer of 1995, Pierre Omidyar, an idealistic young Silicon Valley programmer, was thinking of ways to exploit the new and exciting online marketspace created by the Internet and the Web. Omidyar wanted to create a perfect marketspace where people connected with others in an online community; where anyone could sell and anyone could buy; where all buyers would have the same information on items for sale; and where prices would be set by the marketspace based on the supply of and the demand for each item. Omidyar's solution for a perfect marketspace? An online auction.

In his spare time, Omidyar began creating the software to allow online sellers to post items for sale and online buyers to bid on those items. On Labor Day 1995, Omidyar launched AuctionWeb, a free online auction, as part of his personal Web site. Taking advantage of the network effect, Omidyar began advertising his free online auction through Usenet newsgroups as "The most fun buying and selling on the Web." Group participants discussed the auction service and e-mailed their friends with the news. The first items posted for sale at the site included used computer equipment and a few noncomputer items such as a health-club membership, a couple of autos, and a few autographed posters and other collectibles. Because of the effective exchange of information about the new online auction via newsgroups and e-mail, traffic at AuctionWeb grew rapidly. In its first three months, AuctionWeb hosted hundreds of individual auctions and garnered several thousand buyer bids.

During 1995, Omidyar operated the free AuctionWeb service as a hobby. In February 1996, however, his ISP complained about the level of traffic to the site and began charging Omidyar $250 a month for a commercial account. To cover his increased expenses, Omidyar began charging sellers a fee based on a percentage of the final sales price for each item. And the money rolled in. By the end of February, the AuctionWeb site had generated more fees than the $250 charged by the ISP. AuctionWeb's fee revenue continued to grow from $1,000 in March 1996, to $10, 000 in June 1996 — and a new profitable e-business with no inventory, no warehouse, no responsibility for order fulfillment, and no liability for item returns was born.

On September 1, 1997, AuctionWeb became eBay and by October 1998, eBay was hosting new auctions at the rate of more than 1,000 per day. eBay now posts more than 12 million items for auction on any given day at its U.S. Web site and at local sites around the world in countries such as Australia, the U.K., Belgium, Singapore, Sweden, and Germany. The value of all the merchandise sold at eBay in 2002 was more than $14.5 billion.

With more than $250 million in net income in 2002, eBay is one of the few early e-businesses to enjoy profitability almost from inception. Over time, the original eBay C2C e-business model has evolved to include both individual consumer and business auction participants; revenue generation from listing fees, sales commissions, and advertising; and sales of fixed-price items via its Buy-It-Now feature and through its subsidiary, Half.com.

For more information about eBay, visit the Discovering the Internet Chapter 8 Web page (**scsite/internet/ ch8**) and click a link below eBay.

Amazon.com: An Evolving E-Business Model
@Issue

First, think about South America's Amazon River — huge, with thousands of branches and tributaries, completely dominating its rain forest environment. Now think about Amazon.com, the e-business named for the river — huge, selling thousands of products from books to bath soap, toys to tools, and DVDs to dresses, completely dominating its online retail environment.

In 1994, Amazon.com's founder Jeff Bezos (Figure 8-37), reportedly observed the huge growth in the number of people using the Web and decided to create an e-business that could capitalize on that growth. Bezos then made a list of several different products that could be sold online. After considerable research, Bezos picked books for a number of reasons, including the enormous selection of available book titles. Bezos also reasoned that because books were inexpensive, his market risk was lower than with other products; that information about each book would fit nicely into a Web page format; and that books were easy to ship. With his research completed, Bezos quit his job as a vice president of D. E. Shaw, a New York investment firm, and headed to Seattle where his new e-business would be close to technology innovators and

a huge book distribution center. Following a business-to-consumer (B2C) e-business model that focused on product selection, customer service, personalization, and discount pricing, Amazon.com opened its virtual doors in July 1995, and within two years registered its 1 millionth customer account.

But growing Amazon.com into the "Earth's biggest bookstore" was only a short-term objective. Bezos's long-term objective was to grow Amazon.com

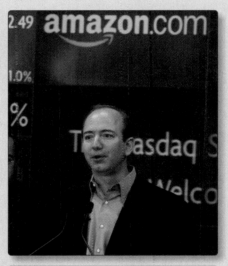

Figure 8-37   Jeff Bezos.

into the online store with the "Earth's biggest selection." In 1998, Amazon .com added music, videos, and DVDs to its offerings and the next year added other retail products including video games, toys, and electronics. To exploit the online auction craze, Amazon .com also opened its auction site in 1999. Today, through acquisitions and partnerships with other retailers such as ToysRUs, Borders, and Circuit City, Amazon.com is a Fortune 500 company that sells thousands of products to millions of customers in more than 200 countries around the world.

And along the way, Amazon.com's e-business model evolved from a single-product B2C e-retailer to a mix of e-business models that allows Amazon.com not only to sell products directly to consumers but also to develop innovative e-business technologies and sell them to other businesses, and to provide a retailing channel for other companies. This successful mix of e-business models underlies annual sales in excess of $3.9 billion as of December 2002.

For more information about Amazon.com, visit the Discovering the Internet Chapter 8 Web page (**scsite/internet/ch8**) and click a link below Amazon.com.

Business-to-Business (B2B)

While B2C and C2C may be the most familiar e-business models, online transactions between businesses, called **business-to-business (B2B)** transactions, account for an ever increasing share of total e-business revenues. Like other e-business models discussed earlier in this section, the B2B e-business model takes a variety of forms and B2B revenues are generated in a number of ways, including:

- Business directory listing fees
- Web site advertising

- Subscription or membership fees
- Referral fees
- Transaction fees
- Sales commissions
- Web site hosting fees
- File storage fees
- Software licensing and rental fees

Some B2B e-businesses aggregate business information for other businesses and generate revenues from directory listing fees and advertising. Examples include the Business.com business search engine and directory and the B2B Yellow Pages (Figure 8-38) that provide business-to-business information similar to a printed telephone business directory.

Figure 8-38　Some B2B e-businesses aggregate business information for other businesses.

Facts@Hand

The term, infomediary, refers to an e-business that gathers and organizes large amounts of data and information and then acts as an intermediary between those who want the information and those who supply the information. Infomediary examples include several B2C e-businesses such as Edmunds.com, Autobytel, Abebooks.com, and BizRate.com. B2B infomediaries include Business.com and the B2B Yellow Pages.

Other B2B e-businesses create online marketspaces to bring buyers and sellers together, operate reverse or forward auctions, provide revenue-generating affiliate programs, sell Web hosting services, sell file storage, or develop and sell e-business technologies.

B2B EXCHANGES   **B2B exchanges** create online marketspaces in which businesses can buy and sell with each other following a predetermined set of exchange rules. These rules determine how buyers and sellers communicate with each other through the exchange, how they negotiate with each other over price, how payment is made, and how products are delivered. B2B exchanges usually generate revenues by charging subscription or membership fees, transaction fees, and sales commissions.

@Issue MetalSite:
The Rebirth of a B2B Exchange

Flat rolled. Master coils. Sheets. Irregular blanks. Although these terms may sound strange to you, they describe just some of the steel products available through the MSA MetalSite B2B exchange. A number of steel industry companies, including Weirton Steel Corporation, LTV Steel, Steel Dynamics, Bethlehem Steel, and Ryerson Tull, originally founded MetalSite in 1998. MetalSite's mission was to provide a single online venue where steel buyers could easily find and purchase specific steel products offered by a variety of steel manufacturers.

MetalSite's services included a product catalog complete with pricing information and a sealed-bid auction service. Through the MetalSite auction service, participating steel manufacturers solicited private sealed bids for their products from steel buyers. MetalSite did not charge buyers to access the MetalSite services; however, it did charge sellers a transaction fee of up to 2 percent for each online sale. To attract customers, MetalSite also provided metal industry news and other related content at its Web site. Unfortunately, the general business slowdown and stock market crash of 2000 also adversely affected MetalSite, and by June 2001, MetalSite's operations ceased for lack of funding.

In October 2001, MetalSite's assets were purchased by Management Science Associates Inc. (MSA), a data management systems developer. MSA refurbished the MetalSite e-business model by adding a request for quote (RFQ) system that allows buyers to post information about their steel needs and sellers to submit quotes based on those needs. MSA further modified the MetalSite e-business model by selling its proprietary B2B technologies to other companies. MSA redesigned and streamlined the MetalSite Web site to focus on the buying and selling process and to make site features easier to use. The new and improved MetalSite B2B exchange was re-launched as MSA MetalSite in November 2002.

MSA MetalSite (Figure 8-39) continues to provide a product catalog and a sealed-bid auction process in addition to the new RFQ system.

MetalSite still does not charge buyers for using the product catalog or bidding in an auction. It does charge buyers a monthly subscription fee, however, to post RFQs. Sellers now pay a subscription fee to list their products in the catalog as well as a transaction fee on products sold through the auction process.

For more information about MetalSite, visit the Discovering the Internet Chapter 8 Web page (**scsite/internet/ch8**) and click a link below MSA MetalSite.

Figure 8-39   MetalSite is a B2B exchange for the steel industry.

Some B2B exchanges, such as Covisint (Figure 8-40), the auto industry B2B exchange, are cooperative efforts backed by major companies in a specific industry. Others, such as CATEX (Figure 8-40), a B2B exchange for the insurance and reinsurance industries, are created by knowledgeable third parties. B2B exchange examples also include GlobalNetXchange (Figure 8-40), which is a B2B exchange for the retail industry and ITParade (Figure 8-40), which is a B2B exchange for the information technology industry.

Figure 8-40   B2B exchanges bring buyers and sellers together in an online marketspace.

AFFILIATE PROGRAMS   B2B revenues also are generated by participating in an affiliate program. An **affiliate program**, sometimes called an associate program, is designed to drive viewer traffic to an e-business Web site. Participants in an affiliate program are called affiliates or associates. An affiliate adds links from its Web site to the sponsoring e-business's Web site. When a viewer clicks-through from the affiliate's site to the sponsoring e-business's site, the affiliate earns a referral fee. That fee may be based on a simple click-through or it may be based on a resulting purchase or some other action taken by the viewer at the sponsoring e-business's Web site.

Amazon.com popularized affiliate programs when it created its Amazon Associates Program. Participants in the Amazon Associates Program are paid a referral fee each time a viewer clicks-through to the Amazon.com site and makes a purchase. For example, Books for Managers, a participant in the Amazon Associates Program, aggregates information about best selling business, management, and technology books from various publications such as *The New York Times*, *Business Week*, and the *Harvard Business Review*. Each book title and cover graphic listed at the Books for Managers site is linked to a related Amazon.com Web page that contains detailed information about the book. The link contains the book's ISBN designation and the Books for

Managers affiliate identification that allows Amazon.com to keep track of click-throughs from the Books for Managers site. Books for Managers receives a referral fee up to 15 percent of the purchase price each time someone clicks-through to the Amazon.com site and makes a purchase. The following steps click-through from a link on an Amazon.com affiliate's Web site to the Amazon.com site.

Steps: To Follow an Affliate Web Page Link

1 Start the browser and visit the Discovering the Internet Chapter 8 Web page (scsite.com/internet/ch8). Click Books for Managers. If necessary, close any pop-up windows. Point to the Featured Books of the Month book cover graphic or text link. Notice the link URL on the browser status bar.

The Books for Managers home page appears (Figure 8-41). Because Web page content is updated continually, the content in the Web page on your screen may vary from that shown in Figures 8-41 and 8-42.

Figure 8-41

2 Click the Featured Books of the Month book cover graphic or link text.

You are now viewing the featured book's page at Amazon.com (Figure 8-42). Amazon.com pays Books for Managers a referral fee if you purchase the book.

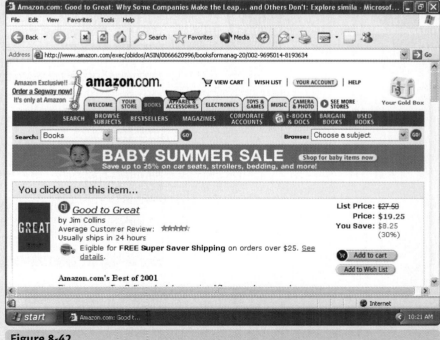

Figure 8-42

TECHNOLOGY PROVIDERS   A large portion of total B2B e-business is conducted between e-businesses and their technology providers — companies that develop and sell the technologies that make e-business possible. Technology providers include ISPs and NSPs such as AOL, EarthLink, WorldCom, Level 3 Communications, and AT&T that provide the Internet communications infrastructure. Other technology providers such as 3Com, Sun Microsystems, Microsoft, IBM, Hewlett Packard, SAP, PeopleSoft, and Cisco Systems develop and sell the networking hardware and application software that enable buyers and sellers to conduct business activities online.

Many early B2C or B2B e-businesses such as Amazon.com and MetalSite modified their original e-business plans to include selling their proprietary e-business technologies. Others such as Yahoo! have added B2B technology sales to their business mix as their original e-business models matured. Still other B2B technology providers including Web hosting companies, online storage companies, Application Service Providers (ASPs), and content delivery networks have created completely new kinds of businesses that use Internet technologies to provide new e-business services.

Thousands of **Web hosting** companies such as Yahoo! Web Hosting and Hosting.com (Figure 8-43) provide e-businesses with Web and database server storage and server administration services at secure, temperature controlled, storage facilities. Many e-businesses find it less expensive to pay for services at a hosting company than to operate Web and database servers at their own facilities. Monthly Web hosting fees can range from a few dollars for a shared hosting service to several hundred dollars for dedicated hosting or co-location services.

Figure 8-43   Three Web hosting company examples.

In a **shared hosting** arrangement, multiple e-businesses share a single Web server owned by the hosting company. Shared hosting services are inexpensive and attractive for small e-businesses that lack the facilities and expertise to manage their own Web servers. Larger e-businesses with hundreds of complex transactions may choose to contract for **dedicated hosting** services, where they have exclusive use of an entire server or servers. Other e-businesses may own their own servers, yet contract with a Web hosting company to store their servers at the hosting company's facilities. This arrangement, called **co-location**, allows e-businesses to reduce server facility costs. Some Web hosting companies, such as Rackspace Managed Hosting provide complete **managed hosting** services by building, customizing, managing, and supporting dedicated e-business servers for which their clients pay a flat monthly fee.

@Issue — Rackspace Managed Hosting: A New E-Business Idea

In 1998, when Web hosting was in its infancy, three technologically-savvy friends from San Antonio, Texas, had a great idea for a new e-business — managed hosting. Richard Yoo, Dirk Elmendorf, and Patrick Condon were former classmates at Trinity University in San Antonio, and were all pursuing careers in IT when they came together to discuss creating a new e-business that would lease and administer customized, dedicated Web servers from a secure, central data center. They named their new company Rackspace Managed Hosting.

Needing to acquire additional funding for their new e-business, the trio pitched their new hosting company to two experienced San Antonio businessmen, Graham Weston and Morris Miller, who immediately liked the managed hosting concept. Weston and Miller invested their own money in the new company and soon took responsibility for its overall management, allowing Yoo,

Elmendorf, and Condon to concentrate on the technical aspects of the business.

One of the first problems the new management team at Rackspace had to solve was how to differentiate Rackspace from the hundreds of other companies that were entering the Web hosting marketspace. To do this, the Rackspace management team asked themselves "What do our customers really want?" Surprisingly, the answer was not rooted in server technologies. The answer was "extraordinarily responsive customer support." The Rackspace management team then developed the company's trademark — Fanatical Support — to express its commitment and unique approach to serving its customers. The Fanatical Support approach includes a 99.999% server uptime guarantee and 24 × 7 customer support provided by highly trained and qualified technicians. And the

powered by **rackspace** MANAGED HOSTING

commitment to Fanatical Support paid off handsomely. In four years, revenues at Rackspace grew from $1.7 million (1999) to $40 million (2002) and the company has been profitable since 2001.

From its early beginning serving small to medium-sized local e-businesses, Rackspace has grown into one of the larger Web hosting companies in the market. Today, Rackspace (Figure 8-43) provides managed hosting services to more than 4,000 customers, including Microsoft, Hershey's, General Electric, U.S. Robotics, Columbia House, and Schlumberger, from four state-of-the-art secure data centers: two in San Antonio, one in Herndon, Virginia, and one in London, England.

For more information about Rackspace Managed Hosting, visit the Discovering the Internet Chapter 8 Web page (**scsite/internet/ch8**), and click a link below Rackspace Managed Hosting.

In Chapter 6, you learned how important it is for a business to create regular backup copies of critical files and then store those files offsite. Storing critical files offsite used to require manually carrying backup disks and tapes to an offsite storage warehouse. Today, for a monthly fee, a business can store backup copies of its critical files at an online storage facility, sometimes called a **Web warehouse**, by renting server space from e-businesses such as Xdrive, IBackup, Anuvio Technologies, and StoragePoint (Figure 8-44).

Figure 8-44   Four Web warehouses, or online file storage sites.

Developing e-business software applications in-house is very expensive; therefore, many e-businesses elect to save time and money by renting their business software from an Application Service Provider. An **Application Service Provider** (**ASP**) develops and maintains business application software — such as accounting, marketing and sales management, personnel management, and employee collaboration software — and then rents the software to its customers. Customers access the software over the Internet via their Web browsers. ASP examples include Digital River and Salesforce.com (Figure 8-45).

Employee collaboration software allows employees to share documents, calendars, contacts, tasks lists, and other information and is very popular and useful. You may be familiar with employee collaboration software such as Microsoft Outlook, which is part of the Microsoft Office suite. E-businesses also can rent employee collaboration software from an ASP such as Intranets.com. In the following steps, you learn more about how an ASP works by taking a tour at the Intranets.com Web site. (This online tour requires a high-bandwidth Internet connection.)

Figure 8-45 ASPs develop and maintain business applications delivered over the Web.

Steps: To Tour the Intranet Application Offered by an ASP

1 **Start the browser and visit the Discovering the Internet Chapter 8 Web page (scsite.com/internet/ch8). Click Intranets.com. If necessary, close any pop-up windows. Point to the Pricing link in the navigation bar near the top of the page.**

The Intranets.com home page appears (Figure 8-46). Intranets.com collaboration applications includes document management, online calendar, task management, discussion forum, and database management software that can be accessed via employees' Web browsers. The Web content on your screen may vary from that shown in Figures 8-46 through 8-49 on pages 491 through 493.

Figure 8-46

(continued)

2 Click the Pricing link. Scroll the page to see the different pricing plans. Point to the View NEW Tour link in the navigation bar.

The Intranets.com Pricing page appears (Figure 8-47). Intranets.com prices its software rental service based on the number of users at a customer's site.

Figure 8-47

3 Click the View NEW Tour link. If necessary, scroll down to display the animation toolbar.

The Intranets.com product tour begins playing (Figure 8-48). You can pause the tour, advance to a different place in the tour, turn the sound on or off, or rewind the tour by clicking the buttons in the toolbar below the tour viewing area.

Figure 8-48

4 Continue to view the tour until you are ready to stop. Then, click the pause button below the tour viewing area to pause the tour and minimize or close the browser.

You may view the tour until it ends or pause the tour at any point if you are ready to stop (Figure 8-49).

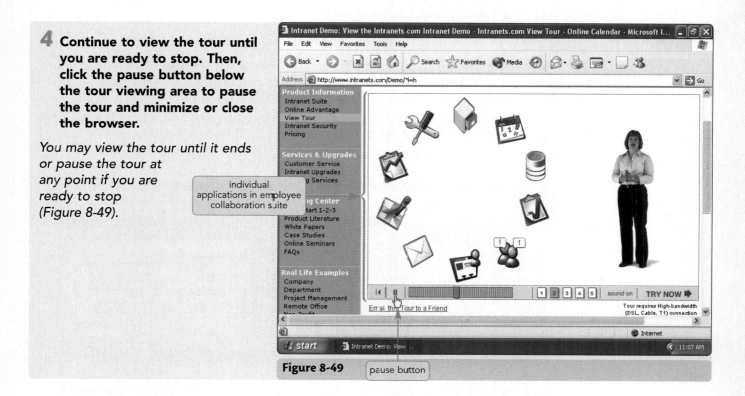

Figure 8-49 pause button

A **content delivery network** (**CDN**) is a dedicated network of servers located in different geographical areas of the country that store, or cache, Web page content from high-traffic Web sites for a fee. The content delivery network's servers quickly *serve up* the cached content upon request. For example, high-traffic Web sites such as MSNBC.com, Edmunds.com, and NASDAQ eliminate traffic congestion at their sites by distributing their Web page content via the Akamai content delivery network. When a viewer requests a Web page from one of these sites, that request is redirected to the Akamai server geographically closest to the viewer allowing the content to be *served up* more quickly.

SUPPLY CHAIN MANAGEMENT B2B transactions go far beyond selling products and services. Internet technologies are fostering a revolution in the way businesses interact with their suppliers. Today businesses can connect with their suppliers via the Internet to exchange product information, purchase orders, shipping reports, invoices, payments, and other B2B transactions. A **supply chain** consists of all the entities — raw material providers, manufacturers, distributors, wholesalers, retailers — involved in creating and distributing products to end users. Many businesses conduct B2B transactions across their supply chains via an extranet. An **extranet** is a private network that uses Internet technologies to connect a business with its suppliers and business partners. Using Internet technologies and extranets to exchange information among trading partners is a less-expensive option than the value-added networks (VANs) you learned about earlier in this chapter.

Business-to-Government (B2G)

The **business-to-government** (**B2G**) e-business model, sometimes called the B2G e-procurement model, is similar to the B2B exchange model. E-businesses following the B2G model provide other businesses with information on bidding opportunities for government agency contracts and sell the technologies used to manage the bidding and procurement process. Onvia, BidNet, Bidmain, and Fedmarket (Figure 8-50) all participate in the B2G online marketspace.

Figure 8-50   B2G e-businesses provide other businesses with government contract bidding opportunities.

Facts@Hand

In Chapter 6, you learned about intranets. Internal business activities related to employees conducted over a company intranet sometimes are called business-to-employee, or B2E, transactions.

Creating an Online Store

An **entrepreneur** is someone who both assumes the risks and responsibilities associated with starting his or her own business and receives the opportunity to earn a profit from this business. Jeff Bezos (Amazon.com), Michael Dell (Dell, Inc.), and Reed Hastings (Netflix) are three famous e-business entrepreneurs you learned about earlier in this chapter. Thousands of other men and women become e-business entrepreneurs each year, many by starting and operating their own online e-retail store. In this section, you learn about the storefront software that you need to create an online store and the payment gateway service and merchant account that you need to process credit card payments.

Storefront Software

A typical e-retail transaction (Figure 8-51) consists of several steps. First, you access the online store's Web site and view the store's product catalog, which is a listing of products complete with descriptions and pricing. Next, you select items from the product catalog, provide your billing and shipping information, and specify a payment method — usually by credit card. Before the order can be filled, the online store must verify that your credit card number is valid and have the transaction authorized. After the transaction is authorized, the online store then must process your credit card payment, fulfill your order, and ship it. Creating and maintaining a complex online store that can handle all these steps can be very expensive. Some very large e-retailers spend thousands of dollars to develop their own custom online store software in-house. Other e-retailers choose to outsource that development by licensing storefront software packages from third-party vendors.

1 buyer accesses online store and product catalog

2 buyer adds items to electronic shopping cart

3 buyer enters name, address, and credit card payment information

4 credit card information is validated and payment is authorized

5 online store processes order

6 order is fulfilled at warehouse

7 order is shipped

Figure 8-51 The path of an authorized e-retail transaction.

Storefront software, sometimes called **e-commerce software** is used to build and maintain Web pages and the underlying product databases that contain product pictures, descriptions, and prices. Storefront software also contains shopping cart software. **Shopping cart software** tracks items selected for purchase and handles the checkout process including summarizing the order, calculating shipping and taxes, calculating the order's total, and processing the order's payment. High-end storefront software also may provide a number of other features such as an interface to order fulfillment and accounting systems or personalization features. Less expensive storefront software may be limited to a product catalog and shopping cart.

 @Source

To learn more about the e-businesses discussed in this section, visit the Discovering the Internet Chapter 8 Web page (**scsite.com/ internet/ch8**) and click a link below Online Stores.

✋ Facts@Hand

An e-business whose Web site already has product pages but lacks online shopping capability can license only shopping cart software instead of a complete storefront software package. Adding shopping cart functionality to existing Web pages is sometimes called *bolting on* the shopping cart software.

Choosing the right storefront software package depends on the complexity of an online store and the specific features required. Medium- to large-sized e-retailers may license storefront software from vendors such as Actinic, MerchandiZer, and ECmerchant (Figure 8-52) for a few hundred dollars. Sometimes called **installed storefront software**, this customizable storefront software is installed on an e-retailer's Web server and then the e-retailer uses it to create and manage a complex e-retail site.

Figure 8-52 Installed storefront software is customizable software installed on an e-retailer's server.

Smaller e-retailers with simple online store requirements often choose to use **hosted storefront software** offered by vendors such as Yahoo! Store, BizPlaces, and iCart (Figure 8-53). Hosted storefront software is designed around easy-to-use Web page templates that allow you to create a store and add products to your online catalog in just a few minutes. You access hosted storefront software via your Web browser. Fees for building and maintaining a hosted storefront can include monthly Web hosting fees, per-item fees for adding products to the store's online catalog, and transaction fees.

Figure 8-53 Smaller e-retailers with simple online store requirements often choose hosted storefront software.

Some hosted storefront software vendors provide software demos or allow you to review their software on a free trial basis. For example, you can test drive the Yahoo! Store hosted storefront software by creating a Yahoo! ID and following an online demo at the Web site.

Credit Card Authorization and Processing

Most online store purchases — more than 90 percent by some reports — are paid for by credit card. Credit cards are not the only way to pay for online purchases however. Online auction sites use person-to-person payment methods and many online stores accept electronic checks and prepaid cards. Electronic cash, micropayments, smart cards, and other online payment methods, however, which were expected to change the e-retail payment process have not yet caught on in the U.S. where online shoppers continue to prefer to pay for their purchases via credit card. To accept credit card payments, an e-retailer must have two things: an account with a financial institution for credit card receipt deposits and a service that authorizes and processes credit card transactions.

@Source

To learn more about alternative online payment methods, visit the Discovering the Internet Chapter 8 Web page (**scsite.com/ internet/ch8**) and click a link below Alternative Payment Methods.

MERCHANT ACCOUNT   An e-business account with a financial institution into which credit card receipts are deposited is called a merchant credit card account, or more simply a **merchant account**. Any business — both bricks-and-mortar and online — that accepts credit cards must have a merchant account. While an e-business can withdraw funds from a merchant account, nothing can be deposited to the account except credit card receipts.

An e-business applies for a merchant account at a financial institution — generally a bank that specializes in e-business merchant accounts — by providing information about its size, length of time in operation, credit history, and the type of cards to be accepted. Fees for an approved e-business merchant account may include one-time setup fees, monthly access fees, per item transaction fees, and a **discount rate**, which is a percentage of each transaction that the financial institution will charge the e-business. The actual fees paid by an individual e-business for its merchant account are based on the financial institution's perceived level of risk on the account.

Before approving a merchant account, a bank first assesses its level of risk on the account based on the e-business's financial and operational history. The bank also evaluates its own chargeback history with similar e-business merchant accounts. A **chargeback** is a return of funds to a credit card company resulting from a card holder's refusal to pay a credit card charge. If a chargeback is processed after the bank has released merchant account funds to the e-business, the bank must recover the funds from the e-business. The bank's risk is that it will not be able to recover the funds.

In assessing its chargeback risk, the bank also considers the kinds of products and services the e-business sells. For example, some types of online credit card transactions, such as payments for gambling, pornographic, or other such products or services, historically generate more chargebacks than other credit card transactions. An e-business offering these types of products or services generally is considered a higher risk and, if approved for a merchant account, is likely to pay higher fees.

Another merchant account risk inherent in online credit card transactions occurs because neither the credit card nor the credit card holder is physically present during the transaction. This situation increases the risk of credit card fraud and potential chargebacks. Because of the **card not present/card holder not present risk**, e-businesses typically are charged a higher discount rate than similar bricks-and-mortar stores where the card and card holder are present during the transaction.

PAYMENT GATEWAY   An online store also must be able to connect to a payment-processing service that can verify, authorize, and process secure credit card transactions. You experience a payment-processing service in action when you use your credit card to pay for products or services at a bricks-and-mortar store or restaurant. At a bricks-and-mortar store or restaurant, your card is passed through a card-swipe machine and the transaction authorization is transmitted back to the store or restaurant electronically. While it is possible to use a similar manual process to access a payment-processing service for online credit card transactions, most e-retailers use an online payment-processing service that authorizes the transaction while the customer is waiting. Online payment-processing services, called **payment gateways**, are offered by a number of vendors such as VeriSign Payments Systems, Authorize.Net, and CyberSource (Figure 8-54). For a monthly fee, a payment gateway connects an online store with card processors, card issuers, and its merchant account (Figure 8-55) providing real-time transaction authorization and payment processing.

An important step in selecting storefront software, a payment gateway, and a merchant account is to be certain that all three are compatible. Most storefront software packages come complete with a connection to one or more payment gateway services. Hosted storefront software services, designed for small e-retailers with limited resources and experience, often provide access to both a merchant account and a payment gateway service for an additional fee.

E-retailers must also have a process for packaging and shipping products called **order fulfillment**. Brick-and-click retailers can take advantage of existing fulfillment operations and some large pure-play e-retailers build and manage their own fulfillment operations. Many e-retailers save time and money, however, by contracting with third-party fulfillment or logistics companies to warehouse, package, and ship their orders.

Figure 8-54 Popular payment gateway vendors.

@Source

For more information about fulfillment companies, visit the Discovering the Internet Chapter 8 Web page (**scsite.com/ internet/ch8**) and click a link below Fulfillment Companies.

Figure 8-55 A payment gateway service verifies, authorizes, and processes secure credit and transactions.

What Are the Early Origins of E-Business?

Electronic business transactions began with the **Electronic Funds Transfer** (**EFT**) system and the **Automated Clearing House** (**ACH**) network used by financial institutions to transfer money without the physical exchange of paper money. Other early electronic business transactions between **trading partners** were processed over private **value-added networks** (**VANs**).

 What Are the Unique Factors Inherent in Doing Business Online That Contribute to the Growth and Success of E-Business?

The unique factors inherent in doing business online include the effect of geography, time, and space; the **network effect**; the ability of individual e-businesses to redefine their markets; and the power of **personalization** and **customization**. Geography, time, and space are much less limiting in the online marketspace because buyers can connect with multiple online sellers that may be located anywhere in the world and whose online stores are open 24 hours a day, seven days a week. The network effect — the increasing value of a network as more users are added — can be used to explain the increasing value of the Internet as more and more users connect and the increasing value of e-business and more and more Internet-connected buyers and sellers participate in the online marketspace.

Individual e-businesses can redefine their markets by removing traditional market intermediaries through a process called **disintermediation** and by introducing new types of intermediaries into the marketspace in a process called **reintermediation**. E-businesses can capitalize on the interactive nature of the Web by using Web site personalization and customization features to offer Web page content, products, and services tailored to each customer's needs and preferences.

 What Is a Business Model, How Are E-Business Models Classified, and How Do E-Business Models Generate Revenues?

A **business model** is the form a business takes to generate revenues and remain viable. Companies doing business online often are classified into general e-business model categories. The most common classification method is by the type of customer the e-business targets: for example, **business-to-consumer** (**B2C**), **consumer-to-business** (**C2B**), **consumer-to-consumer** (**C2C**), **business-to-business** (**B2B**), and **business-to-government** (**B2G**). Within each e-business model classification, an individual e-business may generate revenues in a variety of ways, including selling products and services, selling advertising space at their Web sites, charging buyers a subscription or membership fee; charging sellers a listing fee, charging a transaction fee or sales commission, generating referral fees from other e-businesses, and selling or renting technologies to other businesses.

4 What Technologies Do You Need to Create and Operate an Online Store?

To create an online store, you need **installed storefront software** or **hosted storefront software**, both of which include **shopping cart software** that enables customers to select and pay for products. Because most consumers pay for online purchases by credit card, an e-retailer must have a **merchant account** to accept credit card receipts and a payment-processing service to authorize and process credit card transactions. Most e-retailers use an online payment-processing service called a **payment gateway** that connects the online store with credit card processors, issuing banks, and its merchant account.

CHAPTER REVIEW

The Chapter Review section summarizes the concepts presented in the chapter.

TERMS TO KNOW

After reading this chapter, you should know each term.

affiliate program (*486*)
Application Service Provider (ASP) (*490*)
Automated Clearing House (ACH) (*460*)
B2B exchanges (*485*)
banner ad (*477*)
business model (*474*)
business-to-business (B2B) (*483*)
business-to-consumer (B2C) (*475*)
business-to-government (B2G) (*494*)
brick-and-click (*475*)
card not present/card holder not present risk (*498*)
chargeback (*498*)
click-through (*478*)
co-location (*489*)
content delivery network (CDN) (*493*)
consumer-to-business (C2B) (*480*)
consumer-to-consumer (C2C) (*481*)
customization (*467*)
dedicated hosting (*489*)
discount rate (*498*)
disintermediation (*465*)
e-business model (*474*)
e-commerce software (*496*)
Electronic Data Interchange (EDI) (*461*)
Electronic Funds Transfer (EFT) (*460*)

entrepreneur (*494*)
e-retail (*475*)
extranet (*493*)
Flash animation ads (*477*)
forward auctions (*481*)
hosted storefront software (*497*)
installed storefront software (*496*)
intermediary (*465*)
managed hosting (*489*)
merchant account (*498*)
network effect (*463*)
niche market (*477*)
order fulfillment (*499*)
payment gateways (*498*)
personalization (*467*)
pop-up ad (*477*)
pure-play e-retailers (*487*)
reintermediation (*466*)
reverse auction (*480*)
shared hosting (*488*)
shopping cart software (*496*)
storefront software (*496*)
supply chain (*493*)
trading partners (*461*)
value-added networks (VANs) (*461*)
Web hosting (*488*)
Web warehouse (*490*)

True or False

Mark T for True and F for False. (Answers are found on page numbers in parentheses.)

TEST YOUR KNOWLEDGE

Use the Test
Your Knowledge
exercises to
check your
knowledge of
the chapter.

_____ 1. Someone who assumes the risks and responsibilities associated with starting his or her own business is called an entrepreneur. (*494*)

_____ 2. Shopping cart software is used to build and maintain Web pages containing an online store's product catalog. (*496*)

_____ 3. Redefining a market by removing its traditional intermediaries is called reintermediation. (*466*)

_____ 4. An extranet is a private network that uses Internet technologies to connect a business with its trading partners. (*493*)

_____ 5. A business model is the way a company operates to generate revenues and profits and remain a viable business entity. (*474*)

_____ 6. Some small e-retailers avoid competing with larger e-retailers by targeting small niche markets. (*477*)

_____ 7. A chargeback is a fee paid by an e-business to participate in a B2B auction. (*498*)

_____ 8. The risk of a chargeback is greater when neither the credit card nor the card holder is present during the transaction. (*498*)

_____ 9. Priceline.com operates using a B2G e-business model. (*480*)

_____ 10. A B2B exchange is an online marketspace in which businesses can buy and sell with each other following a predetermined set of exchange rules. (*485*)

 Multiple Choice

Select the best answer. (Answers are found on page numbers in parentheses.)

1. The term often used to describe how the growth in the number of online buyers and sellers increases the value of the online marketspace is the _____ effect. (*463*)
   a. personalization
   b. network
   c. affiliation
   d. infomediary

2. The software designed around Web page templates that allows you easily to create an online store via your Web browser is called _____ . (*497*)
   a. installed storefront software
   b. shopping cart software
   c. hosted storefront software
   d. none of the above

3. An example of a B2C e-business that generates revenues by charging subscription fees is _____ . (*478*)
   a. Rackspace Managed Hosting
   b. Hometown Favorites
   c. Netflix
   d. Amazon.com

(continued)

TEST YOUR KNOWLEDGE *(continued)*

4. The C2B e-business model is sometimes called a(n) _____ . *(481)*
   a. reverse auction
   b. forward auction
   c. e-procurement model
   d. subscription model

5. Any retailer or e-retailer that accepts credit cards must have a _____ . *(498)*
   a. chargeback
   b. merchant account
   c. payment gateway
   d. discount rate

6. An example of an e-business that sells its proprietary e-business technologies to other businesses is _____ . *(483)*
   a. Amazon.com
   b. Hosting.com
   c. CNN
   d. Hometown Favorites

7. The program designed to drive traffic to an e-business Web site by paying referral fees to other e-businesses is called a(n) _____ . *(486)*
   a. supply chain
   b. affiliate program
   c. B2B exchange
   d. shared hosting arrangement

8. The percentage of each transaction charged to an e-business by a bank as part of its merchant account fees is a _____ . *(498)*
   a. booking fee
   b. discount rate
   c. subscription fee
   d. cost of doing business expense

9. B2B e-businesses can generate revenues by charging _____ . *(483)*
   a. transaction fees
   b. sales commissions
   c. software rental fees
   d. all of the above

10. An arrangement where an e-business stores its own servers at a Web hosting facility is called _____ . *(489)*
    a. shared hosting
    b. dedicated hosting
    c. co-location
    d. Web warehousing

Instructions: To complete the Learn It Online exercises, visit **scsite.com/internet/ch8** and follow the directions below. Each exercise has instructions for saving your results, either for your own records or for submission to your instructor.

 Chapter Reinforcement

TF, MC, and SA
Click the Chapter Reinforcement link. Print the quiz by clicking Print on the File menu for each page. Answer each question.

 Flash Cards

Click the Flash Cards link. When the first card is displayed, read the instructions. Type 20 (or a number specified by your instructor) in the Number of Playing Cards text box, type your name in the Name text box, and then click the Flip Card button. When each flash card appears, read the question and then click the ANSWER box arrow to select an answer. Flip through Flash Cards. If you score 15 (75%) correct or greater, click Print on the File menu to print your results. If your score is less than 15 (75%) correct, then redo this exercise by clicking the Replay button.

 Practice Test

Click the Practice Test link. Answer each question, enter your first and last name at the bottom of the page, and then click the Grade Test button. When the graded practice test is displayed on your screen, click Print on the File menu to print a hard copy. Continue to take practice tests until you score 80% or better.

 Who Wants To Be a Computer Genius?

Click the Computer Genius link. Read the instructions, enter your first and last name at the bottom of the page, and then click the PLAY button. When your score is displayed, click the Print button to print a hard copy.

 Crossword Puzzle Challenge

Click the Crossword Puzzle Challenge link. Read the instructions, and then enter your first and last name. Click the SUBMIT button. Work the crossword puzzle. When you are finished, click the Submit button. When the crossword puzzle reappears, click the Print Puzzle button to print a hard copy.

To perform the following exercises, you must be connected to the Internet.

 Evaluate Hosted Storefront Software

You are considering opening an online store to sell your unique quilting patterns, imported thread, frames, and other quilting supplies. You have no experience running an online store, so you ask a friend how to get started. Your friend suggests that you consider using hosted storefront software to create and manage your store. (You may assume any other facts not stated here.)

1. Visit the Discovering the Internet Chapter 8 Web page (**scsite.com/internet/ch8**) and click the links below Exercise 1 to review Yahoo! Store, BizPlaces, and iCart hosted storefront software and services. Create a table that compares the three companies' services and fees.

2. Choose one of the three for your online store and give the reasons for your choice.

2 Identify E-Business Models and Revenue-Generation Methods

1. Visit the Discovering the Internet Chapter 8 Web page (**scsite.com/internet/ch8**) and click the links below Exercise 2 to review the following e-business Web sites:
   a. The Vermont Country Store
   b. GradeBeam
   c. B2gmarket
   d. iOffer.com
   e. Siebel Systems

2. Identify each company's e-business model and revenue generation methods.

 Evaluate ASP Time and Billing Software

You own a Web design and consulting business that is growing rapidly. Now you need to automate your project management administration by using a time and billing application. One of your designers suggests that you rent a Web-based time and billing application from an ASP. You think that is a good idea, but need to know more about which ASPs provide project time and billing software. (You may assume any other facts not stated here.)

1. Visit the Discovering the Internet Chapter 8 Web page (**scsite.com/internet/ch8**) and click the ASP directory links below Exercise 3 to locate at least three ASPs that rent time and billing software.

2. Compare the products and services offered by the selected ASPs.

3. Choose an ASP for your project time and billing needs and give the reasons for your choice.

EXERCISES

Use the
Exercises to
gain hands-on
Internet
experience.

 4 Evaluate Affiliate Programs

1. Visit the Discovering the Internet Chapter 8 Web page (**scsite.com/internet/ch8**) and click the links below Exercise 4 to review the affiliate programs offered by the following e-businesses:
   a. 1-800-Flowers.com
   b. Candy Crate
   c. FragranceNet.com
   d. The Franklin Mint

2. Write a brief description of each affiliate program and how it works.

3. Which of these affiliate programs might be a good match for an e-business that sells gift baskets? Why?

 5 Identify B2B Exchanges by Industry

1. Visit the Discovering the Internet Chapter 8 Web page (**scsite.com/internet/ch8**) and click the search tool links below Exercise 5 to identify at least one B2B exchange for each of the following industries:
   a. agricultural products
   b. floral products
   c. paper
   d. energy

2. Write a brief description of each B2B exchange you select. Identify the services provided to buyers and sellers and, if possible, how each exchange generates revenues.

 6 Evaluate Web Hosting Services

You and your business partner operate a small sporting goods store that specializes in extreme sports equipment including skateboards, safety helmets, and clothing. You and your business partner now want to open an online store. You have selected an installed storefront software package, a payment gateway service, and your company already has a merchant account. You do not want to manage your own Web server; therefore, you and your business partner now want to choose a Web hosting company and determine whether a shared hosting or dedicated hosting arrangement is best. (You may assume any other facts not stated here.)

1. Visit the Discovering the Internet Chapter 8 Web page (**scsite.com/internet/ch8**) and click the links below Exercise 6 to identify four Web hosting companies that offer shared and dedicated hosting arrangements.

2. Summarize the Web hosting companies' shared hosting and dedicated hosting services and fees. Then choose one of the hosting companies to host your online store and give the reasons for your choice.

(continued)

EXERCISES

Use the Exercises to gain hands-on Internet experience.

EXERCISES (continued)

7 Review Online Payment Methods

1. Visit the Discovering the Internet Chapter 8 Web page (scsite.com/internet/ch8) and click the links below Exercise 7 to research the following online payment methods:
   a. electronic checks
   b. electronic cash
   c. micropayments
   d. smart cards
   e. prepaid cards
   f. person-to-person (P2P) payments

2. Write a brief description of each payment method and discuss the role each of these payment methods currently plays in e-business.

8 Personalization and Customization

1. Visit the Discovering the Internet Chapter 8 Web page (scsite.com/internet/ch8) and click the links below Exercise 8 to review the following Web sites.
   a. Amazon.com
   b. eDiets
   c. Lands' End
   d. Nike
   e. Advocate Health Care

2. Describe how each site uses personalization and customization.

9 Redefining Markets

1. Visit the Discovering the Internet Chapter 8 Web page (scsite.com/internet/ch8) and click the links below Exercise 9 to review the following Web sites.
   a. Travel.com
   b. Autoweb.com
   c. Southwest Airlines
   d. Powells.com
   e. Marriott.com

2. Write a brief paragraph about each Web site. Is the sponsoring business involved in e-business disintermediation or e-business reintermediation? Give the rationale for your answer.

10 Exploring an Online Auction

1. Visit the Discovering the Internet Chapter 8 Web page (**scsite.com/internet/ch8**) and click the links below Exercise 10 to search each auction Web site for a Star Trek lunch box, Wonder Woman comic book or poster, or other collectible of your choice.

2. Select one of the collectible items, review the details about the item, and answer the following questions:
   a. What is the item's description? What, if any, are the item's distinguishing features?
   b. What are the starting and ending dates and times for the auction?
   c. What is the starting bid?
   d. What is the current bid?
   e. How many bids have been placed?
   f. Who is the seller? What is the seller's rating, if rated? Where is the seller located?
   g. What is the payment method?
   h. Who pays for shipping costs?

EXERCISES

Use the Exercises to gain hands-on Internet experience.

CHAPTER 9
Managing a Web Site

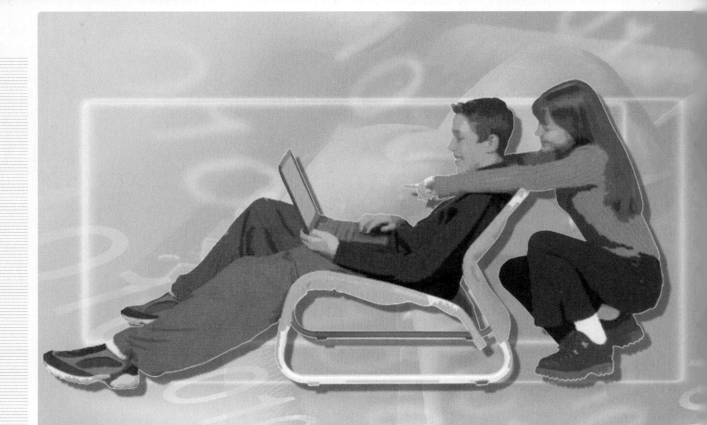

Introduction

As you continue to integrate the Internet and the Web into your daily activities, it is likely that you visit certain favorite sites again and again because the sites contain complex, useful, and timely content. No doubt, some of your favorite sites are portal sites you first learned about in Chapter 2. In this chapter, you learn more about different types of portals and the role they play in ensuring appropriate content is available to various target audiences: the public, employees, vendors, customers, and business partners.

You also learn how some businesses and other organizations manage their portal or other sites' content development, scheduling, and publishing. Finally, you learn how organizations use search tools and other techniques to promote their sites and how they evaluate their sites' performance against planned goals and objectives.

OBJECTIVES

After completing this chapter, you will be able to:

1. Describe and give examples of different types of portals and their target audiences

2. Discuss the importance of managing complex Web content and the benefits of implementing a content management system

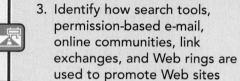

3. Identify how search tools, permission-based e-mail, online communities, link exchanges, and Web rings are used to promote Web sites

4. Describe the benchmarks, Web metrics, and log analysis tools used to measure Web site performance

CONTENTS

Understanding Portals

In Chapter 2, you learned that a portal is a Web site that serves as a gateway to a wide variety of Web content and services. A portal may also be a gateway to information about a specific area of interest or a specific industry. A single Web-based interface to a company's general business information, intranet, and extranet is called a portal. Portals often are classified by their targeted audiences as general consumer portals, vertical portals, industry portals, and corporate portals.

Consumer Portals

General consumer portals offer the visitor a broad range of content including search tools, current news and weather, stock quotes, sports scores, links to reference tools, and links to shopping, and e-mail. By offering varied content, a consumer portal appeals to a very large audience, thus becoming a more attractive venue for other organizations wanting to advertise and promote their sites. Several popular general consumer portals evolved from more humble beginnings. For example, Yahoo!, Lycos, and Excite (Figure 9-1) began as search tools, while MSN and Netscape Network (Figure 9-1) had their origins in the early default home pages for the Internet Explorer and Netscape Navigator Web browsers. By expanding their content, these early search tool and default starting page sites have increased their audience by attracting new users and encouraging users to visit their sites repeatedly. Over time, these sites developed into the general consumer portals with which you are familiar today.

Figure 9-1 General consumer portals offer visitors a broad range of content.

Personal portals, also called **horizontal portals**, are consumer portals whose content you customize to meet your own needs. Personal portals exploit the special interactive nature of the Web and use the personalization and customization features you learned about in Chapter 8 to tailor Web page content to your specific interests. Using your personal preferences to customize a consumer portal makes the portal content more interesting and useful to you and more sticky. My Lycos, My Yahoo!, My Excite, My MSN, and My Netscape (Figure 9-2) are all examples of personal portals. As you learned in Chapter 2, you can change the settings in your Web browser to make a customized personal portal your browser's default home page.

Figure 9-2 Personal, or horizontal, portals are portals whose content is customized to meet individual viewer needs.

Vertical and Industry Portals

Vertical portals, sometimes called **vortals**, provide a Web gateway for viewers with more specific interests such as gardening, women's interests, children's activities, social issues, ethnic interests, and government information, and make it easier for viewers to find information relating to their specific interest. Some of the sites you explored in Chapter 5 such as FirstGov for Seniors and Cancer.gov are vertical portals. Other vertical portal examples include Africana (African American interests), iVillage (women's interests), FirstGov for Kids (Federal pages of interest to children), Export.gov (export issues), EarthTrends (environmental issues), Business Nation (small business owners), and HispaniaNet (Hispanic interests).

Vertical portals that target viewers interested in a specific industry often are called **industry portals**. Some industry portals also function as B2B exchanges by combining information about a specific industry with an online trading marketspace. Other industry portals simply provide industry information, news, links, and advertising. Examples of industry portals include EarthWeb (IT industry), RSX (global insurance and reinsurance industry), Farms.com (agribusiness); Web Host Industry Review (Web hosting industry), MfgGate.com (manufacturing), COMMREX (commercial real estate industry), and the Pest Control Portal (pest control industry). In the following steps, you explore several vertical and industry portals to see examples of the wide range of possible interests vertical portals cover.

Steps: To Explore Vertical and Industry Portals

1 **Start the browser. Visit the Discovering the Internet Chapter 9 Web page (scsite.com/internet/ch9). Click HispaniaNet. If necessary, close any pop-up windows. Scroll the page and review its content. Point to the Change City link.**

The HispaniaNet portal home page appears (Figure 9-3). HispaniaNet provides news, articles, and links to content of special interest to Hispanics. Because Web page content is updated continually, the content and the link locations in the Web pages on your screen may vary from that shown in Figures 9-3 through 9-14 on pages 514 through 519.

Figure 9-3

2 **Click the Change City link. Click the Choose City box arrow and then click Los Angeles. Point to the Business Center link.**

The HispaniaNet page displays links to information of particular interest to Hispanics in the Los Angeles area rather than in the Denver area (Figure 9-4).

Figure 9-4

3 **Click the Business Center link.**

The HispaniaNet Business Center page appears (Figure 9-5). This page features links to business information of special interest to Hispanics.

general business news

Hispanic business news

Figure 9-5

4 **Visit the Discovering the Internet Chapter 9 Web page (scsite.com/internet/ch9). Click FirstGov for Kids. If necessary, close any pop-up windows. Scroll the page and review its content. Point to the Computers link.**

The FirstGov for Kids page appears (Figure 9-6). You can find links to other federal pages directed at children at this portal. Note that the mouse pointer has an animated trail of red stars following it on this page.

links to other federal pages directed toward children

Computers link

Figure 9-6

(continued)

5 Click the Computers link.

The FirstGov for Kids Computers page appears (Figure 9-7). You can find links to various sites directed to children that provide information about the Web and computers on this page.

links to other sites containing information about computers directed toward children

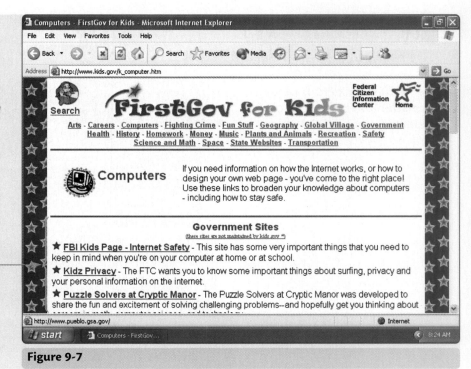

Figure 9-7

6 Visit the Discovering the Internet Chapter 9 Web page (scsite.com/internet/ch9). Click EarthTrends. If necessary, close any pop-up windows. Scroll the page and review its content.

The World Resources Institute EarthTrends environmental portal home page appears (Figure 9-8). You can find links to information about environmental, social, and economic trends at this portal.

navigation links

site description

Figure 9-8

7 **Point to the Climate and Atmosphere navigational link.**

A menu of navigational links appears that links to a searchable database, data tables, country profiles, maps, and other features concerned with climate and atmosphere (Figure 9-9).

Figure 9-9

8 **Click the COUNTRY PROFILES link on the navigation menu.**

A page containing a clickable world map and a list of countries appears (Figure 9-10). You can find climate and atmosphere information for a specific country on this page.

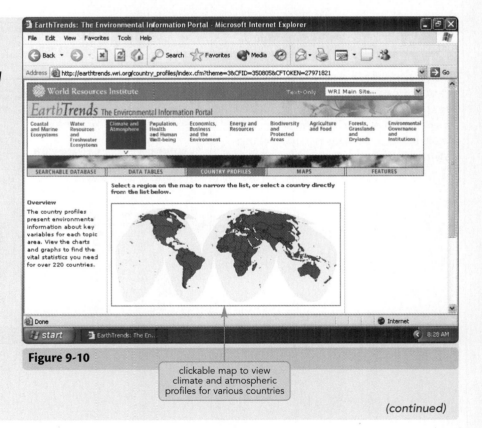

Figure 9-10

clickable map to view climate and atmospheric profiles for various countries

(continued)

9 **Visit the Discovering the Internet Chapter 9 Web page (scsite.com/internet/ch9). Click Farms.com. Point to the Swine Business link.**

The Farms.com agribusiness portal home page appears (Figure 9-11). This page contains links to agribusiness information and sites. Viewers also can create a personal portal by creating a customized myFarms page.

Figure 9-11

10 **Click the Swine Business link.**

The Farms.com Swine Business page appears (Figure 9-12). Swine farmers can read commentary, featured articles, and news about swine farming and link to an online marketspace for buying and selling swine on this page.

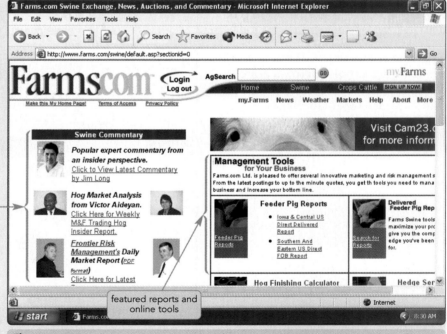

Figure 9-12

11 **Visit the Discovering the Internet Chapter 9 Web page (scsite.com/internet/ch9). Click EarthWeb. Point to the IT Jobs navigation button.**

The EarthWeb IT industry portal home page appears (Figure 9-13). IT professionals can read industry news and reports, link to industry forums, participate in a job search, and find out about different IT industry certifications at this portal site.

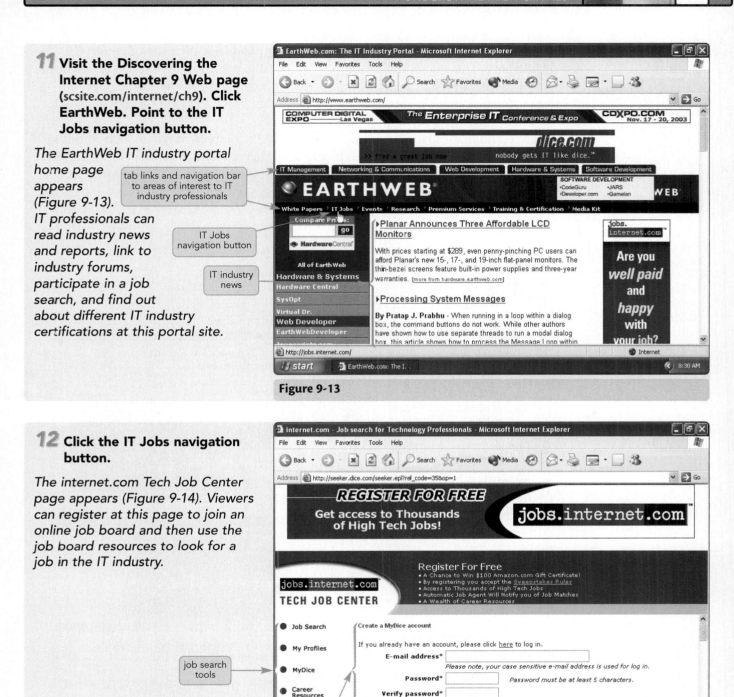

Figure 9-13

12 **Click the IT Jobs navigation button.**

The internet.com Tech Job Center page appears (Figure 9-14). Viewers can register at this page to join an online job board and then use the job board resources to look for a job in the IT industry.

Figure 9-14

Corporate Portals

Corporate portals also are called **enterprise information portals** (**EIPs**). Employees, customers, vendors, and other business partners can use a single corporate portal to access a company's business information, collaborate with others using e-mail and other internal collaboration tools, or conduct business transactions. In Chapter 8, you learned about the value of personalized and customized Web site content. Corporate portals use personalization to control access to company information and business processes based on each user's profile. Some corporate portals also permit customization — news on specific job-related topics, stock trackers on specific stocks, and so forth — based on user preferences.

Portal technologies from vendors such as SAP, PeopleSoft, Vignette, and Plumtree (Figure 9-15) and Yahoo! Enterprise (Figure 9-16) aggregate company-wide data, business information, and applications and then personalize portal pages to ensure that users — employees, vendors, customers, and business partners — have access only to the specific content they need. Figure 9-16 illustrates a sample corporate portal home page found at the Yahoo! Enterprise site.

@Source

To explore the consumer, personal, vertical, industry portals, and portal technology vendors discussed in this section, visit the Discovering the Internet Chapter 9 Web page (**scsite.com/internet/ch9**) and click a link below Portals.

Figure 9-15 Portal technologies aggregate company-wide data, business information, and applications and then personalize portal pages to ensure that users have access only to specific content based on their user profile.

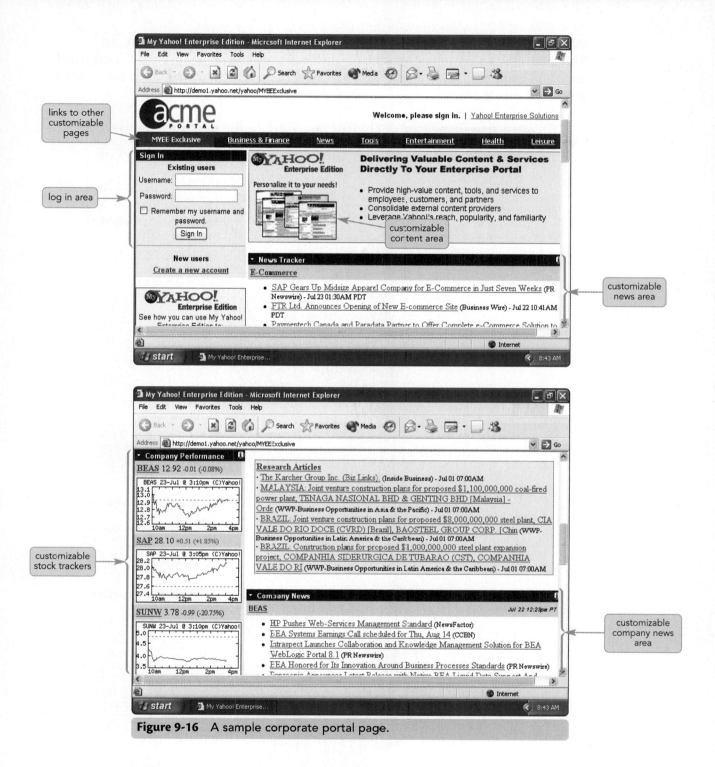

Figure 9-16 A sample corporate portal page.

When an employee uses the corporate portal to log on to the company intranet, the content he or she sees is controlled automatically based on his or her employee profile. By personalizing portal content, an employee in the accounts payable department, for example, can log on and track vendor invoices, company purchase orders, and company receiving reports but cannot access any information from other departments such as accounts receivable or marketing. Other general information such as industry and company news, company stock performance, links to search tools, and general employee information also may be included in the employee's portal content (Figure 9-17). Similarly, when a customer, vendor, or business partner logs on through the corporate portal, personalized content allows access only to specific information based on their profile (Figure 9-18).

Figure 9-17   An employee in the accounts payable department logging on to the corporate portal sees a personalized portal page based on his or her user profile.

Figure 9-18   A vendor logging on to a corporate portal sees a personalized portal page based on the vendor's user profile.

Managing Complex Web Content with a Content Management System

Content at your favorite general consumer or vertical portal and at other business and government Web sites becomes increasingly complex over time as new features are added, viewers demand greater personalization and customization, and both in-house and outside sources generate content for the sites. This increased complexity raises a number of issues for organizations trying to manage their Web site's content. For example, what Web site content issues did these very different real-world organizations have in common: an international agribusiness; a financial services company; an ethnic-oriented news and entertainment portal; an education-oriented charity; a state governor's office; a public television station; and a large law firm? Each of these organizations needed a way to:

- Control the quality, accuracy, and timing of their Web site's ever-growing, dynamic content.
- Ensure that relevant content is presented to the appropriate audience at the right time.
- Integrate content developed from different sources.
- Give all the Web pages at their site a standard appearance.

How did all of these real-world organizations handle their Web site content issues? Each organization implemented a content management system.

A **content management system** (**CMS**) includes all the processes involved in creating and publishing Web site content including authoring, reviewing and editing, approving, and publishing the content *plus* the technologies that tie the processes together. A content management system is effective in integrating content from many different sources. For example, the real-time global and industry news reports, news headlines, weather information, and stock tracker information you see at many portal sites generally is purchased from third-party vendors, such as YellowBrix, in a process called **syndication**. The syndicated content is then integrated with content developed in-house. A CMS is useful to ensure this integration process is timely and smooth. Content that must be updated frequently, such as television schedules, or content that must be personalized for each viewer, such as corporate portal content, also can be controlled through a CMS.

Content management system technologies offered by vendors such as Tridion, Interwoven, Ingeniux, and Documentum (Figure 9-19 on the next page) provide easy-to-use forms that allow nontechnical authors to create or modify Web page content without needing to know HTML. This helps lighten the workload on an organization's technical staff. Additionally, a content management system helps content authors integrate word processing documents, spreadsheets, presentations, and other types of electronic files into their Web pages. A CMS uses Web page templates to standardize the overall appearance of Web pages containing content from different sources.

Content management system technologies also typically provide features that allow Web site administrators to:

- Restrict access to specific pages by creating user accounts and specifying user access rights for each account.
- Track and approve new content or changes to existing content.
- Remove incorrect or inappropriate content.

- Schedule the publishing process so that time-sensitive content such as press releases, news headlines, television schedules, and weather reports can be automatically published and then removed based on a predetermined time frame.
- Archive content so that it can be reused or restored, as necessary.

Figure 9-19   Content management technologies are used to control the quality, accuracy, and timeliness of Web page content.

A content management system (Figure 9-20) uses databases called **content repositories** to store Web page elements: Web page templates that give all the pages at a site a common look and feel; style sheets that control Web page colors and fonts; graphic files such as company logos and other images; text, XML, HTML, and PDF documents; and content syndicated from third-parties. Web pages are built from these reusable items stored in and pulled from a content repository and then published to the site. Other content, such as a banner or pop-up ad or an invitation to try a new product also can be pulled from a content repository as necessary to personalize a Web page for a specific user.

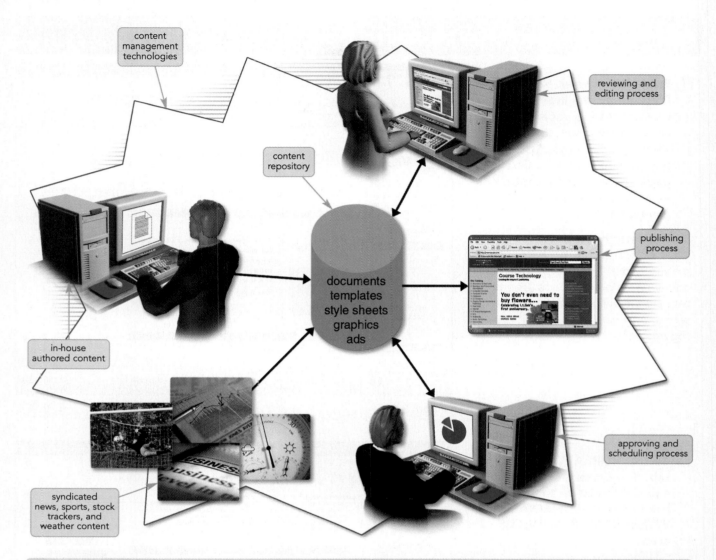

content management technologies

reviewing and editing process

content repository

publishing process

documents templates style sheets graphics ads

in-house authored content

approving and scheduling process

syndicated news, sports, stock trackers, and weather content

Figure 9-20 A content management system includes all the process involved in creating accurate and timely Web page content plus the technologies that tie the processes together.

Many major content management technology vendors offer marketing demos and Webcasts that describe content management concepts and discuss the vendors' proprietary technologies. In the steps on the next page, you view a short Flash content management demo at the Vignette Web site that describes how organizations can benefit from content management. (**Note**: you must have Flash Player installed to view this demo.)

⟫ Steps: To View a Content Management Demo

1 **Start the browser. Visit the Discovering the Internet Chapter 9 Web page (scsite.com/internet/ch9). Click Vignette. If necessary, close any pop-up windows. Scroll the page and review its content. Point to the LIBRARY navigation tab.**

The Vignette home page appears (Figure 9-21). You can link to information about Vignette products and services on this page. The content on the Web pages on your screen may vary from that in Figures 9-21 through 9-24.

Figure 9-21

2 **Click the LIBRARY navigation tab. If necessary, scroll down and then point to the Demos link in the MULTIMEDIA & INTERACTIVE RESOURCES area.**

The Vignette Library page (Figure 9-22) appears. You can learn more about portals and content management systems as well as more about Vignette's products by reviewing a variety of Vignette media including Webcasts, demos, brochures, and white papers using links on this page.

Figure 9-22

3 Click the Demos link. If necessary, scroll down and then point to the Managing Information Across the Enterprise or other content management Start the Demo link of your choice.

The Vignette Demos page appears (Figure 9-23). You can link to a currently available demo on this page.

content management Start the Demo link

demo window

Figure 9-23

4 Click the content management Start the Demo link and view the demo.

The Vignette content management demo is opened in its own window (Figure 9-24).

5 Close the demo window after viewing the demo.

demo controls

Figure 9-24

Promoting a Web Site

The Web contains millions of sites and billions of pages all competing for viewers' attention. Finding ways to get an individual Web site noticed in this crowd can be quite challenging especially for an individual's personal or hobby site or a small e-business site. Traditional promotion tools such as including the site's URL on business cards,

@Source

For more information about content management systems, visit the Discovering the Internet Chapter 9 Web page (**scsite.com/internet/ch9**) and click a link below Content Management.

stationery, and other printed material; buying print ads in trade journals and newspapers; issuing press releases; buying radio and television ads; and good, old-fashioned word of mouth can all be effective in promoting a Web site.

The Web site promotion tools available online, however, also can help get the right information to the right people in a timely manner by getting a Web site noticed by its target audience. As you learned in Chapter 8, online methods such as e-mail, news-groups, Web site advertising, and Web affiliate programs can play an important role in promoting a Web site. In this section, you learn more about using e-mail and online communities to promote a Web site. You also learn how you can use search tools, link exchanges, and Web rings to promote a Web site.

Search Tools

In Chapter 3, you became familiar with a number of popular Web search tools. You also learned how these search tools build their indexes and directories: (1) by using a bot to browse the Web looking for unindexed pages and then automatically adding the pages to the tool's index; and (2) by allowing individuals or organizations to submit Web site information. You can use search tools to promote a Web site in several ways: by proactively submitting site information to several search tools; by paying to position a Web site near the top of a search results list; by purchasing ads that appear on search results list pages; and by optimizing Web pages to make sure they are accessible to search engines.

SEARCH TOOL SUBMISSIONS   Waiting for a number of search engines to locate and index a Web site may take some time. Most organizations, especially e-businesses, pre-fer to speed up the process by proactively submitting site information to targeted search engines. Additionally, as you have learned, individuals and organizations can submit their Web site information to popular directories such as Yahoo! or Google, as well as to specialized search tools such as Business.com, the B2B search engine and directory. The fees, submission guidelines, and listing agreements at each search engine or directory vary. For example, a noncommercial Web site may be submitted without charge at some search tools, while to submit a commercial Web site, a fee may be required. Some search tools may offer accelerated submission and listing services for both noncommer-cial and commercial Web sites for a fee in a process called **paid inclusion**. You gener-ally provide some or all of the following information when submitting a Web site to a search tool:

- Name and e-mail address of person responsible for the listing.
- Site title.
- Site URL.
- Geographic location of the site, if relevant to its listing.
- Brief description of the contents of the site, usually about 150 characters.
- Preferred category for a directory listing and additional information that would assist the editors in properly categorizing the listing.
- Credit card number to pay for a submission fee, if necessary.

Figure 9-25 illustrates the Web site submission forms for Yahoo!, and Figure 9-26 illustrates the Web site submission form for AlltheWeb.

Figure 9-26　The AlltheWeb Web site submission form.

Figure 9-25　The Yahoo! Web site submission form.

Paying a fee to submit a Web site, however, does not always guarantee that the site will be added to the search tool's directory or index. For example, directories use human editors who review Web site submissions to ensure that submitted sites meet the directories' guidelines. Those sites that do not meet the guidelines are not accepted and, in most cases, the submission fee is nonrefundable if the site is not accepted. The three top directories to consider for submission are LookSmart, Yahoo!, and the Open Directory. Because search engine bots follow links when browsing the Web looking for pages to index, having links to pages included in these three top directories may help ensure that search engine bots locate and index the Web pages more quickly.

A number of e-businesses, such as Microsoft bCentral Submit It! and Marketleap.com, offer to submit Web site information to search engines and directories for an annual fee. That fee often includes periodic management reports describing how the submitted Web pages are being ranked in various search results lists and what keywords viewers are using to find the pages.

PAY-FOR-PLACEMENT AND PAY-PER-CLICK PROGRAMS   Most viewers who use search tools commonly look at only the top 20 to 30 items returned in a search results list because of the enormous number of potentially relevant Web pages in most lists. Therefore, to ensure that a Web page will be noticed in a search list, it is important that it be placed near the top of the search results list. One way to be certain this will happen is to participate in a **pay-for-placement program**, which means paying a search tool to position a Web page high in search results lists for specific keywords. Overture, FindWhat.com, ah-ha.com, goClick.com, and Kanoodle.com are all examples of search tools that offer such pay-for-placement programs.

@Source

For more information about Web site promotion, visit the Discovering the Internet Chapter 9 Web page (**scsite.com/ internet/ch9**) and click a link below Web Site Promotion.

For example, to participate in Overture's pay-for-placement program, an e-business selects one or more keywords and then submits a bid for each keyword. The higher the bid, which may be from a few cents to a few dollars, the higher the search results placement. The top three Overture bids for any keyword, called Premium Listings, also appear as links on Overture's business partner pages including Yahoo!, MSN, AlltheWeb, Netscape, AltaVista, Lycos, and AOL. For example, a Premium Listing at the Overture site appears as a *Sponsored Search Listing* at AlltheWeb; as a *Sponsored Link* at AOL Search; as a *Products and Services* link at AltaVista; and as a *Sponsor Matches* link at Yahoo!. A Web page with a Premium Listing bid at Overture thus substantially increases its visibility across a number of top search tools. Overture is paid on a per-click basis. Each bid indicates how much the bidder is willing to pay when a viewer clicks through from the Overture search results list or an Overture business partner link to the bidder's Web site.

Facts@Hand

When you search using the Overture search tool, the search results list is built largely from Overture's business partners' directories and indexes.

In the following steps, you explore how a pay-for-placement program affects search results by searching for Web pages at the Overture site using the keyword, coffee.

Steps: To Explore a Pay-for-Placement Program

1 Visit the Discovering the Internet Chapter 9 Web page (scsite.com/internet/ch9). Click Overture. Type coffee in the Search the Web text box. Point to the SEARCH button.

The Overture home page appears (Figure 9-27). You search for coffee-oriented Web pages at this page.

Figure 9-27

2 **Click the SEARCH button. Observe the sponsored listing indicator at the end of each URL for each of the top three listings. Point to the (sponsored listing) indicator for the first item in the search results list.**

*A search results list appears (Figure 9-28). The top three items in the search results list, as well as other top items in the list, are sponsored listings. A **sponsored listing indicator** means that Overture is being paid on a per-click basis to list that Web page in one of the top positions in its search results list. The higher the per-click payment, the higher the placement in the search list. Because the bidding process at Overture is dynamic, the search results list and bids you see on your screen may vary from those shown in Figures 9-28 through 9-31 on pages 531 and 532.*

Figure 9-28

3 **Click the sponsored listing indicator for the first item in the search results list. Read the explanation and then point to the View Bids Tool link.**

An explanation of the sponsored listing designation appears in its own window (Figure 9-29). You can learn more about how Overture works, participate in the Overture pay-for-placement program, or view the current bids for a search keyword with links in this window.

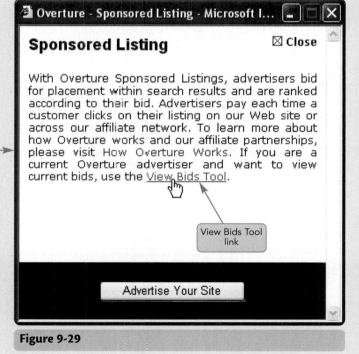

Figure 9-29

(continued)

4 **Click the View Bids Tool link. Type `coffee` in the search term text box. Type the security code in the security code text box. Point to the Search button.**

The View Bids Tool opens in its own window (Figure 9-30). You can view the current bids for the keyword coffee in this window. The security code you see in the View Bids Tool window will vary from that shown in Figure 9-30.

Figure 9-30

5 **Click the Search button. View the top two bids for the keyword coffee. Scroll the page to view other, lower bids.**

The top two bids for the keyword coffee are $1.65 and $1.64 (Figure 9-31). The organizations that sponsor these two Web sites are willing to pay more than $1.50 each time a viewer clicks-through to their site from the Overture search results list or from an Overture-sponsored link at one of Overture's business partner sites. Again, because the bidding process is dynamic, the top two bids you see may vary from those in Figure 9-31.

6 **Close the View Bids Tool and Sponsored Listings windows.**

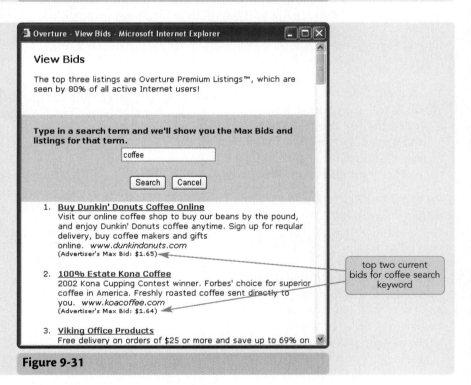

Figure 9-31

Coffee-oriented Web sites that do not participate in the Overture pay-for-placement program are still listed. These sites, however, are positioned far down the Overture search results list — beginning at position 100 or so — certainly well below the point at which most viewers stop reading a search results list.

Arranging **pay-per-click ads** with search tools is another way an e-business can get its Web site highlighted on a search results page. For example, the Google AdWords program allows an e-business to create its own ad, specify keywords that tie to the ad, and then have the ad appear on relevant Google search results pages or Google business partner pages. The e-business pays a fee each time a viewer clicks the ad. Figure 9-32 illustrates a Google search results list for the coffee keyword plus relevant Google AdWords advertisements.

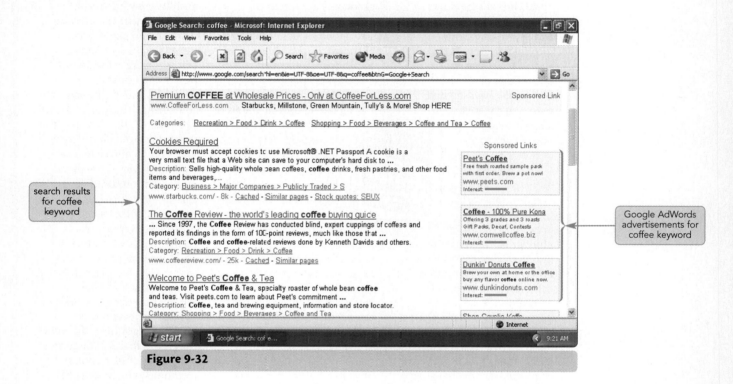

search results for coffee keyword

Google AdWords advertisements for coffee keyword

Figure 9-32

Search Tools: Paid Content versus Editorial Integrity

@Issue

A study by the Markle Foundation, a private philanthropy that works to advance emerging information and communications technologies, found that the word, library, was the number-one metaphor for the Internet and, as you have learned, searching the Web for information is one of the more important ways the Internet is used. As the number of people connected to the Internet increases and the number of Web pages grows into the billions, search tools become ever more critical in navigating the Web. In the early days of search tools — from the mid- to late-1990s — paying a fee to have a Web site included in a search results list was virtually unknown. Search engine users came to expect that Web sites appearing in a search results list were included and ranked based on purely objective factors relevant to search keywords.

In 1998, however, a new company named GoTo.com turned the Web search world upside down by allowing e-businesses to bid on search results rankings for selected keywords. Next, GoTo.com began partnering with other search tools to distribute links to the Web sites that generated its top three bids for each keyword. Within the next three years, more and more search tools began including links to Web sites in search results lists or on search results pages based on paid placement generated by GoTo.com (renamed Overture) and similar companies. While some of the search tools were careful to segregate these paid placements away from the nonpaid search results or were careful to label the paid placements clearly as sponsored links, not all search tools did so, deliberately blurring the line between objective search results and paid search results. Further compounding the problem was the fact that many search tools also offered a paid inclusion program where, for a fee, companies could submit their Web sites for inclusion in the search tools' indexes or directories. Search results lists generally made no distinction between objectively generated items and paid inclusion items.

By 2001, it became increasingly more difficult to tell the difference between objectively generated listings in search results and paid listings. Many users were not even aware of the existence of paid listings. For example, according to a 2001 Consumers Union survey, 87 percent of survey respondents used search tools to find information online; however, 60 percent of the survey respondents did not know that search tools were being paid fees to feature certain Web sites more prominently in search results lists or on search results pages.

Consumer watchdog groups and many Internet industry analysts grew increasingly concerned that the blurring of nonpaid and paid search results listings violated the editorial integrity of search results and bordered on deceptive and misleading advertising. Finally, in 2001, Commercial Alert, a consumer watchdog group founded by Ralph Nader, filed a formal complaint with the Federal Trade Commission (FTC) against eight top search tools alleging that the search tools "inserted advertisements in search results without clear and conspicuous disclosure that the ads were ads" and that "such listings look like information from an objective database selected by an objective algorithm. But really they are paid ads in disguise." In 2002, the FTC responded by recommending that search tools provide a "clear and conspicuous disclosure" of all paid content. Since the FTC recommendation, the disclosure practices at many search tools has improved; however, pay-for-placement and paid inclusion content still might not be disclosed fully by some search tools.

For more information about the paid content versus editorial integrity controversy, visit the Discovering the Internet Chapter 9 Web page (scsite.com/internet/ch9) and click a link below Paid Content versus Editorial Integrity.

SEARCH ENGINE OPTIMIZATION   **Search engine optimization** involves designing Web pages to ensure that they are easy to access and index by search engine bots and that the Web pages are positioned, or ranked, as high as possible in a search results list. Search engines determine the relevancy of indexed Web pages to a specific keyword or keywords and then rank the relevant pages in a search results list in many different ways. That is why the same keyword can produce very different search results lists using various search engines. Many search engines, however, do take into consideration some common elements in the relevancy and ranking process, such as keyword location and frequency, internal links, HTML titles, and HTML meta tags.

Some search engines look for the location and frequency of keywords in a page when determining a page's relevancy. A page with more keywords in more important locations may thus be deemed more relevant and ranked higher in a search results list. In Chapter 7, you learned about the importance of adding a meaningful HTML title to each Web page. Search engines may rank a Web page as more relevant if a keyword related to the page's contents is included in the HTML title. Additionally, search engines may rank pages higher if relevant keywords appear more frequently and in body text closer to the top of the page.

Carefully constructing navigation links from the home page to subsidiary pages and among all pages at a site can make it easier for search engine bots to follow the links and thus index all the pages at a site. For example, some search engine bots may not be able to follow image map links, so it is important to include text links as well as image map links. Some search engine bots may not be able to follow frames links correctly; therefore, as you learned in Chapter 7, many Web designers recommend avoiding using frames when possible.

Also, in Chapter 7, you learned about the HTML heading tags. Along with the HTML title tag, HTML meta tags (<META>) are positioned on a Web page between the <HEAD> and </HEAD> HTML heading tags. Meta tags provide a browser or search engine with additional information about a page such as a page description, search keywords, or an instruction not to index the page. While some search engines use meta tag descriptions in search results listings and meta tag keywords to index a Web page, not all do so. Adding meta description and meta keywords tags, however, can be helpful in exercising more control over how a page is described and indexed with the search engines that do use them.

In Chapter 8, you learned about the Hometown Favorites B2C e-business that sells hard-to-find food products. The Hometown Favorites home page uses an HTML title, meta description, and meta keyword tags to help optimize the page in some search results rankings. In the steps on the next page, you view the title, meta description, and meta keywords used on the Hometown Favorites home page.

◈◈ *Steps:* To View a Title Tag and Meta Tag Example

1 **Visit the Discovering the Internet Chapter 9 Web page (scsite.com/internet/ch9). Click Hometown Favorites. Point to View on the menu bar.**

The Hometown Favorites home page appears (Figure 9-33). You can view the page's HTML tags by opening the page in Notepad.

View menu name

Figure 9-33

heading section

2 **Click View on the menu bar and then click Source. Observe the title, meta description, and meta keyword tags.**

The Hometown Favorites home page appears in the Notepad window (Figure 9-34). The HTML title, meta description, and meta keyword tags use words and phrases to emphasize the products Hometown Favorites sells.

title

meta description

meta keywords

3 **Close the Notepad window.**

Figure 9-34

 In Netscape

In Netscape, you can click the Page Source command on the View menu to open a window similar to Notepad in which you can view the HTML tags.

Permission-Based E-Mail, Online Communities, Link Exchanges, and Web Rings

Individuals and organizations can use a number of online Web site promotion tools to get a Web site noticed, including sending e-mail and newsletters to targeted viewers, indirectly promoting a site through online communities, exchanging links with other Web sites, or joining a Web ring.

PERMISSION-BASED E-MAIL AND NEWSLETTERS Unlike spam, the **unsolicited bulk commercial e-mail** (**UBCE**) you learned about in Chapter 4, **permission-based e-mail** is legitimate commercial e-mail or newsletters sent to recipients who have previously agreed to receive them. Permission-based e-mail can be an effective way to promote a commercial Web site and acquire new customers. For example, a study by the e-business marketer DoubleClick indicates that 69 percent of U.S. e-mail users made online purchases, 59 percent made offline purchases, and 39 percent made catalog purchases — all after receiving permission-based e-mail marketing messages. A similar study by eMarketer indicated 67 percent of U.S. consumers had a favorable attitude about companies that effectively used permission-based e-mail to promote their Web sites and market their products and services.

Some companies that use permission-based e-mail to market their products and promote their Web sites gather e-mail addresses by encouraging viewers to complete and submit a Web-based form in order to receive additional information on new products or information about industry updates. This type of permission-based e-mail is called variously **opt-in e-mail**, **single opt-in e-mail**, or **safe opt-in e-mail**. Viewers who sign up to receive marketing messages or newsletters via e-mail are subscribing, or opting in, to the company's permission-based e-mail marketing program and their e-mail addresses are added to the company's database. In the following steps, you explore an opt-in link and form at the Equal Sweetener Web site.

⟫ Steps: To Explore an Opt-In Form

1 **Visit the Discovering the Internet Chapter 9 Web page (scsite.com/internet/ch9). Click Equal Sweetener. If necessary, close any pop-up windows. Scroll to view the bottom of the page. Point to the Sign up for the latest Equal news via email link.**

The Equal Sweetener home page appears (Figure 9-35). You can find out more about the Equal product, explore health-related information, and find recipes using the Equal product on this page.

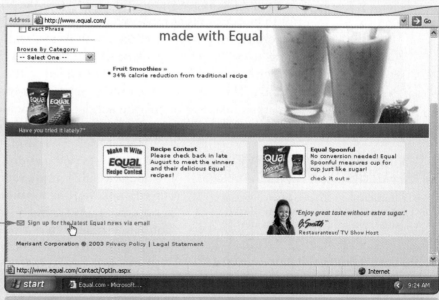

Figure 9-35

(continued)

2 Click the Sign up for the latest Equal news via email link. Scroll the page and review the online form.

An Opt-In Form window appears (Figure 9-36).

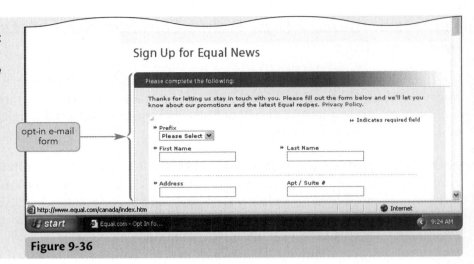

Figure 9-36

To protect a viewer who may have opted in unintentionally to a permission-based e-mail marketing program, some companies immediately send an e-mail confirming the opt-in subscription. Included in the e-mail are instructions on how to unsubscribe, or opt out, if desired. The recipient does not respond to the confirmation e-mail unless he or she wants to opt out. This type of permission-based e-mail program is called **confirmed opt-in e-mail**.

👋 Facts@Hand

Because of the ongoing concerns about unsolicited bulk e-mail, or spam, many individual users, businesses, and ISPs now use some type of spam filtering software to delete messages that appear to be spam before the messages reach users' mailboxes. Unfortunately, the filtering processes often culls out legitimate permission-based e-mail. A study by Assurance Systems, an e-mail monitoring services provider, indicates up to 20 percent of permission-based e-mail messages fail to reach destination mailboxes because of filtering.

Because of the ongoing controversy about spam and the negative consumer attitudes it can produce, many companies that use a permission-based e-mail marketing program want to be certain that those who opt in do so willingly. These companies therefore require the recipient of a confirmation e-mail to respond to the e-mail signifying his or her willingness to participate. This type of permission based e-mail is called **double opt-in e-mail**. The recipient's e-mail address is not added to the company's database until he or she responds. Thus, in a double opt-in permission-based e-mail marketing program, participants must take *two* deliberate actions to be included. The major advantages of a double opt-in permission-based e-mail program are higher response rates and fewer complaints.

👋 Facts@Hand

While individual e-mail users often consider all unsolicited e-mail to be spam, business e-mail users take a slightly different view. According to a survey by the Public Opinion Strategies research firm, 54 percent of business respondents believe that unsolicited e-mail from a company with which they have a prior or ongoing business relationship is not spam. The business e-mail user respondents overwhelmingly classified all other forms of unsolicited e-mail as spam.

The least effective and most controversial type of e-mail marketing is called **opt-out e-mail**, which usually is found in unsolicited bulk commercial e-mail. Recipients of opt-out e-mail who do not want to continue receiving messages must take an action, such as clicking a link in an e-mail message, to opt out. Companies using an opt-out e-mail marketing program often rent mailing lists from e-mail marketers. Some of these lists are legitimate opt-in lists and some are not. Unfortunately, unscrupulous e-mail marketers gather e-mail addresses in a variety of ways — most often without the owners' consent — and then rent the lists to other companies, resulting in floods of universally disliked spam.

Unsolicitied Bulk Commerical E-Mail

@Issue

Open your e-mail inbox on any given day and you are likely to find you have been bombarded with unsolicited bulk commercial e-mail (UBCE), or spam, touting everything from drugs to get-rich-quick schemes. Some analysts estimate that up to 50 percent of all e-mail messages are UBCE. While some of this e-mail is generated from legitimate opt-in mailing lists, most is not. Much of this UBCE, especially the most offensive, is sent by unprincipled e-mail marketers called spammers who use forged names and addresses to hide their real identities and use third-party domain names or false ISP routing information to mask the messages' origin. For example, the FTC collected over 11 million examples of UBCE messages, of which more than 40 percent had false From addresses.

The public outcry by individuals, businesses, and legitimate e-mail marketers against UBCE is galvanizing state and federal legislators to take action. Today, more than 25 states, including Arkansas, California, Illinois, Kansas, Maryland, Minnesota, Ohio, Tennessee, and Virginia, have enacted statutes to make some forms of UCBE illegal. While the state statutes vary, the majority make sending UBCE messages illegal when the identity of the sender and/or the routing information is falsified. Most statutes also require that opt-out instructions be prominently displayed in messages. In addition, states with existing regulations are getting tougher on spammers. For example, on April 29, 2003, the State of Virginia, whose previous regulations made falsifying ISP routing information illegal, enacted a law requiring a jail sentence for spammers convicted of falsifying their identity or sending 10,000 or more copies of an e-mail message.

Federal legislators also are taking action. A number of Senate bills have been introduced that would set limits on or provide stiff penalties for spammers. For example, Senator Conrad Burns (MT) and nine other Senate cosponsors reintroduced the Can Spam Act (S.877). The Can Spam Act requires that all UBCE messages have a valid return address and an accurate subject line. Additionally, spammers would be banned from sending more e-mail if a recipient opts out.

For more information about UBCE issues, visit the Discovering the Internet Chapter 9 Web page (**scsite.com/internet/ch9**) and click a link below UBCE.

ONLINE COMMUNITIES In Chapter 3, you learned how the Internet encourages the growth of online communities whose members share common interests. Participants in these online communities can communicate via newsgroups, Web-based discussion forums, and online chat. Another type of online community in which members share a common interest, often related to a specific industry or technology, is called a **special interest group (SIG)**. SIG members also use online communications tools to share information. For example, a Web designer may participate in a special interest group whose focus is using specific design tools. Because newsgroup, forum, and SIG members use the Internet to share information, individual participation can be a good way to promote a Web site indirectly.

For instance, participating in newsgroups, forums, and SIGs can create opportunities to build relationships with the other participants, identify you as a knowledgeable resource, and enable you to stay up-to-date with industry news or competitors. Any Web site promotion through an online community, however, must be indirect and must occur because of the normal exchange of information by the groups' membership. Today, blatant Web site promotion or advertising is not acceptable in most online communities.

LINK EXCHANGES   Individuals with personal or hobby sites, e-businesses, and other organizations can promote their Web sites by exchanging links, called **reciprocal links**, with sites that offer similar or complementary content. For example, a beachfront hotel might exchange Web site links with the Web sites for local restaurants, shops selling beachwear, or shops renting scuba diving equipment. By exchanging reciprocal links, both sites have an opportunity to increase the number of viewers at their respective sites. One way to exchange links with another Web site is first to identify an appropriate site and then contact the Webmaster or other responsible party listed at the site and ask if he or she is interested in exchanging links. Another way is to contract with an e-business that assists in identifying appropriate sites and arranging the reciprocal links with them for a fee.

Another reason to arrange reciprocal links with high-quality complementary sites is to increase a Web site's relevancy and ranking in a search results list. A measure of the number and quality of the links to a site is called the site's **link popularity**. Several search tools such as Google, AltaVista, Excite, Infoseek, and HotBot also evaluate a site's link popularity when determining its pages' relevancy to specific keywords and their ranking in a search results list. Checking a Web site's link popularity can help determine how many and what type of sites are linking to it and how the site's pages might be ranked in a search results list.

In the following steps, you look at the link popularity (the number of quality links) of two different B2C e-business sites.

Steps: **To Explore Link Popularity**

1   **Visit the Discovering the Internet Chapter 9 Web page (scsite.com/internet/ch9). Click Link Popularity.**

The LinkPopularity.com home page appears (Figure 9-37). You can enter the URL for a Web site and then see the number of links to that site reported by Google, AltaVista, and HotBot. Because Web page content is dynamic, the content you see on your screen may vary from that in Figures 9-37 through 9-41 on pages 540 through 542.

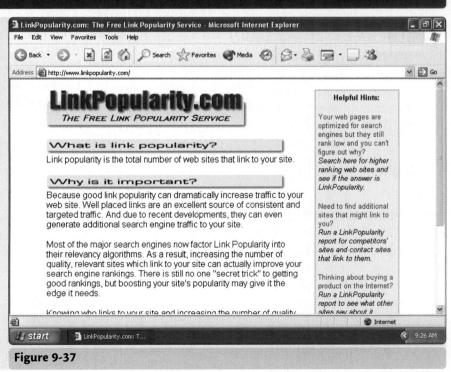

Figure 9-37

2 **Click the Enter Web Site URL text box and then type amazon.com as the entry. Point to the Tell me my popularity! button.**

The screen appears as shown in Figure 9-38.

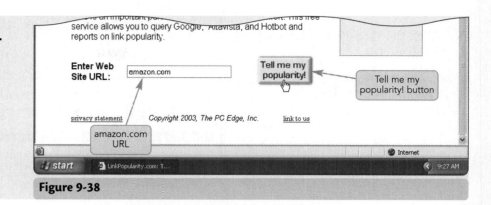

Figure 9-38

3 **Click the Tell me my popularity! button. Point to the Back button on the Standard Buttons toolbar.**

The amazon.com Link Popularity Report page appears (Figure 9-39). The three selected search tools have millions of quality links to the very popular and well-known amazon.com Web site.

Figure 9-39

4 **Click the Back button. Type hometownfavorites.com in the Enter Web Site URL text box and then click the Tell me my popularity! button. Point to the Google link labeled click to view.**

The hometownfavorites.com Link Popularity Report page appears (Figure 9-40). The less well-known Hometown Favorites Web site still has several hundred quality links to its site at these three search tools.

Figure 9-40

(continued)

5 Click the Google link labeled click to view.

The Google Search: link:www.hometownfavorites.com search results page appears (Figure 9-41). You can view different links to the Hometown Favorites site and how they are ranked in the Google search results on this page.

Google list of quality links to Hometown Favorites site

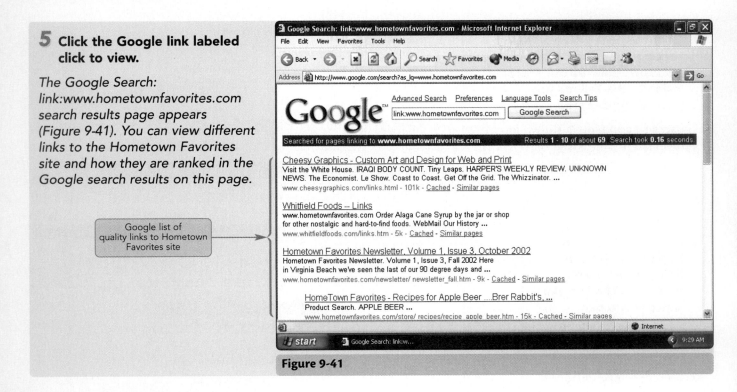

Figure 9-41

WEB RINGS   Individuals and organizations can promote their Web sites by joining a Web ring. A **Web ring** is a group of Web sites with a common topic that are linked together in such a way that a viewer can start at one site, click a Next link to view the next site in the Web ring, click a Previous link to return to the previously viewed site, and so forth until he or she ultimately returns to the original starting site. Figure 9-42 illustrates the Web ring concept.

linked sites with a common theme

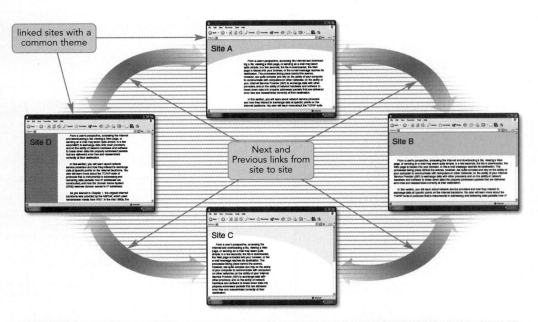

Figure 9-42   A Web ring links sites that have a common topic in a ring structure so that a viewer can move around the ring from site to site and, ultimately, return to his or her starting point.

Web rings provide an easy way for viewers with a specific interest to view quickly several sites focused on that interest; therefore, joining an appropriate Web ring can expose a site to additional viewers. For example, assume that your hobby is refurbishing antique clocks. Suppose you decide to open a small antique clock e-business and you launch a Web site. One way to promote the Web site to others in the antique timepiece community and increase the number of viewers at your site could be to join a Web ring that focuses on antique and collectible timepieces. In the following steps, you explore a Web ring that focuses on collectible timepieces.

Steps: To Explore a Web Ring

1 **Visit the Discovering the Internet Chapter 9 Web page (scsite.com/internet/ch9). Click WebRing. Close any pop-up windows. Scroll the page to view its links, WebRing lists, and WebRing directory. Point to the Collecting link below the Hobbies & Crafts link in the Browse Our Directory of Rings area of the page.**

The WebRing home page appears (Figure 9-43). You can learn more about joining a Web ring and view links to existing Web rings and forums on this page. The Web pages you see on your screen may vary from those in Figures 9-43 through 9-47 on pages 543 through 545.

Figure 9-43

2 **Click the Collecting link. Scroll to view the subdirectory of links to collecting Web rings. Point to the Timepieces link.**

The WebRing Collecting page with a subdirectory of collecting WebRings appears (Figure 9-44).

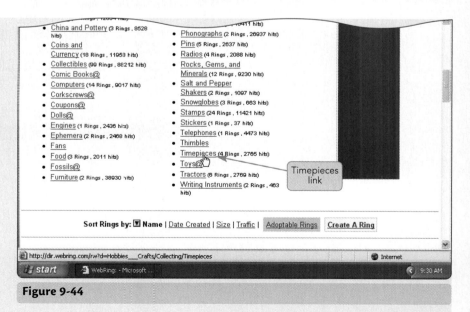

Figure 9-44

(continued)

3 Click the Timepieces link. Point to the Antique Clocks Web Ring link.

A list of the Web rings within this category is displayed (Figure 9-45).

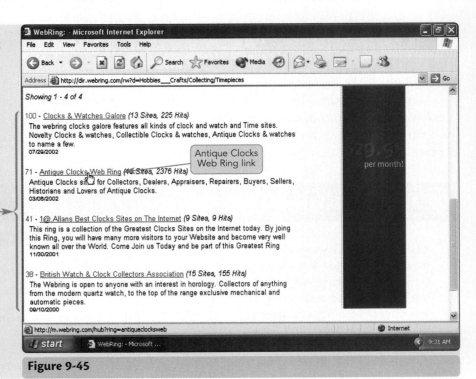

Figure 9-45

4 Click the Antique Clocks Web Ring link. Point to the first link in the list.

The Antique Clock Web Ring hub page appears (Figure 9-46). You enter the Web ring by clicking the link to any site in the Web ring.

Figure 9-46

5 Click the first link in the list. Scroll to view the Web ring links at the bottom of the page.

You can join the Web ring, return to the WebRing hub page, view a random page in the Web ring, or move forward or back in the Web ring to view other pages using these links (Figure 9-47).

Figure 9-47

Measuring Web Site Performance

Assume, for a moment, that you have planned, designed, and launched a new e-business Web site. You have implemented a content management system to monitor and control carefully the content on your site's pages; submitted your site to all the major search tools; verified that your site's pages are designed for search engine optimization; and are using a variety of online and offline methods to promote your site. With all this planning and implementation in place, your work should prove successful.

Nothing remains for you to do with your Web site now but operate your e-business and reap the rewards, right? Not quite. Part of the ongoing management of a Web site, especially an e-business site, is measuring the site's performance and effectiveness over time. You do this by setting performance standards for the site and then measuring actual results against those standards. In this section, you learn about setting Web site performance standards and about commonly used Web site performance measures. You also learn about the role Web server logs play in evaluating a site's performance and about the tools available to analyze the data accumulated in Web server logs.

Web Site Performance Standards

In Chapter 7, you learned that the first part of the Web site development process is to establish the site's overall goals. To determine whether a site is accomplishing these goals over time, you also must set interim, measurable operating goals, also called standards or **benchmarks**. Then you must compare actual operating results with these benchmarks. For example, suppose increasing sales is one stated goal for your e-business Web site. You might then set an operating benchmark that specifies a 20 percent increase in sales attributable to the site over a 12-month period. Comparing actual sales growth with the 20 percent benchmark would be one way to evaluate the site's performance.

The process of setting goals, establishing benchmarks, and comparing actual results with those benchmarks is an ongoing process. In the previous example, if the actual sales increase was less than 20 percent or if sales did not increase, then you might look at ways to make it easier for site visitors to locate products at the site, make the online purchasing process easier, find new ways to promote the site, and so forth. If the sales increase was greater than 20 percent then perhaps your first sales increase benchmark was set too low. After making any changes to the Web site deemed necessary, you might set new benchmarks and again begin the process of comparing actual results with the benchmarks.

Benchmarks for other types of Web site performance also are important. For example, a B2B exchange site whose business customers are using the site to reduce supply chain costs might set a usability benchmark for how quickly customers can log on to the site and complete a transaction. Actual logon and transaction completion times then are compared with the benchmark and appropriate adjustments made to the logon and transaction processes, if necessary.

Web Site Metrics

Knowing how many viewers visit your Web site, how long they stay at the site, and what they do or do not do while there are all important measures of your Web site's performance. These types of measures are called **Web site metrics**. No single Web site metric can measure a site's performance; instead, several common Web site metrics (Figure 9-48) often are used together to detect patterns and trends in Web site traffic. Further review of these patterns and trends can provide valuable information about your site's viewers and can help you determine what changes, if any, you need to make at your site.

Term	Description
Conversion rate	Estimates the percentage of e-retail shoppers that actually make a purchase.
Page views	Measures the number of times a Web page is viewed.
Page views per visitor	Measures the number of pages a visitor looks at on each Web site visit.
Referring URLs	Indicates the link, search engine, ad, or typed URL used by a visitor to reach a Web site.
Unique visitors	Measures the number of visitors who visit a Web site at least once during a specific period.
Repeat visitors	Measures the number of visitors who visit a Web site more than once during a specific period.
Visit (Session)	Indicates the link, search engine, ad, or typed URL used by a visitor to reach a Web site.

Figure 9-48   Common Web site metrics used to evaluate Web site performance.

 Facts@Hand

Some analysts estimate that the rate of shopping cart abandonment — online shoppers who fail to complete the purchase of items in a shopping cart — may be more than 60 percent.

Which metrics you use depends on your Web site and its operating goals. For example, the **page views** metric measures the number of times a page is viewed in a browser. If your site is an e-retail site, you might use the page views metric to determine which product pages are most popular with viewers and which are least popular. The **conversion rate** metric, which estimates how many online shoppers actually become buyers, is another important e-retail Web site metric. For example, if your e-retail site has 100 visitors in a specific period, but only 20 of those visitors actually *complete* a purchase, then the conversion rate is 20 percent. Online shoppers may fail to complete purchases for any number of reasons: perhaps they are just comparison shopping, or maybe they find the cost of shipping too high when they get ready to check out, or perhaps they simply change their minds. A consistently low conversion rate, however, might signify that the site's checkout process is too confusing, is too difficult to navigate, or possibly takes too long.

Suppose your site is an infomediary or media site that focuses on providing quick access to information. Two important Web site metrics you might use in evaluating your site's performance are unique visitors and repeat visitors. The **unique visitors** metric measures the number of visitors who visit a Web site at least once during a specific period. A large number of unique visitors, usually identified by IP addresses or information in cookies, can help estimate the total size of the site's target audience. A large number of **repeat visitors** suggests that visitors are successful in finding useful information at the site and, therefore, return to the site frequently. A small number of repeat visitors indicates visitors often do not return to the site, perhaps because of poor site organization, inadequate navigational tools, or a lack of links to useful information.

You can use other Web site metrics (Figure 9-48) to analyze site traffic by identifying who visits your site, where they came from, how they navigate between pages at the site, and how many pages they view. For example, the **referring URL** metric indicates how a visitor reached your site: by clicking a link at another site, by clicking an ad, by clicking a link in a search engine results list, or by typing the URL in the Web browser. You can use this type of information to evaluate the effectiveness of your Web site advertising programs, link exchanges, and search engine placement and optimization. **Page views per visitor** measures how many pages a visitor views at your site. The more pages each visitor views, the more time they spend at the site, and the stickier your site.

Web Server Logs

The data recorded in a Web server log forms the basis for calculating visitors, unique visitors, conversion rates, page views, page views per visitor and other Web site metrics. A Web server records every request as an **event** in a log file. For example, when a browser requests a Web page or an image, downloads a file, or submits a form, the event is recorded in the server's log file (Figure 9-49).

While the type of data and the log file format can vary, the data typically recorded for an event includes the:

- IP address, browser, and operating system of the computer making the request.
- Date and time of the request.
- URL of the requested page.
- Protocol used to make the request (HTTP, FTP).
- Referring URL.
- Event status code.

Figure 9-49   Data captured from a Web server log forms the basis for calculating Web site metrics.

The thousands of event entries in a server log then are analyzed to determine visitors, unique visitors, page views, and other Web site metrics. Additionally, IP address data is used to identify visitors' networks and countries of origin. The browser type and operating system data is used to verify that pages at the site are viewed properly in the most common browsers and operating systems used by visitors. The event status code data is used to determine whether the event went smoothly or if an error occurred. Error messages then are analyzed to discover broken links or other Web site trouble spots.

Web Server Log Analysis Tools

Attempting to analyze server log data consisting of thousands of events can be overwhelming. Although you could download your server logs into a spreadsheet application such as Microsoft Excel and then manipulate the data, it may be easier and more practical to use **server log analysis tools** developed by vendors such as NetIQ (WebTrends), Sawmill, WebSideStory, DeepMetrix, and ClickTracks (Figure 9-50). These analysis tools often combine data from server log files with customer databases and other sources to create reports that help you monitor your site's traffic and evaluate its performance.

Figure 9-50   Server log analysis tools are used to create reports that help monitor Web site traffic.

For example, WebSideStory offers the ASP-based HitBox Professional Web server log analysis tool you can use via your browser to determine page views, reloaded pages, visits, new visitors, unique visitors, and much more. In the following steps, you use an online demo to explore the HitBox Professional Web server log analysis tool.

Steps: To Explore a Web Server Log Analysis Tool

1 **Visit the Discovering the Internet Chapter 9 Web page (scsite.com/internet/ch9). Click WebSideStory. Point to the products box arrow in the HitBox area.**

The WebSideStory home page appears (Figure 9-51). You can link to an online demo of the HitBox Professional Web site traffic analysis software on this page. The Web pages you see on your screen may vary from those in Figure 9-51 through 9-56 on pages 549 through 551.

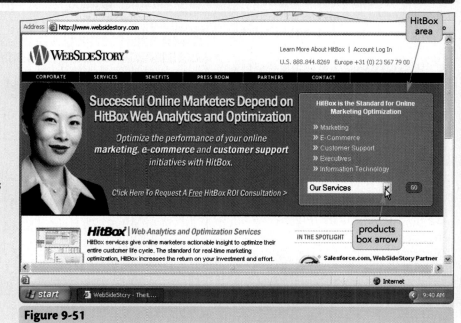

Figure 9-51

2 **Click the products box arrow and then click HitBox Professional in the products list. Point to the GO button.**

The HitBox Professional product is selected (Figure 9-52).

Figure 9-52

3 **Click the GO button. Point to the View Demo link in the HitBox Professional navigation menu.**

The HitBox Professional page appears (Figure 9-53).

HitBox Professional

Essential Web Traffic Analysis for Small and Mid-Sized Sites

When it came time for the editors of *PC Magazine* to hand out their prestigious Editors' Choice Award for Best Web Traffic Analysis Service, one name rose to the top: HitBox Professional.

View Demo link

Figure 9-53

(continued)

4 Click the View Demo link. Click the OK button or a link to view the demo over a secure connection, if prompted to do so. If necessary, maximize the browser demo window. Scroll the page to view the entire sample Traffic Summary report and charts. Point to the Help button in the upper-right corner of the page.

In a few seconds, the HitBox Professional Demo page appears (Figure 9-54). You can view the sample Traffic Summary report that provides an overview of a site's total views, visits, referring URLs, and other metrics on this page.

Figure 9-54

5 Click the Help button.

The HitBox Professional Help window appears report and displays Help information for the Traffic Summary report (Figure 9-55). You can display online Help for each traffic report you view.

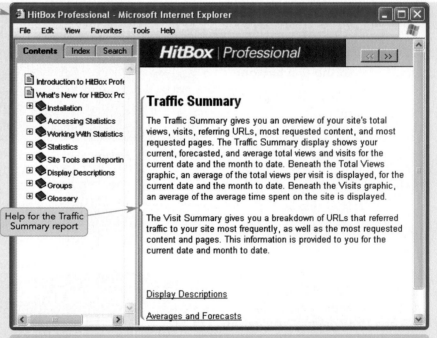

Figure 9-55

6 **Close the Help window. Point to Traffic on the Site Statistics navigation menu and then click Page Views on the Traffic submenu.**

The Page Views report appears (Figure 9-56). HitBox defines a page view as the number of times a particular page is viewed by site visitors (not including a reloaded page). The HitBox page views metric does not include views by search engine bots. The report indicates page views per hour for a specific starting and ending period.

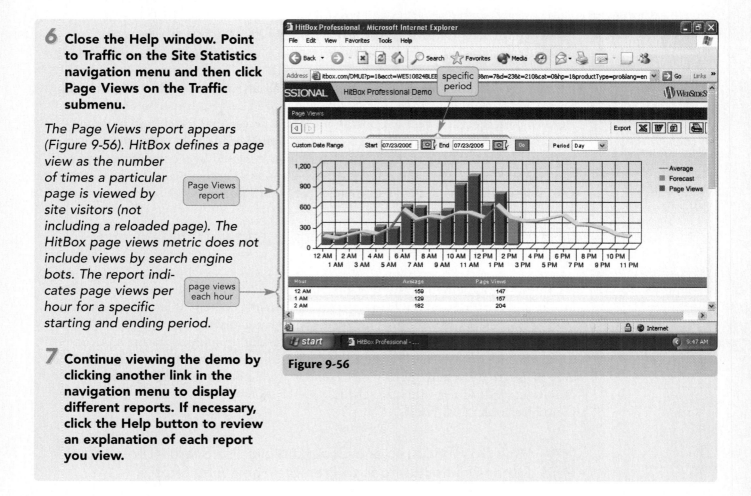

Figure 9-56

7 **Continue viewing the demo by clicking another link in the navigation menu to display different reports. If necessary, click the Help button to review an explanation of each report you view.**

Finally, setting Web site performance benchmarks and then measuring actual results against those benchmarks, as well as using a number of Web site metrics to identify site visitors and track their actions, are only part of the process. The next step is to draw reasonable conclusions about the comparisons and analyses and then decide what changes, if any, should be made to Web site operations. The entire process of setting Web site benchmarks and then comparing actual results against those benchmarks, together with using Web metrics to evaluate a Web site's performance, are all part of the overall process of getting the right information to the right people in a timely manner.

@Source

For more information about measuring Web site performance, visit the Discovering the Internet Chapter 9 Web page (scsite.com/internet/ch9) and click a link below Web Site Performance.

✋ Facts@Hand

According to Jupiter Research, e-business spending on tools to measure Web site performance will reach $1 billion within the next few years, and ASP-based services will account for 29 percent of this spending.

CHAPTER REVIEW

The Chapter Review section summarizes the concepts presented in the chapter.

1 What Are Different Types of Portals and Which Audiences Do They Serve?

A **general consumer portal** offers the public a broad range of content. A **personal portal** is a general consumer portal with customized content based on an individual viewer's preferences. A **vertical portal** is a Web gateway that focuses on more narrow interests. A vertical portal that focuses on a specific industry often is called an **industry portal**. Finally, a single Web-based interface used by a company's employees, customers, vendors, and other business partners to access business information and conduct business activities is called a **corporate portal**.

2 What Is a Content Management System and What Are Its Benefits?

A **content management system** (**CMS**) includes all the processes and technologies involved in creating and publishing complex, dynamic content at large Web sites such as portals. A CMS controls the quality, accuracy, appearance, and timeliness of Web site content developed from multiple sources and in multiple formats. A content management system also allows Web site administrators to control access to specific Web pages; to track and approve new content or changes to existing content; to remove content as necessary; to schedule publication of time-sensitive content; and to archive content for reuse.

3 How Do Individuals and Organizations Use Search Tools and Other Online Methods to Promote Their Web Sites?

Individuals and organizations can submit their Web site information to Web directories. Most search engines also accept Web site submissions. The fees and guidelines for submitting Web site information vary; however, most search tools charge a nonrefundable fee for submitting a commercial site. This fee accelerates the review process but generally does not guarantee inclusion in the search tool's index or directory. Some search tools offer a **pay-for-placement** program, which accepts bids for Web site placement in search results. Others may offer **pay-per-click ads** tied to specific search keywords.

Web pages should be designed to ensure that they are easy to access and index by search engine bots and then ranked as high as possible in a search results list by using HTML titles, the effective placement and frequent use of keywords, and HTML meta description and meta keyword tags. Careful construction of internal links also may help search engines locate and index all the pages at the site.

Permission-based e-mail can be an effective way to promote a Web site and its products and services. Companies using legitimate permission-based e-mail marketing programs use **opt-in e-mail**, **confirmed opt-in e-mail**, and **double opt-in e-mail** programs to make certain the e-mail message recipients have previously agreed to receive e-mail messages or newsletters. Unsolicited bulk commercial e-mail is not appropriate for legitimate e-mail marketing and, under some circumstances, is illegal in many states.

Online communities such as newsgroups, discussion groups, chat rooms, and online special-interest groups may be a good venue for indirectly promoting a Web site through individual participation and relationship-building with other members. Individuals and organizations can promote their Web sites by exchanging links with other sites that have relevant content. Participating in link exchanges increases the number of links to a Web site and may boost the site's **link popularity**. Individuals and organizations can promote their Web sites by adding them to **Web rings**, which are communities of linked Web sites focused on the same topic.

 4 How Are Benchmarks, Web Metrics, and Log Analysis Tools Used to Evaluate a Web Site's Performance?

Evaluating a Web site's performance involves setting standards, or **benchmarks**, and then comparing actual results against those benchmarks. Monitoring Web site traffic by using **Web site metrics** to determine who visits a site, how long they stay, and what they do while they are there also can help evaluate Web site performance. Web **server log analysis tools** use Web server logs and other sources to determine patterns and trends in Web site traffic. You evaluate benchmark comparisons and traffic patterns and trends to make appropriate decisions about Web site operations.

CHAPTER REVIEW

The Chapter Review section summarizes the concepts presented in the chapter.

benchmarks (*545*)
corporate portals (*519*)
confirmed opt-in e-mail (*538*)
content management system (CMS) (*523*)
content repositories (*524*)
conversion rate (*546*)
double opt-in e-mail (*538*)
enterprise information portals (EIPs) (*519*)
event (*547*)
general consumer portals (*512*)
horizontal portals (*513*)
industry portals (*514*)
link popularity (*540*)
opt-in e-mail (*537*)
opt-out e-mail (*538*)
page views (*546*)
page views per visitor (*547*)
paid inclusion (*528*)
pay-for-placement program (*530*)

pay-per-click ads (*533*)
permission-based e-mail (*537*)
personal portals (*513*)
reciprocal links (*540*)
referring URL (*547*)
repeat visitors (*547*)
safe opt-in e-mail (*537*)
search engine optimization (*535*)
server log analysis tools (*548*)
single opt-in e-mail (*537*)
spammers (*539*)
special interest group (SIG) (*539*)
sponsored listing indicator (*531*)
syndication (*523*)
unique visitors (*547*)
unsolicited bulk commercial e-mail (UBCE) (*537*)
vertical portals (*513*)
vortals (*513*)
Web site metrics (*546*)
Web ring (*542*)

TERMS TO KNOW

Instructions for the Terms to Know section would go here.

TEST YOUR KNOWLEDGE

Use the Test Your Knowledge exercises to check your knowledge of the chapter.

True or False

Mark T for True and F for False. (Answers are found on page numbers in parentheses.)

_____ 1. A single, personalized Web-based interface to a company's general business information used by employees, customers, vendors, and other business partners is called a general consumer portal. (*512*)

_____ 2. Fees charged by search tools to list a commercial Web site or to expedite the submission process generally are refundable if the submitted site is not accepted for listing. (*529*)

_____ 3. An enterprise information portal provides a gateway to information about a specific industry. (*519*)

_____ 4. Another term for permission-based opt-in e-mail is spam. (*537*)

_____ 5. A benchmark is a performance-based standard. (*545*)

_____ 6. Paying a fee to submit a Web site to a search tool always guarantees the site will be listed in the search tool's index or directory. (*529*)

_____ 7. One good way to promote a Web site is to post a message to a newsgroup advertising the site or to send an e-mail advertising the site to all members of an online community. (*539*)

_____ 8. The conversion rate Web site metric indicates the number of shoppers at an e-retail site that actually complete a purchase. (*546*)

_____ 9. Organizations can implement a content management system to ensure that relevant Web site content is presented to the appropriate audience at the right time. (*523*)

_____ 10. Search tool pay-for-placement programs allow an e-business to submit a per-click bid for higher placement in a search results list. (*530*)

Multiple Choice

Select the best answer. (Answers are found on page numbers in parentheses.)

1. A keyword-related advertisement that appears on a Google search results page is a result of a _____ program. (*533*)
   a. pay-for-performance
   b. pay-per-click
   c. pay-for-placement
   d. pay-per-view

2. A _____ portal is a gateway to Web sites containing information about a narrow area of interest. (*513*)
   a. corporate
   b. horizontal
   c. vertical
   d. customer

3. A measure of the number and quality of links to a Web page that is used by some search tools to determine the page's relevancy to a specific keyword and ranking in a search results list is link _____ . (540)
   a. relevancy   b. reciprocity
   c. popularity   d. none of the above

4. E-mail marketing programs require participants to both sign up and then take action to confirm their participation are called _____ programs. (538)
   a. opt-out
   b. single opt-in
   c. double opt-in
   d. safe opt-in

5. My Lycos and My Yahoo are examples of _____ portals. (513)
   a. general consumer
   b. vertical
   c. enterprise information
   d. personal

6. The _____ Web site metric indicates the number of visitors who return to a site during a specific period. (546)
   a. visits (sessions)
   b. page views
   c. repeat visitors
   d. unique visitors

7. Designing Web pages to ensure that they are easy to access and index by search engines and ranked as high as possible in a search results list is called search engine _____ . (535)
   a. submission
   b. optimization
   c. placement
   d. none of the above

8. _____ is (are) not part of a content management system. (523)
   a. Content reviewing and editing
   b. The content approval process
   c. Scheduled content publishing
   d. All of the above

9. The _____ Web site metric indicates how visitors reach a site. (547)
   a. page views per visitor
   b. referring URL
   c. unique visitors
   d. conversion rate

10. The databases used by a content management system to store Web page elements are called content _____ . (524)
    a. databases
    b. repositories
    c. vortals
    d. none of the above

LEARN IT ONLINE

Use the Learn It Online exercises to reinforce your understanding of the chapter concepts and terms.

Instructions: To complete the Learn It Online exercises, start your browser, click the Address bar, and then enter the Web address **scsite.com/internet/ch9**. Follow the instructions in the exercises below. Each exercise has instructions for printing your results, either for your own records or for submission to your instructor.

 Chapter Reinforcement

TF, MC, and SA

Click the Chapter Reinforcement link. Print the quiz by clicking Print on the File menu for each page. Answer each question.

 Flash Cards

Click the Flash Cards link and read the instructions. Type 20 (or a number specified by your instructor) in the Number of playing cards text box, type your name in the Enter your Name text box, and then click the Flip Card button. When the flash card is displayed, read the question and then click the Answer box arrow to select an answer. Flip through Flash Cards. If your score is 15 (75%) correct or greater, click Print on the File menu to print your results. If your score is less than 15 (75%) correct, then redo this exercise by clicking the Replay button.

 Practice Test

Click the Practice Test link. Answer each question, enter your first and last name at the bottom of the page, and then click the Grade Test button. When the graded practice test is displayed on your screen, click Print on the File menu to print a hard copy. Continue to take practice tests until you score 80% or better.

 Who Wants To Be a Computer Genius?

Click the Computer Genius link. Read the instructions, enter your first and last name at the bottom of the page, and then click the Play button. When your score is displayed, click the Print Results link to print a hard copy.

 Crossword Puzzle Challenge

Below Chapter 9, click the Crossword Puzzle Challenge link. Read the instructions, and then enter your first and last name. Click the SUBMIT button. Work the crossword puzzle. When you are finished, click the Submit button. When the crossword puzzle is redisplayed, click the Print Puzzle button to print a hard copy.

To perform the following exercises, you must be connected to the Internet.

1 Exploring Real-World Portal and Content Management System Solutions

1. Visit the Discovering the Internet Chapter 9 Web page (scsite.com/internet/ch9) and click the links below Exercise 1 to search each vendor Web site for real-world examples of portal and content management system implementations. Use case studies, white papers, demos, Webcasts, and similar content at each site to locate the real-world examples.

2. Select two real-world portal and/or content management system implementation examples and write a brief paragraph describing each organization, its Web site or content management needs, and how implementing a portal and/or content management system satisfied those needs.

2 Status of Unsolicited Bulk Commercial E-Mail Legislation

1. Visit the Discovering the Internet Chapter 9 Web page (scsite.com/internet/ch9) and click the links below Exercise 2 to review the status and provisions of state and federal statutes regulating unsolicited bulk commercial e-mail or spam and then answer the following questions:
   a. What is the status of senate bill S.877, the Can Spam Act?
   b. How do the statutes in the following states attempt to regulate spam?
      i) North Carolina
      ii) Utah
      iii) California
      iv) Iowa

3 Submitting a Web Site to the Yahoo! Directory and Business.com

1. Visit the Discovering the Internet Chapter 9 Web page (scsite.com/internet/ch9) and click Yahoo! below Exercise 3. Then click the How to Suggest a Site link. Use information on suggesting a site to answer the following questions:
   a. How do you submit the URL for a noncommercial site to the Yahoo! directory?
   b. What is Yahoo! Express and how is it used to add Web sites to the Yahoo! directory?
   c. Is a fee required for submitting a commercial Web site to the Yahoo! directory? If yes, how much is the fee?
   d. Can you list a noncommercial site free?
   e. Does submission of a noncommercial or commercial site to the Yahoo! directory guarantee that the site will be added to the directory?

(continued)

EXERCISES

Use the
Exercises to
gain hands-on
Internet
experience.

EXERCISES *(continued)*

2. Visit the Discovering the Internet Chapter 9 Web page (**scsite.com/internet/ch9**) and click Business.com. Use information at the site's FAQ page to answer the following questions:
   a. What are five criteria for inclusion in the Business.com directory?
   b. What are the guidelines for writing a listing's description?
   c. What is the Standard Listings fee and does payment of the fee guarantee a site will be listed in the Business.com directory?
   d. What are multi-links and what are their benefits?
   e. Can you list a noncommercial account free at Business.com?

4 Identifying Vertical Portals

1. Visit the Discovering the Internet Chapter 9 Web page (**scsite.com/internet/ch9**) and click the links below Exercise 4 to locate at least one example of a vertical portal focused on each of the following interests:
   a. women's interests
   b. gardening
   c. hip-hop music
   d. aerospace industry
   e. kids' interests
   f. bioinformatics industry

2. Write a brief paragraph giving the URL for each example and a description of the portal's contents.

5 Promoting a Web Site in an Online Community

You and your business partner have started a Web design business, just launched your Web site, and you are looking for ways to promote it. Your business partner suggests that participating in several online communities might be a good way to do this.

1. Visit the Discovering the Internet Chapter 9 Web page (**scsite.com/internet/ch9**) and click the links below Exercise 5 to find at least three online communities (newsgroups, special interest groups, forums, and so forth) that might be appropriate.

2. Write a brief description of each online community. Include a discussion of why it is appropriate for your participation and how you plan to promote your new Web site indirectly.

6 Using Permission-Based E-Mail

You and your business partner are operating a small B2C e-business and you want to find a way to attract more customers. Your business partner suggests renting an e-mail address list and mailing a marketing message to everyone on the list.

1. Visit the Discovering the Internet Chapter 9 Web page (**scsite.com/internet/ch9**) and click the links below Exercise 6 to research permission-based e-mail and unsolicited bulk commercial e-mail.

2. Use your research to answer the following questions:
   a. What are the legal restrictions on unsolicited bulk commercial e-mail in your state?
   b. What are the advantages and disadvantages of renting an e-mail address list and sending unsolicited e-mail advertising to everyone on the list?
   c. Should your e-business use unsolicited bulk commercial e-mail? Explain the reasons for your answer.

7 Exploring Pay-for-Placement Search Engines

1. Visit the Discovering the Internet Chapter 9 Web page (**scsite.com/internet/ch9**) and click the search engine links below Exercise 7 to review each search engine's pay-for-placement program. Write a brief paragraph about each search engine describing how its pay-for-placement program works.

2. Using each search engine, search using the keyword, florist. Then, use the results of your searches to answer the following questions:
   a. What were the top three bid amounts for the keyword, florist?
   b. How much would you bid to have a floral business listed in one of the top three positions in a search results list? Why?

8 Link Exchanges

You and your business partner recently opened a small bed-and-breakfast on Key West in the Florida Keys. You also just launched a new Web site for your bed-and-breakfast and need to begin promoting it. Your business partner suggests that exchanging links with other, appropriate Web sites might be a good place to start.

1. Visit the Discovering the Internet Chapter 9 Web page (**scsite.com/internet/ch9**) and click the links below Exercise 8 to select at least three Web sites that would be appropriate for reciprocal linking. List each site's URL and add a brief description of the site. Next, indicate why the site would be a good choice for a link exchange with your bed-and-breakfast site.

EXERCISES

Use the Exercises to gain hands-on Internet experience.

9 Joining a Web Ring

Now that you have exchanged links with other complementary Web sites (see Exercise 8), you think joining a Web ring might be another good way to promote your bed-and-breakfast Web site.

1. Visit the Discovering the Internet Chapter 9 Web page (**scsite.com/internet/ch9**) and click the links below Exercise 9 to identify a Web ring that you can join.

2. Write a brief description of the Web ring and list at least five other sites that currently are part of the Web ring. Write a brief paragraph describing why joining this Web ring would be a good way to promote your Web site.

10 Evaluating Web Site Performance

You and your business partner own and operate a small business that sells team sports hats, T-shirts, patches, and trophies. Six months ago, you added an online store to increase sales and increase your customer base. Now you want to know how well the new Web site is performing. (You may assume any other facts not stated here.)

1. Set two benchmarks you can use to evaluate how well your Web site is performing against the original goals for the site.

2. Identify at least three Web site metrics you can use to help evaluate the site's performance. Describe each metric and explain why it is an important measure for your Web site.

3. Visit the Discovering the Internet Chapter 9 Web page (**scsite.com/internet/ch9**) and click the links below Exercise 10 to review Web log analysis tools. Then, select one of the tools for your business. Give the reasons for your selection.

APPENDIX A
Alternate Netscape Steps

The Internet Explorer browser is used for the Steps hands-on projects in this text. In most cases, the step-by-step instructions also are applicable for the Netscape browser. In some cases, however, the difference between the Internet Explorer and Netscape browsers requires a separate set of alternate Netscape steps. This appendix provides those steps.

Chapter 2 — Browsing the Web

Steps: To Create and Use Bookmarks

1 If necessary, start the browser. Type weather.com in the Location Bar. Press the ENTER key. Point to the Bookmarks button on the Personal Toolbar.

The Weather Channel home page appears (Figure 2-1). The content of the Web pages on your screen will vary from that shown in Figures 2-1 through 2-29 on pages APP2 through APP15.

N Figure 2-1

2 Click Bookmarks. Point to Bookmark This Page.

The Bookmarks menu contains a number of commands, as well as a list of existing bookmarks (Figure 2-2).

N Figure 2-2

3 **Click Bookmark This Page.
Point to the Home button
on the Personal Toolbar.**

*The Home button (Figure 2-3)
redisplays the default home page.*

Figure 2-3

4 **Click Home. Click Bookmarks
on the Personal Toolbar.
Point to weather.com on
the Bookmarks menu.**

*The default home page appears
and the Bookmarks menu is displayed (Figure 2-4). The Bookmarks
menu now contains a bookmark for
the Weather Channel page.*

Figure 2-4

(continued)

5 **Click the weather.com bookmark.**

The Weather Channel page appears (Figure 2-5).

revisited Weather Channel page

N **Figure 2-5**

▶▶▶ Steps: To Use the History List to Revisit a Web Page

1 **If necessary, start the browser, and click the Home button on the Personal Toolbar. Point to Go on the menu bar.**

The default home page appears (Figure 2-6).

Go menu name

N **Figure 2-6**

2 Click Go. Point to the History command.

The Go menu (Figure 2-7) contains commands you can use to navigate among recently viewed Web pages.

N Figure 2-7

3 Click History. Point to the Today folder.

The History window appears and contains the History list (Figure 2-8). The History list may display collapsed folders. The folders you see on your screen may vary from those shown in the figure.

N Figure 2-8

4 Double-click the Today folder, if necessary, to expand it. Point to the Weather Channel folder (weather.com).

The Today folder expands to display a list of folders for Web sites visited today using this computer (Figure 2-9). Your list of folders may be different than those shown in the figure; however, you should have a folder for the Weather Channel site.

N Figure 2-9

(continued)

5 Double-click the Weather Channel (weather.com) folder. Point to the weather.com link.

The Weather Channel folder expands and displays a list of pages viewed at the weather.com Web site (Figure 2-10). Your list of pages may vary from that shown in the figure.

Figure 2-10

6 Double-click the weather.com link. Click the History button on the taskbar. Point to the Close button on the History window title bar.

The Weather Channel page appears (Figure 2-11). When you are finished with the History window, you should close it.

7 Click Close.

The History window closes.

Figure 2-11

>> Steps: To Create a Desktop Shortcut

1 If necessary, start the browser. Type scsite.com/ internet/ in the Location Bar. Press the ENTER key. Point to the Restore Down button on the title bar.

The Discovering the Internet – Home page appears (Figure 2-12).

Figure 2-12

2 Click the Restore Down button. Point to the Web page icon in the Location Bar.

The Netscape window is sized to allow some of the Windows desktop to appear (Figure 2-13). The mouse pointer resembles a five-fingered hand.

Figure 2-13

(continued)

3 Drag the Web page icon from the Location Bar to the desktop. Point to the Close button on the browser title bar.

The shortcut to the Discovering the Internet – Home page is created on the desktop (Figure 2-14).

new desktop shortcut

Figure 2-14

4 Click Close. Point to the Discovering the Internet – Home page shortcut on the desktop.

The browser closes (Figure 2-15). You can use the new shortcut to open the browser and display the Discovering the Internet – Home page.

desktop shortcut to Discovering the Internet - Home page

Figure 2-15

5 **Double-click the Discovering the Internet – Home page shortcut on the desktop. Point to the shortcut.**

The browser starts and displays Discovering the Internet – Home page (Figure 2-16). You can delete the shortcut by dragging it to the Recycle Bin.

Recycle Bin

desktop shortcut

reopened browser with Discovering the Internet - Home page

Maximize button

N **Figure 2-16**

6 **Drag the shortcut to the Recycle Bin. Point to the Maximize button on the browser's title bar.**

The shortcut is deleted from the desktop (Figure 2-17).

N **Figure 2-17**

(continued)

7 **Click Maximize.**

The browser window is maximized (Figure 2-18).

maximized
browser window

 Figure 2-18

Steps: **To Show and Hide Toolbars**   View menu name

1 **If necessary, start the browser. Click the Home button on the Personal Toolbar, if necessary, to display the default home page. Point to View on the menu bar.**

The View menu contains commands you can use to show or hide browser window elements (Figure 2-19).

 Figure 2-19

2 **Click View. Point to the Show/Hide command. Point to the Personal Toolbar command.**

The View menu commands and the Show/Hide submenu commands appear (Figure 2-20). The check mark beside an element's name, such as the Personal Toolbar, indicates the element is visible in the window. The elements visible in your Netscape window may vary from those indicated on the Show/Hide submenu in the figure.

Figure 2-20

3 **Click Personal Toolbar.**

The Personal Toolbar is hidden from view (Figure 2-21).

Figure 2-21

(continued)

4 **Click View. Point to Show/Hide. Click Personal Toolbar.**

The Personal Toolbar is again visible in the browser window (Figure 2-22).

Figure 2-22

Steps: To Change the Default Home Page

1 **If necessary, start the browser. Click the Home button on the Personal Toolbar, if necessary, to view the current default home page. Point to Edit on the menu bar.**

The default home page appears (Figure 2-23).

Figure 2-23

2 Click Edit. Point to the Preferences command.

The Edit menu commands appear (Figure 2-24). The Preferences command opens the Preferences dialog box.

N Figure 2-24

3 Click Preferences. Point to the Location text box in the Home Page area of the dialog box. Write down the current default home page's URL.

The Preferences dialog box opens with the Navigator preferences category expanded (Figure 2-25). You can select a different category and change a variety of preferences in this dialog box.

N Figure 2-25

(continued)

4 Select the contents of the Location text box. Type yahoo.com. Point to the OK button.

This URL (Figure 2-26) changes the default home page to the Yahoo! portal page.

Figure 2-26

5 Click OK. Click the Home button on the Personal Toolbar. Point to Edit on the menu bar.

The new default home page, the Yahoo! portal page, appears (Figure 2-27).

Figure 2-27

6 **Click Edit. Click Preferences. Type the original default home page URL in the Location text box. Point to the OK button.**

This URL (Figure 2-28) returns the default home page back to its original page.

N Figure 2-28

7 **Click OK. Click the Home button on the Personal Toolbar.**

The default home page that appears (Figure 2-29) is the original default home page.

original default
home page

N Figure 2-29

Chapter 3 — Searching the Web

Steps: To Search Using the Browser

1 If necessary, start the browser. Click the Home button on the Personal Toolbar, if necessary, to display the default home page. Point to the Open My Sidebar button.

The Open My Sidebar button (Figure 3-1) opens the My Sidebar pane. The content in the Web pages on your screen will vary from that shown in Figures 3-1 through 3-12 on pages APP16 through APP21.

Figure 3-1

2 Click Open My Sidebar. Point to the Search tab.

My Sidebar appears with the last tab used expanded (Figure 3-2). The expanded sheet on your screen may vary from the expanded Bookmarks sheet shown in Figure 3-2.

Figure 3-2

3 Click the Search tab.

The Search tab expands and the previously expanded sheet collapses (Figure 3-3). The insertion point appears in the Search text box ready for you to enter keywords. You may see the results of a previous search in the Search Results list box in the Search sheet.

N Figure 3-3

4 Type fastest growing jobs in the Search text box and press the ENTER key. Point to the hit of your choice in the Search Results list on the Search sheet.

The default search engine, Google, performs the search and presents the search results list of hits in the browser display area and an abbreviated list of hits in the Search Results box in the Search sheet (Figure 3-4). Your default search engine may be different.

N Figure 3-4

(continued)

5 **Click the hit link. View the resulting page that appears in the display area. Point to the Close My Sidebar button.**

The Web page appears in the display area (Figure 3-5). The search results list remains in the Search sheet with the followed link you clicked a different color.

Figure 3-5

6 **Click Close My Sidebar.**

The My Sidebar pane closes (Figure 3-6).

Figure 3-6

Steps: To Customize Browser Search Options

1 If necessary, start the browser. Click the Home button on the Personal Toolbar, if necessary, to display the default home page. If necessary, click the Open My Sidebar button. Click the Search tab. Point to the using search engine down arrow.

The using search engine down arrow (Figure 3-7) displays a list of search engine choices. Your current default search engine may be different than the default Google search engine shown in the figure.

N Figure 3-7

2 Click the down arrow. Point to Lycos.

You can select a different search engine from the using search engine list (Figure 3-8).

N Figure 3-8

(continued)

3 **Click Lycos. Point to the OK button.**

A prompt window appears asking you to verify whether you wish to change the default search engine (Figure 3-9).

Figure 3-9

4 **Click OK.**

The Lycos search engine is now the default search engine (Figure 3-10).

new default search engine

Figure 3-10

5 **Type fastest growing jobs in the Search text box. Press the ENTER key. Point to the using search engine down arrow.**

A new search using the Lycos search engine is performed (Figure 3-11). The Lycos search results appear in the display area and an abbreviated list of hits appears in the Search Results list in the Search sheet.

search results list in Search tab

Figure 3-11

search results list in display area

6 **Click the using search engine down arrow. Click Google or your original default search tool. Click OK. Point to the Close My Sidebar button.**

The search engine choice is returned to its original default (Figure 3-12).

7 **Click Close My Sidebar.**

Figure 3-12

Chapter 5 — Getting More Out of the Internet

Steps: Viewing an Online Banking Demo

1 If necessary, start your Web browser. Visit the Discovering the Internet Chapter 5 Web page (scsite.com/internet/ch5). Click Citibank. Point to the learn more take a tour link.

The Citibank home page appears (Figure 5-1). This page includes links to open an account, view Citibank's personal or business banking services, or view an online banking demonstration. The content on the Web page on your screen may vary from that shown in Figures 5-1 through 5-13 on pages APP22 through APP28.

tools to help users look for products and services

N Figure 5-1

2 Click the learn more take a tour link. Point to the start button.

The Welcome to Citi start page appears in its own window (Figure 5-2). You can start the demo or close the demo window with links on this page.

start page

N Figure 5-2

3 Click the start button. Point to the next button.

The Welcome to Citi page appears (Figure 5-3) providing both a menu and a Select A Topic list of links to pages that illustrate individual demo topics. You can quickly view a specific demo page by clicking a topic in the menu or by clicking a topic in the list. You can view the demo pages in order by clicking the next button in the lower-right corner of the window.

Figure 5-3

4 Click the next button. Observe the contents of the new demo page. Point to the next button.

The My Citi – Your Home Page appears (Figure 5-4) containing an example of a personalized banking page used to view balances, schedule bill payments, track stock portfolios, and so forth. You can now move back and forth between the demo pages using the back and next buttons.

Figure 5-4

(continued)

5 **Click the next button. Point to the next button.**

The See Things Your Way page appears (Figure 5-5) illustrating areas of the personal banking page that can be customized.

N Figure 5-5

6 **Continue to review the online banking demo by clicking the next button in the lower-right corner of each page until you reach the Thanks for Taking the Tour! page. Point to the close link.**

The Thanks for Taking the Tour! page appears (Figure 5-6) at the completion of the online banking demo. You can click the back button to return to previously viewed pages or close the demo.

7 **Click the close link.**

The online banking demo window closes and the Citibank home page again appears.

N Figure 5-6

Steps: Accessing the Library of Congress

1 If necessary, start your Web browser. Type `ftp://ftp.loc.gov` in the Location Bar, and press ENTER. If necessary, close any pop-up windows. Point to the pub/ subfolder icon or text link.

The FTP site's URL appears in the Location Bar (Figure 5-7). The Web browser automatically logs you on to the anonymous FTP site hosted by the Library of Congress. The root directory (index of ftp://ftp.loc.gov) at the Library of Congress public FTP site contains several subfolders.

N Figure 5-7

2 Click the pub/ subfolder icon or text link to view the folder's contents. Point to the README file icon or text link.

The pub/ subfolder has several subfolders containing files on various topics of public interest, in addition to individual documents that you can open and view from the site or download (Figure 5-8).

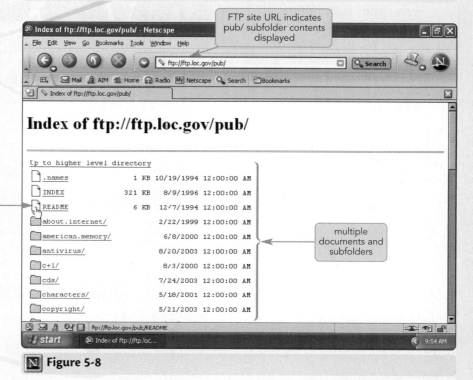

N Figure 5-8

(continued)

3 Click the README file icon or text link and scroll down the document to view its contents. Point to the Back button on the Navigation Toolbar.

The README file (Figure 5-9) lists the contents of the various files and subfolders in the pub/ directory.

Figure 5-9

4 Click the Back button to return to the pub/ subfolder's directory that displays the README file icon and text link. Right-click the README file text link and then point to the Save Link Target As command.

You can download a copy of this document and save it to a folder on your hard drive or a floppy disk (Figure 5-10).

Figure 5-10

5 Click Save Link Target As. When the Save As dialog box opens, switch to the folder on your hard drive specified by your instructor. Point to the Save button.

The Save As dialog box allows you to specify the destination folder (Figure 5-11) on your hard drive. Your Save in folder name will vary from the one shown in the figure.

Figure 5-11

6 Click the Save button. Click the Close button in the 100% of README Saved dialog box, if necessary, after the file is saved. Point to the american.memory/ subfolder or text link in the pub directory.

The README file is saved to the specified folder on your hard drive. The american.memory/ subfolder (Figure 5-12) contains information about the Library of Congress American Memory Project.

Figure 5-12

(continued)

7 Click the american.memory/ subfolder icon or text link. Click the docuview subfolder icon or text link. Point to the libcong.zip file text link.

The docuview folder contains two compressed files, both with a .zip extension (Figure 5-13). Very large files or sets of files often are **compressed** *to save storage space.*

8 Right-click the libcong.zip file text link. Click Save Link Target As. When the Save As dialog box opens, switch to the folder specified by your instructor. Click the Save button. Close the 100% of libcong.zip Saved dialog box, if necessary, after the file is saved.

The libcong.zip file is saved to the specified folder on your hard drive.

libcong.zip file

Figure 5-13

APPENDIX B
HTML Quick Reference

HTML Tags and Attributes

HTML is the original language used for publishing hypertext on the World Wide Web. It is a non-proprietary format based on Standard Generalized Markup Language (SGML). HTML documents can be created with a wide variety of tools, from simple plain text editors, such as Notepad, to sophisticated WYSIWYG authoring tools, such as FrontPage. HTML uses tags such as <H1> and <P> to structure text into headings, paragraphs, lists, hypertext links, and so on.

Many HTML tags have attributes that can be defined in different ways to alter the look of the Web page even more. The following table lists HTML tags and their associated attributes. The list provides a brief description of each tag and its attributes. The default value for each attribute is indicated by bold text. For a comprehensive list, more thorough descriptions, and examples of all HTML tags, visit the World Wide Web Consortium Web site at www.w3.org.

As the World Wide Web Consortium updates the current HTML specifications, HTML tags constantly are being added to, deleted, and replaced by newer tags. In this list, deprecated elements — that is, tags that can be replaced with newer elements — are indicated with an asterisk. Deprecated elements still are available for use, and most browsers still support them. Obsolete elements are elements that no longer are in use or supported by common browsers. This appendix does not list obsolete elements.

HTML Tags and Attributes

HTML Tag and Attributes	Description
<A>....</A>	Anchor; creates a hyperlink or fragment identifier
CHARSET=*character set*	Specifies the character encoding of the linked resource
HREF=*URL*	Hyperlink reference that specifies the target URL
NAME=*text*	Specifies a name for enclosed text, allowing it to be the target of a hyperlink
REL=*relationship*	Indicates the relationship going from the current page to the target
REV=*relationship*	Indicates the relationship going from the target to the current page
TARGET=*name*	Defines the name of the window or frame in which the linked resource will display
<ADDRESS>....</ADDRESS>	Used for information such as authorship, e-mail addresses, or addresses; enclosed text displays italicized and indented in some browsers
No attributes	
<AREA>....</AREA>	Creates a clickable area, or hotspot, on a client-side imagemap
COORDS=*value1, value2*	Specifies the coordinates that define the edges of the hotspot; a comma-delimited list of values

(continued)

HTML Tags and Attributes *(continued)*

HTML Tag and Attributes	Description
<AREA>....</AREA> *(continued)*	
HREF=*URL*	Hyperlink reference that specifies the target URL
NOHREF	Indicates that no link is associated with the area
SHAPE=*shape*	Identifies the shape of the area (CIRC, POLY, RECT)
TARGET=*name*	Defines the name of the window or frame in which the linked resource will display
<B>....</B>	Specifies text to display in bold
No attributes	
<BASE>	Identifies the base in all relative URLs in the document
HREF=*URL*	Specifies the absolute URL used to resolve all relative URLs in the document
TARGET=*name*	Defines the name for the default window or frame in which the hyperlinked pages display
<BIG>....</BIG>	Increases the size of the enclosed text to a type size bigger than the surrounding text; exact display size depends on the browser and default font
No attributes	
<BLOCKQUOTE>....</BLOCKQUOTE>	Sets enclosed text to display as a quotation, indented on the right and left
No attributes	
<BODY>....</BODY>	Defines the start and end of a Web page
ALINK=*color*	Defines the color of an active link
BACKGROUND=*URL*	Identifies the image to be used as a background
BGCOLOR=*color*	Sets the document's background color
LINK=*color*	Defines the color of links not yet visited
VLINK=*color*	Defines the color of visited links
<BOLD>....</BOLD>	Sets enclosed text to display in bold
No attributes	
** **	Inserts a line break
CLEAR=*margin*	Sets the next line to start in a spot where the requested margin is clear (LEFT, RIGHT, ALL, NONE); used to stop text wrap
<CAPTION>....</CAPTION>	Creates a caption for a table
ALIGN=*position*	Sets caption position (TOP, BOTTOM, LEFT, RIGHT)
<CENTER>....</CENTER> *	Centers the enclosed text horizontally on the page
No attributes	

HTML Tags and Attributes

HTML Tag and Attributes	Description
<CITE>....</CITE>	Indicates that the enclosed text is a citation; text usually displays in italics
No attributes	
<CODE>....</CODE>	Indicates that the enclosed text is a code sample from a program; text usually displays in fixed width font such as Courier
No attributes	
<COL>....</COL>	Organizes columns in a table into column groups to share attribute values
ALIGN=*position*	Sets horizontal alignment of text within the column (CHAR, CENTER, TOP, BOTTOM, LEFT, RIGHT)
SPAN=*value*	Sets the number of columns that span the <COL> element
VALIGN=*position*	Specifies vertical alignment of text within the column (TOP, MIDDLE, BOTTOM)
WIDTH=*value*	Sets the width of each column in the column group
<COLGROUP>....</COLGROUP>	Encloses a group of <COL> tags and groups the columns to set properties
ALIGN=*position*	Specifies horizontal alignment of text within the column (CHAR, CENTER, TOP, BOTTOM, LEFT, RIGHT)
CHAR=*character*	Specifies a character on which to align column values (e.g., a period is used to align monetary values)
CHAROFF=*value*	Specifies a number of characters to offset data aligned with the character specified in the CHAR property
SPAN=*number*	Sets the number of columns the <COL> element spans
VALIGN=*position*	Specifies vertical alignment of text within the column (TOP, MIDDLE, BOTTOM)
WIDTH=*value*	Sets the width of each column spanned by the COLGROUP statement
<DD>....</DD>	Indicates that the enclosed text is a definition in the definition list
No attributes	
<DIV>....</DIV>	Defines block-level structure or division in the HTML document
ALIGN=*position*	Specifies alignment of the content block (CENTER, LEFT, RIGHT)
CLASS=*name*	Assigns the class name to each class of divisions
ID=*name*	Assigns a unique name to a specific content block
<DL>....</DL>	Creates a definition list
No attributes	
<DT>....</DT>	Indicates that the enclosed text is a term in definition list
No attributes	

(continued)

HTML Tags and Attributes *(continued)*

HTML Tag and Attributes	Description
<EM>....</EM>	Indicates that the enclosed text should be emphasized; usually displays in italics
No attributes	
<FIELDSET>....</FIELDSET>	Groups related form controls and labels
ALIGN=*position*	Specifies alignment of a legend as related to the fieldset (TOP, BOTTOM, MIDDLE, LEFT, RIGHT)
<FONT>....</FONT> *	Defines the appearance of enclosed text
SIZE=*value*	Sets the font size in absolute terms (1 through 7) or as a relative value (e.g., +2)
COLOR=*color*	Sets the font color; can be a hexadecimal value (#rrggbb) or a word for a predefined color value (e.g., navy)
FACE=*list*	Identifies the font face; multiple entries should be separated by commas
POINT-SIZE=*value*	Sets the point size of text for downloaded fonts
WEIGHT=*value*	Sets the weight of the font, ranging from 100 (lightest) to 900 (heaviest)
<FORM>....</FORM>	Marks the start and end of a Web page form
ACTION=*URL*	Specifies the URL of the application that will process the form; required attribute
ENCTYPE=*encoding*	Specifies how the form element values will be encoded
METHOD=*method*	Specifies the method used to pass form parameters (data) to the server
TARGET=*text*	Specifies the frame or window that displays the form's results
<FRAME>....</FRAME>	Delimits a frame within a frameset
FRAMEBORDER=*option*	Specifies whether the frame border displays (YES, NO)
MARGINHEIGHT=*value*	Adds *n* pixels of space above and below the frame contents
MARGINWIDTH=*value*	Adds *n* pixels of space to the left and the right of the frame contents
NAME=*text*	Specifies the name of the frame
NORESIZE	Prevents the user from resizing the frame
SCROLLING=*option*	Defines the URL of the source document that is displayed in the frame
SRC=*URL*	Adds scroll bars or not – always (YES), never (NO), or add when needed (**AUTO**)
<FRAMESET>....</FRAMESET>	Defines a collection of frames in a frameset
COLS=*value1, value2,...*	Defines the number and width of frames within a frameset
ROWS= *value1, value2,...*	Defines the number and height of frames within a frameset
FRAMEBORDER=*option*	Specifies whether the frame border displays (YES, NO)
<H*n*>....</H*n*>	Defines a header level *n*, ranging from the largest (H1) to the smallest (H6)
ALIGN=*position*	Specifies the header alignment (**LEFT**, CENTER, RIGHT)

HTML Tags and Attributes

HTML Tag and Attributes	Description
\<HEAD\>....\</HEAD\>	Delimits the start and end of the HTML document's head
No attributes	
\<HR\>	Inserts a horizontal rule
ALIGN=type	Specifies the alignment of the horizontal rule (LEFT, **CENTER**, RIGHT)
NOSHADE	Specifies to not use 3D shading and to round the ends of the rule
SIZE=value	Sets the thickness of the rule to a value in pixels
WIDTH=value or %	Sets the width of the rule to a value in pixels or a percentage of the page width; percentage is preferred
\<HTML\>....\</HTML\>	Indicates the start and the end of the HTML document
VERSION=data	Indicates the HTML version used; not usually used
\<I\>....\</I\>	Sets enclosed text to display in italics
No attributes	
\<IFRAME\>....\</IFRAME\>	Creates an inline frame, also called a floating frame or subwindow, within an HTML document
ALIGN=position	Aligns the frame with respect to context (TOP, MIDDLE, **BOTTOM**, LEFT, RIGHT)
FRAMEBORDER=option	Specifies whether a frame border displays (1=YES; 0=NO)
HEIGHT=value	Sets the frame height to a value in pixels
MARGINHEIGHT=value	Sets the margin between the contents of the frame and its top and bottom borders to a value in pixels
MARGINWIDTH=value	Sets the margin between the contents of the frame and its left and right borders to value in pixels
NAME=text	Assigns a name to the current frame
NORESIZE	Prevents the user from resizing the frame
SRC=URL	Defines the URL of the source document that is displayed in the frame
WIDTH=value	Sets the frame width to a value in pixels
SCROLLING=option	Adds scroll bars or not – always (YES), never (NO), or add when needed (**AUTO**)
\<IMG\>....\</IMG\>	Inserts an image into the current Web page
ALIGN=type	Defines image alignment in relation to the text or the page margin (TOP, MIDDLE, BOTTOM, RIGHT, LEFT)
ALT=text	Provides a text description of an image if the browser cannot display the image; always should be used
BORDER=value	Sets the thickness of the border around the image to a value in pixels; default size is 3

(continued)

HTML Tags and Attributes *(continued)*

HTML Tag and Attributes	Description
<IMG>....</IMG> *(continued)*	
HEIGHT=*value*	Sets the height of the image to a value in pixels; always should be used
SRC=*URL*	Specifies the URL of the image to be displayed; required
USEMAP=*URL*	Specifies the map of coordinates and links that defines the HREF within this image
WIDTH=*value*	Sets the width of the image to a value in pixels; always should be used
<INPUT>....</INPUT>	Defines controls used in forms
ALT=*text*	Provides a short description of the control or image button; for browsers that do not support inline images
CHECKED	Sets radio buttons and check boxes to the checked state
DISABLED	Disables the control
MAXLENGTH=*value*	Sets a value for the maximum number of characters allowed as input for a text or password control
NAME=*text*	Assigns a name to the control
READONLY	Prevents changes to the control
SIZE=*value*	Sets the initial size of the control to a value in characters
SRC=*URL*	Identifies the location of the image if the control is set to an image
TABINDEX=*value*	Specifies the tab order between elements in the form, with 1 as the first element
TYPE=*type*	Defines the type of control (**TEXT**, PASSWORD, CHECKBOX, RADIO, SUBMIT, RESET, FILE, HIDDEN, IMAGE, BUTTON)
USEMAP=*URL*	Associates an imagemap as defined by the <MAP> element
VALUE=*data*	Sets the initial value of the control
<INS>....</INS>	Identifies and displays text as having been inserted in the document in relation to a previous version
CITE=*URL*	Specifies the URL of a document that has more information on the inserted text
DATETIME=*datetime*	Date and time of a change
<KBD>....</KBD>	Sets enclosed text to display as keyboard-like input
No attributes	
<LABEL>....</LABEL>	Creates a label for a form control
FOR=*data*	Indicates the name or ID of the element to which the label is applied
<LEGEND>....</LEGEND>	Assigns a caption to a fieldset element, as defined by the <FIELDSET> tags
No attributes	

HTML Tags and Attributes

HTML Tag and Attributes	Description
<LI>....</LI>	Defines the enclosed text as a list item in a list
VALUE=*value1*	Inserts or restarts counting with value1
<LINK>....</LINK>	Establishes a link between the HTML document and another document, such as an external style sheet
CHARSET=*character set*	Specifies the character encoding of the linked resource
HREF=*URL*	Defines the URL of the linked document
NAME=*text*	Names the current anchor so that it can be the destination to other links
REL=*relationship*	Indicates the relationship going from the current page to the target
REV=*relationship*	Indicates the relationship going from the target to the current page
TARGET=*name*	Defines the name of the frame into which the linked resource will display
TYPE=*mime-type*	Indicates the data or media type of the linked document (e.g., text/css for linked style sheets)
<MAP>....</MAP>	Specifies a client-side imagemap; must enclose <AREA> tags
NAME=*text*	Assigns a name to the imagemap
<META>	Provides additional data (metadata) about an HTML document
CONTENT=*text*	Specifies the value for the <META> information; required
HTTP-EQUIV=*text*	Specifies the HTTP-equivalent name for metadata; tells the server to include that name and content in the HTTP header when the HTML document is sent to the client
NAME=*text*	Assigns a name to metadata
SCHEME=*text*	Provides additional context for interpreting the information in the content attribute
<NOFRAMES>....</NOFRAMES>	Defines content to be displayed in browsers that do not support frames; very important to include
No attributes	
<OBJECT>....</OBJECT>	Includes an external object in the HTML document such as an image, a Java applet, or other external object, not well-supported by most browsers
ARCHIVE=*URL*	Specifies the URL of the archive containing classes and other resources that will be preloaded for use by the object
CLASSID=*URL*	Specifies the URL of the embedded object
CODEBASE=*URL*	Sets the base URL for the object; helps resolve relative references
CODETYPE=*type*	Identifies the content type of the data in the object
DATA=*URL*	Identifies the location of the object's data
DECLARE	Indicates the object will be declared only, not installed in the page

(continued)

HTML Tags and Attributes *(continued)*

HTML Tag and Attributes	Description
<OBJECT>....</OBJECT> *(continued)*	
HEIGHT=*value*	Sets the height of the object to a value in pixels
NAME=*text*	Assigns a control name to the object for use in forms
STANDBY=*text*	Defines the message to display while the object loads
TABINDEX=*value*	Specifies the tab order between elements, with 1 as the first element
TYPE=*type*	Specifies the content or media type of the object
USEMAP=*URL*	Associates an imagemap as defined by the <MAP> element
WIDTH=*value*	Sets the width of the object to a value in pixels
<OL>....</OL>	Defines an ordered list that contains numbered list item elements (<LI>)
TYPE=*option*	Sets or resets the numbering format for the list; options include: A=capital letters, a=lowercase letters, I=capital Roman numerals, i=lowercase Roman numerals, or 1=Arabic numerals
<OPTION>....</OPTION>	Defines individual options in a selection list, as defined by <SELECT> element
LABEL=*text*	Provides a shorter label for the option than that specified in its content
SELECTED	Sets the option to be the default or the selected option in a list
VALUE=*value*	Sets a value returned to the server when the user selects the option
DISABLED	Disables the option items
<P>....</P>	Delimits a paragraph; automatically inserts a blank line between text
ALIGN=*position*	Aligns text within the paragraph (LEFT, CENTER, RIGHT)
<PARAM>....</PARAM>	Passes a parameter to an object or applet, as defined by <OBJECT> or <APPLET> element
ID=*text*	Assigns an identifier to the element
NAME=*text*	Defines the name of the parameter required by an object
TYPE=*type*	Specifies the content or media type of the object
VALUE=*data*	Sets the value of the parameter
VALUETYPE=*data*	Identifies the type of parameter used in the value attribute (DATA, REF, OBJECT)
<PRE>....</PRE>	Preserves the original format of the enclosed text; keeps line breaks and spacing the same as the original
No attributes	
<Q>....</Q>	Sets enclosed text as a short quotation
LANG=*option*	Defines the language in which the quotation will display

HTML Tags and Attributes

HTML Tag and Attributes	Description
<SAMP>....</SAMP>	Sets enclosed text to display as sample output from a computer program or script; usually displays in a monospace font
No attributes	
<SCRIPT>....</SCRIPT>	Inserts a client-side script into an HTML document
DEFER	Indicates that the browser should defer executing the script
SRC=*URL*	Identifies the location of an external script
TYPE=*mime-type*	Indicates the data or media type of the script language (e.g., text/javascript for Javascript commands)
<SELECT>....</SELECT>	Defines a form control to create a multiple-choice menu or scrolling list; encloses a set of <OPTION> tags to define one or more options
NAME=*text*	Assigns a name to the selection list
MULTIPLE	Sets the list to allow multiple selections
SIZE=*value*	Sets the number of visible options in the list
DISABLED	Disables the selection list
TABINDEX=*value*	Specifies the tab order between list items, with 1 as the first element
<SMALL>....</SMALL>	Sets enclosed text to display in a smaller typeface
No attributes	
<SPAN>....</SPAN>	Creates a user-defined container to add inline structure to the HTML document
No attributes	
<STRONG>....</STRONG>	Sets enclosed text to display with strong emphasis; usually displayed as bold text
No attributes	
<STYLE>....</STYLE>	Encloses embedded style sheet rules for use in the HTML document
MEDIA=*data*	Identifies the intended medium of the style (**SCREEN**, TTY, TV, PROJECTION, HANDHELD, PRINT, BRAILLE, AURAL, ALL)
TITLE=*data*	Indicates the title of the style sheet
TYPE=*data*	Specifies the content or media type of the style language (e.g., text/css for linked style sheets)
_{....}	Sets enclosed text to display in subscript
No attributes	
^{....}	Sets enclosed text to display in superscript
No attributes	

(continued)

HTML Tags and Attributes (continued)

HTML Tag and Attributes	Description
<TABLE>....</TABLE>	Marks the start and end of a table
ALIGN=*position*	Aligns the table text (LEFT, RIGHT, CENTER, JUSTIFY, CHAR)
BORDER=*value*	Sets the border around a table to a value in pixels
CELLPADDING=*value*	Sets padding around each cell's contents to a value in pixels
CELLSPACING=*value*	Sets spacing between cells to a value in pixels
SUMMARY=*text*	Provides a summary of the table's purpose and structure
WIDTH=*value* or %	Sets table width in pixels or a percentage of the window
FRAME=*option*	Defines which parts of the outer border (frame) to display (VOID, ABOVE, BELOW, HSIDES, LHS, RHS, VSIDES, BOX, BORDER)
RULES=*option*	Specifies which inner borders are to display between the table cells (NONE, GROUPS, ROWS, COLS, ALL)
<TBODY>....</TBODY>	Defines a groups of rows in a table body
ALIGN=*option*	Aligns text (LEFT, CENTER, RIGHT, JUSTIFY, CHAR)
CHAR=*character*	Specifies a character on which to align column values (e.g., a period is used to align monetary values)
CHAROFF=*value*	Specifies a number of characters to offset data aligned with the character specified in the CHAR property
VALIGN=*position*	Sets vertical alignment of cells in a group (TOP, MIDDLE, BOTTOM, BASELINE)
<TD>....</TD>	Defines a data cell in a table; contents are left-aligned and normal text by default
BGCOLOR=*color*	Defines the background color for the cell
COLSPAN=*value*	Defines the number of adjacent columns spanned by the cell
ROWSPAN=*value*	Defines the number of adjacent rows spanned by the cell
WIDTH=*n* or %	Sets the width of the table in either pixels or a percentage of the whole table width
HEADERS=*IDREFS*	Defines the list of header cells for the current cell
ABBR=*text*	Provides an abbreviated version of the cell's contents that browsers can use if space is limited
SCOPE=*option*	Specifies cells for which the element defines header cells (ROW, COL, ROWGROUP, COLGROUP)
ALIGN=*position*	Specifies horizontal alignment (LEFT, CENTER, RIGHT, JUSTIFY, CHAR)
CHAR=*character*	Specifies a character on which to align column values (e.g., a period is used to align monetary values)
CHAROFF=*value*	Specifies a number of characters to offset data aligned with the character specified in the CHAR property
VALIGN=*position*	Sets vertical alignment of cells in the group (TOP, MIDDLE, BOTTOM, BASELINE)

HTML Tags and Attributes

HTML Tag and Attributes	Description
\<TEXTAREA\>....\</TEXTAREA\>	Creates a multiline text input area within a form
COLS=*value*	Defines the number of columns in the text input area
NAME=*data*	Assigns a name to the text area
ROWS=*value*	Defines the number of rows in the text input area
DISABLED	Disables the element
READONLY	Prevents the user from editing content in the text area
TABINDEX=*value*	Specifies the tab order between elements, with 1 as the first element
\<TFOOT\>....\</TFOOT\>	Identifies and groups rows into a table footer
ALIGN=*position*	Specifies horizontal alignment (LEFT, CENTER, RIGHT, JUSTIFY, CHAR)
CHAR=*character*	Specifies a character on which to align column values (e.g., a period is used to align monetary values)
CHAROFF=*value*	Specifies a number of characters to offset data aligned with the character specified in the CHAR property
VALIGN=*position*	Sets vertical alignment of cells in a group (TOP, MIDDLE, BOTTOM, BASELINE)
\<TH\>....\</TH\>	Defines a table header cell; contents are bold and center-aligned by default
BGCOLOR=*color*	Defines the background color for the cell
COLSPAN=*value*	Defines the number of adjacent columns spanned by the cell
ROWSPAN=*value*	Defines the number of adjacent rows spanned by the cell
WIDTH=*n* or %	Sets the width of the table in either pixels or a percentage of the whole table width
\<THEAD\>....\</THEAD\>	Identifies and groups rows into a table header
ALIGN=*position*	Specifies horizontal alignment (LEFT, CENTER, RIGHT, JUSTIFY, CHAR)
CHAR=*character*	Specifies a character on which to align column values (e.g., a period is used to align monetary values)
CHAROFF=*value*	Specifies a number of characters to offset data aligned with the character specified in the CHAR property
VALIGN=*position*	Sets vertical alignment of cells in a group (TOP, MIDDLE, BOTTOM, BASELINE)
\<TITLE\>....\</TITLE\>	Defines the title for the HTML document; always should be used
No attributes	
\<TR\>....\</TR\>	Defines a row of cells within a table
BGCOLOR=*color*	Defines the background color for the cell
ALIGN=*position*	Specifies horizontal alignment (LEFT, CENTER, RIGHT, JUSTIFY, CHAR)

(continued)

HTML Tags and Attributes *(continued)*

HTML Tag and Attributes	Description
\<TR>....\</TR> *(continued)*	
CHAR=*character*	Specifies a character on which to align column values (e.g., a period is used to align monetary values)
CHAROFF=*value*	Specifies a number of characters to offset data aligned with the character specified in the CHAR property
VALIGN=*position*	Sets vertical alignment of cells in a group (TOP, MIDDLE, BOTTOM, BASELINE)
\<TT>....\</TT>	Formats the enclosed text in teletype- or computer-style monospace font
No attributes	
\<U>....\</U> *	Sets enclosed text to display with an underline
No attributes	
\<UL>....\</UL>	Defines an unnumbered list that contains bulleted list item elements (\<LI>)
TYPE=*option*	Sets or resets the bullet format for the list; options include: CIRCLE, **DISC**, SQUARE
\<VAR>....\</VAR>	Indicates the enclosed text is a variable's name; used to mark up variables or program arguments
No attributes	

Index

Photo Credits

Front Matter, *Opening Art,* Background, Creatas © 2002 Dynamic Graphics; Woman and man looking at flat screen, Photodisc © Copyright 1999-2003 Getty Images, Inc. All rights reserved; *Chapters,* Icons, Copyright © CSA Images www.csaimages.com; **Chapter 1,** *Opening Art,* Woman with laptop, Bill Cannon/© 2003 Getty Images, Inc. All rights reserved; *Opening Spread Art,* Background, Creatas © 2002 Dynamic Graphics; *Figure 1-2a,* Woman writing viewing laptop. man at bookshelf, Photodisc © Copyright 1999-2003 Getty Images, Inc. All rights reserved; *Figure 1-2b,* Kissed women with laptop, Photodisc © Copyright 1999-2003 Getty Images, Inc. All rights reserved; *Figure 1-2c,* Laptop computer, Courtesy of Apple Computer, Inc.; *Figure 1-2d,* HR businessman with laptop, Courtesy of © 2003 ACCO Europe; *Figure 1-2e,* i-Pod, Courtesy of Apple Computer, Inc.; *Figure 1-2f,* Laptop computer, Courtesy of Apple Computer, Inc.; *Figure 1-2g,* HR research on laptop, Courtesy of © 2003 ACCO Europe; *Figure 1-2h,* Businessman writing viewing computer, Photodisc © Copyright 1999-2003 Getty Images, Inc. All rights reserved; *Figure 1-2i,* Woman talking on phone viewing computer, Photodisc © Copyright 1999-2003 Getty Images, Inc. All rights reserved; *Figure 1-7a,* VW dealership, Lon C. Diehl/© PhotoEdit, Inc. All rights reserved; *Figure 1-7b,* Woman on automobile website, Courtesy of © Siemens AG 2003; *Figure 1-7c,* Hospital, ©2002-2003 ArtToday, Inc. All rights reserved; *Figure 1-7d,* Lab examination, ©2002-2003 ArtToday, Inc. All rights reserved; *Figure 1-7e,* Oakland Airport, Courtesy of © 2001 Port of Oakland. All rights reserved; *Figure 1-7f,* Airline personnel with passengers, Courtesy of © Siemens AG 2003; *Figure 1-7g,* Man at computer with eBay screen, David Young-Wolff/© PhotoEdit. All rights reserved; *Figure 1-7h,* Couple at grocery store., Mark Richards/© PhotoEdit. All rights reserved; *Figure 1-9,* Leonard Kleinrock, Fred Prouser/© Reuters New Media Inc./CORBIS; *Figure 1-10,* Internet pioneers, © 2003 Getty Images, Inc. All rights reserved; *Figure 1-11,* Ray Tomlinson: Inventor of Email, Courtesy of © 2001 BBN Technologies. All rights reserved; *Figure 1-13,* Gopher session, Courtesy of University of Minnesota, College of Natural Resources Gopher; *Figure 1-14,* Tim Berners-Lee, Elise Amendola/© 1998 AP Photo Archive. All Rights Reserved; *Figure 1-15,* Berners-Lee's early WWW browsers screen shot, Courtesy of WBG Links; *Figure 1-17a,* GA621 1000 Mbps Fiber Gigabit Ethernet Card, Courtesy of Copyright © 1998-2003 NETGEAR™; *Figure 1-21a,* Wi-Fi card, Courtesy of Copyright © 1998-2003 NETGEAR™; *Figure 1-21b,* Man communicating through laptop, Courtesy of © 2000-2002 TeleSym Inc. All rights reserved; *Figure 1-22a,* Woman and man using Wireless-LAN laptop, Courtesy of © Siemens AG 2003; *Figure 1-22b,* Sierra Wireless AirCardÆCourtesy of Copyright © Sierra Wireless, 2003; *Figure 1-22c,* Laptop and hand holding cellular phone Courtesy of © Siemens AG 2003; *Figure 1-23a,* PC-EPhone, Courtesy of © 2001 PC-EPhone. All rights reserved; *Figure 1-23b,* Woman holding cellular phone with mobile Internet, Courtesy of Copyright © Telefonaktiebolaget L M Ericsson, 2001. All rights reserved; *Figure 1-23c,* Wireless-LAN Card inserted into a Jornada 560, Courtesy of © Copyright 2001-2003, Socket Communications, Inc. All rights reserved; *End of Chapter,* Icons, Copyright © CSA Images www.csaimages.com; **Chapter 2,** *Opening Art,* Man with laptop, Photodisc © Copyright 1999-2003 Getty Images, Inc. All rights reserved; *Opening Spread Art,* Background, Creatas © 2002 Dynamic Graphics; *Figure 2-2,* © 2002-2003 ArtToday, Inc. All rights reserved; *Figure 2-65,* Boy at desktop computer, Photodisc © Copyright 1999-2003 Getty Images, Inc. All rights reserved; *End of Chapter,* Icons, Copyright © CSA Images www.csaimages.com; **Chapter 3,** *Opening Art,* Man with laptop, Photodisc © Copyright 1999-2003 Getty Images, Inc. All rights reserved; *Opening Spread Art,* Background, Creatas © 2002 Dynamic Graphics; *Figure 3-1,* Woman at computer researching, ©2002-2003 ArtToday, Inc. All rights reserved; *Sidebar art on page 116,* Woman looking at monitor, ©2002-2003 ArtToday, Inc. All rights reserved; *Figure 3-12,* © 2002-2003 ArtToday, Inc. All rights reserved; *Figure 3-14a,* Jerry Yang, Courtesy of Copyright © 2003 Yahoo! Inc. All Rights Reserved; *Figure 3-14b,* David Filo, Courtesy of Copyright © 2003 Yahoo! Inc. All Rights Reserved; *Figure 3-32,* © 2002-2003 ArtToday, Inc. All rights reserved; *Figure 3-63,* Boy sitting on yellow pages, © 2002-2003 ArtToday, Inc. All rights reserved; *Figure 3-64,* Man reading financial newspaper looking at a monitor, © 2002-2003 ArtToday, Inc. All rights reserved; *End of Chapter,* Icons, Copyright © CSA Images www.csaimages.com; **Chapter 4,** *Opening Art,* Woman sitting on desk with laptop, ©2002-2003 ArtToday, Inc. All rights reserved; *Opening Spread Art,* Background, Creatas © 2002 Dynamic Graphics; *Figure 4-78,* Crowd of people looking up, Photodisc © Copyright 1999-2003 Getty Images, Inc. All rights reserved; *Figure 4-91,* Boy on mountain bike with cell phone, ©2002-2003 ArtToday, Inc. All rights reserved; *Figure 4-92a,* Teleconferencing, Andreas Policik/© Stone; *Figure 4-92b,* Cam meeting from desktop computer, Jon Feingersh/© CORBIS; *End of Chapter,* Icons, Copyright © CSA Images www.csaimages.com; **Chapter 5,** *Opening Art,* Man sitting operating laptop, ©2002-2003 ArtToday, Inc. All rights reserved; *Opening Spread Art,* Background, Creatas © 2002 Dynamic Graphics; *Figure 5-1a,* Basketball players, Creatas © 2002 Dynamic Graphics; *Figure 5-1b and 5-1c,* ©2002-2003 ArtToday, Inc. All rights reserved; *Sidebar art on page 256,* Boys looking at laptop, ©2002-2003 ArtToday, Inc. All rights reserved; *Sidebar art on page 261,* Librarian, Faces Vol. 2, © RubberBall Productions 2003; *Sidebar art on page 264,* Courtesy of Copyright © 1999-2002 PostcardsFromtheRoad.net; *Figure 5-46,* Restaurant, Courtesy of Zaytinya/ HeatherFreeman.com PR; *Figure 5-47,* ©2002-2003 ArtToday, Inc. All rights reserved; *Figure 5-48,* ©2002-2003 ArtToday, Inc. All rights reserved; *Figure 5-49,* ©2002-2003 ArtToday, Inc. All rights reserved; *Figure 5-64,* ©2002-2003 ArtToday, Inc. All rights reserved; *Figure 5-65,* ©2002-2003 ArtToday, Inc. All rights reserved; *Figure 5-66a,* X-ray technician at monitor, Courtesy of © Siemens AG 2002-2003; *Figure 5-66b,* Siemens mobile solutions for a service technician, Courtesy of © Siemens AG 2002-2003; *Figure 5-66c,* Group meeting at laptop, ©2002-2003 ArtToday, Inc. All rights reserved; *Figure 5-66d,* Siemens Teleperm XP I&C system manned by power plant operator, Courtesy of © Siemens AG 2002-2003; *Figure 5-66e,* Mechatronic engineering students Courtesy of © Siemens AG 2002-2003; *Figure 5-66f,* Woman with SIMpad SL4 computer, Courtesy of © Siemens AG 2002-2003; *Figure 5-66g,*

Security Consulting and Management personnel working on laptop, Courtesy of © Siemens AG 2002-2003; *Figure 5-69*, Preproduction vehicle, Courtesy of Chevrolet © 2003 General Motors Corp.; *Figure 5-69*, Disney MoonBeam^SM Service, Courtesy of © 2003 Newstream.com/The Walt Disney Company; *Figure 5-69*, Kodak digital camera, Courtesy of © 2003 Newstream.com/Copyright © Eastman Kodak Company, 1994-2003; *Figure 5-76*, Cards, checkers, chess pieces, domino, ©2002-2003 ArtToday, Inc. All rights reserved; *End of Chapter*, Icons, Copyright © CSA Images www.csaimages.com; **Chapter 6**, *Opening Art*, Asian woman laying down looking at laptop, ©2002-2003 ArtToday, Inc. All rights reserved; *Opening Spread Art*, Background, Creatas © 2002 Dynamic Graphics; *Figure 6-11*, Bluetooth transmission between two women in a city, Courtesy of © 2001 Bluetooth. All rights reserved; *Figure 6-35a*, Treo, Courtesy of Copyright © 1999-2003 Handspring; *Figure 6-35b*, Communicator, Courtesy of Copyright © Copyright 1994-2003 Telefonaktiebolaget LM Ericsson; *Figure 6-35c*, Palm Tungsten, Courtesy of © Copyright 2003 Palm, Inc. All rights reserved; *Figure 6-35d*, Blackberry, Courtesy of Copyright © 2003 Research In Motion Limited; *Figure 6-35e*, Motorola ST7760, Courtesy of © Copyright 1994-2003 Motorola, Inc. All rights reserved; *Figure 6-35f*, Cell Phone, Courtesy of Copyright ©2001-2003 Sony Ericsson Mobile Communications AB. All rights reserved; *Figure 6-35g*, Cell Phone, Courtesy of Copyright © Copyright 1994-2003 Telefonaktiebolaget LM Ericsson; *Figure 6-36a*, Man taking picture using MMS, Courtesy of © Siemens AG 2003; *Figure 6-36b*, Man text messaging on cell phone, Photodisc © Copyright 1999-2003 Getty Images, Inc. All rights reserved; *Figure 6-36c*, Gaming on a cell phone, Courtesy of © Nokia 2003; *Figure 6-36d*, Man accessing internet via PDA, Courtesy of Copyright ©2001-2003 Sony Ericsson Mobile Communications AB. All rights reserved; *Figure 6-36e*, Cyclist accessing internet via watch, Courtesy of Copyright ©2001-2003 Sony Ericsson Mobile Communications AB. All rights reserved; *Figure 6-39*, Photodisc © Copyright 1999-2003 Getty Images, Inc. All rights reserved; *Figure 6-40*, Photodisc © Copyright 1999-2003 Getty Images, Inc. All rights reserved; *Figure 6-45a*, Video images producing contoured face mask, Courtesy of © Siemens AG 2003; *Figure 6-45b*, Identification via digital signature, Courtesy of © Siemens AG 2003; *Figure 6-48a*, ZoneAlarmÆ Pro, Courtesy of © 1999-2003 Zone Labs, Inc. All rights reserved; *Figure 6-48b*, BlackICE PC Protection, Courtesy of Copyrighted material of Internet Security Systems, Inc.; *End of Chapter*, Icons, Copyright © CSA Images www.csaimages.com; **Chapter 7**, *Opening Art*, Two girls, one with laptop, Photodisc © Copyright 1999-2003 Getty Images, Inc. All rights reserved; *Opening Spread Art*, Background, Creatas © 2002 Dynamic Graphics; *Figure 7-80*, Adobe GoLive 6.0, Courtesy of Copyright 2003 Adobe Systems Incorporated. All rights reserved; *Figure 7-82a*, Adobe Photoshop 7.0, Courtesy of Copyright 2003 Adobe Systems Incorporated. All rights reserved; *Figure 7-82b*, Macromedia Flash, Fireworks and Freehand, Courtesy of ©1995-2003 Macromedia, Inc. All rights reserved; *End of Chapter*, Icons, Copyright © CSA Images www.csaimages.com; **Chapter 8**, *Opening Art*, Man standing inputting on laptop, Photodisc © Copyright 1999-2003 Getty Images, Inc. All rights reserved; *Opening Spread Art*, Background, Creatas © 2002 Dynamic Graphics; *Figure 8-7*, Radisson, Courtesy of © Radisson; *Figure 8-7*, British Airways, Courtesy of © 2001 Calgary Airport Authority; *Figure 8-9*, United, ©2002-2003 ArtToday, Inc. All rights reserved; *Figure 8-9*, Hotel, ©2002-2003 ArtToday, Inc. All rights reserved; *Figure 8-52*, Store front, ©2002-2003 ArtToday, Inc. All rights reserved; *Figure 8-53*, Shopping carts, ©2002-2003 ArtToday, Inc. All rights reserved; *Figure 8-54*, Money, ©2002-2003 ArtToday, Inc. All rights reserved; *End of Chapter*, Icons, Copyright © CSA Images www.csaimages.com; **Chapter 9**, *Opening Art*, Boy and girl viewing laptop, Photodisc © Copyright 1999-2003 Getty Images, Inc. All rights reserved; *Opening Spread Art*, Background, Creatas © 2002 Dynamic Graphics; *Figure 9-15*, Front desk, ©2002-2003 ArtToday, Inc. All rights reserved; *Figure 9-15*, Army computer, ©2002-2003 ArtToday, Inc. All rights reserved; *Figure 9-19*, Group at table, Photodisc © Copyright 1999-2003 Getty Images, Inc. All rights reserved; *Figure 9-19*, Two women, Photodisc © Copyright 1999-2003 Getty Images, Inc. All rights reserved; *End of Chapter*, Icons, Copyright © CSA Images www.csaimages.com; **Appendix A**, Backgrounds, Creatas © 2002 Dynamic Graphics.